Massachusetts

AN EXPLORER'S GUIDE

Massachusetts

AN EXPLORER'S GUIDE

CHRISTINA TREE & WILLIAM DAVIS

Second Edition

The Countryman Press
Woodstock, Vermont

Library of Congress Cataloging-in Publication Data
Tree, Christina.
Massachusetts: an explorer's guide : Beyond Boston and Cape Cod /
Christina Tree & William Davis. — 2nd ed.
p.   cm.
Includes indexes.
ISBN 0-88150-405-X (alk. paper)
1. Massachusetts—Guidebooks. I. Davis, William, 1932– II. Title.
F62.3T733 1998
917.4404'43—dc21   97-43869

Cover painting *Sunderland View from Mount
Sugarloaf* by Lewis Bryden, courtesy of
R. Michelson Galleries, 132 Main Street,
Northampton, MA 01060
Cover design by Sue Wheeler and Hugh
Coyle
Text design by Glenn Suokko
Maps by Mapping Specialists, © 1998 The
Countryman Press

Published by The Countryman Press, P.O.
Box 748, Woodstock, Vermont 05091
Distributed by W.W. Norton & Company, 500
Fifth Avenue, New York, NY 10110
Printed in the United States of America
10 9 8 7 6 5 4 3 2 1

Explore With Us!

Massachusetts: An Explorer's Guide was originally published in 1979 as the first in a series of travel books that now includes guides to Maine, New Hampshire, Vermont, Cape Cod, Rhode Island, Connecticut, and the Hudson Valley of New York. This new edition has been reworked and rewritten from scratch: It's an entirely new book!

We hope you'll find its design attractive and easy to read. Although the organization is simple, the following points will help get you started on your way.

WHAT'S WHERE

In the beginning of the book you'll find an alphabetical listing of special highlights and important information that you may want to reference quickly. You'll find advice on anything from where to find the best artists and craftspeople to where to write or call for camping reservations and park information.

LODGING

Prices: Please don't hold us or the respective innkeepers responsible for the rates listed as of press time. Some changes are inevitable. The state rooms and meals tax is 5.7 percent as of this writing, but that rate varies with each town. Be sure to inquire.

RESTAURANTS

In most sections, note a distinction between *Dining Out* and *Eating Out.* By their nature, restaurants in the *Eating Out* group are generally inexpensive.

KEY TO SYMBOLS

☞ The special value symbol appears next to lodging and restuarants that combine quality and moderate prices.

✐ The kids-alert symbols appears next to lodging, restaurants, activities, and shops of special appeal to youngsters.

& The wheelchair symbols indicates restaurants, lodgings, and attractions that have handicapped access.

We would appreciate your comments and corrections about places you visit or know well in the state. Please address your correspondence to Explorer's Guide Editor, The Countryman Press, PO Box 748, Woodstock, Vermont 05091.

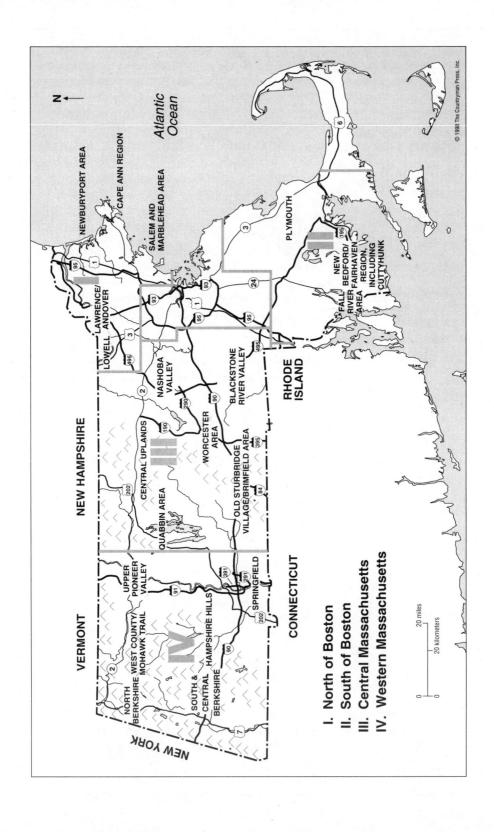

N ←

VERMONT

NEW HAMPSHIRE

NEW YORK

CONNECTICUT

RHODE ISLAND

Atlantic Ocean

© 1998 The Countryman Press, Inc.

NORTH BERKSHIRE WEST COUNTY/ MOHAWK TRAIL

SOUTH & CENTRAL BERKSHIRE HILLS

UPPER PIONEER VALLEY

CENTRAL HAMPSHIRE HILLS

SPRINGFIELD

QUABBIN AREA

CENTRAL UPLANDS

WORCESTER AREA

OLD STURBRIDGE VILLAGE/BRIMFIELD AREA

NASHOBA VALLEY

BLACKSTONE RIVER VALLEY

LOWELL

LAWRENCE/ ANDOVER

NEWBURYPORT AREA

CAPE ANN REGION

SALEM AND MARBLEHEAD AREA

PLYMOUTH

NEW BEDFORD/ FALL RIVER FAIRHAVEN AREA REGION, INCLUDING CUTTYHUNK

I. North of Boston
II. South of Boston
III. Central Massachusetts
IV. Western Massachusetts

IV

III

20 miles

20 kilometers

0

0

Contents

Introduction

We hope you will view this guide as a recipe book for many memorable days. We have attempted to convey a sense of why you should explore "the other Massachusetts" and then to supply the necessary ingredients.

If the less-populated, less-touristed three-fourths of Massachusetts beyond Boston and Cape Cod were a state in its own right, it would probably be recognized as the cultural heart and visual soul of New England.

But what would you call it?

One previous edition of this book was titled *The Other Massachusetts,* but only the people who lived there seemed to know what it meant.

Put another way: Although physically just one-seventh of New England, Massachusetts accounts for almost half the region's population. Half the state's residents live within easy commuting distance of Boston, however, and often seem oblivious to the fact that most of Massachusetts lies beyond the arc of Route 128.

For decades we have puzzled over why many Bay Staters know so little about—and comparatively few visitors discover—the beautiful byways of the North Shore or southeastern Massachusetts, let alone inland regions such as the orchard-rich Nashoba Valley; the immense expanse of Quabbin; the many places to walk and bicycle, as well as dine and shop, in the Upper Pioneer Valley and the Berkshire Hilltowns—as picturesque as any part of Vermont, let alone Berkshire County (they are in neither).

One major reason why so many residents and visitors assume that there's not much worth exploring west of Concord, we think, is that most of the state beyond the crescent of I-495 is so broadly and blandly described. Labels like "western Massachusetts" and "central Massachusetts" conjure up few images likely to lure anyone.

Over the years, between us, we have written thousands of travel stories on virtually every corner of the world; yet we feel strongly that, despite its lack of a clear image, this "other Massachusetts" constitutes one of the country's most beautiful and underrated travel destinations.

That the region eludes precise definition is a tribute to its topographical and human diversity and its quirky, indomitable, and unhomogenized character. To make this "other Massachusetts" more comprehensible and easier to explore, this guide divides it into areas based on geography and the way residents define where they live, rather than on the political boundaries usually applied.

For example: "Springfield and the Pioneer Valley" is the way the 50-mile-wide, 50-mile-long swath of the state's most topographically—and in every other way—varied region is usually labeled. This name, which was coined in the 1940s, implies that the entire area is a combination of city and valley when in fact it includes the hilliest and least populated parts of the state. Within this book we divide it into several very specific and different regions.

The Massachusetts Turnpike, that 123-mile ribbon of double-barreled asphalt slashing across the width of the state, was completed in 1965, cutting the time it takes to drive across Massachusetts to less than 2½ hours. But exits are often so few and far apart, especially west of Worcester (of the Pike's 25 exits, 14 are east of I-495), that you tend to assume there's no reason to leave the highway. The impression is that most of the state is a black hole, prudently bridged by the Turnpike Authority.

Actually, we love the Mass. Pike. It's well maintained in all weather, a quick way home after a day or two of exploring. But frequently we prefer taking Route 2 west from Boston; the eastern end of this route was recently dubbed the Johnny Appleseed Trail and finally blessed with a hospitality center (westbound in Lancaster).

Even from this initial stretch of Route 2, country roads branch like so many veins off the stem of a leaf, leading north to classic villages like Groton and Townsend, Ashby and Ashburnham, south to the orchard country around Harvard (home of the exceptional Fruitlands Museums) and west to Princeton, a popular 19th-century resort (it once boasted 13 hotels, including one on top of Wachusett Mountain) that's still a great place to walk and bird, to dine, to spend the night or ski.

Massachusetts is full of surprises. No other state, for instance, offers so many rural museums: world-famous art museums as well as historical museums and museum villages. It harbors dozens of truly spectacular waterfalls, miles of magnificent ridge trails and ocean walks, and hundreds of thousands of square miles of landscape preserved by old guard groups like the Massachusetts Audubon Society and the Trustees of Reservations (both founded in Massachusetts in the 1890s and dedicated to acquiring only land with exceptional appeal), as well as by the Department of Environmental Management (which alone maintains more than 100 properties within the scope of this book, ranging from beaches, campsites, and bicycle paths to the 12,500-acre Mount Greylock reservation and surprisingly elaborate Heritage State Parks), and thousands more by burgeoning land trusts like Essex Greenbelt.

Just a dozen years ago many of the more beautiful parts of Massachusetts attracted few visitors because they offered few places to stay. When *Massachusetts: An Explorer's Guide* first appeared in 1979, it included Boston, Cape Cod, and the Islands, and yet was shorter than this guide. It was in 1987 that we jettisoned Boston and Cape Cod, attempting to fly without them—the better to help spread the news about proliferating B&Bs, visitor-geared shops, and new pastimes, ranging from local resident theater companies and art centers to white-water rafting, mountain biking, and sea kayaking. All these changes add up to myriad getaways for harried urbanities (or suburbanites) looking for a complete change of pace and scene.

"Change" is the operative adjective for the Massachusetts landscape. It's like that old new England weather adage: "If you don't like it, wait a minute."

This leads us to an admission: Massachusetts is patchy. In contrast to Maine, Vermont, and northern New Hampshire—all of which are essentially rural with very small exceptions—Massachusetts frequently presents to the visitor a facade of highways and road rash. Locals, of course, know where to turn off to find tranquil lakes and shore roads, but they aren't sure they want to share that information with "tourists." Visitors centers are still relatively rare, and scant information about much of Massachusetts is available.

The chronic lack of detailed maps for Massachusetts doesn't help, either. While we are accustomed to using official state highway maps to research the *Explorer's Guides* to northern New England, in Massachusetts we are constantly on roads—usually the more beautiful roads—that are not on the official map.

In this edition of *Massachusetts: Beyond Boston and Cape Cod* we have focused on areas as genuinely appealing as any we know anywhere, and we have tried to pay special attention to mapping them accurately and in a way that conveys the variety of accessible open space.

We invite you to explore Massachusetts from the windswept island of Cuttyhunk (accessible by ferry from New Bedford) to the top of Mount Holyoke (where a restored Summit House serves as the setting for summer sunset concerts), from the dramatic granite rocks on Cape Ann's Halibut Point to the town of Mount Washington (which rises like a green island above valleys in three states). We suggest that you don't try to tour it all in a day or two, especially if you are lucky enough to live within easy distance and can strike out in different directions on different days and times of year.

But please don't just day-trip. Beyond Boston, lodging tends to be reasonably priced, and spending the night in South Dartmouth, Princeton, Rockport, or even Hamilton can provide a sense of change that's deeply satisfying, even if you live less than an hour away. Many visitors from other parts of the country and world have discovered the advantages of basing themselves on the North Shore or west of Boston and taking the commuter rail into the city. Thanks to the proliferation of bike trails and rental bike sources, it's also increasingly possible to come by bus or train (take the commuter rail to Manchester-by-the-Sea or Gloucester; the bus from Boston; or AMTRAK from Manhattan to Amherst) and reach beaches, restaurants, and mountain trails with ease.

The original *Massachusetts: An Explorer's Guide* was the first in a series that now includes guides to Maine, New Hampshire, Vermont, Cape Cod, Rhode Island, Connecticut, and the Hudson Valley. Chris continues to coauthor four of these.

This, however, is the only book that we write together. We first met over the typewriter we shared in the *Boston Globe* city room and subsequently worked together, Bill as *Boston Globe* travel editor, Chris as assistant travel editor, for several years. Chris resigned as a full-time *Globe* staffer when our first son was born (maternity leave in the early '70s was limited to 3 weeks), but she has continued to contribute New England travel stories to the *Globe* on a regular basis. Bill remains a *Boston Globe* feature writer, and our articles still frequently appear together on the front page of the *Globe*'s Sunday travel section. Massachusetts is still our home.

We are grateful to all the people who took the time to contribute their expertise on particular parts of Massachusetts. For help with the North of Boston area we owe thanks to Janice Ramsden, Janice Bell, and Michelle Meehan. We couldn't have done a decent job on Bristol County without Ed Camara's help; or the Johnny Appleseed Trail area without Tom Meyers and Stephanie Corby; the Old Sturbridge/ Brimfield region without Emily Faxon; the Quabbin region without help from Tom Kussy, Jim Fairbanks, and Alain Beret; Springfield without input from Marianne Gambara; Amherst without Steve Calcagnino; Northfield without help from Andrea Dale; or Connecticut Valley *Green Space* without Terry Blunt. Ann Hamilton was a never-failing source of support throughout Franklin County and beyond. Carol and Arnold Westwood, Eleanor Hebert, and Richard Matthews all helped with the Berkshire hilltowns, and Betty Noble saved the day with her skillful update on South Berkshire. More than ordinary thanks to our editors at Countryman: to Helen Whybrow for her unstinting support; to Ann Kraybill for her patient editing; to Doris Troy for copyediting that was actually much more; and to Cristen Brooks for her help with Worcester as well as with production.

What's Where in Massachusetts Beyond Boston and Cape Cod

AGRICULTURAL FAIRS

An up-to-date list of fairs is available from the **Massachusetts Department of Food and Agriculture** (617-727-3018). The Hardwick, Topsfield, and Three-

County (Northampton) fairs all claim to be the oldest. There are a number of genuine, old-style fairs with ox pulls and livestock judging. Our favorites include those held in Middlefield and Cummington. The Eastern States Exposition, held every September in West Springfield, is in a class by itself, a six-state event with thousands of animals competing for prizes along with a midway, concessions stand, big-name entertainment, and the Avenue of States. The MDFA also publishes a seasonal Farm-City Calendar that's well worth requesting.

AIRPORTS

There are 50 public airports and seaplane bases in the state. The **Massachusetts Aeronautics Commission** (617-973-8881) in Boston is currently compiling a database that will include anything you can possibly think of asking about. Scenic rides are currently available (see descriptions within the chapters) in Newburyport, Barre, Orange, and Great Barrington.

AMUSEMENT PARKS

Unfortunately, almost all the state's amusement parks (all founded in the late 19th century by trolley companies as an inducement to ride the cars out to the end of the line) have bitten the dust. The only survivors are **Riverside Park** near Springfield—the state's largest—**Whalom Park** in Lunenburg (see "The Nashoba Valley and Central Uplands"), and small but very special **Salem Willows,** with its antique carousel, in Salem. There is also always the boardwalk in **Salisbury Beach** (see "Newburyport Area").

ANIMALS

New England's largest collection of animals is caged at Southwick's **Wild Animal Farm,** down a back road in Mendon (see "Blackstone River Valley"). New Bedford and Springfield both have respectable small city zoos, and Worcester's **New England Science Center** features two (mother and daughter) polar bears. Also see the **Buttonwood Zoo** in New Bedford, **Forest Park** in Springfield, and in Ipswich **New England Alive** and **Wolf Hollow**. Many farms are now appealing to younger children with their barnyard petting areas. Check out **Davis' Farmland/Family Farm Adventure** in Sterling, **Smolak Farms** in North Andover, and **McCray's Country Creamery** in South Hadley.

ANTIQUES

The **Brimfield Outdoor Antiques Show,** New England's largest antiques show, is held in the Sturbridge-area town of Brimfield three times per year: May, July, and September. More than 4000 dealers set

up shop in the open meadows on both sides of Route 20, drawing patrons from throughout the country. The best-known antiques centers in the state are in **Essex** on the North Shore and in and around **Sheffield** in the Berkshires' South County. **The Berkshire County Antiques Dealers Association** (PO Box 594, Great Barrington, 01230) publishes its own guide to member shops.

ANTIQUARIAN BOOKSELLERS

For a descriptive listing of the 165 members of the Massachusetts and Rhode Island Antiquarian Booksellers (MARIAB), write

them at PO Box 1324, Springfield, 01101, or check their Web site at: www.tiac.net/users/mariab.

APPALACHIAN MOUNTAIN CLUB (AMC)

Founded in 1876 and better known for its extensive presence in New Hampshire's White Mountains, the Appalachian Mountain Club (617-512-0636; 5 Joy Street, Boston) not only is based in Boston but also maintains **Bascom Lodge** on top of Mount Greylock (see "North Berkshire"). It offers a variety of workshop, family, and outdoor programs in the Berkshires.

APPLES

Contact the **Massachusetts Department of Food and Agriculture** (617-727-3018) for the *Pick-Your-Own Apples* guide. Note that there are three prime orchard areas in the state: the Nashoba Valley, the Sturbridge area, and the Hampshire Hilltown/Mohawk Trail country towns.

AREA CODES

No fewer than five area codes now apply in Massachusetts. Western Massachusetts is **413** but around Quabbin Reservoir the pattern begins to get complicated. The North of Quabbin towns, Central Uplands, Nashoba Valley, and North Shore towns (all but Marblehead) are **978.** Marblehead and a semicircle of towns around Boston—including Duxbury and Pembroke on the South Shore—are **781.** The remainder of the state—from the Sturbridge/Brimfield area east to the island of Cuttyhunk—is **508.** Greater Boston itself is **617.**

ART MUSEUMS

Williamstown is a pilgrimage point for art lovers from around the world. The **Sterling and Francine Clark Art Institute** has an exceptional collection of French Impressionists and late-19th-century American artists, a collection that the **Williams College Art Museum** complements with its American pieces and wealth of works by Maurice Prendergast. The **Worcester Art Museum** also has superb 19th-century American paintings, and in Springfield both the **Museum of Fine Arts** and the **George Walter Vincent Smith Art Museum** are well worth visiting. In the Five College area, the **Mount Holyoke College**, **Amherst College**, and (especially) **Smith College** museums all hold surprises. The **Berkshire Museum** in Pittsfield also has its share of American masterpieces, and the new **Norman Rockwell Museum** in West Stockbridge probably draws the biggest crowds of all. In the Nashoba Valley, **Fruitlands Museums** have among their exhibits American primitives and landscapes; the **Addison Gallery of American Art** in Andover is yet another trove of Copleys, Sargents, and Whistlers (but displays vary, so check). The **Fitchburg Art Museum** has an interesting collection of American paintings, as well as special exhibits. The recently expanded **Cape Ann Historical Association** is perhaps the state's most underappreciated art trove, with local scenes painted by Prendergast, Homer, John Sloan, Milton Avery, and other prominent American Impressionist artists as well as a splendid collection of marine paintings by Gloucester artist Fitz Hugh Lane.

BALLOONING
The Balloon School of Massachusetts in Brimfield, **Balloon Adventures** of New Bedford, and **Paul Sena** in Worthington all offer rides. See descriptions of each within their towns' respective chapters.

BASKETBALL
The **Basketball Hall of Fame** in Springfield, where the game was invented, celebrates it in a variety of ways.

BEACHES
In this book we have listed most of those strands to which public access is clear. On the saltwater side check out **Crane Beach** in Ipswich, **Singing Beach** in Manchester, **Duxbury Beach** (described in "Plymouth"), and both **Horseneck Beach** and **Demarest Lloyd** in Bristol County. Our pick of the freshwater strands is **Wallum Lake** in Douglas (see "Blackstone River Valley").

BED & BREAKFASTS
A B&B used to be just a private home in which guests paid to stay and to breakfast. The definition has broadened in recent years to include farms and fairly elaborate and formal lodging places that resemble inns but do not serve dinner. Happily, B&Bs are now widely scattered throughout the state and, especially in less touristed areas, remain reasonably priced. Many are run by longtime residents who are knowledgeable about the surrounding area and delighted to orient their guests. Our lodging focus in this book is on B&Bs because motels and motor inns are well covered in the **AAA** and **Mobil Guides.** In the process of updating this edition, we once more visited hundreds of B&Bs. We do not charge for listings in this book and include only those that we would like to stay in ourselves. We should also note that the bed & breakfast reservation service **Berkshire Bed & Breakfast Homes** (413-268-7244), based in Williamsburg, is a handy way to book more than 100 B&Bs throughout the state. Owner Eleanor Hebert also personally checks out all the facilities she represents.

BICYCLING
We have noted rentals and outstanding bike routes in most sections. The 8½-mile **Norwottuck Rail Trail** between Northampton and Amherst is a popular bike path, and it's possible to come from New York City to Amherst on AMTRAK's *Vermonter* (which carries bikes) and pedal off to a B&B

in either town. A glossy **Massachusetts Bicycle Guide** pamphlet available from the **Massachusetts Office of Travel and Tourism** (1-800-227-MASS) lists state forests with bicycle facilities. For questions about the 22-mile **Southern New England Trunkline Trail,** evolving along a defunct railbed between Franklin and Uxbridge, phone the **Bikeway Coordinator** (617-727-3180, ext. 470). In the southeastern corner of the state, shore roads in the towns of Dartmouth and Westport are also popular with bicyclists. Cyclists should secure copies of the **Rubel Bike Maps,** which are published for both eastern and western Massachusetts and are available in most bike stores ($4.25 each) and from PO Box 1035, Cambridge 02140. New in 1997, these maps finally supply the kind of detailed information that both touring and mountain cyclists really need. The Massachusetts map in the **Topaz Outdoor Travel Maps** series is also useful (see *Maps*).

BIRDING

The **Massachusetts Audubon Society,** headquartered in Lincoln (781-259-9500) and founded in 1896 to discourage the use of wild bird plumage as hat decorations, is the oldest of the country's Audubon groups. Massachusetts Audubon also pioneered the idea of wildlife sanctuaries. While the concept of conserving land was nothing new, the use of an estate in Sharon to encourage and interpret wildlife was so novel in 1920 that it attracted a large number of foreign visitors. Massachusetts Audubon presently maintains 34 wildlife sanctuaries, including 16 staffed "nature centers." It also owns and/or manages more than twice that many properties, a total of more than 24,000 acres, making it the largest private conservation organization in New England. Sanctuaries described in this guide are found in Ipswich,

Marblehead, Princeton, Easthampton, Barre, Shelburne, Pittsfield, and Lenox; request a pamphlet guide. Perhaps the most famous birding spot in the state is **Plum Island** in Newburyport, the proposed site of Massachusetts Audubon's biggest visitors center. The prime eagle-watching spot is from **Quabbin Park** in Belchertown. Hawk-watching is also a popular September pastime in the Pioneer River Valley and from the top of Mount Wachusett.

BOAT EXCURSIONS

Harbor tours are available in Gloucester, Newburyport, Salem, and Plymouth. Ferries sail from Plymouth (to Provincetown) and New Bedford (both to Martha's Vineyard and to Cuttyhunk), from Gloucester to Martha's Vineyard, and from Boston to

Gloucester. Day sails on vintage and classic sailing vessels are also increasing, notably out of Gloucester. You can also tour the canals and Merrimack River in Lowell and cruise a reach of the Connecticut from Northfield Mountain, the Merrimack River (see "Newburyport"), and the Essex marshes. (Also see *Whale-Watching* and *Fishing.*)

BOAT LAUNCHES

Sites are detailed in brochures on salt- and freshwater fishing available from the **Massachusetts Division of Fisheries and Wildlife** (617-727-1843), 100 Cambridge Street, Boston 02202.

BUS SERVICE

Bonanza Bus (1-800-556-3815) runs from Boston to Fall River. **Greyhound Bus Lines** (1-800-231-2222) serves Worcester and Springfield out of Boston. **Peter Pan Bus Lines** (1-800-237-8747) connects Boston with Worcester, Springfield, Holyoke, Northampton, Amherst, Lee, Lenox, and Pittsfield. **Plymouth and Brockton Bus Lines** (508-746-0378) connects Boston with Plymouth.

CAMPING

The **Department of Environmental Management** (DEM; 617-727-3180) lists state camping areas in its *Massachusetts Forests and Parks Recreational Activities* brochure. Call or write to the DEM at 100 Cambridge Street, Boston 02202. You can now reserve campsites at eight of the public campgrounds described in this book. They are the **DAR State Forest** in Goshen (413-268-7098); **Mohawk Trail State Park** in Charlemont (413-339-5504); **Savoy Mountain State Park** in Savoy (413-663-8469); **Tolland State Forest** in East Otis (413-269-6002); **Lake Dennison State Recreation Area** in Baldwinville (508-939-5960); **Wells State Park** in Sturbridge (508-347-9257); **Salisbury Beach State Reservation** in Salisbury (978-462-4481); and **Harold Parker State Forest** in North Andover (978-686-3391). Campsite reservations can be made as much as 6 months prior to arrival for stays of 7 consecutive days or longer; for fewer than 7 days, they can be made as much as 3 months in advance. The cost of the reservation is a deposit equal to 2 nights.

A *Massachusetts Campground Directory* to commercial campgrounds is available from the **Massachusetts Association of Campground Owners** (617-544-3475).

CANALS

The country's first canal was supposedly built in South Hadley in 1794 (scant trace remains). The country's first major canal was the **Middlesex,** built to connect Boston and Lowell and opened in 1808. The **Blackstone Canal,** which once connected Worcester and Providence, Rhode Island, is now evolving into a linear park (see "Blackstone River Valley"). The **Farmington Canal,** which ran from Northampton through Westfield and Southwick on its way to New Haven, is still visible in parts. In Holyoke and Lowell, power canals have become important parts of Heritage State Parks; in **Turners Falls** both power and transportation canals are still visible.

CANOEING

The canoe is making a comeback. Early in this century it was a common sight on Massachusetts rivers, and within the last decade canoe lessons and rentals have proliferated. We detail specific canoe routes and rentals for the Ipswich, the Blackstone, and the Housatonic Rivers; they're also noted in "The Nashoba Valley and Central Uplands."

CHILDREN, ESPECIALLY FOR

Children's museums are found in Dartmouth and Holyoke. Within this book we describe attractions such as amusement areas, waterslides, and mini-golf under the heading *For Families.* Note our ✐ sign, indicating child-friendly lodging, dining, and attractions.

CHRISTMAS TREES

The **Massachusetts Department of Food and Agriculture** (617-727-3018), 100 Cambridge Street, Boston 02202, supplies a list of farms at which you can cut your own.

COVERED BRIDGES

See Charlemont, Colrain, Conway, Greenfield, Pepperell (Groton Street, over the Nashua River), Sheffield, and Old Sturbridge Village for examples.

CRAFTS

The country's largest concentration of craftspeople is reportedly in the Five College area and the hills just to the west. **Northampton's Main Street** showcases much of their work, as does **Salmon Falls Artisans** in Shelburne Falls. The region's

outstanding crafts fairs are the **Paradise City Arts Festival** held Columbus Day weekend at the Three-County Fairground in Northampton and the **Deerfield Crafts Fairs** showcasing traditional crafts in June and September at Memorial Hall in Old Deerfield.

CRANBERRIES

The Pilgrims called these berries, introduced to them by the Native Americans, "crane berries," since the pink blossoms reminded them of the heads of cranes. Harvesting in Plymouth County gets under way in late September and is especially colorful when the bog is flooded, making billions of berries bob to the surface. The **Cranberry World Visitors Center** in Plymouth presents the history of the industry and serves as an information source about annual harvest events (early October).

FACTORY OUTLETS

Fall River and nearby New Bedford in southeastern Massachusetts pride themselves on inventing the factory outlet, at least in this region. With the proliferation of outlet malls—such as the **Worcester Common Fashion Outlet Mall** in downtown Worcester and the **Berkshire Outlet Village** in Lee—their appeal has somewhat lessened, but they still represent outstanding values, especially the **VF Outlets** (admittedly, part of a national chain) in Dartmouth (right off I-195) and the **Tower Mill Complex** in Fall River.

FALL FOLIAGE FESTIVALS

The most colorful fall festivals in the state (ranking right up there with the most colorful in all of New England) are the **Conway Festival of the Hills** and the **Fall Foliage Festival** in Ashfield on Columbus Day weekend (see "West County/Mohawk Trail").

FARMER'S MARKETS AND FARM STANDS

Lists for both are available from the **Department of Food and Agriculture** (617-727-3018).

FARMS

"Agritourism" is big in Massachusetts. A number of farms scattered from the Nashoba Valley through central Massachusetts—and concentrated most densely in the Hilltowns—offer bed & breakfast. A few more offer cottage rentals on their property. Many more farms have pick-your-own (apples, strawberries, blueberries, for example), depending on the season; still others invite you in to watch them milk. A couple sell their own goat cheese, and one (see "Cape Ann Region") makes its own wine, as well as offering just about everything else you can think of. Farms in South Hadley, Sterling, and North Andover feature petting zoos. A visit

to a farm invariably gets you off the main drag and into beautiful countryside you might otherwise not find. Request a *Massachusetts Down on the Farm Directory* and a *Massachusetts Blueberry/Raspberry Pick-Your-Own Farms* directory from the **Department of Food and Agriculture** (617-727-3018). However, unquestionably the best and most widely available map/guide to Massachusetts farms we've seen is *Farms in Thirteen Towns of Hampshire and Franklin Counties.* No less than 60 farms are mapped and described in this area that still supports 1046 farms totaling 127,00 acres.

FISHING
Freshwater fishing options range from mountain streams in the Berkshires and Hilltowns to the wide Connecticut and Merrimack Rivers. In all there are more than 28,000 stocked lakes, ponds, and reservoirs in the state. For a listing of stocked fishing sites, best bets, and areas with handicapped access, call 1-800-ASK-FISH (275-3474). Also check *Fishing* under each of the chapters in this guide. For pond listings and maps, send a self-addressed, stamped envelope to the Information and Education Section, Division of Fisheries and Wildlife, Field HQ, Westborough 01581, or call 508-792-7270. For deep-sea fishing charters and party boats, check *Boating* and *Fishing* in the "North Shore" chapter and "South of Boston" section.

GOLF
More than 200 golf courses in Massachusetts welcome visitors. We have listed golf courses under *To Do* in each chapter.

GUIDANCE
Phone the Boston-based **Massachusetts Office of Travel and Tourism** (MOTT; 617-727-3201) to access a recorded events line ("Great Dates in the Bay State") and to request information about free publications; for a copy of the free *Massachusetts Getaway Guide* phone 1-800-447-6277. MOTT's Web site is: www.mass/vacation.com.

HERITAGE STATE PARKS
Conceived and executed by the Department of Environmental Management (DEM) as a way of revitalizing old industrial areas, each "park" revolves around a visitors center in which multivisual exhibits dramatize what makes the community special. Though they have served as prototypes for similar parks

throughout the country, the six Heritage State Parks within the scope of this book have all suffered severe financial cutbacks under recent administrations. Only the **Holyoke** and **Lawrence** parks seems to have rallied enough local volunteer support to continue operating as envisioned. The film in the **Fall River** park remains the most compelling. But be sure to visit the exhibits at the **Western Gateway Heritage State Park** in North Adams, the **Gardner Heritage State Park,** and the **Riverbend Farm Visitors Center** at the **Canal Heritage State Park** in Uxbridge. All are detailed within their respective chapters.

HIKING AND WALKING

The Department of Environmental Management (DEM) maintains thousands of miles of hiking trails in more than 100 state parks and preserves within the scope of this book. Trails worth special note include the **Midstate Trail,** traversing ridges that run much of the way from Ashby on the New Hampshire line, over Mount Wachusett, and on down to the Connecticut line; and the section of the **Appalachian Trail** that winds 90 miles through Berkshire County. The **Taconic Skyline Trail,** originally blazed by the Civilian Conservation Corps (CCC) in the 1930s, offers many spectacular views along its 21-mile route, also in the Berkshires. Another dramatic, but not easy, hike follows the ridgeline of the east–west Holyoke Range (accessible from the state-run Notch Visitors Center in Granby). Elsewhere in the Five College area, the Amherst Conservation Commission maintains some 45 miles of walking and hiking trails. Many miles of trails are maintained by the **Essex County Greenbelt Association** on the North Shore and throughout the state by the **Trustees of Reservations**. Within this book dozens of walks are suggested in each chapter (see *Hiking* and *Green Space*). The

bible for hiking throughout the state is the Appalachian Mountain Club's *Massachusetts and Rhode Island Trail Guide,* which appeared in its seventh edition in 1995. *Fifty Hikes in Massachusetts,* by John Brady and Brian White (Backcountry Publications), is also a nicely written guide to trails throughout the state.

HORSEBACK RIDING

Over the past decade a number of Massachusetts livery stables have closed or limited themselves to lessons and clinics. See "The Nashoba Valley and Central Uplands," "Old Sturbridge Village/Brimfield Area," "South and Central Berkshire," and "North Berkshire" for operating stables.

HOSTELING

The American hosteling movement began in Northfield, where there is still a summer hostel, in 1934. Although geared to bicyclists, hostels are not limited to serving them. For a mapped guide to New England hostels send a stamped, self-addressed envelope to the Greater Boston Council, AYH, 1020 Commonwealth Avenue, Boston 02215 (617-731-5430 or 617-731-6692 weekdays). Also see "The Nashoba Valley and Central Uplands."

HUNTING

The source for information about licenses, rules, and wildlife management areas is the **Massachusetts Division of Fisheries and Wildlife** (617-727-3151), 100 Cambridge Street, Boston 02202. Request the current "Abstracts" and a list of the division's wildlife management areas.

LIGHTHOUSES

The Bay State boasts at least two dozen light houses between Newburyport and Gay Head. Eleven fall within the purview of this guide. Look for them in Newburyport,

Annisquam (Gloucester), Cape Ann (two on Thachers Island), Salem, Beverly, Marblehead, and Mattapoisett. Check with the **Lighthouse Preservation Society** (1-800-727-BEAM), based in Rockport, for details.

LAKES

The state's largest lake is the human-made **Quabbin Reservoir,** offering fine fishing; **Wachusett Reservoir,** the next largest, is also artificially constructed and also good for fishing. The largest lake with public swimming is Lake Chargoggagomanchauggagogchaubunagungamaug in Webster; unfortunately, it is not in this book because it falls between the Blackstone Valley and the Old Sturbridge Village area, but it is very much there, complete with bathhouse. Other lakes with public access have been described in each chapter.

MAPLE SUGARING

Native Americans reportedly taught this industry to early settlers in Tyringham (South Berkshire) in the early 18th century. Sugaring is thriving today, primarily in the Hilltowns, an area with more sugarhouses than the rest of the state put together. During sugaring season in March, visitors are welcome to watch producers "boil off" the sap, reducing it to the sweet liquid that is traditionally sampled on ice or snow. The *Massachusetts Maple Producers Directory*, listing dozens of sugarhouses that welcome visitors when they are "boiling" in March and that cater to customers year-round, is available from the **Massachusetts Maple Producers Association** (413-628-3912), Watson–Spruce Corner Road, Ashfield 01330.

MAPS

Most of the Massachusetts this book explores has been backroaded by the limited access highways—the Massachusetts Turnpike, I-95, I-91, and 495—and the free state road map available at this writing is of limited use. In this edition we have made a special effort to provide detailed maps to the areas that merit them, striving for accuracy both in the way back roads run and in the extensive amount of open space accessible to visitors (within each chapter we detail it under Green Space). We recommend, however, that readers secure copies of three extremely helpful maps, published for the first time in 1997. The Massachusetts edition of **Topaz Travel Maps** ($8.95) is a real beauty, printed on waterproof paper and furnishing the kind of topographical information not found elsewhere. In addition, it provides a clear, full-color rendition of highways and byways, hiking and bicycle trails, and green space. For bicyclists we also recommend the more detailed **Rubel Bicycle and Road Maps,** both to eastern and western Massachusetts (see *Bicycling*).

MASSACHUSETTS TURNPIKE

It's impossible to explore much of Massachusetts without encountering the "Mass. Pike" (I-90). Completed in 1965, this superhighway cuts as straight as an arrow 123 miles across the state from Boston to the New York line, with just 25 exits, 14 of them east of I-495. Unlike other Massachusetts roadways, the turnpike receives no state or federal money and charges accordingly. At this writing, the toll is $3.10 from the Newton tolls in the east to Springfield and points west. In 1997 tolls west of Springfield were eliminated. It was the first road in Massachusetts on which you can officially drive 65 miles per hour (between Auburn and Ludlow and again between Westfield and the New York line). Eleven service centers (most with fast-food restaurants) are scattered along the route, and four of these include information desks. They are located near the intersection with I-84 in Charlton (eastbound 508-248-4581; westbound 508-248-3853); in Lee (413-243-4929); and in Natick (508-650-3698).

MOUNTAINS

Mount Greylock is the state's highest, and you can get to the top (3491 feet) by car. You can also drive up **Mount Everett** ("South and Central Berkshire"), **Mount Wachusett** ("The Nashoba Valley and Central Uplands"), **Mount Sugarloaf**, **Mount Tom,** and **Mount Holyoke** (all in "Upper Pioneer Valley: Five College Area"). All these offer hiking trails, as do **Mount Toby** ("The Pioneer Valley: Greenfield/Deerfield Area") and **Mount Grace** ("Quabbin Area"). For some dramatic ridge trails, see *Hiking*. Note that you can stay on top of Mount Greylock (see "North Berkshire"—*Lodging*).

MUSEUM VILLAGES

Old Sturbridge Village in Sturbridge recreates New England rural life in the 1790s–1830s. It is one of New England's biggest tourist attractions and has spawned thousands of adjacent "beds," dozens of shops, restaurants, and some smaller museums in town. **Plimoth Plantation** in Plymouth is a smaller but equally painstaking reconstruction of the Pilgrim village. **Hancock Shaker Village** is a restored Shaker complex in Central Berkshire, and **Historic Deerfield** near Greenfield preserves more than a dozen 18th- and 19th-century homes. In West Springfield, **Storrowton** is small but represents one of the country's earliest recreated villages; **Greenfield Village,** just west of Greenfield on Route 2, is one man's collection, housed in a building he constructed himself.

MUSIC

Music festivals are a growing phenomenon.

The oldest (since 1858) is the **Worcester County Music Association Festival** in October. The best known is the **Tanglewood Music Festival** during July and August in Lenox. Other summer series of note include the **Aston Magna Festival** in Great Barrington, the **Berkshire Choral Festival** in Sheffield, the **Sevenars** concerts in South Worthington, the **Mohawk Trail Concerts** in Charlemont, the **Castle Island Festival** in Ipswich, and the popular series of **organ concerts** at Hammond Castle, in Gloucester, and in the Methuen Memorial Music Hall.

PICK-YOUR-OWN

Listings of places where you can pick your own apples, blueberries, and strawberries are available from the **Massachusetts Department of Food and Agriculture** (617-727-3018), 100 Cambridge Street, Boston 02202.

KIMBERLY GRANT

RAIL SERVICE AND EXCURSIONS

The **Massachusetts Bay Transportation Authority** (MBTA; 617-722-3200) offers daily commuter service north to Salem, Gloucester, Rockport, and Ipswich, and west to Fitchburg and Worcester. **AMTRAK**'s (1-800-USA-RAIL) *Lake Shore Limited* from Boston to Chicago stops in Springfield and in Pittsfield every evening (departing Boston at 4:20, arriving in Springfield at 6:35); reservations are required. The **Mystic Valley Railway Society** (617-361-4445) runs a variety of excursions throughout New England every year. The **Providence and Worcester Railroad** (508-799-4000) runs occasional excursions over the line on which it hauls freight on weekdays, and the **Berkshire Scenic Railway** (413-637-2210) offers short, narrated train rides from the grounds of its Lenox railroading museum.

ROOM TAX

In contrast to most states, which impose one state tax throughout, Massachusetts has given local communities the option of adding an extra 4 percent—theoretically for local promotion—to the basic 5.7 percent room tax. Although resort towns tend to add the extra 4 percent, there is no hard-and-fast rule: Salem does, while neighboring Rockport doesn't; Great Barrington does, and neighboring Egremont doesn't. It's worth asking. It's also worth noting that B&Bs with only two or three rooms are exempt from room tax.

SAILING

For sailing lessons and rentals, see "Salem and Marblehead Area" and "Cape Ann Region."

SCENIC DRIVES

Acknowledging that Massachusetts can boast some of both the most beautiful and the most boring roads in New England, we have made a special effort in this edition to detail specific routes that we know and love. Look for these especially in "Southeastern Massachusetts," "The Nashoba Valley and Central Uplands," "Quabbin Area," "Upper Pioneer Valley," and "The Berkshire Hilltowns."

SEA KAYAKING

Several outfitters are described in the "Cape Ann Region." Also see "Southeastern Mas-

sachusetts." Kayakers might also be interested in the lessons offered by the **Berkshire Sculling Association** based in Pittsfield ("South and Central Berkshire") and the "funyaks" at **Crab Apple White Water** in Charlemont (see "Hampshire Hills").

SKIING, CROSS-COUNTRY

A couple of dozen years ago the Finns of Fitchburg were about the only Bay Staters skiing through the Massachusetts woods. There are currently more than a dozen commercial touring centers and hundreds of miles of marked cross-country trails in the state. Trails are noted throughout the book under *Cross-Country Skiing* and *Green Space*. The state's most dependable snow conditions are found in the western Massachusetts snowbelt, which runs north–south through Stump Sprouts (a lodge and touring center) in East Hawley; the Windsor Notch Reservation in Windsor; and Hickory Hill Ski Touring Center in Worthington.

SKIING, DOWNHILL

A *Ski Massachusetts* brochure is available from the **Massachusetts Division of Tourism** (617-727-3201), 100 Cambridge Street, Boston 02202. Within this book we have described each area. In the Berkshires there are Jiminy Peak, Brodie, Bousquet, Catamount, Butternut Basin, and Otis Ridge.

There's also Berkshire East in Charlemont, Mount Tom in Holyoke, and Mount Wachusett in Princeton.

THE SOCIETY FOR THE PRESERVATION OF NEW ENGLAND ANTIQUITIES (SPNEA)

Founded in 1910 to protect New England's cultural and architectural heritage, SPNEA maintains four properties described in this

KIMBERLY GRANT

book, two of which—**Beauport** in Gloucester and the **Spencer-Pierce-Little Farm** in Newbury—are as spectacular as historic houses can be. **Cogswell's Grant,** an 18th-century house set in 125 Essex acres, opens in 1998. For a copy of the *Visitors Guide* to all SPNEA house museums in five states and a list of current events, phone 617-227-3956.

SPAS

Lenox is the spa capital of New England. Admittedly, there are relatively few spas in New England, and only one of the two major facilities in Lenox **(Canyon Ranch)** is technically a spa. The second, the **Kripalu Center for Yoga and Health** is, however, also a mainstream mecca for thousands seeking physical and mental renewal. The staff requirements of both of these centers have drawn a large number of both New Age and traditional fitness practitioners to the area; several have opened small day spas catering to patrons of the many local inns, a situation worth noting, especially in winter and spring, when inn prices drop well below Tanglewood-season rates.

STATE FORESTS AND PARKS

Would you believe that Massachusetts has the eighth largest state park system in the country? The Department of Environmental Management (DEM) is responsible for more than a quarter of a million acres of public forests and parks. It's the largest single landholder in the state. The system began in 1898 with the gift of 8000 acres around Mount Greylock; in 1915 the DEM acquired the Otter River State Forest in Winchendon. Initially its mandate was to purchase logged-over, virtually abandoned land for $5 per acre, and during the Depression the Civilian Conservation Corps (CCC) greatly expanded the facilities (building roads, trails, lakes, and other recreation areas). The DEM continues to expand and diversify its holdings. This book describes roughly 100 forests, parks, and reservations under *Green Space,* suggesting opportunities for camping, canoeing, swimming, skiing downhill (at Mount Wachusett and Butternut) and cross-country, rock climbing, and hang gliding—not to mention hiking. *The Massachusetts Forest and Park Map/ Guide* is a cryptic but indispensable key to this vast system, available, along with an excellent pamphlet guide, *Massachusetts Historic State Parks,* from the DEM (617-727-3180, ext. 482), 100 Cambridge Street, Boston 02202. For specific information, it's best to contact the regional offices: in the Berkshires, 413-442-8928; for the Connecticut River Valley, 413-545-5993; for the central region, 978-368-0126; for the northeast, 617-369-3350; and for the southeast, 508-866-2580.

THEATER

Summer theaters are described in Beverly ("The North Shore"), Stockbridge ("South and Central Berkshire"), Williamstown ("North Berkshire"), South Hadley ("Upper Pioneer Valley"), Gardner and Fitchburg ("The Nashoba Valley and Central Uplands"), and Greenfield ("The Pioneer Valley"). **StageWest** in West Springfield is a year-round theater company, and the **Little Theater** of Chester offers small but superb off-Broadway drama.

TRACKING

With or without snowshoes, tracking is proving to be a new way into the woods year-round for many people. The idea is to track animals for purposes other than hunting. The tracking guru in Massachusetts is naturalist/photographer **Paul Rezendes** (978-249-8810), who offers workshops and guided tours in the Quabbin area. **Massachusetts Audubon Sanctuaries** (see *Birding*) throughout the state also now offer tracking programs.

TRUSTEES OF RESERVATIONS

A nonprofit organization founded in 1891 to preserve the public use and enjoyment of historic places and beautiful tracts of land, the Trustees of Reservations now owns and manages more than 40 properties described in this book. Several of these are beautifully maintained historic houses (in Stockbridge, New Ashford, and Cummington), but most are exceptional pieces of land, several of which include waterfalls. Check under *Green Space* throughout the book; details about properties and special events are available from the Trustees of Reservations (508-921-1944), 572 Essex Street, Beverly 01915.

VINEYARDS

The number and quality of Massachusetts wineries have increased substantially in the past decade; we have described them in Ashburnham, Bolton, Colrain, Ipswich, Raynham, Westport, and West Dudley. **Westport Rivers Winery** is New England's largest vinifera grape vineyard and continues to garner national awards for its white and sparking wines.

WATERFALLS

Someone should make a poster of Massachusetts waterfalls not only because there are so many, but also because most are so little known and varied. We have visited and described them all. Check out Ashfield, Barre, Becket, Blandford, Cheshire, Chesterfield, Dalton, Middlefield, Mount Washington, New Marlboro, North Adams, Royalston, Sheffield, Shelburne Falls, Williamsburg, and Worthington.

WHALE-WATCHING

More than a dozen major whalewatching operators now offer thousands of trips spring through fall to watch the whales that congregate to feed on **Stellwagen Bank,** a dozen miles off Cape Ann. Check the listings for Newburyport, Cape Ann, and Plymouth. If you are inclined to seasickness, Dramamine is very helpful; you might also opt for a larger, newer boat. Be sure to bring a sweater and windbreaker on even a hot day. For many landlubbers these excursions are their first encounter with a small boat on the open sea.

WHITE-WATER RAFTING

Since 1989, when New England Electric began releasing water on a regular basis from its Fife Brook Dam, white-water rafting has become a well-established pastime on the Deerfield River. **Zoar Outdoor** in Charlemont pioneered the sport in this area and offers lodging and a variety of programs. Maine-based **Crab Apple** now has its own attractive base on the river (down the road): stiff competition.

I. NORTH OF BOSTON

The North Shore
The Merrimack Valley

KIMBERLY GRANT

Annisquam lighthouse

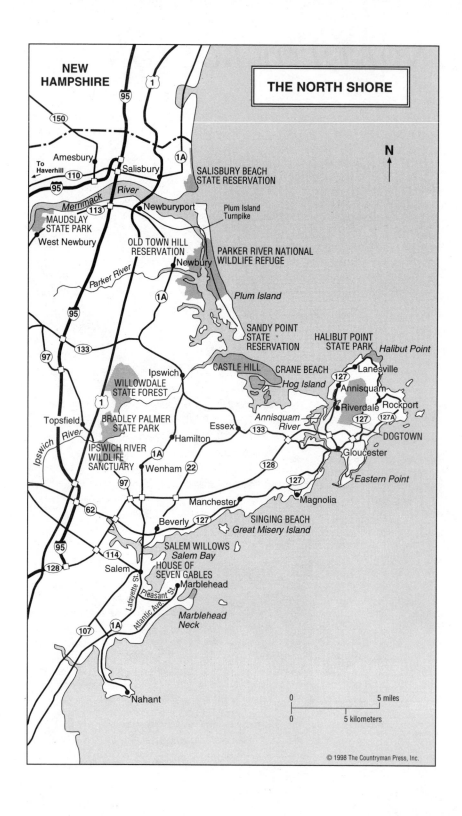

NEW HAMPSHIRE

THE NORTH SHORE

N

95
1
150
To Haverhill
Amesbury
110
95
Salisbury
1A
SALISBURY BEACH STATE RESERVATION
Merrimack River
113
Newburyport
Plum Island Turnpike
MAUDSLAY STATE PARK
West Newbury
OLD TOWN HILL RESERVATION
Parker River
Newbury
PARKER RIVER NATIONAL WILDLIFE REFUGE
1A
95
Plum Island
133
SANDY POINT STATE RESERVATION
HALIBUT POINT STATE PARK
Halibut Point
97
Ipswich
CASTLE HILL
CRANE BEACH
Lanesville
127
WILLOWDALE STATE FOREST
Hog Island
Annisquam
1
Riverdale
Rockport
Topsfield
BRADLEY PALMER STATE PARK
Annisquam River
127
127A
Ipswich River
Essex
133
DOGTOWN
IPSWICH RIVER WILDLIFE SANCTUARY
Hamilton
1A
Gloucester
Wenham
22
128
Eastern Point
97
127
Manchester
Magnolia
62
Beverly
127
SINGING BEACH
Great Misery Island
95
SALEM WILLOWS
Salem Bay
114
HOUSE OF SEVEN GABLES
128
Salem
Marblehead
Lafayette St.
Pleasant St.
Atlantic Ave.
107
1A
Marblehead Neck

Nahant

0   5 miles
0   5 kilometers

© 1998 The Countryman Press, Inc.

The North Shore

For touring purposes, Boston's North Shore begins in Marblehead and runs 30 miles or so, tacking and jibbing around Cape Ann and along the ragged edge of Ipswich Bay to Newburyport at the mouth of the Merrimack River. Here old families, old money, and the purest of Massachusetts accents prevail.

What strikes visitors is the way old seaports remain much the way they did in their heyday—a time that varied from place to place. Ipswich, with its sheltered harbor and vast salt marshes, prospered in the 17th century and boasts the greatest number of houses from that era of any town its size in this country. In Marblehead many buildings along narrow streets were built just prior to the Revolution on profits from the Triangle Trade. Both Salem and Newburyport are distinguished by their unusual number of graceful Federal mansions built by the sea captains and merchants who pioneered trade with the Far East after the Revolution, while Gloucester's look dates from the late 19th century, an era when it ranked as one of the world's foremost fishing ports.

In the late 19th century, all of these old ports emerged as summer havens. Trains, ferries, and trolleys linked the shore to Boston. Beaching and yachting came into vogue. Blue-collar workers flocked to the boardwalks at Salisbury Beach and Salem Willows, and millionaires built summer mansions on Marblehead Neck and Gloucester's Eastern Point. Summer cottages mushroomed on Plum Island and on Little Neck in Ipswich. Hotels appeared along the length of the North Shore—from Swampscott to Salisbury. The 750-room Oceanside in Magnolia billed itself as the largest resort hotel in New England.

By the middle of this century, most of the hotels had vanished, summerhouses were winterized, and the North Shore communities, many of them connected by commuter trains and buses with Boston, were suburbanized. Cape Cod—a bit farther from home and offering more sand, warmer water—supplanted the North Shore as Boston's preferred summer spot.

Quietly, however, the North Shore is evolving again as a tourist destination, one of the most interesting in the Northeast. The area now offers many miles of public shore and woods paths, a choice of ways to kayak and canoe as well as to go whale-watching and sportfishing. Several shops now specialize in fly-fishing gear and advice, others in birding paraphernalia and information about burgeoning birding programs. Mountain bikers can find maps to many miles of wooded trails, and we can all choose from dozens of excursion boats, both with and without motors.

The area's outstanding museums—notably the Peabody Essex Museum in Salem and the Cape Ann Historical Society in Gloucester—have substantially expanded in recent years, and lodging options have proliferated with the spread of small inns and B&Bs. Rockport remains a resort town, and, as their traditional industries fade, Salem, Gloucester, and Newburyport are also turning to tourism. Bostonians haven't yet caught on. They still think of the North Shore as a place to day-trip.

GUIDANCE

The National Parks Service maintains a visitors center just off the Salem common, with a film dramatizing the history of Essex County.

The North of Boston Convention & Visitors Council (978-977-7760; 1-800-742-5306) also publishes a useful guide to the entire region.

Old Byfield Tourist Information Center. I-95 southbound at exit 55. Open daily, 9-5.

Note: Visitors centers are also listed within each specific area described here.

Salem and Marblehead Area

Although Salem and Marblehead abut, the old town centers are several miles apart, positioned on opposite sides of Salem Harbor. Both are bordered on three sides by water and pervaded by a sense of the sea.

Salem is a city of 40,000 people with fine Federal-era mansions, a very walkable downtown, and an immense, superb museum. The Peabody Essex is New England's ultimate treasure chest of exotica, all of it brought from the farthest points of the globe by Salem sea captains and "supercargoes." The Salem Maritime National Historic Site on the waterfront also recalls the era between the Revolution and the War of 1812, when Salem's merchant fleet numbered 185 proud vessels.

Oh, yes, Salem also has witches: wax witches, multimedia witches, candy witches, witch houses, and real witches. Back in 1692, Salem was the site of the infamous "witch trials," during which hundreds of men, women, and children were accused by their neighbors of practicing witchcraft.

It was actually in what is now Danvers, part of Salem at the time, that the slave Tituba captured the imagination of two adolescent girls by telling them ghost stories. The girls then accused village women of witchcraft, sparking the "Salem witch hunt." They also created a virtual industry. Today Salem's busiest season—it's been extended to three weeks of "Haunted Happenings"—is Halloween.

Half the size of Salem, Marblehead has a delightfully walkable historic district that's a tangle of crooked streets, with old houses perched like so many seabirds above the harbor. Most of the older homes are modest, clustering around the Old Town House (1727), their token gardens recalling that only fishermen, not farmers, were permitted to live downtown. Today Marblehead is still synonymous with sailing vessels, but fishermen have been upstaged by yachtsmen for more than a century—ever since the Bay State's most prestigious yacht clubs located here. Once known for its summer hotels as well as mansions, Marblehead Neck is still a great spot from which to watch the thousands of boats competing each July during Marblehead Race Week or just to sit a spell any day and smell the sea.

Beverly claims to have seen the birth of the American navy (a claim disputed by Marblehead and Whitehall, New York). It also claims

America's oldest house (disputed by Dedham) and says it put a stop to Salem's witch hysteria. The town itself was transformed in the 19th century by the shoe industry, but Prides Crossing and Beverly Farms still harbor a number of old private estates. The summertime North Shore Music Theater and the year-round magic of Le Grand David, whose troupe has restored two vintage Cabot Street theaters, draw large audiences.

AREA CODES
978 for Salem, Beverly, and Danvers; 781 for Marblehead.

GUIDANCE
National Park Visitors Center (978-740-1650), 12 Liberty Street, Salem. Open daily 9–6. This major center features a film dramatizing the history of Essex County and information for the entire region.

Salem Office of Tourism; 1-800-777-6848 is the number to call to order the area's map/guide.

Salem Chamber of Commerce (978-744-0004), Old Town Hall, 32 Derby Square. This friendly walk-in information center is open weekdays 9–5.

Marblehead Chamber of Commerce (781-631-2868), PO Box 76, Marblehead 01945. This unusually friendly office at 62 Pleasant Street is open weekdays 9–3; request copies of its guides to lodging, dining, and shopping, and the downtown walking tour. A seasonal information booth at the corner of Pleasant and Essex Streets is open from Memorial Day on weekends, and daily July through Columbus Day, 10–6.

GETTING THERE
By train: **MBTA** (617-722-3200 or 1-800-392-6100) commuter trains connect Salem with Boston's North Station.

By bus: **MBTA** (see numbers above) buses from Boston's Haymarket Square (daily, at least once every half hour).

Airport shuttle: **North Shore Shuttle** (781-631-8660) connects the Salem/ Marblehead area with Logan Airport.

By car: Marblehead is 17 miles north of Boston via Route 1A to Lynn, then Route 129 North. The alternate route from Boston to Salem is Route 128 to exit 25A (Route 114 east). Within Salem, signs lead you to the Park Service Visitors Center and downtown parking.

GETTING AROUND
The Salem Heritage Trail. A 1.7-mile red line down the center of Salem sidewalks links most of the obvious sights to see here. Begin in East India Square with the visitors center and Peabody Essex Museum and walk the short way down Hawthorne Boulevard to Derby Street and the Maritime National Historic Site. The **House of the Seven Gables** (see *Historic Houses*) is a few blocks beyond. Inquire about a printed guide to the **Samuel McIntire Trail.**

The Salem Trolley (978-744-5469) operates July through October, stopping at all the obvious tourist sites, including Salem Willows Park and the House of Seven Gables, every half hour. $8 adults, $7 seniors, $4 children

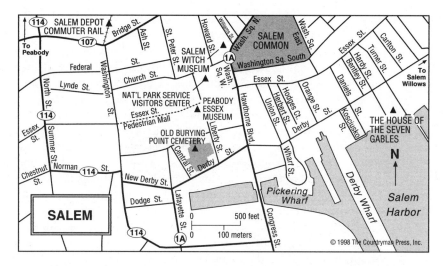

and students. Good for one entire day. You might want to take an initial hour-long tour and then use it for transportation the rest of the day.

PARKING

In Salem: The ubiquitous "P" signs lead to the municipal parking garage ($8 all day and free on weekends) adjoining the National Park Visitor's Center and Peabody Essex Museum. The Church Street lot, also free on weekends, isn't quite as central but more user friendly. Beware the town's zealous meter maids.

In Marblehead: Aside from summer weekends you can usually find curbside parking, and there are limited lots on Rockaway Street, Harris Street, Fort Sewall, and, if it's your lucky day, the Town Landing. Pick up a walking map from the chamber of commerce or information booth; shops, museums, restaurants, and parks are all within walking distance, and during the summer it's better to take a bike than a car onto Marblehead Neck; to find it, head south on Route 114 and turn left onto Ocean Avenue.

MEDICAL EMERGENCY

North Shore Medical Center (978-741-1200), 81 Highland Avenue, Salem; for ambulance: 508-744-4414.

TO SEE

In Salem

MUSEUMS

Peabody Essex Museum (978-745-9500; 1-800-745-4054), East India Square. Open Monday through Thursday and Saturday 10–5, Sunday noon–5, Friday evenings until 8. Closed major holidays. Adults $7.50, $6.50 seniors and students, $4 children ages 6–16, family rate $18. Free admission first Friday of every month, 5–8. In 1992 the Peabody Museum, one of New England's leading maritime museums and a treasure chest of exotica, and the Essex Institute—which for a century and a half stood aloof across from each other on Essex Street—finally merged. The resulting complex, spread over two city blocks and several off-campus sites, includes more than 30 galleries, a research library, 28 historic properties, four period gardens, two museum shops, and a café.

The Peabody was founded in 1799 by 22 of the city's overseas traders as the East Indian Marine Society. The idea was to share navigational information, to support the widows of those lost at sea, and "to form a museum of natural and artificial curiosities such as are to be found beyond the Cape of Good Hope and Cape Horn." Almost 200 years later the Peabody Essex Museum's collection totals more than 400,000 objects and some 3 million books, manuscripts, and works of art.

Thousands of visitors come each year from Japan and China to see priceless porcelain, silver, ivory, and the lacquered screens and exquisite furniture made in their countries during the 16th through 19th centuries (an entire Asian Export Art wing was added in 1988 when the Peabody absorbed the former Museum of the American China Trade in Milton). We are always particularly struck by the 18th- and early-19th-century paintings of the "Hongs," or trading houses in Hong Kong and Canton, and of the traders themselves. The maritime art and history department is also impressive, ranging from a horn fashioned from the penis of a sperm whale to works by artists such as Fitz Hugh Lane and Gilbert Stuart.

The natural history regional collection, with rare examples of the flora and fauna of Essex County, includes a 750-pound turtle found in Ipswich some 200 years ago and still exuding oil. The Arts of Asia and the Pacific gallery continues to delight kids with its huge, fierce (and authentic) sculptures of South Pacific gods, and the heart of the museum remains the grand, 1820s East Indian Hall, lined with ships' figureheads and the kind of old-fashioned "cabinets of curiosities" that the museum's founders envisioned.

The former Essex Institute was founded in 1848 and houses a collection of portraits, period rooms, local silver, and county archives—including the actual records of the 1692 witch trials in Salem. This era is dramatized through exhibits within the museum and, in summer months, through role playing outside the 17th-century **John Ward House,** one of several historic houses on the museum grounds. The neighboring **Gardner-Pingree House** (1804) is a 14-room mansion generally believed to represent Samuel McIntire's work at its best. (McIntire is known for the airy, four-square mansions garnished throughout with delicately carved detailing, arches, and stairways. The lineup of these homes makes Chestnut Street one of the handsomest streets in America.) The heart of this museum remains its two-story, balconied hall, containing period rooms and a wide assortment of local memorabilia. Inquire about the museum's elaborate changing exhibits and about daily guided tours. See the museum's café under *Dining Out.* The **Ropes Mansion and Garden** is open only seasonally and on a reduced schedule at this writing, but well worth inquiring about.

Salem Maritime National Historic Site (978-740-1660), 174 Derby Street. Open daily year-round 9–5. The site includes the Narbonne House (1671), a simple wooden home continuously occupied for 300 years; the brick Custom House (1819), in which Nathaniel Hawthorne worked; a Bonded Warehouse and West India Goods Store; and the brick mansion (1762) built by Elias Hasket Derby, better known as King Derby, who pioneered a new sailing route around the Cape of Good Hope and is said to have been America's first millionaire. A maritime video is shown in the visitors center at the head of Derby Wharf, which dates from 1752 and is the last of some 50 wharves that were once lined with warehouses.

HISTORIC HOUSES

⬦ **House of the Seven Gables** (978-744-0991), 54 Turner Street. Open daily for 45-minute guided tours year-round except major holidays and the last two weeks in January, 10–4:30, and July through Labor Day, 9–6. Adults $7, students $3. No one should leave Salem without a visit to this very special place, a waterside complex that includes the dark clapboard, vintage-1668 house (complete with hidden staircase and penny-candy shop) that inspired Nathaniel Hawthorne's gloomy novel. The complex also contains the house in which Hawthorne himself was born and two more 17th-century homes. A new visitors center with interactive videos and a continuous audiovisual representation, along with a snack bar and garden café, eases you into the site and the story of how it was restored as a tourist attraction back in 1910 as a way of supporting the settlement house across the street, a cause the site still benefits. $7 adults, $4 ages 6–17. Combination ticket with Salem 1630 Pioneer Village (see below) is $10 for adults, $6 for children ages 6–17.

Stephen Phillips Memorial Trust House (978-744-0440), 34 Chestnut Street. Open Memorial Day to mid-October, Monday through Saturday 10–4:30. $3 adults, $2 children under 12. The only house open to the public on Chestnut Street displays paintings, Chinese porcelain, and Oriental rugs. There is also a carriage house with antique cars and carriages.

Pickering House (978-744-1647), 18 Broad Street, Salem. Open Monday, year-round, 10–3, and by appointment. Built in 1651, it is the oldest house in America to be continually occupied by the same family. $4 adults.

⬦ **Salem 1630 Pioneer Village** (978-744-0991 or 745-0525), off Route 114 and West Avenue in Forest River Park. Open Memorial Day through October, Monday through Saturday 10–5, Sunday noon–5. Adults $4.50, $3.50 seniors, $2.50 students. The town's initial settlement was recon-

structed for the city's 300th anniversary and is now staffed by costumed interpreters. Visitors are invited to churn butter, spin wool, and play the era's games. There are barnyard animals, and ducks in the adjacent reeds.

WITCHES

Salem Witch Museum (978-744-1692), Washington Square. Open year-round, daily 10–5, until 7 in July and August. With computerized sound and light, this popular so-called museum tells the whole lurid tale of how 14 women and 5 men were executed in 1692, of the 4 who died in jail, and of the 55 more who saved their necks by accusing others. $4.50 adults, $4 seniors, $3 children ages 6–14. (Under 6 should not be admitted.)

The Witch House (978-744-0180), corner of Essex and North Streets. Open mid-March through June and September to December 1, 10–4:30; July through Labor Day, 10–6. Restored and furnished by the City of Salem in the 1930s, this 1642 building was the home of Magistrate Jonathan Corwin, a judge in the 1692 witch trials. Pretrial examinations of many of the accused were held here. $5 adults, $2 children 5–16.

The Witch Dungeon Museum (978-741-3570), 16 Lynde Street. Open May through October, 10–5. Yet another dramatization of the witch trials, this one with mannequins. $4.50 adults, $3.50 seniors, $3 children 5–12.

Salem Wax Museum & Witch Village (978-740-2929), 282–288 Derby Street. Open daily 10–5 January through April and September through November; 10–6 May and June; 10–7 July, August, and October. $6.95 adults, $4 children. The story of the witch hysteria and the 17th-century maritime community where it happened is told with wax figurines, a multimedia presentation, and hands-on exhibits.

In Marblehead

HISTORIC HOUSES AND SITES

Jeremiah Lee Mansion (781-631-1069), 161 Washington Street. Open mid-May to mid-October, Monday through Saturday 10–4, Sunday 1–4. Adults $4, $3.50 seniors and students; age 10 and under free. Lee was a shipowner who could import his own building materials: mahogany from Santo Domingo for the grand staircase and wallpaper from England. Today the striking building is headquarters for the Marblehead Historical Society, with third-floor exhibits that include bright early-20th-century primitives of Marblehead scenes by J.O.J. Frost and early-19th-century portraits by William Bartoll.

King Hooper Mansion (781-631-2608), 8 Hooper Street (diagonally across from the Lee Mansion). Open Monday through Saturday 10–4, Sunday 1–5. Free. The rare, five-story section of this remarkable house dates from 1728; the three-story, block-front facade and front rooms were added in 1745. The building now serves as headquarters for the Marblehead Arts Association. Changing exhibits are in the former third-floor ballroom.

Abbot Hall (781-631-0000) Washington Square. Open year-round, Monday, Tuesday, Thursday, and Friday 8–5; Wednesday 7:30 AM–7:30 PM;

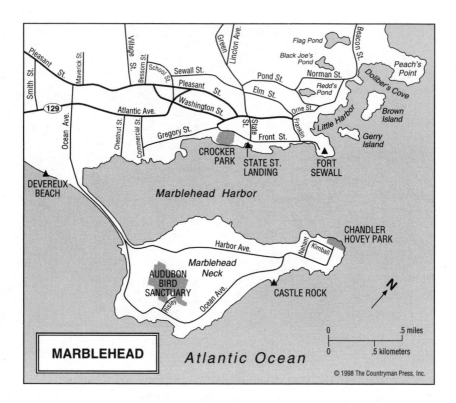

MARBLEHEAD

Saturday 9–6; and Sunday 11–6. A brick Victorian town hall that stands on the highest point of land and towers over the town. Hanging in the Selectmen's Room is the famous (and not disappointing) *Spirit of '76,* which depicts three generations of patriots: a fifer, drummer, and flag bearer. Commissioned for the 1876 centennial exposition in Philadelphia, the painting was given to the town by a Marblehead native. Other paintings in the room depict Washington being rowed across the Delaware by General Glover's "Marblehead Marines," an army unit composed of hardy local fishermen. In the lobby is the 17th-century deed to the town, complete with totem signatures of the local Native American sachems.

Old Town House, Market Square. No longer open to the public, this bright yellow building was built in 1727, designed like Boston's Faneuil Hall to house butcher and produce stalls on its ground floor, with a meeting hall on its second floor (it was here that General Glover organized his regiment). It is an unusually graceful building but compromised by the heavy granite first floor added in 1830.

The Lafayette House (privately owned) at the corner of Hooper and Union Streets is a local landmark because its lower corner was obviously cut out to make passage for carriages and wagons. According to legend, it was altered to allow the Marquis de Lafayette to pass in 1824.

Old Town House, Marblehead

In Beverly

The Beverly Historical Society (978-922-1186), 117 Cabot Street, maintains three outstanding houses, all open mid-May through mid-October, Wednesday through Saturday 10–4, Sunday 1–4. $2 adults, $.50 children; $4 adult admission to all three, $1 children. **The Balch House,** 448 Cabot Street, is a Tudor-style clapboard house built in 1636, now within sight of the mammoth United Shoe factory. It is reportedly the home of the first male born in the Massachusetts Bay Colony, and it has its own witchcraft story. **Cabot House,** 110 Cabot Street, is a handsome brick Federal home built for John Cabot, shipowner and co-founder of America's first cotton mill. There are relics here from the city's privateering and Far Eastern trade, and antique toys. The **John Hale House,** 39 Hale Street (off Route 22), was built partially in 1694 by a minister who was involved in the Salem witch trials, until his own wife was accused of being a witch; he quickly helped end the trials.

In Danvers

Rebecca Nurse Homestead (508-774-8799), 149 Pine Street. Open mid-June to September, Tuesday through Sunday 1–4; weekends through October. $4 adults, $2 children under 16. The vintage-1678 house is starkly silhouetted against its old pastureland, and Rebecca's body lies buried on the grounds, only because her family risked their own necks to retrieve it by night from Gallows Hill in Salem. The 72-year-old mother of eight stoutly refused to say that she was a witch.

TO DO

BICYCLING
Salem Cycles (978-741-2222), 316 Derby Street, Salem, rents bicycles.
BOATING
Note: For whalewatching options see "Cape Ann Region" and "Newburyport Area."
East India Cruise Company (978-741-0434), 197 Derby Street, Salem, offers seasonal harbor cruises from Pickering Wharf; also shuttle service to Marblehead and back, and 10 AM daily whalewatching cruises to Stellwagen Bank. **Coastal Sailing School** (781-639-0553), Commercial Street, Marblehead. Sailboat rentals and sailing lessons. Afternoon and evening excursions available. **Moby Duck Tours** (978-741-4386). Departs hourly 10–4 from the Visitors Center, New Liberty Street, Salem, May through Halloween. A landing craft–type vehicle provides a 55-minute tour of Salem by sea and land. $12 adults, $8 children. **Kayak Learning Center** (978-922-5322), Beverly. Summer programs at Woodbury Beach in Lynch Park (see *Swimming*) using youth kayaks and Hawaiian outrigger canoes. Six-person outriggers, with an instructor-guide, can be rented for coastal cruises. $75 for 2 hours. **Sun Line Ltd.** (978-741-1900), Salem Willows Pier, Salem. Private charters on weekends. Lunch cruises at noon $2. Afternoon tours, $7 adults, $4 children.
SWIMMING
Devereux Beach, Ocean Avenue, at the causeway to Marblehead Neck; rest rooms, covered seating, barbecue grills. $3 weekdays, $5 weekends.
Forest River Park, off Route 114 at West Avenue, Salem. Two small beaches and "the largest outdoor swimming pool in the state." City owned; nominal fee.
Lynch Park, Ober Street off Route 127, Beverly. Once part of a grand estate, this park includes two beaches as well as a grassy expanse for sunning; also a sunken rose garden, rest rooms, concession stands, picnic tables, and a great sledding hill. Band concerts in the shell Sunday evening 6–8. Parking is $5 per car on weekends, $10 weekdays.

GREEN SPACE

PARKS
✍ **Salem Willows** (978-745-0251), Salem. Follow signs out along Derby Street to Fort Avenue. This is one of New England's few surviving old-fashioned amusement areas, and it's set in a landscaped park overlooking the Beverly waterfront on one side, Salem Sound and the coast from Marblehead to Cape Ann on the other. The willows were planted in 1801

The Mall in Salem

to form a shaded walk for patients at the smallpox hospital. Note the round-roofed **Hobbs Pavilion,** still a source of burgers, popcorn, hot peanuts, taffy, and ice cream cones. (Everett Hobbs is said to have introduced the ice cream cone to New England in 1905.) The carousel in neighboring **Kiddieland** dates from the same era; the arcade and **Cappy's Fried Clams** are also local institutions.

Derby Wharf, Derby Street in front of the Customs House, Salem. The wharf itself extends some 2000 feet into Salem Harbor and, now grassed over, forms a great picnic and relaxing spot. It is now part of the Salem Maritime National Historic Park.

Winter Island Maritime Park (978-745-9430), 50 Winter Island Road, off Derby Street just before you get to Salem Willows. This is a former Coast Guard station with some fairly ugly buildings left from that chapter in its history. You'll find RV campsites, a boat launch, and beach; $2 for nonresidents, but the snack bar validates 2 hours of parking.

Crocker Park, Front Street, Marblehead. This park includes a grassy rise with a harbor view and old-fashioned stone seats, all found up beyond a house designed to look like a Viking castle. Bring a sketch pad.

PICNICKING

Old Burial Hill and Fountain Park, Pond Street, Marblehead. Gravestones surround the site of the town's 1638 meetinghouse and mark the resting places of some 600 Revolutionary War soldiers. There is a great view of the town and harbor, and you can picnic just up the way (turn right) at **Fountain Park,** the site of a Revolutionary-era fort. Below Fountain Park (access off Orne Street) is a small, sandy beach, and at low tide you can walk out to a little island. **Redd's Pond,** nearby on Norman Street, is also a place to picnic in summer and to watch skaters in winter.

WALKS

Massachusetts Wildlife Sanctuary, Marblehead Neck, Risley Road. Massachusetts Audubon maintains 15¼ acres here; the pond is used for winter skating.

Chandler Hovey Park and Lighthouse Point, tip of Marblehead Neck; a great spot to picnic, get your bearings, and watch summer boat races.

Fort Sewall, Marblehead, at the eastern end of Front Street. Begun as an earthwork during the 17th century and improved as the Revolutionary-era fortification that still stands, it is now a pleasant park.

Misery Islands (978-356-4351), Beverly Farms. Owned by the Trustees of Reservations, the Misery Islands at the east end of Salem Bay are a relaxed haven, ideal for walking or picnicking. Boats run on Mondays and Tuesdays in June, July, and August. Call for trip schedule and to make reservations. Adults $10, children $5.

Long Hill (978-921-1944), 572 Essex Street (Route 22), Beverly, is a brick mansion built as a summer home for Ellery Sedgwick, author, editor, and publisher of *The Atlantic Monthly* from 1909 to 1938. The mansion itself now houses the offices of the Trustees of Reservations, and the 114-acre grounds are open to the public. The big draw here is **Sedgwick Gardens,** a remarkable collection of trees, shrubs, and flowers, including Japanese maples, weeping cherries, rhododendrons, and azaleas. Walking trails thread through fields, forest, and wetland.

Hospital Point, Beverly. Driving north from the city on Hale Street (toward Route 127), turn right onto East Corning Street for a short detour to an 1871 lighthouse overlooking Salem and Marblehead. This was also the site of a Revolutionary fort, and later of a smallpox hospital.

SPECIAL SPACES

Salem Common (Washington Square). Set aside for public use early in the 1700s, this once swampy, hilly space was leveled in the early 19th century into the classic common that survives today, complete with benches and bandstand.

Derby Square and Essex Street, Salem. From Washington Square you can now walk down Essex Street, a pedestrian way lined with museums and shops, to Derby Square, the original market area around the Old Town Hall. At East India Square, stone benches surround a large fountain.

State Street Landing, Marblehead. A landing since 1662, this is a place to watch people and boats (some 3000 sailing craft summer in the sheltered inner harbor).

LODGING

Note: Local tax on lodging varies—in Marblehead it's 5.7 percent, and in Salem 9.4 percent.

HOTEL

Hawthorne Hotel (978-744-4080; 1-800-729-7829), 18 Washington Square West, Salem 01970. A fine six-story, three-sided, 89-room hotel that was built by public subscription in the 1920s and has managed to keep its standards high in an era during which few small city hotels survived. By far the tallest building around, it also has the best views in town. The lobby, with its fluted columns and potted palms, is quite elegant, and rooms are furnished in reproduction antiques; all have private bath. Facilities include the **Tavern on the Green** (an oak-paneled bar) and **Nathaniel's Restaurant.** $92–162 per room, $225–275 per suite.

BED & BREAKFAST INNS

Two remarkably similar facilities, one in Salem and the other in Marblehead, offer the feel and facilities of a full-service inn but serve only breakfast.

The Salem Inn (978-741-0680; 1-800-446-2995), 7 Summer Street, Salem 01970. A four-story, brick double town house built in 1834 with 21 rooms, private baths. Dick and Diane Pabich have created an appealing place in keeping with its surroundings. There's a comfortable living room with fireplace and suitable ancestor hanging above it. Rooms vary widely, from spacious, bright doubles with working hearths (Duraflame logs), to top-floor family suites with cooking facilities, to smaller rooms (some with fireplace) with baths down the hall. Around the corner at 331 Essex Street, **The Curwen House,** a nearby vintage 1854 Italianate-style house, has recently been added to the inn. It has its own living room and a meeting room plus the guest rooms, six with working fireplaces and three of these with two-person whirlpool and canopy beds. A recent acquisition is **Peabody House** at 15 Summer Street, an 1870s house with six luxury suites. All rooms and suites have cable TV and phone. Breakfast, served in the inn's **Courtyard Cafe** restaurant and on the patio, is included in the rates: rooms $109–179, suites $129–179, higher during Haunted Happenings (see *Events*).

The Harbor Light Inn (781-631-2186), 58 Washington Street, Marblehead 01945. Two Federal-era mansions have been joined to create this elegant 21-room inn. It's flush to the sidewalk of a narrow, busy street near the heart of old Marblehead, with parking and a small, landscaped pool in the rear. Owner Peter Conway has a sure touch. There's ample common space between the formal living rooms and the dining room (a continental breakfast is served 7:30–9:30). A dozen of the guest rooms have a working fireplace; five have Jacuzzis; all have phone, TV, and private bath, and many have canopy beds. $95–150 for rooms to $165–245 for suites.

BED & BREAKFASTS

In Salem 01970

Amelia Payson House (978-744-8304), 16 Winter Street. The feel inside this striking, vintage-1845 Greek Revival house is bright, crisp, and friendly. Ada and Don Roberts have been welcoming guests for more than a decade and obviously enjoy what they do. Guests are invited to gather in the living room with its baby grand and around the dining room table for breakfast (an expanded continental, served 8:30–10). The four rooms consist of two doubles and two with an extra bed, one a studio. There are a microwave and a fridge in the second-floor sitting room for guests' use; $65–125 double.

The Stepping Stone Inn (978-741-8900), 19 Washington Square North. A handsome 1846 house, built for a customs official, looking out on the Salem common and next door to the Witch Museum (see *Witches*).The eight period-furnished guest rooms all have cable TV, air-conditioning, and private bath. $75–125 with continental breakfast.

Morning Glory (978-741-1703), 22 Hardy Street. Hosts Bob Shea and George Pena have lavished a lot of care on this elegant 1808 Federal mansion. Each of the four guest rooms has cable TV, private bath, and distinctive decor. (The Jackie O. Room also has a large fireplace.) A rooftop deck looks out on Salem Harbor. $85–120, including "deluxe" continental breakfast and high tea in the afternoon.

The Stephen Daniels House (978-744-5709), 1 Daniels Street. This is a real find for people who appreciate a vintage-1667 house with a 1745 wing that's furnished with period antiques. Owned for two centuries by one family, the house stood vacant until restored and reopened as a tearoom in 1945. Kay Gill has owned the house for 30 years, taking in guests long before "B&B" was a concept in Salem. Several of the five guest rooms have working fireplaces, and the hearths in the common room and original kitchen are huge. There are period ceilings and paneling throughout. Common space includes the old kitchen and a parlor, as well as the dining room and the pleasant garden with flowering shrubbery and wisteria. Children under 10 are welcome—but should be closely supervised in this antiques-stuffed house—and so (amazingly enough) are pets. Baths can be private or shared. $65–95 per room, $135–175 per suite (two rooms with a connecting bath). *Note:* If no one answers when you call, try again. There's no answering machine or call-waiting, but persevere; it's worth it.

In Marblehead 01945

47 Front Street (1-800-569-6138). Conveniently sited between the Town Landing and Crocker Park, this 1750s house with the eye-catching, lilac-colored door has been meticulously restored by hosts Cathy and Bob Fletcher. The two large guest rooms have fireplaces and there are four more in the house. This was the birthplace of the local folk artist J.O.J. Frost, and prints of his bright scenes of turn-of-the-century Marblehead decorate most rooms. $90–$100 with full breakfast, served in summer in the pleasant back garden.

The Seagull Inn B&B (781-631-1893), 106 Harbor Avenue. This is the last remaining segment of a waterside hotel on Marblehead Neck that functioned from 1893 to 1940. It has been owned by Skip and Ruth Sigler for more than 20 years and modernized to create some great spaces, including the kitchen and the living room. Choose from three suites, all with TV, VCR, air-conditioning, phone, and bath. The largest sleeps five and has a real kitchen and two baths. Our favorite is the third-floor aerie. Guests have free access to a health club and the fax machine. Rates, which include an expanded continental breakfast, are $100–200.

Spray Cliff (781-637-6789; 1-800-626-1530), 25 Spray Avenue. It would be hard to beat the location of this rather grand mansion right on the rocks, overlooking open ocean. Most of the seven rooms have water views and are unusually large, with ample bathrooms, and three have a working fireplace. Although you have to drive into town (or bring a bike), you can walk to Preston Beach. The common room is a sunny former library with an ocean view. Our only problem with this beautiful place is that paying guests must use the old tradesmen's side entrance. $175–200 with breakfast. (Less off-season).

Brimblecomb Hill B&B (781-631-3172 evenings; 632-6366 days), 33 Mechanic Street. Nicely located in the center of the Old Town, this vintage-1721 house has three comfortable first-floor guest rooms. The one with a private bath, a tall four-poster, and its own library is a beauty. The remaining two are smaller and share a bath but are pleasant and have private entrances. The living room features its original hearth and a blue piano (guests are invited to play). Continental breakfast is served here or, weather permitting, in the garden. Gene Arnould, who owns a nearby frame shop/gallery, has been hosting visitors for some years and knows how to make you comfortable. $65–85.

Harborside House (781-631-1032), 23 Gregory Street. Susan Livingston's talents as a professional dressmaker are evident in the bright and neat guest rooms; the look is tailored rather than frilly, and the feel is very comfortable. The front room with twin beds has a water view, and the back room is a double. The living and dining rooms are gracious, and there's a third-story sun deck. Livingston, a Marblehead resident for more than three decades, tunes in guests to what the area offers and also lends a couple of bikes. Tea, as well as breakfast, is included in $60–80, cheaper off-season.

Herreshoff Castle (781-631-3083), 2 Crocker Park. This B&B rents only one suite but it's unique: the two-story carriage house of a fantastical building—a 1920s recreation of a medieval Norse castle. The site is special, too, since Crocker Park both overlooks the harbor and is where most outdoor events in Marblehead occur. The suite consists of living room, bath, and kitchenette on the ground floor and a large bedroom on the second floor. The rate is $150 a night, including a stocked refrigerator and daily breakfast pastries. Two-day minimum stay. Open May–October.

Compass Rose (781-631-7599), 36 Gregory Street. Carol and Bob Swift's waterside house offers just one room, but it's a gem: a snug studio apartment with a great view of the harbor. Facilities include a kitchenette and use of the garden just outside the door. $90. The Swifts also rent out **Compass Rose on the Avenue** at 61 Atlantic Avenue. A compact (15 by 21 feet) but attractive and recently refurbished turn-of-the-century cottage, it has an eat-in kitchen on the ground floor and a bedroom and bath on the second floor. Rent is $125 a night, $750 a week. Three-day minimum stay in high season.

☞ **The Nesting Place B&B** (781-631-6655), 16 Village Street. Louise Hirshberg caters to frazzled women looking for a soothing getaway, but really everyone (families included) is welcome in this cheery house, which offers two rooms with shared bath and outside hot tub (great for stargazing). Can provide a spa-style getaway that includes massage, facials, and stress consultations. $65–75 (less off-season).

In Beverly 01915

Beverly Farms Bed and Breakfast at the John Larcom House (978-922-6074), 28 Hart Street. Nicely situated to take advantage of both the Cape Ann area and Marblehead/Salem sites, yet off the beaten track, within walking distance of the train and a beach. Two of the three bedrooms have fireplaces, and all feature feather beds and handmade quilts. Breakfast and afternoon tea are included. $65–100.

WHERE TO EAT

DINING OUT

Lyceum Bar & Grill (978-745-7665), 43 Church Street, Salem. Open daily for lunch and dinner. Housed in the city's 19th-century Lyceum, there are now a number of different dining rooms, ranging in atmosphere from the brick-walled barroom to the back glass-walled area overlooking Salem's Green. The à la carte dinner menu features entrées such as grilled Maine salmon steak with warm watercress and sesame-soy vinaigrette ($14.95).

Pellino's (781-631-3344), 261 Washington Street, Marblehead. Open daily 4:30–10:30. Early-dining specials, Sunday through Thursday 4:30–5:30. Free parking. This is a small place specializing in fine Italian cuisine. Try the slow-roasted lamb with fresh mozzarella ($11.95) or the roasted duck breast with apple and herb honey ($15.95).

The Red Raven (978-745-8558), 75 Congress Street, Salem. Salem's "bistro" features an eclectic menu and atmosphere that locals rate highly.

Peabody Essex Museum Cafe (978-745-1876), East India Square, Salem. Open Tuesday through Friday 11–4, also for a Tea Buffet 3–4:30; Sunday brunch noon–3. We don't have an "elegant lunching out" or "brunch" category, but if we did, this place would be in it. The relatively small café with its rare china within built-in cabinets has a distinctly elegant feel and the service is formal. Most entrées are in the $6–10 range. Our only complaint is that in this palace built largely on the tea trade tea comes in packets. You don't have to pay a museum admission to eat in the café.

Trattoria Il Panino (781-631-3900), 126R Washington Street, Marblehead. Authentic Tuscan and Mediterranean cuisine. Homemade pastas and risotto are a specialty, and there are also daily specials. Extensive list of Italian wines. Outdoor dining area. Most entrées $10–15.

Michael's House (781-631-5255), 26 Atlantic Avenue, Marblehead. Open for lunch and dinner daily, Sunday brunch. A local landmark, this 17th-century house has low-beamed ceilings and fireplaces. Sandwiches run $3–9, and the Italian/Continental dinner menu $9–16. Live entertainment Thursday through Sunday.

EATING OUT

Between Salem and Marblehead

The Rockmore (781-639-0600), Salem Harbor. A seasonal, floating eatery with seafood, local specialties, and regional beers. It's smack in the middle of the harbor, accessible by launch service from Village Street Landing in Marblehead and from Pickering Wharf in Salem. Entrées are $5–12.

In Salem

Red's Sandwich Shop (978-745-3527), 15 Central Street. Open Monday through Saturday 5 AM–3 PM, Sunday 6 AM–1 PM. Just off Essex Street and around the corner from the Old Town Hall, this shop is housed in an ancient-looking building with a plaque stating that it was once the London Coffee House, established 1691. Breakfast possibilities range from one egg any style to a corned beef omelet, and beverages range from frappes to Millers.

Victoria Station (978-745-3400), Pickering Wharf. Open daily for lunch and dinner, Sunday brunch. It's difficult to beat the tip-of-the-wharf location.

Stromberg's Restaurant (978-744-1863), 2 Bridge Street. Open daily 11–8:30 except Monday (open Monday holidays). Claiming to be the oldest restaurant on the North Shore, Stromberg's proudly displays its 1935 menu. There is a water view, and although fresh fish is featured, the nightly special can be lamb, New England boiled dinner, or prime rib.

Dodge Street Bar & Grill (978-745-0139), 7 Dodge Street. Open noon–1 AM. Billing itself as "Salem's friendliest neighborhood pub," the grill is good for ribs, burgers, and seafood; live music nightly.

In Marblehead

Flynnie's at the Beach, Devereaux Beach. Open daily May through November for all three meals (from 6 AM on weekends). You can park (no small matter on weekends) and enjoy the view from the deck or beach; fried seafood is the specialty.

Driftwood (781-631-1145), 63 Front Street. Open daily 5:30 AM–4 PM. Noted locally for fresh, moderately priced seafood, this is a great place to get an affordable lobster roll or plate of clams (and to hear authentic North Shore accents). No credit cards.

The Barnacle (781-631-4236), 141 Front Street. Open daily for lunch and dinner (closed Tuesday in winter), right on the water. No reservations, checks, or credit cards. Seafood, of course, including broiled scallops and jumbo shrimp sautéed in butter, herbs, and white wine. This place is so popular that it's wise to come early in the lunch and dinner hours.

Maddie's Sail Loft (781-631-9824), 15 State Street. Open for lunch Monday through Saturday; full menu 5–10 PM, but not on Monday. No credit cards. A neighborhood bar with good chowder and blackboard specials; really hops on yachting weekends. Try the fish-and-chips or Marblehead Seafood Pie ($14.95).

The King's Rook (781-631-9838), 12 State Street. Open Monday through Saturday for lunch and dinner; closed Monday evening. This is a café and wine bar in a vintage-1747 building, the place for a curried egg sandwich or gourmet pizza with a glass of wine, or a lemon tart and espresso. Cocktails.

ENTERTAINMENT

✐ **North Shore Music Theatre** (978-922-8500), 62 Dunham Road, Beverly, off Route 128, exit 19. April through December: professional performances, popular plays, musicals, concerts, and children's theater.

✐ **Cabot Street Cinema Theater** (978-927-3677), 268 Cabot Street, Beverly. A jewel of a 750-seat theater restored and owned by Le Grand David and his own Spectacular Magic Company, which has been performing every Sunday (3 PM) year-round since 1976. The company has also restored the 500-seat **Larcom Theatre** up the street, scene of another 2-hour program on selected Saturdays (2 PM) since 1985. Adults bring their children and grandchildren to see these shows, and then come back again. Art films are shown weeknights at the Cabot Street Cinema Theater.

Marblehead Summer Music Festival (781-631-3421), Washington Street. A series of Saturday performances by the Cambridge Chamber Players in the Old North Church.

Marblehead Summer Stage (781-631-4238), a series of performances by a resident repertory company in varied locales.

Summer Jazz (781-631-6366), a series of summer concerts in the Unitarian Universalist Church, Marblehead.

SELECTIVE SHOPPING

Salem's **Pickering Wharf** and Marblehead's historic district both harbor a number of specialty shops, galleries, antiques shops, and bookstores.

BOOKSTORES

The Spirit of '76 Bookstore (781-631-7199), Pleasant and School Streets, Marblehead. A superb bookstore guided with the personal touch of owner Bob Hugo. **Derby Square Bookstore** (978-745-8804), 215 Essex Street, Salem. General and regional books in abundance. **Book Shop of Beverly Farms** (978-927-2122), 40 West Street, Beverly Farms. Frequented by North Shore readers and authors. **Much Ado About Books** (781-639-0400), 7 Pleasant Street, Marblehead. Rare and out-of-print books.

CANDY

Ye Olde Pepper Companie (978-745-2744), 122 Derby Street, Salem, near the House of the Seven Gables. Open daily. Established in 1806, this is billed as America's oldest candy company, specializing in blackjacks, Gibraltar, and other 19th-century treats. **Harbor Sweets** (978-745-7648), 85 Leavitt Street, Salem. Handmade chocolates like Sweet Sloops (chocolate, almond, butter crunch sailboats) are made here and distributed throughout the country. **Stowaway Sweets** (781-631-0303), 154 Atlantic Avenue, Marblehead. Open daily 9:30–5:30, noon–5 Sunday. A name known to candy connoisseurs: 87 varieties of candy, much of it hand-dipped chocolate. In business since 1929, shipping throughout the country.

OCCULT AND PSYCHIC

Crow Haven Corner (978-745-8763), 125 Essex Street, Salem. Founded by Laurie Cabot, "official witch of Salem," and now run by her daughter, Judy Cabot. Tarot card readings, psychic consultations, and love readings. The shop claims to be "purveyor to witches around the world."

Pyramid Books: The New-Age Store (978-745-7171), 214 Derby Street (across from Pickering Wharf), Salem. Open daily until 7. Metaphysical books, music, audios, gifts, jewelry, quartz, healing stones, crystal balls, incense, oils, herbs, and tarot decks.

Angelica of the Angels (978-745-9355), 7 Central Street, Salem. Psychic and medium readings, tarot cards and tea leaves, healing through angels, angelic collectibles.

SPECIAL EVENTS

July: **Independence Day celebrations** in Marblehead (fireworks and harbor illumination); also **Marblehead Festival of the Arts.**

Mid-July: **Salem Maritime Festival** at Salem Maritime National Historic Site (see *Museums*) includes maritime crafts demonstrations and workshops, chantey singing, and a gathering of tall ships.

Late July: **Marblehead Race Week** draws thousands of boats to compete.

August: **Beverly Homecoming Week** (first week); **Heritage Week** in Salem, a citywide festival that includes concerts, exhibits, sidewalk sales, fireworks, parade.

October: **Haunted Happenings** in Salem—three weeks of dances, parties, tours, concerts, and spooky events climaxing with Halloween.

December: **Marblehead Christmas Walk.**

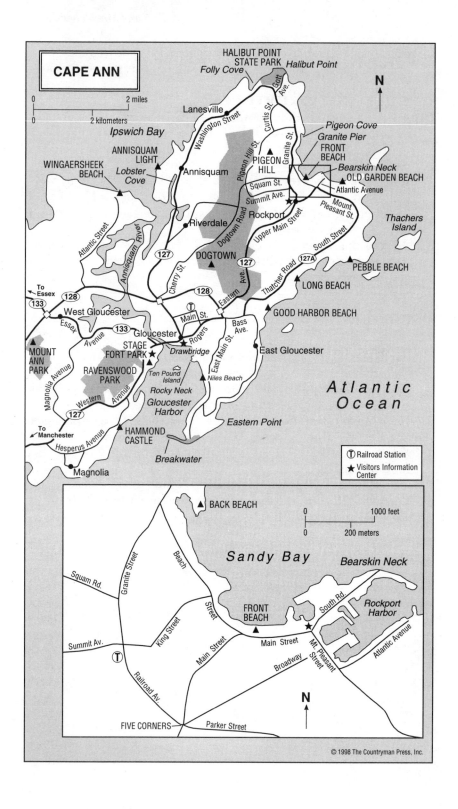

CAPE ANN

Cape Ann Region

Cape Ann is a rocky fist of land thrusting from the North Shore up and out into the Atlantic. It's virtually an island circled by a 15-mile road that we challenge anyone to drive in less than a day—ignoring the beaches, shops, seafood restaurants, and smooth oceanside rocks obviously made for sunning.

Cape Ann has a split personality; it's divided between the very different towns of Gloucester and Rockport.

Founded by fishermen back in 1625, Gloucester prides itself on being the "oldest continuous working harbor in America." Around the turn of this century, Gloucester was the country's leading fishing port, and in the 1930s it still boasted 400 proud, graceful, two-masted fishing schooners. A typical crew included the Yankees, Italians, and Portuguese fishermen portrayed in Rudyard Kipling's *Captains Courageous*.

Gloucester remains home for 200 draggers and trawlers. Current federal regulations threaten to reduce the fleet drastically, though, and there's understandable dismay over the idea that tourism rather than fishing and fish processing may soon be the city's mainstay.

Tourism has, however, been part of the Gloucester mix for more than a century. In 1880 artist Winslow Homer spent the summer on Ten Pound Island in the middle of the harbor, recording and popularizing what he saw. Other artists, including Childe Hassam and John Sloan, summered on Rocky Neck, converting fishermen's shacks into studios. A large hotel and summer theater soon followed, and by the turn of the century a half-dozen hotels lined the shore in East Gloucester. In Magnolia, just south of Gloucester, the 750-room Oceanside billed itself as the largest resort hotel in New England. Elaborate summer mansions, which continued to be built into the '30s, included 40-room Beauport on Eastern Point and John Hays Hammond Jr.'s fantasy castle across the harbor.

Rockport, one-third the size of Gloucester and on the opposite (ocean) side of Cape Ann, also began as a fishing village. Early in the 19th century it grew as a granite quarrying center, and as early as the 1840s it, too, began attracting summer people and artists. Rockport remains primarily a resort—but on its own terms. Since 1856 the town has been "dry," and guests at the North Shore's largest concentration of inns and B&Bs are advised that local dining rooms are BYOB. In contrast to Gloucester, beaches are free, but parking is extremely limited; summer day-trippers are encouraged to come by train and trolley or to stay at one of the many inns and B&Bs within walking distance of the shops, restaurants, and beaches.

Essex, just a few miles west of Gloucester, is another appealing anomaly. Having produced more vessels per capita over the past three centuries than any other community in America, it has also been catering to day-trippers since the 1870s—when Sunday excursion trains began running to the town's Centennial Grove. Today the causeway that once supported 15 shipyards is top-heavy with restaurants (including two claiming to have invented the fried clam) and the North Shore's largest concentration of antiques shops. The Essex Shipbuilding Museum preserves the town's amazing history.

Neighboring Ipswich boasts more 17th-century homes than any other American town its size. It still prides itself on the fact that in 1686 its residents refused to pay taxes without representation, a gesture hailed locally as the "birth of American Independence." Most visitors, however, pass quickly through the village on their way to Crane Beach. Richard T. Crane was a Chicago plumbing magnate who acquired the North Shore's most beautiful beach and built the 59-room Great House. Luckily the mansion (site of summer concerts and theatrical productions) and some 1400 surrounding acres of beach, garden, woodland, and salt marsh are preserved by the Trustees of Reservations.

This may be the best known, but it's just one among dozens of spectacular preserves in Essex County. Despite having been settled since the early 1600s and lying within 40 miles of Boston, dozens of waterfront preserves are open to the public, thanks to a half-dozen groups ranging from "The Trustees" (founded in 1891) to the Essex County Greenbelt Association (founded in 1961).

Still, the Cape Ann region is known primarily as a place to set out on a whalewatching or fishing expedition or to go to the beach. To date, it seems few visitors explore the areas described here under *Green Space* or take advantage of the relatively new ways out into the salt marshes via excursion boats and sea kayaks. The ocean- and riverside inns and B&Bs in this area remain little known and reasonably priced. This beautiful heart of the North Shore is, in fact, far less of a destination than it was a century ago, but is still just as beautiful and hospitable.

AREA CODE: 978
GUIDANCE
Cape Ann Chamber of Commerce (283-1601), 33 Commercial Street, Gloucester. Open May through October weekdays 8–6, Saturday 10–6, Sunday 10–4; otherwise weekdays 8–5; this is a walk-in information center with rest rooms on the waterfront across from St. Peter's Park.
City of Gloucester Visitor's Center (281-8865; 1-800-649-6839), Stage Fort Park, Route 127. Open June to mid-October 9–5 daily. A shingle-

and-stone building in landscaped grounds overlooking Gloucester Harbor, the center is manned by helpful staff and is well stocked with maps, menus, brochures, and rest rooms. Pick up a map/guide to the Gloucester Maritime Trail.

Rockport Chamber of Commerce (546-6575; 1-888-726-3922) maintains a seasonal information center (with rest rooms) on Route 127 just south of town. It's open daily mid-May to mid-October, 11–5, Sunday 1–4; the chamber office at 3 Main Street (just off Dock Square) is open weekdays 10–5. Web site: www.rockportwa.com.

Ipswich Visitor's Center at the Hall-Haskell House (356-8540 May–October; 356-4400 November–April), South Main Street. Open May through October, Wednesday through Sunday, 9–3.

GETTING THERE

By train: The T commuter trains serve both Gloucester and Rockport from North Station (617-227-5070; 1-800-392-6099), and **Cape Ann Transit Authority** (CATA; 283-7916) buses meet some weekday trains; from the Rockport station it's an easy walk to the beach and shops. There are also Gloucester-based taxis: **Cape Ann Yellow Cab** (283-9393), **Atlantic Taxi** (281-5550; 1-800-720-TAXI), and **Charlie's Cabs** (281-4747).

By car: From Boston there are several satisfying approaches to this area. The first two are via Gloucester: (1) Take Route 128 to Grant Circle (the first rotary) and follow signs for downtown and the MUSEUM sign to the Cape Ann Historical Society. Keep going and signs also direct you to the **Cape Ann Visitors Center** on the waterfront. (2) Take exit 15 (see *Scenic Drives*) and approach Gloucester along the shore via Manchester and Magnolia, stopping at the **City of Gloucester Visitors Center** in Stage Fort Park.

For Rockport, continue on Route 128 beyond the second rotary to Route 127 and follow signs. For Essex take Route 128, exit 14, and Route 133 west; for Ipswich take Route 128, exit 20 (Route 1A north) through Wenham and Hamilton and follow signs.

GETTING AROUND

The Cape Ann Transit Authority (CATA; 283-7916) offers frequent daytime service around Cape Ann. June through mid-September CATA runs **Salt Water Trolleys,** circulating all day (10–10, until 11 on Saturday) within Rockport and among Rockport, Gloucester, Magnolia, and Essex. Until September 1, CATA also runs a water shuttle (10–6) from the Gloucester waterfront (Harbor Loop and Seven Seas Wharf) to Rocky Neck and Ten Pound Island.

PARKING

In Gloucester: Try Stage Fort Park, the chamber of commerce, St. Peter's Park, four more lots off Rogers Street on the waterfront, and another metered lot on Pleasant Street.

In Rockport: In addition to in-town metered parking (adequate except on summer weekends), there is a large lot at Blue Gate Meadow Park (across from the Sandy Bay Motor Inn on Route 127; see *Motels*), with summer weekend shuttles connecting with downtown. Several lots are "residents only"; beware. On summer weekends it can make more sense to come by train or to stay in a B&B within walking distance of a beach. Metered parking is enforced.

REST ROOMS

In Gloucester: Check out the Gloucester Visitors Center in Stage Fort Park, City Hall on Warren Street and the Fitz High Lane House on Harbor Loop off Rogers Street (see *Historic Homes*), and the Sawyer Free Library across from Gloucester City Hall.

In Rockport: The seasonal visitors center on Route 127 includes rest rooms, as does the former firehouse right on Front Beach, and there is yet another at the bandstand farther east on Beach Street. Year-round facilities can be found on T-wharf.

MEDICAL EMERGENCY

Call 911

TO SEE

MUSEUMS

In Gloucester

Cape Ann Historical Association (283-0455), 27 Pleasant Street. Open Tuesday through Saturday 10–5; $3.50 adults, $3 retirees, $2 students, free ages 6 and under. This is one of New England's outstanding small museums, founded in 1873, now filling an 1804 house, an attached formal museum, and another attached (via an atrium) three-floor brick building added in 1993. The pride of the collection continues to be the 35 paintings plus sketches and lithographs by Gloucester-born marine artist Fitz Hugh Lane (1804–56), but there are also paintings of mostly local scenes by Maurice Prendergast, Winslow Homer, John Sloan, Milton Avery, and Augustus Buhler, among many other exceptional artists who painted on and around Cape Ann in the late 19th and early 20th centuries. In addition, fine china from China, silver by Paul Revere, and early-19th-century furniture and furnishings contrast with the Fisheries and Maritime collections, which tell the story of the city's Sicilian population. This collection includes antique photos and tools of the fishing industry and several historic boats: the dory *Centennial,* in which a young Gloucester fisherman sailed solo to England in 1876, and the 25-foot Gloucester sloop *The Great Republic,* in which the city's Howard Blackburn, a fisherman whose hands had been reduced to stumps in a previous, seemingly superhuman adventure at sea, sailed solo from Gloucester to Portugal in 1901 (in 1899 he had sailed to England). With its mix of paintings and a sense of the city's very human history, this place is one in which you will tend to linger longer than you had intended. An exhibit on

GEORGE M. CUSHING PHOTOGRAPHY

News from the Fleet (1918) by Augustus W. Buhler is in the Cape Ann Historical Association's Collection.

the Cape's granite-quarrying history and an imaginative children's room are also part of this unusual museum.

Beauport (283-0800), Eastern Point in East Gloucester, off Route 127A. Open for guided tours on the hour mid-May to mid-September, weekdays 10–4; also weekends mid-September to mid-October 10–4. Adults $6, $5.50 seniors, $3 children 6–12. Even historic-house haters shouldn't pass up this one: a mansion of some 45 rooms, most of them representing a phase in American history. "Beauport," incidentally, is the name that Samuel de Champlain gave Gloucester Harbor when he charted it in 1604. This Beauport evolved between 1907 and 1934 and is the work of one of America's leading interior decorators of the 1920s, Henry Davis Sleeper. His arrangement of his carefully collected treasures (which include Lord Byron's bed) is said to have inspired Delaware's Winterthur Museum. It is maintained by the Society for the Preservation of New England Antiquities. To get there, you must ignore the PRIVATE signs at the entrance to Eastern Point. Inquire about afternoon teas, evening concerts, and a sunset tour.

⊘ **Hammond Castle Museum** (283-2080; events line: 283-7673), 80 Hesperus Avenue, Magnolia (5 miles south of Gloucester off Route 127, or take Route 128, exit 14, east on Route 133). Open Memorial Day weekend through September, daily 10–4; otherwise, weekends 9–4; adults $6, $5

for seniors and college students, $4 children 4–12. This castlelike mansion was built in the 1920s by John Hays Hammond Jr., an eccentric inventor who held more than 800 patents including breakthroughs in radio, radar, and remote control. More of a stage set than a home, its props include artificial rain and a Roman bath; its centerpiece is a cathedral-like, 60-foot-high grand hall housing a 10,000-pipe organ that Hammond designed himself (he is not, however, the Hammond of Hammond organs). Organ concerts ($15) are scheduled regularly throughout the year and usually sell out well in advance (so if you are interested, call ahead), and it's worth inquiring about other scheduled concerts and functions. From the grounds you can see the pile of offshore rocks known as Norman's Woe, immortalized by Longfellow in his poem *The Wreck of the Hesperus*.

Essex Shipbuilding Museum (768-7541), housed in an 1830s schoolhouse at 28 Main Street (Route 133) in the center of the village. Open daily year-round, 10–5, Sunday 2–5. Adults $5, $4 seniors, $3 for children. Over three centuries some 4000 vessels are said to have been built within a few miles of each other along the tidal Essex River in this town with a population that never topped 1500. In the 1700s it launched Chebacco boats, then dogbodies, pinkies, and finally schooners. From 1850 until 1900, a period during which Gloucester ranked as one of the world's top fishing ports, Essex built its fishing schooners, and the town's fame spread as the place to get a vessel built reasonably and well. In 1852 the tiny town had 15 different shipyards, and by the 1870s the ships were so big that it frequently took a number of tides to make it down the river. Steamers and yachts as well as schooners were sent to sea by the hundreds. The Causeway, the former site of most of the boatbuilding yards, is now top-heavy with restaurants and antiques shops, but the museum tells the town's story well through photographs, ship models, tools, dioramas, and hands-on exhibits. At the museum's **Story Shipyard** (66 Main Street), the *Evelina M. Goulart*, one of five currently surviving Essex-built fishing schooners, is being restored. This is also the location of the museum shop and offices.

HISTORIC HOMES AND SITES
In Gloucester

The Sargent House Museum (281-2432), 49 Middle Street. Open June through Columbus Day, Friday through Monday noon–4, and by appointment other times of the year. Adults $3, $2 seniors, free 12 and under. Built in 1783, this late-Georgian house tells a fascinating story about Judith Sargent, the first American to have a play produced in this country (it ran two nights in Boston in 1793). The house is preserved, however, because Judith's second marriage was to John Murray, the founder of Universalism in this country. A superb staircase and paneling, paintings by John Singer Sargent, locally crafted highboys and lowboys, and a wealth of period furnishings grace this historic site.

Gloucester Fishermen's Statue, on Western Avenue or Stacy Boulevard (as Route 127 is known at this point) near the Blynman Bridge. This stalwart seaman at the wheel honors the more than 10,000 Gloucester fishermen who have died at sea and all "that go down to the sea in ships." The nearby drawbridge ("oldest in the country") spans an 18th-century canal between Gloucester Harbor and the Annisquam River.

Stage Fort Park, Western Avenue. This is where the fish stages were set up by the Dorchester Company in 1623. It's the site of the city's major seasonal information center and of summer Saturday and Sunday 7 PM band concerts (see *Entertainment*). Pathways climb the smooth rocks overlooking the harbor.

Gloucester Waterfront. Hidden beside Gloucester House Restaurant (see *Dining Out*), **Gus Foote Park** is a great place to watch boats unload between 4 and 6 AM and again between 4 and 6 PM.

Harbor Loop. Heading east along Rogers Street, you can't help but notice the tall granite house standing alone on a green knoll with a side street looping around it. This is the **Fitz Hugh Lane House,** in which the famous painter actually lived and worked. It now houses public rest rooms, among other things. Note the statue of the artist by sculptor Al Duca, sitting on the slope and painting the harbor—an invitation to sit down beside him with a picnic or sketch pad. The Schooner *Adventure,* built in Essex in 1926 and the very last dory schooner when she retired from fishing in 1953, is currently under restoration at the adjacent marine railway. The docks here are also departure points for excursion boats and for the water shuttle to Rocky Neck and Ten Pound Island (see *Getting Around*).

Independent Christian Church (283-2410), Middle and Church Streets. Now Unitarian-Universalist, this is the mother church of Universalism in this country. Built in 1804, it is a graceful building with a Wren-style steeple, a Paul Revere bell, a Willard clock, and a Sandwich-glass chandelier.

Our Lady of Good Voyage Church (283-1490). The church with twin blue domes has unusual warmth and grace, modeled on the cathedral of San Miguel in the Azores, the place of origin of much of its congregation. Models of fishing vessels are mounted on the walls, and its carillon is the oldest in this country. Carillon concerts, every Tuesday at 7 PM July through mid-August, attract top bell players from throughout the country. The church is locked but visitors are welcome; ring the rectory doorbell.

Gloucester City Hall, Warren Street, between Pleasant Street and Dale Avenue. This 1869 brick Victorian building is worth stepping into to see the heroic WPA-era murals and the very moving *Gloucester Fishermen Lost at Sea Memorial* mural, a hand-painted list of 4000 names of mariners lost at sea just between 1874 and 1978; these are inscribed between and around the multistory Gothic windows overlooking the harbor. It's estimated that between 8000 and 10,000 men have perished fishing out of Gloucester since 1623. The city's present population is just 28,000.

Eastern Point Light and Dog Bar Breakwater. See directions for Beauport (see *Museums*), but ignore the PRIVATE signs at the entrance to Eastern Point. Marking the entrance to Gloucester Harbor, the lighthouse is owned by the US Coast Guard and dates from 1890; the breakwater marks the presence of a treacherous sandbar beneath. This is a great spot to clear your lungs and head. The view is of Gloucester's rocky shoreline and of Boston's skyscrapers hovering improbably above the horizon.

In Rockport

Sandy Bay Historical Society and Museum (546-9533), 40 King Street (corner of Granite, near the train station). Mid-June through mid-September. Adults $3, $2 seniors and children. The museum is located in the **Sewall-Scripture House,** an unusual Federal-style granite home built in 1832. It holds an extensive collection of town memorabilia. The historical society also offers tours, by appointment, of the **Old Castle** (set back from Route 127 north of Rockport in Pigeon Cove), a 1715 garrison-style saltbox.

Paper House (546-2629), Pigeon Hill Street. Open July and August 10–5. $1 ages 15 and over; $.50 ages 6–14. North of Rockport on Route 127, turn up Curtis Street. At first you might think this house is just a modest summer cottage set in a rock garden. On closer inspection, though, you find that even the exterior walls are made of newspaper: 215 layers of paper, compacted under two tons of pressure. Inside, a fireplace, a piano (the casing), a grandfather clock, chairs, tables, a desk, and more are all made of "newspaper mâché." The creator was Elis F. Stedman, a Swedish immigrant who read a half-dozen newspapers a day.

James Babson Cooperage Shop, Route 127 midway between Gloucester and Rockport. Open July and August, Tuesday through Sunday 2–5. This small, shedlike building is a restored barrel-repair shop, displaying early tools; also good for local information.

Bearskin Neck. This rocky, natural neck extends off Dock Square and has always formed the heart of Rockport, first as a fishing center, then an artists' enclave, and now a tourist magnet. **Motif #1,** a much-painted red fish shed at the end of Tuna Wharf off Bearskin Neck, has become the symbol of Cape Ann.

In Ipswich

Note: The **John Whipple House** and the **John Heard House** are both described under *Scenic Drives*. **Castle Hill** is described under *Green Space* and *Entertainment*.

ART CENTERS

Since the mid-19th century artists have gathered on Cape Ann to paint its fishing boats and beaches. The cape's special, luminous light, as well as its land- and seascape, continues to draw them. The best display of "local" painters past and present is at the **Cape Ann Historical Association** (see *Museums*).

Rocky Neck, off Route 127A in Gloucester. There is a parking lot at the entrance to this picturesque peninsula, traversed by a narrow, one-way (no parking anywhere in summer) road. Home of one of the country's oldest art colonies, it is also the place where Rudyard Kipling wrote *Captains Courageous* in the company of seamen at the marine railway that's still there. Fairly quiet these days, it sports a colorful jumble of art galleries and restaurants. It's accessible directly from Boston via excursion boat *Virginia C.* (see *To Do*) and from the Gloucester waterfront by water shuttle (see *Getting Around*).

The North Shore Art Association (283-1857), 197 East Main Street near the entrance to Rocky Neck, in Gloucester. Open June through late September, daily 10–5, Sunday 1–5. Housed since 1922 in a large wharf building, the association features an unusual number and variety of juried work in changing exhibits; an annual auction is held in July.

Rockport Art Association (546-6604), 12 Main Street, Rockport. Open daily 10–5 (10–4 off-season), Sunday noon–5. In this former tavern galleries meander off into the skylighted barn out back. The works of art on display are by association members. Art classes and concerts are also held here, and the small gift shop sells cards, books, and gift items.

Local Colors (283-3996), 142 Main Street, Gloucester, is a cooperative gallery showcasing work by a variety of outstanding local artists, sculptors, potters, jewelers, and toymakers

The Patron's Museum and Educational Center (281-6437), 92 Thatcher Road (Route 127A across from the turnoff for Long Beach), Gloucester. Open most afternoons 1–4. This small blue building is a nonprofit gallery focusing both on work by artists like Emile Gruppe (director of the Gloucester School of Painting, 1940–1970), Hugh Breckenridge and Ken Gore (represented by a large '50s mural of Gloucester Harbor), and Frederick Malhaupt, all of whom have taught art on Cape Ann over the past 150 years. Some 70 current artists and craftspeople are also represented.

SCENIC DRIVES

Gloucester

Route 128, exit 15, approach to Gloucester. You quickly find yourself in **Manchester-by-the-Sea,** a picturesque village that still looks like the resort it was in the 19th century. The inns and summer hotels have disappeared, however, and much of the choicest waterfront is now open to residents only. Still, splendid **Singing Beach** (see *Swimming*) is open to anyone willing to walk the little more than a mile from the commuter rail stop or (limited) parking in the village. This seaside town separated from Salem in 1645, and traded with Europe and the West Indies in the 18th century, as evidenced by **The Trask House** (526-7230, 10 Union

Street, open July and August, Wednesday through Saturday 2–5); a curbside, Federal-style home that houses the **Manchester Historical Society** collection. It was owned originally by Abigail Trask, wife of a sea captain who traded with Russian Czar Nicholas I (Abigail was happily married, but insisted that the house remain officially hers). Along Central Street, note the **Orthodox Congregational Church,** a graceful 1809 classic. The **Manchester Memorial Library** next door was designed by Charles McKim. Seaside "1" on Central Street, a fanciful building erected in 1885 to house the town's first steam fire engine, is open Saturdays in summer (10–4), displaying vintage steam engines. **Masconomo Park** on Beach Street is the site of periodic concerts and a good picnicking spot, with a view of Manchester's largely hidden harbor and two yacht clubs. Also note the **Old Burial Ground** on Summer Street (junction with Washington), a beautiful plot with 17th- and 18th-century headstones.

Continue east along Route 127 (Summer Street) and veer off along Raymond Street into **Magnolia,** a village in the town of Gloucester. What's missing here is the 750-room Oceanside Hotel, billed around the turn of the century as the largest coastal resort in New England. (It burned to the ground in 1958.) Shops built to serve the resort still stand but this is now a year-round suburban community with a pleasant restaurant (**The Patio;** see *Eating Out*) at its heart. The **Magnolia Historical Society and Museum** (525-3070), housed on the second floor of the Magnolia Library Center, corner of Lexington and Norman Avenue, displays memorabilia from the village's grand resort era. Continue along the shore, which becomes Norman, then Hesperus Avenue as it passes **Hammond Castle Museum** (see *Museums*). Next you pass **Ravenswood Park** (see *Green Space*) and, next, **Stage Fort Park** and the **Gloucester Visitors Center** (see *Guidance*).

Gloucester to Rockport

The quickest way from Gloucester to Rockport is Route 127, but 127A— the shore route—offers views of the harbor and open ocean, access to beaches, smooth rocks, and to Eastern Point and the Dog Bar Breakwater (see *Historic Homes and Sites*). At the eastern end of Rogers Street, bear right on East Main Street through East Gloucester. Note the access to **Rocky Neck,** then **Niles Beach** (a great place to park and walk) and just beyond it the stone pillars that discourage access to Eastern Point. Beyond them lie **Beauport Museum** (see *Museums*), the **Eastern Point Massachusetts Audubon Sanctuary** (see *To Do— Birding*) and the **Eastern Point Light and Dog Bar Breakwater.** As it rounds the corner to run along the open ocean, Route 127A becomes Atlantic Avenue. Note possibilities for parking, at least briefly, along the water at **Bass Rocks.** Continue on Route 127A, but you may want to double back (it's one-way the other direction) to walk the wooden bridge to **Good Harbor Beach** (see *Swimming*). Off-season parking isn't a problem, and it's a beautiful spot. Continue on Route 12A as it follows the coast (see **Good Harbor Beach, Long Beach,** and **Pebble Beach** under *Swimming*). Offshore note **Thachers Island,** marked by twin lights (1851); it's named for a couple who survived the 1625 shipwreck in which they lost four children. Continue into Rockport.

Rockport to Annisquam

From **Dock Square** follow Beach Street or Route 127 north to the Granite Pier. Across from the quarry, accessible by car, is this great spot to enjoy the view. **Pigeon Cove,** farther along Route 127, is hidden behind Cape Ann Tool Company. It's a quiet inlet where fishing boats tie up. The **New England Lobster Company** (see *Selective Shopping*) at the end of the pier has a reasonably priced selection of fish and lobster. At the next major bend in the road be sure to take a right on Gott Avenue and follow the signs to **Halibut Point State Park** (see *Green Space*). **Folly Cove,** farther along Route 127, is a good spot to pull off and walk the rocks. Next you pass through the small villages of Lanesville and Bayview and come to Annisquam. This village within the town of Gloucester is known for its narrow streets and crooked old homes dating from its improbable 18th- and early-19th-century status as a thriving port. The **Annisquam Village Church** was built in 1830, and the **Village Hall,** as a Baptist meetinghouse, in 1828. On the green is the Old Leonard School, now the **Annisquam Exchange and Art Gallery** (open mid-June to mid-September except Sunday). Also note the **Lobster Cove Bridge,** built in 1847. The footbridge spans Lobster Cove, the easy way down from Route 127 to the heart of the village. The **Annisquam Market and Restaurant** (283-3070), at 33 River Road here, is open May through October for breakfast, lunch, and dinner, with a waterside deck as well as dining room.

Essex to Ipswich

As noted in the **Essex Shipbuilding Museum** (see *Museums*) some 4000 vessels are said to have been built within a few miles of each other here along the tidal Essex River, most along the stretch of Route 133 now known for its seafood restaurants and antiques shops (see *Eating Out* and *Selective Shopping*). You might want to park (in the public lot beside the architecturally amazing vintage-1894 **Town Hall** and **Memorial Library** just off Route 133 on Route 22 south) and explore the Old Chebacco Parish graveyard behind the Shipbuilding Museum. Also note **Cogswell's Grant** (SPNEA), 135 acres that have been farmed continually since 1636 and a splendid vintage-1735 house filled with Americana due to open in August of 1998, with tours Wednesday through Sunday 11–5. Continue west along the marshes into Ipswich and north on Route 1A to the town's south village green with its striking **John Whipple House** (356-2811), 53 South Main Street, open April to mid-October, Wednesday through Saturday 10–4, Sunday 1–4. Adults $5, $2 child and students; admission covers the Heard and Whipple houses (see below).

The major part of this weathered, double-gabled house—one of the old-est buildings in New England—was built in 1640 by "clothiers of good estate." It remained in the Whipple family for two centuries and in 1898 became one of the country's first houses to be restored. It is well fur-nished, and the herb garden contains 60 varieties of medicinal plants. Follow 1A to the **John Heard House** (356-2541), 40 South Main Street. Built in 1795, this stately Federal mansion is crowned with four corner chimneys. Maintained, as is the Whipple House, by the Ipswich Histori-cal Society, it is filled with China-trade treasures; there is also a collection of carriages, from a doctor's surrey to a funeral rig. For hours and admis-sion, see Whipple House.

Most of the town's late-17th- and 18th-century houses are grouped around **Meeting House Green** (the meeting house itself burned and has been replaced by a modernistic church). The **Old Burying Ground** on High Street contains stones dating from 1634, and the carv-ings on many gravestones are outstanding. Also note the **Choate Bridge,** in the middle of the village, said to be the oldest stone-arched bridge (1764) in English-speaking America.

Back to the south green, turn left on Argilla Road, one of the pretti-est roads on the North Shore, past **Goodale Orchards** with its winery (see *Selective Shopping*), on through the salt marshes to Castle Neck and **Castle Hill** (356-4351), Argilla Road. **The Great House**, a majestic, 59-room brick mansion built by Chicago plumbing magnate Richard Crane, is open for tours Wednesdays and Thursdays, May to October 10–4 ($7 adults, $5 children under 12, and free under 6). The house is maintained by the Trustees of Reservations and is the scene of summer concerts, plays, Circus Smirkus, an antique-auto show, and other happenings in July and August, as well as spring and Christmas house tours. The setting is 200 acres that include a Grand Allée and the North Shore's most spec-tacular beach. (Also see the **Crane Wildlife Refuge** under *Green Space* and **Crane Islands Tour** under *Boat Excursions*.) On your way back down Argilla Road take Heartbreak Road to Route 133 and turn right. Just before the Essex line you pass **Wolf Hollow** (356-0216), open week-ends (1–5; presentations at 1:30 and 3:30), which exhibits pure wolves.

Essex to Hamilton

From Essex (see description above, also *Museums, Green Space, Antiques Shops,* and *Eating Out*), turn south onto Route 22 through Essex Falls. Bear right when Essex Street splits and follow it through farms as it turns into Larch Row. Turn left onto Route 1A into Wenham, site of the **Wenham Museum** (468-2377) at 132 Main Street; it's open year-round daily 10–4, Saturday and Sunday 1–5; $4 adults, $3.50 children, $2 se-niors). Substantially expanded in the fall of '97, this surprisingly large and sophisticated museum space houses changing exhibits and an ex-tensive exhibit of working model trains; the doll and toy soldier collec-tion is also justly famous and a "Play and Learn" room is themed to current exhibits. The attached 17th-century **Claflin-Richards House** contains period rooms. The **Wenham Tea House** at the corner of Monument and Main Streets is a North Shore tradition (see *Eating Out* and *Snacks*); it's also a classic gift shop. Turn back north on Route 1A through Hamilton, an aristocratic town known for its polo matches (Memorial Day weekend through Columbus Day every Sunday at 3; phone the **Myopia Hunt Club** at 468-1402). Note **Appleton Farms** on your left as you head north into Ipswich; a portion of this 123-acre estate, which has been in the Appleton family since 1638, is open. The Trustees of Reservations maintains 5 miles of mowed paths—"Grass Rides" for hiking and ski touring. Continue on Route 1A to its junction with Route 133 and return to Essex.

TO DO

BICYCLING
Although the roads are heavily trafficked, in many places they border the water. You can park your bike in spots where you cannot park a car and clamber onto the rocks or browse in shops, where you will pay far less than at the beaches. Bikes can be rented from **Harborside Cycle** (281-7744) in Gloucester and **Seaside Cycle** (526-1200) in Manchester. Bicycle shops are good sources of information about the many local mountain biking possibilities. **Bradley Palmer State Park** (887-5931), in Topsfield, is particularly popular with bicyclists; inquire about the 11-mile segment of the **Bay Circuit Trail** between Ipswich and Rowley (470-1982) and inquire in Gloucester about trails in **Dogtown**, a 3,600-acre conservation area (see *Green Space*).

BIRDING
Ipswich River Wildlife Sanctuary (887-9264), 87 Perkins Row, Topsfield. From Route 1 turn east at the lights onto Route 97, and then left at the first intersection. This is the largest of 16 staffed sanctuaries maintained by Massachusetts Audubon: some 2800 acres of marsh, pond, and upland with 5 miles of frontage on the Ipswich River. An estate developed around the turn of the century as an arboretum by horticulturist Thomas Proctor, it includes the Rockery, an elaborate garden featuring large boulders carted from neighboring towns and plantings imported from around the world. The entire sanctuary is known as a great place to come in May to see migrating birds, specifically the brightly plumed warblers. There are 10 miles of paths, which are marked for skiing in winter. Year-round admission. Massachusetts Audubon also maintains **Eastern Point Sanctuary** at the tip of Eastern Point, Route 127A, East Gloucester. These 26 acres include a pebbly beach, rocky shore, salt marsh, and woods, with a spectacular view of Boston.

Also see *Green Space*, especially the **Cornelius and Mine S. Crane Wildlife Refuge**.

Rockport Harbor

BOAT EXCURSIONS
Water Shuttle

From late June to September 1 the **Cape Ann Transportation Authority** (CATA) operates frequent daily water taxi service from Harbor Loop and Seven Seas Wharf, Gloucester, to Ten Pound Island in the middle of the harbor (some people bring picnics and spend the day) and to Rocky Neck. Weekends only in September.

Harbor and Cape Ann Tours

Moby Duck Tours (281-DUCK), Rogers Street, Gloucester. Mid-May through Labor Day, on the hour, 10–4. Fifty-minute narrated harbor/land tours on amphibious vessels. **Harbor Tours, Inc.** (283-1979), Harbor Loop, Gloucester. Cape Ann Lighthouse cruise, 2½ hours around Cape Ann; shorter hands-on lobster hauling tours. (Also see *Sailing*.)

Longer cruises

The Virginia C. (617-261-6633), 290 Northern Avenue, Boston, Sunday through Wednesday, runs from Boston to Rocky Neck. Bikes permitted. **Gloucester to Provincetown Boat Express** (283-5110), late June through September 1 from Rose's Wharf, Gloucester. A 2½-hour cruise to the tip of Cape Cod and back, with 4 hours in Provincetown.

Lobster-Hauling Cruises

Lobstering "cruises" are offered by **Lobster Hauling Cruise** (283-1979) from Harbor Loop, Gloucester and by **"Dove" Lobstering Trips** (546-3642) from Town Wharf in Rockport.

Others

Essex River Cruises (768-6981), 35 Dodge Street, Essex Marina. April through October; scheduled cruises aboard the 34-foot pontoon boat *Essex River Queen* to Crane Beach and Hog Island. Clambakes available on charters. Cliff Amero narrates the 90-minute tours, pointing out osprey nests, egrets, and local landmarks. **Crane Islands Tour** (356-4351), Crane Wildlife Refuge, Argilla Road, Ipswich. Memorial Day through October, 1½-hour boat and wagon; $12 per adult, $5 children 12 and under; call for hours. The *Osprey*, a 22-passenger pontoon boat, runs twice daily (three times on weekends) to Hog and Long Islands, scene of the 1996 movie, *The Crucible*—which has left the islands slightly tidier (brush cleared, roads graded) but much as it was before 23 houses were built for the set (all but one have been razed). From the *Osprey*, visitors tour the islands on a unique contraption: a tractor hitched to a beach wagon, fitted with a canopy and, if needed in high greenhead-fly season, with side screens. It's also equipped with field glasses and bird and flower guides. See *Green Space* for more about these islands. **Tiny Tug Tours and Charters** (281-1572), Lighthouse Marina, Parker Street, Gloucester. *Time Being*, a 23-foot, six-passenger miniature tugboat designed with a shallow draft to cruise the salt marshes, tours the Annisquam River and harbor several times daily in summer.

BOAT RENTALS

Old Harbor Yacht Club (596-9411), Wharf Road, Rockport. Powerboats and a variety of sailboats are rented. **Sun Splash Boat Rental** (283-4722), East Main Street, Gloucester. **SeaTopia Dive Ventures** (546-9411), Bearskin Neck, Rockport. Here you can rent motor boats, kayaks, sailboats.

CANOEING

The Ipswich River is navigable for 30 miles. Rental canoes and put-in advice are available from **Foote Brothers Canoes** (356-9771), 230 Topsfield Road, Ipswich; reservations for rentals are recommended.

FISHING PARTY BOATS

The Yankee Fleet (283-0313), Cape Ann Marina, 75 Essex Street, Gloucester, offers all-day, half-day, and overnight deep-sea fishing trips. All-day trips leave at 6 and 7 AM, returning at 3 and 4 PM. Bait is supplied, and tackle can be rented. Inquire about cruises to Nantucket. **Capt. Tom Luke's Deep Sea Fishing** (281-5411), Town Dock, St. Peter's Park, Gloucester. The 56-foot *Nicole Renee* departs regularly at 6:30 AM for 9-hour fishing days on Jeffrey's Ledge, Tilly's Bank, and Stellwagen Bank. $38 per adult, $20 for children and seniors. **Coastal Fishing Charters** (283-5513), aboard the 22-foot *Larivee;* customized trips in search of striped bass and bluefish. **Sea Smoke Charters** (282-4940), a 36-foot Sportfisher available for up to six passengers.

FLY-FISHING
Fin and Feather (768-3245), 103 Main Street, Essex, is a source of where-to advice as well as equipment.

FOR FAMILIES
✐ **New England Alive** (256-7013), 163 High Street, Ipswitch (Routes 1A and 133 north of the village), open daily April through November, weather permitting. Admission. This petting farm has barnyard and woodland animals ranging from pheasants and skunks to coyotes and bears, with some exotic snakes.

GOLF
Rockport Golf Club (546-3340), South Rockport; nine-hole course. **Candlewood Golf Club** (356-5377), Route 133, Ipswich; nine-hole public course. **Cape Ann Golf Course** (768-7544), Route 133, Essex; public nine-hole course.

SAILING
The *Thomas E. Lannon* (281-6634), the first schooner to be built in Essex in 50 years, offers 2-hour sails from Gloucester. The *Chrissy* (768-7035), a Gloucester-based, vintage-1910 Friendship sloop captained by Harold Burnham (who built the *Thomas E. Lannon*), offers tours and charters.

SCUBA DIVING
Cape Ann Divers (281-8082), 17 Eastern Avenue, Gloucester. Rentals, boat charters, dive trips, instruction, snorkeling equipment. **SeaTopia Dive Ventures** (546-9411), Bearskin Neck, Rockport.

SEA KAYAKING
Essex River Basin Adventures (768-ERBA; 1-800-KAYAK-04), based at the Essex Shipbuilding Museum boatyard, Route 133, Essex, offers a variety of guided tours. We can vouch for the beauty of paddling with owner Ozzie Osborn out through the Essex basin to Crane Beach or Hog Island for a swim or walk. **Kayak Cape Ann** (282-1370), based in Gloucester, specializes in guided tours from a variety of Cape Ann venues. **Ipswich Bay Ocean Kayaking** (356-2464) specializes in the waters between Ipswich Bay and Plum Island.

SWIMMING
In Gloucester: All beaches forbid the use of inflated tubes and the like. Lifeguards are on duty 9–5, and the nonresident parking fee (charged 8–4) is $15 per car. All have bathhouses and snack bars. On weekends it's best to be there before 10 to ensure a spot. **Good Harbor Beach,** Thatcher Road, is the most popular, and **Wingaersheek Beach** on Atlantic Street (exit 14 off Route 128) is favored by families with small children (great climbing rocks and relatively small surf). **Half Moon** and **Cressy Beaches** at Stage Fort Park are city beaches.

In Rockport: Beaches include **Long Beach** (lined with cottages) and **Cape Hedge Beach** (one parking area serves both); also **Old Garden Beach,** accessible by foot from many Rockport inns; **Front** and **Back Beaches** on the other side of the village; and well-named **Pebble Beach** on Penzance Road. There are rest rooms at Front Beach, which,

Good Harbor Beach in Gloucester

along with Back Beach, is accessible to anyone who can find a legal parking space. Most people come by trolley or on foot from local inns and B&Bs.

In Ipswich: **Crane Beach** (356-4354) is part of the **Richard T. Crane Jr. Memorial Reservation,** Argilla Road. Open daily 8 AM–sunset, the summer services include lifeguards, bathhouses, and refreshment facilities. Admission in 1998: January to mid-May, $5 per car weekdays, $8 weekends; Memorial Day through Labor Day, $15 per car; weekends, $9 per day; midweek, shoulder prices in shoulder seasons. $2 per bicycle year-round. This property, maintained by the Trustees of Reservations, includes more than 4 miles of sand on Ipswich Bay. The superb, dune-backed beach never quite fills, but the parking lot frequently does, despite the stiff fee. Overflow parking is at Steep Hill Beach (a section of the main strand), entailing a fair walk down a steep hill; not ideal if you are trying to manage both gear and small children. Both sides of the beach are also plagued by greenhead flies in late July and early August. (See *Scenic Drives* and *Entertainment* for more on **Castle Hill**, also part of this reservation.)

In Manchester: **Singing Beach** is a wide, smooth beach now backed by mansions. There is an elegant little beach house with a weather vane and fanlight. Anyone can use the snack bar and rest rooms, but changing rooms are for just Manchester residents. Parking is by sticker only, but you can leave your car in town or come by train from Boston and walk the mile or so to the beach.

WHALE-WATCHING

Whales fast all winter and feast during the months that conveniently coincide with tourist season. They feed on sand eel—a tiny, wormlike creature that thrives on Stellwagen Bank, a dozen miles off Cape Ann. Some

200 whales—humpbacks, minkes, finbacks, and right whales—feed here from April through October. They add up to the world's greatest concentration of whales, not only in numbers but also in species. The massive mammals seem to respond to whale-watchers by breaching (flinging their entire bodies—up to 50 feet and 40 tons' worth—out of the water). They also "spy-ho" (shove their massive snouts out of the water) and "lob-tail" (wave their huge tails in the air). All the Cape Ann boats offer half-day trips with naturalists aboard to narrate the whale story. **Cape Ann Whale Watch** (283-5110; 1-800-877-5110), Rose's Wharf at the eastern end of the Gloucester waterfront. Capt. Fred Douglas was the first (in 1979) to take whale-watchers out from Gloucester. **Yankee Whale Watch** (283-0313; 1-800-942-5464), at Cape Ann Marina, 79 Essex Avenue, Gloucester. Two trips daily, three on summer weekends. **Seven Seas Whale Watch** (283-1776; 1-800-238-1776) departs from the wharf behind the Gloucester House Restaurant (see *Dining Out*). A 90-foot Privateer, five-hour narrated cruises.

GREEN SPACE

WALKS

We recommend securing a copy of the *Passport to Essex County* ($15), published by the **Essex County Greenbelt Association** (768-7241); you can find it in local bookstores or pick it up at the association's headquarters, the farm at the **Cox Reservation** on Route 133 in Essex. Since its 1961 founding, Greenbelt has preserved some 8000 acres of land in the county. The guide details walks to 17 of its 200 properties. Inquire about monthly guided walks.

Walking Cape Ann, by Helen Naismith ($11.95), is also a handy tool, containing 22 maps and written descriptions of dozens of widely varied trails running the length and breadth of the cape. Descriptions are based on **Walks with Ted Tarr**. For the past 20 years Tarr has been meeting with anyone wishing to take a long walk (the trail varies each week) at the Whistlestop Mall on Railroad Avenue in Rockport, Sunday at 10 AM, year-round. A direct descendant of a Rockport founding father, Tarr says he "inherited the job" from Dorothy Luce when she was 80; Luce had been leading Sunday-morning walks since the '30s.

In Gloucester

Ravenswood Park, off Western Avenue (Route 127), southwest of Gloucester; the parking lot is some 2 miles west of the junction with Route 133. The 300-acre park was laid out in 1889 and contains miles of wide, wooded paths, good for jogging and cross-country skiing. This spot is reportedly the northernmost point that the wild magnolia grows in.

Dogtown. Best accessed from Cherry Street in the Riverdale section of Gloucester. A 3000-acre tract that's best explored on a guided Sunday-morning walk (see above). No houses survive, but there are a few dozen cellar holes, the traces of the 80 families who lived here between the early 1700s and the 1830s. The Essex County Greenbelt Association has been instrumental in acquiring land, removing trash, and improving signs to this area. It's a superb place for birding in spring and fall and for blueberrying in July, but it can be confusing. Detailed trail descriptions can be found in both guidebooks listed above, and a Dogtown Map ($5) is sold at the Gloucester Visitors Center. Do not come without a guide or a companion.

Stony Cove and Presson Reservation, exit 13 off Route 128, Gloucester, near the confluence of the Annisquam and Little Rivers. This 45-acre property includes a granite pier, tidal inlet, salt marsh, and upland white pine, oak, and sweet birch. Detailed directions and descriptions are in the *Greenbelt Passport.*

Back Shore, Atlantic Avenue, Gloucester. From Route 128, turn left at the second light after the second rotary. Follow Bass Avenue to the ocean for a wonderful dune walk to view the rocky shoreline and large summer homes. Great surf-watching after storms.

In Rockport

Note: A Rockport Guide to Public Paths & Town Landings, available from the Rockport Chamber of Commerce (see *Guidance*) and in local bookstores, offers clear maps and detailed directions to shoreline paths, headlands, and beaches.

Halibut Point, Gott Avenue off Route 127. North of Rockport a narrow path leads down to one of the most dramatic sites on the eastern seaboard. First there is the 12-acre Halibut Point property maintained by the Trustees of Reservations; a path leads through low scrub to flat rocks and a fine view across Ipswich Bay. The adjoining 54-acre Halibut Point State Park (546-2997) section commands the same view (on a clear day, Mount Agamenticus in York, Maine, looms at the end of the sweep of coastline) and includes deep granite quarries (a sign says NO SWIMMING; admission is $3 per car). This rocky headland forms the northern tip of the cape, off which sailing vessels have always had to tack ("haulabout"). This spot is great for picnics, and there are tidal pools to explore; also a self-guided trail detailing the granite industry.

In Essex

The Cox Reservation, Route 133, Essex (first driveway west of J.T. Farnham's Restaurant; see *Eating Out*). The headquarters for the Essex County Greenbelt Association is in an old farmhouse, former home of Allyn Cox (his murals grace Grant's tomb). A path leads down past the gardens and orchard, through marsh to a landing on the Essex River with a fine view of Hog Island and Crane Beach (see *Swimming*) in the distance. Bring paper and paints.

James N. and Mary F. Stavros Reservation, Island Road off Route 133 (just west of Cape Ann Golf Course; see *To Do—Golf*). A short foot trail leads to the top of White's Hill, just 116 feet high but with a view that takes in Castle Hill, Hog Island, and the meanderings of the Castle Neck River. The 53-acre refuge includes a salt marsh and pine, cedar, and cherry trees. A great spot to sketch or picnic.

In Ipswich

Cornelius and Mine S. Crane Wildlife Refuge (356-4351), Argilla Road, Ipswich. Open Memorial Day–October 21, 9–3:30, maintained by the Trustees of Reservations. Day-use fee: $2 adults, $1 children 6–12. Of all the 78 Trustees' properties in Massachusetts, the most spectacular are two reservations that once formed this 2000-acre estate. Amassed in 1909 by Chicago plumbing baron Richard T. Crane, the property includes most of the 4-mile-long barrier beach protecting the Essex and Ipswich river estuaries (see *Swimming*) and the 59-room mansion above it (see *Historic Homes*). A mile-long interpretive trail explores the barrier-beach system, leading to a woodland where sand dunes are slowly engulfing pine trees. The 680-acre wildlife refuge is accessed from Castle Neck, just before the beach parking area. Theoretically it's composed of five islands but what you access are Hog Island and Long Island, linked by a bridge and accessible in summer via the *Osprey* (see *Boat Excursions* for details about seasonal boat/wagon tours). These islands are magical. On our tour, right on the dock, a tree swallow thrust its iridescent blue-green head from a birdhouse, and up the road snowy egrets and a glossy ibis rested beside the salt pans. White terns dive-bombed for minnows in a tidal creek. Bobolinks and meadowlarks perched, and brightly colored butterflies flitted in meadows carpeted with purple clover, buttercups, daisies, and oats (also poison ivy). Stone walls are overgrown with wild roses. The tractor tugs you up through the pine forest, planted in 1935 by Crane's son Cornelius, who lies buried on the open summit, from which the view extends down the coast to the Isles of Shoals.

Greenwood Farm (356-4755), Jeffrey's Neck Road. Another Trustees of Reservations treasure: 213 acres of salt marsh and upland meadows. Good birding. To find it, continue straight ahead, if you are coming up Route 1A at South Green (instead of heading into the village); this is County Road, which turns into East Street. About a mile after the Ipswich Town Landing, bear left on Jeffrey's Neck Road. Fieldstone pillars on the right mark the entrance to the property 0.7 mile farther. Turn into the driveway and park in the lot. A path leads down to the shore.

Also see the **Ipswich River Wildlife Sanctuary** under *Birding*.

BEACHES

Whittemore Marsh. Open only October through May, this 75 acres of salt marsh and barrier beach is owned by Greenbelt. Access is from Wingaersheek Road in West Gloucester.

Coolidge Point Reservation, Manchester, off Route 127 just past its junction with Hesperus Avenue. Small parking lot. Easy trail leads through woods, past salt marshes, and by a salt marsh pond to Magnolia Beach. Great birding.

(Also see *Swimming*.)

PICNICKING

Lumber Wharf, Rockport. Right off Dock Square but totally hidden behind the Lumber Wharf Building, down the alley by the Rockport Chamber of Commerce office (see *Guidance*). Picnic tables and a great view of Sandy Bay.

Pigeon Hill, Landmark Lane off Route 127 near Pigeon Cove, Rockport. A great picnic spot above Sandy Bay if you don't mind sharing it with a water tank.

The Headlands, Atlantic Avenue, Rockport. This rocky point at the entrance to Rockport Harbor has benches great for boat-watching.

Rafe's Chasm, Magnolia; off Hesperus Avenue, about ¼ mile after Hammond Castle heading toward Magnolia (see *Museums*). There's a small parking area and a short, easy path leading to spectacular rock perches.

Agassiz Rock in Manchester, east side of School Street, Essex; ½ mile north of Route 128, exit 15. This 106-acre property is wooded upland with two glacial boulders said to have been discovered by Harvard naturalist Louis Agassiz. A great spot for a picnic. From Route 128, exit 15, take School Street north ½ mile. The entrance and parking are on the right.

STATE FORESTS

Bradley Palmer State Forest (887-5931) in Topsfield (from Route 1, turn right at the second light north of the Topsfield Fairgrounds, then onto Hamilton Road) offers picnic areas, fishing, and canoeing on the Ipswich River; 35 miles of hiking and ski trails; mountain biking on snowmobile trails.

Willowdale State Forest (887-5931), Linebrook Road in Ipswich, is 2400 acres with 40 miles of trails, canoeing, and fishing.

LODGING

INNS

In Rockport 01966

✐ **Seaward Inn and Cottages** (546-3471; 1-800-648-7733), Marmion Way. Open April through October. Jane Fiumara carries on the traditions of Rockport's most appealing resort. The 39 rooms (all with private bath) are scattered among the main house, The Breakers (directly on the water), Carriage House, and assorted small cottages, some with fireplace and/or kitchen. A path winds along the shore of a sheltered, spring-fed pond (with a small sandy beach) and into a small wood. Old Garden Beach (see *Swimming*) is a 5-minute walk, and the village is a mile away. The main house itself offers a spacious, comfortable sun porch, a fairly formal living room with a grand piano, and an old-fashioned dining room that is open to the public as the Sea Garden (see *Dining Out*). $115–175, $100–140 off-season with breakfast; $20 for extra person in room, no charge for cribs and children 3 and under.

Yankee Clipper (546-3407), PO Box 2399, Route 127 north of the village. The main inn is hedged off below the road, facing Sandy Bay and, across the bay, the village. The living room is carpeted in Oriental rugs, richly paneled, and decorated with ginger jars, ship's models, and the portrait of Mehitable Lamon, great-grandmother of innkeeper Barbara Wemyss Ellis. Barbara's parents opened the Yankee Clipper in 1946. There is a sense of tradition here, and of everything in its place. A total of 29 rooms are scattered among the inn, its annex, the Captain's Quarters, and the Bulfinch House across the road (named for its architect), which caters to more transient guests. Grounds are terraced in flowers, and rocky promontories overlook the water. There is an outdoor pool. $109–249 with breakfast, less in the off-season; midweek packages available. See *Dining Out*.

Ralph Waldo Emerson House (546-6321), Green Street. Open mid-April through November. Off by itself beyond Pigeon Cove, this grand 1850s summer hotel is hanging in there but is currently up for sale. It offers large common rooms and a sub-lobby recreation area (table tennis, large-screen TV, whirlpool, and sauna); also a heated saltwater pool. Rooms are old-fashioned, all with private bath; $96–137 in season; from $85 Labor Day through October and less off-season. Breakfast and dinner are served.

BED & BREAKFASTS
In Gloucester 01930

Harborview Inn (283-2277; 1-800-299-6696), 71 Western Avenue (Stacy Boulevard). Open year-round. The six guest rooms have all been wall-papered and painted by *Better Homes & Gardens* magazine and are bright, crisp, and flowery to the max. Rooms vary from the small Rockport Room with shared bath to the Boulevard Penthouse, which fills the entire third floor and has two baths and a living room, as well as a bedroom. The Gloucester Suite features a working fireplace, and most rooms have ocean views. Note the painting of the fishing boat above the mantel; it belonged to innkeeper John Orlando's father. A continental breakfast is included in $79–185, cheaper off-season.

☞ **Williams Guest House** (283-4931), 136 Bass Avenue. Betty Williams is the delightful host of this shingled house overlooking salt marsh, tidal water, and Good Harbor Beach. Open May through October. Accommodations range from the neighboring cottage and two apartments with ocean views to four second-floor guest rooms with and without private baths. High-season rates are $54 and $64 for rooms, from $66 per night for apartments; off-season rates begin at $42. A complimentary light breakfast is served.

✐ **Samarkand Inn** (283-3757), 1 Harbor Road. Open year-round, a pleasant house with views of the water and Good Harbor Beach (see *Swimming*) across the road and plenty of comfortable common space: a long, glassed-in porch and big comfortable living room. There are five guest rooms, three with private bath; $40–50 plus tax includes a breakfast of home-made muffins. Families welcome.

Gray Manor (283-5409), 14 Atlantic Road. Open May through late October. This is a longtime B&B within walking distance of Good Harbor Beach (see *Swimming*). Madelaine Gray has three guest rooms and six kitchenettes, all with private bath, air-conditioning, cable TV, refrigerator, some decks. Movies are offered in the lounge, and continental breakfast is served in the new sun room. $45–52 off-season, $59–65 in season; kitchenettes $450 per week.

The Thomas Riggs House (281-4802), 27 Vine Street. Billed as the oldest extant house on Cape Ann, this structure was built between 1660 and 1720 of dovetailed squared logs. It remained in the Riggs family until Barbara Lambert acquired it a few years ago. She installed running water and heat (although the original six fireplaces remain) and added a back wing. The house now includes three guest rooms, each with an unattached bath. All are furnished with antiques. Not far from Wingaersheek Beach and Annisquam. $125 includes breakfast.

In Rockport 01966

Addison Choate Inn (546-7543; 1-800-245-7543), 49 Broadway. Although the 1860s house is right downtown on Broadway, it offers peace: a deep garden with a nicely landscaped swimming pool, six rooms and three suites artfully decorated with a mix of antiques and modern furniture and original art. The coach house has the feel of a country cottage and sleeps four, and the Celebration Suite is fit for honeymoons and anniversaries. Shirley and Knox Johnson are exceptionally helpful and friendly hosts. The buffet breakfast features homemade granola; it's served either in the dining room or on the long, flower-filled porch. $85–125 per couple for rooms, more for suites, breakfast included.

Eden Pines Inn (546-2505), Eden Road. This is a real find, a gracious B&B with rooms right on the open ocean, overlooking Thachers Island and its two lighthouses. It's a classic, shingled, turn-of-the-century mansion, 2 miles south of the village. The seven upstairs bedrooms have luxurious baths and ocean views (several are large enough to accommodate four people). There is a paneled living room with a stone hearth and a bright breakfast room overlooking the ocean. Best of all are the porch and patio, and the smooth rocks below are great for sunning. $100–165 includes an ample breakfast. Inquire about the four-bedroom oceanfront house up the road available May through October ($230–380 per day).

Rocky Shores (546-2823; 1-800-348-4003), 65 Eden Road. Open mid-April through October. This is one of those unusual places that is equally good for families, singles, and couples. A brown-shingled 1905 mansion forms the hospitable centerpiece for 11 two- and three-bedroom housekeeping cottages. Renate and Gunter Kostka encourage guests to mingle in the living room and on the porch, which commands a splendid view of the ocean and twin lighthouses on Thachers Island. Guests in the main house also meet over breakfast. If you opt for a cottage, choose one in front instead of in back of the main house. Beaches are within walking distance. $76–117 per couple for rooms; cottages run $640–825 per week.

Inn on Cove Hill (546-2701; 1-888-546-2701), 37 Mount Pleasant Street. Built in 1791, this classic Federal-style house has a curving staircase with 13 steps, representing the 13 original colonies. Legend has it that it was built with pirate gold found at nearby Gully Point. John and Marjorie Pratt offer 11 guest rooms, most of them doubles, one with an extra bed. There's also a bright little single on the third floor. The wide-planked floors gleam, and moldings and doors have been preserved. Rooms are papered in designer prints and furnished with family antiques, comforters, and canopies made by forebears. $47 for a room with shared bath, $65–101 with private, including continental breakfast, less off-season.

Old Farm Inn (546-3237; 1-800-233-6828), Pigeon Cove. This 1799 saltwater farm offers low-beamed common rooms and three pleasant guest rooms in the inn itself, four in the Barn Guesthouse (one with a kitchenette, the others with fridge and hotpot). All have private bath and TV. There is a comfortable sitting room for guests in the inn, and continental breakfast is provided in the sun room. It's a bit far from the village, but set in 5 acres of lawn and meadow and adjacent to Halibut Point (see *Green Space*). $90–135 (for a two-room suite) in summer, less off-season. It's up for sale at this writing, so check to see if new ownership has worked changes.

Peg Leg Inn (546-2352; 1-800-346-2352), 2 King Street. Open mid-April to late October. Five 19th-century houses, clustered within steps of each other, offer a total of 33 rooms, all with private bath and TV. Owned by the Welcome family as long as anyone can remember, this cluster obviously offers a variety of rooms and views, the best in the Coakley House right at the head of Front Beach, with views back toward the village and an expansive front lawn (shared by all guests) on Sandy Bay. Guest rooms are all crisply impersonal but immaculate and comfortable: white bedspreads, ruffled curtains, wallpaper, a couple of inviting chairs. The Main Inn and Office offers spacious common rooms in which a continental breakfast is laid out. Families are accommodated in three of the houses and there is a game room. Also see *Dining Out*. $85–130 double, $150 for a two-bedroom ocean-view unit for up to four people.

Pleasant Street Inn (546-3915; 1-800-541-3915), 17 Pleasant Street. Open year-round. The view from the expansive porch is across town to the bay, unquestionably one of the most pleasant places in town to sit on a summer day. The eight rooms are also comfortable, all with private bath and all different, from spacious tower rooms and a snug double under the eaves to a private basement-level room with its own entrance and a Jacuzzi. Inquire about the Carriage House apartment. Roger and Lynn Norris have nicely renovated and landscaped this large Victorian house that sits high above town, within walking distance of shops and restaurants. $88–98 includes a buffet breakfast, less off-season.

Seven South Street (546-6708), 7 South Street. Open February into December. This 18th-century house offers six attractive rooms in the house itself, three with private bath, also a cottage and a one-bedroom suite with kitchenette. The front room doubles as the owner's gallery and all rooms are hung with interesting, mostly local art. Common space includes a back deck as well as a small pool and garden; Old Garden Beach (see *Swimming*) is a short walk. The rest of the village is just up South Street (Route 127A). In summer, rooms are $60–85 double; less off-season; inquire about the appealing little back room—it's a real bargain.

Beach Knoll Inn (546-6939), 30 Beach Street. The core clapboard house was one of the first on Sandy Bay, and it has a wide old hearth with a hidden passage. Rooms all have private bath, some have fireplace and refrigerator. Back Beach (see *Swimming*) is just across the street. $63–87 for a room, more for two-room and three-room apartments, also weekly rates. Cheaper off-season.

The Captain's House (546-3825), 69 Marmion Way. This large, white-stucco, vintage-1913 house is sited right on the ocean, 1½ miles from the center of town. Open March through mid-December. The five bedrooms, with private baths, are all pleasant. A continental breakfast is laid out in the seaside sun room. $90–110, less off-season.

Seafarer Inn (546-6248), 50 Marmion Way. Open May through September. This homey, gambrel-roofed inn has ocean views from every room. There are eight airy guest rooms hung with paintings by local artists. The best views are from the two third-floor rooms with breakfast nooks and efficiency kitchenettes. Most rooms have their own bath. A continental breakfast is included in $65–95 in summer. An apartment rents for $1500–1800 per month.

Linden Tree Inn (546-2494; 1-800-541-3915), 26 King Street. This Victorian home and converted carriage house is on a quiet street within easy walking distance of both railroad station and beaches. There are 18 nicely decorated rooms, some ideal for families, and a spacious living room; also a sun porch. Continental breakfast is included in the $63–98 per room, less off-season. Inquire about efficiency units.

Tuck Inn B&B (546-7260; 1-800-789-7260), 17 High Street. Open year-round. An early-19th-century home on a quiet corner with nine nicely furnished rooms, including one suite that can accommodate four. In winter, fireplaces warm the common rooms, and in summer there's a pool; beaches and shops are all within walking distance. Continental breakfast is served. $77–107 double, less off-season.

✑ **The Blueberry** (546-2838), 50 Stockholm Avenue. Open year-round. Nicely sited in Pigeon Cove, just two bedrooms sharing a bath, reasonably priced and with a great breakfast. Families welcome, handy to shore walks. $75 double, $65 single, $10 for an extra roll-away cot; less off-season.

In Magnolia 01930

The White House (525-3642), 18 Norman Avenue. This gracious Victorian house has 8 rooms, also 10 in a motel-style wing (open all year). It is within walking distance of Magnolia shops and restaurants and offers access to a private beach. Continental breakfast featuring home baking is included in $75–90 per couple.

In Essex 01929

George Fuller House (768-7766), 148 Main Street (Route 133). Tucked amid the seafood restaurants and antiques shops, between the main drag and the salt marshes, this cheerful old house is unusually welcoming. The snug, square parlor with paneling and Indian shutters is in the Federal (1830) part of the house, but rooms ramble off into Victorian-era spaces and porches. All six guest rooms have private bath, phone, air-conditioning, and color TV, but each is different. Some have canopied beds; four have working fireplaces. Generally speaking, we prefer the second- and third-floor rooms in back because the view is off across the salt marshes, but the downstairs rooms are also attractive. The penthouse, with its efficiency sink and stove, is a real find. Breakfast might include French toast drizzled with brandied lemon butter or piña colada pancakes. Bob and Cindy Cameron are genial hosts with plenty of suggestions about local options. From $90 for the Story Room off-season to $145 for the penthouse in summer. Most rooms are $115. The Andrews suite, two rooms with a working fireplace, is $135. $15 for extra person in room.

In Hamilton 01936

✑ **The Miles River Country Inn** (468-7206), 823 Bay Road (Route 1A). This is a genuine North Shore estate and one on which you are made to feel like an invited (not just paying) guest. Gretel and Peter Clark's home is a 24-room mansion dating from a number of periods between 1774 and the 1920s, set in lawns and spectacular flower gardens stretching back to the river. Four of the eight guest rooms are named for the Clarks' children, and each has a different feel. Most have private baths; half have a working fireplace. The common rooms are luxurious, most again with working fireplaces. A study is paneled with 19th-century wooden bedsteads from Brittany. The full breakfast features eggs laid by the resident hens and honey from the apiary. Gretel delights in sharing her garden with guests and in directing them to other little-known show gardens in the area. Needless to say, this is a great place for a wedding (but only outside). Children welcome. $110–165 in season, $90–145 off-season.

In Ipswich 01938

Town Hill Bed & Breakfast (356-8000; 1-800-457-7799). An 1850 house on Meeting House Green with 11 guest rooms. One is downstairs, most in a back wing, nine with private bath. $75–135.

In Manchester 01944

Old Corner Inn (526-4996), Route 127, Manchester. A former mansion with nine guest rooms with private baths, some with working fireplace. $75–125, less in winter.

MOTELS

In Gloucester 01930

The Anchorage Inn (283-4788), 5-7 Hawthorne Lane. Open March through December. A motor inn with some of the best harbor views in Gloucester; 14 units that get nicer as you get higher; try for #6 on the second floor, or best of all #9 on the third. Most rooms have balconies and one includes a kitchenette. Walk to Niles Beach. $59–$119 includes continental breakfast.

Cape Ann Marina Resort (283-2112; 1-800-626-7660), 75 Essex Avenue. Right at the marina, this 53-room facility is geared to those who are setting out on 7 AM fishing expeditions or morning whale-watches, but it still maintains a nice seaside atmosphere. Facilities include a swimming pool, hot tub, and seasonal restaurant. $70–110 per room, more for the penthouse; less off-season.

Cape Ann Motor Inn (281-2900), 33 Rockport Road. This three-story motel stands right on Long Beach and includes a pleasant lobby with fireplace and a parrot. Open year-round. $108 double in summer, $25 for each extra person, $15 extra with kitchenette, less off-season. Rates include continental breakfast.

Good Harbor Beach Inn (283-1489), Salt Island Road. Open spring through fall. This place has charm. The check-in desk is a pine-paneled living room with a fireplace. The 17 rooms are pine-walled too, furnished in traditional beach cottage style, and each has two double beds and full bath. Good Harbor Beach (see *Swimming*) is steps away and a part of the view from most of the rooms; $89–95 in summer, less in shoulder seasons.

In Rockport 01966

Captain's Bounty (546-9557). Open April though late October. This three-story, shingled motel has 25 basic units, most with balconies overlooking Front Beach, an unbeatable location on the edge of the village. $98–120 (for the efficiency suite) in summer, $10 for each additional person. Less in spring and fall.

Sandy Bay Motor Inn (546-7155), 173 Main Street. The rooms are basic: two double beds, a phone, and TV, but facilities include an attractive indoor pool and whirlpool and outside tennis courts; also a pleasant coffee shop where breakfast and lunch are served daily. $96–166 in season, from $76 in spring and fall.

CAMPING

Cape Ann Camp Site (283-8683), 80 Atlantic Street, West Gloucester. Open May to October. Sited on 100 wooded acres overlooking salt marsh and inlets. Handy to Wingaersheek Beach (see *Swimming*); 300 tent and trailer sites.

WHERE TO EAT

DINING OUT

In Gloucester

The White Rainbow (281-0017), 65 Main Street. Open daily for dinner only, closed Monday. The dining room is candlelit and low beamed in a vintage-1800 commercial building. Long established and generally regarded as the best restaurant in town, with prices to match ($18–25 for entrées) for dishes like lobster Monte Carlo and seafood capellini. The **Cafe Wine Bar** offers lighter fare and lower prices (lobster stew $6.50) and an outdoor garden.

Thyme's on the Square Cafe (282-4426), 197 East Main Street. Open daily for dinner only. An elegant storefront dining room with a menu featuring starters such as blackened sea scallops with cheese grits and tomatillo salsa ($7) and entrées ranging from polenta lasagna with wild mushrooms, red peppers, arugula, and asiago cheese ($11) to Black Angus ribeye marinated in beer with garlic mashers and ginger onions ($18).

Cafe Beaujolais (282-0058), 118 Main Street. Open for dinner only, closed Monday. A variation on a previous local dining landmark (same owners, new location and menu). The atmosphere is French but still reasonably priced. On the September day we stopped by we might have started with a butternut squash soup ($3.95) and dined on crispy-skinned salmon over lentils with a carrot ginger reduction ($16.95) or pasta with smoked duck breast, duck confit, and preserved lemon ($19.95).

Passports (281-3680), 110 Main Street. Open Monday through Saturday for lunch and dinner. Patrons are greeted with complimentary hot popovers, and the Adriatic stew we sampled for lunch was thick and well seasoned. Dinner entrées include pan-seared chicken finished with chipotle peppers, spring onions, mushrooms, and sun-dried tomatoes, served over linguine ($11) and hand-pounded medallions of veal dipped in egg and sautéed with shallots and mushrooms, topped with fresh mozzarella and finished with Marsala ($14.50). Fresh fish always figures in the daily specials. Beer and wine are served.

✐ **Evie's Rudder** (283-7967), 73 Rocky Neck Avenue. April through October, lunch weekdays, dinner until 12:30. A waterfront restaurant on Smith Cove to which Bostonians drive for dinner and to see the Parsons family— mother (Evie) and daughters Susan and Paula—perform. Built in the 1880s as a fish-packing and -processing plant, it subsequently served as studio space and has been under its present ownership for more than 30 years. Specialties include roast leg of lamb, and shrimp, clam, and scallop farci. Piano music and after-dinner sing-alongs. From $12.95 for steamers as an entrée to $17.95 for lamb farci; children's menu items are $7.95.

✐ **The Studio** (283-4123), 51 Rocky Neck Avenue. Seasonal. Open daily for lunch and dinner. Built in the 1880s as a fish house, then an isinglass

factory, and then a summer art school, the building now houses a large, airy dining space with an open hearth, windows, a piano bar in the evening, and a deck on Smith Cove. Entrées range from spinach fettucine and fish-and-chips ($9.95) to baked lobster casserole ($17.95), and the Little Sailors menu includes a grilled frankfurter ($2.95).

Gloucester House Restaurant (283-1812), Seven Seas Wharf on Rogers Street. A large, waterfront fish restaurant with views of the boats out the windows and from the open-air **Cafe Seven Seas** on the back deck, as near to the water as you can get. Geared to groups and tourists but locally respected. Open daily for lunch and dinner; entrées $5.95–27.

McT's Lobster House & Tavern (282-0950), 25 Rogers Street. Open year-round for lunch and dinner. Fine waterfront view, best on a day when you can sit out and take advantage of the deck. The huge menu ranges from burgers to pasta with lobster Alfredo ($19.95).

In Rockport

Note: Rockport is dry; all restaurants are BYOB.

My Place By-the-Sea (546-9667), tip of Bearskin Neck. Open most of the year Thursday through Sunday for lunch and dinner. Sited at the very end of Bearskin Neck, with an outdoor deck and a view from the inside. Sandwiches, salads, and omelets at lunch; dinner is the time to come here—for marinated shrimp kebob ($17.50) or tuna Mediterranean, baked with fresh tomato, onion, shiitake mushrooms, garlic, wine, and herbs ($16.50)—as the sun sinks over the water.

Sea Garden (546-3471), Seaward Inn, Marmion Way. In season, open daily for dinner except Monday (open Thursday through Sunday only in the off-season); reservations requested. This inn dining room serves some of the most interesting food in town. A four-course $35 prix fixe (tax and gratuity included) dinner includes many choices. You might begin with crabcakes or lobster ravioli with pine nut sauce, then a salad of roasted eggplant and spinach with mushroom ranch dressing. Your entrée might be pan-seared salmon with Asian sauce and cellophane noodles or rack of lamb with sweet plum sauce. A lighter bistro menu is available on the sun porch.

Peg Leg Restaurant (546-3038), 18 Beach Street. Open late April until late October, dinner nightly, Sunday all day. A long-established place with views over Front Beach through large windows and a converted greenhouse. The traditional menu features scallop pie ($13.95), baked stuffed shrimp ($15.95), and Peg Leg's chicken pie ($9.95). Children's menu, $6.95.

Veranda at the Yankee Clipper (546-7795), Route 127, north of Rockport village. Open daily for breakfast and dinner. Oceanfront dining, creative New England cuisine. Dinner entrées from $12 for vegetarian strudel to $22 for crabmeat royale.

In Manchester

Seven Central Publick House (526-4533), 7 Central Street, opposite Manchester Town Hall. Open daily for lunch and dinner, patio dining in season. Housed in a former farmers' market dating from 1753, with a patio overlooking Mill Brook. The menu is large; specialties include seafood and prime rib. Entrées $6.95–18.95.

In Magnolia

The Patio (525-3230), 12 Lexington Avenue. Open year-round weekdays for lunch, daily for dinner. A family-owned, locally favored place priced for area residents; fish-and-chips at lunch is $4.95; dinner entrées from $9.95 for marinated charbroiled chicken salad to $17.95 for filet mignon. Try the haddock Portuguese-style ($12.95). Entrées come in junior and regular sizes.

Taormina Ristorante (525-4900), 56 Raymond Street. Open for dinner. A dining room with hand-hewn beams, fieldstone fireplace, and a classic Italian menu.

In Essex

Tom Shea's Restaurant (768-6931), on the causeway. Open for dinner from 4 PM daily, brunch on weekends. The atmosphere is casual, with antique decor and a view of the marshes. Generally rated as the best of the more expensive seafood places on the causeway. Scallop-stuffed shrimp ($17.95) and Cajun blackened salmon ($18.95) are particular favorites. Pasta dishes begin at $14.95, steak entrées average $20.

Jerry Pelonzi's Hearthside (768-6002), Route 133. Open 11:30–5:45 Monday through Friday, until 5:15 Saturday. You dine in the loft of a converted barn or in the fireplaced dining areas of a 250-year-old farmhouse overlooking the marshes. Leisurely lunches are the specialty of the house; seafood dishes include deep-fried smelts ($12.95) and baked finnan haddie with egg sauce ($14.95); filet mignon Hearthside is $18.95.

In Ipswich

Chippers River Cafe (356-7956), at the Choate Bridge. Open daily for breakfast (from 6 AM on weekdays), lunch, and dinner; a seasonal deck. Omelets, Belgian waffles, interesting sandwiches, salads, dinner entrées like mustard-lemon chicken and Chippers Cioppino (seafood simmered in marinara sauce); entrées from $9.95.

Steep Hill Grill (356-0774), 40 Essex Road (at Bruni's Marketplace on Route 133). Closed Monday, otherwise open for dinner from 5. Soups and unusual salads (like lamb and feta cheese on mixed greens) are specialties, along with a wide variety of appetizers. Entrées might include grilled shrimp and scallops with a lime-chervil beurre blanc ($14.95) and roast orange-glazed duck with chutney ($15.95).

Stone Soup (356-4222), Mitchell Road (turn off Route 1A/Route 133 on the road across from the Dairy Queen). Open Tuesday through Friday 7–2, Saturday and Sunday 7–midnight. Thursday through Saturday reservations are a must for one of the two dinner sittings (6 and 8). Very small, very popular. Italian specialties, dinner entrées from $7.50.

1640 Hart House (356-9411), 51 Linebrook Road (off Route 133/1A). Open for lunch, dinner, and Sunday brunch. Dating in part to the 17th century, this is presently a local dining landmark with live music on weekends. The menu ranges from escargots to potato skins for appetizers and from burgers to filet mignon ($13.95) for entrées.

EATING OUT

In Gloucester

Halibut Point (281-1900), 289 Main Street. Open daily 11:30–11. Occupying the original tavern built by Howard Blackburn in 1900 after his amazing voyage (see the Cape Ann Historical Society under *To See*), the place has a pub atmosphere and is a favorite with residents. Specialties include a spicy Italian fish chowder, burgers, deli-style sandwiches, and reasonably priced entrées like spicy shrimp (cooked on the grill, and seasoned with garlic, dill, and shallots).

Jalapeños (283-8228), 86 Main Street. Open for lunch and dinner daily. Authentic Mexican fare, dishes like the *pollo mole* (chicken in a spicy chocolate sauce), chile relleno (stuffed poblano chilies), and Tampiqueña (marinated steak) draw patrons from near and far.

Charlie's Place (283-0303), 83 Bass Avenue near Good Harbor Beach. Open daily year-round, 7 AM–8 PM. A bright, Formica place with a counter and tables, Styrofoam cups, paper plates, a huge fried shrimp roll, luscious crabmeat, a haddock plate. Breakfasts are a specialty (fresh-squeezed orange juice).

Gull Restaurant (283-6060), 75 Essex Avenue at the Cape Ann Marina. Open seasonally 5:30 AM–9:30 PM; geared to the owners of the motor yachts tied up here and passengers on the Yankee fleet's fishing and whalewatching expeditions. A great old standby on the Annisquam River. Cocktails served.

✐ **Captain Carlo's Seafoods** (283-6342), Harbor Loop. A fish store and popular restaurant, especially with families or anyone who simply wants to be on the working waterfront and eat flapping fresh, reasonably priced fish (but you can get a hot dog and chips for $1.50). Fish and chips are $5.95 and char-grilled swordfish is $10.95.

✐ **Amelia's** (281-8855), Thatcher Road (Route 127A) across from Good Harbor Beach. This popular family restaurant expanded into larger quarters in the fall of '97, still serving linguiça bombs (a hot sub), chowders, steak tip dinners ($6.99), and pu pu platters like eggplant, broccoli, sausage, and meatball (with spaghetti, garlic bread, and tossed salad) for two ($14.95).

Sailor Stan's Drift-In (281-4470), 24 Rocky Neck Avenue at the entrance to Rocky Neck. Open April through December for breakfast (from 7 AM) and lunch. Never changes. Always good.

Glass Sail Boat Cafe (283-7830), 3 Duncan Street. Open year-round, 7 AM–4 PM. A health food market with a pleasant café featuring soups, sandwiches, and muffins.

In Rockport

✐ **Brackett's Ocean View Restaurant** (546-2797), 27 Main Street. Open most of the year for lunch and dinner; this is the real heart of town, with picture windows overlooking Sandy Bay. Despite the tablecloths and

attentive service, this is very much a family-geared place with a traditional Yankee menu and seafood specialties. The menu is much the same for lunch and dinner, ranging from my personal lunch favorite, Cajun chicken roll-ups ($5.95 for lunch, $6.95 for dinner), to baked stuffed chicken ($8.95 at lunch, $9.95 at dinner); lobster and crab dishes are priced daily. The kids get their own brightly colored menu.

Ellen's Harborside (546-2512), T Wharf. Open April through October, daily from 6:30 AM for breakfast, lunch, and dinner. Right on the harbor, a family-owned (three generations) eatery with open counter and tables, authentic atmosphere, seafood specialties, but hamburgers too; dinner specials.

Portside Chowder House (546-7045), Bearskin Neck. Open 11–8 in summer, year-round for lunch. A pleasant place with a hearth that's lit in winter, water view, good chowder, lobster stew, daily specials.

The Greenery (546-9593), 15 Dock Square. Closed November through March; open daily in season for lunch and dinner, also Sunday breakfast. A bright, casual place with a great harbor view, salad bar, gourmet sandwiches, fresh fruits, lobster. Dine on seafood linguine, mussels in tomato herb sauce, or grilled swordfish.

In Essex

Woodman's (768-6451), Route 133. The most famous clam house on the North Shore. Open daily for lunch and dinner. The claim is that "Chubby" Woodman invented the fried clam more than 75 years ago, and the house specialty remains fried seafood by the plate and bucket. Patrons eat at picnic tables, in the rough. As with most legendary places, you hear it's too crowded, not as good as it used to be, but judge for yourself; everyone has to try it at least once. Beer on tap. This is also one of the few places that cater old-fashioned clambakes.

J.T. Farnham's (768-6643), 88 Eastern Avenue (Route 133). Open March through October for lunch and dinner. Wooden booths and windows that overlook the Essex marshes; chowder, famous fried clams.

Village Restaurant (768-6400), 55 Main Street (junction of Routes 22 and 133). Closed Monday, otherwise open for lunch and dinner. The Riccis began with five booths and seven counter stools 30 years ago, and they now seat 225. They specialize in local seafood; an Essex River Sampler includes sautéed haddock, shrimp, and clams.

Fortune Palace II (768-3839), 99 Main Street, Essex. Open for lunch and dinner. Enthusiastically recommended by locals. No MSG; a wide choice, including salads and pan-fried dishes; try the plum-flavored crispy duck. White tablecloths, bright, cheerful atmosphere.

In Manchester

The Coffee Cup (526-4558), 25 Union Street. Open daily 6 AM to 9 PM. Greek specialties, homemade soups, grinders, and pizza. $3.25–4.95.

The Edgewater Cafe (526-4668), 69 Raymond Street. Open daily 5–10 PM. Specializing in Mexican food; casual atmosphere. BYOB.

Woodman's clam shack in Essex

In Ipswich

The Clam Box, High Street on Route 1A just north of the village. Open March through Memorial Day daily except Monday, then daily until Labor Day; closed Monday again until Columbus Day, then open Wednesday through Sunday until December 15. This landmark dates back to the '30s and derives its name from its original shape: a 15- by 15- by 30-foot clam box. There is now space for eating in as well as taking out.

Choate Bridge Pub (356-2931), middle of the village at the bridge. Open daily 11–10. A comfortable village pub like too few villages have. There's a smoky bar side and a dining room with booths and blackboard specials. The burgers are outstanding, and in the evening you can also feast on a kielbasa pizza.

In Wenham

Wenham Tea House (468-1398), 4 Monument Street. Just of Route 1A across from the Wenham Museum (see *Museums*). Opened in 1915 by the Wenham Village Improvement Society (itself founded in 1893), this was once one among hundreds of similar teahouses and now is one of the few survivors. Lunch (11:30–2:30) and tea (see *Snacks*) are served in the brightly painted sun room, filled with cream-colored wooden chairs positioned at tables covered with flower-patterned oilcloth and set with fresh flowers. Entrées include creamed chicken on toast with a choice of jellied or green salad and "soup-r-boule"—lobster bisque served in a hollow French boule. The building also houses a variety of shops and is part of the complex (see *Scenic Drives*) that includes the Wenham Museum; proceeds support worthwhile community causes.

TAKEOUT

Virgilio's Grocery (283-5295), 29 Main Street in the West End, Gloucester, features sandwiches made to order with "fisherman's bread" fresh from the oven (request the St. Joseph's); also pizza by the slice. **Destino's Submarine Sandwiches** (283-3100), 129 Prospect Street, Gloucester, opposite Our Lady of Good Voyage Church, may just offer the best lunch deal in town; every sub comes with a free side order of slaw, macaroni salad, or three-bean salad, plus (weekdays only) soup. **Bruni's Market** (356-4877), 36 Essex Road, Ipswich (Route 133, just east of Route 1A). A great deli, source of sandwiches for picnics; some benches on the premises. (Also see *Selective Shopping—Seafood*.)

SNACKS

Caffe Sicilia (283-7345), 40 Main Street, Gloucester. Outstanding espresso and Sicilian pastry. **Donut Jim's** (283-3383), 24 Washington Street, Gloucester. Very good doughnuts and pastries. Locally loved. **The Glass Sailboat** (283-7818), 3 Duncan Street (just off Main), Gloucester. Open 8–5:30 and Thursday evenings. A café/deli in the back of a natural foods store serves croissants, homemade soups, and pocket-bread sandwiches. **Helmut's Struedel** (546-2824), 49 Bearskin Neck, Rockport. Memorable pastries, also coffee and sandwiches, with seating on an outside deck. **Wenham Tea House** (468-1398), 4 Monument Street (just off Route 1A). *The* place for tea on the North Shore, served 3:15–4:15 daily except Sunday. Try the cranberry scones! **Captain Dusty's Ice Cream** (526-1663), 60 Beach Street, Manchester. Right where you need it, across from Masconomo Park on the way to Singing Beach, a picturesque seasonal stand selling homemade ice cream and frozen yogurt.

BREAKFAST

Eating breakfast out is a popular local custom around Gloucester and a good way of tuning in. **Sailor Stan,** off Route 127A at the entrance to Rocky Neck, is open for breakfast and lunch; counter and tables, good chowder, local gossip center, bargain priced. **Lee's,** corner of East Main

Street and Eastern Avenue, **Gull Restaurant,** and **Charlie's** (noted above), as well as **Captain's Lodge** at 237 Eastern Avenue in Gloucester, **Flav's Red Skiff** in Rockport, and **The Firehouse** in Lanesville, are all popular morning spots. **MoJack's,** 16 Beach Street, across from Front Beach in Rockport, opens at 7 AM and serves breakfast until 2 PM.

ENTERTAINMENT

MUSIC

Rockport Chamber Music Festival (546-7391), the Rockport Art Association, Rockport. From mid-June to early July, distinguished chamber musicians perform at the art association and other local places. Performances are Thursday, Friday, and Saturday at 8; Sunday at 5.

Hammond Castle Organ Concerts (283-2080), Hesperus Avenue, Gloucester. Performances on the 10,000-pipe organ, housed in the 100-foot-long Great Hall with its 85-foot tower, are scheduled throughout the year (see *Museums*).

Castle Hill Festival (356-7774), Argilla Road, Ipswich. A July and August series of concerts and other special events at the Concert Barn; all events are at 5 PM, with picnicking permitted beforehand on the Grand Allée of the Great House.

Band concerts in July and August, Sunday at 7:30, at the bandstands in Rockport (near Back Beach) and Gloucester (at Stage Fort Park).

Annual **Essex Music Festival** at Chebacco Lake (468-6581), late August.

THEATER

Gloucester Stage Co. (281-4099), 267 East Main Street, Gloucester. Mid-May through December, Wednesday through Sunday. Staged in a 150-seat theater in a former Gorton's Fish Company warehouse near Rocky Neck. Affordably priced.

FILM

Little Arts Cinema (546-2548), 18 Broadway, Rockport, shows a variety of classic and popular films, nightly.

Gloucester Cinema (283-9188), 75 Essex Avenue (Route 133), Gloucester.

NIGHTSPOTS

In Gloucester

Check out **Cameron's** (281-1331), 206 Main, for live bands Thursday through Saturday; Sunday is open mike. **Dockside Bar and Grill** (281-4554) on Rocky Neck offers entertainment and dancing nightly. **Gloucester House** (283-1812), Seven Seas Wharf, has live entertainment Thursday through Sunday. **Rhumb Line** (283-9732), 40 Railroad Avenue, offers live music every night but Tuesday. **Evie's Rudder** (283-7967) features piano and specializes in "spontaneous entertainment." **The Studio** (283-4123), 51 Rocky Neck Avenue, has a piano bar Thursday through Saturday, starting at 8. The **Blackburn Tavern Pub** (282-

1919), 2 Main Street, offers live entertainment on weekends, as well as Sunday brunch.

In Essex

Both the **Red Barrel Pub** (768-7210), 171 Eastern Avenue, and **Lobster Trap Pub** (Route 133 on the causeway) have live music on weekends.

SELECTIVE SHOPPING

ANTIQUES

In Essex

Essex styles itself "America's Antique Capital" and counts at least 40 dealers, 16 right on Main Street (Route 133). **The White Elephant** (768-6901), 32 Main Street, bears special mention because it was the village's first antiques shop (when it opened in 1952, the legend is that someone found a Winslow Homer painting here for $10 and an original Rembrandt sketch for $1). It's still one of the best, a clutter of everything from sleds and vases to license plates, beds, radios, quilts, and almost anything else you can think of; the outlet is up Route 133 near Essex. **Main Street Antiques** (768-7639) in Essex is four floors, and **Robert C. Coviello Antiques** (768-7365) is three floors. Needless to say, antiques dealers are also scattered around Cape Ann itself.

In Rockport

Rockport also offers a half-dozen antiques shops within a few blocks. Pick up an *Antiques in Rockport* flier. **The Rockport Trading Company** (546-8066), 67 Broadway, features a wide variety of fun stuff and is open year-round. **Rockport Quilt Shoppe** (546-1001), 2 Ocean Avenue, features quilts dating from 1820 to 1930 and antique linens, pillowcases, tablecloths, and bedspreads, and restores vintage quilts.

In Gloucester

There's good antiquing along Main Street in Gloucester.

ART GALLERIES

Rockport is home to more than two dozen art galleries, all within a mile or so of each other. Pick up a copy of *The Rockport Fine Arts Gallery Guide* from the Rockport Chamber of Commerce (see *Guidance*). (Also see *To See—Art Centers.*) **Gloucester,** too, is a genuine arts center. Check out **Menage Gallery of Fine Artists & Artisans** (283-6030), 134 Main Street; **Local Colors** (283-3996), 142 Main Street, a cooperative gallery with new works mounted every six weeks; **Bodin Historic Photo** (283-2524), 82 Main Street, featuring pottery, original art, and carved decoys, as well as stunning vintage photographs of the area. (Also see *To See—Art Centers.*)

SPECIAL SHOPS

In Rockport

Bearskin Neck, a finger of land dividing Sandy Bay from Rockport Harbor, is one of the pleasanter places along the eastern seaboard to stroll, nosh, and browse. As in Ogunquit, Maine, the several dozen seasonal

KIMBERLY GRANT

White Elephant Antiques in Essex

shops and restaurants here are housed in former fish shacks. The **Sun Basket** specializes in Native American Indian crafts. The **Pewter Shoppe** is deservedly a landmark, and **Half Moon Harry**'s hand-painted clocks are truly special. In Dock Square, **Too Fortunate Pottery** is a combination studio/shop specializing in attractive hand-painted lamps, vases, soap dishes and such. The **John Tarr Store,** Main Street, is an old-fashioned haberdasher with a bargain corner and women's wear. If you keep walking (Main Street turns into Beach Street), **The Enchanted Dove** is a year-round trove of ornaments and Scandinavian items.

In Gloucester

Gloucester's Main Street has become one of New England's more interesting shopping streets in recent years. Begin with **Bananas** (283-8806), 78 Main Street, a rare trove of antique clothing including flashy sequined numbers and amazing hats, along with an extensive collection of costume jewelry. At **Hibiscus** (283-3848), 114 Main Street, Sandy and Michael Koolkin offer an interesting mix of furnishings, women's clothing, and gifts. **Glass Sail Boat Wearhouse,** 199 Main Street, is good for women's clothing: natural-fiber, nicely styled skirts, dresses, jumpers, sweaters, and other things woven; cosmetics. (Also see *Art Galleries* and *Antiques.*)

In Ipswich

Check out **Ocmulgee Pottery** (356-0636), a clay studio and showroom for a distinctive pottery.

BOOKSTORES

Toad Hall Bookstore (546-7323), 51 Main Street, Rockport. Open daily, evenings in summer. Housed in an old granite bank building and walled with inviting titles, this exceptional store donates net profits to cultural and ecological projects. **The Bookstore** (281-1548), 61 Main Street, Gloucester. A pleasant store with a particularly good selection of children's books, books on boating, cooking, poetry, outdoors, antiques, and art. There's also a selection of greeting cards, and a rear view of the harbor. **Bookends** (281-2053), 132 Main Street, Gloucester. A good selection of paperbacks, and the best magazine rack in town. **The English Book Shop** (283-8981), Rocky Neck, Gloucester. Owned by a British transplant married to a local fisherman, this shop features British publishers and titles, also children's fairy tales and nautical subjects, and a general stock of used books.

FARMS

Goodale Orchards (356-5366), Argilla Road, Ipswich. Open June through December 24, a 179-acre farm on the verge of the marshes with an orchard store in an 18th-century barn. The Russell family specializes in fruits, vegetables, and flowers all grown on the farm, pick-your-own strawberries in June, raspberries in July, blueberries in August, apples and tomatoes in September; also fruit and dandelion wines, cider (hard as well as regular), and a daily barn menu of soups and sandwiches. In October, visit the haunted barn.

Marini's Farm Stand (356-0430), 259 Linebrook Road. Open April through October. Pick-your-own strawberries and tomatoes; farm stand with seasonal fruits, vegetables, pumpkins, cider.

SEAFOOD

Steve Connolly Seafood (283-4443), 431 Main Street, Gloucester, is a purveyor of fish to the White House.

Captain Carlo's Fish Market (283-6342), Harbor Loop, Gloucester, stays open until 6.

Gleason's Fish & Lobster (283-4414), 42 Eastern Avenue, Gloucester. Open daily year-round 8–8. Reasonably priced crab and lobster rolls, boiled as well as fresh lobster to go.

Moore Lobster Co., Bearskin Neck in Rockport, sells lobster cooked to order that you can eat "in the rough" outside at round wooden tables (the kind formerly used for spooling cable).

New England Lobster Co., in Pigeon Cove (north of Rockport, hidden behind Cape Ann Forge), offers flapping fresh fish, shrimp, and lobster. The boats dock a few feet away.

SPECIAL EVENTS

May: **Prince of Whales Ball** to celebrate the return of the whales. Five-mile road race. **Motif No. 1 Day Celebration** in Rockport. **Essex Shipyard Festival**, usually mid-May.

June: **Rockport Chamber Music Festival** (546-2825), a series of concerts by prominent performers at the **Hibbard Gallery** in the Rockport Art Association. **Rocky Neck (studios) Open House. St. Peter's Fiesta**—biggest event of the year in Gloucester. A week of music, sporting events, parades, a blessing of the fishing fleet. **Swedish Midsummer Festival** of Swedish dances, foods in Rockport.

July: **Independence Day parades** in Gloucester, Rockport, and Manchester. **Renaissance Fair** at Hammond Castle.

August: **Olde Ipswich Days** includes a block dance, marathon, public dinners. **Gloucester Waterfront Festival**—art and crafts show, weekend fish fry. **Manchester Sidewalk Bazaar**—races, parade of sail. **Annual Crane Beach Sand Castle Contest.**

September, Labor Day: **Gloucester Schooner Festival** and 15-mile **Cape Ann Road Race** around the cape. **Essex Clamfest,** usually the second Saturday, the annual tribute to the town's best-known product.

October: **North Shore Antiques Show**—major display by area dealers at Woodman's Function Hall in Essex. Columbus Day weekend: **Round the Cape Arts and Crafts Studio Tours. Amateur Art Festival,** Rockport. **The Topsfield Fair,** Route 1 in Topsfield (just off I-95, on the way to Ipswich), is one of the largest, oldest, and most colorful agricultural fairs in the state. **Annisquam Arts and Crafts Show,** Annisquam Village Hall. **Haunted Halloween Nights** at Hammond Castle (see *Museums*).

December: **Christmas in Rockport**—ice sculpture, tree lighting, strolling carolers and minstrels, climaxing with a Christmas pageant; the Christmas tree in the middle of Dock Square is itself worth a trip. Second Saturday: **"Where the Past is Present,"** Holiday Open House up Middle Street, Gloucester. Also **Annual Santa Claus Parade** in Gloucester, **Victorian Christmas Festival** at Hammond Castle. December 31: **First Night,** Gloucester.

Newburyport Area

The Bay State's smallest city contains the country's largest collection of Federal-era buildings. Sited at the mouth of the Merrimack River, Newburyport was an early shipbuilding center and by the outbreak of the Revolution was the fourth largest town in America. Thanks to its privateers, fortunes were made during the War for Independence, and the ensuing decades—judging from its present look—were unusually prosperous. Architecturally, Newburyport is frozen in the 1790s to 1830s.

Driving into town along High Street you can't help but notice the 2-mile lineup of white, wooden, "Federal-style" homes with their distinctive three stories, spare, symmetrical lines, and shallow-hipped roofs. The commercial buildings down along State Street and around waterfront Market Square are also older and more graceful than those of most other American downtowns. They were built of brick after a fire in 1811.

The Federal era also bred a deep split between High Street residents and the craftsmen and mariners who lived above their shops down by the river. Each party supported its own fire company, bank, Masonic lodge, and militia company. A century later in 1930, when a five-volume study focused on Newburyport as Yankee City, the "upper-uppers" were still living on High Street, and social status sloped downward through five distinct strata to the "lower-lowers" along the waterfront. Hometown novelist John P. Marquand satirized the study and its subject in *Point of No Return*, a story about a city in which "everyone instinctively knew where he belonged."

This picture altered, however, in the 1960s, when urban renewal razed the old distilleries and post–Civil War factories along 20 acres of the city's waterfront and turned menacingly to the city's early brick commercial rows. Newburyporters of every ilk rallied in protest, attracting many preservation-minded newcomers in the process.

Today more than a hundred shops—a mix of basics, boutiques, and antiques—are housed in waterfront complexes like the Inn Street Mall, the Tannery, and Merrimac Landing, and mellow brick buildings run the length of State Street. On the river itself the granite Custom House, a Greek Revival temple designed in 1835 by the architect of the Washington Monument, is now a museum, and the vintage-1823 firehouse is a combined theater and gallery. The waterfront itself is a landscaped place to walk and watch river traffic, as well as to board whalewatching, fishing, and excursion boats.

Plum Island, an 8½-mile, stringbean-shaped barrier island minutes from downtown, offers miles of beach and wildlife refuge trails known to birders around the world. Although the Massachusetts Audubon chapter owns some 23,000 other acres in the state, it has chosen to buy 3 acres on the Plum Island Turnpike as a site for its most elaborate visitors center, and guided bird walks are offered by an increasing number of groups, both commercial and private, year-round. Maudslay State Park, on the other arm of town, beckons with hiking and biking trails on the Merrimack River. Newburyport is a hinge between the Merrimack River Valley and the North Shore, a logical hub from which to explore both.

AREA CODE: 978

GUIDANCE

Greater Newburyport Chamber of Commerce (462-6680), 29 State Street, Newburyport 01950. Open weekdays 9–5, Saturday 10–4, Sunday noon–4. A seasonal information booth in Market Square, with rest rooms, welcomes visitors June through mid-October daily 10–4, Sundays noon–4; until 7 on Fridays, Saturdays in summer.

The **Salisbury Chamber of Commerce** (465-2581) is a friendly source of local information for the town.

GETTING THERE

By bus: **Commuter Coach** (1-800-874-3377) offers frequent service to Boston during commuter hours. **C&J Trailways** (465-2277; in Boston, 617-426-6030) also offers frequent service to Boston and Logan Airport. Inquire about progress of commuter train service from Boston.

By boat: Dockage downtown.

By car: I-495 is the most common approach; Route 113 exit.

PARKING

Free parking in Newburyport lots off Green and Merrimack Streets.

MEDICAL EMERGENCY

Anna Jacques Hospital (462-6601), Highland Avenue, Newburyport.

TO SEE

MUSEUMS

Cushing House (462-2681), 98 High Street, Newburyport. Open May through October, Tuesday through Saturday 10–4. $4 adults, $1.50 students; free 10 and under. This brick mansion, housing the town's historical collection, was built in 1808 and served as home to Caleb Cushing, our first ambassador to China. Twenty-one rooms are filled with elegant furnishings, silver, paintings, and vintage clothing. The 1700s French-style garden is under restoration.

◇ **Custom House Maritime Museum** (462-8681), 25 Water Street, Newburyport. Open April to late December, Monday through Saturday 10–4, Sunday 1–4. Adults $3, $2 children. Built in 1835 of Rockport granite and designed by Robert Mills, architect of the Washington Monument and the US Treasury, this building was sold in 1913 and used for hay storage and, eventually, as a junk shop. This handsome building is now a fine museum with a permanent collection of ship models, marine paintings, portraits of sea captains, and artifacts from around the world. It also houses the Marquand Library, furnished and filled with the novelist's treasures. Major exhibits dramatizing some aspect of the city's history change each year. Touchpool Treasures, a hands-on exhibit about local creatures, is geared to kids.

HISTORIC HOUSES

◇ **Spencer-Pierce-Little Farm** (462-2634), 5 Little's Lane, Newbury (Route 1A just south of the light at Rolfe's Lane, a way to the Plum Island Turnpike). Open June to October 15, Wednesday through Sunday, tours on the hour 11–4. $4 adults, $3.50 seniors. Hauntingly beautiful and set in 240 acres of meadow and salt marsh, this house is one of New England's oldest and the only grand Jacobean-style manor built of stone and brick. Built in the late 1600s, it has been restored at a cost of $1 million by the Society for the Preservation of New England Antiquities (SPNEA). Although still unfurnished, the mansion is skillfully interpreted on tours that begin by introducing you to the family who lived here in the 20th century. You then move back through the rooms and generations, into the wooden Federal-era wing and back again to the second-floor, 17th-century kitchen. Don't miss the attic, with its early-19th-century graffiti. The fields, presently leased to local farmers, stretch to the Plum Island Turnpike. Inquire about special events.

Coffin House (227-3956), 14-16 High Street (Route lA), Newbury. Open June through mid-October, weekends, tours on the hour 11–4; adults $4, $3.50 seniors. This weathered house was begun circa 1654 and grew considerably over the next two centuries. Its old kitchens and early wallpaper, as well as its furnishings, are interesting. Owned by the Society for the Preservation of New England Antiquities.

HISTORIC SITES

Bartlett Mall, High Street, Newburyport. The high-splashing fountain here is known as Frog Pond; the mall as a whole was the gift of a merchant in 1800. The adjacent brick courthouse was designed by Charles Bulfinch. The **Old Hill Burying Ground** across the way contains many of Newburyport's most memorable residents.

The Old Jail (north end of the mall), built of Rockport granite, dates from 1823. The cornerstone was laid by Lafayette.

Newburyport Public Library (465-4428), 94 State Street, Newburyport. Patrick Tracy's 1771 brick mansion has hosted George Washington, the Marquis de Lafayette, Aaron Burr, and Benedict Arnold. During the

KIMBERLY GRANT

Revolution, Patrick's son Nathaniel made a fortune from his privateers (selling cargo from the captured ships for more than $4 million), but eventually he lost it all and was forced to sell both this house and his country property (now the Spencer-Pierce-Little Farm; see *Historic Houses*). This mansion has been a library since 1865 and contains marine paintings and a model of the clipper ship *Dreadnought*, built in Newburyport.

Unitarian Church (465-0602), 26 Pleasant Street, Newburyport. This 1801 structure is thought to have been designed by Samuel McIntire and has an unusually graceful facade and spire with a Paul Revere bell. The interior is also graceful and airy. Services are held every Sunday.

Old South Presbyterian Church (465-9666), 29 Federal Street, Newburyport. Built in 1756 with a bell cast by Paul Revere, this dignified church has a whispering gallery; at one time it boasted a sea captain "at the head of every pew on the broad side."

FOR FAMILIES

Salisbury Beach Amusement Area (465-3581), Salisbury Beach, Route 1A. An old-time carnival boardwalk atmosphere prevails adjacent to 5 miles of beach: arcades, family entertainment center, midway. In the course of researching a *Boston Globe* story on this area in the '60s, Chris was told by a fortune teller here that she would write books, marry a stubborn man, and have three sons; all have come to pass.

SCENIC DRIVES

Amesbury

From Newburyport, drive out Merrimac Street to the Chain Bridge. After the bridge, bear left onto Main Street and look for **Lowell's Boat Shop**

(462-0162), open year-round weekdays 9–5, at 459 Main Street; it's brown shingled and wedged between the road and river. Founded by Simeon Lowell in 1793, it is the country's oldest boatbuilding shop and has produced some 150,000 boats over the years. Dories and small wooden sailing skiffs are the specialty of the house. It's a sweet-smelling place, filled with boats and men working on them; inquire about workshops and special programs (388-0162). The shop is administered by the Custom House Maritime Museum (see *Museums*), and visitors are welcome. Beyond the shop lies the picturesque, small village of Point Shore. Continue along Main Street into the middle of town. The **Bartlett Museum** (388-4528), 270 Main Street, open Memorial Day to Labor Day, Friday through Sunday 1–4, houses an interesting town historical collection, including Native American artifacts. You learn that Amesbury was known as the Carriage Center of the World in the late 19th century. The former carriage-mill buildings are under restoration as a shopping and restaurant complex adjoining the Amesbury Chamber of Commerce (388-3178) at 5 Market Square (open weekdays 9–3). Also worth searching out, the **Whittier Museum** (388-1337), 86 Friend Street (open May through October, Tuesday through Saturday 10–4), the home of John Greenleaf Whittier for 46 years, conveys a genuine sense of the poet and his poems.

West Newbury and Haverhill

From Newburyport, drive west on Route 113 to the village of West Newbury. This was a bustling spot until the 19th-century construction of the Chain Bridge prevented larger vessels from sailing this far upriver. Take either Bridge or Church Street to the Rocks Village Bridge (it still has to be opened manually with a capstan for boats to pass) and follow Country Bridge Road (note the old houses in Rocks Village) to Route 110. West on Route 110 you come to the **John Greenleaf Whittier Birthplace** (373-3979) at 305 Whittier Road (open May through October, Tuesday through Saturday 10–5; Sunday 1–5; November through April Saturday 10–5, also Tuesday through Friday and Sunday 1–5), and then to the entrance to **Winnekenni Park,** a former 214-acre estate with **Winnekenni Castle** (open for special exhibits, concerts, and other events; 521-1681). At the junction with Route 113, continue west to the **Buttonwoods Museum** (374-4626) at 240 Water Street; this complex includes a shoe shop, an 1814 home furnished to period, and Tenney Hall, housing Native American relics and town exhibits. It's open Wednesday, Thursday, Saturday, and Sunday 1–4:30; $5 adults; $3 students; free under age 7. Continue along the river past 19th-century brick mills and shops all compressed into a relatively small area; this Washington Street Shoe District is billed as the finest Queen Anne–style industrial street in America. Try contacting the Greater Haverhill Chamber of Commerce (373-5663).

TO DO

AIR RIDES

Air Plum Island (462-2114), Plum Island Turnpike, offers sightseeing rides. Inquire about helicopter rides, flight instruction, charters, plane rentals; private planes are accommodated and serviced.

BICYCLING

The bike paths in **Maudslay State Forest** and the 7-mile road (6 miles are now hardtopped) through the Parker River reservation on Plum Island are particularly popular. A Rail Trail suitable for mountain bikes begins in Salisbury at the Merrimack River (parking at Braedon Road, off Route 1A).

Aries Sports and Bikery (465-8099; 1-800-501-BIKE), Route 1, one mile south of the Newburyport traffic circle. Sales, service, and rentals.

BIRDING

The 4,662-acre **Parker River National Wildlife Refuge** on Plum Island is recognized as one of the world's better places to view a wide variety of shorebirds and migrating waterfowl. More than 300 species of birds have been seen in the immediate area. Newburyport's place on the global birding map dates from the 1985 sighting of the Ross's gull, a rare species associated with Siberia. Dan Rather and the front page of *The New York Times* featured the story, and birders, as well as birds, have been flocking to Newburyport ever since (see Plum Island under *Green Space*).

In winter snowy owls, northern shrikes, and many ducks migrate into the Plum Island area. During spring migration it's alive with warblers, and summer residents include great and snowy egrets, great blue herons, glossy ibises, Wilson's phalaropes, swallows, martins, and several species of warblers and shorebirds. In the fall it is once more thick with warblers and shorebirds moving south. Massachusetts Audubon is presently constructing a major interpretive facility on the Plum Island Turnpike, due to open in the year 2000. The **Birdwatcher of Newburyport** (462-2473) at 50 Water Street (the Tannery) is a shop catering to birders; it sponsors both guided walks and birding boat tours on the Parker River.

BOAT EXCURSIONS

Yankee Clipper Harbor Tours (948-2375) aboard a 49-passenger vessel captained by Bill Taplin depart from the Boardwalk (wharf next to Hilton's) in Newburyport; the 45-minute narrated cruise runs from 11–6:30, sunset cruises and charters are also offered.

Merrimack Queen Riverboat (372-3420), a 150-passenger paddle wheeler, sails Sunday (Memorial Day weekend to mid-October) from the Route 197 bridge in Haverhill. The 4-hour cruise to Newburyport and back costs $15 adults, $7.50 children.

FISHING

Hilton's Fishing Dock (465-7165; 1-800-848-1111), 54 Merrimac Street, Newburyport. There is ample free parking on the wharf and a shop from which you can set out for a full day of fishing. (Also see *Whale-Watching*.) **Captain's Fishing Parties** (462-3141; 1-800-427-1333), April through October, Plum Island. Fishing and whale-watching, also weekly dinner cruises. **The Clipper Fleet** (465-7495) offers fishing charters from Salisbury.

GOLF

Evergreen Golf Course (465-3609), 14 Boyd Drive, Newburyport. Nine holes open to the public daily. **Ould Newbury Golf Club** (462-3737) Route 1, Newburyport. Nine holes, open to the public weekday afternoons.

SEA KAYAKING

Adventure Learning (346-9728; 1-800-649-9728), 67 Bear Hill, Merrimac. One-day clinics, weekend tours. The specialty here is outdoor education; patrons are invited to come paddle with the whales.

SWIMMING

Salisbury Beach State Reservation (462-4481), off Route 1, Salisbury, is a 3.8-mile-long expanse of sand, frequently crowded in summer. Facilities include bathhouses, picnic areas, boat launch, and interpretive programs (ranging from guided walks to live entertainment). (Also see "Plum Island" under *Green Space*.)

WHALE-WATCHING

Hilton's Newburyport Whale Watch (465-9885; 1-800-848-1111), Hilton's Fishing Dock, 54 Merrimac Street, Newburyport. April through October. One of the oldest and best known of the region's whalewatch excursions, founded by Scott Mercer, who does much of the narrating. Naturalist-narrated runs depart twice daily July through mid-September, weekends in spring and fall; the vessel is 100 feet.

GREEN SPACE

BEACHES

Plum Island. This stringbean-shaped, 8½-mile-long barrier island is accessible via Water Street, which turns into the Plum Island Turnpike. Beginning in the 1890s, when a horsecar line reached Plum Island from downtown Newburyport, this area has been a colony of summer cottages. Since the 1940s the southern two-thirds of the island has been maintained as the **Parker River National Wildlife Refuge** (465-5753), a natural landscape of dunes, bog, tidal marsh, and beach. The refuge is open dawn to dusk, year-round; $5 per car, $2 per bicycle or walk-in during warm-weather months. A 7-mile road bisects the refuge, with parking areas strung along its length and access both to the beach and to Parker River at scattered intervals. The beach is closed April through June (tern nesting season), and when it opens parking spaces tend to fill by 10 AM, even in greenfly season (mid-July to mid-

KIMBERLY GRANT

Plum Island

August). The beach is famous for surf fishing but is not a good place to bring small children: It's a hike over the dunes, and the surf and undertow are unusually strong. In spring (through early June) and fall (beginning in August and especially in September and October), the refuge makes a good place to watch migrating wildfowl: Some 300 species of birds have been sighted (see *To Do—Birding*). In winter there is still a surprising number of birds, as well as deer and rabbits. A self-guiding wildlife trail at Hellcat Swamp (Parkinson #4) is rewarding any time of year. *Warning:* Parking throughout the refuge is limited to 300 cars.

Sandy Point State Reservation (462-4481), at the end of the 7-mile gravel access road on Plum Island (see above), is a 72-acre area with a sandy beach backed by rolling dunes and a small hill called Bar Head. Parking is limited to 50 cars (attendants at the gate to the national wildlife refuge keep tabs on availability).

Town of Plum Island Beaches. The 3½ miles of sand north of the wildlife refuge on Plum Island is public, accessible from parking lots scattered among the cottages and a larger one at North Beach at the mouth of the Merrimack River. This is a popular area for fishing and wading out onto the sandbar; beware of currents near the jetty.

Salisbury Beach State Reservation (462-4481) is open year-round. A long barrier beach, good for walking, swimming, fishing, and birding. Camping is available year-round.

THE RIVER

The Merrimack River Watershed Council (617-363-5777; 1-800-422-6792), West Newbury, promotes the entire Merrimack River Watershed. It's a source of map guides to walking trails and boating, also of organized events.

WALKS

✐ **Maudslay State Park** (465-7223), West Newbury. Marked from Route 113: Take Story Lane 1 ⅔ miles to its junction with Geoffrey Hoyt's Lane; turn right and follow signs. Open year-round, 8–sunset. This 480-acre property includes 19th-century estate gardens, rolling agricultural land, and mountain laurel. It also includes 2 miles of frontage on the Merrimack River in one of its loveliest segments. The mansions (one had 72 rooms) are gone, but the formal gardens, designed by Charles Sprague Sargent (who also designed Harvard's Arnold Arboretum in Boston), remain, along with the glorious mountain laurel that inspired John Greenleaf Whittier to write a number of poems, among them "The Laurels" and "June on the Merrimack." More than 16 miles of carriage roads and trails provide hiking, biking, cross-country skiing, and horseback riding. Guided walks are offered spring through fall, and performances by a resident group called Theater in the Open, along with children's theater and concerts, are also staged.

Old Town Hill Reservation. In Newbury turn left off Route 1A at Newman Street—at the far end of the Green, the first left after crossing the Parker River. The Trustees of Reservations own these 230 acres. The steep path takes less than a half hour round-trip, and it is one of the most delightful walks in the state: You climb gradually, following old stone walls and wild rose bushes. Benches are scattered along the way, and the view is not only of Newbury and Plum Island but also as far north as Mount Agamenticus in Maine and south to Cape Ann.

Mosely Pines (465-7336), Merrimac Street near the Chain Bridge; tennis courts, fireplaces for cookouts, swings, play equipment.

Waterfront Park. Two acres and boardwalk at Market Square, landscaped and fitted with benches and gas-style street lights, a favorite spot from which to watch boat traffic.

Newbury Perennial Gardens (462-1144), 18 Liberty Street, Newburyport. Open mid-April through June 8–6 daily, Friday until 8; July through September 10–5 daily. Nominal fee. Begun in 1974, 20 theme gardens are scattered throughout the grounds of a private estate; the Garden Store sells seeds, bulbs, and garden accessories.

LODGING

INNS AND BED & BREAKFASTS

Note: All listings are in Newburyport 01950.

Morrill Place (462-2808), 209 High Street. A three-story, Federal-style mansion built in 1806, Morrill Place offers nine guest rooms (five with private baths). The decor is a mix of formality and fun. Some rooms have sleigh beds, others, four-posters and canopies; a few have fireplaces, and most have a third bed tucked discreetly in a corner. Guests gather for breakfast and tea around the formal, lace-covered table in the rose-colored dining room but otherwise spread throughout the house. There's a formal parlor, a wicker-filled upstairs TV room, a luxurious library with hearth, a glass-sided winter porch, and a wraparound veranda. Innkeeper Rose Ann Hunter is a warm host who also conducts workshops on innkeeping and brokers inns. Continental breakfast and afternoon tea are included in $72–95 per couple.

Clark Currier Inn (465-8363), 45 Green Street. Another classic, three-story Federal mansion, built in 1803, near the heart of Newburyport. The parlor features graceful window arches and a Samuel McIntire mantel and is furnished with wing chairs and appropriate antiques. Guests can also relax in the upstairs library or in a comfortable skylighted sitting room off the garden—itself another inviting space, with a gazebo and fish pond. A light breakfast of muffins, bread, and fresh fruit is served by the hearth in the dining room. The eight guest rooms all have private baths but vary in shape, decor, and size. The Merrimac Room is fitted for families, the Hale Room features a Franklin stove, and several rooms have canopied beds. Your hosts are Mary and Bob Nolan and their daughter Malissa. $95–145.

The Windsor House (462-3778), 38 Federal Street. Guests gather for full English-style breakfasts around the table in the kitchen of this 18th-century brick house. Afternoon tea is served in the formal common room beneath the portrait of Queen Elizabeth II. Innkeeper Judith Harris is an enthusiastic lecturer on Neolithic and Celtic Britain, and her husband John hails from Cornwall. The five guest rooms are all large, and three have private bath. The Merchant Suite, originally a chandlery and now a pleasant ground-level room with its own entrance, is usually reserved for guests with pets or children, and upstairs the Bridal Suite honors the original couple for whom the house was built in 1786. $95 per couple with shared bath, $135 with private, $180 for a two-room suite sharing a hall bath. Additional persons in a room are $25; off-season, $85–99. Rates include tax as well as a full breakfast and tea. Children and pets by special arrangement only.

Garrison Inn (465-0910), 11 Brown Square. The atmosphere is that of a small, formal hotel (with an elevator and a handicapped-accessible room); built as a residence in 1803, it has been an inn of one sort or another since the turn of the century. The 24 guest rooms (private bath, color TV) are furnished with reproduction antiques; six suites have lofts with spiral or Colonial-style staircases, and a number of rooms have fireplaces. Although the downstairs level is devoted to dining areas (see *Dining Out*), staff are helpful in orienting and otherwise serving guests. From $97.50 per room, $135 per suite.

Essex Street Inn (465-3148), 7 Essex Street. Feels like an apartment house rather than an inn (no public space), but all 17 rooms are air-conditioned, with private baths, antiques. One-room suites have a fireplace and whirl-pool; two-room suites have fireplace, kitchen, and deck. $85–175; less off-season.

CAMPGROUNDS
Salisbury Beach State Reservation (462-4481), Route 1A, Salisbury, offers some 500 campsites for trailers on a first-come, first-served basis.

WHERE TO EAT

DINING OUT
Note: Restaurants are in Newburyport except where indicated.

Scandia Restaurant (462-6271), 25 State Street. Open Monday through Friday for lunch and dinner; Saturday, dinner only; Sunday, brunch and dinner. This storefront dining room is elegant with white tablecloths and fresh flowers, blue walls, and antique mirrors. It's a popular spot for soups, salads, and sandwiches at lunch, and the weekday buffet (not offered every day) is one of the best values in town. Dinner entrées range from $14.95 for boneless chicken breast with prosciutto and fontinella cheese to $17.95 for veal and lobster sauté. A Sunday brunch buffet ($14.95 adult, $6.95 for children over age 3) is served Columbus Day through Mother's Day.

✐ **David's Restaurant** (462-8077), 11 Brown Square. Downstairs, in the brick-walled basement, the mood and menu are informal; upstairs it's quite elegant. Here is a place you can bring the kids anytime because there's a nursery with a big-screen TV, games, and kid food (children must be 18 months; the charge is $5). You might dine on oysters baked with sun-dried tomatoes and spinach cream, followed by crisp boneless breast of duck carved over apple sage stuffing and dressed with cranberry port wine sauce; entrées are $15.95–21. At this writing, David's is offering a $40 dinner for two (a four-course meal), including a bottle of wine.

The Bayou (499-0428), 50 State Street. Open daily except Monday for lunch and dinner. The atmosphere varies in the dining rooms on each of the three floors in this narrow old building, but each is fun. We like the top floor best (smoking permitted) and intend to come back for the blues band. You can lunch on Louisiana seafood gumbo and po-boys (sandwiches made with southern fried shrimp, oysters, or alligator and served on French bread) and dine on portobello ribeye ($18.95) or pe-can-crusted catfish ($13.50).

Cafe France (463-8220), 27 State Street. Open for dinner; reservations suggested. We have not sampled this relatively new, small storefront restaurant but if the fare is as authentic as the accent of the family (from Lyon, a city famed for its cuisine) who own it, then it should be good. The menu is varied. You might start with vol-au-vent d'homard (puff pastry filled with fresh lobster in a light mushroom cream sauce; $12.50) or *salade des haricots blancs et crevettes* (a white bean salad with shrimp). Then dine on roasted quail stuffed with mashed garlic and parsley potatoes served with braised cabbage ($20.95) or salmon with aioli and tomato coulis served with fresh vegetables and potato ($18). Save room for profiteroles or crème brûlée.

Joseph's Winter Street Cafe (462-1188), 22 Winter Street. Open Monday through Saturday from 5:30, Sunday from noon. The food and atmosphere are Italian. A locally favored dining place with standout veal dishes, along with choices like grilled shrimp and prosciutto, calamari, and penne pasta. Jazz piano nightly.

Ten Center Street (462-6652), 10 Center Street. Open for lunch and dinner daily. An 18th-century mansion with the informal **Molly's Pub** downstairs and a more formal white-tablecloth dining room upstairs with specialties like veal Firenza ($19.95); entrées range from pastas ($14.50) to twin filet mignon béarnaise ($21.95).

Glenn's Galley (465-3811), 44 Merrimac Street, Newburyport. "World class cuisine in a funky casual atmosphere," clean and modern with exquisite food and plating; specializes in dishes cooked on a wood-fired grill, such as bourbon pecan chicken.

Amesbury House (388-5249), 62 Haverhill Road (Route 110), Amesbury. Open for lunch and dinner weekdays, dinner on weekends. Fine dining and an extensive wine list; specialties include fresh seafood, beef, and poultry. $11.95–16.95 for dinner.

EATING OUT

Note: All establishments are in Newburyport except where indicated.

The Grog (465-8008), 13 Middle Street. Open for lunch and dinner daily. Usually crowded in the less formal pub space downstairs; slower-paced but the same menu upstairs in a living room setting with a hearth. You can lunch on pasta or burgers, dine on a selection of seafood, pasta, and Mexican dishes; try the Key lime pie. Nightclub entertainment downstairs after 8 PM.

Michael's Harborside (462-7785), Tournament Wharf (under the Salisbury Bridge). Open daily for lunch and dinner. An informal place right on the water; fried and broiled seafood, chowder. Mixed reviews.

✐ **The Mall** (465-5506), corner of High and Green Streets. Open daily for lunch and dinner. Pronounced Mal, this local dining landmark caters to families, with tablecloths that kids can draw on; reasonably priced, varied menu ranging from West Indian to Mexican.

Ciro's Restaurant (463-3335), 1 Market Square. Open daily for lunch and dinner. One in a chain of local Italian restaurants: slick, good food, reasonable prices, great location in the firehouse with outside dining on the waterfront park in season. Pizza, calzones, and pasta dishes.

✐ **Jacob Marley's Restaurant** (465-5598), 23 Pleasant Street. Open daily for lunch and dinner. A large, family-geared place with a large menu ranging from Mexican through pizza and pastas to burgers, sandwiches, lots of greens, children's menu. Sunday buffet brunch 11–2.

Main Street in Newburyport

KIMBERLY GRANT

Angie's Food (462-7959), 7 Pleasant Street. Open 6 AM–4 PM, Monday
through Thursday, weekends 6 AM–3 PM. A great old-fashioned coffee
shop with a counter and blue Formica tables; as satisfying to visitors as
to its many regulars.

The Agawam Diner (948-7780), Route 1, near the junction with Route
133, Rowley. Open daily 5 AM–12:30 AM. A chrome classic. Breakfast is

served all day, and there are blue-plate specials, homemade cream and fruit pies, reasonably priced fried clams and shrimp.

Abraham's Bagels (465-8148), 11 Liberty Street. Open 6 AM to early afternoon. A distribution bakery—great bagels and other bakery basics.

Szechuan Taste & Thai Cafe (463-0686), 19 Pleasant Street. Open daily for lunch and dinner until midnight, until 1 AM Friday and Saturday. This attractive restaurant does not use MSG and offers an unusually wide choice of Chinese dishes, especially seafood. Try the fresh scallops with ginger sauce.

Taffy's (465-9039), corner of State Street and Prince Place. Open Monday through Saturday 4 AM–2:30 PM, in winter, 4 AM–2 PM. Little changed since it opened 45 years ago, this old-fashioned luncheonette with a counter and booths is clean, friendly, and cheap. Try the soups of the day or luncheon special.

SNACKS

Fowle's Restaurant (465-0141), 17 State Street. This '30s tobacco store with a soda counter features an art deco fountain. It's now a café specializing in freshly roasted coffees and pastries.

Gretta's Great Grains (465-1709), 24 Pleasant Street. Open 7:30–5. This bakery features fragrant, good-for-you breads and muffins; some tables; and coffee.

ENTERTAINMENT

*The Firehouse Center for the Performing Arts** (462-7336) is a vintage-1823 firehouse in Market Square, Newburyport, that now includes a 195-seat theater, two art galleries, and a restaurant (Ciro's; see *Eating Out*). Year-round productions (Wednesday through Sunday) include a wide variety of concerts and plays, also children's theater. Contact the box office (open daily, varying hours) for a current calendar.

The Playhouse Dinner Theater (388-9444), 109 Main Street, Amesbury (town parking lot off Route 150), near the junction of I-95 and I-495 (exit 54). Performances by a resident troupe of 60 actors; classics like *Arsenic and Old Lace* and *Can-Can*.

The Screening Room (462-3456), 82 State Street, Newburyport. A small, unusually comfortable cinema specializing in classic flicks.

SELECTIVE SHOPPING

ANTIQUES

In Newburyport, no fewer than 15 antiques stores can be found within a half-dozen downtown blocks: Federal, Water, State, and Merrimac Streets. Pick up a list at any store. Salisbury, too, is an antiques center.

ART GALLERIES

The Newburyport Art Association (465-8769), 65 Water Street, Newburyport. Open March through December, 1–5 daily except Monday.

The gallery shows and sells works by members. We counted more than a dozen other galleries in Newburyport on our last visit. **Piel Craftsmen Company** (462-7012), 307 High Street, Newburyport. Open weekdays 8:30–noon, 1–4:30. Visitors are welcome to watch shop models of 1800s ships made by hand.

BIRDING

The Birdwatcher of Newburyport (462-2473), 50 Water Street in the Tannery. Birding supplies, bird feeders; guided walks and boat tours on the Parker River.

BOOKSTORES

Jabberwocky (465-9359), the Tannery, 12 Federal Street, Newburyport. Open Monday through Saturday until 9, Sunday noon–6. A large, full-service bookstore with an adjoining café. **Middle Street Bookstore** (463-2000), 3 Middle Street, Newburyport. A small store with a large selection of titles. **The Book Rack** (462-8615), 52 State Street, Newburyport. A full-service bookstore. **Old Port Book Shop** (462-0100), 18 State Street, Newburyport. Open daily. In addition to 18,000 of its own antiquarian titles, 15 dealers from around New England are also represented.

FARMS AND FARM STANDS

Long Hill Orchard (363-5545), Main Street (Route 113), West Newbury. Open daily, year-round. Pick-your-own vegetables in-season, apples, cider, peaches, pears, blueberries, jams, honey. **Tender Crop Farm** (462-6972), High Road (Route 1A), Newbury. Open spring through Christmas. Home of Buffy the Buffalo as well as homegrown fruits, seasonal vegetables, dried flowers, nursery plants. **Pettingill Farm** (462-3675), 121 Ferry Road, Salisbury. Open daily April through June, weekends in July and August, daily except Saturday in September, October. A more than 200-year-old farm featuring perennials and dried flowers. Gardening classes.

SHOPPING COMPLEXES

State Street and the Inn Street Mall, Newburyport. The lower State Street shops back onto delightful pedestrian courts and more shops. The buildings themselves, all built of sturdy brick after an 1811 fire destroyed this area, are wonderful places to browse. **The Tannery** (465-7047), 12 Federal Street, Newburyport, is a pleasant indoor mall with some 30 specialty shops: antiques, flowers, books, and clothing.

SEAFOOD

David's Fish Market (462-2504), Bridge Road (Route 1 a mile or so beyond the bridge), Salisbury. Open daily 8–6. This white cinder-block building should be the last stop on every day-tripper's list; the fish is flapping fresh and includes fish stock, chowder fish, lobster, and shellfish.

SPECIAL EVENTS

Note: All events are in Newburyport.

May: **Spring Wildlife Plover Festival** at Parker River National Wildlife Refuge, Maudslay State Park, and throughout the city. **Custom House Antique Show** at Plum Island Airport. **Salmagundi Fair**—craft fair Sunday and Monday of Memorial Day weekend, includes food, dancing.

June: **Garden Tour**, sponsored by Cushing House (see *Museums*).

July through August: **Yankee Homecoming**—last week in July, climaxing first weekend in August. Races, contests, sidewalk sales, concerts, buggy rides, fireworks.

September: **Annual Country Auction** at Upper Green, Newbury. High-quality antiques, collectibles, and books attract bidders from throughout New England.

October: **Fall Harvest Festival**, Sunday and Monday of Columbus Day weekend—craftspeople, performances, food, farm exhibits.

November: Santa parade, tree lighting.

December: Choral concerts and candlelight services, caroling, and open houses at shops. **First Night**.

The Merrimack Valley

LOWELL

Because Lowell was the country's first completely planned manufacturing city—a utopian concept in the 19th century—its more than 5 miles of canals and several of its mammoth brick mills have been restored to form a National Historical Park. Old-fashioned trolley cars shuttle visitors from one site to another and in summer tour boats ply the canals.

An introductory film at the park visitors center dramatizes the way Boston merchant Francis Cabot Lowell memorized the mechanics of the power looms he viewed on a visit to Britain in 1810. At the time, only cotton yarn—not cloth—was being manufactured in the United States, and upon his return Lowell was able to produce cloth—from bale to bolt—in a factory in Waltham on the Charles River. His Boston Manufacturing Company quickly outgrew its power source, and in 1821 some 400 acres surrounding a major drop in the Merrimack River was selected as the site for an entire company-planned town of mills.

By 1836 Lowell boasted eight major textile mills, employing 7500 workers. By 1855, after completion of the world's largest waterpower canal system, 9000 women and 4000 men were producing more than 2 million yards of cloth a week. The women were Yankee girls who had come from upcountry farms to live together in tidy boardinghouses; they were well paid and spent their limited free time attending lectures, reading, and writing. This was the Lowell that drew sightseers from Davy Crockett to Charles Dickens, but it was short-lived.

By the 1850s other mill towns had emerged, many established by the same Boston Associates who had developed Lowell. Competition soon forced longer hours and lower wages. Yankee mill girls were replaced at the looms by immigrant families willing to accept work at any pay and to live in the flimsy wooden tenements that mushroomed around town. Irish families arrived in the 1850s; French Canadians in the 1860s and 1870s; and Greek, Polish, and East European families in the 1890s and early 1900s. By the turn of the century, mill hands were working a 72-hour week for $5 or less. A major strike in 1912 brought some concessions. The city's population, with its 40 nationalities, peaked during World War I at 126,000.

Textile companies, however, soon began transferring their operations to the South to take advantage of cheaper labor. Then came the Depression, and one mammoth mill after another closed. The World War II demand for cloth and munitions brought a short reprieve, but by the 1950s Lowell itself looked like a war zone, filled with crumbling brick

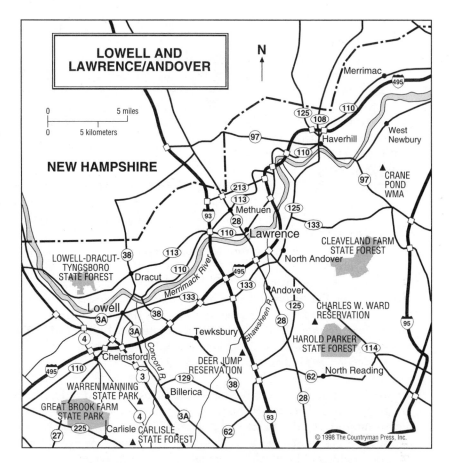

buildings—obvious targets for urban renewal.

It was school principal Patrick J. Mogan who first fired residents with the idea that Lowell had a history so special that it deserved a national park. Business leaders and local politicians rallied to the cause, and the Lowell National Historical Park was established in 1978. In the 1980s more than 100 downtown buildings were rehabilitated, attracting a variety of tenants. The University of Massachusetts at Lowell (formed in 1975 when Lowell State College and Lowell Technological Institute merged) also expanded, becoming a palpable downtown presence.

Beyond its restored core, however, Lowell remains a city of recent immigrants. The latest arrivals are from Cambodia, Laos, Latin America, and the Caribbean.

Visitors today are surprised by the present quality and quantity of the national park exhibits. In Building #6 in the Boott Mills, the centerpiece of the national park, visitors are greeted with the deafening clatter of 88 belt-driven power looms and must pass through this "weave room" to reach the elaborate displays upstairs. Exhibits in the neighboring Boarding House are devoted to Lowell's workers from the 1830s up to today.

Park rangers offer a variety of narrated tours year-round. Seasonal tours combine boat and trolley rides. You might request self-guiding walks to the canals and the river (be sure to at least drive by mighty Pawtucket Falls) and to sites in town connected with Lowell-born and -bred Jack Kerouac, author of *On the Road* and a number of novels set in his birthplace.

AREA CODE: 978

GUIDANCE

The National Park Visitors Center (970-5000), 246 Market Street, open daily 8:30–5. The place to phone before you come and to check into as soon as you arrive for an idea of the day's tour and events schedule.

GETTING THERE

By train and bus: **MBTA Commuter Service** offers frequent daily service from Boston's North Station (227-5070) to the Charles A. Gallagher Transportation Terminal (459-7101) on Thorndike Street, also the local depot for **Trailways** and **Vermont Transit.** Shuttle service to downtown Lowell runs every 15 minutes Monday through Saturday.

By car from Boston: Either Route 128 to Route 3 or I-93 to I-495; either way, exit onto the Lowell Connector and follow signs for the park visitors center at Market Mills; free parking in back.

GETTING AROUND

From March through November, replica 1901 trolleys, powered by an electric overhead line, shuttle between the visitors center and other points of interest like the Boott and Suffolk Mills and Lower Locks; open-sided cars are used in warmer months. The distance between the visitors center and Boott Mills is actually just a short and interesting walk.

MEDICAL EMERGENCY

St. Joseph's Health Care Center (453-1761), 220 Pawtucket Street (west end of Merrimack Street), 24-hour emergency service.

TO SEE

MUSEUMS

Note: All places are in Lowell unless otherwise indicated.

National Park Visitors Center and Tours (470-5000), 246 Market Street, in the former Lowell Manufacturing Company Mill Complex, now called Market Mills. A 20-minute film, *Lowell: The Industrial Revelation* (presented twice each hour), describes the dramatic rise of Lowell as well as its factory system, its turn-of-the-century excesses and rich ethnic life, and its subsequent decline. Here you also sign up for one of the day's tours (call ahead to reserve a spot).

✐ **Boott Cotton Mills Museum.** Open daily 9:30–4, admission $5 adults, $4 seniors, $2 youths, children 5 and under free. Visitors are startled by the noise and vibration of the 88 looms (earplugs are available). Walk the length of the room reading quotations by workers. Just six looms here now actually produce cloth, reproduction Boott Mills towels that are sold in the museum store. These particular looms were first used in Fall River and later in Tennessee. You learn that when the Boott Mills first opened, in the 1830s, each weaver tended a pair of looms, but a century later it was common to assign 20 looms to each weaver. At the far end of the Weave Room, stairs lead to the second floor (there's also an elevator), with its elaborate displays describing the transition from preindustrial to industrial society; *Wheels of Change,* a 24-minute, nine-projector slide program, also tells the story, and another exhibit, "Lowell Heyday: Bale to Bolt," details the production process. Another room depicts an empty mill room, and videos present workers' memories of the city in decline. The final room is an upbeat, optimistic presentation on Lowell as is today.

Elsewhere in the Boott Mills: Check to see whether the **New England Folklife Center** (970-5190), located on the fifth floor, is open. Note that the **Tsongas Industrial History Center** (970-5080) offers a variety of hands-on, experiential exhibits.

Working People Exhibit at the Patrick J. Mogan Cultural Center, 40 French Street. Open noon–5. Free. Housed in the vintage-1836 boardinghouse adjacent to the Boott Mills, this is one of 70 boardinghouses built and operated by Lowell's original textile corporations. The tables are set for a meal, and you hear invisible girls discussing their lives. Extensive exhibits upstairs draw you into another part of the center, all depicting actual workers, from mill girls through a variety of immigrants; part of the gallery is devoted to changing exhibits.

The American Textile History Museum (441-0400), 491 Dutton St. Open Tuesday through Friday, 9 AM–4 PM; Saturday through Sunday, 10 AM–4 PM. Adults $5, $3 seniors and students. Free parking. Founded in North Andover in 1960, the world's largest and most comprehensive textile museum—its collection includes 5 million fabric samples—moved to Lowell in 1997 and now occupies an 1860s canalside textile machinery factory elegantly remodeled at a cost of $7 million. Exhibits such as the re-creation of a 1700s felting mill, an 1870s woolen mill, and a working 1950s factory weave room tell the story of how textiles have shaped the lives of Americans from colonial times to the present. Along with often fascinating exhibits of costumes, fabrics, and tools, the museum displays nearly 300 different spinning wheels, the largest such collection anywhere. The museum shop sells beautiful high-quality fabric products, some handmade and others woven on the premises. The **Gazebo Cafe** off the museum's dramatic atrium (open 10–3 Tuesday through Sunday) is a real restaurant serving such trendy dishes as Cajun braised rabbit and chicken pirouette. Brunch on Sunday.

Lowell

The New England Quilt Museum (452-4207), 18 Shattuck Street. Open Monday through Saturday 10–4 and Sunday noon–4. Closes Sunday November to May. $4 adults, $3 seniors and students. The only quilt museum in the northeast features changing exhibits on regional, national, and international quilting. A gift shop has quilting books and supplies.

Whistler House (452-7641), 243 Worthen Street, one block from the National Park Visitors Center. Open June through August, Tuesday through Saturday 11–4, Sunday 1–4; September through May, Wednesday through Saturday 11–4, Sunday 1–4; closed major holidays. Adults $3, students and seniors $2; children free. Built in 1823, this house served as home for three years to Maj. George Washington Whistler, the engineer charged with supervising construction of the locomotives for a rail line between Lowell and Boston. His son James Abbott was born here in 1834, but never returned when he left at age 3. Here you learn that James's artistic training began in St. Petersburg (his father supervised construction of the railroad from there to Moscow beginning in 1843) and that he later attended West Point (like his father) but was discharged for failing chemistry and getting too many demerits. He went on to become a celebrated artist, living in Paris and London. Since 1908 this building has housed the **Lowell Art Association;** rooms display late-19th-century landscapes and portraits from the collection, and the adjacent **Parker Gallery** stages changing exhibits.

The Sports Museum of New England (452-6775), 25 Shattuck St. Open Monday through Saturday from 10 AM, Sundays noon–5 PM. Adults $4, seniors and students $2, children free. Exhibits, artifacts, and videos on New England's sports heritage.

WALKING TOURS

Jack Kerouac's Lowell. At the National Park Visitors Center, pick up a descriptive map/guide to sites associated with Jack Kerouac, born March 12, 1922, in the Centralville section of Lowell. The writer's Underwood typewriter and backpack are exhibited, with copies of some of his most famous works (*On the Road* and *Mexico City Blues*) in the Working People Exhibit at the **Patrick J. Mogan Cultural Center** (see *Museums*). He frequented the **Pollard Memorial Library,** and often lifted a glass at the **Old Worthen Tavern** on Dutton Street (see *Where to Eat—Other*) and **Nicky's Bar** (now Luna d'Oro Restaurant; see *Dining Out*) on Gorham Street. Kerouac's grave is in the Sampas family plot at the **Edson Cemetery** (corner of Gorham Street and the Lowell Connector). The **Jack Kerouac Commemorative,** a sculpture park with eight granite columns inscribed with quotations from his works, is at the intersection of Bridge and French Streets. Kerouac, who died in 1969, draws to Lowell an increasing number of fans from around the world. For details about the series of exhibits, poetry readings, and musical performances honoring him in October, call the Lowell Cultural Commission (441-3800).

Pawtucket Falls. This 30-foot drop is impressive, best viewed from the Pawtucket Canal Gatehouse, School Street.

The Acre bounded by Merrimack and Dummer Streets. The city's oldest and most densely settled immigrant neighborhood is constantly changing. Begin with the **Whistler House** (see *Museums*) and walk a couple of blocks, checking out the ethnic restaurants and markets.

The Butterfly Place (392-0955), 120 Tyngsboro Road, Westford. (Take exit 34 on Route 3 north from Lowell. Also accessible from I-495, exit 32; call for directions.) Open mid-April to Columbus Day. $6 adults, $5 seniors and children over age 3. A 3100-square-foot atrium with 22-foot-high walls that then taper to make a 27-foot-high peak is filled with flowering plants and some 500 live butterflies representing as many as 40 species.

CHURCHES

St. Anne's Episcopal Church, corner of Merrimack and Kirk Streets. Built in 1825, the church is supposedly haunted by the ghost of its first minister, who sided with the rebellious mill girls (who refused to pay tithes to the church as they were ordered). It's also said to be built from stone excavated during the construction of the Merrimack Canal. Note the stained-glass windows by Tiffany.

St. Joseph The Workers Shrine in the Lee Street Church (between Kirk and John Streets, one block north of Merrimack). Built in 1850 of the same stone as St. Anne's, the shrine was originally a Universalist church but later was bought by the Boston archdiocese to be the state's first French Canadian parish.

St. Patrick's Church (459-0561), 282 Suffolk Street. The city's oldest church and the center of the Irish community; inquire at the National Park Visitors Center (see *Guidance*) about periodic tours.

TO DO

Lowell National Historical Park Tours (970-5000). Programs are offered year-round, departing from the visitors center (see *Guidance*). Reservations are strongly advised. Walking tours follow parts of the canalway trails, explore ethnic neighborhoods and churches, and include boat rides on portions of the canal system. Narrated boat and trolley tours offered several times daily June through Columbus Day. Adults $4, seniors $2, youths (6–16) children free.

SWIMMING

Privately operated **Wyman's Beach** (692-6287) in Westford offers swimming, camping, and picnicking. A public beach on the Merrimac at the Bellegrade Boathouse is due to open.

CROSS-COUNTRY SKIING

Great Brook Farm Ski Touring Center (369-6312), Lowell Street, Carlisle. Open in ski season daily 9–4:30, until 9 PM Tuesday and Thursday; 12 miles of groomed trails, instruction, rental equipment, night skiing on a 1.5K loop. Located on a working dairy farm.

GREEN SPACE

Vandenberg Esplanade River Front Park, Pawtucket Boulevard, Lowell, is a 2½-mile paved walkway with benches and landscaped lawns along the north bank of the Merrimack River, maintained by the Department of Environmental Management (DEM). The Sampas Pavilion stage is the site of live performances, and the boathouse offers community sailing and rowing programs.

Lowell Waterpower Trail. A system of trails, called canalways, has been laid out to guide you around the canal system. This 3-mile walk links the visitors center and the Boott Cotton Mills (see *Museums*) via two spurs along the canals and travels past the mills to Pawtucket Dam and the Vandenberg Esplanade. Request the printed guide from the visitors center.

Lowell-Dracut-Tyngsboro State Forest (452-7191), Trotting Park Road off Varnum Avenue, Lowell. This 997-acre park sports a 30-acre lake for skating and fishing; picnicking; and scenic trails for hiking, cross-country skiing, and bicycling. A spring and the springhouse were used by a former bottling works. Granite from the forest's quarries was a resource for mill foundations and canal embankments.

Great Brook Farm State Park (369-6312), Lowell Road, Carlisle. From Lowell, take Route 110 south to Route 4 through Chelmsford. South of the village the road splits; bear right where Route 4 bears left (Lowell Road). The 950-acre park is on the left just over the Carlisle line. Open meadows, wooded trails, and a scenic pond. There are 15 miles of hiking trails, a working dairy that sells ice cream, and a ski-touring center in winter.

Carlisle State Forest (369-6312), Forest Road, Carlisle. A 22-acre area, this former estate is webbed with hiking and touring trails.

Warren Manning State Park (369-6312), Chelmsford Road (Route 129), Billerica. A 380-acre wooded spread with picnic tables, a children's spray pool, bridle paths, hiking trails.

LODGING

HOTELS

Sheraton Inn, Lowell (452-1200), 50 Warren Street, Lowell 01852, at the Lower Locks. This 251-room hotel overlooks the Pawtucket Canal, within walking distance of all the park sites and downtown shops. Facilities include a swim and fitness club, two restaurants, and two lounges. Doubles $80–$110.

Lowell Courtyard by Marriott (458-7575), 30 Industrial Avenue East, Lowell 01852. A 120-room hotel with motel-like amenities. Limited room service and only breakfast served in the dining room. Doubles $50–100.

BED & BREAKFASTS

Note: The following B&Bs are located in Lowell's two posh Victorian neighborhoods, Belvedere and the Highlands (both 01851), set high above the downtown.

Coddington Hall (454-1763), 353 Wilder Street. Linda Coddington offers one or two rooms in her large Victorian house. One room has a double bed and private bath; the small second room is good for an accompanying child. Breakfast served, kitchen privileges. $65 and up.

Commonwealth House (459-8418), 87 Nesmith Street. A Federal-style house built in 1843 and listed on the National Register of Historic Places. The four guest rooms share two baths. From $60.

WHERE TO EAT

DINING OUT

Note: All restaurants are in Lowell. Be forewarned that the names of places change frequently here but the quality and value of the ethnic restaurants—which actually serve the communities they represent—remain.

La Boniche (458-9473), 143 Merrimack Street. Open for lunch Tuesday through Friday and dinner Tuesday through Saturday. Located on the

ground floor of the restored former Bon Marché department store, this
is a tastefully simple but culinarily sophisticated French-style bistro.
You can lunch handsomely on quiche or escargot sautéed in a Dijon
and tarragon cream sauce, or dine on sherried roast duckling or stuffed
pork medallions. The wine list is exclusively French. Dinner entrées in
the $18–22 range. There are classical music and jazz performances Sat-
urday nights; reservations recommended.

Luna d'Oro (459-8666), 110 Gorham Street. An attractive restaurant serving Mediterranean (mostly Portuguese and Spanish) cuisine, this was
once a blue-collar bar called Nicky's and supposedly Kerouac's favorite
of the several local pubs he regularly patronized. (His picture hangs on
the wall.) Specialties include garlic sausage in port wine sauce, paella,
and roasted rack of lamb with sweet potato pancakes. Entrées in the
$15–22 range.

Athenian Corner (458-7052), 207 Market Street. Open daily for lunch and
dinner, boasting the "largest variety of fine Greek food in New England."
Handy to the National Park Visitors Center (see *Museums*), the Athenian
Corner has daily luncheon specials; dinner entrées average $8–15.

Cobblestones (970-2282), 91 Dutton Street, near the Merrimack
Gatehouse and St. Anne's Church (see *Churches*). A former mill agent's
mansion is now a large, fairly formal restaurant that's surprisingly reasonable in price for dinner. Smoked chicken and wild mushrooms tossed
with fettucine and cashews in cream is $11.95, and roast pork loin is
$9.95. The bar side is pleasant.

EATING OUT

Southeast Asian Restaurant (452-3182), 351 Market Street. Open daily 8
AM–7:30 PM. Thai, Laotian, Cambodian, and Vietnamese specialties are
all made from scratch here. Descriptions of the exotic dishes are detailed on the menu. Bargain-priced luncheon and dinner buffets.

Xamsanthai Restaurant (446-0977), 368 Merrimack Street. An unpretentious, family-run restaurant serving Thai, Laotian, and Chinese cuisine. Across from City Hall, it's popular with politicians as well as the
Asian community. Entrées in the $9–15 range; $5.95 luncheon buffet.

Bombay Mahal (441-2222), 45 Middle Street. Authentic Indian menu. Monday through Saturday, northern Indian traditional dishes are the specialty,
but Sunday brunches feature southern Indian food. Beer and wine.

Dubliner (459-9831), 197 Market Street. Open daily (except Sunday) for
lunch and dinner, around the corner from the park's visitors center. An
Irish pub atmosphere featuring sandwiches, steaks, and seafood—all day.

Brewhouse Cafe (937-2390), 201 Cabot Street. Open weekdays for lunch,
Tuesday through Saturday for dinner, noon–8 on Sunday. A pleasant
pub with good food and brew.

The Old Worthen Tavern (441-3189), 141 Worthen Street, open Monday
through Saturday for lunch. The city's oldest tavern and bar; a genuine
neighborhood pub but conscious of its status as a former Jack Kerouac
haunt. Inquire about Kerouac nights.

M.L. Shaw's (937-0100), 11 Kearney Square. Serves breakfast and lunch but locally renowned for its ice cream, made daily with fresh milk from the Shaw family's own dairy farm in Dracut.

DINERS

Arthur's (452-8647), 112 Bridge Street. Also known as the Paradise Grill. A shabby but friendly and clean diner, this is the source of one of the best pastrami sandwiches we've ever had; the Boott Mill sandwich will set you up for the day.

Club Diner (452-1679), 145 Dutton Street, across from the visitors center. Open 24 hours Monday through Friday, closing Saturday at noon, then open 11 pm Saturday to noon Sunday. The yellow-bodied classic, here since 1933, was owned by Mademoiselle le Vasseur from 1928 until 1962 and is still in the family. Red Jell-O, baked stuffed haddock, stuffed peppers, coffee in heavy mugs; clean and friendly.

Four Sisters Owl Diner (453-8321), 244 Appletown Street. Open 6 AM–2 PM. Diner buffs will recognize this place as a "semi-streamer," and in Lowell it's an institution. Note the artwork in the dining room. Reliable food, generous portions (breakfasts are massive), and a friendly atmosphere.

ENTERTAINMENT

Note: The **Lowell Office of Cultural Affairs** (441-3800) publishes a bimonthly calendar of events and serves as a constant source of information about ongoing entertainment.

Merrimack Repertory Theatre (454-3926), Liberty Hall, 50 East Merrimack Street, Lowell. A professional Equity theater presenting a full program of plays; also special summer events.

University of Massachusetts/Lowell Center for the Arts (934-4444), Durgin Hall, South Campus, Pawtucket and Wilder Streets. A performance series that includes top-flight Broadway productions, children's entertainment, and musical groups.

Boarding House Park Summer Performance Series (441-3800), French Street at Boott Mills (see *Museums*). The outdoor stage here serves as a lively performance center on summer weekends.

Lowell Memorial Auditorium (454-2854), East Merrimack Street, Lowell. The theater seats 1200 and is the frequent stage for nationally known groups and Broadway shows, as well as for world-class wrestling matches.

SELECTIVE SHOPPING

Note: Unless otherwise indicated, all shops are in Lowell.

Brush Art Gallery and Studios (459-7819), 246 Market Street, across the courtyard from the park's visitors center, includes 12 working artists' studios, a gallery, and a gift shop. Open Tuesday through Saturday 11–5,

Sunday noon–5. **The Design Place** (970-0203), 44 Palmer Street. Fabrics, furnishing, accessories, and other interior design products, as well as good advice. **Wells Emporium** (454-4401), 169 Merrimack Street. Hand-crafted gifts. **Hub Mills Factory Outlet** (937-0320), 12 Perkins Street (off Cabot Street). Closed Sunday and Monday. Wool, mohair, cotton, and silk yarns; wool sweaters, blankets, and lingerie. **George's Textile Company** (452-0878), 360 Merrimack Street. A find for anyone looking for fabric; great selection and prices. Note the wall of old Lowell photographs. **Cote's Market** (458-4635), Salem Street. A French Canadian market with prepackaged specialties like bread pudding and baked beans. **Center City Farmer's Market**, 45 Palmer Street. There's a little bit of everything for sale in this former firehouse, including antiques and crafts, fresh fruit and vegetables, baked goods, pizza, espresso, butter and eggs, and Lowell High School memorabilia.

BOOKSTORES

Barnes & Noble Booksellers (458-3939), 151 Merrimack Street. This large, full-service downtown bookstore on the street floor of the landmark former Bon Marché department store building is also the official bookstore of the University of Lowell. Good selection of books about Lowell and the Merrimack Valley. Also, of course, every book by Jack Kerouac. **Summer Street Books** (256-3514), Summer Street Crossing Mall, Chelmsford. General selection of hardcover and paperback books.

SPECIAL EVENTS

April: **Thoreau's Portage White-water Invitational Slalom**—the New England championships, with members of the US White-water Racing Team and other kayak and canoeists running the rapids on the Concord in Lowell; a great spectator event.

Mid-April: **Cambodian New Year** is celebrated with a 3-day festival of rituals, music, and games.

July: **July 4th Celebration. Lowell Folk Festival** (last weekend), the largest free folk festival in the country, draws thousands of visitors for traditional folk music, dance, parades, crafts, ethnic food; performances are on five outdoor stages, along the canals, on downtown streets.

September: **Banjo** and **Fiddle contests** at Market Mills (Saturday after Labor Day).

October: **Lowell Celebrates Kerouac!** Exhibits, poetry readings, musical performances.

November: **Lowell's City Lights Celebration** begins the weekend after Thanksgiving.

December 31: **Family First Night.**

LAWRENCE/ANDOVER

In 1845 the Essex Company selected a rural stretch of land along the Merrimack River, known as Deer Jump Falls, as a site on which to build a planned mill town. By 1847, Lawrence (named for Abbot Lawrence, a partner in the company) was incorporated, and its population zoomed to 3550. By 1848 the company had already built the Great Dam, which still stands, as well as two canals, a machine shop to build locomotives, the Prospect Hill reservoir, 50 brick buildings, a large boardinghouse, and the Atlantic Cotton, Pemberton, Upper Pacific, and Duck Mills. The Essex Company also conscientiously planted elms, laid out a common and parks, and built its mills and workers' boardinghouses solidly. By 1850 the 6-square-mile town boasted 11 schools and a lecture series that drew Emerson and Melville.

This town was the Lawrence that attracted trainloads of Bostonians to breathe its clean air and stroll its handsome streets—and it vanished quickly. In 1860 the five-story Pemberton Mill collapsed, killing 88 and seriously injuring 116 more, an ominous sign of things to come as the town doubled and redoubled its size. Cramped wooden "four-deckers" housed immigrants from Italy, Germany, Britain, Russia, Austria, Poland, and Syria, among other places. Those born in the city rarely lived beyond 40, if they survived infancy. The whole sorry scene became one of national concern with the Bread and Roses Strike of 1912.

At the time of the strike, the city was the "worsted center of the world," a city of 86,000, in which 74,000 were foreign born or of foreign parentage. In the wake of the strike, wages increased slightly and immigration dropped off, largely because an investigation of conditions in Lawrence led to the passage of a federal quota law.

The city's population today is 73,000, and it continues to attract new arrivals from Southeast Asia and Latin America. Hispanics now account for more than 40 percent of the total population. It remains one of the country's most vividly ethnic cities.

This park is one of the most successful among the nine Heritage State Parks founded in Massachusetts since the late 1970s. Housed in a canal-side, 1840s mill boardinghouse, it tells the city's story and also serves as a visitors information center for the area and a community center for Lawrence.

From the Heritage State Park, request directions to the museums and historic houses across the river in Andover and North Andover. Within a few miles of the city's colossal brick mills, you can pick peaches on a centuries-old farm or view Americana at a prestigious prep school museum or in a colonial-era house set in a rural Yankee village.

AREA CODE: 978

GUIDANCE
Lawrence Heritage State Park Visitors Center (794-1655), One Jackson Street, corner of Canal. Open daily 9–4.

Merrimack Valley Chamber of Commerce (686-0900) in Lawrence furnishes publications and information by phone.

GETTING THERE
By train: The **T Commuter Service** (617-722-3200; 1-800-392-6100) terminal is a reasonable walk across the Casey Bridge from the canal-area sites.

By car: I-495, exit 45, follow DOWNTOWN and HERITAGE STATE PARK signs.

PARKING
The **Heritage State Park** has a parking lot; follow signs.

MEDICAL EMERGENCY
Lawrence General Hospital (683-4000), 1 General Street.

TO SEE

Lawrence Heritage State Park (794-1655), One Jackson Street, Lawrence. Open daily 9–4. The 1847 brick boardinghouse contains two full floors of exhibits depicting life from the point of view of the various immigrant groups (totaling more than 50) that have worked in the mills. A video depicts the 1912 Bread and Roses strike, and displays include a tenement kitchen. The third floor doubles as a gallery, with changing exhibits.

Phillips Academy, Main Street (Route 28), Andover. Founded in 1778, this academy is one of the country's leading prep schools, with a college-sized (450 acres) campus and two excellent museums: **Addison Gallery of American Art** (749-4015), closed August, is otherwise open Tuesday through Saturday, 10–5, Sunday 1–5. Free. The collection includes only American art, and you might want to call ahead to ask what's on display; shows change frequently. Don't miss the collection of exquisite ship's models in the basement. **Robert S. Peabody Museum of Archeology** (749-4490), Phillips and Main Streets. Open Tuesday through Friday 10–5, Saturday 10–1 (closed most holidays). Collections of shards and Native American implements unearthed in digs around the region and in the Southwest. This is a teaching museum and only 1 percent of the collection is on view at any one time.

HISTORIC HOUSES
Andover Historical Society (475-2236), 97 Main Street, Andover. Open Monday through Saturday 9–5 and by appointment. Adults $4, students $2. The early 19th century is featured in the **Blanchard House** and **Barn Museum.** Five period rooms illustrate the decorative arts of that period; you can also see extensive archives, a tool collection, and an early pumper. Ask about changing exhibits and walking tours.

North Andover Historical Society (686-4035), 153 Academy Road, North Andover. The **Johnson Cottage** (open year-round Tuesday through

Friday, 10–noon and 2–4; $2 adults, $1 students) is a vintage-1789 artisan's cottage. The **Parson Barnard House** (1715), open June through September, Tuesday through Thursday and by appointment, is a mustard-colored saltbox with some unusual features, like a Federal-era mantel that folds away to reveal the original hearth, and panels displaying successive wall coverings.

Stevens-Coolidge Place (682-3580), Andover Street, North Andover. Open April through October, Sunday 1–5, Wednesday 2–4. Gardens open daily from 8 AM to sunset. Adults $3, children free. An exceptional summer mansion, actually two older buildings transformed around the turn of the century by noted Colonial-revival architect Joseph Chandler. Furnishings include Chinese porcelain, early American pieces, Oriental rugs, and cut glass. Many personal mementos convey a sense of its owners, Helen Stevens Coolidge (a North Andover native who inherited this farm) and John Gardner Coolidge (a Boston Brahmin who, after graduating from Harvard, spent almost 20 years traveling). The couple devoted immense energy to the estate. The 90-acre grounds contain elaborately landscaped gardens, including a sunken-walled rose (36 varieties) garden.

HISTORIC SITES

Great Stone Dam, Lawrence. The largest in the world, at 35 feet high, when it was completed in 1848. Descend below the John W. Casey Bridge to Pemberton Park; drive or walk beyond the parking lot to the viewing platform.

Ayer Mill Clock Tower. The pride of Lawrence and the world's largest mill clock: The dial is just 6 inches smaller than that of Big Ben. Installed in 1909 and abandoned in the 1950s when the mill closed, it was recently restored with $750,000 largely raised from former mill workers and their children.

Immigrant City Archives (686-9230), 6 Essex Street, Lawrence. Open Monday through Thursday 9–4 and by appointment. Former offices for the Essex Company, which built and managed the city for much of a century, this is the place to research genealogies of the city's social history or simply to see the big old safes and collection of record books.

First Church Congregational (687-1240), 26 Pleasant Street, Methuen. Open September through May, weekdays 9–3, also Sunday services and by appointment. An opaque glass window depicts the resurrection by Robert LeFarge; it's set above an altarpiece designed by Augustus Saint-Gaudens. Below the church is a Civil War monument with lions smiling toward the North, scowling toward the South.

Shawsheen Village, junction of Route 28 and Route 133 in Andover. A classic, early-20th-century mill village built by the American Woolen Company with shops and suburban-style housing as well as mills.

TO DO

BOATING

The Greater Lawrence Community Boating Program (681-8675), Eaton Street, off Andover Street, Lawrence. There's a seasonal fee, and a swimming test is required to take out a sailboat or canoe; inquire about the Sunday excursion-boat cruises in July and August.

Merrimack River Watershed Council (681-5777), 56 Island Street, Lawrence. This nonprofit group, dedicated to promoting the entire length of the river, has published a detailed map showing launch areas. It is also the source of a pamphlet guide to canoeing, fishing, and bicycling along the river, and of guided canoe trips and special events. *A Guide to Trails from Canada to the Atlantic Ocean* includes details about the New Hampshire Heritage Trail as well as a section on hiking the Merrimack River Trail.

CANOE RENTALS

Moor & Mountain (475-3665), Railroad Street, Andover.

FISHING

The Shawsheen River is stocked with trout. For details about the Merrimack, consult the Merrimack River Watershed Council's guide (see *Boating*).

GOLF

Rolling Green (475-4066); nine holes in Andover. **Hickory Hill** (686-0822); 18 holes in Methuen.

GREEN SPACE

STATE FOREST

Harold Parker State Forest (686-3391), Middleton Road, North Reading. A 3000-acre preserve with a total of 135 campsites, 11 ponds (9 artificially created), picnic grills, and 35 miles of trails and woods roads.

WALKS

Charles W. Ward Reservation, Prospect Road, east of Route 125, North Andover. A self-guided interpretive trail explores a typical northern bog; hiking and cross-country ski trails traverse woodland. The 640-acre reservation includes Holt Hill, the highest hilltop (just 420 feet) in Essex County, with views from Boston to Maine.

Deer Jump Reservation, River Road west of I-93, Andover. A 130-acre area on the river with trails leading west (follow the blue blazes) along the river to the Tewksbury line. This land belongs to the Andover Village Improvement Society and accesses 5.1 riverfront miles. (See *Boating* for details about the Merrimack River Watershed Council's guidebook that describes the Merrimack River Trail.)

Merrimack River Trail System, Lowell, consists of three trails of several miles each along sections of both banks of the river. The trails go through Riverfront Park, Dogwood Park and to sites associated with the 1912 Bread and Roses strike. See "Guidebook to the Merrimack River Trail" (available at the state park visitors center) for details.

LODGING

Andover Inn (475-5903; 1-800-242-5903), Chapel Avenue, Andover 01810. This columned brick inn is an integral part of the Phillips Academy campus, but it sits on the edge of the campus, almost like a gatehouse. It dates from 1930, the gift of an alumnus. The lobby is formal, and the dining room, elegant and popular (see *Dining Out*). There are 23 rooms and suites. Although it caters to Phillips Academy parents, other travelers are welcome. Double rooms $99, suites $120–140. All rooms have phone, color TV, radio, and air-conditioning.

WHERE TO EAT

DINING OUT
Bishop's (683-7143), 99 Hampshire at Lowell Street, Lawrence. Open weekdays for lunch and dinner, Saturday from 4 PM, Sunday from 2 (from 4 in summer). The atmosphere and menu are Middle Eastern, but lobster and roast beef are also specialties. Friday evenings offer music and dancing, bar until 1 AM. Average $8–10 for lunch, $15–22 for dinner.

The Andover Inn (475-5903), Phillips Academy, Chapel Avenue, Andover. The dining room is formal: white tablecloths, chandeliers, courteous service. You might lunch on chicken with asparagus ($11) or chicken salad on a croissant ($7) and dine on medallions of veal with Calvados and apple chutney ($23) or scampi flambé ($22). The dinner specialty on Sunday (and only then) is an authentic Indonesian rijsttafel ($23.50): dry steamed rice with an indefinite number of side dishes such as roast chicken on sticks, marinated cucumbers, and pork in soy sauce and ginger. Reservations a must.

Top of the Scales (681-8848), 4 Johnson Street, North Andover, center of the village. Open daily from 7 AM except Monday; Sunday brunch. A downstairs crafts center, with upstairs dining inside and on the sun porch: fresh-baked croissants, quiches, soups, salads for lunch, and specializing in seafood and chicken at dinner. Entrées $10–15. Full liquor license.

Vincenzo's (475-7337), 12 Main Street, Andover. Open for lunch and dinner weekdays, dinner only on weekends. This is a pleasant upstairs restaurant in the middle of Andover's brick shopping street. You might lunch on zuppa di cozze rosso o Bianco (fresh mussels poached in your choice of white broth or spicy marinara sauce over angelhair pasta) and dine on pollo al limone (chicken medallions sautéed with shiitake mushrooms and finished with lemon and fresh rosemary). Entrées in the $15–20 range.

EATING OUT

Note: All establishments are in Lawrence unless otherwise indicated.

Lawton's Hot Dog Stand, corner of Broadway and Canal Streets, features hot dogs deep fried in flavored oil (the formula is a closely guarded secret). Devoted local clientele. This stand evolved from a pushcart and was asked to move when first a street, then a walking path ran right through it. Popular support kept it where it is. Note the original sidewalk and fire hydrant inside the stand.

Ellie's Restaurant (688-7587), 76 South Broadway, South Lawrence. Lunch and dinner, lounge. This cheerful little Lebanese restaurant serves great combo platters and specialties like *kafta* (lean ground beef mixed with onions, parsley, and spices), stuffed grape leaves, lamb skewers, and eggplant dishes. You can also have chicken soup or a turkey dinner.

Ye Loft and Ladle Tavern (687-3933), 337 Essex Street. Open Monday through Wednesday 7:30–5, Friday until 9, Saturday until 2 PM. This is a great downtown lunch spot with good, reasonably priced sandwiches, soups, and salads; also dinner specials. The anadama bread and muffins are baked fresh daily, and the beer list is extensive.

Cafe Azteca (689-7393), 180 Common Street. Open for breakfast and lunch Monday through Saturday; closes at 5 PM. This is the real thing, not just Tex-Mex. You can start the day with sincronizada (a cheese, ham, and flour tortilla melt), lunch on tacos or flautitas, and finish with chilis rellenos de puebla (cheese-covered green peppers filled with egg batter and topped with red salsa) or steak fajitas. Nothing is more than $8.

Cedar Crest Restaurant (685-5722), 187 Broadway (Route 28). Open for breakfast, lunch, dinner. Family restaurant, reasonable prices, daily specials.

Al's Diner (687-9678), 297 South Broadway, Lawrence. A classic diner, great meat pies.

Lobster Den (686-7494), 255 Merrimack Street, Methuen. Open Monday through Saturday 9–8, Sunday noon–8. A great Cajun chicken sandwich and good fried seafood.

ENTERTAINMENT

Methuen Memorial Music Hall concerts (685-0693), 192 Broadway (Route 28), Methuen. You have to see this cathedral-shaped hall and the magnificent organ it houses to believe it. Built in 1863 in Germany for the Boston Music Hall, the organ is huge and baroque. After 21 years, it was sold to make room on the stage for the Boston Symphony Orchestra and eventually acquired by Methuen native and millionaire Edward Searles. The hall that Searles commissioned has a 65-foot vaulted ceiling, marble floors, and rich paneling. Concerts here are events, especially the Mai Fest, a pops-style concert with Bavarian dancing that's always held the third week in May. Starting in June, recitals are held on 18 consecutive Wednesdays, 8 PM. There are also frequent screenings of classic silent movies with organ accompaniment.

SELECTIVE SHOPPING

SHOPPING STREET
Main Street, Andover. A number of small specialty stores add up to interesting shopping. **Andover Bookstore** (475-0143), 89 Main Street, Andover. Exceptionally well stocked, and offers a crackling fire and coffee in winter.

FACTORY STORES
Note: All listings are in Lawrence unless otherwise indicated.

KGR (659-1221), 189 Canal Street. Classic women's suits and separates. Faye and Chet Sidell have created a thriving business employing upward of 1000 men and women who cut, stitch, and in other ways help produce the clothing sold only in this handsome mill store—which is open only one Saturday a month, and not at all in February or July. The trick is to get on their mailing list and to be in line early the day of the sale; savings are at least 50 percent below retail. Missy, petite, and women's sizes. **Blotner Woodworks** (682-9412), 60 Pine Street, Methuen. Open Monday through Friday 9–5. A pilgrimage point for parents and nursery school teachers: piles of wooden balls, beads, tubes, rings, cubes, and pegs for creating. **Malden Mills** (557-3242), 530 Broadway. Open Monday through Saturday 8–3; Sunday 11–3. Full line of Polartec and Polarfleece as well as cotton fleece and upholstery fabrics. **Cardinal Shoes** (686-9706), 468 Canal Street. Monday through Friday 10–5, Saturday 10–3. Great savings on women's shoes: sizes 6–10, medium width only, made here. **New Balance** (682-8960), 5 South Union Street. Open 9:30–5, Monday through Wednesday; 9:30–7 Thursday; 9:30–6 Friday and Saturday; noon–5 Sunday. Running shoes and apparel for men, women, and children. **Southwick** (794-2474), 50 Island Street. Open Wednesday through Saturday 9–5. Men's fine suits, sportcoats, trousers, shirts, ties, outerwear. **Hampshire Printed Fabrics** (683-5433), 300 Merrimack Street. Open Monday through Thursday 8:30–5, Friday until 4, Saturday until 5, Sunday noon–4. Designer fabrics and accessories. **Merrimack Fashions** (683-3362), 350 Merrimack Street. Women's wool and cashmere coats and blazers; yarns and fabrics. Open weekends 10–4.

FARM

Smolak Farm (688-8055), 315 South Bradford Street, North Andover. Open 7–6 daily. A 155-acre, 300-year-old farm with 35 acres of apple trees (including 20 antique varieties), a total of 2700 fruit trees, cut-your-own Christmas trees, walking trails, barnyard petting animals, a greenhouse, hayrides, haunted barn at Halloween. The farm stand is known for its baked goods as well as produce. Pick-your-own apricots, cherries, peaches, nectarines, and pumpkins, as well as apples and flowers.

SPECIAL EVENTS

Note: All events are in Lawrence.

June: **Hispanic Week.** Eight-day celebration of 25 Central and South American countries.

June through September: **Organ Recital Series** at Methuen Memorial Music Hall.

September: Labor Day weekend—**Bread and Roses Celebration.** This event is big, with multistages in major parks. The **Common Street City Block Festival** and the **Feast of the Three Saints** are the same weekend.

October: **Octoberfest.**

II. SOUTH OF BOSTON

Plymouth
Southeastern Massachusetts

KIMBERLY GRANT

The Huntington sculpture in New Bedford's Tonnessen Park

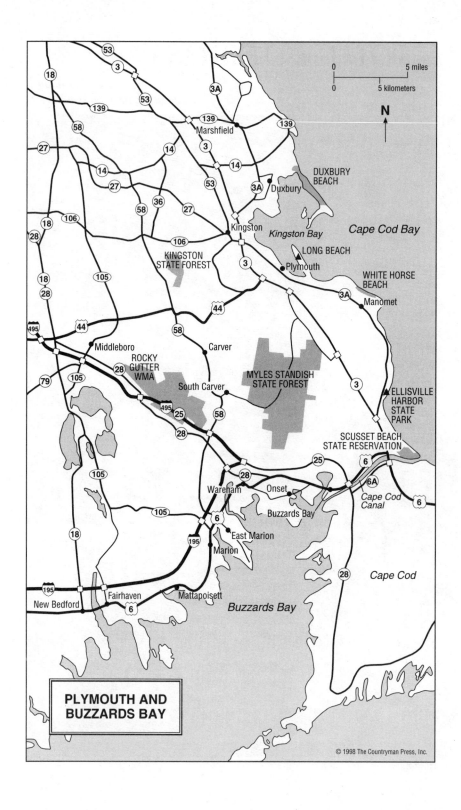

PLYMOUTH AND
BUZZARDS BAY

© 1998 The Countryman Press, Inc.

Plymouth

As you might suspect, "America's Home Town" is a mix of tourist-geared attractions and authentic historic landmarks. During the busy summer season it can be hard to see the town for the visitors, but if you look past the tour buses and souvenir shops clustered around Plymouth Rock, you'll find a genuinely interesting community with some well-preserved colonial-era homes and one of America's best museum villages.

Plymouth is actually the state's biggest town in terms of area, dotted with ponds and lakes and with large expanses of forest and cranberry bog. An old summer resort, both its bay and its lakeshores are lined with summer cottages and offer public beaches. A fleet of fishing boats is based at Town Wharf.

Duxbury, a short drive up the coast, has its own Pilgrim sites, stately historic homes, and outstanding beach, and the tiny inland hamlets of Carver and Middleboro represent the state's largest concentration of cranberry bogs. They also harbor enormous state forests.

AREA CODES

508 for Plymouth; 781 for Duxbury.

GUIDANCE

Massachusetts Tourist Information Center (508-746-1150), exit 5 (Long Pond Road) on Route 3 south, Plymouth. Open year-round, 8:30–5. An information clearinghouse with a large selection of maps and brochures from local hotels, motels, restaurants, museums, and other attractions. The staff are ready to answer questions from visitors in person as well as over the phone. The large facility has lots of parking, rest rooms, and picnic tables.

Plymouth Visitors Information Center/Discover Plymouth (508-747-7525; 1-800-872-1620), Water Street. Open daily April through December, 9–5, and June through August, 9–9. Right on the waterfront, this visitors information center has a broad selection of tourist-oriented literature and a knowledgeable staff. There are public rest rooms, too, and baby-changing stations in each bathroom.

GETTING THERE

By car: To reach Plymouth from Boston, drive south on Route 3 (approximately 45 minutes) and follow signs from the highway. The fastest approach is from exit 6 on Route 44 east. If you're not in a rush, take Route

3A south from Duxbury. The scenic road winds along the coastline through affluent commuter villages, beside lovely coves and harbors, and in view of lighthouses, fishing boats, and graceful old homes.

By bus: **Plymouth and Brockton Street Railway Company** (508-746-0378) isn't a train line; it's a bus company that runs frequent trips between Plymouth and the rest of the South Shore to Boston, including Logan Airport. One-way fare is $7.75.

By train: **Old Colony Lines Rail Service** (617-222-3200; 1-800-392-6100). Serving Plymouth from nearby Middleborough, this recently restored commuter-oriented rail has four weekday morning trains (5:25–7:25 AM) to Boston's South Station and four returning in the afternoon and early evening (4–6 PM). One-way fare is $4.75.

By boat: Private boats can dock at **Brewer's Plymouth Marina** (508-746-4500).

GETTING AROUND
Plymouth is eminently walkable. Other than Plimoth Plantation, most of the sites you'll want to see are within 10 minutes' walk from one another. If you get tired of walking, or if you'd rather see everything quickly, the **Plymouth Rock Trolley** (508-747-3419), 22 Main Street, is an excellent resource. In 45 minutes, the trolley stops at all the major sites, including the Rock and the *Mayflower II*. During the summer months it goes all the way to Plimoth Plantation and Long Beach. It operates from the first weekend in May through Thanksgiving weekend, 9–5, and until 8 PM during the summer. Per-day tickets are $7 for adults, $6 for seniors, and $3 for children. You may get off and on the trolley as often as you'd like—and there'll be another one along in 30 minutes.

MEDICAL EMERGENCY
Jordan Hospital (746-2000), 275 Sandwich Street (exit 5 off Route 3), Plymouth.

TO SEE

Note: The following listings are in Plymouth unless otherwise indicated.

MUSEUMS
✍ **Plimoth Plantation** (508-746-1622), Route 3A, Warren Avenue. $15 adults, $9 children 5–12, under 5 free. A two-day ticket for both the plantation and the *Mayflower II* is $18.50 adults, $11 children. Open April through November, 9–5. Three miles south of downtown Plymouth, this extraordinary living history museum is populated by men and women in period costume who live the lives and play the parts of the residents of the Pilgrim village in the year 1627. Within the diamond-shaped stockade, small wooden houses with thickly thatched roofs straggle along a dirt road to the fortified meetinghouse. The "settlers" (wearing the bright-

Mayflower II

colored clothing the real Pilgrims favored, not the somber shades of our stereotype) speak only Elizabethan English and are as much a part of the museum as the tools they use and the lives they lead. They are eager to answer your questions about their daily activities—never using an anachronism or letting their accents slip. Plimouth Plantation has been a pioneer among living history museums, stressing historical accuracy to the point of backbreeding modern farm animals to their original 17th-century appearance. Outside the stockade is **Hobbamock's Homesite,** a Wampanoag tribal encampment typical of those of the same period as the plantation and with skin- and fur-clad Native Americans in residence. The large visitors center has a snack bar and restaurant; an elaborate museum shop with a bookstore and separate shops for children's and Native American crafts; exhibition areas; and a theater where an introductory film is shown.

Pilgrim Hall Museum (508-746-1620), 75 Court Street. Open daily 9:30–4:30. Adults $5, children $2.50. Continuously operating since 1824 and the oldest public museum in the country, the Greek Revival building houses the largest collection of Pilgrim possessions, including richly styled Jacobean furniture and the relic of the *Sparrow-Hawk,* one of the many ships that brought the early colonists to Plymouth. The ship's hull is especially fascinating for modern viewers: It was hewn from naturally curved tree trunks and branches. The museum also owns the only known painting of a *Mayflower* passenger, Edward Winslow.

HISTORIC HOMES

Mayflower Society Museum (508-746-2590), 4 Winslow Street (mailing address: PO Box 3184, Plymouth 02361). Admission fee. This striking white building, built in 1754, boasts a fabulous double staircase and a wealth of stories. Here are three tidbits from the house's history: The original owner was Edward Winslow, a Tory leader who was forced to flee to Canada during the Revolution; Ralph Waldo Emerson got married in the front parlor in 1835; and ether was supposedly discovered here in 1842. If you think you may be a descendant of one of the *Mayflower* passengers, you may research your own genealogical history in the library, which is run by the General Society of Mayflower Descendants.

Spooner House (508-746-0012), 27 North Street. Admission fee. The 1749 Spooner House is more humble than many historic houses, but its vast collection of five generations of Spooner family possessions is truly impressive.

Richard Sparrow House (508-747-1240), 42 Summer Street. Donations requested. The Sparrow House was built in 1640 by Richard Sparrow and his family. It's now Plymouth's oldest surviving wooden-frame house. The spartan furnishings and primitive construction provide an honest glimpse into 17th-century life. A gift shop sells pottery, jewelry, and glass.

Hedge House (508-746-9697), 126 Water Street. Open daily, late June to Labor Day, 10–5 Monday through Saturday, noon–5 Sunday; weekends in June and September to mid-October; closed mid-October through May. Admission fee. Next to the visitors information center (see *Guidance*) is this stately 1809 Federal building, originally the home of a shipping family. It's filled with period pieces, including fine quilts and Chinese porcelain.

Jabez Howland House (508-746-9490), 33 Sandwich Street. Open late May to mid-October and Thanksgiving weekend, 10–4:30. In a town full of "oldests," the Howland House is the only surviving house to have been inhabited by *Mayflower* passengers. John Howland and Elizabeth Tilley arrived in Plymouth in 1620, married soon after, and produced 10 children. Their youngest son, Jabez, purchased the house in the late 1660s; his parents lived here during the winters in order to be close to their church, and Elizabeth continued living with Jabez and his family after John died in 1673 (at the age of 80). The John Howland Society, formed by Howland descendants, has restored the building, finishing it with many fine examples of period chairs, tables, and beds.

HISTORIC SITES

Most first-time visitors to Plymouth head straight for **Plymouth Rock** on Water Street, on a hill overlooking the harbor. Purported to be the landing place of Plymouth's first European settlers, and considerably reduced in size by souvenir hunters over the years, the smallish boulder is now inside a protective neo-Grecian portico within Massachusetts's smallest state park.

Cranberry harvest

✏ ***Mayflower II*** (508-746-1622), State Pier. $5.75 adults, $3.75 children 5–12, under 5 free (see **Plimoth Plantation** under *Museums* for special boat-and-plantation rates). Down the street from the Rock is the *Mayflower II*, a reproduction of the original. By modern standards, the boat seems incredibly small to have carried a crew and 102 passengers—along with their domestic animals, tools, and supplies—across the Atlantic from England to the New World. In summer costumed guides conduct tours, worth the wait.

1749 Court House and Museum (508-830-4075), Town Square. Open year-round. Free. The site of several cases tried by none other than John Adams, before he became the second president of the United States, the building today is the oldest wooden courthouse in the country. The first floor is a museum, and the second floor is a re-creation of the courtroom as it looked during the mid-18th century. Items on view in the museum include a hand-drawn suction pumper from 1828 used by Plymouth's early firefighters, and an intricately carved 1740 oak bench.

FOR FAMILIES

✏ **Cranberry World Visitors Center** (508-747-2350), 225 Water Street. Open May through November. Free. Sponsored by Ocean Spray, the cranberry growers cooperative, the center displays a scaled-down "bog" used for harvesting demonstrations, exhibits on the history of cranberry cultivation around the world, daily cooking classes, concerts, and free samples.

✏ **The Children's Museum of Plymouth** (508-747-1234), 46-48 Main Street. Open daily mid-April to Labor Day; Labor Day to mid-April, open weekends, holidays, and during school vacations. Admission. The

Children's Museum is a kid-sized version of everyday places in and around America's Home Town. Kids may take part in a variety of activities, such as operating the weather station at Gurnet Lighthouse, driving a fire engine, DJ-ing at a radio station, and even working behind the counter at Dunkin' Donuts.

Plymouth National Wax Museum (508-746-6468), 16 Carver Street. Open March to December. $5 adults, $2 children 5–12. The depictions of Pilgrim life at this museum are fanciful and, at times, even awkward; they're geared more toward kids than adults. Bring your sense of humor, and you'll probably have a good time, too.

TO DO

BICYCLING

Biking trails: **Myles Standish State Forest** (508-866-2526), Cranberry Road, South Carver. Open mid-April through Columbus Day weekend. Miles of bike trails wind through the 15,000-acre reservation area. To get there, take Route 3 to exit 5, turn south on Long Pond Road, and look for the sign to the forest, approximately 2.5 miles south. For **Scusset Beach State Reservation**, take Route 3 to the rotary before the Sagamore Bridge, then follow the signs. The park has 7 miles of paved bike trails.

Rentals: **Bike Line** (508-830-0100), 127 Samoset Street, Plymouth, has standard, mountain, racing, and hybrid bicycles for rent, as well as helmets, carriers, locks, and other equipment. **Martha's Bicycles and Fitness** (508-746-2109), 300 Court Street, Plymouth. Bikes repaired and rented by the half-day, day, week, or month. Family rate for rentals of three or more bikes.

BOAT EXCURSIONS

Plymouth-to-Provincetown Ferry (1-800-242-2469), State Pier, Plymouth. Late May through late September. Adults $22, seniors $18, $14 for children under 12, bikes $2. The 90-minute ferry ride across Cape Cod Bay to Provincetown on the *Cape Cod Clipper* saves you the drive, and it's twice as fast. Reservations recommended. **Cape Cod Canal Cruises** (508-295-3883), Onset Bay Town Pier, Onset. Spring through fall. Two- and three-hour narrated round-trip cruises through the canal. Adults $7–8; children $3.50–4. Jazz, cocktail, dance, and other specialty cruises on weekends. **Splashdown Amphibious Tours** (508-747-7658; 1-800-225-4000). Harbor Place, Plymouth. One-hour tour of Plymouth by land and water in an amphibious landing craft–type vehicle. Adults $12, children $8. (Kids under 3 are 50 cents.) **Lobster Tales** (508-746-5342), Town Wharf, Plymouth. One–hour excursions around Plymouth harbor in a converted lobster boat. Participants get to help haul traps and handle live lobsters. Adults $10, seniors $8, children $5. (Also see *Fishing* and *Whale-Watching*.)

Off Onset

FISHING

Massachusetts's waters support a world-class striped bass fishery, and the South Shore is one of the country's most overlooked striper hot spots. Migratory striped bass enter area waters here at the beginning of May and stay well into November. The area also sees good fishing for such game species as bluefish and blue shark. **Henry Weston Outfitters** (781-826-7411), 15 Columbia Road (Route 53 at Pembroke Crossing), Pembroke, can supply you with tackle, information, and guides. Shop owner Jim McKay retains the services of Coast Guard–licensed guides who specialize in fly-fishing and light spin-fishing for striped bass and bluefish. Also books charters for blue shark using both conventional and fly tackle. **Andy Lynn Boats** (508-746-7776; 1-800-540-3474), Town Wharf, Plymouth. A full-service fleet of boats that offer sportfishing, off-shore fishing, and year-round deep-sea fishing. Trips of various lengths are available, from 4 hours to overnight.

GOLF

Plymouth Country Club (508-746-0476), Warren Avenue, Plymouth. 18 holes. **Squirrel Run** (746-5001), Route 44 (5 miles west of Route 3), Plymouth. 18-hole course, rentals, pro shop, carts, and sandwich shop.

KAYAKING

Billington Sea Watercraft (508-746-5444), 14 Union St., Plymouth. Guided kayak tours of the Plymouth waterfront.

PARASAILING

Plymouth Parasail and Water Sports (508-746-1415), 14 Union Street, Plymouth. No experience or special equipment necessary.

SWIMMING
See **Duxbury Beach, Long Beach, White Horse Beach**, and **Myles Standish State Forest** under *Green Space.*

📖 **Nelson Street Beach,** off Water Street, Plymouth, just north of Cranberry World, is a pleasant beach with good swimming. Parking is free, but limited. Since the beach is part of a park with a playground, there are lots of kids.

📖 **Stephens Field Beach, Park, and Playground** are at the end of a dead-end lane called Stephens Field, just off Route 3A, 1 mile south of Plymouth; take the first left after the fire station. Playground, picnic tables, a small duck pond, a short beach, tennis courts, and free parking (limited number of spaces).

WHALE-WATCHING
Captain Tim Brady and Sons (508-746-4809), Town Wharf, Plymouth.

Captain John Boats (508-746-2643; 1-800-242-2469), Town Wharf, Plymouth.

GREEN SPACE

BEACHES
Duxbury Beach (781-837-3112 for information), accessed via Route 139 through Marshfield's Green Harbor area, is a 5-mile-long stretch of clean white sand that juts out into the ocean. Be cautious: The surf on the Cape Cod Bay side of the beach can be rough at times. A few areas of the beach are accessible by four-wheel-drive vehicle only. Lifeguards, rest rooms, showers, changing rooms, and snack bar. Late May through early September; $8 parking on weekends, $7 weekdays.

Long Beach, also known as Plymouth Beach, on Route 3A, 3 miles south of Plymouth center. Located in a half-rural, half-residential area, this popular beach has lifeguards (June through Labor Day), rest rooms, showers, a snack bar, excellent fishing, and good swimming. Part of the beach is roped off to protect nesting terns and sandpipers. Parking is $10 per car on weekends, $7 weekdays.

White Horse Beach, Manomet. South of Plymouth center, take Route 3A south, then follow signs when you get to Manomet. The locals keep it quiet, but they love this beach. It's just as popular with the folks who rent the beachside cottages summer after summer. Parking is hard to find: It's off-street only, usually in a resident's driveway for approximately $7–10 per car.

STATE FORESTS
Myles Standish State Forest (508-866-2526), Cranberry Road, South Carver. Take Route 3 to exit 5, turn south on Long Pond Road, and look for the sign to the state forest, approximately 2.5 miles south. The roads, walking trails, and bike paths that wind through this 14,635-acre park's forest and meadows seem to go on forever. Even during the busiest

Duxbury Beach

summer weekends, visitors can easily find some space to be alone. The park, Massachusetts's first state forest when it was created in 1916, has 15 ponds and two freshwater beaches (at Fearing and College Ponds). Motorcycle, bicycle, bridle, and hiking paths; fishing; picnic areas; rest rooms; camping; bathhouses; swimming; and interpretive programs. Picnic tables, fireplaces, and parking ($5). Open mid-April through Columbus Day weekend.

LODGING

Probably because it's a popular holiday destination for families, Plymouth has plenty of motels that are unremarkable in decor and budget oriented. For travelers who are looking for more pleasant and unusual lodgings several nice bed & breakfasts are available.

INNS AND BED & BREAKFASTS

Note: Listings are in Plymouth (02360) unless otherwise indicated.

Foxglove Cottage (1-800-479-4746), 101 Sandwich Road. An impeccably restored 1820 Cape-style house, this is a gem of a B&B just a short drive inland from Plimouth Plantation (see *Museums*). The many antiques—furniture, paintings, decorative porcelain—are early Victorian and fit the house perfectly. The three rooms all have private bath and working fireplace. Guests have the use of a cozy living room. Full breakfast, served in summer on a deck looking out on a grassy meadow. Owners Charles Cowan and wife Michael (yes—a woman!) are hospitable and helpful hosts. Open year-round. $75–90.

Windsor House Inn (617-934-0991), 390 Washington Street, Duxbury 02332. Some 15 minutes north of Plymouth is this inn/restaurant, a black-shuttered white building in a neighborhood that's filled with houses that are on the National Register of Historic Places. The inn's two bedrooms and two suites are gracefully decorated with light blue paneling and pretty, blue-and-white stenciling; furnishings are a mix of Shaker and Federal reproductions. Rates for two are $137–221, including full breakfast served in the restaurant (see *Dining Out*).

The Jackson-Russell-Whitfield House (508-746-5289), 26 North Street. Just a 5-minute walk from Plymouth Rock (see *Historic Sites*), this elegantly proportioned, red-painted brick mansion was built in 1782. Owner Brian Whitfield has restored the original paneling and decorative woodwork and filled the house with antique furniture and art. There is a grand piano in the living room that Whitfield, a gifted amateur musician, often plays. There are three large rooms: one with a queen-sized bed, another with two twins, and a suite. All have private bath. $80–140.

The Mabbett House (1-800-572-7829; fax 508-830-1911), 7 Cushman Street. Three large, sun-filled bedrooms sharing two bathrooms in a home that's surrounded by gardens. Breakfast is served in the screened-in porch. $85–170.

The Thornton Adams House (1-888-747-9700), 73C Warren Avenue. Modern Colonial Revival house with tasteful reproduction period furniture and decor. Facing the ocean and just down the road from Plimouth Plantation (see *Museums*). Three pleasant rooms, one with Jacuzzi and another with a balcony, all with private baths. Hosts Aldine and Bob Thornton are very knowledgeable about the area. $75–95 with full breakfast.

Plymouth Bay Manor (1-800-492-1823), 259 Court Street. An expansive, turn-of-the-century shingled house, renovated from top to bottom by enthusiastic young owners, Larry and Cindi Hamlin. The three rooms are large and attractively furnished. All have ocean views and private baths and are air-conditioned; two have a fireplace. A full breakfast is served in the sunroom looking out on the bay. Rates are $85–$110.

Seaview (508-830-1781), 123B Warren Avenue. Within walking distance of Plimouth Plantation (see *Museums*), this pleasant sun-filled house looks out on Plymouth Bay. There are three rooms, one (The Captain's Room) with a Jacuzzi. A full breakfast with Scandinavian touches. Rates are $75–85; Captain's Room, $95.

MOTELS

The John Carver Inn (508-746-7100; 1-800-274-1620; fax 508-746-8299), 25 Summer Street. A large, imposing motel on the south side of Burial Hill that attracts tour groups during the summer months. The 79 rooms are decorated in tans and beiges, furnished with Colonial-style reproductions. There is a restaurant, lounge, gift shop, and pool. $65–135.

Cold Spring Motel (phone/fax 508-746-2222), 188 Court Street. Among Plymouth's many motels, this one is probably the most attractive, with its cheerful yellow awnings and carefully landscaped grounds. The rooms are exceptionally clean, if not inspiringly furnished or decorated, but the very reasonable rates make up for lack of atmosphere. $49–89.

Pilgrim Sands (508-747-0900; 1-800-729-7263), 150 Warren Avenue/ Route 3A. The prime attraction of this oceanside motel is its private beach, which is an extension of Long Beach (see *Swimming*). It's also very close to Plimoth Plantation (see *Museums*). Various sizes of rooms (some with kitchenette) are available to accommodate families and groups. Most rooms have a balcony. Facilities include indoor and outdoor pools and a whirlpool. $75–120.

CAMPGROUND

Myles Standish State Forest (508-866-2526), Cranberry Road, South Carver 02566. Open mid-April through Columbus Day weekend. The state forest has 470 tent/RV sites (no hookups) with rest rooms, hot showers, and a fireplace and picnic table at each site. Rates are $6 per night with showers, $5 per night without showers. To get there, take Route 3 to exit 5, turn south on Long Pond Road, and look for the sign to Myles Standish State Forest, approximately 2.5 miles south.

WHERE TO EAT

DINING OUT

Crane Brook Restaurant (508-866-3235), 229 Tremont Street, South Carver. Open year-round except for one week in January and the last week in June; lunch Wednesday through Friday, dinner Wednesday through Sunday. Located in a former iron foundry that's surrounded by a mix of forests, pastures, and cranberry bogs, this restaurant is a terrific spot for lunch or dinner. The dining room looks out over a pond. Lunch entrées include grilled duck breast sandwich; dinner might be rack of lamb or spicy pork loin roast. Reservations required. Most entrées in the $10–20 range.

Bert's Cove (508-746-3330), Warren Avenue (Route 3A), Plymouth. A large, cheerful, very popular barn of a place on Long Beach. Often a wait for dinner in high season but patrons rate it highly. Fresh seafood specials daily. Entrées include Cajun blackened swordfish steak, and lobster, shrimp, scallops, and mussels in citron cream sauce and are in the $11–16 range.

Isaac's on the Waterfront (508-830-0001), 114 Water Street, Plymouth. A local institution (it sponsors the Thanksgiving Day parade), this restaurant has a great view that includes the Plymouth waterfront and the Mayflower. Sautéed jumbo shrimp is the house specialty. Entrées in the $10–15 range.

Cafe Nanina (508-747-4503), 14 Union Street, Plymouth. Menu is basically Italian but seafood is served daily. A deck overlooks Plymouth harbor. Entrées $4–8 lunch, $10–20 dinner.

Martha's Galley (747-9200), 179 Court Street (Benny's Plaza), Plymouth. Don't be put off by this small restaurant's unpretentious appearance and location. (It's in the back of a shopping plaza between a pet store and a Radio Shack outlet.) The menu is creative, prices are moderate, and many locals think it's the best restaurant in town. Menu standards include baby back ribs and clam fritters as well as Mediterranean dishes such as pasta rusticana and chicken stuffed with prosciutto, broccoli, and Swiss cheese. Always interesting specials. Wine and beer served. Entrées $5–$11.

Windsor House Inn (781-934-0991), 390 Washington Street, Duxbury. Open year-round for dinner. Established in 1803, this black-shuttered white inn is a favorite celebration-dinner destination for South Shore residents. Dine in the elegant main dining room (weekends only) or in the carriage house (daily). Typical entrées include marinated tomato and eggplant pizza and lobster in saffron cream sauce on a puff pastry. Most entrées $15–22.

EATING OUT

1620 Restaurant (508-746-9565), 158 Water Street, Plymouth. Open year-round for lunch and dinner. Perched on one of the busiest street corners in Plymouth, this second-floor restaurant is a good place to have a meal and watch the harbor traffic. The dining room has vaulted ceilings and glass walls on three sides; try to get a table with a view of the water. Appetizers include lobster tartlet; entrées include turkey dinner and baked tortellini with scallops. $5–13.

Iguana's (508-747-4000), 170 Water Street, Plymouth. Open for lunch and dinner. A Mexican/southwestern restaurant in the Village Landing complex, with good quesadillas, taco salads, and fajitas with your choice of fixings. Try to sit in the glassed-in addition on the north side; you'll have a view of the harbor. $5–10.

Persy's Place (781-585-5464), 117 Main Street, Route 3A, Kingston. Open daily for breakfast and lunch. You may be distracted by the old-time country store decor and feel of the place, but take a few minutes to read the lengthy list of offerings; this family-oriented eatery asserts that it has "New England's largest breakfast menu." There's something for everyone here, from fish cakes to chipped beef on toast, from catfish and eggs (no-cholesterol eggs are available) to thick pancakes. $3–12.

All-American Diner (508-747-4763), 60 Court Street, Plymouth. Open daily 5:30 AM–2 PM for breakfast and lunch; takeout also available. This cheerfully decorated restaurant serves traditional as well as unusual egg dishes, crunchy French toast (their invention), and sandwiches with a choice of home fries or rice pilaf. $1.55–5.90.

Wood's Seafood and Fish Market (508-746-0261), end of Town Wharf, Plymouth. Open year-round for lunch and dinner, weekdays 11–8, weekends until 9; closed in January. Sit indoors or at an outdoor picnic table on Town Wharf and feast on a clam roll, fresh fish sandwich, or a cup of fish or clam chowder. Fresh fish and lobster sold at the adjacent market. $4–15.

The Lobster Hut (508-746-2270), Town Wharf, Plymouth. It's slightly more crowded with bus traffic than Wood's, but the atmosphere is still authentic New England seaside, as is the cuisine: clam rolls, lobster salad, and lots of fries. $4.95–15.95.

Star of Siam (508-224-3771), Route 3A, Manomet. High-quality, take-out Thai food may not be what you expect to find in staid old Plymouth/ Manomet, which makes this place such a pleasant surprise. Do what the locals do—pick up a spicy pad Thai lunch or dinner and bring it to the beach. $4.95–12.95.

SNACKS

Farfar's Danish Ice Cream Shop (781-934-5152), Millbrook Station, St. George's Road, Duxbury. In a converted train depot, the proprietors make all ice cream daily, served at wooden benches and tables inside and on the big porch out back.

Corner Bakery and Deli (508-747-2700), Court Street (corner of Brewster Street), Plymouth, offers several flavors of gourmet coffee and fresh-baked scones, croissants, and enormous cookies.

ENTERTAINMENT

MUSIC

Village Landing Marketplace (508-746-3493), Water Street, Plymouth. During the summer months, free concerts here range from swing music to Irish ballads, with special performances for kids.

THEATER

Priscilla Beach Theatre (508-224-4888), Rocky Hill Road, Manomet. June through mid-September. The country's oldest summer-stock barn playhouse presents children's shows Friday and Saturday at 10:30 AM, performing-arts day camps throughout the summer (1-week and 2-week programs only), and adult shows Monday through Saturday at 8:30 PM. Call for specific show schedule.

NIGHT SPOTS

The Pub at the Sheraton Plymouth (508-747-4900), 180 Water Street, Plymouth, offers live music on weekends.

The Full Sail (508-224-4478) is beside White Horse Beach, Manomet (see *Beaches*) in an innocuous building that looks like a ranch house. Its clientele are locals and summer folks who love this beach, which is bordered by tiny beach houses. No food is served here, just beverages.

SELECTIVE SHOPPING

ANTIQUES SHOPS

Simon Hill Antiques (781-934-2228), 453 Washington Street, Duxbury. Located in the scenic Snug Harbor area of Duxbury, this shop carries a fine selection of antique furniture and decorative pieces, as well as antique jewelry.

BOOKSTORES

Westwinds Bookshop (781-934-2128), 45 Depot Street, Duxbury. Charming atmosphere and location. Splendid children's books section. **Yankee Books and Antique Shop** (508-747-2691), 10 North Street, Plymouth. Open year-round, Monday through Saturday 11–5, Sunday noon–4. Specializes in hard-to-find books and Pilgrim history.

FACTORY OUTLETS

Cordage Park Marketplace (508-746-7707), Route 3A, North Plymouth, is a former cordage rope factory that's surrounded by ponds, fountains, gazebos, lawns, and flower gardens. Manufacturers with discounted merchandise include American Tourister, Van Heusen, and Maidenform.

FARM STANDS

On Route 3A in Manomet, just south of the Purity Supreme grocery store, you'll see a farm stand that some locals swear by as their primary source of fresh vegetables and fruits. The only sign next to this weathered white building said ROSES $6.99.

Carvelli's Farm Stand. On Route 44, approximately 5 miles west of Route 3A, a large farm tops a hill. Set back from the road, a small, red, wooden building serves as the farm stand for a brisk business in corn and other fresh produce, all sold in a setting that looks like a bit of Iowa right here in Plymouth.

SPECIAL SHOPS

Little Shoes (508-747-2226), 359 Court Street, Plymouth, has—you guessed it—shoes for kids. A great selection and some bargains, too. **Plimoth Plantation** (see *Museums*) has an extensive gift shop and bookstore. **Scarecrow** (508-747-6776), 8 Main Street Extension, Plymouth, is a specialty shop indeed—it features snowboards and skateboards as well as the requisite baggy padded clothing. **The Stencil Shoppe** (508-830-1163), 16 Court Street, Plymouth, has a selection of ready-made stencils and other materials you'll need if you decide to try your hand at stenciling; there's plenty here to inspire you. **Village Landing Marketplace,** Water Street, Plymouth. Housed in a group of clapboard buildings, this seaside mall contains T-shirt shops, crafts stores, ice cream shops, a deli, and restaurants.

WINERIES

Plymouth Bay Winery (508-746-2100), 170 Water Street. A family winery overlooking Plymouth Bay, it produces fruit wine using cranberries, raspberries, blueberries, peaches, and grapes. Wine tastings.

Plymouth Colony Winery (508-747-3334), Route 44 west. Open year-round. Free wine tastings and tours of a working cranberry bog. Since this is cranberry country, cranberry wine is one of the 14 varieties they make.

SPECIAL EVENTS

June: **John Carver Day,** Carver.

July: **Waterfront Festival**, Plymouth.

October: **Cranberry Harvest Festival.** Second week in October, at the Cranberry World Visitors Center, Plymouth (see *For Families*) and at Edaville Bog, South Carver.

November: **Thanksgiving** observances, Plymouth. Reasonably priced turkey and fixings served continuously in Memorial Hall 11–5. Square dancing and other entertainment.

December: **Christmas on North Street,** Plymouth.

Southeastern Massachusetts

The apron of land jutting seaward between Buzzards and Narragansett Bays forms a beautiful byway between Cape Cod and Rhode Island. Billed as "The South Coast of Massachusetts" by *The New Bedford Standard Times,* the extraordinarily scenic and sleepy shoreline stretches from Marion on the east to Westport on the west. It's backroaded by interstates and known only for its two small but distinctive cities, Fall River and New Bedford.

New Bedford is a genuinely interesting destination, one of New England's oldest and largest fishing ports. Its early-19th-century waterfront is now home to the Whaling National Historical Park, with an outstanding museum at its center. Fairhaven, just across the Acushnet River, has its own story, suggested by its amazing architecture.

New Bedford's backyard is one of New England's best-kept secrets. In neighboring Dartmouth the distinctive farmland between the yachting villages of Padanaram and Westport Point is exceptional bicycling country. Corn and dairy fields stretch to the water, webbed with narrow roads between stone walls and hedgerows reminiscent of England's countryside. This small area also offers some of the state's best birding, kayaking, sailing, and swimming.

Fall River, a 19th-century city with mammoth granite mills, is also well worth a stop, at least to tour the Heritage State Park and Marine Museum and to shop an outlet or two.

New Bedford/Fairhaven Region, Including Cuttyhunk

The physical size and shape of Manhattan Island, New Bedford has a population that's smaller than that of Cambridge, a heady mix of Portuguese, old-line Yankee, and a couple of dozen ethnic groups. In the 19th century, New Bedford—first as the world's leading whaling port and subsequently as a major textile center—drew workers from all the world's corners.

"I'm an Irishwoman who married a Greek, and I run a Jewish delicatessen," is the way our tour guide introduced herself. "That's the way it is in New Bedford. Everyone's very ethnic, but we're all mixed up together, very friendly." The summer walking tours are led by local volunteers.

Generally perceived as a pass-through place, New Bedford is actually well situated to serve as a hub from which to day-trip to Newport, the islands of Martha's Vineyard and Cuttyhunk (both accessible by ferry), and Cape Cod.

In Dartmouth, southwest of the city, quiet, shady roads wind through farms and salt marshes to public beaches and conservation land, and the yachting village of Padanaram offers some unexpected dining and shopping. In nearby Westport, the state's number-one dairy town, fields sweep to tidal rivers, and one farm is now an outstanding winery. On the island of Cuttyhunk you can walk for an hour and meet only birds, and maybe a rabbit.

Across the Acushnet River from New Bedford, Fairhaven is a genuinely salty town with large boatyards and splendid public buildings funded by Henry Huttleston Rogers, a local boy who made his fortune in Pennsylvania petroleum rather than in whale oil.

While New Bedford's famous fishing industry is flagging, down from 300 fishing boats just a few years ago to around 160 at this writing, the city continues to find new ways to focus on the sea: One of the world's largest aquariums, which will include a major aquatic research center, is presently slated to fill that monster old waterfront power station by the year 2000.

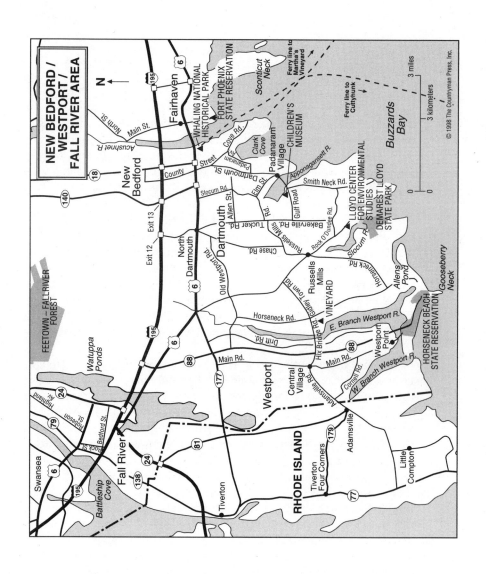

NEW BEDFORD /
WESTPORT /
FALL RIVER AREA

N

© 1998 The Countryman Press, Inc.

3 miles

3 kilometers

Buzzards Bay

Ferry line to Martha's Vineyard

Ferry line to Cuttyhunk

Sconticut Neck

Fairhaven

WHALING NATIONAL HISTORICAL PARK

FORT PHOENIX STATE RESERVATION

North St.

Main St.

Acushnet R.

New Bedford

Cove Rd.

Clark Cove

CHILDREN'S MUSEUM

Padanaram Village

Apponagansett R.

County Street

Dartmouth St.

Padanaram

Smith Neck Rd.

18

140

Slocum Rd.

Allen St.

Elm St.

Gulf Road

LLOYD CENTER FOR ENVIRONMENTAL STUDIES

Exit 13

Exit 12

North Dartmouth

Dartmouth

Tucker Rd.

Bakerville Rd.

Russells Mills

Rock O'Dundee Rd.

Slocum R.

DEMAREST LLOYD STATE PARK

Chase Rd.

Old Westport Rd.

6

Russells Mills VINEYARD

Horseneck Rd.

Gidley Town Rd.

Allens Pond

Gooseberry Neck

FEETOWN – FALLRIVER FOREST

195

Horseneck Rd.

E. Branch Westport R.

Drift Rd.

Hix Bridge Rd.

Westport Point

HORSENECK BEACH STATE RESERVATION

88

Watuppa Ponds

6

88

Main Rd.

177

Westport

Central Village

Main Rd.

88

W. Branch Westport R.

Cornell Rd.

24

Highland Av.

79

Hobson St.

Bedford St.

81

Adamsville Rd.

RHODE ISLAND

179

Adamsville

Swansea

6

Rock St.

Fall River

138

24

Tiverton Four Corners

77

Little Compton

195

Battleship Cove

Tiverton

New Bedford's waterfront recently became the Whaling National Historical Park with the vintage-1854 New Bedford Institution for Savings building as its visitors center, complementing the city's waterfront visitors center (with parking) on Pier 3. Increasingly visitor-friendly, New Bedford is, however, still a genuine fishing port, with real seamen's bars and real seamen.

AREA CODE: 508

GUIDANCE

New Bedford maintains two visitors information centers. The **Waterfront Visitors Center** (979-1745; 1-800-508-5353), Pier 3, Monday through Friday 9–5, also Saturday and Sunday 10–4, April through November, occupies the former Wharfinger Building, for many decades the scene of daily fish auctions; it offers free parking and rest rooms. **The Whaling National Historical Park Visitors Center** (991–6200), open 9–4, year-round, corner of William and Second Streets, was built in 1852 as a bank. It housed the Third District Court of Bristol County from 1899 to 1914 and was subsequently auctioned to the Nonquiet Tribe of Red Men. It served a number of unlikely purposes until it was eventually reclaimed as a bank (1979–1994) and works well as headquarters for New Bedford's evolving National Historic Park. This is the departure point for walking tours, mid-June to mid-September. See *Getting There* for directions.

Town of Fairhaven Office of Tourism & Visitors Center (979-4085), 27 Center Street. Open daily 8:30–4 (closed Wednesday and Sunday).

Bristol County Convention and Visitors Bureau (997-1250), 70 North Second Street, New Bedford; in the Historic District, handy to the Elm Street Garage. Good for information on the entire county.

GETTING THERE

By car: From the west and New York, take I-95 to I-195 east, exit 15 to Route 18, downtown exit. From points north and Boston, take Route 24 to 140 to I-195 east to exit 15 (Route 18) to the downtown exit. For the National Park Visitors Center and the Whaling Museum, park in the Elm Street Garage, a right just off the exit. For the Waterfront Visitors Center, take the downtown exit but continue straight ahead to Union Street, then turn left onto Frontage Road (second traffic light) and right onto Fisherman's Wharf (Pier 3).

By bus: **Bonanza** (1-800-556-3815) offers service to Providence and New York. **American Eagle Coach Company** (1-800-453-5040) offers frequent service to Boston.

By air: New Bedford Regional Airport is served by **Cape Air** (flying to Nantucket and Martha's Vineyard). **Bayside Air Charter** (636-3762) also offers seaplane service to Cuttyhunk and the other islands.

By ferry: See *To Do—Ferries and Excursions*.

GETTING AROUND

Although the Downtown Connector (Route 18) disconnects the historic district with the water, there are pedestrian crossways to the wharves, where

Westport Point

KIMBERLY GRANT

scallopers and draggers are docked. Guided tours of the area depart from the **National Park Visitors Center,** corner of William and Second Street (cater-corner to the Custom House; see *Historic Sites*).

PARKING
The **Elm Street Garage** (on your right just off the downtown exit) costs less than a meter, maximum of $5 per day.

MEDICAL EMERGENCY
St. Luke's Hospital (997-1515), 101 Page Street, New Bedford.

ISLANDS

Cuttyhunk Island. Accessible by the M/V *Alert II* (see *To Do—Ferries and Excursions*) from Pier 3 in New Bedford, and by air with Bayside Air (see *Getting There*). Cuttyhunk is the westernmost of the 16 Elizabeth Islands that together form the town of Gosnold. The islands trail off in a line from Woods Hole, dividing Buzzards Bay from Vineyard Sound, and Cuttyhunk is one of only two not owned by Boston Brahmin families. It is little more than 2 miles long and an irregular ¾ mile wide, home for fewer than 30 people in winter, maybe 400 in summer. It's best known for bass fishing.

From the dock you walk past the old life-saving station and, skirting the village, find the footpath through the cemetery and up the bluff. The panoramic view is off across the neighboring, very private islands to the dramatic cliffs at Gay Head on Martha's Vineyard. It's difficult to imagine a more perfect picnic spot, unless it's the observation platform on the island's height of land, overlooking the village, the harbor, and the sandy public beach on Copicut Neck.

In Cuttyhunk's one-room schoolhouse, the pupils (who seldom number more than three) learn that their island was the site of the Bay State's first English settlement. Bartholomew Gosnold built a stockade here in 1602 and set about planting a garden and gathering sassafras (valued for medicinal uses). Native Americans, lurking in the brush, made the settlers jumpy, however. After a 22-day stay, the would-be colonists sailed away. A singular stone tower, erected in 1902, now marks the event on a mini-island in the middle of a salt pond (in which oysters are presently being cultivated) at the western tip of the island.

From town it is a pleasant hour's or day's walk to the monument, depending on how frequently and long you pause on the smooth boulders to watch the surf breaking or the sun glinting on beach grass. (It's advisable to wear socks and long pants against wood ticks.)

Kris Lombard's **Cuttyhunk Bed & Breakfast Inn** (993-6490) in the center of the village offers three guest rooms, and cottages can be rented by the day, weekend, week, or month; contact **Cuttyhunk Boat Lines** (992-1432). You might also inquire about bass boats, "with tackle, boat, and the guidance of their owners," which can be rented by the day or the tide. There's a small general store, and in summer the **4 Corners** serves meals.

If you can't spend the night, Cuttyhunk is still worth a day trip. The hour's ride down Buzzards Bay is a pleasant interlude, but the absolute peace of the island comes as a jolt.

Martha's Vineyard. This isn't the place to describe New England's largest island and one of its most popular tourist destinations. (Contact the **Martha's Vineyard Chamber of Commerce:** 693-0085). The Vineyard is generally accessed by car ferry from Woods Hole on Cape Cod, but getting a reservation for your car is frequently difficult, not to mention expensive, and traffic to Woods Hole can be impossible. The 600-passenger ferry *Schamonchi* (see *To Do: Ferries and Excursions*) from New Bedford docks in Vineyard Haven (as do ferries from Cape Cod). Day-trippers can bring bikes and spend up to 8 hours on the island, taking the bike path along the shore and into Oak Bluffs and Edgartown, then back the short way to Vineyard Haven. Rental bikes and cars are also available, and you can step right from the boat onto a tour bus or take advantage of the island's (seasonal) visitor-geared bus system. This is a beautiful ride on a calm day, far preferable to the shorter crossing (longer, more trafficked car ride) from Falmouth. It's notoriously rough, however, in bad weather.

Note: Watch for news about the steamer *Nobska*, a vintage 1925 ferry that plied the waters for 50 years between Woods Hole and the islands and is presently under restoration at the Charlestown Navy Yard, due to begin passenger and dining service between New Bedford and Martha's Vineyard by 1999. Check out the New England Steamship Foundation's

Nobska display in the Sundial Building, corner of Water and Union Streets.

TO SEE

MUSEUM
The New Bedford Whaling Museum (997-0046), 18 Johnny Cake Hill, New Bedford. Open daily 9–5, Thursday until 8 June through Labor Day. Internationally known for its scrimshaw collection (more than 2000 pieces), the museum displays vivid paintings of life aboard whaling vessels from Tahiti to the Arctic Circle. Whaling voyages are illustrated on a quarter-mile-long panorama (produced in 1848 to show in traveling tents), etched on whale teeth, and dramatized in movies (shown regularly in the museum theater). You can clamber aboard the world's largest ship model—a half-scale model of the New Bedford bark *Lagoda*, fully equipped. The museum showcases more than the whaling chapter in the area's history. There is a room full of the ornate art glass for which New Bedford was known beginning in the 1880s, and there are always major changing exhibits. $4.50 adults, $3.50 seniors, $3 children 6–14. Inquire about frequent special programs and twice-daily films.

HISTORIC SITES
In the Waterfront Historic District of New Bedford
Seamen's Bethel (992-3295), 15 Johnny Cake Hill. Open May through October, weekday afternoons and weekends. The pulpit, shaped like a "ship's bluff bow," as Melville put it, was actually installed after the publication of *Moby-Dick*. The remainder of the 1830s chapel conveys a sense of the men who have prayed here (and continue to) before setting out to sea. The walls are covered with memorial tablets to men who have died in every watery corner of the earth, cenotaphs from the 1840s side by side with those from the 1970s and '80s. It is a Quaker-plain, moving place. It's also a popular place for weddings because of the lore that marriages made here last. The **Mariner's Home** next door, like the Bethel, is run by the Port Society, founded in 1830 "for the moral and religious improvement of seamen." The building itself dates from 1787, and there is a nominal charge to fishermen for a night's lodging (not open to the public).
Double Bank Building, 56-60 North Water Street. One of the city's most distinctive buildings, built in 1831–35 as a classic Greek Revival temple of finance, originally for two different banks (notice the two kinds of pillars); it now houses the Fishermen's Union and related firms.
Custom House (994-5158), corner of William and Second Streets, built in 1834–36, is impressive both inside and out. It is still operating as the oldest custom house in the country.
Dock Walk
From the **Waterfront Visitors Center** on **Fishermen's Pier (Pier 3)** (see *Guidance*), walk left along the water to **Tonnessen Park,** with its statue

of a man holding a cod in his left hand and a sturgeon in his right. The statue itself was the work and gift of Anna Hyatt Huntington (she was 86 at the time) to the city as a memorial "to those seamen whose only graves are the ocean floor." Panels here tell the story of the vintage-1894 schooner *Ernestina,* which may or may not be at her dock here. Walk out along the **State Pier** to view the Coast Guard lightship *New Bedford.* This retired lightship saw long service in Atlantic waters until 1971 and is a waterfront landmark awaiting restoration.

Along Pleasant Street, New Bedford

City Hall, Pleasant, William, and Sixth Streets. Dating from the city's whaling era (it was built in 1856), the building contains an ornate 1906 open-cage elevator, said to be the oldest functioning elevator in the United States.

New Bedford Free Public Library, Pleasant Street next to City Hall. The building dates from 1837, constructed of native granite with Egyptian Revival detailing (boasting the world's only Egyptian Revival elevator). The Melville Whaling Room includes a superb collection of logbooks and other whaling-era material. Note the handsome 1905 rotunda and, outside, the Whaler's Memorial.

Along County Street, New Bedford

"Nowhere in America will you find more patrician-like houses," Herman Melville wrote about **County Street;** "brave houses and flower gardens, . . . harpooned and dragged hither from the bottom of the sea." One of the oldest streets in the city, County Street runs along the crest of the hill from which the city slopes down to the harbor. It was the obvious place to build for the wealthiest whaling merchants, followed by textile-mill owners.

Rotch-Jones-Duff House and Garden Museum (997-1401), 396 County Street. Open Tuesday through Saturday 10–4, Sunday 1–4. One of New Bedford's finest mansions, built in 1834 by Nantucket whaling merchant William Rotch Jr. at age 72 for his second wife. The 28 rooms are filled with furnishings illustrating the lifestyles of the three different families who lived here and their respective eras. We found the locally made Pairpoint glass chandeliers, the extensive costume collection, and Captain Jones's study particularly interesting. The formal gardens, which occupy an entire city block, are an oasis filled with boxwood hedges, a dogwood allée, wildflowers, and roses. In July and August there are Friday-evening concerts; guests are invited to spread blankets and to picnic in the garden beforehand. Admission $4 adults, $3 seniors; $1 age 12 and under. Concerts $7; $1 for children 12 and under.

In Fairhaven

Just across the Acushnet River (take the Route 6 bridge) from New Bedford, **Fairhaven** is a proud old shipbuilding and whaling town, distinguished today by its elaborate public buildings—virtually all the gifts of Henry Huttleston Rodgers. A multimillionaire who made his fortune in Pennsylvania petroleum rather than in whale oil, H.H. Rodgers donated the huge, castlelike high school (Route 6 and Main Street), the Masonic Hall, the splendid Unitarian church (102 Green Street), and, most notably, the library.

The Millicent Library, 45 Centre Street, dedicated to the memory of Rodgers's daughter, who died at age 17, is worth a stop simply to see its ornate Victorian interior. Many Japanese visitors come to see its collection of memorabilia relating to Manjiro Nakahama, a shipwrecked Japanese boy who was rescued by a Captain William Whitfield in 1841. The Fairhaven captain brought the boy home and sent him to private school. Nakahama later returned to Japan, serving as interpreter for Admiral Perry in negotiating the 1853 treaty that opened Japanese ports. The late emperor of Japan stopped at the library in 1987, and Japanese tourists continue to come to sign their names in the same book that he used. The library also displays memorabilia of Joshua Slocum, who set sail from Fairhaven in his small boat, *The Spray,* to circumnavigate the world. Samuel Clemens (Mark Twain), who dedicated the library in 1894, pronounced it "the ideal library, I think. Books are the liberated spirits of men, and should be bestowed in a heaven of light and grace and harmonious color and sumptuous comfort, like this." H.H. Rodgers is said to have saved Clemens from bankruptcy.

Fort Phoenix, on the bay (from Route 6, Green Street runs south to the fort), is the other Fairhaven site to see: Pre-Revolutionary in origin, it claims the first naval engagement of the Revolution (May 14, 1775). The fort maintains its original shape. One cannon (still here) had been captured by John Paul Jones in the Bahamas. The fort was overcome in 1778 but fended off a British invasion party in 1814, and again saw service in the Civil War. The smooth rocks and small beach below the fort at the base of the Acushnet River breakwater are free and locally favored for sunbathing. (Also see *Swimming.*)

Also in Fairhaven: For a sense of the town's active waterfront, stop by the Public Boat Landing across from **Cushman's Park** (Middle Street), and check out the scallopers at **Kelley Boat Yards** and in the **Fairhaven Ship Yard.** Note that most boats here and in New Bedford bear the letters *F.V.* ("Fishing Vessel").

Between New Bedford and Fairhaven

No fewer than four islands spot the bay between New Bedford and Fairhaven; Popes Island is worth pausing on (eastbound) to view the many pleasure boats and the striking new statue of Prince Henry the Navigator. The park here includes a waterside walk and children's play area. *Note:* The antique turn-bridge here may be an engineering marvel, but it can also be a pain; locals tend to cut around on I-95 to avoid it.

FOR FAMILIES

✐ **Children's Museum** (993-3361), 276 Gulf Road, South Dartmouth. Open year-round, Tuesday through Saturday 10–5, Sunday 1–5. Housed in a huge old dairy barn, it is now filled with a kaleidoscopic range of hands-on exhibits: a fishing boat; a fantastical revolving pillar of trucks, cranes, and mechanical contrivances; a plethora of blocks and Legos; and, outside, a "windfarm" and 60 acres of conservation land. Inquire about frequent special events. Admission $3.75 per person.

🖉 **New Bedford Fire Museum** (992-2162), corner of Bedford and South Sixth Streets, New Bedford. Not far from the center of town, but a fire engine shuttles visitors up from the visitors centers. Open July and August only, daily 9–5. Housed in a former stable next to 19th-century Fire Station #4, this museum maintains a collection of antique equipment: shiny pumpers, buckets, horns, and more. There is a corner for children to dress up in firemen's uniforms and a pole for them to slide down (grown-ups, too, are permitted to slide). It is staffed by veteran firefighters. $1 adults, free for children 12 and under.

(Also see **Demarest Lloyd State Park** under *To Do: Swimming* and the **Lloyd Center** under *Green Space*.)

SCENIC DRIVE OR BIKE RIDE

Just southwest of New Bedford lies some of the most beautiful seaside farmland in the state. From the New Bedford historic waterfront area, the easiest route is Route 6 west to Slocum Road (the Bishop Strong Catholic High School is set back on the corner here); and bear right at the Y onto Russells Mills Road for 200 yards and then left across from the Police Station (that's the tricky part I always miss) onto Elm Street, which brings you right into **Padanaram Village.** This marks the spot of a 17th-century settlement and 19th-century saltworks and shipyards. Now it is a fashionable yachting resort with some fine restaurants. The view of the yacht-filled harbor from the bridge and causeway across Apponagansett Bay is exceptional, as is the ride along Smith Neck Road, one of the area's more prestigious summer addresses. Note Salt Marsh Farm B&B (see *Lodging*) and not far beyond it, **Round Hill,** an estate built by the son and daughter of Hetty Green, known as the Witch of Wall Street and supposedly the richest and most miserly woman in the world around the turn of the century. Round Hill is now a private condominiums complex. The huge satellite dish resembling a fountain is a legacy from the mansion's past ownership by MIT.

Follow Little River Road along the salt marsh to the **Lloyd Center** (see *Green Space*). Continue north to Rock O'Dundee Road, on through the stop sign. Straight into **Russell Mills Village** in which houses are scattered, each on its own rise of land, around an old millpond (note Davoll's General Store and Salt Marsh Pottery under *Selective Shopping*). Ask directions to the **Apponagansett Friends Meeting House,** a weathered building built in 1790 (closed except for a Sunday meeting in summer months). The graveyard is a quiet, moving place with the same names on the plain tombstones that appear on local mailboxes: Allen, Slocum, Gifford, Russell.

The Alert II *of New Bedford*

From Russells Mills, drive south to **Demarest Lloyd State Park** (see *Swimming;* but this is also a great place to walk), then Allens Neck Road to Old Horseneck Road, then left on Horseneck Road. Note the **Bayside** restaurant (seasonal lunch and dinner; see *Eating Out*) at the point that the road meets the shore, and across from it, the Massachusetts Audubon Sanctuary at **Allens Pond,** another great place to walk and to bird. The other great walking/birding spot here is **Gooseberry Neck** (next left, beyond the lineup of trailers); park and walk the path around this point.

Horseneck Beach (see *Swimming*), a state camping and day-use area, lies beyond, along West Beach Road. This area was an upscale resort (FDR convalesced here from polio) with a large hotel until the 1938 hurricane savaged it. Cherry & Webb Lane leads to **Moby-Dick** restaurant (see *Dining Out*) and Route 88 leads north across the river. Take the first left after the bridge and go left again into **Westport Point,** one of the oldest settlements between Newport and Plymouth and a major shipbuilding village in the 1850s. It's now a quiet, gray-shingled village with a main street that ends at the fishing pier and **Lees Wharf Fish Market.** Shops, farmstands and **Ellie's Place** (see *Eating Out*) cluster along Main Street in Central Village, several miles up Main Road, just beyond the turnoff for Hixbridge Road. This is a decision point. I strongly recommend detouring a few miles east of Hixbridge to the **Westport River Winery**, a major sights-to-see in this area (see *Selective Shopping*). You might also want to turn west from the village on Adamsville Road to Adamsville, with its millpond, **Gray's Store** (billed as the oldest general store in America), shops, and two restaurants. Both Route 88 from Westport and Route 81 from Adamsville lead back to Route 6, I-195, and Fall River.

TO DO

BALLOONING
Balloon Adventures of New Bedford (636-4846), 564 Rock O'Dundee Road, South Dartmouth. One-hour champagne flights available year-round, specializing in coastal flights; 17 years' experience. $200 per person, $225 on weekends.

BICYCLING
The route described under *Scenic Drives* is eminently suited to bicycling. **Salt Marsh Farm B&B** (see *Lodging*) offers use of bikes to its guests and specializes in mapping routes of varying distances. Fairhaven, too, lends itself to touring by bicycle, perhaps the reason the town publishes a *Bicycling in Fairhaven* brochure. Construction of a bike path along an old railbed connecting Ferry Street in Fairhaven with Mattapoisett began in 1997.

Bicycle Rentals are seasonally available from the **Westport Point Market** (636-3732).

CANOEING AND KAYAKING
Palmer River Canoe & Kayak (336-2274; 1-800-689-7884), 206 Wheeler Street, Rehoboth. Sited on the Palmer River, canoe and kayak rentals, guided trips on the Taunton and Nemasket Rivers. **Sakonnet Boathouse** (401-624-1440), 169 Riverside Drive, Tiverton, Rhode Island. Just over the Rhode Island line in Tiverton Four Corners; guided tours and instruction. Also contact the **Lloyd Center** (see *Green Space*) about scheduled trips on the Slocum River.

FERRIES AND EXCURSIONS
Cape Island Express Lines, Inc. (997-1688), Billy Wood's Wharf, New Bedford. The 600-passenger *Schamonchi* departs mid-May to mid-October, making one to four runs (depending on the day and month) to Vineyard Haven on Martha's Vineyard. Parking is $7 per day at the southern end of the city (not the midtown waterfront). Round-trip fare to the Vineyard is $16 adults, $7.50 children; $9 and $4.50 one-way; $2.50 for bicycles. This can be a beautiful ride up through the bay and by the Elizabeth Islands, but it's not advisable in rough weather. Follow directions to the downtown exit 15, then Route 18 south to fifth set of lights; turn left and follow signs.

Cuttyhunk Boat Lines, Inc. (992-1432; 992-6076), Fisherman's Wharf/Pier 3, New Bedford. Mid-June to mid-September daily; Tuesday, Friday, and weekends in spring and fall; Tuesday and Friday only in winter.

Obviously designed as much for freight as for people, this 60-passenger, aluminum-hulled ferry serves as the life and information line to Cuttyhunk. On summer weekends prepaid reservations are suggested. $16 adults round-trip, $11 one-way, and $9 for children round-trip. Inquire about harbor tours and other excursions. Follow directions for the city's visitors center next door.

FISHING

Captain Leroy (992-8907) departs from the Fairhaven Bridge (Route 6) April through November daily at 7:30 AM, returning at 4. His 50-foot and 65-foot party boats are equipped with fish and depth finders; rods and reels available for $7. (Also see Cuttyhunk Island under *Islands.*)

Captain Brad Sherman (636-2730) offers fishing and sight-seeing charters from Westport Point.

GOLF

Emerald Park Golf Club (992-8387), North Dartmouth, 18 holes. **Whaling City Country Club** (996-9393), New Bedford, 18 holes. **Marion Golf Club** (748-0199), nine holes.

SWIMMING

Demarest Lloyd State Park (636-8816), Barney's Joy Road, South Dartmouth. This is one of our favorite state beaches, crowded on Sunday but otherwise relatively deserted, ideal for small children since there is no surf. There are roughly 2 miles of beach with a view of Cuttyhunk; picnic tables, grills, and fireplaces. A large spit of sand jutting into the mouth of the Slocum River is a pleasant place to walk. There is a parking fee in season.

Horseneck Beach (636-8816), Westport Point, accessible from I-195 by Route 88. The highway stretches almost to the blacktopped parking lot and camping area and nearly to the futuristic concrete shower/restroom/snack-bar complex. There is even a blacktop strip between the dunes and the beach. The vast expanse of beach is spectacular, and the surf is just challenging enough. Nominal admission.

Apponagansett Point Beach (parking fee for nonresidents) is a small, pleasant beach on Gulf Road, South Dartmouth, near the Children's Museum (see *For Families*).

New Bedford beaches. Follow Route 18 south to Rodney French Boulevard. **Hazelwood Park** and **East Beach** both have changing rooms and snack bars; open late June until Labor Day, 9–6; free.

Fort Phoenix State Beach (992-4524), Fairhaven. Take Green Street from Route 6. This beach can be windy, but it is otherwise pleasant and uncrowded on weekdays; an urban beach with bathhouse, lifeguards, parking fee.

GREEN SPACE

Buttonwood Park (993-5686), Route 6, New Bedford. Designed by the prestigious firm of Olmsted/Elliot in 1894, this 97-acre park includes tennis courts, picnicking space, and paddleboats. Scheduled to reopen in 1998 after a three-year remake.

✐ **Brooklawn Park** (995-6644), Acushnet Avenue, New Bedford, has a kiddie pool, tennis courts, and picnicking facilities.

Lloyd Center for Environmental Studies (990-0505), 430 Potomska Road, South Dartmouth. This former home has been fitted with touch tanks, aquariums, an environmental library, and a third-floor observatory overlooking a 55-acre preserve on the Slocum River. The nature trails are varied, snaking through wooded hills, sloping through large holly stands to Osprey Point, and winding around a swamp filled with salamanders and spotted turtles. Inquire about canoe trips and frequent guided walks.

Fort Phoenix, Fairhaven. See *Historic Sites.*

Fort Taber, Rodney French Boulevard (the end), New Bedford. At the far southern end of the city, this massive granite complex was designed by Captain Robert E. Lee in 1846, long before his command in the Confederate Army.

LODGING

BED & BREAKFASTS

☞ **Edgewater Bed & Breakfast** (994-1574), 2 Oxford Street, Fairhaven 02719. Parts of this unusual house, on Poverty Point, were built as a store in the 1760s. It is now a rambling 1880s home with some of the best views of New Bedford across the Acushnet River, which seemingly surrounds the house and moves so quickly by its many windows that you actually feel afloat. There are five rooms, each with a TV and private bath. The Captain's Suite has a private sitting room with a working fireplace and water views on three sides. The Clara Anthony Room has water views and a claw-foot tub. The Joshua Slocum Suite (good for families) in the 1760 part of the house has a private entrance and deck, a sitting room, and a kitchenette. The Eldridge Room and East Indies Room in the old part of the house lack views but are nicely furnished. A muffins-and-juice breakfast is served in the formal dining room, and guests have full access to the handsome sunken living room. Kathy Reed, a college professor, is a warm host and is knowledgeable about local restaurants and sights. $70–90 double; $5 less single.

☞ **Salt Marsh Farm** (992-0980), 322 Smith Neck Road, South Dartmouth 02748. The hip-roofed Georgian farmhouse dates from 1727, and it's set in its own 90 acres, with access to a nearby beach. The homestead has been in Sally Brownell's family since World War II, and she shares with guests her special sense of the area. There are two small guest rooms with private bath, antique and handmade quilts, each room with its own hall and stairway besides. The living rooms and dining room are slant-floored, furnished in comfortable antiques. Larry Brownell nurtures an extensive garden and Sally prides herself on fairly spectacular breakfasts:

Dutch Babies (puffy shells and waffles topped with fresh strawberries and syrup), omelets from fresh-hatched eggs served with nasturtiums, fabulous scones, and freshly squeezed orange juice. Guests are welcome to use the house bikes (or to bring their own) and follow a variety of routes through the countryside (see *Scenic Drive*). $75–95 per couple, including tax and breakfast, depending on the day of the week and the season; two-night minimum on weekends, May through October. No smoking. Children welcome but parents must rent both rooms.

The Saltworks, A Bed and Breakfast on Padanaram Harbor (991-5491), 115 Elm Street, South Dartmouth 02748. An 1830s house, Victorianized and expanded—with whole new wings and a huge welcoming porch—in Padanaram's 1890s gilded resort era. The two guest rooms are upstairs, one with a big brass bed, private bath, and working fireplace, the second with a fine four-poster and vintage, skylighted shower. Downstairs there's a sense of comfort and space, books and exceptional art, much of it by host Sandra Hall. Both rooms are $95 plus $10 for a small bedroom that adjoins one. Rates include a buffet breakfast. Closed mid-December to mid-January.

1875 House (997-6433), 36 Seventh Street, New Bedford 02742. Just off County Street, within the historic district, is a long-established B&B in a Victorian home with three rooms, private baths. Contact Cynthia and Steve Poyant; $55–65 includes a breakfast of fresh fruit and muffins.

23 Water Street (758-9733), PO Box 361, Mattapoisett 02739. We have to confess to never having gotten there the day we tried, but the location is prime, right across from Town Wharf in a picturesque village, steps from a waterside park and from fine dining at the Mattapoisett Inn. This is a Victorian house with three guest rooms and an apartment. $90–120 for the rooms, $850 per week for the apartment.

The Mattapoisett Inn (758-4922), 13 Water Street, Mattapoisett 02739. Open April through November. This classic old summer hotel offers three rooms, each with private bath, all with harbor views, but you may want to inquire about dining room noise.

The Little Red House (996-4554), 631 Elm Street, Padanaram Village 02748. Meryl Zwirblis offers two rooms in a gambrel-roofed house within walking distance of village shops and dining. The rooms, one with twin beds and the other with a queen, share a bath. $70 per couple includes a full breakfast.

The Paquachuck Inn (636-4398), 2056 Main Road, Westport 02791. This shingled 1827 building, obviously a former store, sits right across from the dock in the village of Westport Point. Common space includes a large studio, dock, and beach. $95 with two-night minimum or $105 per night. Seasonal. (This was closed when we came by but looks interesting.)

MOTELS

Days Inn (997-1231), 500 Hathaway Road, intersection of Route 140 (exit 3) and I-195, New Bedford 02719. This is a 133-room, recently refurbished motel with a locally respected restaurant, indoor pool. $89 double.

Comfort Inn (996-0800 or 1-800-228-5150), 171 Furnace Corner Road, exit 12A off I-95 in North Dartmouth 02747. An 85-room motel with cable TV, an outdoor pool, and continental breakfast; handy to VF Outlet complex (see *Factory Outlets*). $84.65 for a room with two double beds.

Hampton Inn (990-8500), Bridge Street and Alden Road, Fairhaven 02719. A half-mile south of I-95, exit 18. A 77-room, thee-story motor inn with cable TV, outdoor swimming pool; $89 per couple, less off-season.

CAMPGROUND

Horseneck Beach (636-8816) offers 100 campsites (see *Swimming*).

COTTAGES

For waterside summer rentals, especially on Sconticut Neck; check with the **Fairhaven Office of Tourism**. (See *Guidance*).

WHERE TO EAT

DINING OUT

Worden's (999-4505), 7 Water Street, Padanaram Village. Open Wednesday through Sunday, 5–9, also lunch Thursday through Sunday. Owner-chef Steve Worden has an enviable reputation for regional American dishes and fresh, local ingredients. Large windows overlook the yacht harbor and tables are white-clothed; specialties include sautéed rainbow trout with three-bean succotash, grilled barbecued Atlantic salmon with organic pea greens, and oven-roasted rack of lamb with cool mint pesto. You might start with smoked bluefish cakes with a mustard-horseradish sauce ($6) and dine on sautéed veal medallions with eggplant and tomato ($18); entrées: $17–22.

Bridge Street Cafe (994-7200), 10-A Bridge, South Dartmouth. June to Labor Day, open Tuesday through Saturday for lunch and dinner (brunch on Sunday). A garage turned restaurant, specializing in fresh, local ingredients and in "bridging the gap between the mundane and the much too fancy"; Greg and Sally Morton feature ginger chicken, barbecued baby back ribs, soft-shell crab, grilled lamb, a variety of homemade pasta and seafood dishes, and Sally's outrageous desserts. Dinner entrées $17.95–21.

Freestone's City Grill (993-7477), 41 William Street, New Bedford. Open daily 11–11 , Sunday noon–10. This is both a casual and a serious dining spot, depending on the time of day and what you order. In 1979 Debbie Sequin and Kerry Mitchell dislodged a raunchy bar and restored this early-19th-century bank building, preserving the original mahogany paneling and working fireplace. Specialties include prizewinning fish chowder, grilled Louisiana scallop and crabcakes, and a wide choice of salads, sandwiches, and seafood. For dessert, try the chocolate walnut pie. Dinner entrées range $14–17.

Huttleston House (999-1791), 111 Huttleston Avenue, Fairhaven. Open daily for lunch and dinner. Traditional American fare, friendly service. Complete dinners average less than $20 and daily specials are less than $10.

Candleworks (992-1635), 72 North Water Street, New Bedford. Open for lunch and dinner Monday through Saturday, 4–9 on Sunday. Regional fish, Italian dishes. Housed in a granite building built by Samuel Rodman in 1810 to produce spermaceti candles, this has an attractive main dining room, as well as a sun porch and patio dining. Dinner entrées $14–22.

Moby-Dick (636-6500), Westport Point (the last right off Route 88 before Horseneck Beach). Open May through December for lunch and dinner. This old dining landmark was expanded and upscaled when it was rebuilt (after a fire) several years ago. Accessible by boat as well as car. The menu ranges from pizza and fried calamari to smoked salmon rolls and almond-crusted cod; entrées $10.95–$19.95. More formal dining indoors than out.

The Mattapoisett Inn (758-4922), 13 Water Street, Mattapoisett. Open April through November for lunch and dinner, Sunday brunch. Entertainment Friday and Saturday. An old summer hotel with low-beamed dining rooms, atmosphere, early-bird specials. The menu includes Cajun dishes, frogs' legs, and roast duckling.

EATING OUT
In New Bedford

✐☞**Davy's Locker** (992-7359), 1480 East Rodney French Boulevard. Open daily 11–10. A large dining landmark at the south end of the city, overlooking the water, this is generally agreed to be the best reasonably priced place to eat fish in New Bedford. The clam chowder is outstanding. Note the nightly dinner specials. Steaks and other meat staples are part of the extensive menu.

Rosie's (990-3700), 380 Hathaway Road, New Bedford. A local favorite with a pleasant atmosphere and nicely presented, imaginative fare at reasonable prices. You might begin with fried calamari or mussels Provençale ($5.95) and dine on chicken and broccoli with penne pasta ($9.95) or chicken breast with a lemon garlic sauce ($10.45).

Antonio's Restaurant (990-3636), 267 Coggeshall Street. Open Sunday through Thursday 11:30–9:30; Friday and Saturday until 10. One of the best places for Portuguese food in the state; an informal, friendly place with a bilingual menu. You smell the spices the moment you walk in. Of course you start with kale soup and make a satisfying, reasonably priced meal of the Cacoila Platter; the specialty of the house is Mariscada a Antonio's, a seafood casserole usually split between two. From I-195 west, take exit 17 (Coggeshall Street) and turn left. Go through the traffic light, and the restaurant is on your right. Free parking is in the lot across the street. No credit cards or reservations. Try the Sagres (Portuguese) beer while waiting for a table. The Seafood Antonio satisfies two starving adults ($17.95). Entrées begin at $5.50.

Cobblestone's Restaurant (999-5486), 7 South Sixth Street. Open for breakfast and lunch, Sunday brunch, dinner Thursday and Friday. Housed in the former storefront of a 19th-century building that's been a Turkish bathhouse and an undertaker's parlor, this attractive, brick-walled space with mismatched antique oak tables and chairs offers imaginative egg dishes, salads, and sandwiches.

Maxie's Deli, Purchase Street across from City Hall. Open 4 AM–2:30 PM. A bright, friendly eating and gossip spot with exposed brick walls and hanging plants; the day's paper is stacked for guests. Bargain-priced breakfasts and Jurassic-sized New York–style deli sandwiches.

Shawmut Diner (993-3073), Shawmut Avenue. Open 5:30 AM–7 PM daily, until 8 Thursday through Saturday. A chrome classic, but owners Phil and Celeste Paleologos feature leg of lamb. $5.95 buys dinner; $2.99 for fish-and-chips.

Spearfields Restaurant (993-4848), 1 Johnny Cake Hill. Open daily 7–4. Cheerful and handy, steps from the Whaling Museum, good for omelets, salads and sandwiches, patio dining in season.

In Fairhaven

Mike's (996-9810), 714 Washington Street (Route 6). No reservations; cash only. Usually a wait in the lounge until your name is called. The attraction here is steak and seafood—lots of both at bargain prices: clam chowder, a full, boiled lobster, and side order of potato (or spaghetti) for $9. Also good for thin-crust pizza, and where else can you get an Italian pu pu platter?

Margaret's, corner of Main and Water Streets. Closed Tuesday, otherwise open from 7 AM for breakfast and lunch, dinner Friday and Saturday. A hangout for locals and boatyard workers. Coffee-shop atmosphere, but fresh flowers and café-style food: Norwegian fish cakes; Portuguese-style codfish salad; sautéed chicken with tomato, garlic, spinach, and feta; and, if you must, peanut butter with jelly and fluff. Desserts the day we stopped by included almond torte and apricot meringue cream cake.

Morgan's (997-4443), 58 Washington Street. Open weekdays from 6 AM–2 PM, weekends, 6 AM–noon. The kind of neighborhood eatery every town used to have but few now do. Small, friendly, local.

Pumpernickel's (990-2026), 23 Centre Street. The menu is printed on a paper bag. Good for chowder or kale soup, linguiça, or a seafood medley; fabulous desserts.

The Phoenix Restaurant (996-1441), 140 Huttleston Avenue. Open 11 AM–
2 PM. Breakfast is the specialty here; try scrambled eggs with linguiça and
home fries. Cheese rolls, Portuguese and Greek specialties.

The Fairhaven Chowder House (996-4100), Sconticut Neck Road at
Droun Boulevard. Open daily; a locally owned fish market with a modern, squeaky-clean dining room, seafood specialties. Full liquor license.

Tofu Chinese (990-2888), 9 Popes Island (Route 6 on the New Bedford/
Fairhaven causeway). Good Mandarin and Szechuan dishes (no MSG);
we recommend the crispy whole fish and lunch and dinner buffets Monday through Thursday.

In Dartmouth, Westport, and in Rhode Island

The Bayside (636-5882), 1253 Horseneck Road, Westport. Open 11–9
weekdays, 8–8 weekends, closed off-season. This family-owned oasis is
sited on a particularly inviting piece of the shore. We were disappointed
with the quahog chowder on our last visit but can recommend the codfish cakes and johnnycakes. The menu ranges from hamburgers to scallops Provençale or Cajun mussels served over linguine. BYOB.

Riverhouse Grille (992-8148), 3 Water Street, South Dartmouth. Open
weekdays 11–11, weekends 9 AM–11 PM. A shingled, waterside pub specializing in micobrews and casual dining.

Ellie's Place (636-5590), 1403 Main Road, Westport. Open 7:30 AM–8 PM
except Monday year-round. A friendly local eatery featuring stuffed
quahogs and quahog chowder, johnnycakes with bacon, Portuguese-
style fish broiled in a special marinade, fried smelts, and whiffleburgers
(scrambled hamburger with onions, tomatoes, peppers, mushrooms,
and melted cheese). Beer and wine are served.

Abraham Manchester's Restaurant (401-635-2700 or 635-2006), Stone
Church Road, Adamsville, Rhode Island. A half-dozen miles from
Westport Central Village, open daily, year-round, 11:30 AM–10 PM. A
dining landmark with a comfortable atmosphere and solid local following, known for seafood like littlenecks steamed in garlic butter and wine
($10.25) and family-priced dinners like the roast turkey plate ($8.50).

The Barn Restaurant (401-635-1985), Stone Church Road, behind Abraham
Manchester's in the middle of Adamsville, Rhode Island. Open weekdays 6
AM–11:30 AM, weekends, 7 AM–12:30 PM, also Wednesday dinner. Breakfast
is not only served but also elevated to an art (BYOB).

Not Your Average Joe's (992-5637), Route 6 next to Baker's Books, west
of Slocum Road, Dartmouth. Open for lunch and dinner. Pizza chefs
toss dough deftly in the air and bake it in a wood-fired oven, centerpiece of a kitchen open to view from a long, undulating counter. There's
also plenty of seating in the raspberry-colored dining room and a large,
varied menu featuring pastas and pizza but including plenty else, from
(wood-baked) Black Angus sirloin meat loaf to pot-au-feu, all reasonably priced.

ENTERTAINMENT

✎ **Zeiterion Theatre** (997-5664), 684 Purchase Street, New Bedford. All-vaudeville theater. Its restoration has been a community effort, a symbol of the new New Bedford. The Zeiterion now has a professional summer and performing arts season, featuring musicals, jazz, dance, classical concerts, productions by the New Bedford Festival Theater, the New Bedford Symphony Orchestra, and children's performances. Call for seasonal schedule.

UMass Dartmouth (999-8000), Old Westport Road, North Dartmouth, stages cabaret theater July through August.

Heritage Concert Series at the Rotch-Jones-Duff House (see *Historic Sites*) in July and August (Friday evenings). Guests are invited to picnic in the garden beforehand.

SELECTIVE SHOPPING

ANTIQUES SHOPS

Brookside Antiques (493-4944), 44 North Water Street, New Bedford, specializes in Pairpoint glass and other things local. **New Bedford Antiques Company** (993-7600), 85 Coggeshall Street, New Bedford, right off Route 195, exit 17 heading west, exit 16 heading east. Open daily 10–5, Sundays 1–5. Huge (260 dealers), an eclectic mix of good-quality antiques.

ART GALLERIES

Bierstadt Art Society Gallery (993-4308), 179 William Street, New Bedford. Hours vary. Area painters exhibit in changing shows. **New Bedford Art Museum** (961-3072), 608 Pleasant Street, New Bedford. Open Wednesday through Sunday 12–5, Thursday until 7. Adults $2 (over 17). Housed in the 1918 Vault Building, this is a small, new, but ambitious museum founded to show paintings and prints from the New Bedford Free Public Library collections—works by Bierstadt, Bradford, and Gifford. It features changing exhibits. **Gallery X** (992-2675), 169 William Street, New Bedford. Open Wednesday through Sunday, 11–3. A nonprofit, locally geared showcase for visual and performing artists and writers. Admission fee. **Norton Gallery** (997-9674), 330 Elm Street, Padanaram Village. Nautical prints, sculptures by locally known artists. **Artisans Cooperative Gallery** (993-0411), 338 Elm Street, Padanaram. Open Monday through Saturday 10–5, Sunday 1–5. Functional and sign art. **Arthur Moniz Gallery** (992-6050), 28 Smith Street, Fairhaven. Original paintings, limited-edition prints, framing; features local artists.

BOOKSTORES

Baker Books (992-3749), 69 State Road, North Dartmouth. Open Monday through Saturday 9–9, Sunday noon–6. A pseudo-Tudor facade distinguishes this large bookstore from the road rash along Route 6. This independent bookstore moved from downtown New Bedford several years ago and has a wide range of titles, including books of local, regional, and nautical interest as well as maps, guides, and children's books. Includes a café. **The Village Bookshop,** 294 Elm Street, Padanaram Village. This cheerful, welcoming store has an extensive collection of yachting and children's books, greeting cards. **Barnes & Noble** (997-0701), Dartmouth commons off Route 6, North Dartmouth. Open Monday through Saturday 9–9, Sunday noon–6. Huge and well stocked; general titles plus discount books, maps, guides, periodicals.

FACTORY OUTLETS

When petroleum replaced whale oil in the 1860s, New Bedford merchants put their money into cotton mills. These mills grew as whaling waned, reaching their peak prosperity in the 1920s. Then came a very long depression for the city. Factory-outlet shopping was supposedly invented here in the 1950s, when clothing manufacturers opened a few square feet of factory floor space to the general public for direct sales. One outlet led to two and today there are relatively few "stand-alone" factory outlet shops. Most of them have gathered to form centers, usually in former mill buildings.

VF Factory Outlet (998-3311), 375 Faunce Corner Road (the road is an exit off I-195; exit 12B) in North Dartmouth. Open Monday through Saturday 9–9. This is a vast, hangarlike building filled with some of the best clothing outlets around. In the section shared by Jantzen, Vanity Fair, and Lee there are ample changing rooms and mirrors, a great selection of jeans (including odd sizes), and sportswear for the whole family, all at 50 percent off. A dozen outlets in this complex include such popular brand names as Cape Isle Knitters, Van Heusen, American Tourister, and Bannister Shoes.

Bedspread Mill Outlet (992-6600), Mt. Pleasant Street, New Bedford. Open Monday through Saturday 9:30–5:30, Thursday until 8. Blinds, balloon shades, drapes, sheets, comforters, blankets at 30 to 50 percent savings.

Gourmet Outlet (999-6408; 1-800-423-8333), 2301 Purchase Street. Open Tuesday through Saturday 10–5. Looking for truffle juice? White asparagus out of season? Banana leaves? Nine varieties of fresh mushrooms, six kinds of fresh olives, five kinds of Russian caviar, daily fresh sourdough bread from San Francisco? Even if you aren't a foodie, this huge warehouse—in which fresh produce turns over twice a day on its way to fine restaurants throughout the world—is a fascinating stop. We came away with purple potatoes (surprisingly sweet), a large, bargain-priced bottle of French champagne vinegar, and several kinds of rice and grains.

FISH
Your final stop in New Bedford should invariably be at **Kyler's Catch** (984-5150), 2 Washburn Street, just off I-195, exit 16. Tony Cardoza has spent his life selling fish and this splendid shop is the result, a showcase for a wide range of the freshest local seafood at prices well below your neighborhood fish market.

PORTUGUESE SPECIALTIES
Note: All listings are in New Bedford.

Several local companies make linguiça sausage right in front of your eyes. It's definitely different from what's available in supermarkets. But be careful: Hot is hot!

Amaral's Sausage Company (993-7645), 433 South Second Street. Open 7–3:30 weekdays, 8–11 Saturday. Linguiça and chouriço at wholesale prices. **New Bedford Linguiça Company** (992-9367), 56 Davis Street (North End). Smoked linguiça is the specialty here; walk in and the aroma hits you; watch it made through a glass window in the doors. **Lydia's Bakery** (992-1711), 1656 Acushnet Avenue. Open 7–5 daily. Portuguese breads and pastries baked daily. **Carmen's Portuguese Bakery** (996-9066), 478 Riet Street. Open 7–5 daily. Giant handmade Portuguese breads, malassadas (fried and sugared dough), and sweets. **Economy Bakery** (992-9138), 1685 Acushnet Avenue. Open 7–3 Monday through Saturday, 6–noon Sunday. Popular spot for "pops," small handmade Portuguese rolls, great for sandwiches or with dinner.

FARMS, GREENHOUSES, AND A WINERY
Westport River Vineyard and Winery (636-3412), 417 Hixbridge Road, New Bedford. Open daily April through December noon–5; tours Saturday and Sunday (winter tours by appointment). The source of genuinely distinguished vinifera wines: Chardonnay, Johannisberg Riesling, Pinot Noir Blanc, Methode Champenoise Sparklers, and special releases. "We made a climatic study and discovered that this area between Newport and Cape Cod offered the longest, sunniest growing season in New England," says Carol Russell about why she and her husband, Robert, chose Westport for their vineyard. More than 40 of the 110 acres (making this the physically largest vineyard in New England) on this former farm are now planted in vinifera grapes. There's a tasting room, small gallery, and gift shop. Inquire about frequent special events at the winery and about the **Long Acre House Wine and Food Education Center,** which offers programs in food and wine pairings.

Fisher Farms (636-3814), 784 Fisher Road, Dartmouth. Open seasonally, Monday through Friday 1–7, weekends 9–7. Fruits, vegetables, antiques, flower arrangements, crafts. **Figuerido's Greenhouses** (636-4084), 417 Hixbridge Road, Westport. Open weekdays 8–7:30, weekends 8–4:30.

Davoll's General Store

Working greenhouses specialize in herbs and plants. **Alan Haskell** (993-9047), 782 Shawmut Avenue, New Bedford. Generally acclaimed as a gardening guru whose clients come from around the country to find unusual plants and flowers. **Avant Gardens** (998-8819), High Hill Road, North Dartmouth. A source of unusual perennials.

SPECIAL SHOPS

Davoll's General Store (636-4530), 1228 Russells Mills Road in the middle of Russells Mills village. You can buy coffee and cornflakes here, but also a variety of glass, metal, pottery lamps, antique and reproduction furniture, century-old quilts, handwoven woolen and cloth rugs, collectibles, and, most surprising of all, a selection of autographed children's books. Beyond the basic general store are five more rooms crammed with merchandise. Inquire about special events. **Salt Marsh Pottery** (636-4813; 1-800-859-5028), 1167 Russells Mills Road on the edge of the village of Russells Mills. Open Monday through Saturday 10–6, Sunday noon–5. Housed in a vintage-1913 schoolhouse, the pottery employs some 20 artists producing handmade, hand-painted, decorative dishes, tiles, clocks, lamps, and tiled mirrors, all with wildflower impressions; distinctive magnets; seconds. Warning: It's difficult to leave without buying something. **Adriance Furnituremakers** (997-6812), 288 Gulf Road, Padanaram Village. Fine handcrafted Shaker and Colonial-style furniture, next to the Children's Museum (see *For Families*), very special. **Bedford Merchant** (997-9194), 28 William Street, New Bedford. Open Monday through Saturday 9–5. Quality gifts and home furnishings at modest prices; frequent sales and specials. **Dorothy Cox's Candies** (996-2465), 115 Huttleston Avenue (Route 6), Fairhaven. Open daily 10–8, until 9 in summer. All recipes are made in small batches and cooked in heavy copper kettles. The specialties are buttercrunch and a variety of hand-dipped chocolates. In business since 1928; ships throughout the United States.

SPECIAL EVENTS

Early May: Annual **WHALE Auction** at the Zeiterion Theatre, New Bedford (see *Entertainment*)—artwork and antique furniture to benefit the **Waterfront Historic Area League**.

Memorial Day: Probably the country's most moving day of the year in New Bedford. More than 300 names are read out at the harborside, each the name of a fisherman lost at sea since 1950. A bell is rung after each name, and family and friends throw flowers into the harbor.

June: **Padanaram Days**—sidewalk sale, trolley rides, music, Padanaram Village.

July: **Whaling City Festival** in Buttonwood Park, New Bedford, sunrise to sunset—giant flea market, car show, train rides.

Weekend of July 4: **Summerfest**—a waterfront festival featuring seafood, a tugboat rally, children's events, Blessing of the Fleet. Brewfest and winefest, Pier 3, New Bedford.

August, first weekend: The **Feast of the Blessed Sacrament,** music, dancing, and FOOD—you rent a skewer and brown your own meat over a pit. There are fava beans, bacalhau (dried cod fish) in a variety of sauces, linguiça sausage and other Madeiran delicacies, and plenty of Madeiran wine. Midway at Madeira Field in the North End, New Bedford.

September: Labor Day weekend, **Feast of Our Lady of Angels,** Fairhaven:

Portuguese foods, live entertainment, religious procession down Main Street.

October: **Westport Harvest Festival,** the weekend after Columbus Day, at Westport River Winery, Westport.

Early October, biennial (odd-numbered years): **John Manjiro Festival**— A Japanese cultural festival celebrating the 1841 rescue of a Japanese boy by a Fairhaven sea captain; the boy was raised in New Bedford and became a prominent citizen in his own country; in alternate years the festival is in Tosashimizu, Japan.

December: Celebrations at the **Rotch-Jones-Duff House** (specially decorated for Christmas) and a downtown, outdoor **choral sing. Christmas Shops,** sponsored by WHALE in New Bedford. **First Night** celebration, downtown New Bedford.

Fall River Area

From its source in the Watuppa Ponds, the Quequehan River (said to mean "Falling Water") drops 132 feet in less than a mile. You can see the river in very few places today—it's been built over—but its effect has been dramatic. Fall River remains one of the state's outstanding monuments to the textile industry. Its mammoth, five- and six-story granite mills rise in tiers above Mount Hope Bay. Its first power loom was set in motion in 1817, and by the turn of the century, the city boasted more than 100 mills and 4 million spindles. In 1900 Fall River produced enough yardage to wrap the earth at the equator 57 times.

In 1927 the industry sagged. Over the next few years millions of square feet of factory space were abandoned, and fire wiped out the city's business core. Fall River went into receivership in the 1930s and was governed by a state-appointed finance board for a decade. The last mill shut down in 1965.

Today Fall River's mills are filled by "needle trades"—electronics and metals firms—and also by some 80 factory outlets and off-price stores. While the outlets draw bargain hunters, Battleship Cove draws families with its lineup of naval vessels, restored carousel, and maritime museum. The Heritage State Park here has exhibits and landscaped, riverside grounds.

The Fabric of Fall River, a film shown at the Heritage State Park Visitors Center, tells how dozens of ethnic groups intermingled to form this unusual city. More than half of Fall River's residents are still classified as of "foreign stock." The spires of St. Anne's Church (a symbol for French Canadian residents) tower above the factory domes, and Columbia Street is lined with Portuguese shops, bakeries, and restaurants. The city is still divided into the dozen ethnic neighborhoods that began as self-contained mill villages.

AREA CODE: 508

GUIDANCE

Bristol County Visitors Bureau maintains a toll-free fulfillment line (1-800-288-6263) for requesting printed guides and brochures and a visitors center (675-5515) on I-195, eastbound between exits 1 and 2 in Swansea, open daily 9–5 (extended hours on Friday during holiday weekends).

Fall River outlets

The Fall River Chamber of Commerce (676-8226), 200 Pocasset Street, is increasingly visitor-friendly.

The Fall River Heritage State Park (675-5759), Battleship Cove. Open year-round 9–4:30 daily except Monday; daily Memorial Day to Labor Day. Staff answer questions about local sights, restaurants, and lodging.

GETTING THERE

By bus: **The SRTA Bus Terminal** (679-2335), 221 Second Street, Fall River, is served by **Bonanza,** connecting with Boston and New York, New Bedford, Padanaram Village, and Fairhaven.

By car: From Boston, take Route 24 to Route 79; the Battleship Cove exit is not well marked. From I-195 it's exit 4, just east of the Braga Bridge; from Route 79 south, take the Davol Street exit.

GETTING AROUND

Fall River is confusing. The three areas of interest—Battleship Cove, the historical society, and the factory outlets—are in three different parts of town. We suggest you begin at any of the sites in Battleship Cove and pick up a map and current pamphlet guides at the Heritage State Park (see *Guidance*). The Portuguese restaurants and bakeries on Columbia Street are nearby, and the Lizzie Borden Bed & Breakfast Museum (see *Museums*) is in the same neighborhood. Get directions to the historical society (more extensive Lizzie Borden exhibits), which is in the fancy, mill-owned neighborhood set just above downtown and overlooking the Taunton River. Most outlets are marked from I-95, exit 8A.

MEDICAL EMERGENCY

Charlton Memorial Hospital (676-0431), 7363 Highland Avenue, Fall River.

TO SEE

MUSEUMS

Fall River Heritage State Park (675-5759 or 675-5773), Battleship Cove. Open year-round 10–4. The handsome, brick visitors center stands in an 8½-acre landscaped park, the scene of frequent concerts and special events; the adjacent boathouse offers rental paddleboats. *The Fabric of Fall River* is shown at 2 PM. The film traces the city's history vividly, dwelling on the rigors of immigrants working 6 AM–6 PM shifts and on the accidents and deaths that befell child workers. It also dramatizes the vitality of the city in 1911, when President Taft visited for the Cotton Centennial. Exhibits include a loom and a variety of historical photo blowups. (Note the adjacent merry-go-round under *For Families*.)

Marine Museum (674-3533), 70 Water Street, Battleship Cove. Open daily year-round; Memorial Day through October, 9–5 weekdays, noon–5 Saturday, noon–4 Sundays and holidays. $4 adults, $3.50 seniors, $3 children. Housed in a former mill building of the American Print Works, this museum holds a fascinating collection of ship's models. It tells the story of the Fall River Line, from 1847 until 1937 the city's proudest advertisement. Exhibits include the 1880s Fall River Liner *Puritan*, which carried 1000 passengers and boasted electric lights, rich carpeting, mirrors, potted palms, and a full band to drown the thunder of paddle wheels. Many passengers slept in open berths, but the 360 staterooms cost only $1 more. A four-course dinner, served on the boat's personalized china, included steak and lobster for $1.50; a glass of wine was $.15 extra. The minicruise was favored by business tycoons bound for Newport and New York, and by honeymooners and young swingers just for the live bands. On the northbound route, $4 bought steerage and a new life. In all there are more than 100 ship's models on display, including the 28-foot *Titanic* built by 20th Century–Fox for a 1952 movie. Special slide presentations on the Fall River Line and the sinking of the *Titanic* are shown.

Fall River Historical Society (679-1071), 451 Rock Street. Open April through December, Tuesday through Friday 9–4:30 (but closed noon–1 for lunch); June through September, also weekends 1–5. $5 adults, $3 children 10–16. Built in 1843 for a mill owner near his mill, the building was moved in 1870 to this height of land, acquiring a mansard roof. The rich woodwork, elaborately carved doors, period chandeliers, and 14-foot ceilings in the front and back parlors are exceptional; displays fill 16 rooms and include exhibits on the mills and the Fall River Line and (what everyone comes to see) photos and descriptions of Lizzie Borden and her trial.

Lizzie Borden Bed & Breakfast Museum (675-7333), 92 Second Street, Fall River. Open for tours on the hour 11–3; $7.50 adults, $3.50

per child. Room rates—$150-200 per night—include a two-hour tour as well as breakfast! This grim-looking brown, mid-19th-century house across from the city bus terminal is a pilgrimage point for Lizzie Borden fans from the world over. You can now sleep in the rooms (complete with heavy Victorian furnishings) in which Andrew Jackson Borden and his wife, Abby, were found brutally murdered on August 4, 1892. Room rates include a breakfast similar to the one the Bordens ate on the morning they were murdered. The question of whether Lizzie was responsible (she was tried and acquitted) continues to be debated. Museum–B&B owner Martha McGinn inherited the house from her grandfather. No fewer than 45 "gifts," ranging from hatchet-shaped sugar cookies to a brick from the Borden home chimney ($100) are available by mail order as well as in the "museum."

FOR FAMILIES

✐ **USS *Massachusetts*** (678-1100; 1-800-533-3194), Battleship Cove. Open year-round 9 AM–sunset. $9 adults, $4.50 children 6–14, admission to all the boats. The "Big Mamie" was saved from the scrap pile with $300,000 in nickels and dimes contributed by Bay State residents. Children now swivel the 40mm gun mounts and clamber in and out of turrets. Women gawk at the 80-gallon stew pots. This onetime home for 2400 men has a soda fountain, three dental chairs, a sick bay, repair shops, and four mess halls. Groups (mostly Scouts) can spend the night, September through June 1, aboard the World War II attack submarine **USS *Lionfish***, moored next door. You can inspect the cramped living quarters for 120 men, the torpedo rooms, and the conning tower. The destroyer **USS *Joseph P. Kennedy, Jr.*,** also here, is the official state memorial to the 4500 who died in the Korean and Vietnam conflicts. Two World War II torpedo boats are also moored here. Gift store.

✐ **Fall River Carousel** (324-4300), Battleship Cove, adjacent to the Heritage State Park (see *Guidance*). Open seasonally. A restored, vintage-1920 merry-go-round that stood for many years in the local amusement park, to which trolleys ran from the city for many decades. Its 48 hand-painted horses and two chariots are now working again, housed in an elaborate pavilion with a snack bar.

✐ **HMS *Bounty*** (676-8226), Battleship Cove. Open seasonally 10–6, until 8 Friday and Saturday. Built specially for the MGM film *Mutiny on the Bounty*, this 412-ton replica was launched from Lunenberg, Nova Scotia, and sailed to Tahiti for filming. Visitors can explore the three levels and 120-foot length of the vessel. Admission fee.

✐ **Old Colony and Fall River Railroad Museum** (674-9340), Battleship Cove at Central and Water Streets. Open late June through Labor Day, daily noon–5, Saturdays 10–5, weekends in spring and fall. Nominal admission. Antique rail car exhibiting memorabilia, equipment, model trains, and steam engine.

✐ **Dighton Rock** (822-7537) in Dighton Rock State Park, Bay View Road, Berkley (Route 24, exit 10 west; left on Friends Street; follow signs). The building that shelters the rock is closed. In 1677, Cotton Mather was impressed by the rock but puzzled by its meaning, and scholars have yet to agree on who drew the pictographs, still clearly visible. The most popular explanation in this heavily Portuguese region is that they were drawn by Miguel Cortereal, a Portuguese explorer who disappeared in 1502 while sailing to Newfoundland in search of his brother Gaspar, who had failed to return from a voyage the year before. Miguel's signature, the Portuguese cross, and the year 1511 are said to be clearly visible on the rock (it depends on how you look at it). There are picnic tables, and a parking fee when someone is there to collect it.

TO DO

GOLF
Fall River Country Club (678-9374), 18 holes. **Fire Fly Country Club** (336-6622), Seekonk, 18 holes. A number of former farms in Rehoboth are now golf courses, among them **Rehoboth Country Club** (252-6259) and **Sun Valley Country Club,** both with 18 holes.
SWIMMING
The big beach is **Horseneck** (see "New Bedford Region"). In Swansea, visitors can also pay to swim at the town beach.

GREEN SPACE

Fall River's park system was designed by the firm of Frederick Law Olmsted in the 1870s. It includes Ruggles—North and South (now John F. Kennedy)—Parks (both include picnic space, tot lots, and wading pools), as well as the Durfee Green in the Highlands, Bradbury Green in the South End, and Northeastern Avenue.

Freetown State Forest (644-5522), Slab Bridge Road, Assonet. (Route 24, exit 10; bear left onto South Main Street; follow signs). More than 5000 acres of woodland, a wading pool, hiking paths, picnic tables with fireplaces. As you pass through Assonet (a picturesque old village with a millpond), note signs for **Profile Rock,** a wooded state reservation where paths lead to a striking profile of a Native American jutting out from an 80-foot-high pile of granite.

LODGING

Perryville Inn (252-9239), 157 Perryville Road, Rehoboth 02769. A 19th-century restored Victorian house sited on more than four wooded acres with a brook, mill pond, stone walls, and shaded paths, this B&B overlooks an 18-hole golf course. The four rooms are furnished with antiques and accented with handmade quilts; all have a private bath. Bicycles, including a tandem, are available for guests to explore nearby country roads. A horse-drawn hayride and hot-air balloon rides can be arranged. $65–95 includes a generous continental breakfast.

WHERE TO EAT

DINING OUT

T.A. Restaurant (673-5890), 408 South Main Street, Fall River. Open 11–10 daily, Sunday noon–9. Parking (handy in this part of town) in the rear. "T.A." stands for Tabacaria Acoreana, and you will hear more Portuguese than English spoken in this tastefully decorated restaurant. You might begin with kale soup and lunch on a chourico sandwich or marinated pork bits with steamed littlenecks and potatoes, and dine on shrimp St. Michael–style or steamed octopus. Most entrées are less than $10. The Portuguese wines are reasonably priced. Service is formal and courteous, the kind you would expect in a far more expensive restaurant.

White's of Westport (675-7185 or 993-2974), 66 State Road (Route 6), Westport. Open daily 11:30–10. Overlooking Lake Watuppa, the large SS *Priscilla* dining room replicates the grand salon of the Fall River Line's most luxurious boat. Good for seafood dinners ($12 range) and for reasonably priced luncheons.

Sagres Restaurant (675-7018), 181 Columbia Street, Fall River. Open Monday through Thursday 11–10, Friday and Saturday until 11, Sunday noon–10. A family-owned place specializing in a mix of Portuguese and Spanish dishes. Come for the *fado* singing on weekends. $6.50–13.

Venus de Milo (678-3901), Route 6, Swansea, I-195, exit 3. Open daily for lunch and dinner, noon–9. A long-established, family-owned restaurant, it's known for chowder and baked lobster. Excellent for seafood, but also good for prime rib and veal dishes. Entrées average $10.

Eagle (677-3788), 35 North Main Street, Fall River. Open daily for lunch and dinner. The gracefully curving, columned, vintage-1929 dining room is paneled in mahogany and studded with stained-glass windows. The extensive menu features pasta, seafood, and steak. Sunday brunch buffet (10–2) features 20 dishes. Dining and dancing on weekends. Dinner $11–20, early-bird specials from $5.95.

Public Clam Bakes at Francis Farms (252-3212), Rehoboth. Ten summer Sundays and holidays, rain or shine (but call to check). The 125-acre farm dates from the 1820s, and the public clambakes from the 1870s. Two pavilions can together accommodate around 1000 guests, and the clambakes are happenings done the traditional way, with lobsters, clams, corn, and so on. $21.75 adults, $7.75 children. Also inquire about Drovers Roasts and other special events; private clambakes can be scheduled anytime.

EATING OUT

Al Mac's Diner (679-5851), corner of President Avenue and Davol Street, Fall River. Open most days 6 AM–3 AM. A '50s replica of an original diner, with a Formica counter, heavy coffee mugs, and plenty of chrome. Norman and Joyce Gauthier are known for French meat pie (sausage and hamburger) and hearty basics like American chop suey and turkey dinners, as well as three-egg omelets and great pies such as blueberry–cream cheese and banana cream.

Water Street Cafe (672-8748), 36 Water Street Fall River. Open in summer Tuesday through Saturday for lunch; dinner Thursday through Sunday; Sunday brunch; inquire about off-season hours. Handy to the Battleship Cove sites, a good bet for grilled eggplant and hummus in a pocket, spinach fettucine, and shrimp or spicy cashew ginger pork medallions. Dinner entrées range $12.95–$14.95.

Le Page's Seafood Restaurant and Market (677-2180), 439 Martine Street (Route 6), Fall River. Open 7 AM–9 PM daily except holidays. Lebanese and local seafood dishes overlooking Watuppa Pond; outdoor terrace in season.

SELECTIVE SHOPPING

BOOKSTORE

Partners Village Store (636-2572), 999 Main Road, Westport. Small but choice selection of books.

FACTORY OUTLETS

Only a couple of decades ago, "factory outlet" meant a small room selling half-price "seconds" in the actual factory in which the product was made. Fall River was the first New England town to augment these traditional outlets with other off-price stores, the first (long before Kittery, Freeport, and North Conway) to cluster such stores for the convenience of bus groups. Fall River remains a shopping destination, with some 50 stores gathered within a few blocks just off Route 24 and I-195 in the **Heart District** (general information: 1-800-424-5519). The major complexes here are: **Tower Outlet Mill** (674-4646), 657 Quarry Street. Open daily 9–6, Friday until 8, Sunday noon–5. Includes the Burlington Coat Factory, Champion-Hanes, Izod-Monet sportswear, Luxury Linens, and Stetson Hats. **Wampanoag Mill Factory Outlet Center** (678-5242), 420 Quequechan Street. Open 9–5 weekdays, Friday until 8, Sunday noon–5. Includes Bay State Trading Co., the Curtain Factory Outlet, and Dress Express. **Quality Factory Outlets** (677-4949), 638 Quequechan Street. Open daily 9–6; Friday until 8, Sunday noon–6. Includes the Book Warehouse, Bugle Boy Factory Store, Corning/Revere, Levi's, Swank Jewelry, and Libbey Glass.

SPECIAL EVENTS

June: **Fall River Festival.**

Late June: **Santo Christo Feast,** Columbia Street, Fall River.

July: **Feast of St. Anne,** annual procession to the shrine of St. Anne. Dighton Indian Council Somerset Pow-Wow (phone: 401-941-5889).

August, second weekend: **Fall River Celebrates America**—waterfront festival includes parade, fireworks, live entertainment.

III. CENTRAL MASSACHUSETTS

The Nashoba Valley and Central Uplands
Worcester Area
Blackstone River Valley
Old Sturbridge Village/Brimfield Area
Quabbin Area

New Salem

KIMBERLY GRANT

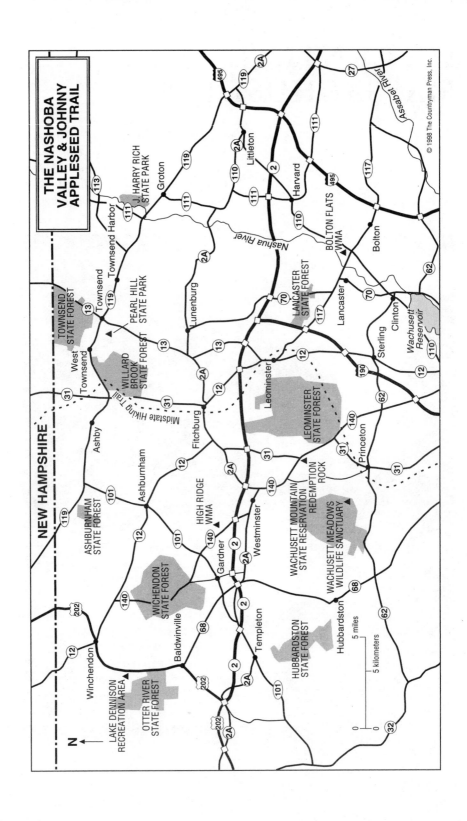

THE NASHOBA
VALLEY & JOHNNY
APPLESEED TRAIL

NEW HAMPSHIRE

© 1998 The Countryman Press, Inc.

The Nashoba Valley and Central Uplands

The Nashoba Valley and the Central Uplands are two distinct regions that complement each other beautifully. The Valley is a rolling and rural swath of farmland between the Nashua and Assabet Rivers. Beyond it lies the northern tier of Worcester County, a physical extension of New Hampshire's Monadnock region; both are hilly and forested. Each area is characterized by classic New England villages clustered companionably around classic commons.

Here there are two distinct and equally beautiful foliage seasons. In mid-May hundreds of thousands of apple trees blossom, and in mid-October the forested hillsides blaze with color. Apple orchards are, in fact, the single most striking feature of this landscape, an appropriate birthplace for John Chapman, better known as Johnny Appleseed, recently resurrected as the area's official symbol.

Despite creeping suburbanization, the Nashoba Valley remains a genuinely rural place. It is easily accessed from Boston via Route 2 to Harvard, and then onto country roads (great for bicycling) that meander south along the Nashua River and west along Route 62 through Bolton and Sterling to the town of Princeton, with Mount Wachusett—the state's second highest mountain—at its heart. Princeton boasted no fewer than 13 inns and hotels in the late 19th century, one of them atop the mountain summit (still accessible by road and hiking trails). Wachusett Mountain State Reservation now includes a popular ski area and many miles of hiking and cross-country trails.

North of Route 2, up Route 111 from Harvard to Groton or Route 13 to Townsend and then west on Route 119 to Ashby and the back roads into Ashburnham are all favorite bicycle routes, through countryside that's notably steeper and more forested than that to the south.

The country's furniture industry was centered here in the 19th century because of a fortuitous combination of skilled labor, ample water, and great stands of hardwood trees. There is still some furniture manufacturing, but the great 1938 hurricane wiped out most of the hardwoods, and many companies have since relocated. The story of the local furniture industry's entrepreneurs, inventors, and artisans is well told at the

Gardner Heritage State Park.

By the turn of the century, Gardner was known as Chair City, exporting its cane-seated, stenciled, and bentwood rocking chairs throughout the world. There are still about a dozen furniture makers in the Greater Gardner area and many furniture outlets.

The eastern part of this region—the countryside around Fitchburg— is known as Montachusett, a name coined by a Fitchburg newspaperman from the area's three visible mountains: Monadnock (just over the New Hampshire line) and Watatic on the north, and Wachusett on the south. Sited beyond the Boston commuter belt, this area is genuine country, a fact evident in the size of the small cities of Gardner and Fitchburg as well as in the byways of Ashburnham and Townsend.

The area's many public forests and lakes offer camping and swimming, and its back roads are well known to wheelmen. The Mid-State Hiking Trail traverses the ridgeline that runs down the center of the region.

Fitchburg, like most other New England factory towns, contains considerable ethnic diversity, although French Canadians (mostly Acadians from New Brunswick) and Scandinavians are the major groups. The Finnish community here is one of the oldest in the country. Thanks to a tradition of philanthropy and a relatively healthy economy based on plastics and electronics, Fitchburg has been able to raise money for a first-rate library, an excellent small art museum, a planetarium, and a civic-center complex that's frequently used for both amateur and professional sports and entertainment.

AREA CODE: 978

GUIDANCE

Johnny Appleseed Trail Visitors Center (534-2302), Route 2 westbound, between exits 34 and 35. Web site: http://appleseed.org. This is the visitor-oriented information source for the area. While its focus at this writing is a shade west of the Nashoba Valley, it is the only information source for this area as well.

Department of Environmental Management, Region 3 (368-0126), can furnish details about area forests and reservations.

GETTING THERE

By train: **The MBTA Commuter Rail** (1-800-392-6100) extends to Gardner on a limited basis, with more frequent runs to Fitchburg.

By bus: **Vermont Transit** (1-800-552-8737) serves Fitchburg, Gardner, and Winchendon. **Trailways–Peter Pan** (1-800-343-9999) serves Fitchburg from the Trailways Terminal from South Station, Boston.

By car: This region is an hour's drive west of Boston. Route 2 runs east– west, while I-495 arcs south–north.

MEDICAL EMERGENCY

Clinton Hospital (365-4531), 201 Highland Street, Clinton; the emergency room is open daily around the clock.

Burbank Hospital (343-5000), 275 Nichols Road, Fitchburg. **Heywood Memorial Hospital** (632-3420), 242 Green Street, Gardner.

VILLAGES

Ashby, Route 31 and Route 119. The First Parish meetinghouse, now the Unitarian church, has a Willard clock that has to be wound by hand. Also note the Town Library, Grange Hall (old town hall), Congregational church, town pump, watering trough, and bandstand where the Ashby Band, organized in 1887, holds forth on the common Wednesday evenings in summer.

Harvard. This town's common is often used for local festivities and is classically surrounded by white-steepled churches, a handsome library building, and a general store. The town's meandering rural roads, lined with orchards and gentlemen's farms, are ideal for bicycling. A Shaker community was established in Harvard in 1791 and lasted until 1919. The Shaker brothers and sisters rest under simple markers and in orderly rows in the old **Shaker Cemetery** on Shaker Road. A nearby nature trail leads to the top of Holy Hill, where in the mid-19th century the Shakers held outdoor services at which they danced and sang ecstatically and claimed to glimpse paradise. All that can be seen from the hill today is the Nashoba Valley—maybe not heaven, but not bad either. Some of the community's buildings still stand on Shaker Road, but one of the original 1790s structures was moved to **Fruitlands Museums** (see *To See—Museums*) in the 1920s, restored, and now houses an extensive Shaker crafts collection.

Lancaster. The first town in Worcester County, Lancaster was founded in 1642 by Thomas King, who had a trading post on what is now George Hill Road. Native Americans sacked the town in 1676, during King Philip's War, and carried off a number of prisoners, including Mary Rowlandson, the minister's wife. Her gripping account of captivity includes a vivid description of camping out with her captors under a rock on George Hill, now Rowlandson's Rock. Burned twice more by Native Americans before the settlement finally took root, Lancaster today is a notably serene and peaceful place. Its **First Church of Christ,** designed by Charles Bulfinch and built in 1816 of local brick laid in Flemish bond, has a Paul Revere bell and preserves its handsome horse sheds, the venue of an annual fall crafts festival (see *Special Events*). One of Bulfinch's finest efforts, the church reflects the beginning of classical Greek influence on American architecture. The **Lancaster Library,** also on the green, was built as a Civil War memorial, with a dome above its octagonal center and a luxurious 1920s children's room designed to look like a gentleman's study. Many of the old houses along Main Street belong to Atlantic Union College, operated by the Seventh-Day Adventist Church.

Groton

Groton. Founded in 1655, Groton was named for Puritan leader John Winthrop's ancestral home. Like so many other Nashoba Valley settlements, Groton was burned during King Philip's War; however, a Native American attack in 1694 was beaten off, and the town went on to prosper, as the elegant, tree-lined Main Street attests. In 1884 the Reverend Endicott Peabody, a Massachusetts Brahmin who had been a preacher on the Wild West frontier, founded **Groton School** and made the town a household name—at least in many well-to-do households. The prototypical elite American preparatory school, Groton was modeled after great British public schools. The campus complex, a quadrangle of ivy-covered buildings surrounded by playing fields, wouldn't look out of place in Sussex. Not as famous, but older by almost a century and more visible in town, is Groton's other prep school, **Lawrence Academy.** This school was founded in 1793 and named for its 19th-century benefactors, the wealthy industrialist brothers William and Amos Lawrence. The academy's attractive campus fronts on—and beautifies—Main Street (Route 119). Also on Main Street is the Old Groton Inn, now called the **Stagecoach Inn** (see *Lodging* and *Eating Out*). An inn has been at this spot, off and on, for more than 300 years. The present one incorporates the foundations of a tavern built in 1678.

Princeton, Route 31 and Route 62. The village frames an exceptional common at the southern foot of Mount Wachusett. The white-steepled Congregational church dates just from 1883 but has a Paul Revere bell. The ridge road from the village to Mount Wachusett is lined with 1890s country mansions and former inns. (Also see **Redemption Rock** and

Wachusett Mountain State Reservation under *Green Space* and
Wachusett Meadows under *To Do—Birding.*)

Templeton. Templeton common is unusually beautiful, the site of the
Narransett Historical Society, open July to September 1 on Saturday afternoons from 2–5; also the first Sunday afternoon of July and
August. Tea is served Saturday afternoons in the garden. Admission is
free, and it's a wonderful brick Federal house (vintage 1810) that's fully
furnished and includes a replica of an old country store, complete with
cracker barrel, cheese box, dry drugs, etc. Across the common a genuine 18th-century country store houses **Rubber Stampleton** (939-
5737), a shop specializing in unusual and design-your-own rubber
stamps and cards. **Country Mischief** (939-5460), also on the common,
is a Federal-era brick mansion, its 18 rooms filled with antiques and
imaginatively crafted items. Its **Country Cupboard Tearoom** (939-
1199; open Thursday through Monday 7–3, Wednesday 9–3) offers surprisingly full breakfast and lunch menus. Templeton common is just
one mile from Route 2.

Townsend, West Townsend, and **Townsend Harbor,** Route 119.
Townsend itself is a classic center with a steepled white church (built in
1731 with a slave balcony), brick mill, Victorian town hall, lineup of
shops in 19th-century wooden buildings, and common complete with
bandstand. In West Townsend the **Old Brick Store** was constructed as
a meetinghouse for the Universalist Restoration Society in 1849—with
the meeting hall on the second floor, stores and post office on the street.
The steeple is long gone, and the effect is unsettling but nice (the general store hasn't been fancied up). Townsend Harbor, east of Townsend,
contains some unusually handsome houses. It's unclear whether the
town's name stems from the fact that its three forts harbored settlers
from 18th-century Native American attacks or from its status as a stop—
and safe haven—on the Underground Railroad.

Winchendon is still known as Toy Town, a name earned when it was a
center for the wooden-toy industry and shipped its rocking horses all
over the world. The toy factories are gone, but a giant wooden horse
still dominates the small common.

TO SEE

MUSEUMS

Fruitlands Museums (456-3924), 102 Prospect Hill Road, Harvard. Open
10–5, Tuesday through Sunday and Monday holidays, from mid-May to
mid-October. (Grounds and walking trails are open year-round, 10–5.)
Admission $6 adults, $5 seniors, $3 children. Fruitlands is a complex of
four museums centered on the 18th-century farmhouse in which
Bronson Alcott—Louisa May Alcott's father and the model for Dr.
March in *Little Women*—and fellow transcendentalists attempted to

create a "New Eden" based on absurdly high principles. The group was not just vegetarian but would only eat "aspiring vegetables" that reached toward the sky (no carrots or potatoes), eschewed cotton (raised by slaves in the Deep South), and wouldn't wear silk or wool (which would exploit helpless creatures). Hungry, cold, and disillusioned, the group disbanded before the first winter was over. The old farmhouse is now a museum on the transcendentalist movement, with pictures, books, and relics of Alcott, Ralph Waldo Emerson, and other leaders, as well as exhibits about the New Eden experiment. Fruitlands was founded by Clara Endicott Sears, a Boston grande dame who was a collector ahead of her time; she began acquiring Shaker furniture and crafts, American portraits and landscape painting, and Native American artifacts in the 1920s, well before they were fashionable. Her remarkable collections are housed in several buildings. The picture gallery contains outstanding portraits by itinerant, early-19th-century artists and Hudson River School–style paintings of New England scenes by Thomas Cole, Albert Bierstadt, and Frederick Edwin Church. The Native American museum displays Henry David Thoreau's personal collection of arrowheads and projectile points. There is also King Philip's war club, stolen from Fruitlands in the 1970s and found at a yard sale in 1995. The grounds are beautiful, and the view of the Nashoba Valley from Prospect Hill is inspiring, especially in spring, when orchards are in bloom, and during fall foliage season. There are picnic tables, a gift shop, and a very pleasant "tearoom."

Fitchburg Art Museum (345-1157), 185 Elm Street, Fitchburg. Open Tuesday through Saturday 11–4, Sunday 1–4. Closed Monday and major holidays. Admission $3 (students and children free). Founded by Fitchburg native Eleanor Norcross, who spent most of her life in Paris, the museum has a permanent collection of some 1000 American and European paintings, prints, drawings, and sculptures, including works by George Bellows, Edward Hopper, Rockwell Kent, Raoul Dufy, and Edouard Vuillard. A spacious new wing is used for changing exhibitions.

Gardner State Heritage Park Visitors Center (630-1497), 26 Lake Street, Gardner. Open Tuesday through Saturday 9–4; noon–4 Sunday and Monday. Multimedia exhibits depict the history of furniture production, silversmithing, and the precision timing instruments invented and manufactured in town. There are also displays about the diverse ethnic groups—Swedish speakers from Finland and French-speaking Acadians from New Brunswick, for instance—who made up the labor force. The Heritage Park includes Dunn's Pond on Pearl Street, about a half mile east; it has a picnic area, beach, and changing facilities.

Gardner Museum (632-3277), 28 Pearl Street, Gardner. Open Tuesday through Friday 1–4. Housed in the town's brick Romanesque Revival former library, donated by furniture baron Levi Heywood. (The en-

Fruitlands Museums

trance was designed to resemble a chair.) A small permanent collection and changing exhibits on local history and crafts.

Fitchburg Historical Society (345-1157), 50 Grove Street, Fitchburg. Open Monday through Thursday 10–4, Sunday 2–4; closed summers. The collection includes a 300-year-old hurdy-gurdy and a rare 1777 "Vinegar" Bible, so called because of its misspelling of "vineyard."

Leominster Historical Society (537-5424), 17 School Street, Leominster. Open Tuesday through Thursday, 9–12; Friday 1–3. Leominster calls itself "Comb City" because of its long history of comb manufacturing, and the society has the country's largest comb collection. There are combs made of ivory, jade, silver, wood, and plastic, and some encrusted with rhinestones or precious gems. One particularly beautiful piece from China is shaped like a dragon.

National Plastics Center and Museum (537-9529), 210 Lancaster Street, Leominster. Historical exhibits detail the history of plastics, especially in Massachusetts. Hands-on plastics science education, current uses, "environmental" gallery.

FOR FAMILIES

✐ **Wallace Civic Center and Planetarium** (343-7900), John Fitch Highway, Fitchburg. Open daily 9–5.

✐ **Whalom Park** (342-3707), on Route 13 in Lunenburg (just east of Fitchburg). Open daily Memorial Day to Labor Day except Monday; weekends in spring and September. A family amusement area with a water slide, mini-train rides, some 50 carnival-style rides, and a beach and bathhouse on Whalom Lake. Admission $10.95 for all rides, $14.95 for rides and slide.

✐ **The Giant Chair,** on Elm Street in Gardner in front of Elm Street Elementary School. The city's most photographed object, this item is a replica of the chair that stood by the railroad depot in Gardner's furniture-making heyday. Twenty feet, 7 inches high, it weighs 3000 pounds and is believed to be the world's largest chair.

&⊘**Farmland Petting Zoo** (422-6666), Redstone Hill Road, Sterling (marked from Route 62 in Sterling). Open mid-May through October. The boast here is that the zoo contains one of North America's largest collections of endangered farm animals. The snack bar is open noon–2; picnickers welcome. Pony rides; birthday parties are a specialty. November through March hay- and horse-drawn sleigh rides are offered. $6.50 per child and adult, $6 senior.

TO DO

AERIAL LIFT
The **Skyride at Wachusett Mountain Ski Area** (464-2355) operates regularly in summer and fall. $4 round-trip ($3 one-way).

BICYCLING
Route 119, Route 12, and Route 31 are all popular, and there are endless possibilities along side roads. Cyclists long ago discovered the beauty of the Nashoba Valley's winding country roads and sweeping views. **Friendly Crossways,** a youth hostel on the Harvard-Littleton line (see *Lodging*), has been catering to bikers since 1947 and is a good source for route information. Particularly scenic in apple blossom and foliage seasons are Route 110 in Harvard; Route 117 in Bolton; Route 62 through Sterling and Princeton; Route 70 through Boylston; Route 119 through Townsend and Groton; and the 17-mile loop around Wachusett Reservoir.

BIRDING
Wachusett Mountain State Reservation (464-2987) is a birding mecca, especially in September, when thousands of hawks can be spotted in a single day.

Massachusetts Audubon Society properties include: **Wachusett Meadows Wildlife Sanctuary** (464-2712), Goodnow Road off Route 62, west of the common in Princeton. A 907-acre preserve with a boardwalk "swamp nature trail" and a variety of other walks through uplands, meadows, and woods. Admission fee. **Flat Rock Wildlife Sanctuary in Fitchburg** (537-9807); 315 acres with an excellent trail system. Enter from Flat Rock Road, the first right off Scott Road, which is off Ashby West Road. **Lincoln Woods Wildlife Sanctuary** (537-9807), 226 Union Street, Leominster; a 65-acre site with several ponds and pronounced glacial topography.

CANOEING
Nashoba Paddler (448-8699), PO Box 385, West Groton. Located on Route 225 on the banks of the unspoiled Nashua River, Nashoba Paddler rents canoes, gives instruction, and has a tour program for a variety of New England rivers.

GOLF

Gardner Municipal Golf Course (632-9703), Eaton Road, 18-hole public course. **Grand View Country Club** (534-9685), Wachusett Street, Leominster, 18 holes. **Maplewood Golf Course** (582-6694) in Lunenburg, nine holes.

FISHING

Fishing is permitted in **Wachusett Reservoir** from April 1 through October. A state license is required. Access points are Route 70, Gates 6–16; Route 140, Gates 17–24; Route 12/110, Gates 25–35; and Thomas Basin, West Boylston.

HIKING

The Mid-State Trail, utilizing and expanding a number of old trails, begins at Mount Watatic north of Route 119 in Ashby (you can park at the presently closed ski area). It follows the Waumpack Trail. (Also see *Green Space.*)

HORSEBACK RIDING

Bobby's Ranch (263-7165), off Route 2A in Littleton (behind Acton Mall). Open Wednesday through Sunday 9–6. Trails are through a 2000-acre conservation area around Kennedy Pond.

SWIMMING

Dunn's Pond in Gardner and **Whalom Lake** (see *To See* for both), as well as **Beaman Pond** in Ashby and **Wyman Lake** in Westminster, are all popular spots. (Also see *Green Space—Parks and State Forests.*)

CROSS-COUNTRY SKIING

Wachusett Mountain State Forest (464-2987), Princeton, is webbed with high-altitude cross-country trails. Rentals are available from the alpine area; see *Downhill Skiing.* There are trails at **Nashoba Winery** in Bolton and **Sterling Orchards** in Sterling (see *Lodging: Bed & Breakfasts*). (Also see *Green Space;* and inquire locally about conservation land trails.)

DOWNHILL SKIING

Wachusett Mountain Ski Area (464-2300), Mountain Road, Princeton. This is a privately operated ski area on a state reservation. A good mountain for families and for night skiing, with a vertical drop of 1000 feet. Facilities include an unusually attractive full-service restaurant and lounge as well as a cafeteria, nursery, rentals, and a ski shop. *Vertical drop:* 990 feet. *Terrain:* 18 trails. *Lifts:* One detachable quad, one triple, one double, one pony lift, one rope tow. *Ski school:* SKIwee program for children 5–12 offered weekends and holidays. *Rates:* $29 adult, $24 children weekdays; $35 adult, $27 children on weekends. Special rates for night skiing .

Nashoba Valley (978-692-3033), Powers Road, Westford (between Route 2A/119 and Route 110). Open late November through late March. A learners hill and local ski area, with only a 204-foot vertical drop but an extensive trail system, night skiing, and considerable lift capacity. *Lifts:* Three triple chairs, one double chair, one bar, four tows. *Snowmaking:*

100 percent. *Ski school:* Strong. *Rates:* $29 adults weekends, $20 weekdays; seniors $24 weekends, $15 weekdays; juniors $27 weekends, $18 weekdays.

GREEN SPACE

J. Harry Rich State Forest (597-8802), Route 119, Groton. An undeveloped 508-acre park with more than 6 miles of dirt roads and walking trails; canoeing.

New England Forestry Foundation properties in Groton include **Groton Place** (Route 225), a 54-acre former estate with a notable avenue of trees and walking and cross-country ski trails; and **Sabine Woods,** a 146-acre forest reserve with a nice swimming hole (adjoining Groton School and about 6 miles east of Groton village on Route 40).

Wachusett Reservoir (365-3272), Route 70 in Clinton and Boylston, was created in 1906 with a 206-foot-high dam across the south branch of the Nashua River. The reservoir has 37 miles of shoreline. South Dike extends 2 miles out into the water and has a footpath.

Redemption Rock, Route 31 in Princeton, is maintained by the Trustees of Reservations. In the pines sits a huge, flat table rock where, according to legend, King Philip's Native Americans agreed to ransom Mary White Rowlandson and her children. That event was in 1676, and Mrs. Rowlandson, wife of the first minister of Lancaster, wrote a best-seller about her kidnapping. The Mid-State Trail (see *To Do—Hiking*) passes through this spot and continues south to the top of Wachusett Mountain. (Also see the wildlife sanctuaries under *To Do—Birding.*)

PARKS AND STATE FORESTS

Ashburnham State Forest (939-8962), 2000 acres accessible from Route 119 in Ashburnham, is good for fishing, hiking, and hunting.

Willard Brook State Forest (597-8802), Route 119 in Townsend and Ashby, has 21 campsites and four year-round cabins; there's a sandy beach at Damon Pond. The miles of hiking and ski trails include one to **Trapp Falls.**

Lake Dennison State Park (297-1609), accessible from New Winchendon Road in Baldwinville, is part of the Otter River State Forest. It offers 150 campsites in two distinct areas, a swimming beach with bathhouse, 197 picnic tables and grills, fishing for bass and trout, and cross-country skiing.

Otter River State Forest (939-8962), accessible from New Winchendon Road, Baldwinville, has 119 campsites; also offers picnicking and swimming and a summer interpretive program, centered on Beaman Pond.

Pearl Hill State Park (597-8802), accessible via New Fitchburg Road from West Townsend; 1000 acres with 51 campsites; swimming, fishing, and picnicking; hiking and ski touring trails.

WALKS

Wachusett Mountain State Reservation (464-2987), with a full visitors center. At 2006 feet, Wachusett Mountain is the highest point in Massachusetts east of the Connecticut River. In the late 19th century a road was built to the summit, the site of a summer hotel until 1970. From the summit you can see Boston to the east, Mount Tom to the west, and Monadnock to the north. This spot is a popular hiking goal for local Scout groups. There are 20 ways to the top, but most people favor the 1½-mile Jack Frost Trail. The 1950-acre reservation also includes 17 miles of hiking and cross-country ski trails, as well as picnic facilities. (Also see *Downhill Skiing.*)

LODGING

INN

Stagecoach Inn (448-5614), Main Street (intersections of Route 40 and Route 119), Groton 01450. There has been an inn or a tavern on this spot for some 300 years, and the Stagecoach claims to have been "established" in 1678. The main building dates from early in this century, however, and has 17 comfortable but simply furnished units. The tavern attached to the inn serves breakfast, lunch, and dinner. An unusual amenity is a resident ghost, supposedly that of a Revolutionary War soldier, who is occasionally spotted by guests. $75–85 for rooms, $120 for suites, with full breakfast.

BED & BREAKFASTS

&. **Fernside** (464-2741; 1-800-545-2741; fax: 464-2065), 162 Mountain Road, Princeton 01541. An 1830s house to which wings and porches were added in the 1890s by the Girls' Vacation House Association of Boston, this was for a century a subsidized vacation retreat for working girls, mostly shop girls. Princeton residents Jocelyn and Richard Morrison have lovingly, painstakingly renovated the old place from top to bottom, preserving the unusual amount of common space on the first floor, now tastefully decorated with seating around several hearths. Still the most dramatic thing about this fabulous place is the view. Walk in the front door and on a beautiful day you are looking out onto the back terrace—with its more than 50-mile view extending east to Boston. Upstairs, many small rooms have been reduced to the original four, each luxuriously large, elegantly furnished, with working fireplaces and luxurious baths. Downstairs are two two-room suites, one handicapped accessible. Try to arrive in time for sunset, and inquire about making reservations at one of the two outstanding local restaurants (see *Dining Out*). Breakfast is a sumptuous, multicourse event served in the formal dining room, and there are many nearby paths on which to walk it off. $105–135 Sunday through Thursday, $125–155 Friday and Saturday.

The Rose Cottage (835-4034), 24 Worcester Street (Route 12), West Boylston 01583. A Gothic Revival (1850) house within sight of Wachusett Reservoir. Michael and Loretta Kittredge have been inn-keepers since 1985. There are five guest rooms, all furnished with antiques. The Carriage House, moved to its present site when the reservoir was created, has two apartments on the second floor and meeting space below. Rooms are $69.95 plus tax with full breakfast; the apartment is $325 a week.

☞ **Marble Farm** (827-5423), 41 Marble Road, Ashburnham 01430. Elizabeth and Dick Marble have restored the extended 18th-century farmhouse that's been in his family for five generations. It sits on 200 acres that include a pond good for fishing and swimming and is within walking distance of the Mid-State Trail (see *Hiking*). There are three rooms, including a first-floor double with private bath. $55–60 with "hearty country" continental breakfast.

The Maguire House Bed & Breakfast (827-5053), 30 Cobb Road, Ashburnham 01430. This unusually large and handsome house incor-porates an 18th-century tavern built by Captain Deliverance Davis, a Minuteman at Concord and Lexington. A local historian noted that un-der the next owner it was known as Uncle Tim's Tavern and "renowned from Canada to Boston"; the specialty of the house was fresh pickerel from nearby Upper Naukeag Lake. You can still walk down to the lake (where a rowboat awaits) through present owners Paul and Terry Maguire's 44 acres. There's a view of Mount Monadnock from the Wist-eria Room and the Rose Room, both inviting guest rooms with private bath. At this writing a first-floor guest room is evolving. Common space includes a large, comfortable living room and the dining room in which a "hearty" continental breakfast is served; $100–120.

Carter-Washburn House (365-2188), 34 Seven Bridge Road, Lancaster 01523. A classic Federal-style mansion built in 1812 for a local physi-cian. Quite grand. Rooms are high-ceilinged, and there are four con-necting parlors guests can use. There is a sunny exercise room and a gazebo that overlooks tranquil little Angel Pond. The three large guest rooms all have fireplaces and are furnished with antiques and original artwork. $55–70 with full breakfast.

Sterling Orchards (422-6595), 60 Kendall Hill Road, Sterling 01564. Bob Smiley offers two suites, each with a sitting room and private bath, in the 1740 homestead of his 100-acre farm. There is a seasonal farm stand and walking and cross-country ski trails. $65 with full country breakfast.

Amerscot House (897-6915), 61 West Acton Road, Stow 01775. An el-egant 1730s house with two guest rooms (private baths) and a suite. Homey touches include fresh flowers and handmade quilts. Owners Jerry and Doreen Gibson often invite guests to join them for Scottish country dancing (Doreen was born in Scotland). $95–115 (the high end is for the suite, which has a Jacuzzi), includes a full breakfast, frequently featuring fresh-baked scones.

The Harrington Farm Country Inn (464-5600), 178 Westminster Road, Princeton 01541. Accessed by a winding country road, the inn—a 1763 farmhouse—sits on the western slope of Mount Wachusett looking west toward the Berkshires, convenient to Mount Wachusett Ski Area and the hiking-trail system of the state reservation. Six pleasant upstairs rooms (three with private bath) and a suite have a comfortable, unfussy decor but there is no common space because this is primarily a justly popular restaurant (see *Dining Out*). $57.50–100 with continental breakfast.

Wood Farm (597-6477), 41 Worcester Road (Route 113), Townsend 01469 (¾ mile from the common). The oldest house in town: The old cape section dates from 1716 and has hardly changed since. Guests have the run of the 17-room house, in winter usually gathering around the fire in the keeping room, with its 8-foot-wide hearth. Owners Eric and Vi Stanway are hospitable and helpful. There are 13 acres with a stream running through them; there's a pond, too, good for both skating and swimming. There are bass in the pond, and the nearby Squanacook River is a famous trout stream. Three rooms share two baths. $45–65 with full, cooked-to-order breakfast.

MOTOR INN

Westminster Village Inn (874-5351; 1-800-342-1905), 9 Village Inn Road, Westminster 01473. Just off Route 2, this facility has recently received a total remake by its new owners, Wachusett Ski Resort. The core of the 11-building compound is a New England–style red-clapboard building that wanders a distance from the living room–like lobby (with fireplace) at its heart. Amenities include both indoor and outdoor pools, and steam, game, and exercise rooms. The 74 units are divided evenly between this main building and clusters of cottages in back. At this writing, rooms in the main building have been redecorated with reproduction antiques; a number of rooms have working fireplace. The Mid-State Trail crosses Route 2 on a new overpass at this point; it continues on the inn's property along a ridge and down to Redemption Rock in Princeton (see *Green Space*). $95–169 for a double, and guests receive discounts on dining. Inquire about frequent packages.

YOUTH HOSTEL

Friendly Crossways Youth Hostel and Conference Center (456-3649), 247 Littleton County Road, Harvard 01460. A large, comfortably furnished farmhouse set on a country road and 50 acres of land. This has been an American Youth Hostel since 1947, and managers Keith and Mary Veseenka Turnen are upholding the tradition of service and hospitality established by the previous long-term owners—Mary's parents. Hostelers pay $10–25 for a night in dorms or semiprivate rooms; other guests pay $13–30.

CAMPGROUNDS

Note the total of almost 250 campsites in the adjoining Lake Dennison, Otter River, Pearl Hill, and Willard Brook State Parks and Forests (see *Green Space*). Private campgrounds include **Howe's Camping** (827-4558) in Ashburnham, **Peaceful Acres** (928-4288) in Hubbardston, **Peaceful Pines** (939-5004) in Templeton, and **Pine Campgrounds** (386-7702) in Ashby.

WHERE TO EAT

DINING OUT

The Harrington Farm Restaurant (464-5600), 178 Westminster Road, Princeton. Open Wednesday through Sunday 5:30–9 by reservation. Chef-owner John Bomba, a graduate of the Hyde Park Culinary Institute and a veteran of top hotel kitchens, creates his own dishes. Driving up and up the winding road along a flank of Wachusett Mountain, you feel like Little Red Riding Hood on the way to Grandmother's house. It's well worth the trip! The setting is farmhouse traditional (a series of low-beamed rooms, well-spaced tables with fresh roses on each) but there's nothing traditional about the menu, which changes daily. Be warned that many of the appetizers can be as filling as a regular entrée; i.e., roasted quail and seared New York State foie gras with a warm salad of roasted beets and apple-cider vinaigrette ($8), or maple-cured salmon with sweet potato pancakes, cranberry and pear chutney, and maple crème fraîche ($7.75). Try purée of autumn squash soup with almonds and roasted garlic, and the roasted, semi-boneless, soy-marinated duckling (a half duck) with fried rice and ginger brandy–soaked apricots ($18). The selection of wines is good and remarkably reasonably priced. Most patrons do not pass up the dessert, maybe a chocolate soufflé topped with raspberry purée and crème fraîche or praline tuile. Entrées: $16.75 to $23.50.

The Victorian House (827-5646), 16 Maple Avenue (off Route 12), Ashburnham. This elegant restaurant, operated by the Saccone family since 1987, has a devoted following. Occupying a redbrick, mansard-roofed, 19th-century building, the restaurant has Victorian decor and an international menu. The menu changes with the season but often includes specials such as lobster Savannah and beef tournedos. Entrées are in the $20–35 range.

Sanoma (464-5775), Princeton Village (Route 140/31). Open for dinner Wednesday through Saturday, Sundays 12–7. A small chef-owned restaurant with a huge local reputation. Dimly lit and decorated with interesting art (for sale), a setting for serious dining. Appetizers include Louisiana crayfish and tasso cakes (ingredients include spicy Cajun ham) served with zucchini, summer squash, and onion confit splashed with a tangy Dijon-chili oil cream ($9), and steamed dim sum. Dinner might be a portobello mushroom and salmon roulade ($21), mushroom-crusted rib chops of venison ($28), or pan-roasted Cornish hen with merlot-cassis sauce ($18). The wine list is extensive.

The Brass Pineapple (297-0312), Route 12, Winchendon. Open Wednesday through Saturday for lunch and dinner, Sunday for brunch. Exotic dishes like ostrich and kangaroo but more traditional entrées too; extremely popular locally.

The 1761 Old Mill Restaurant (874-5941), Route 2A, Westminster. Open daily for lunch and dinner; Sunday breakfast and brunch from 9 AM. An area institution with an attractive old mill (a sawmill established in 1761) setting on a pond; small guests are given bread to feed the ducks. This is a busy, high-volume restaurant (very popular with wedding parties) but moderately priced, friendly, and welcoming. New England specialties include duck and prime rib. Entrées in the $12–18 range.

The Sterling Inn (422-6592), Route 12, Sterling. Closed Monday, otherwise open for lunch and dinner. This is a popular eating spot and has an authentic 1920s atmosphere. Dinner entrées include chicken supreme, broiled filet mignon with mushroom sauce, and prime rib. There are daily lunch and dinner specials, and daily baked desserts like midnight chocolate cake and Indian pudding. Dinner entrées: $11–23.

EATING OUT

Johnson's Drive-In (448-6840), Route 119, Groton. Open 6 AM daily year-round, until 10 PM in summer, until 9 in spring and fall, until 3 in winter except Thursday, Friday, and Saturday, when it's open until 8. This is a handy place to eat breakfast if you are setting out for a day of cross-country skiing or exploring; anytime for a basic burger or homemade ice cream. Also try the nightly specials such as roast turkey or fried haddock.

Slattery's Back Room (342-8880), 106 Lunenburg Street, Fitchburg. Open for lunch and dinner. A full menu from soup and sandwiches to lobster and prime rib, casual atmosphere, reasonably priced.

Sully's Eating and Drinking Place (632-7457), 74–76 Parker Street, Gardner. Open daily for lunch and dinner. This large family restaurant has an adjacent pub. Extensive menu; live comedy acts on Saturday night.

Skip's Blue Moon Diner (632-4333), 102 Main Street, Gardner. An authentic Worcester Lunch Car Company diner, circa 1950, in mint condition with a dining room in back. Nice atmosphere, reasonable prices, traditional family diner menu (the meat loaf is reliable; the pie is good).

Old Traveler's Restaurant (297-0740), 102 Front Street, Winchendon. Homestyle cooking and informal, friendly atmosphere.

Moran Square Diner (343-9549), 6 Myrtle Avenue (Route 2A), Fitchburg. A classic, much photographed 1940s diner. Besides fried chicken, burgers, and joe, you can also buy diner T-shirts.

Coffee on The Common, in the Village Country Store, on the Princeton common. Open 7 AM–3 PM, a cheerful small lunchroom with good soup, sandwiches, specials.

Jeanie's Lunch (939-8956), Route 2A/Route 202 in Templeton. Breakfast from 6 on weekdays, from 7 on Saturday, and from 8 on Sunday, open until 2. Clean, cheerful, and reasonably priced.

4 Corners Restaurant (448-3358 or 448-3359), junction of Route 119 and Route 225, Groton. Open daily for lunch and dinner. This Cantonese restaurant looks a little out of place in a Yankee woodscape, but it's a popular institution. The menu features chop suey, chow mein, and egg foo young. Sweet-and-sour shrimp and a variety of meat and seafood dishes are in the $7–10 range.

Stagecoach Inn (448-5614), Main Street (intersection of Route 40 and Route 119), Groton. Open for lunch and dinner. The inn's restaurant is a popular local watering hole and dining spot.

Fruitlands Museums Tea Room (456-3924), Prospect Hill, Harvard. Open early May through late October. Lunch served 1–3. The dining area, both inside and out, is one of the most pleasant spots around; the menu includes some Shaker recipes. Lunch in the $7–10 range. (See also *Museums*.)

Tish's Dishes, intersection of Route 62 and Route 140, a great spot on a nice day. A seasonal trailer serving good stuffed sandwiches and about anything you could want for lunch. Picnic tables.

ENTERTAINMENT

Thayer Symphony Orchestra (368-0041) stages six concerts (three classical and three popular) over the October-to-May season. Concerts are in Machlan Auditorium on the campus of Atlantic Union College on Main Street (Route 70), South Lancaster.

Indian Hill Symphony Orchestra (486-9524) presents four classical concerts each season at the Groton Dunstable Performing Arts Center (the Middle School), Route 119, Groton.

Sunset Concerts at Fruitlands Museums (456-3924), 102 Prospect Hill Road, Harvard. Thursday at 7:30 PM in July and August (see *Museums*).

Groton Center for the Arts (448-3001), Willowdale and Main Streets, PO Box 423, Groton 01450, is an information source about children's and adult performances.

Theatre at the Mount (632-3856), La Fontaine Fine Arts Center, Mount Wachusett Community College, Gardner (Route 140). July and August productions of popular classics by a community theater group.

The Guild Players Touring Company (582-9041), the 50 Main Street Playhouse, Lunenburg. Adult and children's productions are presented in this 100-seat theater during July and August.

High Tor Summer Theater (342-6888). From Fitchburg, take Route 2A/ Route 12 north on Main Street, then south on Route 31 for 100 yards; bear right at the Cumberland Farms and follow the sign. A long-established summer (July and August) theater, High Tor presents works ranging from Shakespeare to Molière, Ibsen, Chekhov, Miller, O'Neill, and more.

SELECTIVE SHOPPING

BOOKSTORE
Village Books (597-5900), 18 Main Street, Townsend. General, Native American, children's books.

A BREWERY AND A WINERY
Nashoba Valley Winery (779-5521), 100 Wattaquadoc Hill Road, Bolton. Open year-round 10–5. In Bolton Center, turn left at the yellow blinking light; the winery is ¼ mile on the left. A 45-acre orchard supplies a portion of the fruit used in these delicious fruit wines, including dry table wines from apples, pears, peaches, plums, blueberries, strawberries, and elderberries. Visitors can pick their own berries in summer and apples in fall. There is a tasting room and gift shop as well as trails through the orchard groves for walking or cross-country skiing. Hard Nashoba Cider is a specialty and owners Cindy and Richard Pelletier maintain a microbrewery (Nashoba Beer). Inquire about frequent special events. **Wachusett Brewing Co. Inc.** (874-9965), 175 State Road East, Westminster. Tours and tastings are offered Saturday at 1 and 3; a variety of fresh ales are brewed, kegged, and bottled.

CANDY
Hebert Candies (779-6586), 47 Sugar Road, Bolton. This justly famed candy and novelties store has a "make-your-own-sundae" bar.

CHEESE
Smith's Country Cheese (939-5738), 20 Otter River Road, Winchendon. Open Monday through Saturday. Award-winning Gouda and cheddar cheeses are made and sold here. **Westfield Farm Goat Dairy** (928-5110), 28 Worcester Road, Hubbardston, welcomes visitors year-round; eight different kinds of goat cheese are prepared for market.

CRAFTS SHOPS
The Museum Store at Fruitlands Museums (see *To See—Museums*) in Harvard sells Shaker and early American crafts reproductions. **Sterling Works of Art & Crafts** (534-9527), Sterling village center, behind the fire station. Open Wednesday through Saturday 10–5, Sunday noon–5:30. A former wooden mill building houses several studios and crafts displays, including a candle-making shop and glassblower.

HERBS
Herbal Acres (365-7841), 320 Harvard Road, Lancaster. Open daily May through October. An herb farm with a garden for viewing; gift shop.

KIMBERLY GRANT

ORCHARDS

Bolton Orchards (779-2733), junction of Route 110 and Route 117, Bolton, maintains a major farm stand/gift shop featuring local produce, baked goods, and crafts. **Carlson Orchards** (456-3916), Route 110, Harvard. Just north of Route 2, this retail farm market has plants, cut flowers, a deli, and a cider press. **Chase Farm** (486-3893), 509 Great Road, Littleton. This retail outlet sells local fruit and produce; open daily. **Clearview Farm** (422-6442), 4 Kendall Hill Road, Sterling. Pick-your-own peaches, pumpkins, pears, and raspberries. **Deershorn Farm Orchard** (365-3691), Chase Hill Road, Lancaster, off Route 62. Pick-your-own apples and strawberries, trailer rides through the orchards, picnic area. The farm stand on Route 62 sells native corn, pumpkins, vegetables, and cider, as well as apples, gifts, and fruit baskets. **George Hill Orchards** (365-4331), George Hill Road, South Lancaster. Open Sunday through Friday in season. Wagon and pony rides, cider-press viewing, face painting, snack bar on weekends and holidays. **Hillbrook Orchards** (448-3248), 170 Old Ayer Road, off Route 119, Groton. Open daily in season; pick-your-own apples.

Meadowbrook Orchards (365-7617), 209 Chace Hill Road, Sterling. Open daily 7–6 year-round. A 120-acre apple orchard with a farm store and bakery. Lunches served daily with soups, sandwiches, and specials. **Nagog Hill Farm** (486-3264), Nagog Hill Road, Littleton. Pick-your-own apples, peaches, and vegetables. Open daily in season. **Honey Pot Hill Orchards** (562-5666), 144 Sudbury Road, Stow. Open daily mid-September to mid-October for pick-your-own. **Flat Hill Orchards** (582-6756), 321 Elmwood Road, Lunenburg, is open daily August through December, selling its apples, peaches, plums, and nectarines. **Pease Orchard** (939-5324), 11 Phillipston Road, Templeton. A family orchard open weekends, Labor Day through Thanksgiving. **Spring Farm** (779-2898), 149 Main Street, Bolton, offers pick-your-own apples and pumpkins, a picnic area, and hot apple dumplings, homemade cider, and spice doughnuts.

FACTORY OUTLETS

In Gardner: **Chair City Wayside Furniture** (632-1120), 372 East Broadway (Route 2A). This four-story, boxlike granite building with a giant ladderback chair out front is just as unusual as it looks. Ladderback chairs are crafted on the premises, with a craftsman weaving fiber seating as you watch. Also a selection of locally made bedroom and dining room furniture. Monday, Wednesday, Thursday, Friday 9–5; Tuesday 9–8; Saturday 9–4. **The Factory Coop** (632-1447; 1-800-828-5556), 45 Logan Street, carries a variety of furniture. Open daily. **R. Smith Colonial Furniture** (632-3461), 289 South Main Street. Colonial-style furnishings and accessories. Open daily. **Gardner Furniture Outlet** (632-9661), 25 Kraft Street. Complete furniture line. Open daily.

Elsewhere: **Winchendon Furniture Co., Inc.** (297-0131), 13 Railroad Street, Winchendon. Furniture, lamps, and accessories. Adjacent discount warehouse. Open daily. **Dan's Pine Shop** (939-5687), 45 Elm Street (Route 302), Baldwinville. A 14-room showroom with an extensive line of Colonial and country furniture and accessories. **Templeton Colonial Furniture** (939-5504), 152 Baldwinville Road, Templeton. Locally manufactured, traditional furniture in cherry, maple, and pine.

SPECIAL EVENTS

May: **Spring Apple Blossom Festival,** held on the Harvard common, usually on the second or third weekend of the month. **May Apple Blossom Festival,** Nashoba Valley Winery, Bolton. Usually coincides with the Harvard festival and includes music, crafts tables, and wine tasting. **Art Walk**—guided tours of the studios and galleries of Groton Center, mid-May.

June (first Saturday): **Johnny Appleseed Day**—Leominster's annual salute to native son John Chapman, the Swedenborgian missionary who planted apple trees along frontier wagon routes.

July (early): The **Arthur M. Longsjo Jr. Memorial Bike Race,** a 50-mile event that attracts international participants, perpetuates the memory of a local Olympian who was both cyclist and speed skater.

October: **Horse Sheds Crafts Festival,** First Church of Christ, Lancaster, first weekend. **Three Apples Story Telling Festival**—a gathering of storytellers and musicians from around New England, the rest of the United States, and Canada. Harvard town common; first weekend.

Note: Inquire about summer and fall events at Wachusett Mountain (464-2300).

December: **Artisans Exhibit**—a juried exhibition of the work of area artists and craftspersons at the Groton Center for the Arts. First weekend.

Worcester Area

Worcester's civic symbol is the heart, representing its location in the heart of both Massachusetts and New England. The city's own heart seems to require major surgery every 20 years or so in the form of large-scale downtown renewal projects.

Currently, 21 acres in the city center are being redeveloped as part of the $255 million Medical City project. When completed, the hospital complex—which will employ thousands of people and attract patients from around the region—is expected to revitalize a somewhat lackluster downtown business district.

With a population of 170,000, Worcester is the second largest city in both the state and New England. It has a lot to boast about, including eight colleges and universities (a major medical school and teaching hospital among them), a first-rate art museum, an elegant concert hall, a resident theater company, a symphony orchestra, the region's premier rock concert facility, one of the country's oldest music festivals, a new $38 million convention center, interesting dining and diverse shopping (including the country's first urban enclosed designer outlet mall). Its proximity to Boston, about an hour's drive away, has had a somewhat inhibiting effect on the city's cultural life, but Worcester has its own special character.

Originally known by its Native American name, Quinsigamond, Worcester was handicapped by not being on a navigable waterway and wasn't permanently settled until 1713. Although the seat of Worcester County, the town was a placid, rural, inland outpost until the mid-19th century, when improved transportation—most importantly the opening in 1828 of the Blackstone Canal, linking Worcester with the port of Providence, Rhode Island—set off a manufacturing boom. With the arrival of the railroad era, Worcester's easy accessibility to markets and raw materials enabled it to blossom into an extraordinarily diversified manufacturing and commercial center.

The old colonial common off Main Street is the traditional hub of the city and a real link with Worcester's past. It has both a Civil War monument and a fenced-in graveyard where early settlers are buried. The city hall (modeled after the civic palace in Siena, Italy) stands on the north side of the common facing Main Street. In the 1970s, the common was modishly redesigned and given a reflecting pool that mirrors the city hall as part of the massive urban-renewal project that created Worcester Center, now the retail shopping complex called Worcester Common Outlets.

Worcester's simple 18th-century meetinghouse stood on the same site as city hall and it was here on July 17, 1776, that the patriot printer Isaiah Thomas—whose newspaper, *The Massachusetts Spy*, is considered the country's first—read the Declaration of Independence to a large crowd assembled on the common. It was the first such reading in New England.

Thomas remained in Worcester after the Revolution and his printing business grew until it was—for a period—the largest in the new United States. A passionate book collector, Thomas founded the American Antiquarian Society. The society's magnificent library, housed in a handsome neo-Federal building on Salisbury Street, holds an estimated two-thirds of all the material printed in the country before 1820.

The middle years of the 19th century were New England's Golden Age, characterized by a sunburst of Yankee ingenuity and creativity. Nowhere was the region's legendary breed of self-taught inventors and tinkerers busier than in Worcester. Within three years of each other in the mid-1850s, for example, Russell Hawes invented the first practical envelope-folding machine; George Crompton designed a revolutionary power loom; Thomas Blanchard developed a lathe for turning irregular forms; and Erastus B. Bigelow produced an improved carpet loom. The story of this extraordinary era is well told at the Worcester Historical Museum.

Factories turning out products of all sorts—grinding wheels, greeting cards, shredded wheat (another Worcester invention), Pullman cars, firearms, wire, carpets, and much more—sprang up around the city. Each factory usually became the focal point of a little world of its own, complete with bands, choral societies, sports teams, and social clubs. The factories had voracious appetites for labor, attracting workers from around the world to give Worcester an ethnic diversity unusual even by the polyglot standards of New England mill towns.

The carpet industry, for instance, employed Lebanese, Syrians, Turks, Assyrians, Albanians, Armenians (the first Armenian church in the country was in Worcester), Greeks, Romanians, and even Yorkshiremen. Swedes, not a major ethnic presence elsewhere in the state, once made up about a fifth of the population. Swedish immigrants began arriving in the 1860s, most going to work for the American Steel and Wire Company and Norton Company, one of the world's largest manufacturers of grinding wheels and abrasives.

Hispanics are the city's newest major ethnic group, arriving in significant numbers only in the last 20 years. Like other immigrants before them, Spanish speakers have mainly settled in tenement neighborhoods once home to other ethnic groups.

Two neighborhoods that still retain a lot of the old immigrant-era flavor are Shrewsbury and Water Streets. Originally an Irish enclave, Shrewsbury Street became Worcester's "Little Italy" early in this century and is still lined with diners and restaurants specializing in Italian cuisine from meatball subs (The Boulevard Diner) to focaccia (**Caffe Dolce**). Once the main drag of Worcester's original Jewish neighborhood, Water Street is now multiethnic, but you can still get a great pastrami sandwich and kosher pickle (Weintraub's Deli) and fresh-baked bagels (**Lederman's Bakery**).

Ethnic bars and social clubs still anchor many Worcester neighborhoods. Older sections are also often dotted with "three-deckers"—flat-roofed, three-story wooden tenements with porches in front and in back—that were first built to meet the needs of large immigrant families. Worcester has one of the greatest concentrations of this distinctively New England housing, once home for about half the city's population.

The redbrick mills of another age still loom large on the cityscape, but these days many have been converted to nonindustrial use. Some are now office buildings, others are restaurants or nightclubs; one (Tatnuck Bookseller) is a huge bookstore.

In the modern era, Worcester played a role in ushering in both the age of space travel and the sexual revolution. Robert Goddard, a professor at Clark University, fired the first liquid fuel rocket in the suburb of Auburn in 1926, and the birth control pill was developed at the Worcester Foundation for Experimental Biology in 1957.

Worcester today is more a service-oriented, white-collar town than an industrial, blue-collar one—the largest employer is the Universty of Massachusetts Medical Center —but its central location is still important. Some 6 million people live within about an hour's interstate drive of the city, which makes it ideal for meetings, conventions, and major musical events.

Once one of the squarest places in the state, Worcester has become the rock and pop music concert capital of New England, the regional venue of choice for the top touring bands and performers. Most popular music performances take place in the Centrum, a sizable multipurpose arena also used for sports events, on downtown Foster Street, adjoining the new (1997) convention center. Because of the restaurants and lounges that have sprung up to serve the Centrum and convention center crowds, a city that used to go to bed early now has some pretty lively nightlife.

WORCESTER-AREA FIRSTS

Pink Flamingo lawn ornaments: These ubiquitous suburban decorations were first produced in the 1950s by Union Products, a Leominster plastics company.

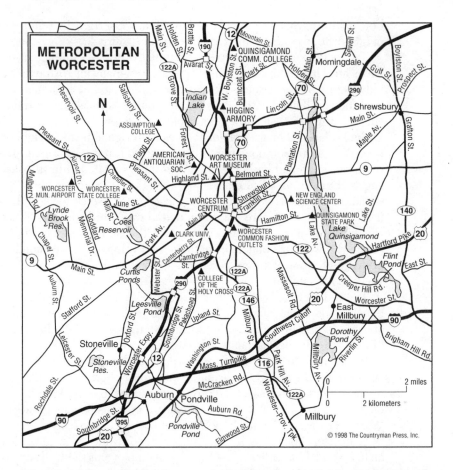

First American disc jockey to air the Beatles: Dick "the Derby" Smith of radio station WORC in Worcester. The Fab Four were so grateful they gave Smith the gold record for their hit "She Loves You."

The monkey wrench: Invented by Loring Coes of Worcester in 1840.

The smiley face: The cheery yellow button was designed by Worcester graphic artist Harvey Ball in 1963 as promotion for a local insurance company.

Shredded Wheat: Invented by Henry Perky in 1890. At the turn of the century, Worcester claimed to be "Shredded Wheat capital of the world."

Drugstore valentines: Esther Howland of Worcester, a pioneer female entrepreneur, founded the New England Valentine Co. in 1874 and mass-produced Valentine's Day cards for the first time.

White chocolate: Developed by Hebert's Candies of Shrewsbury and first sold in the early 1950s.

AREA CODE: 508

GUIDANCE

Worcester County Convention & Visitors Bureau (753-2920), 33 Waldo Street, Worcester 01608.

City Line (792-9400). Free interactive telephone information service operated by the *Worcester Telegram & Gazette,* the daily newspaper. Includes up-to-date information on dining, entertainment, and special events and activities.

Magazines: *Worcester Magazine* (755-8004); *Worcester Phoenix* (832-9800).

GETTING THERE

By car: Worcester is 40 miles from Boston via Route 9 or the Mass. Pike. Coming from Boston, take exit 11 off the turnpike. Use exit 10 if approaching the city from the south or west.

By bus: **Peter Pan–Trailways Bus Lines** (754-4600; 1-800-237-8747). The bus station is at 75 Madison Street.

By train: **MBTA** commuter Worcester-Boston service (722-3200; 1-800-392-6100). The railway station is at 45 Shrewsbury Street.

GETTING AROUND

Worcester's attractions are widely scattered, and a car is necessary to see the city properly.

PARKING

There is a 4300-car garage in Worcester Common Fashion Outlets, between the Centrum and Convention Center complex and the common, and several large municipal lots and garages are located downtown. When completed, the Medical City complex will include a 1000-car garage.

MEDICAL EMERGENCY

University of Massachusetts Medical Center (856-0011), 55 Lake Avenue North.

Memorial Healthcare (793-6611), 119 Belmont Street.

Fallon Healthcare Systems: Hospital, 25 Winthrop Street (852-0600); clinic, 630 Plantation Street (753-0811).

TO SEE

Massachusetts Avenue Historic District, a parkway off Salisbury Street laid out in the late 19th century and lined with stately Victorian and Edwardian homes built in Queen Anne and other period styles by local business and professional men. Teddy Roosevelt paraded down the avenue in an open carriage in 1902.

Goddard Exhibition (793-7572), Goddard Library, Clark University, 950 Main Street. Open Monday through Friday 10–4. The space age was born in 1926 when Dr. Robert Goddard, a physics professor at Clark, fired a rocket 41 feet in the air from a hilltop in Auburn, a Worcester suburb. Goddard's notebooks and patents, along with photos and rocket memorabilia, are displayed in the handsome library his alma mater named for him.

MUSEUMS

Worcester Art Museum (799-4406), 55 Salisbury Street. Open Wednesday through Friday 10–5, Saturday 10–5, Sunday 11–5 (closed Monday and Tuesday). $6 adults; $4 students, seniors, and youths 13–18. Marked from I-290, Lincoln Square exit. First opened in 1898 (and extensively renovated for its centennial celebration in 1998), the museum ranks among the country's best, with the region's second largest permanent collection—more than 30,000 works of art spanning 5000 years. There are fine examples of Greek, Roman, pre-Columbian, Asian, Persian, European, and American art. The Early-American paintings displayed are outstanding. The museum was one of the first to begin collecting photographs as fine art, and there are constantly changing exhibits of photographs from the Civil War era to the present. There is also a complete room from a 12th-century French monastery and a group of splendid Roman mosaics from Antioch. The museum has a gift shop, restaurant, and in summer a pleasant garden café.

Worcester Historical Museum (753-8278), 30 Elm Street. Open Tuesday through Saturday 10–4, Sunday 1–4. Devoted to local history, the museum's handsome brick building is also the headquarters of the Worcester Historical Society. There are interesting displays tracing the city's evolution from frontier village to industrial city, and frequently changing exhibitions. The library has 10,000 volumes. A block away from the museum, at 40 Highland Street, is the **Salisbury Mansion,** residence of the prominent Salisbury family from 1772 to 1852. One of Worcester's few surviving 18th-century buildings, the mansion has been been restored by the historical society to re-create the home life of the Salisburys around 1830.

American Antiquarian Society (755-5221), 185 Salisbury Street. Open for guided tours Wednesday at 2 PM and to qualified researchers Monday through Friday 9–5. Founded by Isaiah Thomas in 1812, the society specializes in American printed materials—books, newspapers, magazines, broadsides, and sheet music—from the mid-17th century through 1876. Thomas's original flatbed press and selections from the society's vast collection of Americana are displayed. The library is superb but open only to scholars working on specific projects.

American Sanitary Plumbing Museum (754-9453), 39 Piedmont Street. Open Tuesday and Thursday 10–2 (closed July and August). The only one of its kind in the country, this museum—the personal collection of a family in the plumbing business for several generations—has a unique perspective on American domestic life. Among its treasures are a replica of the toilet George Washington used at Mount Vernon and a primitive 1920s prototype of the dishwasher called an electric sink. Lots of plumbers' tools and fancy chamber pots, too.

FOR FAMILIES

Higgins Armory Museum (853-6015), 100 Barber Avenue, off Gold Star Boulevard. Adults $4.75, seniors $4, children 6–16, $3.75. Open Tuesday through Saturday 10–4, Sunday noon–4. Located in an industrial section, this unusual museum is the result of the extensive research into ancient metallurgy by local industrialist John Woodman Higgins. While trying to rediscover the techniques that enabled medieval armorers to produce such fine steel, Higgins collected suits of armor—more than 100 of them. Dramatically displayed in a great hall—like that of a castle—the collection includes very rare and beautiful armor, such as the tournament armor of kings and special suits for children and dogs. Also on view are banners, swords, shields, battle-axes, maces, and crossbows, along with period paintings, stained glass, wood carvings, tapestries, and a replica of an armorer's workshop. There is a gallery with armor reproductions that museum visitors can try on, and also a gift shop selling all sorts of knightly memorabilia.

New England Science Center (791-9211), 222 Harrington Way. Open Monday through Saturday 10–5, Sunday noon–5. Adults $6; seniors, children 3-16, and students, $4. A museum and wildlife center set in a 60-acre park that includes a zoo complete with wolves, mountain lions, polar bears—and a miniature railroad. There are also science exhibits, an observatory, a planetarium, and nature trails.

TO DO

Providence and Worcester Railroad (755-4000). This working railroad offers passenger excursions, most frequently in foliage season. Departures from Worcester Railway Station.

GREEN SPACE

Quinsigamond State Park (757-2140), off Lake Avenue on Lake Quinsigamond, consists of two areas: Regatta Point has a swimming beach, changing facilities, and sailboats; Lake Park has swimming and picnic areas as well as tennis courts and other sports facilities. The park is frequently the site of regional and national collegiate rowing competitions.

Rutland State Park (886-6333), a 1900-acre park on Route 122 in Rutland, has swimming and picnic areas on Whitehall Pond and fishing and boat-launching ramps on Long Pond.

Elm Park, off Park Avenue, established in 1854, is the oldest public park—as distinguished from town green or common—in the nation. Generations of Worcesterites have had their wedding photos taken on the ornate Victorian bridge over the pleasing pond.

Moore State Park (792-3969), off Route 31 in Paxton, is a 350-acre former estate with a 19th-century sawmill, fishing, and scenic walks.

Wachusett Mountain State Reservation (464-2987), Mountain Road, Princeton; a 1600-acre park dominated by Mount Wachusett. At an elevation of just over 2000 feet, the summit of the mountain is the highest point in Worcester County, with a view on a clear day that includes Mount

Monadnock, the White Mountains, and the Boston skyline. Hiking, cross-country skiing, and an alpine ski area, open for night skiing, that is the area's largest (see "The Nashoba Valley and Central Uplands").

LODGING

HOTELS

Crown Plaza Hotel (791-1600), 10 Lincoln Square 01608, at the junction of I-21 and Route 9. A 245-room hotel with indoor and outdoor pools, sauna, and exercise room. Standard rooms $109–129.

Beechwood Inn (754-5789), 363 Plantation Street. Adjacent to the Medical Center complex and Biotechnology Park, this distinctive, circular building has 58 deluxe rooms. The excellent restaurant has outdoor dining on the terrace. Standard room $129, junior suite $139.

Holiday Inn (852-4000), 500 Lincoln Street 01065. The 142-room hotel has an indoor pool and a restaurant. Standard rooms $109; suites $160.

Clarion Suites Hotel (753-3512), 70 Southbridge Street 01608. A good downtown location and 105 one- and two-bedroom suites. Single $85, double $95.

BED & BREAKFASTS
See "The Nashoba Valley and Central Uplands," "Old Sturbridge Village/ Brimfield Area," or "Blackstone River Valley."

WHERE TO EAT

DINING OUT

Arturo's Ristorante (755-5640), 411 Chandler Street. Open 11:30 AM– 11:30 PM Monday through Saturday; until 10 PM Sunday. Extensive northern Italian menu. Pleasant dining room. Arturo and Dianne Cartagenova have a winning touch with decor and with light but heavy-on-the-herbs-and-vegetables meat dishes and pastas. $10–20. If you don't want to go the whole three courses, the **Pizzeria** at Arturo's features a wood-fired oven for pizza or roast chicken. $7–10.

Harlequin Restaurant (754-5789), 363 Plantation Street, in the Beechwood Inn (see *Hotels*). Open 6:30–10:30 AM, 11:30 AM–2:30 PM; 6–10 PM for dinner. The long, elegant dining room and terrace are the setting for cuisine that's distinctly American with interesting international touches, such as linguine with smoked chicken in Cajun cream sauce, and ribeye steak served with demiglaze. $20–30.

Struck Cafe (757-1670), 415 Chandler Street. Open Monday through Friday for lunch and dinner, Saturday for dinner only. Simple decor, mismatched china, great food: soups and salads as well as light entrées at noon ($3–8) and an elegant à la carte dinner menu that changes every few months ($15–25). Reservations suggested for dinner.

El Morocco (756-7117), 100 Wall Street. Open 11:30–10 Monday through Thursday, Friday to 10:30, Saturday 4–11, Sunday 4–9 for dinner. Anchoring a hilltop in the old Lebanese neighborhood, "The El" is a local institution, serving authentic Middle Eastern food. Lamb and beef kabobs are a particular specialty. Entrées $10–25.

Maxwell Silverman's Toolhouse (755-1200), 25 Union Street at Lincoln Square. Open 11:30–4 and 5–10 Monday through Friday; until 11 Saturday; 4–9 PM Sunday. Housed in a 19th-century factory building and trendily decorated with old tools and machine parts. Dinner $11–20.

Sole Proprietor (798-3474), 118 Highland Street. Open Monday through Thursday, 11:30–10; Friday, 11–11; Saturday, noon–11; Sunday, 4–9. This very popular seafood restaurant offers more than 30 varieties of fresh fish—the alphabetically arranged menu runs from amberjack to wahoo—served baked, broiled, fried, steamed, grilled, or blackened Cajun style. Entreés $15–22.

Pasta Pantry (756-4560), 806 Pleasant Street. Open 11:30–9, Monday through Saturday; closed Sunday. Relaxed bistro atmosphere. The wide variety of freshly made pasta dishes includes capellini, fettucine, ravioli, and linguine. Most entrées $5–10. BYOB.

Crescent City Steak House (757-1450), 278 Shrewsbury Street. Open Monday through Friday 10–11, Saturday 3–11, Sunday 10–3 for brunch and 3–9 for dinner. Unabashedly dedicated to the proposition that there is nothing like a thick, sizzling steak. Rack of lamb and swordfish tenderloin are also specialties. Entrées $15–25.

Angela's (756-7995), 257 Park Avenue. Open Sunday through Thursday 4–10:30, Friday and Saturday 4–11:30. Homestyle Italian cuisine in a friendly, bistrolike atmosphere. Enormous portions (the homemade manicotti is the size of a burrito) and moderate prices. Pizza like a Neapolitan grandmother would make. Most entrées less than $10. Fried dough served with all meals. No reservations.

O'Connor's Restaurant and Bar (853-0789), 1160 West Boylston Street. Open Monday through Thursday 11:30–10, Friday and Saturday 11:30 AM–midnight. A large, cheerful restaurant with the cozy feel of an Irish pub. The menu is as Celtic as the staff. Among the specialties are Paddy's whiskey chicken and shrimp, Guinness-enhanced beef stew, and Bailey's Irish Cream pie. Entrées $8–12.

Restaurant at Tatnuck Bookseller (756-7644), 335 Chandler Street. Open Monday through Thursday 8–10, Friday from 8 and Saturday from 9 until midnight; Sunday 9–6. Not just a bookstore café, this is a serious restaurant with an extensive, eclectic, and constantly changing menu that usually includes stir-fry and pasta. There is a patio for outdoor dining. Lunch entreés $6–10, dinner $10–15. (Also see *Selective Shopping*).

KIMBERLY GRANT

The Boulevard Diner

DINERING OUT

Once home of the Worcester Lunch Car Company, the country's leading diner manufacturer in its day, Worcester still has more than a dozen old-fashioned diners, more than any other city in the region. The following are the most popular and atmospheric.

Boulevard Diner (791-4535), 155 Shrewsbury Street. Open 7 AM–4 AM. A classic and much photographed 1930s diner, the Boulevard has a mostly Italian menu. The lasagna and meatball subs are particularly good.

Parkway Diner (753-9968), 148 Shrewsbury Street. Open Monday through Thursday 6 AM–9 PM, Friday and Saturday until midnight. This neighborhood institution serves traditional southern Italian dishes. Hot sausages or meatballs with eggs are a breakfast specialty.

Kenmore Diner (753-9541), 250 Franklin Street. A cozy nest for night owls, the Kenmore is open from 11 PM to 11 AM. A remodeled 1940s diner, it retains the original beautiful black marble countertops and old-fashioned ceramic coffee mugs. Great corn muffins, good coffee and breakfast (including steak and eggs) served all night.

Miss Worcester (752-1310), 300 Southbridge Street. Open for breakfast and lunch; closed Sundays. Affectionately known as Miss Woo to its many regulars, this classic 50-year-old diner stands across the street from the former Worcester Lunch Car Company factory, where it was built.

Ralph's Chadwick Square Diner (753-9543), 95 Prescott Street. Open 6 PM–2 AM. An authentic old diner attached to a live music club in a former factory building. Burgers and chili are specialties.

Corner Lunch (755-5576), 133 Lamartine Street. Open 6 AM–3 PM. A shimmering stainless-steel 1950s exterior, cool neon sign, and booths upholstered in glittery gold vinyl. Great home fries.

EATING OUT

East Park Grille (no phone), 172 Shrewsbury Street. Open Tuesday through Saturday 4–10. Casual atmosphere, seafood the specialty. Cash only.

El Basha Restaurant (797-0884), 424 Belmont Street. Open Monday through Saturday 11:30–10. Distinctly unpretentious but noted for savory Lebanese cuisine.

La Patisserie (756-1454), 252 Commercial Street. Monday through Saturday 7 AM–3:30 PM; Sunday 8 AM–2 PM. Known for its homemade soups and sandwiches.

Living Earth Cafe (753-1896), 232 Chandler Street at Park Avenue. Pleasant café restaurant attached to a health food store. Ingredients used are fresh, organic, and locally grown. Great soups (try the tofu stew) and salads but also exotic low-fat meat dishes such as ostrich burger and buffalo chili.

Coney Island Lunch (753-4362), 158 Southbridge Street. Open Sunday, Monday, Wednesday, and Thursday 9:30–8; Friday and Saturday 9:30–10 PM. Hot dog heaven. Perfectly cooked wieners smothered with toppings and served in a warm bun. A Worcester institution since 1918 and worth a visit just to see the restored kitsch classic neon sign: a large hand holding a hot dog dripping bright yellow mustard.

Weintraub's Deli (756-7870), 126 Water Street. Open 9–8 Tuesday through Sunday, until 4 PM Monday. Still doing business in what was the city's first Jewish immigrant neighborhood. An authentic old-style deli with great Romanian pastrami sandwiches. Cash only.

THE PUB SCENE

Brew City Grill and Brew House (752-3862), 104 Shrewsbury Street. Beer central. At any given time at least 30 different beers on tap, including many imported varieties and exotic domestics such as Pilgrim blueberry beer. Pub-style menu. Open noon–midnight, Sunday through Tuesday; until 2 AM Wednesday through Saturday.

Leitrim Pub (798-2447), 265 Park Avenue. A traditional Irish bar that banished "Danny Boy" from the jukebox and now attracts a largely young, collegiate crowd. Open Monday through Friday, 4 PM–2 AM.

ENTERTAINMENT

Centrum (755-6800), 50 Foster Street. Well-designed and centrally located, this auditorium hosts more big-name rock and popular music concerts than any other facility in New England.

Mechanics Hall (752-5608), 321 Main Street. Built in 1857 primarily for lectures (Charles Dickens spoke here), the hall fell on hard times in this century and was long used primarily for wrestling matches and roller derbies. Restored as a bicentennial project, the acoustically superb hall is now used for concerts, balls, and theatrical presentations.

Mechanics Hall

Foothills Theatre (754-4018), Worcester Center, 100 Front Street. The city's resident professional theater company, it stages eight productions during the September through April season.

SELECTIVE SHOPPING

There are a variety of shops along Main Street, but downtown Worcester's shopping magnet is **Worcester Common Outlets** (798-2581) in the impressively spiffed-up former Worcester Center Galleria. Open Monday through Saturday 10–9, Sunday 11–7. The nearly 120 stores in the enclosed, two-level atrium mall—most outlets for designer lines at discounts of 30 to 70 percent—include Saks Fifth Avenue, Polo Ralph Lauren, Filene's Basement, and Barneys New York. There is a large food court and attached parking garage.

Note: All shops are in Worcester unless otherwise indicated.

Spag's Supply (799-2570), Route 9, Shrewsbury. A no-nonsense, barnlike place that carries everything from kitchenware and automotive supplies to beauty aids and fishing tackle. Regionally renowned for its bargains and hard-to-find items, Spag's is always crowded. Open Monday through Friday 9–9; Saturday 8 AM–9 PM; Sunday noon–6.

Worcester Center for Crafts (753-8183), 25 Sagamore Road. One of the country's oldest crafts complexes. The center shop carries quality crafts as well as craft supplies. Open Tuesday through Saturday 10–5.

Charlie's Surplus and Athletic Supply (752-7121), 116 Water Street. Open 10–6 Monday through Saturday, 9–4 Sunday. This unpretentious walk-up emporium looks more like a warehouse than a store but is piled high with boxes of name-brand shoes and sneakers selling at prices often a third less, or better, than those of fancier places. No credit cards.

Tatnuck Bookseller Marketplace (756-7644; 1-800-642-6657), 335 Chandler Street (Route 122). Open Monday through Thursday 8–10; Friday from 8 and Saturday from 9 until midnight; Sunday 9–6. Housed in a cavernous former machine-tool factory, this is the largest independent bookseller in Massachusetts. The more than 5 miles of bookshelves hold some 500,000 volumes. There are separate departments for secondhand, rare, foreign language, and children's books as well as books about Worcester or by Worcester authors. Also candle, stationery, and gift shops, and an excellent full-service restaurant with an outdoor patio (see *Dining Out*).

SPECIAL EVENTS

May: **Eastern Sprints Regatta,** intercollegiate rowing competition at Regatta Point on Lake Quinsigamond.

October: **Worcester County Music Association Festival.** Held annually since 1858, the festival features major ensembles and internationally known artists.

December: **Handel's Messiah,** performed in Mechanics Hall (321 Main Street) by the Worcester Chorus and Orchestra. **First Night,** a community-wide cultural New Year's Eve celebration featuring mime, poetry readings, theater, dance, and music.

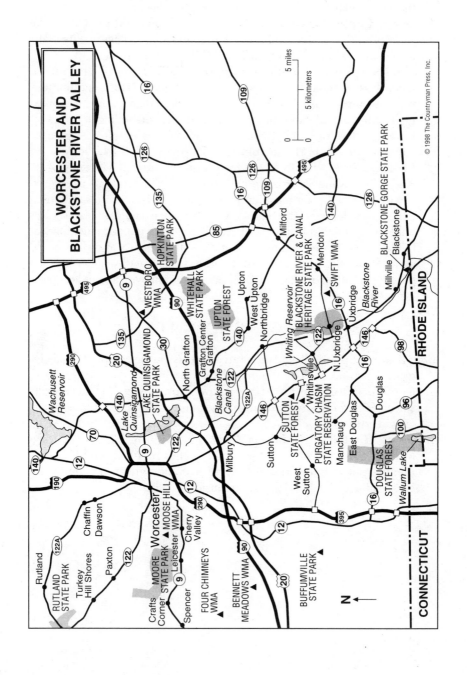

WORCESTER AND
BLACKSTONE RIVER VALLEY

© 1998 The Countryman Press, Inc.

5 miles
5 kilometers

RHODE ISLAND

CONNECTICUT

N

Blackstone River Valley

The fascinating thing about the Blackstone River Valley is the way it looks: woods and pastures spotted with 18th-century meetinghouses and early-19th-century mill villages, each carefully formed like a well-crafted bead strung along the thread of river.

America loves "firsts," and the vintage-1793 Old Slater Mill in Pawtucket, Rhode Island, the first place in which cotton was success-fully spun by machine in America, has been a museum since the 1920s. In 1986 Congress passed an act establishing a bistate Blackstone River Valley National Heritage Corridor, belatedly recognizing that the Slater Mill was just the opening paragraph in the first chapter of America's Industrial Revolution, a chapter that's written all over the face of this 44-mile-long valley.

Park rangers at the Blackstone River and Canal Heritage State Park in Uxbridge explain that by 1810 an estimated 100 cotton mills were peppered along local rivers, most inspired by Slater's design, known as the Rhode Island System. In contrast to the mammoth planned mill cities such as Lowell and Lawrence that first appeared in the 1830s, Blackstone Valley mills were usually run by the owner (rather than by agents and absentee investors), employed entire families for whom they provided housing (rather than mill hands for whom they built board-inghouses), and remained relatively small, compact, and on a human scale.

By the time the Blackstone Canal was completed in 1828, linking Worcester and Providence, dozens of small textile mills and several mill villages already lined the river, which drops 438 feet through innumer-able rapids and falls. This uneven terrain necessitated no fewer than 49 locks on the canal.

In 1839 the fastest way to get from Worcester to Providence was aboard a 50-passenger canal barge. In 1847 the Providence and Worces-ter Railroad came along, reducing travel time from 12 to 2 hours, thus putting the canal out of business. Today only a half dozen of its original miles are still "watered."

The Heritage State Park in Uxbridge represents the most scenic and accessible stretch of the former canal. From the visitors center there, you can walk in one direction along a wooded millpond to high stone cliffs and, in the other, along a shaded towpath to the graceful, sadly now mostly unoccupied, Stanley Woolen Mill (built in 1851) in the middle of Uxbridge.

Some three dozen distinct mill villages survive within the valley. Other local attractions include New England's largest collection of wild animals and Purgatory Chasm, easier to explore than to explain.

AREA CODE: 508

GUIDANCE

Blackstone Valley Chamber of Commerce (234-9090; 1-800-841-0919), 110 Church Street, Whitinsville 01588. The best source of information before you come.

River Bend Farm Visitors Center at the Blackstone River and Canal Heritage State Park (278-7604), 287 Oak Street, Uxbridge 01569. Open daily 10–6 in summer, 10–4 in winter. This is the logical place to begin exploring the Massachusetts segment of the valley: a staffed information center stocked with local tourist literature and furnished with interpretive exhibits and slide presentations. The center schedules walking tours, lectures, and educational programs on local nature and history, and holds special events.

Blackstone River Valley National Heritage Corridor Commission (401-762-0250), One Depot Square, Woonsocket, Rhode Island 02895. Open Monday through Friday 8–5. This is the National Park Service office for the valley, coordinating information for both the Massachusetts and Rhode Island segments of the corridor.

Blackstone River Watershed Association (234-8797), Northbridge Town Hall, Memorial Square, Whitinsville 01588.

Blackstone River Valley Tourism Council (401-334-7773), PO Box 7663, Cumberland, Rhode Island 02864, serves the Rhode Island segment of the valley. Ask about the evolving museum of work and culture in Woonsocket, bike trails, and special events.

GETTING THERE

Less than an hour's drive southwest of Boston, the heart of this bistate "National Heritage Corridor" (see *Guidance*) is Uxbridge, accessible from Boston via I-495 to Milford, then Route 16 west. To follow the canal from Grafton south to Blackstone, exit the Mass. Pike at Route 122 in North Grafton. For Purgatory Chasm in Sutton, take the Mass. Pike to Route 146 south.

MEDICAL EMERGENCY

Milford-Whitinsville Regional Hospital (473-1190), Route 16, Milford.

VILLAGES

Grafton Center. Founded in 1654 as one of John Eliot's Praying Indian villages, it has a classic New England common with a bandstand that is surrounded by 19th-century homes, an inn, and commercial buildings (see *Lodging* and *Where to Eat.*)

East Douglas. A classic, sleepy crossroads with the two-story frame **E.N. Jenckes Store,** preserved by the Douglas Historical Society (open weekends in June and August, 1–4 and by appointment; 476-3856), complete with a dry-goods section, ledgers, and crockery, and looking precisely the way it did in the 1890s.

TO SEE

Blackstone River and Canal Heritage State Park (278-7604), 287 Oak Street (marked from Route 16), Uxbridge. Open daily 10–6 in summer, 10–4 in winter (see *Guidance*). The farmhouse itself is dotted with interpretive exhibits on the history and other aspects of the valley, and from here you can walk a mile or so under arching trees to the Stanley Woolen Mill or walk north to the point at which the river and canal join at the graceful Stone Arch bridges. Muskrats and great blue herons are frequently sighted along the Goat Hill Trail, which continues another couple of miles along the edge of Rice City Pond. A trail on the other side of the pond leads to King Philip's Rock, a high stone stage on which the 17th-century Native American chief should have stood even if he didn't. The view is across rolling green hills and wetlands, punctured by just one smokestack in the distance. Inquire about lectures, walking tours, and special events. (Also see *Green Space.*)

Willard House & Clock Museum (839-3500), 11 Willard Street, Grafton. Signs point the way from Grafton's common, also from Route 30 (it's just a half-mile south) and Route 122. Open Tuesday through Saturday 10–4, Sunday 1–5. Guided tours year-round. Adults $5, $4 seniors, $2 children 6–12. A classic saltbox built in 1718 by the grandfather of four clock-making brothers who made some 7500 timepieces in the late 18th and early 19th centuries. More than 70 magnificent clocks are displayed in nine galleries, which include five original rooms in the house.

✐ **Southwick's Wild Animal Farm** (883-9182), 2 Southwick Street (marked from Route 16), Mendon. Open daily May through Labor Day 10–5, limited hours in April, September, October. Adults $8.50, $6.50 for children 3–12. Given the lack of a first-rate public zoo in New England, this is the next best thing: the largest collection of animals in the region. Begun as a hobby on their 300-acre farm in the 1950s, the Southwicks now regularly care for 500 animals, representing more than 100 species: giraffes, rhinos, lions, tigers, bears, chimps, monkeys, camels, zebras, and giant tortoises. The petting zoo includes llamas, deer, and barnyard animals. Kiddie rides, a snack bar, and picnic tables are also part of the scene.

Quaker Meetinghouses. Many of the valley's first settlers were Quakers, and two of their 18th-century buildings survive. In Uxbridge, on Route

Blackstone River and Canal Heritage State Park

146A (south of town; across from the **Quaker Motor Lodge**), stands a 1770 meetinghouse (open July and August, Sunday afternoons 2–4) with its interior unchanged. The second is the **Chestnut Hill Meeting House** (open by appointment; 883-9409), Chestnut Hill Road between Southwick's Wild Animal Farm and Millville. Built in 1769 with a gallery and box pews, the building has been recently restored; a peaceful place.

SCENIC DRIVES

Mill Villages. Begin in North Uxbridge on Route 16 at the **Crown and Eagle Mill,** which looks more like a Yankee version of a Loire Valley château than a factory. Built in 1826 of local granite with clerestory monitor windows and a handsome bell tower, it spans the Mumford

River and is set in formal parklike grounds. Burned by vandals in 1975, the mill has since been restored as housing for the elderly, and its village still includes a school, the original 1810 Clapp Cotton Mill, handsome brick housing, and a store.

A mile away, the mansard-roofed, brick **Linwood Mill,** built in 1870, overlooks a pond-shaped stretch of river. The mill housing is next door, and the ornate former mill-owner's mansion is just up the road.

Another mile brings you to **Whitinsville** (pronounced *White-insville*), a village built around three mills—a small vintage-1826 red mill with a weather vane on its belfry, a mid-19th-century granite mill, and the larger and later Whitin Machine Works around the corner. Millponds stretch on and on both north and south of the village. **Purgatory Chasm** (see *Green Space*) is 2 miles up North Main Street through **New Village,** the valley's largest cluster of mill workers' housing. In Manchaug, less than 5 miles west of Whitinsville, the granite **B.B. Knight Cotton Mill** is another beauty with an ornate tower and wrought-iron balconies, across from an early dam and waterfall.

Farms and Fudge in Sutton. From Route 146 south, take the Northbridge/Oxford exit and turn right onto Armsby Road at the Pleasant Valley sign. Just off Route 146 you pass **Vaillancourt Folk Art** (see *Selective Shopping*) and in a quarter mile come to the **Pleasant Valley Country Club,** home of the New England Classic Golf Tournament in July, an area landmark that's open to the public for lunch (see *To Do—Golf*). Continue across Boston Road to Burbank Road and, after another quarter mile, note **Eaton's Farm Confectioners,** a former dairy farm that's the source of great fudge and a sinful Lust Bar; this is also a good picnic site (box lunches available; see *Selective Shopping*).

From Eaton's, take a right onto Burbank Road, keeping an eye out for **Freegrace Marble Farm** (on the right, at the second sharp curve in the road). This is a very special farm, little changed over the centuries and harboring a Native American burial ground. Owner Leona Dona (865-2406) has deeded it to the Society for the Preservation of New England Antiquities (SPNEA) and is generally delighted to tell visitors about the Native American relics found on the property and the history of the farm itself. If you want to stop, be sure to call ahead.

Continue on Burbank Road until it intersects with Wheelock Road; turn left onto Wheelock and follow it to the end. Take a left onto Singletary Road and follow it to the junction of Singletary and Boston Roads. The 1890s **Sherman Blacksmith Shop** (open by appointment; 865-2725) is on your left.

Purgatory and Heaven in Sutton. From Route 146 take Purgatory Road to Purgatory Chasm State Park (see *Green Space*), then continue along Purgatory Road to the Central Turnpike and take a left into West Sutton. There, make another left onto Douglas Road and in a half mile turn left again onto Waters Road. This road leads steeply uphill to **Waters Farm** (865-4886), a 1757 homestead, an 1840s barn, and 103 acres of land that have been conveyed to the town of Sutton and are being developed as a living history center. It's worth stopping by just to enjoy the panoramic view of Lake Manchaug, but you might want to call ahead; the farm is the site of frequent events ranging from bluegrass concerts to sleigh rallies (see *Special Events*).

TO DO

BICYCLING
The area's narrow country roads invite biking. From the Department of Environmental Management you might also secure a description of the **Southern New England Trunkline Trail,** a 22-mile bikepath-in-the-making that follows an old railbed from Franklin to Uxbridge and on into Connecticut.

BOAT EXCURSION
The *Blackstone Valley Explorer* (401-724-1500; 1-800-619-2628), a 49-passenger riverboat maintained by the Blackstone Valley Tourism Council, shifts its location throughout the summer. It is usually based in Uxbridge the first half of June.

CANOEING
The *Blackstone River Canoe Guide*, a booklet available from all the guidance sources listed, divides the river into 15 segments of various lengths, 10 of which are in Massachusetts. The most popular is the 6-mile stretch through the Blackstone River and Canal Heritage State Park. Put in at Church Street in Northbridge. Canoes can be rented from **Fin & Feather Sports** (529-3901), Route 140, Upton Center, and **Great Canadian Canoe Co.** (865-0010), Route 146, Sutton.

GOLF
Pleasant Valley Country Club (865-4441), marked from Route 146 in Sutton. A highly rated 18-hole course, for many years host to the New England Classic Golf Tournament (July). It is private, but **Dimples** restaurant (lower level) is open to the public Tuesday through Friday for lunch. Tickets for tournaments must be purchased in advance.

SWIMMING
Wallum Lake, Douglas State Forest, Douglas (see *Green Space*), is exceptionally clear, sandy-bottomed, with a beach large enough to absorb the weekend crowd; relatively empty midweek. Changing rooms, picnic tables. Nominal fee.

✐ **West Hill Recreation Area,** Uxbridge. A glorified mud puddle, great for children. Older kids can swim right across the pond to the opposite beach. Changing rooms, picnic tables.

✐ **Breezy Picnic Grounds and Waterslide** (476-2664), 538 Northwest Main Street, Douglas. Open weekends Memorial Day through mid-June, then daily through Labor Day. $4 adults weekdays, $5 weekends; $3.50 for children. Use of water slides as well as lake, $11.50 adults, $9.50 children. Lake swimming, snack bar, picnic grounds, two 300-foot water slides.

GREEN SPACE

Purgatory Chasm State Reservation (234-3733), Purgatory Road (off Route 146), Sutton. The chasm itself is a series of three 65-foot-deep ravines strewn with jumbles of granite boulders over which you pick your way. You then follow a trail up through the pines along the rim, squeezing through Fat Man's Misery if you can. The 188-acre reservation includes a playground and picnic tables in the pines.

Douglas State Forest (476-7872), Wallum Lake Road (off Route 16), Douglas. Wallum Lake (see *To Do—Swimming*) is one of the state's outstanding swimming and fishing lakes. The recreation area includes a boat ramp, picnic tables and grills, changing rooms, and hiking trails. $3 day-use fee.

Upton State Forest (278-6486), off Route 122, Northbridge. A 2660-acre spread with hiking, snowmobiling, and biking trails; fishing in Dean Pond.

Blackstone State Forest (278-6486), off Route 122, Northbridge, offers canoeing and hiking.

West Hill Dam and Recreation Area, West Hill Road, Uxbridge. This is an Army Corps of Engineers project and includes the dam at the end of one road and a recreation area with swimming, picnicking, and hiking trails at the end of the other. Well posted from Route 16.

Blackstone Gorge State Park. A Rhode Island state park but right on the line. Park in Blackstone near the wide, gently curving waterfall at Rolling Dam and walk south through the pines and maples above the river as it rushes through steep granite walls.

Blackstone River and Canal Heritage State Park (278-7604), 287 Oak Street, Uxbridge. This 1005-acre park lies along some 6 miles of the river, including a dammed portion, Rice City Pond. River Bend Farm here serves as the information center for the Massachusetts segment of the valley (see *Guidance* and *To Do—Canoeing*).

LODGING

BED & BREAKFASTS
☞ **Heritage House** (839-5063), 28 North Street, Grafton 01519. Peg and John Koomey have raised seven children in this gracious house, a vintage-1796 Federal beauty, on a maple-lined street that meanders back along its garden. The three guest rooms, furnished in antiques, feature European feather beds and share two large baths. Peg offers her guests terry-cloth robes (also alarm clocks and hair dryers). Common spaces include the living room, music room, and sitting room, and breakfast is served either in the dining room or in the garden. $65 and up.

✐ **The Putnam House** (865-9094), Putnam Hill Road, Sutton 01590. Dating from the 1730s, carefully restored with original paneling and walk-in fireplaces. Margaret and Martyn Bowden offer one large 20-by-20 room with a working fireplace and a small adjoining room sharing a bath, which can accommodate a family with up to three children. From $45 single to $75, full breakfast included.

The Captain Slocomb House (839-3095), 6 South Street, Grafton 01519. Bob and Judy Maynard offer three attractive guest rooms: Aunt Mary's Room with its own sitting room, the Master Bedroom Suite with its own dressing room, and the West Room, all with private bath, in a fine 19th-century house just off Grafton's common. Large swimming pool in the back garden. $60–70 includes a full breakfast.

Morin's Victorian Hideaway (883-7045), 48 Mendon Street, Blackstone 01504. A large, 1840s house on three acres overlooks the Blackstone River and has been lovingly restored by hosts Chip and Lynn Morin. Three rooms, one with private shower. The Lilac and Rose rooms are themed in those colors; the Almost Heavenly room is bedecked with Victorian angels and cherubs. Reservations required. Guests have access to horseshoes, croquet, and other yard games, as well as a refrigerator stocked with soft drinks. $65–75 with continental breakfast.

The Fieldstone Victorian (883-4647; 1-800-828-0000), 40 Edgewater Drive, Blackstone 01504. A handsome turn-of-the-century fieldstone home overlooking Harris Pond. The two rooms both have pond views. The second-floor room incorporates a turret and the first-floor room is next to the bathroom. Guests have the run of the parlor and dining room, decorated in period style. Rooms come with TV, alarm clock, and bathrobes. Year-round rates are $60–75, with full breakfast. Hosts Joe and Donna Emidy are trained chefs and breakfasts are scrumptious. (Try the stuffed French toast or soufflé-like apple omelet.)

WHERE TO EAT

DINING OUT
Note: Entrées in this section average $10.

Cocke'n Kettle (278-5517), Route 122 south of Uxbridge. Open for dinner nightly except Monday. An imposing mansion, the local place to dine on veal cordon bleu, good early-bird specials ($8.95 for a complete meal).

New England Steak and Seafood (473-9787), Route 16, Mendon. Closed Tuesday, otherwise dinner from 5 nightly, lunch weekdays. A dependable steakhouse featuring live music and karaoke.

Ploughboy Pub at the Grafton Inn (839-5931), 25 Central Square, Grafton. Open daily 11–9, until 11 on Saturday.

EATING OUT

Special Teas (839-7447), Grafton common. Open Tuesday through Thursday 11–4, Saturday and Sunday 10–5, Thursday until 8. A tasteful tearoom serving lunch, weekend breakfasts, cakes, and desserts (to go, too).

Lowell's Restaurant (473-1073), Route 16, Mendon. Open daily 6:30 AM through dinner. A great family find, good for all three meals.

The Elmwood Restaurant (476-2535), Main Street, Douglas. Open daily 7 AM–10 PM, good for fried seafood, sandwiches, Hershey ice cream.

Apple Tree Barn (476-2291), West Street off Route 16, East Douglas. Open for all three meals; rustic but good.

ENTERTAINMENT

A lingering '50s feel in the valley is evidenced by two of New England's last drive-in movie theaters: the **Mendon Drive-In** (473-4958) on Route 16, Mendon, and the **Rustic Drive-In** just over the Massachusetts line on Route 146 in Lincoln, Rhode Island. Also, the **Redwood Drive-In** (473-2125), with a snack bar and picnic area on Route 16 in Mendon, has carhops who bring orders on a tray to patrons sitting in their cars.

SELECTIVE SHOPPING

ANTIQUES SHOPS

David Rose (529-3838), Route 140, West Upton. Carries 18th- and 19th-century furniture and accessories. **Nipmuc Trading Post** (634-8300), Route 16, Mendon. Open Tuesday through Sunday 10–5, Wednesday 10–8. A cooperative with varied quality antiques and collectibles. **Grafton Antique Exchange** (839-2314), 2 South Street, Grafton. Housed in a grand 1880s mill owner's mansion on Grafton's common, this consignment store has an eclectic collection of bric-a-brac, furniture, pottery, and glass made between 1860 and 1940. **Mendon Flea & Craft Market** (478-5484), Route 16 (Hastings Street), Mendon. Open year-round Sunday 8–4. Look for the pink tractor. A weatherproof grab bag.

FARMS AND ORCHARDS

Wojcik Farm (883-9220), 65 Milk Street, Blackstone, sells fruit, vegetables, pick-your-own apples. **Douglas Orchard** (476-2198), 36 Locust Street, East Douglas, offers pick-your-own apples and raspberries. **Cahills Farm** (473-4039), Hartford Avenue, East Mendon, sells fruits and vegetables. **Lazy Acres Farm** (839-2990), 109 Merrain Road, Grafton, sells vegetables and Christmas trees. **K.C. Acres,** 11 George Hill Road, Grafton, offers pick-your-own blueberries. **Hawkhill Orchards** (865-4905), 79 Carleton Road, Milbury, offers pick-your-own apples, peaches, plums, and apricots. **Stowe Farm** (234-6711), 15 Stowe Road, Milbury, sells its apples and peaches. **Foppema's Farm** (234-6711), 1612 Hill Street, Northbridge, offers fruit, vegetables, and pick-your-own strawberries. **Keown Orchards Farm Stand** (865-6706), 9 McClellan Road, Sutton, is open mid-July through December 26, 10–6, selling (depending on the season) fruits, vegetables, herbs, flowers, pick-your-own apples and pumpkins, and Christmas trees. **Silvermine Farm** (865-5335), 96 Eightlots Road, Sutton, offers pick-your-own strawberries, vegetables, and blueberries. **The Amato Farm** (473-3819), 11 East Street, Upton, sells vegetables, fruits, baked goods, and pick-your-own raspberries and strawberries. **Dick Kelly's Farmstand** (529-6258), 10 Gable Street, Upton, sells vegetables, peaches, strawberries, raspberries, and blueberries.

FACTORY OUTLET

Giovannio Ladies Hat Factory Outlet (839-9011), 308 Providence Road, South Grafton. Open Monday through Saturday 10–4:30; women's hats.

SPECIAL SHOPS

Eaton's Farm Confectioners (865-5235; 1-800-343-9300), Burbank Road, Sutton. Open weekdays 8–6, weekends 1–4. A former dairy farm, now a source of homemade fudge, hand-dipped chocolates and "bark candy," and baked goods. **Mendon Country Gift Barn** (473-1820), 24 Hastings Street (Route 16), Mendon. Open daily. Gifts, dinnerware, candies, good for rainy-day browsing. **Vaillancourt Folk Art** (865-9183), 145 Armsby Road, Sutton. Open Monday through Saturday 9–5, Sunday 11–5. Features collectible chalkware Santas and Father Christmases in limited editions; Christmas all year. **Grafton Country Store** (839-4898), 2 Central Square, Grafton. Open Tuesday through Sunday 10–5. Assorted staples and gifts.

SPECIAL EVENTS

June: The excursion boat ***Blackstone Valley Explorer*** is based at the Heritage State Park in Uxbridge. **Canalfest** at the park, the first weekend, features music, guided tours. In late June, inquire about the **Native American Fair** at the Nipmuc Indian Reservation in Grafton.

July: **Wednesday evening concerts** on the common, Grafton. **Native American Indian Pow Wow,** Grafton common.

August: **Wednesday evening concerts** on the common, Grafton.

October: **Waters Farm Days,** open house at Waters Farm in Sutton, first weekend (see *Scenic Drives*).

Old Sturbridge Village/ Brimfield Area

Most Worcester County towns evolved between 1790 and 1830, an era during which churches, taverns, and stores still clustered around the common, and, though not completely self-contained, each community was highly self-sufficient. Today most of these towns retain their steepled old church and common, much as a family preserves its formal head-and-shoulders portrait of a 19th-century forebear.

At Old Sturbridge Village, one of the country's finest museum villages, the portrait is full length, and you explore the mills, shops, homes, and farms that formed the body belonging to that 1830s face. Based on thorough and ongoing research, the museum village offers vivid insights into real life in this heavily romanticized era. Buildings straggle out from the green along dirt roads. The farm animals seem hardier and less domesticated than the current norm, and it is difficult to believe that a family of nine once crowded into the working farm's small house. There is just one mansion in town: a square, Federal home where the leading member of the local gentry, the largest landowner, lives among his Boston-bought furnishings and passes the latest fashions on to his neighbors.

Although the more than 40 buildings in the village have been gathered from throughout New England, the story they tell is that of the surrounding countryside. We suggest that you allow a few days for the area. Save at least one for Old Sturbridge Village (an admission ticket is good for 2 days) and the shopping and attractions lined up just outside the gates along Route 20. A day or two more can be pleasantly spent at local swimming holes, orchards, and antiques shops, as well as exploring the back roads of the Brookfields and Spencer, New Braintree, and Barre.

This is rewarding countryside almost any time of year. We actually prefer the village in winter when there are far fewer people and the Publick House inn stages its Yankee Winter Weekends, packages that offer period food and entertainment at off-season prices.

AREA CODES
413 and 508

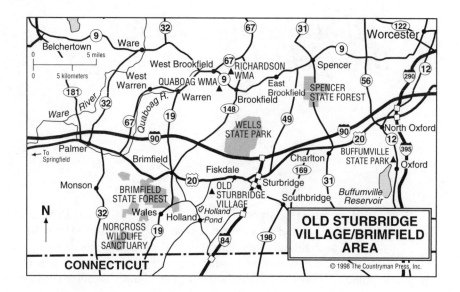

GUIDANCE

Sturbridge Area Tourist Association Information Center (508-347-2761; 1-800-628-8379), 380 Main Street (Route 20), opposite the entrance to Old Sturbridge Village. Open 9–5 daily. Staff answer mail inquiries (the zip is 01566) and help walk-ins. This is an unusually welcoming center with rest rooms, wing chairs, racks of brochures, and a video directory that provides views of local inns, restaurants, and attractions, as well as information about them. Staff make lodging and restaurant reservations on request, sell bus tickets, and offer a wide range of advice about the entire area.

GETTING THERE

By bus: **Peter Pan Bus** (508-752-1717 for Sturbridge area) offers frequent service between Boston and Sturbridge.

By car: Sturbridge is at the junction of the Mass. Pike, I-84 to Hartford (and NYC), and Route 20.

GETTING AROUND

King Courier (508-347-3660; 1-800-366-5466) offers 24-hour limo service to Bradley and Logan airports, also tours (reservations through the Sturbridge information center) to Quabbin Reservation and other local sites, and to Sturbridge museums and restaurants.

Status Limousine (508-347-3660; 1-800-366-5466). Limo service around the clock to major airports and for tours and functions.

MEDICAL EMERGENCY

Harrington Memorial Hospital (508-765-9771), 100 South Street, Southbridge, marked from Route 131.

Old Sturbridge Village

OLD STURBRIDGE VILLAGE

TO SEE

In Sturbridge

Old Sturbridge Village (OSV) (508-347-3362; 1-800-733-1830; hearing impaired 508-347-5383), Route 20. Open year-round (weekends only, January through mid-February). Closed Monday, November through December and mid-February through March. Adults $15, $13.50 seniors, $7.50 children 6–17. Admission ticket is good for two consecutive days. Special rates for groups of more than 15. Leashed pets are welcome, but strollers are not allowed in museum buildings.

A nonprofit museum, Old Sturbridge Village is one of the top attractions in New England. Expect to spend most of a day strolling the unpaved roads that wind around the common and down to the Freeman Farm or through the covered bridge to the Mill Neighborhood. An orientation slide program sets the tone. Be sure to talk with the costumed "interpreters": The shoemaker and printer are delighted to describe their daily lives in the 1830s, and the minister's wife will tell you why she'd like a cookstove like her neighbor, Mrs. Towne. Three water-powered mills are important features, as well as the cider mill, which operates weekends in October.

Notice the care with which the Asa Knight Store has been stocked: English china, foreign fabrics, West India ginger and rum, tooth powder, and 2000 more items drawn from throughout the world. You learn that the storekeeper was the town's link with seaboard cities, the trusted middleman who exchanged his neighbor's produce for manufactured staples and the luxuries of life. There are countless such discoveries here.

In addition to the village buildings and a visitors center with changing exhibits, there is the adjacent T. Cheney Weeks Clock Gallery and displays of glass, textiles, militia equipment, and lighting devices. In the reference herb garden, more than 400 plants bloom between May and October. There is a cafeteria and more formal dining in the Tavern, and an extensive gift shop. Frequent special events are staged, and there are adult and family craft workshops and special theme programs, including hearthside cooking and dining in the parsonage as part of Dinner in a Country Village (winter only).

The story of how Old Sturbridge Village came to be is a typical Massachusetts tale. It was founded through the philanthropy of Albert Wells, a Southbridge optics magnate. His enthusiasm for antiques led him to collect items in such quantities that they eventually outgrew his home, so the family bought this 200-acre tract of meadow and woodlot on the Quinebaug River. Since its 1946 opening the museum has changed substantially, acquiring through dedication to authenticity (the research library includes nearly 35,000 books, periodicals, and manuscripts relating to early-19th-century New England rural towns) a life of its own. You come away with a genuine sense not only of how this area looked but also how it smelled and felt in the early 19th century.

St. Anne's Shrine (508-347-7338). There are two century-old churches just off Route 20—St. Anne's and St. Patrick's—and a museum building that houses a collection of 60 Russian icons, some more than 200 years old, acquired by priests of the Assumptionist order. There are also picnic grounds and an open-air pavilion in which Mass is celebrated on summer weekends.

Beyond Sturbridge

St. Joseph Abbey (508-885-3901), Route 31 in Spencer. This is a Trappist monastery, famed for the beauty of its Gregorian chants (available on tape and CD), for its jams, and as a place to find peace. Visitors are welcome in the side chapel. Daily masses are at 5:45 AM, preceded by the singing of "lauds," a traditional choral service. Evening vespers are at 6:30 weekdays and 7 on Sunday, when they are preceded by a benediction service. For details about staying in the guest house, phone 885-3010.

WINERY

Mellea Vineyard (508-943-5166), 108 Old Southbridge Road, West Dudley. Open Memorial Day to December, Wednesday through Sunday 11–5. The specialty of this house is Colonial Cuvee. No joke—Mellea produces European-style wines from its own vineyards using French-American varieties. Visitors are invited to picnic.

TO DO

BALLOONING
The Balloon School of Massachusetts (413-245-7013), Balloonport at Dingley Dell, 14 Sutcliffe Road, Brimfield. Year-round rides, usually at daybreak. The $200-per-person fee includes a postflight breakfast. The whole adventure takes less than 3 hours, with 1 hour in the air.

BICYCLING
This relatively flat, rural area has some little-trafficked back roads. *Short Bike Rides in Greater Boston and Central Massachusetts*, by Howard Stone (Globe Pequot Press), suggests some specific routes. Westville Recreation Area offers good pedaling opportunities.

BOATING
Two flood-control dams have turned the Quinebaug into a chain of ponds and reservoirs, ideal for canoeing and sailboarding. The Quinebaug River Canoe Trail Map is available from the local state parks and forests (see *Green Space*). A canoe launch and fishing spot can be found in Brookfield, just before the railroad bridge on Route 148.

GOLF
Bay Path Golf Club (508-867-8161) in East Brookfield, nine holes. **Hemlock Ridge** (508-347-9935) in Sturbridge, nine holes. **Heritage Country Club** (508-248-3526; 248-3591) in Charlton, 18 holes. **Oxford Golf and Racquet Club** (508-892-9188), North Oxford, 18 holes.

HIKING
The **Mid-State Trail** passes through Charlton and Oxford. This long-distance trail is described in the *Massachusetts and Rhode Island Trail Guide* published by the Appalachian Mountain Club, 5 Joy Street, Boston 02108. A Mid-State Trail map is also available by contacting the Department of Environmental Management (see *What's Where*).

HORSEBACK RIDING
Rocking M. Ranch (508-248-7075), 120 Northside Road (off Route 20), Charlton, offers trail and pony rides. $18 for an hour. Reservations are recommended.

SWIMMING
Note under *Green Space* that Brimfield State Forest, Buffumville Federal Recreation Area, Lake Siago, and Spencer State Forest all have swimming areas. Other local swimming holes include the **Westville Recreation Area** in Southbridge (take Route 131 east to South Street), the **East Brimfield Dam** area at Long Pond in Sturbridge, the **Cedar Lake Recreation Area** in Sturbridge, and **South Pond** in Brookfield (small but free, with shade trees, off New Boston Road).

CROSS-COUNTRY SKIING
Brookfield Orchards Touring Center (508-6858), 12 Lincoln Road. Adults $5, children $2, seniors free.

The local state parks and forests (see *Green Space*) have many miles of skiable trails.

GREEN SPACE

Brimfield State Forest, Dirth Hill Road, Brimfield. This area is a 4033-acre forest, but most visitors are interested only in the **Dean Pond Recreation Area,** with its 100-foot-long beach and picnic facilities. Fishing, swimming, and boating are permitted, and the **Woodman Pond Group Camping Area** has three bunkroom buildings (for information, call Wells State Park at 508-347-9257).

Buffumville Federal Recreation Area (508-248-5697), Charlton Street, Oxford. From the center of Charlton, turn left onto Muggett Hill Road; after 4 miles, turn right onto Oxford Road; the area is 2 miles on the left. There is a beach here, open 10 AM–8 PM in season. Wildflowers bloom under the White Pine Observatory—lady's slippers and lilies of the valley; also picnic facilities and a self-guided nature trail. Fee.

Lake Siago (413-245-0116), Holland. From Sturbridge, turn west on Route 20 to Holland. Take East Brimfield Road south 4 miles to Day Hill Road. A town-run recreation area with a swimming beach, picnic tables, barbecue grills, and a volleyball court. The pond is stocked with pike and is suitable for canoeing. Fee.

Streeter Point Recreation Area (508-347-9316), Sturbridge. Swimming beach, picnicking, and a boat-launch area. Pleasant but a bit marshy.

Spencer State Forest, Howe Pond Road, Spencer (for information call Rutland State Park, 508-866-6333). Swimming and picnicking at Howe Pond; trails used for hiking and horseback riding.

Wells State Park (508-347-9257), Route 49, Sturbridge. There are 59 campsites, $6 per night. Reservations for more than a week can be made 4 months in advance; for less than a week, 3 months in advance. Swimming beach and picnic facilities.

WALKS

Tantiusques Reservation, Sturbridge, 1 mile west of Route 15 on a not-too-well-marked dirt road. This 55-acre reserve includes a graphite or black lead mine granted by the Native Americans to John Winthrop in 1644. Several open cuts that followed the original veins are still visible. Owned by the Trustees of Reservations.

Norcross Wildlife Sanctuary (413-267-9654), Peck Road, Wales. Open year-round, Monday through Saturday 8–4; closed Sunday, holidays. Free. An exceptional visitors center displays pictures of flowers, ferns, and trees native to the eastern seaboard, and the sanctuary itself has been planted with specimens representing most of the species of this continent's vegetation, including rare wildflowers. Birds and animals, needless to say, are protected within the area. The 3000-acre preserve is a gift of Arthur D. Norcross, a Wales native who founded Norcross Greeting Cards.

LODGING

INNS AND BED & BREAKFASTS

Publick House (508-347-3313), PO Box 187, Sturbridge 01566. The proud white tavern was built in 1771 by Ebenezer Crafts, who gave everything to the Revolution. Impoverished by 1791 (a year after planting the elms that still grace the inn), he was forced to move north (150 neighbors went with him), founding the northern Vermont town of Craftsbury. Positioned at the junction of Boston and New York high roads, the inn prospered. Restored in the 1930s, it offers an extension of the Old Sturbridge Village atmosphere. Although shops, restaurants, and motels have proliferated to form a "strip" along Route 20 outside the museum village entrance, the old inn has remained secure in its pristine setting on the original Sturbridge Village common, complete with town hall and meetinghouse. Behind the inn stretch 60 acres of meadow. Though the Publick House is now known primarily for its dining rooms (see *Dining Out*), there are 18 rooms upstairs and four suites, plus one room in neighboring Chamberlain House. All rooms are furnished with antiques, including wing chairs, four-posters, and canopy beds. There is also an adjacent 100-room motor lodge, nicely furnished with Colonial reproductions and small-print wallpaper. A pool, tennis court, and rental bicycles are available. $74–135 per room, $114–155 per suite in the inn; $59–89 per room, $85–130 per suite in the Country Lodge motel. Inquire about Yankee Winter Weekends, offered January to March— weekend packages that include 18th-century-style feasting, entertainment, and special tours of Old Sturbridge Village.

Colonel Ebenezer Crafts Inn (508-347-3313), Fiske Hill, Sturbridge 01566. Although it is owned by the Publick House, this 18th-century home is off by itself on a hilltop instead of in the middle of the village. There are gracious living and sun rooms and inviting spaces to linger, and tea or sherry is served in the afternoon. Rooms are beautifully paneled and furnished with antiques, and there is a secret panel downstairs behind which runaway slaves were once hidden. The inn has a pool, and guests have access to the Publick House tennis court. $114–135 for a double, $155 for a suite, less off-season.

Misty Meadows (413-245-7466), Allen Hill Road, RR 3, Box 3019, Holland 01521. A deceptively small-looking home that Ron Croke built some 30 years ago, truly delightful within, offering three rooms nicely furnished with Dot's family antiques—which include an iron bedstead and classic cottage furniture. Double rates are $60 with shared bath and $80 with private bath, full breakfast included.

Spencer Country Inn (508-885-9036), 500 Main Street, Spencer 01562. An early country mansion, now primarily a restaurant, but with four guest rooms in the main house and six in an annex. $42 double with private bath.

Sturbridge Country Inn (508-347-5503), 530 Main Street, Sturbridge 01566. Handsome 1840s house extensively renovated. Each of the nine rooms has a fireplace, air-conditioning, cable TV, and private bath with whirlpool tub. Live theater performances are held in the barn mid-June through October. Within walking distance of restaurants, shops, and OSV. Rooms are $69–139; suites $139–159.

Avondo's Bed & Breakfast (413-267-5829), 26 East Hill Road, Monson 01057. There are three guest rooms sharing two baths in this pleasant, gambrel-roofed home, handy to Brimfield's antiques markets (see *Selective Shopping*) and the Brimfield State Forest. $55–75.

Commonwealth Cottage (508-347-7708), 11 Summit Avenue, PO Box 368, Sturbridge 01566-0368. Conveniently located but just far enough off Route 20 to distance it from the noise of the strip. An 1890s gingerbread house nicely restored by owners Wiebke and Bob Gilbert. The six guest rooms all have private bath and are comfortably but unfussily furnished with period antiques. $85–145 for a double, including full breakfast and afternoon tea in the elegant (it has a black marble fireplace) dining room.

The Birch Tree Bed and Breakfast (508-347-8218), 522 Leadmine Road, Sturbridge 01566. Built as a retirement home by Jim and Jane Fischer, the separate guest floor has two bedrooms (each with queen-sized bed and private bath) and an atrium TV lounge. Guests also have access to a private patio. In a quiet country area, about 5 miles from OSV, near Tantiusques Reservation (see *Walks*). $65–75 per night, with full breakfast.

Bethany Bed and Breakfast (508-347-5993), 5 McGregory Road, Sturbridge 01566. A modern Colonial-style house with four double guest rooms, two with private bath. Separate TV and sitting room. British-born hostess Colleen Box is an avid gardener, and there are flower arrangements in all the rooms. Full breakfast. Afternoon tea (or mulled cider in the chilly off-season) and tea in the garden can be arranged. $80–115 per room.

The Red Maple Inn (1-888-257-2474), 217 Main Street, Spencer 01562. A handsome house, the Red Maple was built around 1800 and is listed on the National Register of Historic Places. All four rooms have private bath, fireplace, and period antiques. $79 single, $99 double.

Zukas Homestead Farm (508-885-5320), 89 Smithville Road, Spencer 01562, is a recently built post-and-beam house on a hilltop working farm. Pete Zukas raises heifers, and wife Lynn runs a baking and catering business from the house. The one rental unit is a three-room, top-floor suite with private bath and Jacuzzi, TV and VCR, and wonderful views. $95 per couple with a full breakfast that includes eggs from the farm's chickens and homemade jams and jellies.

(Also see "Quabbin Area" for the Wildwood Inn, Ware, and Winterwood at Petersham.)

MOTELS

Note: Check with the **Sturbridge Area Tourist Information Center** (see *Guidance*) for information about the many motels along Route 20.

Oliver Wight House and **Old Sturbridge Village Lodges** (508-347-3327), Route 20, Sturbridge 01566. The Oliver Wight House is the only building on Old Sturbridge Village property that stands on its original site. In recent years the 1789 mansion has formed the centerpiece for a motel complex and has been restored, offering a genuine inn atmosphere in its 10 rooms (furnished with reproduction antiques from the period). The remaining 50 units are a notch above standard motel design (furnished in Colonial reproductions and Hitchcock chairs, bright chintz), scattered in clapboard-sheathed buildings. Morning coffee and tea available.The inn and hotel are owned by Old Sturbridge Village. $85–110 double in the Oliver Wight House, $60–95 double in the motel units.

WHERE TO EAT

DINING OUT

Salem Cross Inn (508-867-2345 or 867-8337), Route 9, West Brookfield. Open Tuesday through Friday 11:30–9, Saturday 5–10, Sunday and holidays noon–8; closed Monday. The original part of this handsome, four-square house was built in 1705 by the grandson of Peregrine White (the baby born on the *Mayflower*), and it still stands alone, surrounded by its 600 acres. This landmark was in sorry condition when the Salem family (the name actually refers not to the owners but to a traditional design on the inn's front door) acquired it in the 1950s and began the daunting job of scraping away centuries of paint and restoring the 18th- and 19th-century woodwork. Specialties include old New England dishes such as baked stuffed scallops and broiled, herbed lamb steak. Dinner entrées in the $11–20 range. In winter, special Colonial-style Fireplace Feasts include mulled wine, chowder, prime rib (cooked on a rare, 17th-century roasting jack), breads, and pies, all cooked on the wood-fire hearth. Sleigh rides are part of these Friday evening and Sunday (brunch) rituals. There are also outdoor hayrides and drovers roasts in summer. The inn is worth visiting just to see the clutter of old tools, sleds, butter churns, and assorted antiques in the barn, as well as the collection of photos on the "lost towns" drowned to form the Quabbin Reservoir (see "Quabbin Area").

Publick House (508-347-3313), Route 131, Sturbridge. Open Monday through Friday 7–10:30 AM and noon–8:30; Saturday 7–11 and 4–9; Sunday 8–11 and noon–8:30. The original low-beamed, 18th-century tavern is now but one of six dining rooms in this grand old inn. Although 400 patrons can sit down to dine in these various spaces, the service is remarkably personal. There are cranberry muffins and pecan rolls at all meals as well as hearty, all-American fare, from deep-dish apple pie for breakfast to prime rib, stuffed shrimp, and individual baked lobster pies for dinner. Entrées in the $16–24 range. Children's plates. Special yule log dinners in Christmas season.

The Whistling Swan (508-347-2321), 502 Main Street, Sturbridge. Closed Monday, otherwise open for lunch and dinner. Three formal dining rooms in a Greek Revival mansion are the setting for enjoying mussels meunière or frogs' legs followed by medallions of veal in three-mustard sauce or duckling *au poivre,* topped off by Russian cream with strawberries Romanoff or chocolate almond pie. Dinner entrées in the $15–24 range. Lighter (and cheaper) meals are served in the pleasantly informal **Ugly Duckling Loft,** which has a strong local following.

Spencer Country Inn (508-885-9036), 500 East Main Street (Route 9), Spencer. Closed Monday, otherwise open for lunch and dinner, Sunday brunch. A 19th-century mansion with five dining rooms, including the **Hogshead Tavern;** live music Saturday evenings. Dinner entrées run $13–18.

✐ **Charlie's Restaurant** (508-347-5559), Haynes Street, Sturbridge. (Formerly Charlie Brown's Steakhouse). Open daily for lunch and dinner. In the orchard of the Publick House complex, this is a happily unpretentious family restaurant. The decor is zany (chicken coops, stained glass, farm implements), and the prices are reasonable. House specialties, such as steak and prime rib, average $10–17.

Rom's (508-347-3349), Route 131, Sturbridge. Open daily for lunch and dinner, Italian specialties. Wednesday-night buffet is $13.95; Thursday luncheon buffet is $6.75.

Le Bearn Restaurant Français (508-347-5800), 12 Cedar Street, Sturbridge. Owners Leon and Rose Marty are from the south of France and serve classic French cuisine with Provençale touches. Dinner served from 5 PM. Closed Sundays. Entrées average $17–20.

C.J.'s (413-283-2196), Route 20, Palmer. Locals swear by this unpretentious place, noted for inexpensive, full lobster dinners. Entrées average $10–15.

Piccadilly Pub Restaurant (508-347-8189), 362 Main Street (Route 20), Sturbridge. Open daily for lunch and dinner. Large, popular restaurant with extensive menu ranging from fish-and-chips to lobster pie, from burgers to sirloin steaks. Usually busy, but service is fast and cheerful. All menu items less than $10.

Admiral T.J. O'Brien's (508-347-2838), 407 Main Street, Sturbridge. Lively place in the midst of the Sturbridge strip. Mid-American cuisine with dinner entrées in the $8–15 range. Open for dinner Monday through Sunday 11:30–9. Live entertainment Friday and Saturday evenings.

Dinner in a Country Village at Old Sturbridge Village (508-347-3362) is offered Saturday nights, November through March, by reservation; $60 per person. Guests arrive at 5 and are ushered into one of the village homes, where they help prepare the dinner that they then consume. Recipes and atmosphere are as authentically 1830s as possible. Limited to 14 per evening.

EATING OUT

The Sunburst (508-347-3097), 484 Main Street, Sturbridge (corner of Route 20 and Arnold Road). Open daily 7–2. Home-baked muffins are the breakfast specialty—breakfast is served all day—and for lunch there are homemade soups, quiches and salads, fruit-flavored "smoothies," and more muffins. A dining deck is open May through October.

Woodbine Country Store and Restaurant (413-245-3552), Main Street, Brimfield. A friendly, reasonably priced eatery in the middle of this classic New England village.

SNACKS

Westview Farms Creamery (413-267-5355), 111 East Hill Road (off Route 20), Monson. Open daily April through November. A real working dairy farm (about 300 cows) with a great view of the Berkshire foothills. Its creamery serves homemade ice cream and light meals.

Hebert Candies and Ice Cream (508-347-3051), River Road (exit 2 off I-84), Sturbridge. One of the oldest roadside candy shops in the country, Hebert's has been in the same family since 1917. All candies are freshly made, without preservatives. The make-your-own-sundae buffet offers 12 varieties of homemade ice cream and 18 different toppings.

SELECTIVE SHOPPING

ANTIQUES SHOPS

Brimfield Fair, Route 20, Brimfield (7 miles west of Sturbridge). Three times a year—in May, July, and September—more than 4000 dealers gather in the meadows and open space just west of the Brimfield common. The antiques show has its own year-round, 24-hour information tape (413-283-6149) that tells you when the next antiques show will occur and gives directions to Brimfield. Information is also available at the Sturbridge Area Information Center (see *Guidance*) and the Quabog Valley Chamber of Commerce (413-283-2418). The shows are divided into 21 distinct markets, each with 50 to 500 dealers specializing in different kinds of furniture, clothing, jewelry, collectibles, and so on. The crowd usually tops 100,000, and it's a vivid scene that engulfs usually tranquil Brimfield. Stands serving surprisingly good finger food cluster around the markets. For a booklet prepared by the local chamber of commerce, with detailed information about the shows, send $5 to QVCC, PO Box 269, Palmer, MA 01069.

Sturbridge Antique Shop (508-347-2744), about a mile east of OSV on Route 20. Open daily. Houses more than 70 dealers year-round. **Fairground Antiques Center** (508-347-3926), 362 Main Street (Route 20), Sturbridge. Open Monday through Saturday 10–5, Sunday noon–

5. A multidealer center with more than 75 booths and showcases. **Antique Center of Sturbridge** (508-347-5150), 462 Main Street (Route 20), Sturbridge. A number of specialty dealers on two floors. Open 10–5 Monday and Wednesday through Saturday; Sunday noon–5. **Sunday flea markets** are held regularly at the **Auburn Antique & Flea Market** on Route 12 in Auburn, at **Ye Old Brookfield Mill** in Brookfield, and in Spencer on Route 9.

FACTORY OUTLETS

Wright's Mill Store (413-347-2839), 559 Main Street (Route 20), Fiskdale. A large outlet in The Millyard, a recycled former cotton mill. Trims, tapes, ribbons, laces, notions, and more. **North Oxford Mills** (508-987-8521), Route 12, North Oxford. The place to buy braided rugs, all sizes, all shapes; also carpets, remnants. **Maurice the Pants Man** (508-347-7859), Route 20, Sturbridge. A discount store rather than a factory outlet, this is a great place to shop for Woolrich and other name-brand sportswear for the whole family.

ORCHARDS

This is apple country, and the orchards are in some of the most beautiful corners of it. Call ahead to make sure the following are open and set up for visitors.

✐ **Brookfield Orchards** (508-867-6858), Orchard Road, off Route 9, East Brookfield. Set high on a hill, with picnic tables and children's play equipment, the Country Store here sells jellies, gifts, and apple dumplings with an apple baked into each. Owned by the Lincoln family since 1918.

✐ **Breezelands Orchards Farm Stand & Cidermill** (413-436-7100), Southbridge Road, Warren 01083. Pick-your-own peaches and apples, fresh cider. Petting zoo and tractor rides. Open daily from the end of July through autumn.

Cheney's Apple Barn (413-245-9223), Brimfield. Open daily in picking season: cider, fruit stand. **Cheney Orchards** (413-436-7688), marked off Route 148 between Sturbridge and Brimfield. In the family since 1911, an 80-acre orchard and a country store selling 35 varieties of apples, peaches, pears (10 varieties), 8 varieties of honey, frozen apple pies, and more. Here you can also cut your own Christmas tree. **Fay Mountain Farm** (508-248-7237), Stafford Street, Charlton. In the Gilmore family since 1910. Apples and fresh cider, raspberries, blueberries, strawberries, and peaches in season. **Hyland Orchards** (508-347-3416), Arnold Road, Sturbridge. Apples and cider in season. **Baxter Echo Hill Orchard** (413-267-3303), Wilbraham Road, Monson. Apples; shop selling gifts, antiques, and produce.

SPECIAL SHOPS

The Shaker Shop (508-347-7564), 454 Main Street (Route 20), Sturbridge. A restored 1830s house with 10 rooms of Shaker-style furniture, crafts, and accessories. Besides Shaker chairs and the like, the shop sells stencils for decorating walls and a line of milk-based paint, a biodegradable product ecologically minded Shakers invented in the 18th century. **Old Sturbridge Village Gift Shop** (508-347-3362). Strategically positioned at the entrance to the museum village so that you don't have to pay the entry fee, this extensive emporium sells early-19th-century furniture, furnishings, a variety of gifts, and books. Same hours as OSV. **The League of American Crafters** (413-347-2323), 559 Main Street (Route 20), Fiskdale. A permanent crafts show occupying the entire third floor of the Millyard complex, a mile west of OSV. More than 150 craftspeople are represented.

SPECIAL EVENTS

Old Sturbridge Village publishes its own calendar, filled with events dictated by the seasons. The following notes only some of the highlights.

February: **George Washington's Birthday** is celebrated at OSV as it would have been in the 1830s. **Maple sugaring** at OSV.

March: **Hog butchering** at OSV.

April: **Annual Town Meeting** at OSV.

May: **Brimfield Flea Market,** Brimfield. **Muskets, Music, and Merriment** (Militia Day) and **Shearing, Spinning, and Weaving** (Wool Days) at OSV.

July: **Brimfield Flea Market,** Brimfield. **Independence Day celebrations** at OSV.

August: **Wales County Fair,** local exhibits and livestock, Main Street, Wales. **Hardwick Fair,** just off the common.

September: **Brimfield Flea Market,** Brimfield. **Spencer Fair** (Labor Day weekend). **Antiquarian Book Fair** at OSV. Apple-picking and cider-pressing at local orchards.

November: **Thanksgiving** at OSV.

December: **Yule Log celebrations** at the Publick House. **Christmas shows** at Bethlehem in Sturbridge.

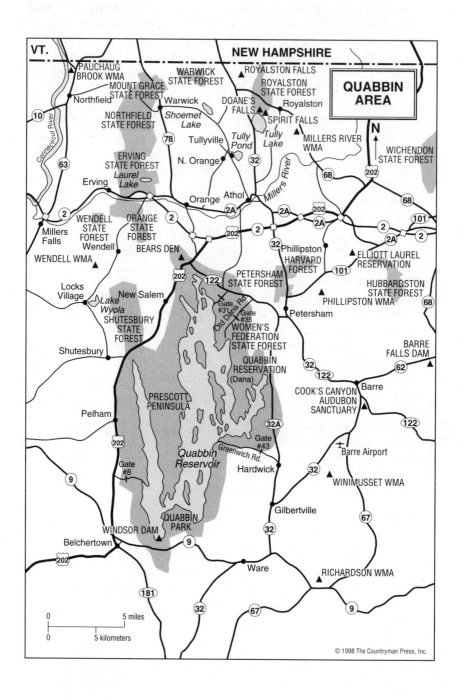

Quabbin Area

The traditional dividing line between central and western Massachusetts, Quabbin is also the centerpiece of one of the state's most rural and hauntingly beautiful areas. Unfortunately, the reservoir itself is elusive. Occasionally you see it; mostly you don't. Accessible by foot from more than 50 gates and by car from three, it requires some sleuthing to penetrate the reserve, and a fishing license, whether you use it or not, to launch a boat. And while the hiking trails are really roads, bicycling on all but a few is forbidden.

Obviously the MDC is in the drinking water business, not the recreation business, but those who take the trouble to explore Quabbin on its own terms are vastly rewarded.

The biggest body of fresh water in the state and one of the largest reservoirs in the world, Quabbin—a Native American name meaning "Land of Many Waters"—is 18 miles long and covers 39 square miles, with an average depth of more than 50 feet; it contains 412 billion gallons of water. Managed by the Metropolitan District Commission (MDC), the reservoir provides pure drinking water to 2.5 million people in 46 communities, including the city of Boston.

The reservoir and the watershed lands around it comprise a remarkable nature preserve. The woods and meadows of the 81,000-acre Quabbin Reservation teem with deer and bird life, some species once rare or extinct in New England. Wild turkeys and bald eagles, for instance, have been successfully reintroduced. The reservoir itself is open for fishing from April to October, and lake trout, bass, perch, and landlocked salmon are abundant.

Quabbin is unquestionably one of the state's great recreational and environmental assets, a haven for endangered wildlife and a boon for those seeking tranquility and unspoiled nature. About 500,000 people visit it annually. Initially, however, the reservoir was widely seen as a social tragedy—an example of big-city imperatives overriding small-town rights.

Quabbin was first proposed at the turn of the century when it had become obvious that, unless new drinking water sources were found, Greater Boston's growing population faced a thirsty future. After surveying the state, engineers concluded that the steep-sided Swift River Valley was the natural location for a reservoir large enough to meet the metropolitan area's needs.

For the residents of the valley, the price of metropolitan Boston's progress came high. Once the Swift River was dammed and the valley flooded, four entire towns would be inundated—Dana, Greenwich, Enfield, and Prescott—along with a number of villages in neighboring communities. The reservoir was bitterly opposed by the residents of the affected towns, who took their case all the way to the Massachusetts Supreme Court, but lost. The state of Connecticut also sued Massachusetts, in federal court, charging that Quabbin would divert water rightfully meant to flow down to the Nutmeg State. After prolonged litigation, the US Supreme Court found in favor of Massachusetts.

The project got under way in 1927. Before actual construction could begin, the MDC had to clear the site, a complex and painful process that involved displacing 2500 residents from 650 homes, exhuming 7500 bodies from 34 cemeteries, and taking up the tracks of the railroad that ran through the valley (trains stopped at so many villages and hamlets that the railway was known as the Rabbit Line). Most buildings were demolished, but about 10 percent of the structures were moved to high ground off the MDC reservation, where many still stand.

Quabbin was completed in 1939, but it took seven years for the reservoir to fill. Not until 1946 did it reach its maximum storage capacity of 412 billion gallons.

The Quabbin story is interestingly told with pictures, maps, models, and dioramas at the interpretive center in the brick MDC administration building at Windsor Dam in Belchertown. The MDC building is also headquarters for Quabbin Park, a 3200-acre reserve at the southern end of the reservoir that has picnic areas, scenic lookouts, 20 miles of hiking trails, and 13 miles of paved road. Also in the park is the Quabbin Cemetery, the final resting place of the deceased of Enfield, Dana, Prescott, and Greenwich.

With time, the painful memories surrounding the clearing and flooding of the valley have largely faded in the area, but the mystique of the four lost towns is still strong. You certainly feel it in the Quabbin Cemetery, where each town has its own section, complete with Civil War monuments and other memorials that once stood on town commons and in parks. Also very moving is the Swift River Valley Historical Society museum in New Salem, where exhibits of household furnishings, tools, crafts, and photographs of valley people at work and play evoke a drowned world with painful clarity.

AREA CODES
978 and 413

GUIDANCE
Quabbin Park Visitors Center (413-323-7221), MDC administration building, 485 Ware Road (Route 9), Belchertown 01007. Maps and in-

formation on fishing, hiking, and wildlife. Open weekdays 9–4:30.

North Quabbin Chamber of Commerce (978-249-3849), 521 Main Street, Athol 01331. Brochures, maps, and tourist information about the nine towns around the northern end of the reservoir.

Franklin County Chamber of Commerce (413-773-5463), PO Box 898, Greenfield 01302. Web site: www.co.franklin.ma.us. A source of information on the area north and west of Quabbin.

GETTING THERE

The Quabbin Reservation is some 65 miles west of Boston, located between Route 2 and the Mass. Pike.

GETTING AROUND

You need a car. You can make a complete loop around the Quabbin reservation on well-maintained and -marked state roads. Route 9 runs along the southern edge of the reservoir, where MDC headquarters, Quabbin Park, and the Quabbin Cemetery are located. Route 32 (which connects with the Mass. Pike to the south at Palmer) and Route 32A run up the eastern side. Route 122 runs along the northern end of Quabbin, between Route 32A and Route 202, the latter route paralleling the reservoir's western shore between Route 9 and Route 2.

MEDICAL EMERGENCY

Athol Memorial Hospital (978-249-3511), 2033 Main Street, Athol.

For emergencies inside the Quabbin Reservation contact the **Quabbin Police** (413-323-7561).

VILLAGES

Barre. A handsome old crossroads town with shops along one side of an immense common with a white Victorian bandstand (the stage for Sunday evening concerts for more than 100 summers). The common is also the summer site of Saturday morning farmers markets as well as a variety of events, from church and craft fairs to car rallies. The **Barre Historical Society** (978-355-4978), 18 Common Street, and the **Barre Playhouse** (see *Entertainment*) are also within steps of the common. The town was named in 1776 for Colonel Isaac Barre, a fierce defender of American autonomy in British Parliament. **Cook's Canyon**, an Audubon Sanctuary on South Street (see *Green Space*) is worth a stop. Barre offers a surprising choice of lodging options and is a good base for exploring much of central and western Massachusetts. Back roads harbor artists' studios (see *Selective Shopping*).

Belchertown At the foot of Quabbin Reservoir, an old town with a large common, with a white clapboard Congregational church and a cemetery dating back to the 18th century. Now a bedroom town for Springfield (its population has more than doubled in the past decade) and a pass-through place for visitors (on a well marked shortcut to Amherst from the Mass. Pike), Belchertown is also the site of **Quabbin Park** (see *Green Space*) and of the **Stone House Museum** (413-323-6573,

Route 202 just west of the center, open mid-May through October, Wednesday and Saturday 2–5 or by appointment: 323-7052; $3 per adult). This historical society collection, housed in an 1827 stone house, includes children's dolls, toys, and board games; its annex, built by Henry Ford, displays the many sleighs, carriages and wagons made in town (there were once 10 carriage factories). The complex also includes the Blackner Print Shop, a vintage 1915 newspaper plant (the *Belchertown Sentinel* is still going). (Also note the **McLaughlin Trout Hatchery** and the **Swift River Wildlife Management Area** under *Fishing.*)

Hardwick. Just west of Quabbin on Route 32A, Hardwick is an agricultural town with a beautiful common framed by churches, the town hall, and a one-room school house. It's the site of one of the state's oldest and most colorful agricultural fairs. Billed as "the oldest fair in the United States," the **Hardwick Community Fair** has been held in mid-August since 1762 (for details about the fair, phone **Hardwick Town Hall:** 413-477-6197). **Quabbin Gate 43,** one of the prime access points to the reservoir, is also here at the end of Old Greenwich Road (see *Boating* and *Fishing*). The two social centers of town are the general store and the handsome **Paige Memorial Library**, both within steps of the common. Look for the **Ware-Hardwick Covered Bridge**, in Gilbertville just off Route 32 at the town line.

New Salem. Although not wiped off the map by the Quabbin Reservoir like the four lost towns, New Salem was drastically affected by it. Today 80 percent of its original land area is owned by the MDC, and the town is almost eerily quiet. The old town center, just off Route 202, is a gem, with an elliptical common and streets lined with 18th- and 19th-century white-clapboard houses. This was once a busy crossroads, but now Main Street, originally part of a major east–west thoroughfare, ends abruptly at a chain-link fence marking the Quabbin boundary. The area around the New Salem common is a historic district that includes the granite assembly hall (once part of New Salem Academy), with its clock tower; the old Town House (1838), now a public library; the Congregational church (1854), and the 1794 Meeting House, now a cultural center (see *Entertainment*); former school rooms now house **The Common Reader Bookshop**. A plaque on the common recalls the scene of April 20, 1775, when, summoned by ringing church bells, the patriotic men of New Salem marched off to Boston to fight the British. The **Swift River Valley Historical Society** (978-544-6882) on Elm Street (marked from Route 202; open Wednesday afternoons in summer and by appointment), housed in the **Whitaker-Clary House,** contains photos and memorabilia of the lost towns. In front of the museum is a much photographed 1880s square "guide post" giving directions to three of the lost towns: Dana, Greenwich, and Enfield.

North Orange. This village is a dignified gathering of old country homes near the **Community Church** of North Orange and Tully, built in 1781.

Goddard Park, in front of the rectory, is the scene of frequent church suppers and community events.

Pelham. Route 202 is the Daniel Shays Highway, named for a farmer from Pelham. Shays served honorably in the Revolution, but then led a rebellion in 1786 against the merchant-dominated Boston state government, which was stripping farmers of their land and clapping them into prison for debts. A marker beside the 18th-century **Pelham Town Hall** (near the junction of Route 202 and Amherst Road) commemorates the site on which Shays camped with half his troops from January 28 until February 3. Displays in the **Pelham Historical Society** (open weekends June through September; check with the town clerk: 413-253-7129) in the neighboring vintage 1839 former Congregational church tell much more about Daniel Shays. **Quabbin Gate 8** off Route 202 at Knights Corner, south of the center, is a prime access (See *Boating* and *Fishing*). The **Pelham Overlook,** Route 202 north of the center, offers the best overview of the reservoir from a main road. We should note that Route 202 and Amherst Road is the quickest as well as most scenic route from Boston to Amherst (take Route 2 to 202).

Petersham. Sited on a high ridge, Petersham (pronounced "Peter's ham") has commanding views of the rolling, wooded central Massachusetts countryside. It's a beautiful place and a quiet one, with one of the state's lowest population density rates: 14 people per square mile. A thriving agricultural town in the 1830s, when fortunes made in sheep farming were spent on white-pillared mansions, Petersham was rediscovered as a summer resort in the 1890s. Architectural examples of both these eras of exuberant prosperity can be seen around the gracious town common. The white-pillared **Petersham Country Store** (978-724-3245) has been purveying varied merchandise since 1842, making it one of the oldest general stores in the state, according to owner Charles Berube. The rambling Nichewaug Inn was Petersham's social center for more than half a century, then served as the Maria Assumpta Academy until 1973. Still the most imposing building on the common, the old inn now has new owners, who have renamed it The Vintage. They plan to restore the place completely and reopen it as an inn and gourmet restaurant. A bronze plaque on the common commemorates the winter morning in 1787 when state troops chased and captured the rebellious Daniel Shays and 150 of his followers. Exhibits about Daniel Shays can be viewed on the common in **The Petersham Historical Society** (978-724-3380; open Sunday afternoons in summer and by appointment year-round). Don't miss the **Petersham Crafts Center** (978-724-3415; open Tuesday through Sunday 11:30–4) just north of the common on Route 32. The non-profit center displays changing art exhibits as well as offering workshops; its shop sells quality crafts. The **Fisher Museum of Forestry** (724-3302), a few miles north on Route 32 (open weekdays 9–5 year-round; also Saturday 10–4 May through

Quabbin Reservoir

October), is maintained by Harvard University, along with the 3000 acres in back. The museum contains a series of dioramas that dramatize the changes in the rural Massachusetts landscape over the past few hundred years. They depict the farms of the 1830s, when 75 percent of the land was cleared; the abandonment of the farms in the 1850s; and the succession of land-use practices to the present day. With a population of roughly 1000, Petersham has more recreational conservation land per capita than any other town in the state. See *Green Space.*

Phillipston. This village center off Route 2A is small enough to fit into the snapshot it demands. The Congregational church here, built in 1785, is a beauty, the site of the annual June bazaar and October pumpkin weigh-in (see *Special Events*).

Royalston. This spookily beautiful town was named for Isaac Royall, a wealthy 18th-century colonist (his Medford mansion is open to the public) who lived up to his name and was a Tory during the Revolution. The village is essentially one street, running along the crest of an 800-foot-high ridge lined with handsome white houses, many dating from its brief era as a 19th-century summer resort. See *Green Space* for details about **Doane Falls, Royalston Falls,** and **Tully Lake.**

Templeton. Falling right on our line between the "Central Uplands" and the "Quabbin Area," Templeton belongs in both. We describe it in detail in "The Nashoba Valley and Central Uplands," but include it here as a suggested approach to Quabbin from Route 2: Route 101 is a beautiful up-and-down ride, as well as a shortcut from Route 2 to Route 32 and Petersham.

Warwick. This perfectly preserved old Hilltown is about as far off the beaten track as you can get in Massachusetts. A three-sided marker notes that it's 20 miles from here to both Keene, New Hampshire, and Brattleboro, Vermont, and 8 (precipitously downhill) miles to Northfield. You seem a century from anywhere in this classic center, which includes a Unitarian Church, library, historical society building, fine old fountain, and the double-porched inn (see *Lodging—Other*).

TO DO

BICYCLING
Within the Quabbin Reservation bicycling is limited to a half dozen designated gates. The circuit around Quabbin outlined in "Getting Around" (Route 32A to Route 122 to Route 202 to Route 9) is actually a popular bicycle circuit; for more detailed routes see the **Western Massachusetts Bicycle and Road Map** by Rubel (see *What's Where—Bicycling*).

BIRDING
Quabbin is known for its nesting eagles and wild turkeys and is considered a prime birding spot by those who know. Check with local Massachusetts Audubon Sanctuaries for guided walks in the reservation.

BOATING
To take out your own boat or to rent a boat at Quabbin, a Massachusetts fishing license is required. It doesn't matter if you don't want to fish. The boating season is also the fishing season, mid-April through mid-October. Boat rentals (with and without motors) are available at Gate 8 off Route 202 at Knights Corner in Pelham, at Gate 43 in Hardwick (accessible via the Greenwich Road from Route 32A), and at Gate 31 off Route 122 in New Salem. The fee to launch a boat is $2 per person; rental boats are 10 horsepower (rates are reasonable, but a deposit is required). Private boats are limited to 20 horsepower. Canoes are permitted in only two designated areas.

FISHING
Quabbin Reservoir is open for fishing mid-April through mid-October, 6 AM to one hour before sunset. To rent a boat you must be 16 years or older and have a Massachusetts fishing license (see *Boating*); licenses and bait are available at local shops such as **Bill and Cathy Martel's bait shop** (413-323-7117) at Gate 8 in Pelham, **Flagg's Fish & Tackle** (978-544-0034), Route 202 in Orange, and **Penn Valley Rods & Reels, Bait & Tackle** (978-355-6134), Route 122, Barre. Much of Quabbin is off limits, but Gate 8 (Route 202 in Pelham) accesses cold salmon and trout-filled water, and both Gate 31 and Gate 43 access warm-water areas good for largemouth bass and chain pickerel as well as colder areas. Shore fishing is possible along all nonrestricted shoreline (Gate 17–21, leading to the Prescott Peninsula, is the only area totally off-limits to the public). For

more detailed information contact the **Quabbin Visitors Center:** 413-323-7221. The **Charles L. McLaughlin Trout Hatchery** (413-323-7671), just east of Quabbin's main gate on Route 9 in Belchertown, is open daily 7:30–4. It adjoins the **Swift River Wildlife Management Area,** which offers good fishing in the Swift River, as well as fields and woodlands webbed with trails.

GOLF

Petersham Country Club (978-724-3388), Petersham, nine holes. **Ellinwood Country Club** (978-249-9836), 1928 Pleasant Street, Athol, 18 holes. **Mill Valley Driving Range** (413-323-0264), 380 Mill Valley Road, Belchertown.

HIKING

Twenty miles of hiking trails in the 3200-acre **Quabbin Park** are open year-round to hikers. Hikers may also use 50 of 55 access gates to the **Quabbin Reservation.** The detailed *Quabbin Reservation Guide* (the paper version is $3.15, plastic is $5.25) is available at the **Quabbin Visitors Center** (see *Guidance*) and from **New England Cartographers,** Box 9369, North Amherst 01059. Trails are typically old roads, but in New Salem's Gate 35 you walk along an old rail bed to the reservoir's edge. The former town common of Dana, accessible by foot and bike from Gate 40 (Route 32A, Petersham), is a favorite destination.

SKYDIVING

Jumptown (1-800-890-JUMP), based at the Orange Municipal Airport, offers lessons and parachute jumps, promising: "With just one class you can make your first jump."

SWIMMING

Laurel Lake in Erving State Forest (413-544-3939) is the most user-friendly place, with rest rooms, a pavilion, and a picnic area. There is also **Ruggles Pond** in Wendell State Forest (413-659-3797).

Town beaches are found at **Lake Ellis** and **Silver Lake** in Athol, **Lake Mattawa** in Orange, **Queen Lake** in Phillipston, and **Moore's Pond** in Warwick. Belchertown's town beach on **Arcadia Lake** is open for a fee ($3), and **Lake Wyola** in Shutesbury is now managed by the DEM.

CROSS-COUNTRY SKIING

Red Apple Farm (1-800-628-4851), 455 Highland Avenue (marked from Route 2, exits 18 and 19) in Phillipston maintains 10 miles of trails and roadways; the **James W. Brooks Woodland Preserve** on East Street, 1 mile east of the Petersham Common, offers superb ski touring along the east branch of the Swift River. Other trails are noted under *Green Space*.

TRACKING

Paul Rezendes (978-249-8810), Bearsden Road, South Royalston, is a well-known local naturalist and nature photographer who offers a variety of programs in tracking local wildlife, year-round.

GREEN SPACE

WALKS

Quabbin Reservation. With 36,000 acres of wooded land, the Quabbin is the biggest green space in the state, offering more than 100 miles of roads to walk, not counting the inaccessible areas.

Women's Federation Club State Forest (978-939-8962), marked from Route 122 near the Petersham–New Salem line. There are picnic tables, fireplaces, wilderness campsites, unmarked trails; also, trout fishing in Fever Brook.

Harvard Forest (978-724-3325), Route 32, Petersham. A 3000-acre property attached to the Fisher Museum (see *Villages—Petersham*). It includes a self-guided natural history trail and Black Gum Trail, which highlight the forest's features. Take the 4½-mile trail to Prospect Hill for a view of the area from a fire tower.

Mount Grace State Forest (978-544-7474), Winchester Road, Warwick. Mount Grace itself, a 1617-foot peak, has long attracted hikers, and for 20 years, beginning in the '40s, the state maintained a four-trail ski area here. There is still a great view from the top. The trail begins at the picnic area.

Elliott Laurel Reservation, Phillipston; off Route 101 just west of Queen Lake. Woodland paths follow stone walls through white pine and hardwood with an extensive understory of mountain laurel.

Bearsden Woods, entrance from Bearsden Road near Athol Memorial Hospital; 1000 acres maintained by the Athol Conservation Commission. From the parking lot, a dirt road continues to the Millers River. There are a total of 10 miles of hiking trails and nice views from Roundtop Mountain.

Cook's Canyon Wildlife Sanctuary (978-355-4638), .5 miles down South Street from the Barre common. $2 per adult, $1 children and seniors. Open dawn to dusk except Mondays and holidays. This is really two adjoining sanctuaries, 47-acre **Cook's Canyon** and 12-acre **Williams Woods.** A trail system leads through meadowlands and forests to a shallow pond. No rest rooms or visitors facilities.

Also see **Swift River Wildlife Management Area** under *Fishing*.

WATERFALLS

Bear's Den Reservation in North New Salem, off Elm Street, ¾ mile from Route 202. This Trustees of Reservations site is a tiny grotto on the Middle Branch of the Swift River with a sparkling waterfall. Local legend states that in 1675 King Phillip met here with his chieftans to plan the attack on Deerfield.

Doane's Falls in Royalston. Athol Road at Doane Hill Road. Owned by the Trustees of Reservations, this site is a truly spectacular series of waterfalls. Lawrence Brook flows through a granite gorge crowned with pine and hemlock. A path leads down along the falls, worth following even in winter when the falls are an ice sculpture.

Spirit Falls, owned by Harvard Forest, is 1 mile west of Royalston Common but another mile hike via a forest road (north from Doane Hill Road) just east of a bridge across Tully River. The falls is also accessible from a forest road from Route 68; look for a small, unmarked turnout where a short footpath leads to a great view of the river.

Royalston Falls. Falls Brook drops nearly 70 feet over granite ledges into a steep gorge, its walls softened by ferns and hemlocks rooted in the cracks of the rocky walls. The Metacomet-Monadnock (M&M) Trail runs through this 205-acre Trustees' Reservation. You can reach it from the junction of Routes 68 and 32. Proceed north to the Newton Cemetery (to the right of Route 32) and follow the white blazes of the M&M trail. You can also drive in on a fairly rough (4-wheel-drive recommended) road from Route 68 north of Royalston Center; bear right on Falls Road and drive 3.2 miles; entrance and parking are marked.

OTHER

Barre Falls Dam (978-249-2547), Royalston. The recreation area on this dam, also managed by the Army Corps of Engineers, is off Route 62 on the Barre/Hubbardston line. Fishing and canoeing as well as picnicking.

Federation State Forest (978-939-8962), Route 122, Petersham. There are a couple of dozen nicely sited picnic tables with fireplaces, from which unmarked trails lead to eight "wilderness" campsites.

Orange State Forest (978-544-3939). Just 59 acres on the western end of Orange. Good for hiking and cross-country skiing.

Royalston State Forest (978-939-8962). Just 776 acres of forested terrain in the western section of Royalston. Good for hiking, snowmobiling.

Tully Lake (978-249-9150), Route 32, north of Athol. This 200-acre reservoir, constructed and maintained by the US Army Corps of Engineers, is bordered by 1250 acres of public land. It offers canoe access as well as hiking and picnicking.

Warwick State Forest (978-544-7474), via Tully Road from Athol or Athol Road from Warwick. **Shoemet Lake** is a beautiful spot, created by Augustus Bliss in the mid-19th century as a millpond. There is a boat-launch ramp good for canoes and rowboats (no motors permitted). The lake is stocked with trout, but no swimming is allowed.

Wendell State Forest (413-659-3797). Take Wendell Road from Millers Falls. There is swimming and picnicking at Ruggles Pond, fishing and canoeing at Ruggles and Wickett Ponds. The miles of roads through this 7566-acre forest are used for the annual September fat-tire race (see *Special Events*); it's ideal for biking.

LODGING

INNS

☞ **Bullard Farm** (978-544-6959), 89 Elm Street, North New Salem 01355. This 1792 farmhouse on 400 acres, just a mile from Quabbin, has been in Janet Krafts's family for many generations. The farm has its own walking and cross-country skiing trails and adjoins the Bear's Den Reservation (see *Waterfalls*). Deer and flocks of wild turkeys from the reservation sometimes wander onto the property. The house offers four large and comfortable guest rooms with period furniture (sharing two baths), and there is ample common space in addition to a meeting/function room in the former barn, good for weddings. Breakfasts are full, and if you come during blueberry season season you will most likely be loaded down with berries to go. Janet delights in turning guests on to birding, bicycling, hiking, and otherwise appreciating this most remote and least touristed part of the Quabbin area—in which Bullard Farm is virtually the only place to stay. Rates are $60 single, $75 double including breakfast.

The Mucky Duck (413-323-9657), 38 Park Street, Belchertown 01007. "It's a smiling name," Annie Steiner replies when asked: "Why Mucky Duck?" Sited on the quiet side of Belchertown's common, this early 19th-century Greek Revival Gothic house is a smiling place to stay, as attractive inside as it is out. The exterior features a sharply peaked roof, a second-floor balcony, and an arched porch; inside it is tastefully, deftly decorated, filled with interesting art, antiques, and sun (no curtains). The two windows flanking the hearth are highlighted with stained glass Steiner has fashioned, and a carved oak armoir complements the hutch and sideboard in the adjacent dining room; both have been in Annie's family for two centuries. Oriental rugs, comfortable seating, and plenty of reading material make it all very inviting. The largest guest room, the Aylesbury (the name of a white duck), is really a suite. The front bedroom is behind that balcony, decorated all in white and delft blue; the bathroom features a refinished claw-foot tub (with shower). The Wood Duck room, also upstairs, has wide pine floorboards and a king bed (that can be separated into twins) and is decorated with colorful mementos the Steiners have collected in their travels. A shower has been tucked into one closet and the bath into another. The third room, the Mallard, is on the first floor, with a full-sized antique bed, hunter green walls, and a full bath. Breakfast is European-style (Annie Steiner is Belgian), with fresh fruit, a selection of cheeses, and the bread Annie bakes fresh every morning. $60–95.

The Wildwood Inn (413-967-7798; 1-800-860-8098), 121 Church Street, Ware 01082. A turreted and shingled 1880s house, built during Ware's heyday as a textile manufacturing center. The house is filled with

American primitive antiques and brightly patterned quilts, and antique photographs (some scenes of the lost towns) decorate the walls. There are nine rooms, seven with private bath, and guests have access to a large antiques-furnished parlor with an ornate fireplace. Owners Fraidell Fenster and Richard Watson help visitors explore the area and will even lend them a canoe. Rooms are $50–80 with full country breakfast.

Winterwood at Petersham (978-724-8885), 19 North Main Street, Petersham 01388. Jane Day's Greek Revival house offers six guest rooms, each with private bath and all but one with a working fireplace. $60–80 includes a continental breakfast.

The Harding Allen Estate Bed & Breakfast Inn (978-355-4920), Route 122, Barre 01005. This expansive white-pillared mansion is set on more than 2 acres of landscaped grounds just off Barre common. Shared space includes a paneled living room/library and a "morning room" with Italian marble flooring, a marble fountain, and a crystal chandelier; in fall and winter, hot tubs bubble in the old greenhouse. The library features amazing tiles and windows. The mansion accommodates just 12 guests in a choice of large, comfortable rooms. The specialty of the house is orchestrating weddings, both the event and reception, and the estate is fully booked for weddings every weekend from May through October. But in winter the character of the place changes, becoming very much the away-from-it-all country inn. Jim Fairbanks and Alain Beret are genial, helpful hosts who enjoy plugging guests into all that's special in the surrounding area. $85–120 plus tax, $140 for the two-room suite. They also sell French antiques.

Jenkins Inn (978-355-6444), 7 West Street, Barre 01005. An attractive Victorian house with five guest rooms (three with private bath) and period decor. Fine dining here is popular and public. $95–135 with full breakfast. Bread and pastries are all homemade.

Hartman's Herb Farm (978-355-2015), Old Dana Road, Barre 01005. Three pleasant rooms (two with private bath) in a Colonial-style house (beamed ceilings and wide floorboards) built to replace the 200-year-old farmhouse that burned in 1989. Still a working herb farm. $65 single, $75 double includes a full breakfast.

Stevens Farm (978-355-2227), 749 Old Coldbrook Road, Barre 01005. This is the real thing: a hilltop, 350-acre working farm that has been in the same family for five generations. Irene and Richard Stevens raise heifers and keep pigs and chickens. There are walking and cross-country ski trails on the property, and Mount Wachusett and Quabbin Reservoir are nearby. Built in 1789, the farmhouse has five comfortable guest rooms sharing two baths, and there's a small swimming pool. $45–55 with breakfast.

The Wholesome Hearth (978-355-6543), 100 Pleasant Street, Barre 01005. A brightly painted 1850s house (the architecture is a mix of

Italianate and Greek Revival) just off the Barre common. Lisa Marselle offers two attractive guest rooms, one a queen, the other with a double and day-bed combination, sharing one bath. $65–80 includes a breakfast that might feature banana-walnut French toast or an herbed omelet; special diets, including vegan, are accommodated. Lisa's **Tapestry Glass Studio** adjoins the house.

Note: See also **Ingate Farms B&B** under *Lodging* in "Upper Pioneer Valley."

OTHER

Insight Meditation Society Center (978-355-4378), Barre 01005. This brick, former Catholic retreat now serves the same purpose for practitioners of the Southeast Asian school of Theavadin Buddhism. The emphasis is on simplicity of lifestyle and personal insights, the latter often gained by long meditative walks. Call ahead for a retreat schedule or to arrange a visit.

The Warwick Inn (978-544-7802), Warwick 01278. This 1827 classic stagecoach inn with its double porch and long ell have almost miraculously survived over the years, but every time we have stopped recently (admittedly we don't pass through Warwick too often; see *Villages*) it has been closed. On the other hand, we have always found a local person willing to vouch that it's still a good place to stay, a resource for local families and potentially for anyone who enjoys adventuring off the beaten track. At present it is divided into suites, each with a queen bed, sitting room, sofa, rocking chair, and newly renovated bath. $70 includes a full breakfast. Please let us know what you think.

WHERE TO EAT

DINING OUT

Also see **Salem Cross Inn** under "Old Sturbridge Village Area"—a destination restaurant with a display of photographs of flooded Quabbin towns.

Mark's New Salem Restaurant (508-544-6618), Route 202, New Salem. Open for all three meals just Friday, Saturday, and Sunday. New chef-owner Mark Antsel has altered this popular little landmark to make it more of an intimate dining room, the setting for memorable meals that might commence with a cup of French vegetable soup with white beans and progress to grilled top sirloin steak with classic béarnaise sauce ($13.95), a fresh spinach tart with lentil pilaf ($12.95), or fresh salmon filet with sorrel sauce ($13.95). Reservations suggested for dinner. Lunch might be a hearty Tuscan salad ($5.95), a roasted pepper and eggplant omelet ($4.55), or a quesadilla ($5.50).

Tully's Boiler Room Grill and Restaurant (978-575-0777), 245 Tully Road, Tully. The Grill is open daily 11–11, and at this writing the slightly more formal upstairs dining room is open Thursday through

Saturday for dinner, Sunday for brunch from 11, dinner after 3. Many locals do not even know where Tully is, but everyone knows about Tully Pond in North Orange, and that's really where this is (take Tully Road north from Route 2A just west of downtown Athol). The mill housing the restaurants is the third to occupy this site; built in 1920, its exterior is not a thing of beauty but the Boiler Room Grill is a great space, filled with a long bar, many deep wooden booths, and many satisfied customers. The large menu ranges from ham and leek pie ($7.25) and stone-baked thin-crust pizza blanco (basil pesto and four cheeses, $7.95) to salmon with a coriander dusting, rolled with matchstick carrots and zucchini and grilled with spinach and chipotle mayonnaise ($11.95). Entrées in the upstairs restaurant run $9.95–$16.95.

The Jenkins Inn & Restaurant (978-355-6444), Route 122, Barre. Open for lunch Wednesday through Saturday, dinner Wednesday through Sunday 5–closing, also Sunday brunch 9–2. This small (maximum 20 people), award-winning restaurant is housed in an attractive B&B just north of the Barre common on Route 122. It's wise to reserve. The menu changes frequently but might range from wild mushroom ravioli ($11.25) to rotisseried half-duckling ($15.95). Lunch might be a spinach and tomato quiche ($6.75) or a Caesar salad with salmon.

Fox Run Restaurant (978-249-8267; 1-800-695-8267), 185 Ward Hill, Phillipston. Open Tuesday through Saturday 5–9, Sunday 12–7. Take exit 19 off Route 2 west; turn left at the stop sign and follow the signs. This converted barn is a dining landmark. The dining rooms are large (there's an upstairs "hayloft" and downstairs "stable"), and the predictable menu ranges from broiled scrod ($11.95) and baked stuffed shrimp ($14.95) to chateaubriand for two ($41).

Colonel Isaac Barre Tavern and Fine Dining (978-355-4629), on the common, Barre. Open daily 11–3 and 5–10.

EATING OUT

Kozy Cabin (978-355-6264), Route 122, Barre. Open daily 5 AM–3:30 PM. A roadhouse exterior but comfortable and friendly family-style restaurant within. The extensive menu includes seafood and locally famous cream pies.

Gouvin's Cafe (413-967-0308), old mill complex, Main Street (Route 9), Ware. Your best bet in Ware at lunchtime: an attractive café in an early-19th-century former textile mill that's part of the town's shopping complex.

Wendell Country Store (978-544-8646), Locks Village Road, Wendell. Light food served from 7:30 AM until 7 or 8 at night (depending on the day); tables inside and out. Inquire about monthly coffeehouses on the Saturday nearest to the full moon, held in the town hall.

Petersham common

Quabbin Woods Restaurant (978-724-3288), junction of Routes 122 and 32, Petersham. Open Monday through Saturday 6 AM–2 PM, Sunday 7:30 AM–2 PM. A good waystop: homemade soups, muffins, and desserts.

The Petersham Country Store (978-724-3245), Petersham village common. Serving daily 7:30–7, Sundays 11–7. The back of this roomy old general store is a cheerful place for homemade soup, pizza, calzone, and sandwiches; dinner specials after 4 PM.

(Also see **Hamilton Orchards** under *Selective Shopping*.)

ENTERTAINMENT

The 1794 Meetinghouse (978-544-5200), New Salem common, is the setting for a program of concerts and theatrical presentations that runs June through September. Tickets are generally $8 in advance, $10 at the door, $7 for seniors and students.

Barre Players (978-355-2096; 1-800-733-2096), at Barre Playhouse on the common, has been the stage for live theater for 75 years; performances year-round.

Full Moon Coffeehouse (978-544-7894), Wendell Town Hall. Monthly concerts on the Saturday night closest to the full moon.

The Quabbin Community Band presents concerts at the Harding Allen Bandstand on Barre common from mid-June through mid-August, 7:30–9:15. Rain throughout the day means a cancellation (cancellations announced at 4:30 PM on radio WARE, AM 1250).

SELECTIVE SHOPPING

The Common Reader Bookshop (978-544-3002), 8 Main Street on the common, New Salem. May through October, Wednesday through Saturday 10–5, Sunday noon–5. Owner Dorothy Johnson has a large collection of general-interest old and used books. Women's history is a specialty.

Country Gourmet Kitchen and Gift Shop (978-355-6999), on the corner of Summer Street & Valley Road, Barre. Cooking and baking times, gifts, freshly ground coffee beans.

Designer Jewelry (978-355-2446), 74 Common Street, Barre. Fine and custom-made jewelry.

Iris Designs (978-355-6375), 260 Chapman Road, Barre. Fiber artist Pat Derry weaves table linens and rugs; she also designs scarves, jackets, and kimonos in her studio. By appointment or by chance.

The Rooster in the Strawberry Patche Gift Shoppe (978-355-2910), Route 122, Barre. Closed Tuesdays. Handcrafted silver jewelry, local pottery, crafts, gifts.

Stonemill Antique Center (413-967-5964), Route 9, Ware. Located in a historic former textile mill, this large consignment store has a variety of antiques and collectibles. Open daily 10–5, Sunday noon–5. Hours are extended until 9 PM during Brimfield antiques fairs.

Wilton Children's Clothing Store (413-967-5811), East Main Street (Route 9/32), Ware. Open daily 9–5, from noon on Sundays. A vast mill space filled with children's clothing of all kinds. Big-screen cartoons for children while parents shop.

FARMS AND ORCHARDS

Hartman's Herb Farm (978-355-2015), Old Dana Road off Route 32 and Route 122, Barre. Open daily 10–6. Reasonably priced plants (175 varieties), dried herbs and teas packaged on the spot; also herb wreaths, potpourri, dried flowers, raffia dolls. You can walk through the gardens and browse in the barn where herbs dry in bunches hanging from rafters and walls.

Sunnyhill Farm Fibers (978-355-2089), 452 Fruitland Road, Barre. Open daily except Fridays, noon–7. A fiber farm, raising wool, angora, and mohair, selling multicolored yarns, knitted goods, knitting and crocheting supplies; spinning lessons offered.

Hamilton Orchards (978-544-6867), Route 202 and West Street, New Salem. Open weekends 9–5, March to Thanksgiving, but daily during apple harvest (Labor Day to mid-October). Closed in June. One of the nicest orchards around: Some 35 acres of trees yield a variety of species that you can pick yourself in season. Cider is also pressed in the fall, and you can pick raspberries from late August until mid-October (blueberries, earlier). Barb Hamilton makes the pies, which are for sale, and the snack bar serves hot dogs and hamburgers as well as the pies and pancakes with Hamilton-made syrup. The view is off across the Quabbin Reservoir, and nature trails meander across the property.

Red Apple Farm (1-800-628-4851), 455 Highland Avenue (marked from Route 2A), Phillipston. There is no pick-your-own; instead a farm store sells pears and peaches, many varieties of apples (shipped anywhere), and cider pressed in season. Specializes in unusual varieties. There is also a bakery and a retail shop, hayrides, and a fall festival. Visitors are invited to hike and cross-country ski.

Quabbin Lamb Farm, 1276 Patrill Hollow Road, Hardwick. Open year-round. A small sheep farm raising lambs and selling lambskins, yarn, knitted goods; cross-country skiing and birdwatching permitted on the property.

SPECIAL EVENTS

January–April: Sunday afternoon lectures at the **Quabbin Visitors Center**.

April: **Athol-to-Orange River Rat Race** (usually held on the third Saturday, but check with the North Quabbin Chamber of Commerce). This is huge, usually attracting more than 300 canoes.

May: **May Day Morris Dancing** in North Orange. **Open House** at **Quabbin Reservoir** during National Drinking Water Week. **Memorial Day Parade** on Barre common.

May–October: **Barre Farmers Market**, Saturdays, 9:30–12:30. **Barre Craft Association** sales on the common, Sunday afternoons.

June: **Phillipston Craft Fair** (last weekend); **Fly-in and Yankee Engineuity in Action** steam engine show at the Orange Municipal Airport; **Athol Summerfest** last weekend in June.

August: **Royalston Day**; **North Orange Village Fair**; **Hardwick Community Fair** ("oldest fair in the country"; see *Villages*).

September: **New England Fat-tire Road Races** in Wendell State Forest. **Fall Festival** in downtown Athol, third Saturday.

October: First weekend: **Back Roads Studio Tour,** Barre/Petersham and Hardwick area. Columbus Day: **Celebrate the Harvest** in Orange; **Phillipston Pumpkin Commission Weigh-in**; **Old Home Days** in Warwick, New Salem, and Wendell.

December: **Christmas on the Common,** sponsored by the Barre Historical Society.

IV. WESTERN MASSACHUSETTS

The Pioneer Valley
The Berkshire Hilltowns
Berkshire County

The Poet's Seat in Greenfield

KIMBERLY GRANT

The Pioneer Valley

Since the 1940s, a 50-mile wide slice of Western Massachusetts has been promoted as the Pioneer Valley, a name underscoring the way settlement along the Connecticut River predated that of Berkshire County to the west and Worcester County to the east. Unfortunately, it also suggests that the entire area is a flat valley when, in fact, it includes the high, hilly plateau between the Connecticut and Berkshire County described by 18th-century settlers as the Berkshire Barrier.

The distinction between the Connecticut River bottomland and its flanking hills is unusually sharp. The valley floor is a distinctive mix of farms, venerable towns, and cities, while the Hilltowns to the west (see "The Berkshire Hilltowns") and gentler hills to the east (see "Quabbin Area") remain among the most rural landscape in New England. These towns were the last in Massachusetts to be settled, and the first to be all but vacated in the 1820s when residents moved west to easier farmland or to valley mill or rail towns. They are also far enough from major cities or resort areas to have changed little since.

The valley was carved by a series of glaciers, the last leaving 2-mile-deep Lake Hitchcock in its wake. Geologists have found that the lake was suddenly released, rushing to the sea all in one day—some 10,000 years ago. Just 5 miles wide up around the Vermont–New Hampshire line, the valley widens to 20 miles down around Springfield. Improbably, an abrupt chain of mountains march east–west across the middle of the valley (do they suggest a mammoth herd of dinosaurs to anyone else?), yielding views from ridge paths and from two especially famous peaks—Mount Tom and Mount Holyoke—on opposite sides of the Connecticut. Both peaks are accessible by car, and both overlook the oxbow and river loop.

New England's longest river, the Connecticut plays a far more obvious role as the boundary between New Hampshire and Vermont and, again, as the centerpiece for the state that bears its name than it does in its 69-mile passage through Massachusetts. Still, its role here has been far greater than you might think.

In the 18th and early 19th centuries Massachusetts's communities along the Connecticut—isolated from the state's coastal capital and

KIMBERLY GRANT

Tobacco fields in the Pioneer Valley

population centers—developed their own distinctive, valley-centered society, architecture, and, most interestingly, religion. In the 1730s and '40s Northampton-based Reverend Jonathan Edwards challenged the theology of Boston-based Congregationalism, trumpeting instead the message that everyone (not just the "elect") could be saved. Edwards's emotionally charged revival meetings launched a "Great Awakening" that rippled throughout New England.

In the valley itself, this fire-and-brimstone brand of Calvinism lingered on well into the 19th century, long after Boston had forgotten its Puritan horror of sin and embraced a more permissive Unitarianism. Puzzling on the themes of death and eternity in Amherst in the 1850s through '70s, poet Emily Dickinson was more a part of her time and place than is generally understood.

The valley's stern religion bred a concern for proper schooling. Deerfield Academy, founded in 1797, quickly attracted female as well as male students from throughout the area. Amherst College was founded in 1821 by town patriarchs, and in 1837 Mount Holyoke College opened in South Hadley. Both contributed more than their share of Protestant missionaries.

Subtly but surely, education became a religion in its own right, and today it represents one of the valley's leading industries. Its heart is the Five College area, home to Smith, Hampshire, Amherst, and Mount Holyoke Colleges and the University of Massachusetts at Amherst. It represents one of the country's largest rural concentrations of students

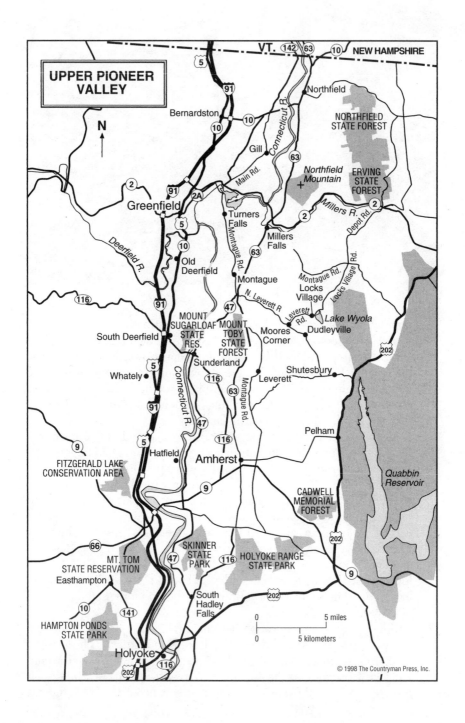

UPPER PIONEER VALLEY

N

VT. 142 63 10 NEW HAMPSHIRE

5

91

Bernardston
10
10

Northfield

NORTHFIELD
STATE FOREST

Gill

63

Northfield
Mountain

ERVING
STATE
FOREST

2
91
2A

Greenfield

Main Rd.

Millers R.

2

Depot Rd.

5

Turners
Falls

Millers
Falls

63

10

Montague Rd.

Montague

Locks
Village

Montague Rd.

Locks Village Rd.

Deerfield R.

Old
Deerfield

91

N. Leverett R

47

Leverett Rd.

Lake Wyola

Dudleyville

116

MOUNT
SUGARLOAF
STATE
RES.

MOUNT
TOBY
STATE
FOREST

Moores
Corner

South Deerfield

Sunderland

116

Shutesbury

202

Whately
5

Connecticut R.

63

Leverett

Montague Rd.

9
91
5

116

Pelham

Hatfield

Amherst

FITZGERALD LAKE
CONSERVATION AREA

9

CADWELL
MEMORIAL
FOREST

Quabbin
Reservoir

47

202

66

MT. TOM
STATE RESERVATION

Easthampton

10

141

47

SKINNER
STATE
PARK

116

HOLYOKE RANGE
STATE PARK

9

South
Hadley
Falls

202

0   5 miles
0   5 kilometers

HAMPTON PONDS
STATE PARK

Holyoke

116

202

© 1998 The Countryman Press, Inc.

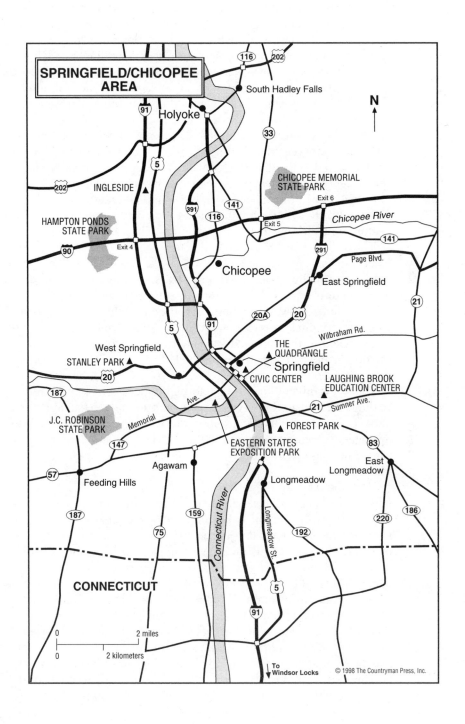

SPRINGFIELD/CHICOPEE AREA

N

116 202

South Hadley Falls

91 Holyoke

33

5

CHICOPEE MEMORIAL STATE PARK

Exit 6

202 INGLESIDE

391

141

116

Chicopee River

Exit 5

141

HAMPTON PONDS STATE PARK

90 Exit 4

Chicopee

291

Page Blvd.

East Springfield

21

5

91

20A

20

Wilbraham Rd.

West Springfield

STANLEY PARK

THE QUADRANGLE

Springfield

20

CIVIC CENTER

LAUGHING BROOK EDUCATION CENTER

187

21 Sumner Ave.

Ave.

J.C. ROBINSON STATE PARK

Memorial

FOREST PARK

83

147

EASTERN STATES EXPOSITION PARK

East Longmeadow

57 Feeding Hills

Agawam

Longmeadow

187

159

Connecticut River

Longmeadow St.

186

220

75

192

CONNECTICUT

5

91

0   2 miles

0   2 kilometers

To
Windsor Locks

© 1998 The Countryman Press, Inc.

and certainly one of its liveliest rural music, crafts, art, and dining scenes.

Perhaps the valley's most striking feature for visitors is the way in which the many layers of its history—from dinosaurs to diners—are visible, far more so than in most other places. The dinosaurs left footprints, lots of them. Many were unearthed during construction of I-91 in the 1960s, and three-toed tracks can be seen in science museums in Springfield and at Amherst College and right in the ground at Smith's Ferry (Route 5 north of Holyoke).

The valley's unusually rich soil—said to have been farmed in some places for 8000 years before the first white settlers arrived—is considered as sacred as the dino tracks by many local preservationists, and despite recent development pressures a number of farms survive. The story of the pioneer in this valley is vividly told in Old Deerfield, a village of 18th- and early-19th-century homes, 14 preserved as samplings of 18th-century rural life, one that was surprisingly rich and sophisticated.

This valley seems to have been a Yankee version of the Garden of Eden: rich soil bordering a waterway to the ocean. The Connecticut served as a highway on which new settlers continuously arrived and crops were exported. Flat-bottomed, square-rigged boats plied this thoroughfare, deftly negotiating a half-dozen patches of "quick water." In 1777 Springfield was chosen for the site of an armory. Skilled workmen flocked to the spot and speedily began turning out guns, paper cartridges, and cartridge boxes for the Patriot cause. These items went downriver too.

Today it is difficult to grasp the former importance of this waterway. In the 1790s transportation canals were built around the falls at Holyoke and at Turners Falls. A number of vessels were built on West Springfield's common around 1800, and at the height of the subsequent canal-building craze, a canal system linked Northampton with New Haven.

With the dawn of the industrial revolution in the 1820s, the waterfalls that had been obstacles in the canal era were viewed as the valley's biggest assets. In the 1820s Boston developers began to build textile mills at Chicopee Falls and in the '30s and '40s developed Holyoke from scratch—a planned, brick town, complete with factories, 4½ miles of power canals, workers' housing, and mill-owners' mansions. Meanwhile, Springfield was booming, thanks to its own homebred inventors and investors, a breed initially drawn to the area by the armory.

Although working and living conditions in the mill towns were dreadful (and well publicized by *Springfield Union* editor Edward Bellamy), the 1890s–1920—the period from which most buildings in its towns and cities still date—was obviously the valley's most colorful and exuberant era. In Springfield public buildings like the magnificent City Hall and Symphony Hall, the soaring Florentine-style campanile, and the

View from Mount Holyoke, by William Henry Bartlett, is in the collection of Springfield's Connecticut Valley Historical Museum.

quadrangle of museums all conjure up this era. So do exhibits in the Holyoke Heritage State Park—dramatizing Sunday picnics on Mount Tom and suggesting the extent of trolley lines that webbed the valley. Also during this period, volleyball was invented in Holyoke (look for exhibits in the Children's Museum complex) and basketball (a three-story Hall of Fame tells the story), in Springfield.

The valley today is distinguished by its number of extensive, manicured parks, its elaborate stone and brick public buildings, and its private school and institutional buildings designed in every conceivable "Revival" style—all gifts of 19th-century philanthropists who refused to be forgotten (each bears the donor's name). Mount Holyoke itself now stands in vast Skinner Park, donated by a family who made its fortune producing satin in the country's largest silk mill. Northampton's 200-acre Look and 22-acre Childs Parks were both donated by the industrialists whose names they bear, and Stanley Park in Westfield was created by Stanley Home Products founder Frank Stanley Bevridge. Although Springfield's 795-acre Forest Park isn't named for its principal benefactor, it does harbor New England's most elaborate mausoleum, built by ice skate tycoon Everett H. Barney.

As early as the 1820s, sophisticated tourists came to view the valley's peculiar mix of factory and farmscape, bottomland and abrupt mountains. In 1836 Thomas Cole, one of America's most celebrated landscape artists, painted the mammoth work *The Oxbow: View from Mt. Holyoke, Northampton, Massachusetts, After a Thunderstorm,* now owned by New York's Metropolitan Museum. The oxbow subsequently became the "motif number one" of western Massachusetts, and the small Mountain House on the summit of Mount Holyoke was soon replaced with a more elaborate hotel (a portion of which still survives), accessed from riverboats and a riverside train station by a perpendicular cog-and-cable-driven railway. Other hotels appeared on Mount Tom and atop Sugarloaf Mountain in South Deerfield.

Even before the Civil War, Old Deerfield's mile-long street of 18th- and early-19th-century houses was drawing history buffs. An 1848 crusade to save the so-called Indian House (still bearing the marks of a tomahawk embedded in it during the 1704 raid) is now cited as the first effort in this country to preserve a historic house. The door, at least, survived and was displayed, along with the first "period room" in America, in Memorial Hall, a museum that opened in 1880. Over the next few years the village's 18th-century tavern was restored as a center and showcase for an arts and crafts movement dedicated to reviving traditional handicrafts—not unlike those for which the area is currently known.

Still linked both physically by I-91 (which superseded old north–south highways Route 5/Route 10, which in turn had upstaged the railway, which had replaced the river) and culturally with Connecticut's cities and Brattleboro (Vermont) more than with Boston, the valley remains a place unto itself.

A case can be made that this Massachusetts stretch of the Connecticut Valley is the cultural heart of New England. The distance from Springfield's Quadrangle of art, science, and heritage museums on the south to Old Deerfield's house and town museums on the north is little more than 40 miles, a straight scenic shot up I-91. Exit midway at Northampton to view theater, film, and world-class art; hear music or lectures at the five local campuses; visit the Emily Dickinson Homestead or the National Yiddish Book Center in Amherst; or simply stroll a Main Street, past more interesting restaurants and galleries than can be found within three blocks anywhere else in New England.

All these cultural attractions are unusually accessible, set in one New England's most intensely cultivated agricultural pockets, a distinctive landscape in which paved roads climb to hilltop lookouts, hiking trails follow ridge lines, and bike paths trace old trolley and rail lines.

The Connecticut itself is recapturing some of its old status as the region's focal point. It has made a dramatic comeback since the federally mandated Clean Water Act began to take effect in the '70s. Now swimmable and fishable, it has been further improved through the protection of more than 4000 riparian acres in Massachusetts. Underpromoted, a 52-mile Riverway State Park is now a reality.

On summer weekends hundreds of powerboats emerge from marinas sited on the deep lakelike stretches of the river above the power dams at Holyoke and Turners Falls, but two particularly beautiful stretches of the river—the dozen miles below Turners Falls and above French King Gorge—are too shallow for powerboating and particularly appealing to canoeists. The easiest way onto the river is aboard *Quinnetukut II*, a snappy riverboat cruising back and forth through the gorge between Barton Cove and Northfield Mountain. The sleepy old roads along both sides of the river are also becoming increasingly popular with bicyclists.

One of the state's most traveled bike paths follows an old railbed linking Northampton and Amherst, two towns that together represent one of the state's largest and most interesting concentrations of shops and restaurants. Lodging ranges from tents within sight of the eagles at Barton Cove to convention hotels in Springfield and includes both longstanding inns and a burgeoning number of B&Bs.

Springfield

Springfield is a 33-square-mile city of 157,000 people, with high rises, shops, and major museums all conveniently grouped within a few blocks of each other. Known locally as Springfield Center, this downtown rewards everyone who stops long enough to find the stately old Court Square, the Quadrangle of art, science, and history museums, and the Springfield Armory museum.

Founded in 1794, the armory became a magnet for skilled technicians during the industrial revolution. With the War of 1812, it turned Springfield into a boomtown. At the time of the Civil War, the population once more doubled as the armory produced more than half the guns for the Union cause, nearby Smith and Wesson turned out 110,000 revolvers, and the Ames Sword Company in Chicopee made 150,000 swords. During the late 19th century, Springfield continued to prosper as a rail, industrial, and commercial center and became known for an impressive array of inventions: the first gas-powered car and first motorcycle, pioneering vacuum cleaners, airplanes, and steel-bladed ice skates, to name a few. Although 19th-century philanthropists bequeathed the Quadrangle museums and grand public spaces like Forest Park, they never established a museum to dramatize all those inventions, so the only "first" anyone remembers is basketball, memorialized in a splendid, three-story Basketball Hall of Fame.

Most of the turn-of-the-century downtown theaters, hotels, department stores, and shops are now just memories, supplanted by the sterile if impressive Baystate West complex (a 29-story office tower and hotel with parking and shopping) and the Civic Center (a sports arena and convention center). In recent decades many old buildings have been restored, a Riverfront Park has opened the downtown to the Connecticut, and the area has become known for good eating.

Springfield is also the birthplace of Dr. Seuss. Born Theodor Geisel in 1904, the son of a park commissioner, the artist grew up following his father around the city's splendid Forest Park, a landscape now known to a world of children. After viewing the displays in the Quadrangle, visit the park itself.

AREA CODE: 413

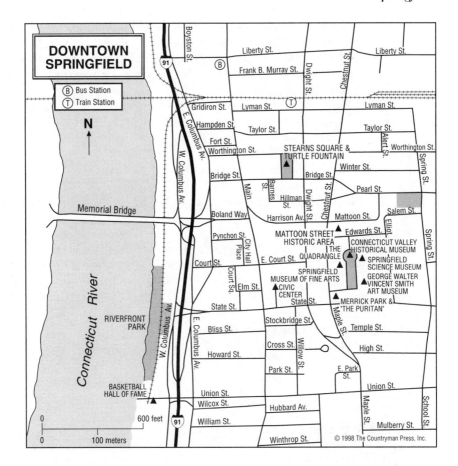

© 1998 The Countryman Press, Inc.

GUIDANCE

Greater Springfield Convention and Visitors Bureau (787-1548; 1-800-723-1548), 34 Boland Way, Springfield 01103. Open 8:30–5 weekdays. Request the *Official Guide to Springfield and the Pioneer Valley*.

Springfield Hospitality Council (732-7467), 338 Worthington Street, Springfield. Open weekdays 9–5.

GETTING THERE

By air: **Bradley International Airport** (203-292-2000) is 18 miles south of Springfield in Windsor Locks, Connecticut. It is served by most national and regional carriers and major car rentals. **Airport Service of Springfield** (739-9999) also connects Bradley with the city.

By train: **AMTRAK** (1-800-USA-RAIL; 785-4230) connects Springfield with Hartford, New Haven, New York City, Philadelphia, Baltimore, Washington, D.C., and Chicago. There is frequent service from New York (change in New Haven). The bus depot is right around the corner from the train station.

By bus: **Peter Pan–Trailways** (781-2900), based in Springfield (with its own terminal at 1776 Main Street), connects with the airport, Boston, Hartford, Cape Cod, Albany, and New York City. **Vermont Transit** (1-800-552-8737) stops en route from New York and Albany to Vermont, New Hampshire, and Montreal.

By car: The route is trickier than you might think. From NYC and points north, take I-91 (exit 4). From Boston, take the Mass. Pike to exit 6, I-291 (a cross-town connector); from Holyoke, I-391 is another connector.

GETTING AROUND

Pioneer Valley Transit Authority (781-7882) serves the Springfield-Holyoke area.

By taxi: **Diamond Cab** (739-9999), **City Cab** (734-8294), and **Yellow Cab** (732-1101).

PARKING

Because downtown Springfield is such a relatively small, congested area of one-way streets, it's best to park as quickly as possible and walk. Reasonably priced parking lots can be found under I-91, in the Baystate West complex (Boland Way), and in the Civic Center Garage (enter from East Court or Harrison Street).

MEDICAL EMERGENCY

Baystate Medical Center (784-3233), Chestnut at Spring Street. Also dial 911.

TO SEE

MUSEUMS

The Quadrangle (236-6800), corner of State and Chestnut Streets, Springfield. At this unique cultural common, four museums and the city's main library are assembled around a grassy green. The museums are open Wednesday through Sunday noon–4; $4 adults, $1 children 6–18, under 6 free; includes admission to all four museums. Inquire about frequent special events. The bronze *Puritan* by Augustus Saint-Gaudens stands in Merrick Park at the entrance, welcoming visitors to the first four of the following museums:

The Museum of Fine Arts (263-6800), the Quadrangle. A 1930s art deco building with a central court, the museum houses a collection ranging from ancient through medieval to modern, with paintings by Winslow Homer, John Singleton Copley, Claude Monet, John Singer Sargent, Georgia O'Keeffe, and several by Erastus Field. The latter was a Leverett portrait painter whose *Historical Monument of the American Republic* is a huge, absorbing fantasy depicting 10 elaborate towers that represent American history, culminating with the triumph over slavery (note Abraham Lincoln rising to heaven in a fiery chariot near the top of the central tower). Completed in 1876, the painting was found be-

MUSEUM OF FINE ARTS

Historical Monument of the American Republic (1876), *by Erastus Salisbury Field, can be viewed at Springfield's Museum of Fine Arts.*

hind a Leverett pigsty in the 1940s and is now enshrined at the center of the museum court. Also note Field's compelling primitive portraits and *The Newsboy,* a moment in 1889 captured by George Newhall, Springfield's leading late-19th-century artist. Be sure to locate *New England Scenery* by Frederic Church. The '20s and '30s are also well represented; note *Church Supper,* by Paul Sample, depicting a small town in 1933. Changing exhibits.

George Walter Vincent Smith Art Museum (263-6800), the Quadrangle. The first museum on the Quadrangle (1896), this is a one-man collection housed in a magnificent palazzo. G.W.V. Smith (always called by his full name locally) amassed a fortune in New York and married Springfield's Belle Townsley, retiring here at age 35. The couple devoted the remainder of their lives to collecting ancient Japanese swords, armor, and art; Islamic rugs; the largest Western collection of cloisonné; and 19th-century landscape paintings. Like Boston's Isabella Stewart Gardner, the Smiths stipulated that the collection not be altered after their deaths, and their ashes are interred in the museum. The couple's portraits are just off the entry hall, surrounded by portraits of stern past captains of valley industry. Note the excellent introductory film about G.W.V.S.

Connecticut Valley Historical Museum (263-6800), the Quadrangle. A Colonial Revival mansion built in 1927 (note the replicated Connecticut Valley front door) houses an excellent genealogical library and increasingly interesting exhibits on Springfield inventions, personalities, and institutions. An imaginative exhibit on Theodor Geisel (Dr. Seuss) matches the sights of the author/artist's boyhood Springfield with the landscape of his books; plenty here for children to relate to and with. Recent special exhibits here have been truly outstanding.

✐ **Science Museum** (733-1194), the Quadrangle. Dinosaur buffs will find a 20-foot-high model of *Tyrannosaurus rex* and the tracks of much smaller dinosaurs. Exhibits also include a vintage-1937 Gee Bee monoplane made in Springfield, a hands-on Exploration Center, an impressive African Hall full of animals, some great old-fashioned dioramas, Native American artifacts, and a new Eco-Center featuring live animals in realistic habitats—lifelike vegetation, fish that walk on land, turtles that look like leaves, and an Amazon rain forest. Planetarium shows daily ($1).

Springfield Armory National Historic Site, Armory Square (enter from Federal Street near the corner of State Street). Open Tuesday through Sunday 10–5. Billed as the world's largest collection of firearms, exhibits include an array of weapons used in every war since the Revolution; also a film with footage from old, wartime-era newsreels. The museum building dates from just before the Civil War in 1847. The handsome brick complex, which occupies more than 15 acres of bluff above the city, was demilitarized in 1968 and is now Springfield Technical Community College.

Basketball Hall of Fame (781-6500), 1150 West Columbus Avenue, Springfield. Open daily 9–6 in summer, 9–5 September through June. A three-story building just off I-91 (the one site that's well marked from the interstate) tells the story of how Dr. James Naismith first threw a soccer ball into a peach basket in 1891. Exhibits include a basketball court, multi-image presentations of the game, and a hall depicting its greats. Newcomers are inaugurated each spring. $7 adults, $4 seniors and students, free under age 7.

Springfield Indian Motorcycle Museum and Hall of Fame (737-2624), 33 Hendee Street, Springfield. Open daily March through November 10–5 and December through February 1–5. From downtown Springfield, take I-291 east to exit 4, then turn right onto Page Boulevard until you see the HISTORIC SPRINGFIELD sign. The museum is a brick, garagelike building in an industrial complex. The collection includes a wide variety of vehicles, from old Columbia bikes to motorized toboggans. You learn that Indian was the first commercially marketed, gasoline-powered motorcycle manufacturing company in the United States; manufacturing ceased in 1953. Admission $3.

Titanic Historical Society Museum (543-4770), rear of Henry's Jewelry Store, 208 Main Street, Indian Orchard. Open 10–4 weekdays, 10–3 Saturdays. The world's largest collection of objects (3600) recovered from the *RMS Titanic*, the world's most famous shipwreck (April 15, 1912, with a loss of 1600 lives). The society's founder and president,

Edward Kamuda, was inspired to begin the collection after seeing the 1953 film *A Night to Remember.*

Storrowton Village Museum (787-0136), 1305 Memorial Avenue, West Springfield, at the Eastern States Exposition grounds (Route 147). Open mid-June through Labor Day, Monday through Saturday 11–3:30. $5 adults, $4 children. The gift shop and the Old Storrowton Tavern are open year-round (closed Sunday). Donated to the Exposition in 1929 by Mrs. James Storrow of Boston (the same family for whom Storrow Drive is named), this grouping of 13 restored 18th-century buildings makes up one of the first museum villages in the country. All buildings were moved here from their original locations.

HISTORIC HOMES AND SITES

Court Square, bounded by Court and Elm Streets, Springfield. Springfield's "Municipal Group" recalls the city's golden era. Completed in 1913, the monumental, many-columned, Greek Revival City Hall and Symphony Hall buildings are separated by a soaring, 300-foot Italianate campanile. The **City Hall** interior is graced by 27 kinds of marble and fine wood paneling and includes a Municipal Auditorium seating 3000. **Symphony Hall** is equally elegant and known for its acoustics. In the columned **Old First Church** (737-1411), check out the art gallery (open Monday through Friday 9:30–2:30 or by appointment), topped with a rooster shipped from England in 1749. The park here, created in 1812 to complement the first Hampden County Courthouse, is the scene of frequent events. Note the Victorian-era courthouse designed by Henry Hobson Richardson.

Storrs House (567-3600 or 567-5500), 697 Longmeadow Street, Longmeadow. Open Wednesday and Thursday 9–noon and by appointment. Originally the parsonage for the First Church of Christ, now headquarters of the Longmeadow Historical Society, with Connecticut Valley furnishings, 18th-century-style grounds.

Josiah Day House (734-8322), 70 Park Street, West Springfield. Open Saturday and Sunday 1–5. Built in 1754 and billed as "the oldest saltbox in America," it houses the collection of the Ramapogue Historical Society.

Historic Springfield neighborhoods. In the late 19th century Springfield became known as the City of Homes, reflecting the quality of the thousands of wooden homes—single- and two-family houses instead of the usual tenements and triple-deckers for the working class, and truly splendid houses for the middle and upper classes. Unfortunately, with the flight of families to the suburbs, several once proud neighborhoods are now shabby, but still well worth driving through. Forest Park, developed almost entirely between the 1890s and 1920, is filled with turreted, Victorian, shingled homes, many built by the McKnight brothers (for whom the McKnight District, boasting some 900 of these homes, is named). Right downtown the Mattoon Street Historic District is a street of 19th-century brick row houses, leading to the 1870s Grace Baptist Church designed by Henry Hobson Richardson.

FOR FAMILIES

⌀ **Riverside** (786-9300), 1623 Main Street (Route 159), Agawam. Open weekends mid-April through May, daily June through Labor Day, weekends in September; hours vary. Largest amusement park in New England; over 50 rides, including the Cyclone roller coaster and three more coasters, a flume ride, midway, arcades, food outlets, live entertainment. $21.99 adults for all rides and shows, $15.99 for juniors 36–48 inches tall. Stock-car races on NASCAR speedway Saturday night March through Labor Day; some off-season races ($10.99 and up).

TO DO

BOAT EXCURSION

⌀ ***Tinker Belle*** (781-3320; 1-800-343-9999), Riverfront Park, State Street, Springfield. May through October, 4–5 cruises daily. Peter Pan's "river bus" offers narrated cruises on the Connecticut River.

GOLF

In Springfield check out the **Franconia Municipal Golf Club** (734-9334) and the **Veterans Municipal Golf Course** (787-6449), South Branch Parkway.

HIKING

See *Green Space*.

SWIMMING

See **Forest Park** and **Chicopee Memorial State Park** under *Green Space*.

J.C. Robinson State Park (786-2877), North Street, Agawam, also offers swimming and picnicking.

GREEN SPACE

⌀ **Forest Park** (787-6440). Three miles south of the center of Springfield, just east of I-91, also off Route 21 (Sumner Avenue). Open year-round. Free for walk-ins, $1 per car ($2 for out-of-state) weekdays, $2 ($3 for out-of-state) weekends. The 795 acres include a wild animal zoo (deer, bear, woodland animals) and a petting zoo (open mid-April to mid-November; $3 adults, $2 seniors and children 5–12). The park also offers paddleboats, 21 miles of nature trails, tennis courts, picnic groves, swimming pools, and summer concerts at the **Barney Amphitheater.** A magnificent, columned mausoleum built by ice skate tycoon Everett H. Barney (his mansion was destroyed to make way for I-91) commands a great view of the Connecticut.

Stanley Park (568-9312), Westfield, open mid-May to mid-October, 8–dusk. Endowed by the founder of Stanley Home Products, the 100-acre park is known for its extensive rose garden (more than 50 varieties), mini–New England village, 96-foot-high carillon tower, Japanese garden with tea house, arboretum, and large fountain. Sunday evening concerts range from singing groups to the Springfield Symphony Pops.

Laughing Brook Education Center & Wildlife Sanctuary (566-8034), 789 Main Street, Hampden (from I-91 in Springfield, take exit 4 (Route 83) to Sumner Avenue, then go 3.6 miles). Off any main route to anywhere, this is a popular destination for families drawn by the onetime home of storyteller Thornton Burgess. The house is now part of a 259-acre preserve owned by the Massachusetts Audubon Society, which includes hiking trails, fields, streams, a pond, caged animals, a picnic pavilion, and a "touch-and-see" trail.

Chicopee Memorial State Park (594-9416), Burnett Road, Chicopee. A 574-acre park with two human-made lakes and the Chicopee and Morton Brook Reservoirs. There is a beach and bathhouse at Chicopee Reservoir; also four separate picnic areas and a 2-mile paved bicycle path. Day-use fee in summer.

Riverfront Park, foot of State Street, Springfield. A 6-acre, riverfront park offers a view of the Connecticut, which is otherwise walled from access by rail tracks and highway. This is the site of summer concerts.

LODGING

The downtown convention hotels include the 264-room high-rise **Springfield-Marriott Hotel** (781-7111) and the 304-room **Sheraton Springfield Monarch Place** (781-1010), both right at the downtown I-91 exit, both with indoor heated pools and full health clubs. Marriott rates are $135 per couple and Sheraton's are $89–160. A 12-story, 252-room, relatively new **Holiday Inn** (781-0900; 1-800-465-4329), 711 Dwight Street (I-291, exit 2A), has an indoor pool and rooftop restaurant. $90–115 double, but inquire about specials.

Berkshire Bed & Breakfast Homes (268-7244), PO Box 211, Williamsburg 01096. This reservation service offers bed & breakfast in a number of Springfield homes. We were delighted with the one we stayed at; our host, a lifelong Springfield resident and enthusiast, insisted on giving us a tour of Forest Park. $45–150.

WHERE TO EAT

DINING OUT
Student Prince & Fort Restaurant (734-7475), 8 Fort Street (off Main), Springfield. Open 11–11, Sunday noon–10. Sandwiches served all day. The Springfield business community's favorite spot since 1935: a grand old downtown beer hall with stained-glass windows, hung with beer steins. Serves imported wine and draft beers and offers a large menu of

hearty German specialties—sauerbraten, Jaeger schnitzel and Wiener schnitzel, hunter's pie, and Hungarian goulash. Seasonal specialties include a February wild game menu (where else can you try young bear or buffalo in wine sauce with spaetzle?). Lunch runs $4.50–12.95; dinner, $8.25–21.

Caffeine's Downtown (788-5546), 254 Worthington Street, Springfield. Open for lunch and dinner. Handy to the Quadrangle Museums and Symphony Hall, a vaguely Mediterranean decor and menu, a good bet either for lunch (try the Cobb salad or marinated artichoke pizza) or dinner— anything from a California white pizza (grilled eggplant with feta, mozzarella, shredded greens, tomato, and onion) to grilled duck with a blueberry Grand Marnier sauce ($17.95) or fresh sea bass grilled and served over a caramelized onion couscous with pineapple jalapeño salsa ($17.95).

Cara Mia (739-0101), 1011 East Columbus Avenue, Springfield. Open Tuesday through Saturday 4–10. An upstairs place with welcoming red velvet decor but, surprisingly, delightfully nonstuffy. Jackets not mandatory, but the food is elegant. The veal and lamb dishes are particularly good; several daily specials. Live music Saturday nights. Entrées run $9.95–22.

Michael's Restaurant (532-2350), 85 Montcalm Street, Chicopee. Open Wednesday through Saturday 5:30–10. Attached to a long-established local function facility (Chateau Provost), this French restaurant gets good reviews. Both the menu and nightly specials are ambitious. You might begin with a paté or baked Brie in puff pastry, dine on roast lamb, and finish with crêpes Suzette. $14.95–22.95. A good wine list.

Hofbrauhaus (737-4905), 1105 Main Street, West Springfield. The dining room features murals of German landscapes, and the atmosphere is quite formal but fun. Try deep-fried sauerkraut balls or goulash soup, a selection of good veal dishes, and a sparkling German wine. Be sure to leave room for a torte. Dinner entrées average $10.

Federal Hill Club (789-1267), 135 Cooper Street, Agawam. Open for dinner by reservation Tuesday through Saturday 4:30–9:30. The atmosphere and history here are that of a private club, but one that has been open to the public for a couple of decades now. The setting is the dignified dining room of a mansion and the extensive menu is recited, not printed. Five courses are the rule, and the wine list is quite impressive. $15.50–32.

Old Storrowton Tavern (732-4188), Eastern States Exposition Grounds, West Springfield (on Route 147). Open daily (except Sunday) 11:30–10. Built as the John Atkinson Tavern in Prescott (one of the towns drowned by the Quabbin Reservoir), it has a traditional Yankee menu, good for chicken pot pie and seafood, veal, and beef dishes. Entrées $10 for lunch, $15–22 for dinner.

EATING OUT

Gus & Paul's (781-2253), Tower Square, 1500 Main Street. A popular breakfast and lunch spot in downtown Springfield. Freshly baked bagels and deli sandwiches are the specialty, also egg dishes like egg and pastrami scramble, knishes, gefilte fish, blintzes, and chopped liver, not to mention knockwurst on a bagel with mustard and kraut. There is also always a choice of freshly made soups, sandwiches, and salads; beverages include Dr. Brown's Soda, including celery flavor (our favorite and seldom seen).

Tilly's (732-3613), 1390 Main Street, Springfield. Open 11:30–9 Monday through Wednesday; open later through Saturday; Sunday noon–8. Great homemade soups, deli sandwiches, quiches, breads and desserts, daily specials, full dinners. Try the Black Forest pie. A popular meeting place for lunch and after work.

Blue Eagle (737-6135), 930 Worthington Street, Springfield. Open from 11:30 daily, until 9 Sunday through Thursday, until 10 on weekends. Diner fans should drive (though not far from Main Street, this isn't a walking neighborhood) up Worthington Street to this popular place with '40s touches like round windows in the door and glass-block windows. The menu is large and better than basic, ranging from a BLT to surf and turf, including lamb shish kabob and fried seafood dinners.

Mom & Rico's Market (732-8941), 899 Main Street, Springfield. Open Monday through Friday 8–5:30. A great Italian deli/grocery with a self-service buffet that usually includes lasagna, sausage and peppers, eggplant Parmigiana (better than your mother's). Pay by the pound or order from the large choice of grinders. This is headquarters for local bocci fans. For cappuccino and a cannoli, step next door to the **Cafe La Fiorentina** (883 Main Street).

Frigo's (731-7797), 1244 Main Street, Springfield. Open Monday through Friday 8–5, until 6 in summer. The blackboard menu features take-out specialties like pizza rustica, veal parmigiana, large and interesting sandwich combinations; a favorite with the downtown lunch crowd. If you have time, step around to **Frigo's Market** at 90 Williams Street, a cheese lover's mecca, also Italian cold cuts and takeout.

Lido (736-9433), 555 Worthington, Springfield. Open Monday through Saturday 11–11. Drive (don't walk) to this Italian favorite, good for the basics like lasagna and eggplant parmigiana and hot or sweet sausage. Best garlic bread in town.

Sitar (732-8011), 1688 Main Street, Springfield. Open Monday through Saturday for lunch and dinner, Sunday for dinner 5–10. Sampler platters and luncheon specials help the uninitiated choose from a large menu of Indian and Pakistani dishes.

ENTERTAINMENT

StageWest (781-2340), 1 Columbus Center, Springfield. Professional theater, November through May. StageWest Summer Series includes concerts, dance, and comedy.

Springfield Civic Center and Symphony Hall (787-6610; box office 787-6600), 1277 Main Street, Springfield. This complex, across from Court Square, stands on the site of the courthouse that Daniel Shays and his friends besieged after the Revolution. It includes a 7500-seat Grand Arena that also serves as a theater, as a basketball court for the NCAA Division II Championship Playoffs, and, with a coat of ice, as the home of the Springfield Indians hockey team and scene of the annual Ice Capades. There is also a Little Arena, scene of a variety of live presentations. Symphony Hall, the classic, columned music hall on Court Square itself, is the home of the Springfield Symphony Orchestra (733-2291). It also stages top-name performers, Broadway shows, children's theater, and travelogues.

Paramount Performing Arts Theater (734-5874), 1700 Main Street, Springfield. A '20s movie palace staging pop, rock, and country music concerts as well as comedy and children's shows.

Bing Theater (733-4273), 716 Sumner Avenue, Springfield. Second-run films at bargain prices.

Palace Cinema (781-4890), 895 Riverdale Road, and **Showcase Cinemas** (733-5131), 864 Riverdale Road, West Springfield; both show first-run films.

Zone Arts Center (732-1995), 395 Dwight Street, West Springfield. Exhibitions, readings, films, and concerts, as well as art exhibits.

SELECTIVE SHOPPING

Baystate West, 1500 Main Street, Springfield. This indoor mall harbors 70 shops and restaurants; the complex is currently slated for a remake as an outlet center.

SPECIAL EVENTS

Note: For event information, call the **Spirit of Springfield** hotline (748-6190).

February: **Spring Flower Show** at the Civic Center, Springfield.

May: **Peach Basket Festival**, includes enshrinement of newcomers to the Basketball Hall of Fame, Springfield. **World's Largest Pancake Breakfast,** Main Street, downtown Springfield (733-3800).

June: The **American Crafts Council's Fair** at the exposition grounds in West Springfield (737-2443). **Laurel Week** in the Westfield River Valley. **Taste of Springfield**, Court Square; more than 30 restaurants participate. (733-3800).

June through August: **Summer Sounds** (free outdoor concerts on Saturday evenings in Riverfront Park, Springfield).

Fourth of July: **Star Spangled Springfield**. Live music, food, an arts festival, and fireworks in Court Square, Springfield (733-3800).

July through August: Sunday performances by **Springfield Pops** in Stanley Park, Westfield. Theatrical and musical performances in Forest Park, Sunday evenings.

Mid-August: **Harambee Festival of Black Culture,** Winchester Square, Springfield.

September: **Glendi**—Greek festival with folk dances, crafts, food at the Greek Cultural Center, Springfield. **Kielbasa Festival**—Polish music, dance, and food at Fairfield Mall, Chicopee. **Eastern States Exposition** ("The Big E"; 732-2361), West Springfield, the biggest annual fair in the East—livestock shows, horse shows, giant midway, entertainment, avenue of states; always runs 12 days including the third week in September. **Quadrangle Weekend** (737-1750)—outdoor festivities, films, lectures, crafts demonstrations, Springfield. **Mattoon Arts Festival**—an outdoor fair on a downtown street lined with brownstones, gaslights; Springfield.

October: **Chicopee Octoberfest. Springfield Arts Festival** (736-ARTS)— hundreds of visual and performing artists display work inside and out in all of Springfield's 18 neighborhoods. **Columbus Day Parade** down Main Street, Springfield, to the Christopher Columbus statue in the South End.

November: **Parade of the Big Balloons**, day after Thanksgiving, downtown Springfield. **Fall Color Festival** in Springfield, day after Thanksgiving.

Late November through mid-January: **Bright Nights at Forest Park**. New England's largest Christmas light display, with themes like Seuss Land, Victorian Village, North Pole Village. Evenings from 6:00. $8 per car weekdays, $10 weekends.

December: **First Night**, New Year's Eve celebration, centered in the Quadrangle.

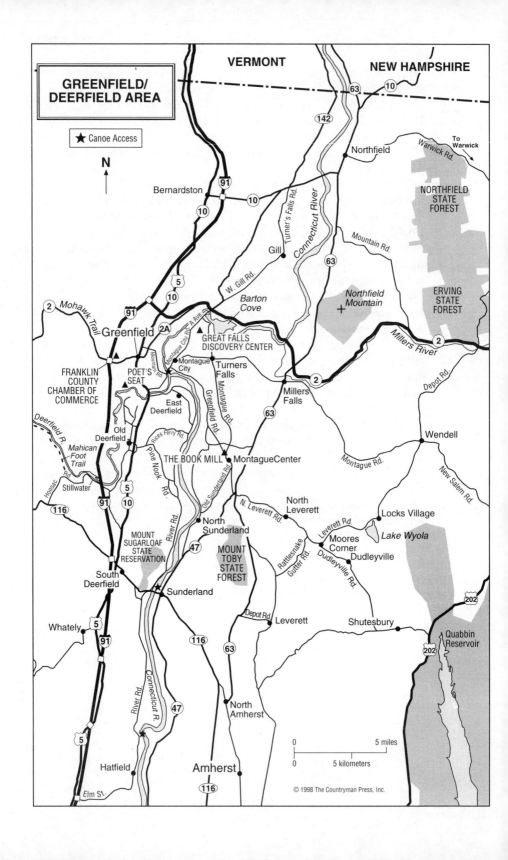

Upper Pioneer Valley

This northern two-thirds of the valley divides into two distinct parts: (1) the most northern, narrow, and rural stretch for which the big sight to see is the village of Old Deerfield and the commercial center, Greenfield; (2) the Five-College Area, with 30,000 students on five very different campuses within an 11-mile radius.

With its mile-long march of 18th- and early-19th-century brick and wood buildings, set starkly against a thousand acres of cornfields, Old Deerfield includes 14 Historic Deerfield buildings open to the public, as well as Memorial Hall, an exceptional town historical museum, and the 1890s Deerfield Inn. The Historic Deerfield houses are open year-round, as rewarding to visit in January as they are in July.

The commercial strip along the combined Routes 5 and 10 in Deerfield has become an attraction in its own right. Yankee Candle, with its Bavarian Village and car museum, counts more than 1.5 million customers a year (compared with Historic Deerfield's quarter of a million visitors). The village of South Deerfield, 4 miles south of Old Deerfield, offers a surprising number and range of restaurants and a view down the valley—from the top of Mount Sugarloaf.

Lewis Brydn's painting on the cover of this book presents the view to the east: the town of Sunderland set against Mount Toby. The view south down the valley is even more memorable: The shimmering ribbon of river stretches as far as the eye can see, flanked by a baffle of trees and broad patchwork of yellow and green fields, spotted with century-old wooden tobacco sheds, and walled on the south by the magnificent east–west march of the Holyoke range.

Bicycle or drive up or down River Road through farmland along the Connecticut in Deerfield or Whately or cross over to Sunderland and drive back down to Hadley on Route 47. Better yet: Get out on the Connecticut. Above Turners Falls the river itself is accessible by excursion boat as well as by rental boats and canoes.

Greenfield is the Franklin County seat and the commercial center of this end of the valley. It remains a classic New England town with some architecturally interesting buildings and a peppering of galleries, shops, and cafés (the new Lunt Design Center combines all three).

The feel is totally different 20 miles downriver in Amherst and Northampton, dual but different hubs of the Five College area. They are sited on opposite sides of the Connecticut and connected by relentless road rash along Route 9 and a 9.75-mile bike path (the Norwottuck Rail Trail) through the flanking farmland.

The four private colleges and the University of Massachusetts at Amherst together enroll some 30,000 students on campuses within an 11-mile radius of each other. In cities, such academic concentrations are less noticeable. Here, against a backdrop of cornfields, apple orchards, and small towns, the visible and cultural impact of academia has been dramatic, especially since the '70s. Between 1961 and 1972, the UMass enrollment tripled, and five 22-story dormitories plus one of the world's tallest libraries appeared above surrounding fields. Innovative Hampshire College opened in an Amherst apple orchard, and the Five College Consortium evolved from a concept into a reality.

During the academic year buses now circulate among the campuses (residents and visitors welcome). Five thousand students annually take courses at the other institutions, and all share a lively calendar of plays, concerts, and lectures. Increasingly, too, graduates have opted to stay on in the valley, establishing the crafts and art galleries, restaurants, shops, and coffeehouses for which the area is now known.

Northampton, the valley's focal point both for students and visitors, is now known not only for the quantity of its attractions (some 75 restaurants, roughly 100 shops, and a dozen major galleries) but also for the quality of the art and crafted work on display. It is increasingly a magnet in its own right for artists, including musicians and filmmakers from throughout the country. Northampton is, besides, an architecturally interesting old county seat, with an outstanding art museum (at Smith College) and the country's oldest and most ornate municipal theater (the Academy of Music).

Amherst retains an appealing but small-town look and feel. The outsized common, framed by the Amherst College campus and 19th-century shopfronts, remains its centerpiece, connected to the UMass campus (curiously invisible, despite the high rises, unless you go looking for it) by one long street of shops and restaurants that offers plenty of good eating, shopping, and book browsing but remains low-key.

Mount Holyoke in South Hadley is the country's oldest women's college and arguably has the most beautiful of the five campuses, an 800-acre spread designed by the firm of Frederick Law Olmsted with two lakes and majestic trees.

The fact that each of the five "colleges" is so different adds, of course, to the beauty of their mix—a phenomenon best experienced during the academic year. Summer is, however, increasingly interesting in the valley. Entertainment options include theater at Mount Holyoke College, concerts at the Summit House atop Mount Holyoke and in the garden at Forty Acres in Hadley, and Jazz in July at UMass. Hiking trails run along the ridge of the Holyoke Range and through many miles of conservation land, a bike trail follows the old railbed between Northampton and Amherst, and canoes can be rented to paddle down the Connecticut River.

We include the small brick-mill city of Holyoke in the Five College area although it's physically—improbably—here, designed from scratch by Boston developers in the 1840s, a foil to the nearby ivy-covered communities. Industrial-architecture buffs will be intrigued by canal-side mill buildings; shoppers will love the genuine galleries and outlets. Families will appreciate the attractions conveniently grouped around the Holyoke Heritage State Park—the Children's Museum and a working antique merry-go-round. Mount Tom offers great views, a wave pool, and water slides.

Thanks to both AMTRAK and bus service (from New York City and frequent buses from Boston and among the campuses), the Five College area in particular is accessible without a car.

AREA CODE: 413

GUIDANCE

Franklin County Chamber of Commerce (773-5463, daily, 24 hours), PO Box 790, Greenfield 01302. The chamber's office at 395 Main Street serves as a walk-in information center year-round. Weekdays June through foliage season an information center at the I-91, Route 2 rotary is also open.

Amherst Area Chamber of Commerce (253-0700), 11 Spring Street (side entrance of the Lord Jeffery Inn), Amherst. Monday through Friday 9–3:30. An information booth on the common is open May through mid-October.

Greater Northampton Chamber of Commerce (584-1900), 99 Pleasant Street (Route 5 south). Open Monday through Friday 9–5.

GETTING THERE

By air: **Bradley International Airport**; see "Springfield."

By bus: **Peter Pan–Trailways** (1-800-343-9999) connects Greenfield, Amherst, South Hadley, and Holyoke with Boston, Springfield, Bradley International Airport, and points beyond. The local departure points are in Amherst, 79 South Pleasant Street (256-0431); in Northampton, 1 Round House Plaza (586-1030). From New York City, **Greyhound** (1-800-231-2222) and **Vermont Transit** (1-800-552-8737) serve Greenfield on north–south routes.

By train: **AMTRAK** (1-800-872-7245), Amherst.

By car: The Mass. Pike and Route 2 offer east–west access, and I-91 runs north–south. From Route 2 the quickest and most scenic way to the Amherst/Northampton area is via Route 202 (exit 16), the Daniel Shays

Highway, running down along the Quabbin Reservoir; turn west at the Pelham Town Hall.

GETTING AROUND

The **Pioneer Valley Transit Authority**, or PVTA (586-5806), connecting Northampton, Amherst, and South Hadley, is free and frequent. It circles among the five campuses from 6:45 AM until 11:35 PM weekdays during the academic year, less frequently on weekends and in summer.

PARKING

In Greenfield: There is metered parallel and angled parking on Main Street and in the lot across from the Chamber of Commerce.

In Northampton: The big parking garage ($.35 an hour) is on South Street behind Thornes Market; parking lots are scattered throughout town with major areas just south of Main Street, accessible from Pleasant Street and from Hampton Road.

In Amherst: In addition to metered street parking, there are four downtown lots. The Boltwood lot (access from Main Street) is the handiest, with access to North Pleasant Street shops. Behind the CVS on North Pleasant Street is another lot, and there are also small lots on Spring Street (adjacent to the common) and Amity Street (across from the Jones Library).

In Holyoke: The downtown parking garage is on Dwight Street, one block from the Heritage State Park.

MEDICAL EMERGENCY

The Cooley Dickinson Hospital (582-2000), 30 Locust Street (Route 9), Northampton.

Providence Hospital (536-5111), 1233 Main Street, Holyoke.

Franklin Medical Center (772-0211), 164 High Street, Greenfield.

VILLAGES, TOWNS, AND CITIES

Amherst. Despite significantly more students than Northampton (the town's population of 35,200 includes 23,000 students at UMass, 1500 at Amherst, and 1200 at Hampshire colleges), Amherst remains a relatively quiet college town with intriguing shops and restaurants limited to two sides of its common and broad North Pleasant Street. As noted in the introduction, the vast and high-rise UMass campus, north of downtown Anherst, is curiously invisible. The far smaller Amherst College campus, just off the common, also eludes visitors but is well worth finding, both for its **Mead** (art) and **Pratt** (science) museums (see *To See*) and for its view down the valley to the dramatic **Holyoke Range**. Emily Dickinson buffs should visit the collection devoted to the poet in the **Jones Library,** as well her house (see *To See*); both are within walking distance of the common. As noted in the Upper Valley introduction, Amherst has direct train service to Manhattan (with a bicycle baggage car) and a direct bus from Boston, as well as excellent local public transport and a bike trail to Northampton. With neighboring Hadley, it also

KIMBERLY GRANT

The octagon at Amherst College

offers the valley's largest concentration (admittedly not huge) of inn and bed & breakfast rooms and a surprising amount of very accessible natural beauty, if you know where to look (see *Green Space*).

Deerfield. Old Deerfield's serene good looks belie its ups and downs during the 19th and 20th, as well as the 17th and 18th, centuries. Founded on a lush plain in 1663, the first settlement here was deserted in 1675 after King Philip's Native Americans killed most of its young men in an ambush that's remembered as the Bloody Brook Massacre. Seven years later, however, the proprietors of Deerfield were back, harvesting crops and listening to Sunday sermons in the square, tower-topped meetinghouse (reconstructed on a smaller scale as the present post office). Then one blustery February night in 1704, Frenchmen and Native Americans swarmed over the stockade, carrying more than 100 villagers off to Montreal. Within three years of this widely publicized event, many of the same families were back again. Today visitors are amazed by the richness and sophistication of life as it was lived here during and after the Revolution—as judged from the quality of the architectural detailing, furniture, silver, and furnishings on view. Ironically, having been wiped out twice, Old Deerfield survives today as a unique sampling of life in the late 18th and early 19th centuries.

By the 1820s, however, Deerfield had been upstaged by Greenfield as the local commercial center. Already it had become the place to come to school (Deerfield Academy was founded in 1797) and to visit "historic" sites. In 1830 an elaborate granite obelisk replaced a vintage-1720s memorial on the North Main Street (in South Deerfield) site of the Bloody Massacre, and in 1848 a campaign was mounted to save the Indian House, which still bore the mark of the hatchet implanted in it during the 1704 raid. Though the campaign failed, it is now cited as the first effort in this country to preserve a historic house; the door was acquired by a Boston antiquarian, which so outraged local residents that he had to return it.

Deerfield's zeal for self-preservation was fanned by George Sheldon, a self-appointed town historian given to raiding his neighbors' attics. Sheldon organized the Pocumtuck Valley Memorial Association in 1870 and a decade later acquired a striking, three-story brick building designed by Asher Benjamin (it had been the original Deerfield Academy building). The society filled this Memorial Hall with local relics ranging from the Indian House door to colonial-era cooking utensils, displayed in what is now recognized as the first "period room" to be seen in any American museum.

Sheldon also enticed his cousin C. Alice Baker back to town. Born in Deerfield, Baker had become a teacher and noted preservationist in the Boston area (she was involved in the campaign to preserve the Old South Meeting House) and was familiar with the then-current attempts to restore colonial buildings in and around the village of York, Maine. Back in Deerfield, Alice Baker acquired the Frary Tavern, restored it, and went on to found two societies dedicated to reviving colonial-era crafts such as weaving, hearth cookery, pottery, and basketry. Visitors came. They came by rail and later by rural trolley, stayed in local farms and several now-vanished hotels (including Jewitt House atop Mount Sugarloaf), and shopped for arts and crafts in local homes and studios.

By the 1920s Deerfield was again forgotten. The 1937 *WPA Guide to Massachusetts* described it as "the ghost of a town, its dimness almost transparent, its quiet almost a cessation, but it is essential to add that it is probably quite the most beautiful ghost of its kind, and with the deepest poetic and historic significance to be found in America."

This time it was Deerfield Academy Headmaster Frank Boyden who came to the rescue of the old houses, persuading Deerfield Academy alumnus and parent Henry Flynt and his wife, Helen, to buy a number of decaying Old Deerfield buildings. The Flynts subsequently restored many of these buildings, incorporating them as the nonprofit Heritage Foundation (now Historic Deerfield) in 1952. The entire town of Deerfield has been remarkably lucky in preserving some 5900 acres of cultivated land. Although tract housing sprouted in several fields in the late 1980s, a Deerfield Land Trust was subsequently established and is now dedicated to preserving local farmland.

The largest property holder in Old Deerfield is **Deerfield Academy,** and there are two more private schools—**Eaglebrook** and **Bement School**—in the village. Also in Old Deerfield: **The Brick Church,** built in 1824, has arched doorways and a closed wooden cupola. It's the scene of frequent special events as well as regular (Unitarian) services. The **Old Burying Ground** (walk along Albany Road) has many 18th-century stones. Sited as it is at the confluence of the Deerfield and Connecticut Rivers, the town enjoys an unusual amount of water frontage (see *Green Space*), and many of the farms that welcome visitors (see *Selective Shopping*) are on river roads, which are good for bicycling. (Also see *Lodging*, *Where to Eat*, and *Special Events*.)

Greenfield. This proud old town of 18,000 is sited at the confluence of the Green and Connecticut Rivers, and also at the junction of Route 2 and I-91. Main Street is distinguished by a number of interesting buildings in a wide variety of styles, several by native son Asher Benjamin, the unsung hero responsible for the architectural look of much of rural New England. In the 1790s, a period when much of western Massachusetts and northern New England was quickly settled, Benjamin was keenly aware of the need for a "do-it-yourself" guide to the new architectural styles being introduced in Boston by Charles Bulfinch. In 1796 Benjamin wrote *The Country Builder's Assistant*, followed by six more books that resulted in the construction of thousands of homes and hundreds of churches—the distinctive three-story houses and high-steepled churches that remain the pride of New England villages. The **Greenfield Public Library** (772-1544), 402 Main Street, said to be the first building designed by Asher Benjamin, has an exceptional children's room and an interesting historical collection. The **Greenfield Historical Society** (774-3663), 3 Church Street (by appointment), offers eight rooms filled with furnishings, portraits, early Greenfield artifacts, and photos. (Also see *Lodging*, *Eating Out*, and *Selective Shopping*.)

Hadley. The filler between Northampton and Amherst, Hadley is easy to miss because it's still predominantly tobacco, onion, and asparagus fields—beyond the Route 9 shops, greenhouses (the Hadley rose, the Talisman rose, and the Hadley gardenia were all developed here), and the many malls. Settled in 1659, it is the mother town of Amherst, South Hadley, Sunderland, Granby, and Hatfield, and was originally known as Norottuck, a name recently resurrected for the bike path that threads its fields. In 1675 a white bearded recluse, reputedly William Goffe (a Charles I regicide), saved the town from an Indian attack and has ever since been known as the Angel of Hadley. Turn off Route 9 at Middle Street to see the pillared **Town Hall** (1841), **Hadley Farm Museum** (see *To See—Museums and Historic Homes*), and the **First Congregational Church** (1808). The **Porter-Phelps-Huntington House** (1742) hidden away on the river (Route 47, north from Route 9; see *To See—Museums and Historic Homes*) is a jewel.

Holyoke. In 1847 Boston investors formed the Hadley Falls Company, buying 1000 acres with the idea of utilizing the waterpower from the magnificent falls here. The company—and its dam—went bust but was soon replaced by the Holyoke Water Power Company, until recently the city's major political and economic force. Holyoke is a classic planned mill city. Its 4½ miles of canals rise in tiers past dozens of mills; the commercial area is set in a neat grid above the mills. Housing changes with the altitude—from 1840s brick workers' housing on "The Flats" near the river, through hundreds of hastily built, late-19th- and early-20th-century tenements, to the mill-owners' mansions above, and above that the parkland on Mount Tom. In the visitors center at **Holyoke Heritage State Park** (534-1723, 221 Appleton Street, open Tuesday through Sunday noon–4:30 [follow the signs for downtown]), a short film conveys a sense of the city's late-19th-century vitality, of the era in which immigrants turned neighborhoods into "Little" Ireland, Poland, France, and a half-dozen more bastions. If the film were remade today, it would note the last two decades' influx of Puerto Ricans, a group first drawn in the '60s to work in the nearby tobacco fields. Specialty papers, from college bluebooks to hospital johnnies, remain Holyoke's most notable product. Inquire about guided and leaflet walking tours and frequent special events. Mill architecture buffs will appreciate the beauty of the canal-side Graham Mill (Second Level Canal near the Route 116 bridge). Inquire about the status of the Holyoke Heritage Park Railroad, dormant but not dead at this writing.

Northfield, bisected by the Connecticut River and bounded on the north by both Vermont and New Hampshire, has an unusually wide and long Main Street lined with many houses built during the heyday of river traffic and sheep farming. Northfield is best known today for the two college-sized campuses of Northfield Mount Hermon, founded as two distinct prep schools by evangelist Reverend Dwight Moody in the late 19th century. Although there is no trace of Moody's grand old summer hotel, there is a summer youth hostel (American Youth Hostel began here in 1934) and two bed & breakfasts representing the town's two most notable eras. The trails at **Northfield Mountain** and rides aboard the excursion boat *Quinnetukut II* also attract visitors, and both golf and bicycling options are outstanding. Stop by the **Northfield Historical Society** (498-5565) to learn more about Dwight Moody and the Stearns brothers, and don't miss Rua's (see *Eating Out*).

Northampton. Despite a population of less than 30,000, this is a city, one with more art and music, film and drama, shopping and dining than most urban centers a dozen times its size. Thanks to **Round Hill,** an 1840s–1860 mineral water spa, Northampton loomed large on New England's pre–Civil War tourist map. In 1851 Jenny Lind, the Swedish Nightingale, spent a three-month honeymoon at Round Hill. She called Northampton Paradise City, a name that's stuck (current local listings include Paradise City Travel, Paradise Copies, etc.). The brick hotel itself survives as part of the **Clarke School for the Deaf** (established 1867) on Round Hill Road, off Elm Street. Northampton is the seat of Hampshire County and home to **Smith College,** as well as to historic figures as different the as fiery 18th-century preacher Jonathan Edwards, 19th-century food faddist Sylvester Graham (as in Graham cracker), and 1920s Northampton mayor and US president Calvin Coolidge.

Northampton also has its share of brick mills, however, and Main Street seemed more blue-collar than collegiate in 1971 when we bought our wedding cake at the Polish bakery near Woolworth's. Certainly it wasn't the current lineup of galleries and restaurants. "Twenty years ago friends told me I was crazy to move my shop from Amherst to Northampton," Don Muller recalls. Muller's is now one of a half-dozen crafts galleries salted among the restaurants, art galleries, and boutiques along the town's five-block-long **Main Street.** The turning point in Northampton's recent history is frequently pegged to the early '70s transformation of vacant McCallum's Department Store into **Thorne's Market,** a 40-shop complex that has incubated many current Main Street enterprises. Now known as Noho, Northampton continues to evolve. One art deco former bank building is now occupied by Silverscapes; it is an appropriate jewel box—complete with stained-glass skylight and artfully designed art deco–style counter— in which to display jewelry. Another is the R. Michaelson Gallery, a handsome two-story-high space seemingly designed to display sculpture, prints, and paintings by nationally known but locally based artists like Leonard Baskin, Barry Moser, and Greg Gillespie.

Northampton these days illustrates synergy like no place we know. It's not unusual to find the city's internationally famed Young At Heart Chorus of senior citizens sharing a stage with the Northampton Gay Men's Chorus, or for visitors to view a Matisse or Picasso in the **Smith College Museum of Art** (free admission) and then stroll down the street to see a concert or a locally produced film at the municipally owned (since 1890) **Academy of Music;** others may have just walked up the street from touring the **Words & Pictures Museum,** brainchild of locally based Teenage Mutant Ninja Turtles cartoonists Peter Laird and Kevin Eastman. Annual events include a Lyric Theater as well as arts and film festivals, and live music is a nightly given in several venues. Restaurants are so plentiful that patrons know they can always find a table within a block or two.

TO SEE

ART MUSEUMS
Smith College Museum of Art (585-2760), Elm Street (Route 9, just beyond College Hall), Northampton. Open July and August, Tuesday through Sunday noon–4, Thursday until 8; September through June, Tuesday, Friday, and Saturday 9:30–4, Wednesday and Sunday noon–4, Thursday noon–8. This is the standout collection of art in the entire

Morning Picture (1890), by Edwin Romanzo Elmer, is set in Ashfield; the painting can be found in the Smith College Museum of Art.

valley, housed in an unobtrusive but spacious three-story museum. Usually on view are works by Picasso, Degas, Winslow Homer, Seurat, and Whistler, and sculpture by Rodin and Leonard Baskin. We've returned time and again to see Rockwell Kent's *Dublin Pond,* Marsden Hartley's *Sea Window,* and two starkly realistic oils by Edwin Romanzo Elmer evoking 19th-century scenes from the nearby Hilltowns. Special exhibits in the adjacent but easy-to-miss wing are frequently also world-class.

Mead Art Museum (542-2335), on the campus of Amherst College, Amherst. September through May, Monday through Friday 10–4:30, Saturday and Sunday 1–5; June through August, Tuesday through Sunday 1–4. The building was designed by McKim, Mead, and White, and although exhibits change there is always the Rotherwas Room, an ornately paneled, vintage-1611 English hall. The college's 9000-piece collection includes paintings by Thomas Eakins, Winslow Homer, Marsden Hartley, and Childe Hassam.

Mount Holyoke College Art Museum (538-2245), South Hadley. Open Tuesday through Friday 11–5, Saturday 1–5. One of the oldest collegiate art collections in the country, but housed in a modern building. Permanent holdings range from ancient Asian and Egyptian works to some outstanding 19th-century landscapes; changing exhibits.

Note: Art lovers should also visit Northampton's major art galleries (see *Selective Shopping*), which represent current artists whose work hangs in many of the world's major museums.

MUSEUMS AND HISTORIC HOMES
In Amherst

Emily Dickinson Homestead (542-8161), 280 Main Street. Guided tours only, Wednesday through Saturday in April through October, Wednesday and Saturday March and November through mid-December; call for specific times and to reserve a place. Adults $4, $3, students, $2 children 6–11. Dickinson was born here, and her second-floor bedroom has been restored to look as it did during the years (1855–86) when she wrote her finest verse here. The only objects known to have belonged to her, however, are the sleigh bed, a hatbox, and the white dress she wore after her father's death in 1874. Unfortunately, much of the poet's furniture and her books are presently in Harvard's Houghton Library, but the quality of the tour at the homestead is now excellent. You learn that less than a dozen of Dickinson's nearly 1800 poems were published during her lifetime, and that she rarely left this house during the 11 years in which she was consumed with writing her honest and intense puzzlings on the grand themes of love and nature, God and death, ragged-edged lines like:

> *"Hope" is the thing with feathers,*
> *That perches in the soul,*
> *And sings the tune without the words*
> *And never stops—at all.*

The garden Dickinson tended remains a pleasant place to sit, and a path still leads next door to her brother Austin's house, **The Evergreens,** an ornate period piece that, through a curious sequence of events, still retains its 1870s decor and feel; let's hope that it will one day soon be open to the public.

Dickinson buffs should also see the display on her life and work at the **Jones Library** (256-4090), 43 Amity Street; open Monday through Saturday. A recent wing includes a handsome research facility with seven panels depicting Dickinson's life (1830–86) in Amherst and original handwritten poems; the collection here includes 8000 items. Also inquire about the Robert Frost collection (Frost lived in Amherst from 1931 to 1938 and returned in the '40s to teach at Amherst College). In **West Cemetery** on Triangle Street, in Amherst, it's not difficult to find the Dickinson family plot, which is bounded by an ornate black iron fence. Here Emily lies surrounded by her grandparents, parents, and sister Lavinia. Note that on the Saturday nearest May 15 (the anniversary of her death), visitors are invited to meet at the homestead and walk to the cemetery. Inquire about periodic workshops held to coincide with this event.

The **Amherst History Museum** at the **Strong House** (256-0678), 67 Amity Street. This 1740 gambrel-roofed house displays decorative arts, clothing, textiles, fine art, period rooms, and changing exhibits; the feel is Victorian and the focus is on the 19th century. The garden is 18th century. In 1899 it was the Amherst Historical Society's colorful founder, Mabel Loomis Todd, who secured this property. A novelist in her own right, Todd was mistress to Austin Dickinson and editor of the first published volume of Emily Dickinson's poetry.

National Yiddish Book Center (1-800-535-3595), Hampshire College campus, Route 116. Admittedly a cultural more than an art center, this handsome wooden complex of work, exhibition, and performance spaces, designed to resemble an Eastern European shtetl, opened in 1997. Credit for the very idea of rescuing Yiddish literature (roughly a century's worth of works in the Yiddish language, beginning in the 1860s) goes to the center's director, Hampshire College graduate Aaron Lansky. This is a clearinghouse for books of a genre presumed almost dead when the center was founded in 1980; at the opening of the current facility in 1997 it had collected 1.3 million volumes, with an average 1000 arriving weekly. Volumes are distributed to shops and libraries throughout the world. Exhibits change but the quality of the artwork on display alone would have been worth our trip; also inquire about frequent lectures and performances.

In Deerfield

Historic Deerfield (774-5581), in Old Deerfield, marked from Route 5, is 6 miles north of Exit 24 off I-91, or 3.5 miles south of Greenfield (off I-91 and Route 2). Open all year 9:30–4:30 daily except Thanksgiving, Christmas Eve, and Christmas Day. May through October: $12 adults, $6 children 6–17, includes admission to Memorial Hall; otherwise $10 adults, $5 children. Tickets (good for 2 consecutive days) are sold in the **Hall Tavern** (be sure to see the upstairs ballroom). Guided tours are presently offered of 13 buildings displaying a total of some 20,000 objects made or used in America between 1630 and 1850. Historic houses include:

The **Wells-Thorn House** (sections built in 1717 and 1751) shows the dramatic changes in the lifestyles in Deerfield through two centuries. The **Ashley House** (1733), with its elegantly carved cupboards and furnishings, depicts the lifestyle of the village's Tory minister (note his 1730s Yale diploma). The **Asa Stebbins House** (1799/1810) is the first brick home in town, grandly furnished with French wallpaper, Chinese porcelain, and Federal-era pieces. The **Wright House** (1824), another brick mansion, is a mini-museum of early furniture and china. The **Sheldon-Hawks House** (1743) is furnished almost exclusively with pieces from the Connecticut River Valley and Boston and is still filled with the spirit of George Sheldon, the town's colorful first historian. **Frary House/Barnard Tavern** (1740/1795), is my favorite because of its classic tavern look, ballroom, and 1890s restoration by C. Alice Baker. The **Ebenezer Hinsdale Williams House** (1750s, re-

KIMBERLY GRANT

Historic Deerfield

built 1816–20), opened in 1993 after 12 years of painstaking restoration, seems surprisingly airy, with touches like the light-toned rag stair rug, "glass curtains," and brightly patterned wallpapers.

Memorial Hall (774-7476), Memorial Street and Route 5/Route 10, Old Deerfield. Open May through October 10–4:30 weekdays, 12:30–4:30 weekends. $6 adults, $3 students, free for children under 6; also see Historic Deerfield for a combination ticket. We have already described much that is special about this museum (see Deerfield under *Villages*). Opened by the Pocumtuck Valley Memorial Association in 1878 to house the wealth of things collected by town historian George Sheldon, it features an extensive collection of Native American relics, early paintings and quilts, and priceless Hadley chests. This is also the place to savor the town's 1890s–1920s revival—through paintings and photographs (note both by the fabulous Fuller family), clothing, and the world's largest collection of work by the Deerfield Society of Blue and White needlework. (Inquire about the society's semiannual crafts festivals and other special events.) The Old Indian House, reconstructed in 1929 and owned by Memorial Hall, is open for special events and can be rented for parties and weddings.

In Hadley

Porter-Phelps-Huntington Historic House Museum (584-4699), 130 River Drive (Route 47, 2 miles north of the junction of Route 9 and Route 47). Open May 15 through October 15, Saturday through Wednesday 1–4:30. **Wednesday Folk Traditions** (ethnic folk music) at 7 PM in June and July. **A Perfect Spot of Tea,** Saturday in July and

August (pastries and music at 2:30 and 3:30); also a **Fall Foliage Festival** (crafts, a barn dance, storytelling, children's games) on a mid-October weekend. Also known as **Forty Acres,** this aristocratic old farm was built right on the banks of the Connecticut River in 1752, and there have been no structural changes since 1799. The furnishings have accumulated over six generations of one extended family.

The **Hadley Farm Museum,** Route 9 and Route 47, Hadley. Open May through October 12, 10–4:30, Sunday 1:30–4:30, closed Monday. Free. The 1782 barn from Forty Acres (see above) was moved in 1930 to its present site near the First Congregational Church and white-pillared town hall. It houses old broom-making machines (broom corn was once the town's chief crop), hay tedders and other old farm implements, pottery, an old stagecoach from Hardwick, and other assorted mementos of life in the valley.

In Holyoke

Wistariahurst Museum (534-2216), 238 Cabot Street. Open Wednesday, Saturday, Sunday, noon–4. A late-19th-century, 26-room mansion built for the Skinner family, owners of the world's largest silk mill. Period rooms feature turn-of-the-century furnishings and decorative arts; changing exhibits.

In Northampton

Historic Northampton (584-6011), 46-66 Bridge Street (Route 9). Open for tours March through December. The **Parsons House** (1730), the **Damon House** (home of architect Isaac Damon), and the **Shepherd House** (a mid-19th-century home) reflect lifestyles over three generations.

Coolidge Memorial Room in the **Forbes Library** (584-8399), 20 West Street. Open Monday through Wednesday 10–1 and by appointment. The only presidential library in a public library, this room contains all of Calvin Coolidge's papers from his years as governor, vice president, and president. The Amherst College graduate (1895) studied law and first hung out his shingle in Northampton. He became city solicitor, met his wife (Grace Goodhue was teaching at the Clarke School for the Deaf in Northampton when she met fellow-Vermonter Cal), was elected a state representative, then mayor of Northampton (two terms). He became state senator, then governor, then vice president, and, when Harding died suddenly (August 3, 1923), president (for six years). The Coolidges returned to Northampton, and Calvin died here in 1933. Personal belongings on display include an electric horse.

In South Hadley

Skinner Museum (538-2085), Route 116. Open May through October, Wednesday and Sunday 2–5. Housed in the 1846 church that once stood in the town of Prescott (flooded by Quabbin Reservoir), this holds a trove of 4000 items ranging from Native American artifacts to medieval sets of armor.

Mount Holyoke College

THE COLLEGES

Amherst College (542-2000), Amherst. Founded in 1821 to educate "promising but needy youths who wished to enter the ministry," Amherst is today one of the country's most selective colleges. The campus is handsome and nicely sited, its oldest buildings grouped around a common overlooking the valley to the south and the Holyoke Range beyond. In addition to the **Mead Art Museum** (see *Art Museums*), the college maintains the **Pratt Museum of Natural History** (542-2165), September through May, weekdays 9–3:30, Saturday 10–4, Sunday noon–5; in summer, Saturday 10–4, Sunday noon–5. This is a terrific, very old-fashioned museum with displays ranging from local "track ways" (dinosaur tracks) to the skeleton of a woolly mammoth, the skeletal legs of an 87-foot-long diplodocus, and an 800,000-year-old human skull.

Hampshire College (549-4600), 893 West Street (Route 116), Amherst. Opened in 1970, this liberal arts college is predicated on cooperative programming with the other four colleges. Its 1200 students design their own programs of study. Inquire about current exhibits at the three campus galleries and events at the Performing Arts Center.

Mount Holyoke College (538-2000), Route 116, South Hadley. Founded in 1837, Mount Holyoke is the country's oldest women's college. The 800-acre campus features ivied buildings in a number of Revival styles, home to some 1800 women. The adjacent **Village Commons,** a complex of restaurants, shops, and a theater, was designed by Graham Gund. Spend some time in the **Talcott Arboretum** (538-2116), open weekdays 9–4, weekends 1–4. This exquisite little Victorian-style greenhouse

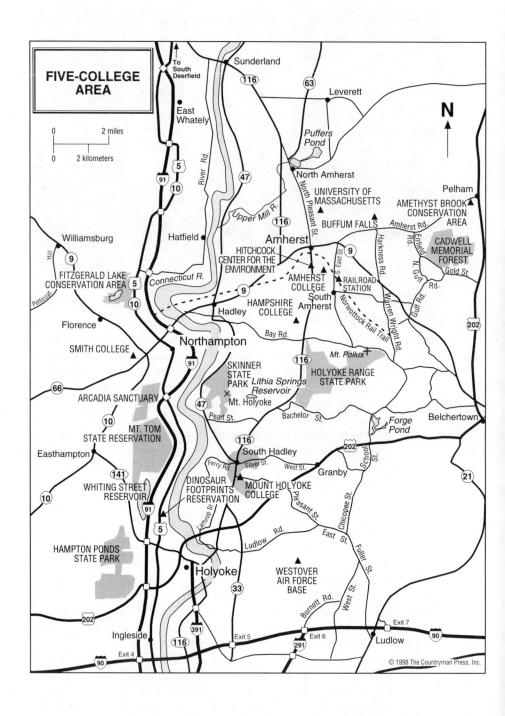

is filled with a jungle of exotic flora, featuring special late-winter and spring flower shows.

Smith College (584-2700), Northampton. Founded in 1875 for "the education of the intelligent gentlewoman," the 125-acre campus now includes 97 buildings, an eclectic mix of ages and styles. Don't miss **Paradise Pond**. The **Lyman Plant House** (585-2740), open daily 8–4:15, is known for its spring and fall flower shows; adjacent are an arboretum and gardens.

University of Massachusetts (545-0111), Amherst 01003. Founded in the mid-19th century as the state's agricultural college, the university doubled its size and suddenly skyrocketed both physically and academically in the 1960s and '70s. It now includes nine undergraduate schools and colleges, also graduate schools, in more than 150 buildings on a 1200-acre campus. Some 5500 courses are offered by 1300 faculty. Sights to see at UMass: **Fine Arts Center and Gallery** (545-3670), changing exhibits. **William Smith Clark Memorial**, a half-acre memorial at the eastern entrance to the campus (off North Pleasant Street) dedicated to the first president of the university and his work in Japan, where he founded Sopporo Agricultural College, now the University of Hokkaido. The unusual memorial encompasses two circles linked by a spiral walk and twin steel walls depicting Clark's Amherst home and the Agricultural Hall at Hokkaido. Clark is widely revered in Japan, and many youth clubs are still dedicated to his memory. The memorial garden is sited on a hill with views extending across the campus to the river and hills. **Durfee Gardens** and **Durfee Conservatory** (545-5234), open weekdays 8:30–4:30. The conservatory dates from 1867 and houses tropical plants such as banana, coffee, and papayas divided by a 40-foot pool with an ornamental bridge and fountain. Five interlocking garden spaces offer benches, paths, and trellised wisteria and morning glories.

FOR FAMILIES

Yankee Candle Company (665-2929), Route 5/10, ¼ mile north of I-91, exit 24, South Deerfield. In 1969 Michael Kittredge used his mother's kitchen to make his first candles. Now billed as "the world's largest candle store," Yankee Candle is a vast, ever-growing complex that includes a Bavarian Village complete with year-round falling snow and make-your-own-country-kitchen candles; it lures more than a million visitors a year. Attractions include a castle courtyard and waterfall, nutcracker castle, year-round Santa's toy factory, giant toy machine, and its own Chandler's Tavern. The complex includes the **Yankee Candle Car Museum** (665-2020), open daily 9:30–6, except Thanksgiving and Christmas. Adults $5, $2 for children 4–11. More than 50 vehicles, from several classic Rolls-Royce limos to a gull-winged DeLorean coupe, from a 1930s BMW Bariolet to current curiosities like the 1963 Amphicar.

Words & Pictures Museum (586-8545), 140 Main Street, Northampton. Open Tuesday through Sunday noon–5. $3 adults, $2 students and seniors, $1 under 18. Founded by the Teenage Mutant Ninja Turtles co-creator Kevin Eastman, this nonprofit museum has transformed a former Main Street commercial building into a four-story happening, a permanent collection in a classic museum on the top floor. You enter through a cave (note the cave paintings) and beam up through the age of hieroglyphics and ancient Chinese illustrations into the world of superheroes. Exhibits change frequently, but cartoons are always featured and would-be cartoonists can always test their skill in a number of satisfying, hands-on ways. Admission necessary for the gift shop.

Old Greenfield Village (774-7138), Route 2 west from Greenfield. Open daily 10–4 May through October, except Tuesdays. This is a genuine, Yankee kind of phenomenon that has disappeared almost as completely as the thousands of artifacts it displays. What's here are the basics found in stores, in dental offices, churches, barbershops, and tool shops around the turn of the century, all collected over 30 years by retired schoolteacher Waine Morse—not a man with a lot of money, but just a sense of where to find what, when. Morse also constructed the buildings by himself. Raising the church steeple alone, he admits, was a bit tricky. Morse also guides visitors around. $5 adults, $4 seniors; $3 ages 12–16, $2 ages 11 and under.

Merry-Go-Round (538-9838), next to the Holyoke Heritage State Park Visitors Center. September through May, weekends noon–4; June through Labor Day, Tuesday through Sunday 11–5. $1 per ride. This vintage-1929 carousel with 48 hand-carved steeds, two chariots, and 800 lights was built for Mountain Park, an old-fashioned amusement park that closed in 1987. It was restored and moved to this handsome pavilion at a total cost of $2 million. Also available for private parties.

Children's Museum (536-KIDS), 444 Dwight Street (across from the Heritage State Park Visitors Center), Holyoke. Open Monday through Friday 9:30–4:30, Sunday noon–5. $3.50 per person. A stimulating space with a Main Street that simulates downtown Holyoke's shops and enterprises (the favorite is a working TV station). There is also usually a large, dramatic exhibit in a lower-level museum (additional admission), a gift store, and a café.

Look Memorial Park (584-5457), Route 9, Florence. Open Memorial Day through Labor Day. The many attractions of this 150-acre park include picnicking; swimming and wading pools; pedal boating and canoeing on **Willow Lake;** a playground; a small zoo with native deer, peacocks, pheasants, and raccoons; the **Pines Outdoor Theater** (summer concerts and theater); the **Picnic Store;** and a miniature replica of an 1863 train that circles the zoo.

Volleyball Hall of Fame (536-0926). Housed in the Children's Museum complex (see above). Open Tuesday through Friday 10–5, Saturday noon–5. Invented in Holyoke in 1895, volleyball is commemorated here in a series of interpretive panels.

✐ **SummerSide at Mount Tom** (536-0416), Route 5, Holyoke. Open 10–8 weekends from Memorial Day; daily in July and August. $15.95 admission. This ski area has replaced its Alpine Slide with Alpine Falls (two tube rides), a huge wave pool, and a water slide. Slopeside café.

✐ **Dinosaur Footprints Reservation**, Smith's Ferry on Route 5, 1 mile south of Mount Tom, Holyoke. Look for a small, unmarked turnout on the river side of the road. An 8-acre stretch of three-toed tracks, each 15 inches long and belonging to a 20-foot-long dinosaur (*Eubrontes giganteus*) who lumbered by 200 million years ago, is visible. Smaller tracks and other fossils have also been preserved.

✐ **McCray Farm** (533-3714), 55 Alvord Street, South Hadley. Open daily, year-round, with a dairy bar open spring through fall. A petting zoo, wagon and sleigh rides depending on the season, maple breakfasts in March, and pick-your-own pumpkins.

✐ **Red-Wing Meadow Fee Fishing** (367-9494), 528 Federal Street, Montague. Open for fee fishing April through November. A fee is charged for fishing and per pound for fish you catch. Pole rentals available. Picnic tables are scattered around the ponds.

✐ **Turners Falls Fish Ladder** (863-3221), off Route 2 in Turners Falls. Mid-May through July, be sure to stop by to view the fish ladder through a glass wall. Shad, striped bass, and salmon are the ladder patrons. A small display also depicts the natural and industrial history of the falls, and Unity Park here offers picnicking facilities and a playground.

✐ **Robert E. Barrett Fishway** (536-9428), Holyoke Dam, Holyoke, just off Route 116 at the South Hadley Falls Bridge. Open in mid-June, Wednesday through Sunday 9–5. Viewing windows and an observation platform overlook American shad and Atlantic salmon as elevators help them bypass the falls on their trip upriver to spawn.

Northfield Mountain Recreational and Environmental Center (659-3714), Route 63 in Northfield. April through October, bus tours take you to the upper reservoir and underground powerhouse of Northeast Utilities' unusual pumped storage hydroelectric plant. A film about the construction and operation of the plant can be viewed in the visitors center. The project utilizes water from the Connecticut, draws it up into an artificially created lake on top of the mountain, and uses the stored water to generate power during high-use periods. The powerhouse itself is hidden in a cavern as high as a 10-story building, as wide as a four-lane highway, and longer than a football field. The center also houses superb displays dramatizing the story of the river's 18th- and early-19th-century flat-bottomed sailing barges for which canals were constructed in the 1790s. The story of steamboating and the advent of the railroad is also told, along with subsequent industrialization, logging, and the present hydro uses of the river's "white gold." The center also offers a series of lectures and workshops on the area's flora and fauna. See *To Do* for June through mid-October cruises on the Connecticut aboard the *Quinnetukut II.*

SCENIC DRIVES

River Road runs along the western shore of the Connecticut all the way from Hatfield north to the confluence with the Deerfield, and it's lined with farms, tobacco sheds, and fields. It's flat except for the monadnock, Mount Sugarloaf, which thrusts up all alone (be sure to drive to the top). See *Selective Shopping* for farms along this road, and note the old headstones in **Pine Nook Cemetery** some 4 miles north of Route 116. River Road in Northfield, south from the landing (off Route 63) at Northfield Mountain to Route 2, is also beautiful.

Route 2 to Montague Center to either Greenfield or Deerfield. Turn off Route 2 at Route 63, to Montague Center, with its common framed by a Congregational church designed by Asher Benjamin and a brick town hall that serves as a summer theater. The **Book Mill,** with its crafts, bookstore, and the **Blue Heron Restaurant,** is just south of the common, over a small iron bridge at the junction of Depot Street and Greenfield Road. Continue on Greenfield Road; take a left on Montague City Road and cross the river. To reach the Poet's Seat (see *Green Space*), turn right on Mountain Road. For Old Deerfield, continue to Routes 5/10 and turn left; Old Deerfield is a mile or so south, on your right.

Route 2 to Turners Falls to Old Deerfield. This is a shortcut rather than scenic drive, but handy to know since it lops off several tedious highway miles. Leave Route 2 at Turners Falls and cross the high bridge onto Avenue A, the main drag of this classic, late-19th-century mill town. You might stop for a meal or at least pie at the **Shady Glen Restaurant;** also stop by the **Great Falls Discovery Center** across the way. Continue south on Avenue A, which turns into the Montague City Road, and cross the iron bridge, bear left to Routes 5/10, and watch for an Old Deerfield sign.

Mohawk Trail. New England's first tourist trail (dedicated in 1914) begins in Greenfield and heads west, abruptly uphill. Shelburne Falls, the hub of the the Mohawk Trail, is just 8 miles west of downtown Greenfield. (See "West County/Mohawk Trail" for details.)

Route 11. From Mt. Sugarloaf in Deerfield, Route 116 climbs almost as steeply and quickly out of the valley as Route 2. (See "Hampshire Hills" for details.)

Route 47. From the lights on Route 9 at Middle Street, head north on Route 47, past the **Porter-Phelps-Huntington Historic House Museum** (see *Historic Museums and Homes*), to **Sunderland,** a classic 18th-century river town with most of its homes strung along Main Street, flanking a brick town hall that was built in 1867 to double as the school. You pass the access road to **Mount Toby** (see *Hiking*), the **Mt. Toby**

The Poet's Seat

Sugar House, and many tobacco barns.

Rattlesnake Gutter and the Peace Pagoda. Assuming that you are coming from Amherst, the easiest way into this web of wooded roads is north from the lights in North Amherst, forking almost immediately right onto the road that becomes Route 63—but just before it does (there's a sign), turn right on Depot Road, then left on Montague. Rattlesnake Gutter Road is the next right, a dirt road that plunges down into a thickly wooded ravine—flanked by far deeper ravines. Continue to Moores Corner, turn left on the North Leverett Road, and in a couple miles turn left again onto Cave Hill Road; left again in .9 mile at a small sign for the Peace Pagoda. Follow the dirt road to a small parking lot, from which you can climb up to the unlikely, white-domed Buddhist shrine and a hilltop view. Cave Hill Road runs back into Montague Road, back down to Depot, etc.

Note: Also see "Views" under *Green Space.*

TO DO

AIRPLANE RIDES AND SKYDIVING

Pioneer Aviation (863-9391) offers scenic flights from Turners Falls Airport.

Massachusetts Sport Parachute Club (863-8362), Turners Falls Airport. Skydiving instruction with three different methods: static line, tandem, and accelerated free fall.

BICYCLING

Given the number of young and young-in-spirit residents of this valley, combined with relatively flat, quiet, unusually scenic rural roads, it's not surprising that bicycle touring is big here. At this writing it's possible to arrive on the AMTRAK Vermonter in Amherst at 4 PM, unload your bike from the bike baggage car, and take off along the **Norwottuck Rail Trail,** an 8.5-mile bike path linking Northampton, Hadley, and Amherst along the former Boston & Maine Railroad right-of-way. You could also, of course, easily find a room within walking distance of the station and rent a bike from **Valley Bicycles** (256-0880), 319 Main Street, Amherst.

Other access points to the Rail Trail are at **Mountain Farms Mall** on Route 9 in Hadley, and at **Elwell State Park** on Damon Road (just north of the Route 9 bridge) in Northampton. It crosses the Connecticut on an old rail bridge and passes through open farmland, with views to the Holyoke Range to the south and to Mount Toby and Mount Sugarloaf to the north. All the scenic drives outlined in this book lend themselves to bike touring, but there are many more loops. Inquire at local bike shops. Mountain biking is also popular in summer on the 40 miles of trails at **Northfield Mountain**. Rentals as well as advice are available from: **Northfield Bicycle Barn** (498-2996), Main Street, Northfield (look for Al's Convenience Store; the Barn is behind the neighboring house). Other bike sources: **Basically Bicycles** (863-3556), 88 Third Street in Turners Falls, **Bicycles Unlimited** (772-2700), 322 High Street, Greenfield, and **Peloton Sports** (584-1016), 15 State Street, Northampton.

BIRDING

Arcadia Wildlife Sanctuary in Easthampton (see *Green Space*) is the area's most obvious birding center, but there are others. The valley represents a major migratory flyway and is known especially for its many soaring hawks in fall. The **Hitchcock Center for the Environment** (see *Green Space—Walks*) offers some birding workshops and is base for the **Hampshire Bird Club.** An exellent guide, *Birding Western Massachusetts: The Central Connecticut River Valley* (1996), edited by Peter Westover for the Kestrel Trust and Hampshire Bird Club, is available in local bookstores. You might also want to check with **Barton Cove** (see *Boating*) about whether American eagles are in residence.

BOATING

   ᕫ **Elwell State Park,** a former junkyard just north of Route 9 at the Northampton end of the Coolidge Bridge, is now a state-of-the-art boat dock, handicapped accessible.

River information: For a copy of the brochure *The Connecticut River Greenway State Park Trail,* detailing information about river access, send a self-addressed, stamped envelope to the Massachusetts Department of Environmental Management, 136 Damon Road, Northampton 01060, or call 586-8706; inquire about guided river trips. **The Connecticut River Watershed Council** (529-9500), One Ferry Street, Easthampton, publishes a canoe guide to the entire river and offers periodic guided canoe trips. **The Great Falls Discovery Center** (863-3221), Avenue A, Turners Falls, is also a source of river information. At **Barton Cove** (863-9300; 1-800-859-2960), Northeast Utilities maintains tent sites, rents canoes and rowboats, and offers shuttle service to put-in places in Northfield.

Boat access points: There is a state boat-launch site on the Connecticut at Pauchaug Brook in Northfield, and below Turners Falls dam you can put in at the Montague City Bridge (off Poplar Street). There is also an informal access point at the Route 116 bridge on the Sunderland side, at a small park in Whately, and at Elwell State Park in Northampton.

BOAT RENTALS

Sportsman's Marina (586-2426), Route 9 at the Coolidge Bridge, Hadley, rents boats April through October (weather permitting): canoes, aluminum outboards, and pontoon boats. Bring a picnic and head for an island. **Brunelle's Marina** (536-3132) in South Hadley has a restaurant and launch area. There is also a state access ramp almost 1½ miles north of Hatfield center, and another is off Route 5 at the Oxbow in Easthampton. The 16-mile stretch of the Connecticut River above the Holyoke Dam is heavily used on summer weekends by water-skiers, fishermen, and powerboat owners as well as canoeists. **Taylor Rental** (773-8643) in Greenfield rents aluminum canoes. **Wildwater Outfitters** (586-2323), Route 9, Hadley, rents canoes and kayaks.

BOAT EXCURSIONS

The *Quinnetukut II* (659-3714) cruises the Connecticut from the Riverview picnic area at Northfield Mountain 6 miles downstream to the Turners Falls dam. Departures are from two to four times per day late May through mid-October. Call for reservations. $7 adults, $3 children under 14, $6 seniors. Inquire about special children's cruises and sunset cruises with live jazz.

CANOEING

Arcadia Nature Center and Wildlife Sanctuary (see *Green Space*), marked from Route 5, Easthampton, but on the Northampton-Easthampton line in Northampton, is a great place for novice canoeists to explore quiet waters. Inquire about guided canoe trips.

The new 52-mile **Connecticut River Greenway Park** (see *Boating*) includes a 12-mile **Connecticut River Water Trail** that runs from the Turners Falls Dam in Montague to the Hatfield state boat ramp. The water along this trail is too shallow for powerboating, so the area is limited to small boats and canoes and to low-impact recreation. A detailed brochure guide to the trail is available from the **Department of Environmental Management** (DEM) (784-1663), 136 Damon Road, Northampton 01060.

Northfield Mountain Recreation and Environmental Center (659-3714), Route 63, Northfield, is the source for information about canoeing sites that Northeast Utilities maintains for public access: **Captain**

Kidds' Island (also good for picnicking), **Munn's Ferry Camp-ground** (with Adirondack shelters and tent sites, accessible only by boat), and **River View,** a float dock, picnic tables, and sanitary facilities on the river across from the entrance to Northfield Mountain. Also see **Barton Cove** under *Boating*.

FISHING

The Connecticut River offers oustanding fishing for bass, shad, yellow perch, all kinds of sunfish, carp, walleye, and trout (check out the mouths of feeder streams). If you don't know how to fish, check out the **Red-Wing Meadow Fee Fishing** (see *For Families*), almost across the road from the **Richard Cronin National Salmon Station**, Route 116 in Sunderland. The **State Fisheries and Game Division** oper-ates a hatchery off Route 116 in Sunderland and a beautiful trout hatch-ery off Greenfield Road in Montague. The oxbow stretch of the area is particularly rewarding year-round (ice fishing too). The most user-friendly put-in places for visitors is **Barton's Cove**; see *Boating* for further rentals. In Turners Falls the **Great Falls Discovery Center** (863-3221) offers information on the river and fishing and **Pipione's Sport Shop** (863-4246) across the street is a source of advice as well as equipment and licenses. See *For Families* for details about the fish lad-ders at Turners Falls and Holyoke.

Note: The nearby Quabbin Reservoir is the state's premier fishing hole, and the Deerfield, West, and Millers Rivers are nationally famed among anglers for fly-fishing.

GOLF

Crumpin-Fox Golf Club (648-9101), Route 10, Bernardston, 18 holes. The front nine were designed by Robert Trent Jones himself and the back nine by his firm. This is a destination golf course with lodging, the neighboring Fox Inn (see *Motels*), and dining at hilltop Andiamo (see *Dining Out*).

Hickory Ridge Country Club (256-6638), West Pomeroy Lane, Amherst, is an 18-hole championship course with a clubhouse and snack bar; **Cherry Hill** (253-9935), Montague Road, Amherst, is a public nine-hole course in North Amherst.

✐ **Western Massachusetts Family Golf Center Practice Range and Miniature Golf** (586-2311), Route 9 in Hadley.

HIKING

See *Green Space* for quick sketches of specific trails that add up to one of the most interesting and accessible hiking centers in New England. *Hiking the Pioneer Valley*, by Bruce Scofield (1995), is a helpful guide.

ICE SKATING

Mullins Center (545-0505), UMass campus, Amherst. Olympic-sized skat-ing rink open to the public. Rentals; call for hours.

CROSS-COUNTRY SKIING

Northfield Mountain Ski Touring Center (583-9073), Route 63, Northfield, offers 40 km of double-tracked trails. Touring equipment and snowshoes can be rented from **Northfield Bicycle Barn** (498-2996), Main Street, Northfield.

DOWNHILL SKIING

Mount Tom (536-0416), Route 5, Holyoke. This is a teaching and, frankly, locally geared mountain with Christmas and February vacation ski camps for area youngsters. *Vertical drop:* 680 feet. *Terrain:* Fifteen trails. *Lifts:* Four chairs and one J-bar. *Snowmaking:* 100 percent. *Facilities:* base lodge, ski shop, large ski school; night skiing. *Rates:* $29 adults weekends, $26 midweek; juniors and seniors $25 weekends,$22 midweek; half-day tickets also available.

SWIMMING

In Amherst the swimming hole is **Puffer's Pond** (off Pine Street in North Amherst) and it's a beauty, with a small beach and woods area (ten minutes north of the common); **Lake Wyola** (367-2627) in Shutesbury is a privately maintained, sandy public beach on a wooded lake; no picnic tables. The **Greenfield Town Beach** (772-1553), Nash's Mill Road (2 miles from Route 2), is open Memorial Day weekend through Labor Day weekend (parking fee).

GREEN SPACE

VIEWS

What sets off this Massachusetts stretch from the rest of the Connecticut River Valley is the number of abrupt mountains thrusting from its floor and the fact that so many old carriage roads, built to serve long-vanished 19th-century hotels, access their summits. Only by taking advantage of these amazing vantage points can you appreciate the valley's unusual mix of farmland and villages, cities, and woods—a mix that has not altered essentially since Thomas Cole painted *The Oxbow* from the top of Mount Holyoke in 1836.

Mount Tom State Reservation (527-4805), Holyoke. Access from Route 5 or from Route 141, Easthampton. This 1800-acre mountaintop woodland contains 30 miles of trails, picnic tables, a lookout tower, and the **Robert Cole Museum** (open May 30 through Labor Day) with nature exhibits. **Goat Peak** has a spectacular view across the valley. In winter the road isn't plowed, but you can ski or snowshoe in. **Lake Bray** offers fishing in summer.

Skinner State Park (586-0350), Route 47, Hadley. **Summit Road** open mid-April to mid-November, the **Summit House** open mid-May to mid-October. "The Paradise of America" is the way Swedish singer Jenny Lind described the view from the top of Mount Holyoke in 1850—the same view of the Connecticut River oxbow, surrounding towns, and distant hills that Thomas Cole popularized in his 1836 painting. One of the first mountaintop inns to be built in New England (the first inn opened in 1821) and the only one preserved in any shape today, the Summit House (also known as Prospect House) is accessible by an

Mount Pollux

auto road and hiking trails. In 1938 Joseph Skinner donated the Summit House and the surrounding 390 acres to the state. It's the setting for sunset concerts in summer.

Mount Sugarloaf State Reservation, off Route 116, South Deerfield. A road winds up this red sandstone mountain (said to resemble the old loaves into which sugar was shaped) to a modern observation tower on the summit, supposedly the site from which King Philip surveyed his prey before the mid-17th-century Bloody Brook Massacre. There are picnic tables and a great view down the valley.

Poet's Seat Tower and Rocky Mountain Trails. Off High Street in Greenfield (or see *Scenic Drives* from Turners Falls). This medieval-looking sandstone tower on Rocky Mountain honors local 19th-century poet Frederick Goddard Tuckerman, who liked to sit near this spot. You can understand why. A Ridge Trail (blue blazes) loops along the top of the hill.

(Also see **Mount Toby** under *Hikes*.)

WALKS AND HIKES

In Amherst and Pelham

The **Amherst Conservation Commission** (town hall, 256-4045) maintains some 1450 acres scattered in 45 distinct holdings, with 60 miles of trails for walking, birding, and ski-touring. It's worth stopping by the town hall or local bookstores to pick up printed maps or guides. The most popular (and most heavily used) areas include **Upper Mill River** and **Puffer's Pond,** State Street off Pine, good for swimming and picnicking. Trails—including one designed for handicapped access and blind walkers—lead upstream from the pond along the Cushman Brook's cascades.

Hitchcock Center for the Environment (256-6006) at the Larch Hill Conservation Area, 1 mile south of Amherst center on Route 116. The 25 acres include hiking trails, formal gardens, and ponds. The center offers a variety of lectures and workshops; it also exhibits local artwork.

Mount Pollux, off South East Street, Amherst, is a favorite spot from which to watch the sunset, a gentle slope to climb through old apple orchards to a summit with a 365-degree view. The entrance is just off South East Street in South Amherst (turn left heading south). It's a very small sign and then a short ways to the parking area, and a short walk to the top of a hill with the memorable view.

Amethyst Brook Conservation Area, Pelham Road, Pelham, is a great spot to walk or ski through woods and fields.

Buffum Falls, Amherst Road, Pelham. Heading east, turn left onto North Valley Road (almost a mile west of Amethyst Brook); look for a parking area on the left. Not particularly well marked but well used, an unusally beautiful spot. A 1-hour hike.

Along Route 2, Millers Falls and Gill

French King Bridge (Route 2 west of Millers Falls) spans a dramatically steep, banked, narrow stretch of the Connecticut, 140 feet above the water. Park at the rest area and walk back onto the bridge (there's a pedestrian walk) for the view. Note the mouth of the Millers River just downstream. The bridge is named for French King Rock below. The king was Louis XV, and the rock was reportedly named by one of his subjects in the mid-1700s. It's funny how some names stick.

Barton Cove Nature and Camping Area (1-800-859-2960), Route 2, just east of Turners Falls in Gill. The office/information center is on Route 2 in the former Rainbow Bend Restaurant. An interpretive nature trail meanders along a rocky ridge overlooking the Connecticut River, and there's a picnic area in addition to tent sites. During nesting season, eagles are usually in residence. Canoe and boat rentals available (see *Boating*).

Between Amherst and South Hadley

Holyoke Range State Park (253-2883), Route 116 between Amherst and South Hadley. Visitors center open daily 9–4 except Tuesday and Wednesday in winter. This dramatic east–west range rises abruptly from the valley floor. It is the most striking feature of the area, visible everywhere from Belchertown to Northampton. Mount Holyoke at its western tip (see Skinner State Park) is the only summit accessible by road, but a trail traverses the entire 9-mile-long ridgeline. From the visitors center at "the Notch" on Route 116, a trail leads east to Mount Norwottuck (connecting with trails to Mount Toby in Sunderland and Mount Monadnock in New Hampshire). Ask about the Horse Caves below Mount Norwottuck in which Daniel Shays and his men supposedly sheltered after raiding the Springfield Armory (the caves are actually so shallow that two Boy Scouts and a pony would have trouble fitting in).

In Deerfield

Channing Blake Meadow Walk in Old Deerfield. A half-mile path through the village's north meadows and a working 700-acre farm begins at the northern end of Deerfield Street; inquire at Historic Deerfield about special family tours and nature activities.

Pocumtuck Ridge Trail, South Deerfield. Take North Main Street to Hillside Drive (across from Hardigg Industries) to Stage Road. Turn left at the top of the hill onto Ridge Road for the trailhead for paths through Deerfield Land Trust's 120-acre preserve.

Mahican-Mohawk Trail. The first mile and a half of this 7.25-mile trail, said to be the actual 10,000-year-old route along the lower Deerfield, is accessible from Deerfield. Request a map at the Hall Tavern in Historic Deerfield (see *Historic Museums and Homes*). Drive south on Deerfield Street and instead of turning back onto Route 5, jog right and then south along Mill Village Road and turn right at the small stone building at the corner of Stillwater Road; at .9 mile take Hoosac Road and you will see the trailhead at .2 miles. The trail follows an abandoned trailbed to the South River. For a description of the rest of the trail, see "West County/Mohawk Trail."

In Northfield

Northfield Mountain, Route 63, Northfield (see *To Do—For Families*)

Bennett Meadow Wildlife Management Area, also maintained by Northeast Utilities, maintains space to park by the west side of the river in Northfield.

In Northampton/Easthampton

Arcadia Wildlife Sanctuary (584-3009). Grounds open dawn to dusk daily except Monday (unless a holiday); the office is staffed 9–3 Tuesday through Friday, 1–4 on Saturday. Accessible from Northampton (take Lovefield to Clapp Street) and Route 10 (off Route 5) in Easthampton. This Massachusetts Audubon Sanctuary owns more than 500 acres of field, woodland, and marsh on the Connecticut River oxbow. Walk out the Cedar Trail and along the Mill River to look out over the Arcadia Marsh from the observation tower. Duckling Trail is a short loop for children. The Conservation Center offers a full program of guided walks, canoe trips, and campouts.

Northampton Conservation Areas include **Robert's Hill** in Florence, overlooking the Lower Leeds reservoir; **Fitzgerald Lake** in Florence; **Childs Park,** 30 acres off Elm and Prospect Streets; and **Look Memorial Park** (584-5457), 150 acres off Route 9 in Florence (see *For Families*).

In North Sunderland

Mount Toby, the tallest mountain in the valley (1269 feet), has great views plus caves and waterfalls. As is the case with Mount Holyoke and Mount Sugarloaf, a hotel once capped its summit but now there's just a fire tower. Access is off Route 47, 4 miles north of Sunderland center. It's a 3-hour round-trip hike, but you can go just as far as the cascades. From Route 47 in North Sunderland, turn right onto Reservation Road; the parking area is a half-mile.

LODGING

Note: Berkshire B&B Associates (268-7244), based just west of Northampton in Williamsburg, is a registration service for many area B&Bs; owner Eleanor Hebert is especially adept at finding space during crunch periods.

Also note: Otherwise inexplicable high rates at some inns take advantage of proximity to expensive prep schools.

HOTELS AND INNS

 ᛦ **Deerfield Inn** (774-5587), 81 Old Main Street, Deerfield 01342. Open year-round. A newcomer by Old Deerfield standards (it opened in 1884), the antiques-filled inn is dignified but not stiff. It is the place to stay when visiting Historic Deerfield, enabling you to steep and sleep in the full atmosphere of the village after other visitors have gone. There are 23 rooms, all with private bath, 12 in an annex added since the 1979 fire (from which townspeople and Deerfield Academy students heroically rescued most of the antiques). Rooms feature wallpaper and fabric from the Historic Deerfield collection, and furnishings are either antiques or reproduction antiques; some canopy beds. Attention to details, phones. Some annex rooms are quite spacious. $140.50–206 plus 10 percent service fee (including a full breakfast). Rates vary with the season, not the room, which strikes us as strange since rooms vary in size and feel, and come with and without ghosts.

 ᛦ **Lord Jeffery Inn** (253-2576; 1-800-742-0358), 30 Boltwood Avenue, Amherst 01002. Built in 1926 by the same architect who designed the matching Colonial Revival Jones Library across the common. College owned and obviously college geared, this is more of a small hotel than an inn. All 50 rooms have private bath, phone, and cable TV; a number also have a balcony overlooking the garden. All rooms are periodically refurbished but look much as we remember them more than 25 years ago when we lodged our wedding guests here. Dining options include informal **Elijah Boltwood's Boltwood Tavern** and intimate high-end dining in the former living room. You can picture Robert Frost rocking on the porch. From $69 (for an economy double, low season) to $168 for the King Suite in high season. Handicap access.

 ᛦ **Hotel Northampton** (584-3100), 36 King Street, Northampton 01060. Built in 1927, this is a proud, redbrick, five-story downtown hotel, handy to all the town's shops and restaurants. The lobby has a hearth, wing chairs, and a soaring ceiling. The glass-fronted **Coolidge Park Café** serves light lunches and dinners, and Wiggins Tavern Restaurant (see

Dining Out) is a valley landmark. The one suite (#500) we've seen is a beauty, complete with Jacuzzi and a view of Mount Holyoke, but most of the standard rooms, though furnished nicely with reproduction antiques, wicker, and duvets, are small. Rates include continental breakfast, parking, and use of the exercise room. $89–195 per couple; "deluxe" rooms and suites are $135–325. Packages available. Two handicapped-accessible suites.

BED & BREAKFASTS

☞ **Clark Tavern Inn Bed and Breakfast** (586-1900), 98 Bay Road, Hadley 01035. A 1740 tavern that stood on the other side of the Connecticut River until 1961 when it was slated for demolition to make way for I-91. Luckily, it was moved and restored. The house retains its "King's Lumber" panels, wide pine floors, and much original detailing. The best news here is, however, the hospitality. Ruth Callahan is a nurse and her husband, Michael, is a physician's assistant, both obviously adept at ministering to the public. "It's so good to be able to make people feel great, not just better," Michael comments. The three rooms are each meticulously but not fussily furnished; the Fireplace Room has both a canopy bed and working fireplace; all have private bath and plenty of reading and relaxing space. Breakfast is served either on the large screened porch overlooking the extensive garden (with swimming pool), or in the Keeping Room, also overlooking the garden. The sound of birds, audible inside as well as from the porch, is so constant that I thought at first it must be a tape, but it isn't. A guest's fridge is well stocked and the Callahans are themselves a fund of local knowledge, happy to lend advice on dining, walking, biking, entertainment, whatever. $100–105 for the smaller room, $115–135 for rooms with working fireplaces. Rates include a very full breakfast and taxes.

Allen House Inn (253-5000), 599 Main Street, Amherst 01002. Peacock feathers in chinoiserie vases, ornate Victorian-era wallpaper on ceilings as well as walls, and antimacassars on intricately carved Eastlake chairs don't usually turn us on, but the Allen House does. This 1880s, stick-style Queen Anne home is a genuine period piece that's never really been on the market. The rush matting is as original to the house as the Eastlake fireplace mantels. Each of the five bedrooms (all with private bath) is papered in hand-silkscreened copies of William Morris, Walter Crane, and Charles Eastlake, and all are furnished with appropriate antique beds and dressers bought locally. Rooms range in size from the back "scullery" to a large front room with three beds. Alan Zieminski first became intrigued with the house while lodging here as a student and secured first option when it came up for sale. Ann Zieminski is a warm hostess and known for spectacular breakfasts, like Swedish pancakes, stuffed French toast, homemade fruit sauces, quiche, and fruit compotes. They're served at the dining room table, but all guests need not gather at the same time.

In 1997 Ann and Alan restored a second house on Main Street, almost directly across from the Emily Dickinson Homestead (see *Historic Museums and Houses*), and were in the process of securing licensing for that property when we stopped by. $55–135.

☞ **Northfield Country House** (498-2692; 1-800-498-2692), 181 School Street, Northfield 01360. The house was built in 1901 on 16 acres along "the ridge" above town as a summer mansion for a prominent Boston family, one among many who attended Dwight Moody's summer Northfield Conferences. Andrea Dale is a hospitable, helpful host. Her dining room is richly paneled and has a quartz-studded mantel to match that in the living room. The latter has a grand piano, an Estey (made in nearby Brattleboro, Vermont) organ, Oriental rugs, and inviting reading nooks. The seven upstairs rooms vary in size, but all are nicely furnished with comfortable antiques. Three have working fireplace and five have private bath; two small back rooms (both atrractive) share a bath. The house is hedged in hydrangeas and set in landscaped grounds complete with pool. The sense of quiet around this place is palpable; I always sleep exeptionally well here. Breakfast is a production. $50–90 per room. No children under 10, please.

☞ **Centennial House** (498-5921), Northfield 01360. Built in 1811 and formerly the headmaster's house for the Mount Hermon School, this handsome old home was designed and built by the town's premier builder, Calvin Stearns. Marguerite Lentz offers three guest rooms (private baths), a gracious parlor and dining room, and—the best part—an expansive view of the river valley. The house sits right on Northfield's long, wide Main Street, which invites strolling. $70–85 including breakfast.

Salt Box B&B (584-1790), 153 Elm Street, Northampton 01060. Opened in '97 across from the Smith College campus, Carol and Craig Melin's 18th-century house makes a great B&B. A mural greets guests in the entry hall; the parlor, though small, has a working fireplace and an air that's both comfortable and gracious. Beyond is a cheery breakfast room. The three guest rooms are decorated with verve. Timothy's Orchard ($85 for one, $100 for two) has its own entrance and patio (good for smokers), but the two that impressed us are the Sabbatical (a suite with a queen-bedded room, full bath, efficiency kitchen and sitting area, and numerous tea cups ($115 for one, $130 for two); and Hester's Retreat, with a four-poster queen, an alcove with an extra daybed, and a bath with two-person whirlpool bath ($110–125). While it isn't fussy, the decorating is unusually imaginative and the general feel of the place is very welcoming. Park your car in back and walk to shops, restaurants, and museums.

The Brandt House (774-3329; 1-800-235-3329), 29 Highland Avenue, Greenfield 01301. Phoebe Compton's expansive, 16-room Georgian Revival house is set on more than 3 acres and offers seven guest rooms,

northhamptonuncommon.com

all with private bath. Common rooms include a tastefully comfortable, plant-filled living room, the dining room with large sash windows (no curtains) overlooking the garden, a game room with a full-sized pool table, a wicker-furnished porch and patio, and an upstairs sun room stocked with local menus, a microwave, and TV; there's also a clay tennis court. Guest rooms are all relatively small but tastefully furnished, two with working fireplace, and the top floor harbors a two-room suite. $127–175 includes a full breakfast. It strikes us as strange that there's also a substantially lower "corporate rate."

☞ **Sunnyside Farm** (665-3113), River Road, Whately 01093. Mary Lou and Dick Green welcome visitors to the big, yellow, turn-of-the-century farmhouse 5 miles south of Deerfield. It's been in their family since it was built and stands on 50 acres of farmland that grew tobacco and is now leased in part to the neighboring berry farm. All five rooms overlook fields. Two spacious front rooms with small TVs face River Road. There's a small but appealing corner double, and a back room has a king-sized bed; baths are shared. Guests have full access to the downstairs rooms, which include a comfortable living room and a dining room in which everyone gathers around a long table for breakfast. Don't miss the porch swing. $55–85.

Yellow Gabled House (665-4922), 111 North Main Street, South Deerfield 01373. Overlooking Bloody Brook (now tamed to a small stream) and the obelisk-shaped memorial to the 1675 massacre on the site, this Gothic Revival house is both snug and elegant. There are three carefully furnished upstairs guest rooms, all with fans and air-conditioning. Two rooms (we like the one with the spool bed) share a bath, and a suite has a canopy bed, adjoining sitting room with TV, and private bath. Host Edna Julia Stahelek is a cartographer and local historian. $75–120 includes breakfast.

Hitchcock House (774-7452), 15 Congress Street, Greenfield 01301. Betty Gott's Victorian-style house sits on a quiet residential street within walking distance of downtown Greenfield. The four second-floor guest rooms are all immaculate, two with private bath. Guests are welcome to try out the electric organ in the living room. $85-100 includes breakfast of fruit cocktail and muffins.

Hannah Dudley House (367-2323), 114 Dudleyville Road, Leverett 01054. Built handsomely in 1797 on a rise surrounded by fields and woods, the house offers four guest rooms, two with working fireplace. As we write, the B&B is up for sale, so the following details may not apply. As stands, our favorite is the lemon-colored Dragon's Lair, and the Kitty Korner suite is ideal for a couple with a youngster in tow. Windows are tall, sunny, and uncurtained. Furniture is comfortable rather than antique. Breakfast, served at 8:30 in the square little dining room, includes homemade granola, muffins, pastries, and fresh fruit.

Facilities include a guest fridge in the game room, an in-ground pool, landscaped grounds with two ponds, and hiking trails through the woods. Lake Wyola (see *Swimming*) and Rattlesnake Ravine are also nearby. The house is 12 miles north of Amherst. $125–185.

Black Walnut Inn (549-5649), 1184 North Pleasant Street, North Amherst 01002. The most imposing house in North Amherst, right in the middle of the village (at the traffic light), this Federal brick house meanders back through an 18th-century wing to a Victorian carriage house. Marie and Edd Twohig have rebuilt much of the house from the floors up, but the integrity of the rooms survive. Furnishings in the seven rooms are handsome (we especially like the Mulberry Room), quilts are handmade, and the baths are private. Breakfast includes hot apple pie as well as other hot dishes like crêpes Suzette, three-cheese quiche, and Belgian waffles. Rooms geared to families are in the back wing; the Carriage House holds a meeting space good for 30 people. $95–125.

Lincoln Avenue B&B (549-0517), 242 Lincoln Avenue, Amherst 01002. This spacious, casual, turn-of-the-century home just a couple of blocks from everything is home for Bonnie Novakov-Lawlor and Lawrence Lawlor, two typical Amherst residents: Larry is a lighting specialist, set designer, and artist, and Bonnie offers acupressure and yoga classes (the reason the living room is so sparsely furnished). Guests tend to gather in the comfortable dining room overlooking the garden. Breakfast is partly self-service and partly served—fruit salad, eggs, toast, juice, granola, and coffee. The guest rooms—two on the second floor (private and semiprivate baths) and several more under the eaves on the third floor (shared bath, robes in rooms)—are all attractive, very much what you would expect to be offered by friends if you were visiting. Children welcome. $65–90.

Pennington Place at Delta Organic Farms (253-1893 or 253-0891), 352 E. Hadley Road, Amherst 01002. Jim and Penny Pitts's attractive new house sits on a quiet road in the midst of cornfields and organic vegetable gardens. It includes a small fridge and microwave, cable TV, its own entrance and phone, and, best of all, lovely views of surrounding farmland. There's a double bed and a pull-out. $95 includes breakfast.

The Knoll (584-8164), 230 North Main Street, Florence 01060. An English Tudor–style home set on 17 acres 3 miles west of downtown Northampton, within walking distance of Look Memorial Park (see *To Do—For Families*). Lee and Ed Lesko offer three rooms, two with double and one with twin beds, sharing two baths. Breakfast is included in $50–55. No smokers, and no children under 12.

Ingate Farms (253-0440), 60 Lamson Avenue, Belchertown 01007 (on the Amherst/Belchertown line). B&B accommodations are in a 250-year-old bobbin factory moved here from land flooded by Quabbin Reservoir. Three of the five pleasant guest rooms have private baths and the others share one. The 500 acres include an Equine Center at which horses can be accommodated and lessons are offered. Because this was a former riding camp (and is still a summer riding day camp), facilities include an Olympic-sized swimming pool. $69–85 depending on room and season. Easy access from the Mass. Pike.

Also see **Bullard Farm** in North New Salem and the **Mucky Duck** in Belchertown ("Quabbin Area") and **Twin Maples** in Williamsburg ("Hampshire Hills").

MOTELS

☞ **Fox Inn** (648-9101), Route 10, Bernardston 01337. An unusually attractive motel just off I-91, exit 28, but with an out-in-the-country feel. Rooms all overlook greenery; request one with peaked ceilings. $58–66 double.

Autumn Inn (584-7660), 259 Elm Street, Northampton 01060. This is a splendidly built and maintained 30-room motel, geared to the parents of Smith students. Rooms are large with double and single beds, TV, phone, and private bath. Breakfast and lunch are served in the coffee shop with a hearth, and there's a landscaped pool. $72 single, $100 double, two non-smoking efficiency suites, $120; charges for extra guests in rooms.

✐ **French King Motor Lodge** (659-3328), Route 2, Millers Falls. A good bet for families, 18 units with a swimming pool and resturant near the French King Bridge. $65–95.

✐ **The Inn at Northampton** (1-800-582-2929), junction of Route 5 and I-91, Northampton 01060. A good bet if you have children along: 125 rooms, an indoor and an outdoor pool, sauna, game room, and lighted tennis court; also a restaurant and lounge. $99–129 for standard rooms.

✐ **Holiday Inn** (534-3311), Holidrome and Conference Center, junction of I-91 and the Mass. Pike at Ingleside, Holyoke. A 219-room, four-story complex featuring a tropical recreational area with 18-foot-high palm trees, a pool, full spa, and, of course, a volleyball court. $79–135 per couple.

CAMPGROUND

Barton Cove Nature and Camping Area (for reservations prior to the season phone 695-3714; otherwise 863-9300), Route 2, Gill. This is an unusual facility maintained by Northeast Utilities on a peninsula that juts into the Connecticut River. Wooded tent sites are available. $15–20 per night.

YOUTH HOSTEL

Isabel and Monroe Smith American Youth Hostel (498-3505 in-season; 498-5983 off-season) at Highland Avenue and Pine Street, Northfield 01360. Open only late June to late August. Named for Isabel and Monroe Smith, founders of AYH, who opened America's first hostel in Northfield in 1934 in the Chateau, a stone mansion (since leveled). The current hostel offers 14 beds, both private and dorm-style rooms, in a Victorian house with a large yard, good for volleyball, croquet, and barbecues. Tennis courts, a pool, golf, and mountain biking are all nearby. $16 per person for nonmembers, $13 for members.

WHERE TO EAT

DINING OUT

This is recognized as one of the liveliest dining areas in New England. Because the largely academic clientele is unusually sophisticated but not particularly flush, many of the top restaurants are not that expensive.

TOPS AND TRENDY

Sienna (665-0215), 6 Elm Street, South Deerfield. Dinner from 5:30, Wednesday through Sunday, reservations a must. An unpretentious storefront is the setting for this chef-owned restaurant that's generally ranked best in the valley. Jonathan Marohn's menu changes frequently and always features local produce. Your entrée might be grilled duck breast perfumed with anise on mesclun greens with toasted garlic vinaigrette at $17.

Green Street Cafe (586-5650), 62 Green Street, Northampton. Open for dinner nightly from 5:30. Owner-chef John Sielski is a valley native who operated a restaurant in Brooklyn before opening this elegant storefront bistro. The plum-colored rooms are hung with original art, and on weekends there's frequently music. The handwritten menu might include such appetizers as mussels stewed in red wine ($7.95) or wild mushroom bisque, with entrées such as salmon baked en papillote with potato soufflé or chicken with apples and hazelnuts; half portions of pasta dishes like spicy noodles with shrimp and vegetables are also available. Inquire whether liquor is served. If the seasonal license isn't in effect, it's BYOB. Entrées $14–17.

Martini's (584-1149), 5 Bridge Street, Northampon. Open for dinner and Sunday brunch. Upscale and interesting, appetizers like Swedish gravlax, grilled quail, pastas such as penne Gorgonzola with spinach ($10.50), seafood specialties like salmon, mussels, and shrimp in a lobster sauce ($17.95). Jazz on the piano Thursday and Friday.

La Cucina di Pinocchio (256-4110), 30 Boltwood Walk, Amherst. Open Monday–Saturday for lunch and dinner; dinner only on weekends (Sunday from 4 PM). Mauro and Claire Aniello specialize in the cuisine of Northern Italy and Tuscany and take pride in the elegant atmosphere, wines, and dishes like risotto primavera ($13.95) and loin of lamb ($19.95).

Del Ray Bar and Grille (586-2664), One Bridge Street, Northampton. Open nightly for dinner; the lounge closes at 1 AM. You can reserve—a plus on busy nights in Northampton where most of the popular places are first-come, first-served—and the food is outstanding; maybe chicken with shallots, morel and Vermont chanterelle mushrooms in riesling wine and cream. Entrées $15–22, $37 for a four-course dinner menu sampling.

Spoleto (586-6313), 50 Main Street, Northampton. Open Monday through Thursday 5–10, Friday and Saturday 5–11, Sunday 4–9. Featuring

Spoleto Festival posters and creative "fine Italian" dishes like eggplant rollatini (sliced eggplant rolled and stuffed with spinach, ricotta, mozzarella, mascarpone, and herbs); entrées run $11.95–$16.95. A local favorite; there can be a wait on weekends.

Blue Heron Restaurant (367-0200), 440 Greenfield Road, Montague Center. Open Wednesday through Sunday for dinner and Sunday brunch. While we lament the passing of the Book Mill Cafe, this full-service restaurant that has taken its place promises to be a plus for the local dining scene. Owners Deborah Snow and Barbara White specialize in American regional cooking. Antipasta and mezze plates for starters, choice of a half-dozen entrées $12–18; Sunday family-style dinners.

Eastside Grill (586-3347), 19 Strong Avenue, Northampton. Open for lunch Monday through Saturday 11:30–2:30, dinner 5–11, Sunday 4–10. A popular place with a pleasant, multilevel dining room (try for a booth), a big menu with something for everyone: garlic salmon ($11.95), pasta with wild mushrooms ($10.95), Cajun burgers ($5).

TRADITIONAL FINE DINING

Deerfield Inn (774-2359), The Street, Old Deerfield. Open daily for lunch, dinner nightly. This is a formal dining room with white tablecloths, Chippendale chairs, and a moderately expensive lunch menu. At dinner you might begin with house smoked salmon ($8) or wild mushroom hash ($7), then dine on breast of chicken wrapped in puff pastry filled with creamed spinach and goat cheese and served with a roasted shallot demiglaze ($18), or on jumbo shrimp sautéed with fresh herbs and orzo pasta ($18). Wine is available by the glass (from $3.50), and the wine list itself is extensive. Inquire about late-afternoon carriage rides as part of the dinner package.

Whately Inn (665-3044; 1-800-WHATELY), Chestnut Plain Road, Whately. The dining room in this chef-owned, white-clapboard, center-of-town inn is large and rather funky, but the food is reputedly good, service slow. Entrées are priced from $11.95 for broiled stuffed scrod to $19.95 for lamb dijonnaise; roast crisp duckling ($15.95) is a favorite. Prices include soup to nuts.

Falls River Inn (648-9904), Main Street, Bernardston. Open Wednesday through Saturday for dinner from 4:30, Sunday from noon. This restaurant is in a classic, century-old, three-story inn; under the current ownership of Kathleen Kerber, the food is reputedly good, but it always seems to be closed when we stop by. Let us know what you think.

Seasons Restaurant (253-9909), 529 Belchertown Road, Amherst. Open Sunday through Thursday 5–9, Friday and Saturday 5–10, Sunday buffet brunch 10:30–3. A restored post-and-beam barn with a deck overlooking hills. Specializes in prime rib, Italian dishes, and seafood; plenty of pasta. Dinner entrées $9–17, sandwiches and lighter fare available.

Wiggins Tavern Restaurant (584-3100), 36 King Street, Northampton. Open Wednesday through Saturday 5:30–9:30, Sunday 3–8. An authentic low-beamed, 18th-century tavern with a large hearth that was incorporated into the original hotel (now the Hotel Northampton) when it was built. Traditional New England fare ranges from Yankee pot roast ($14.95) to roast rack of lamb ($21.95).

The Lord Jeffery Inn (253-2576), 30 Boltwood Avenue, Amherst. Open daily for breakfast, lunch, and dinner. Admittedly, we haven't dined here lately, but our survey reveals that the food in this formal main dining room has improved vastly in the past couple of years and is now fully commensurate with prices like $18.95 for grilled duck breast and $19.95 for seafood le crème Dijon (lobster, scallops, shrimp, sea clams, and mussels sautéed in a roasted garlic white wine cream sauce with mushroom, scallions, and a touch of Dijon on linguine). Specials change daily; dinner entrées from $13.75.

The Delaney House (532-1800), Route 5 at Smith's Ferry, Holyoke. Open Monday through Saturday from 5 PM, Sunday from 4. Everyone's favorite large, special-occasion place, four different dining rooms and an extensive menu that might include native Cornish game hen with cornbread stuffing and blackberry glaze ($17.95) and a veal chop with Black Forest ham, Gorgonzola cheese, and shallots ($21). A favorite dessert is fresh strawberries in maraschino cream served in a pastry shell with candied violets; specialty drinks are featured. Children's menu.

Windows on the Common (534-8222), 25 College Street, Village Commons, South Hadley. Open Monday through Saturday for lunch and dinner, Sunday 10:30–2 for a brunch buffet ($10.95). Decor is contemporary elegant, and the menu is large; early dinner specials (5–7) are $7.99–9.99, otherwise you're talking $9.50–16.95.

Yankee Pedlar Inn (532-9494), 1866 Northampton Street (Route 5 near I-91, exit 16), Holyoke. A landmark with a number of function rooms and a small, richly paneled dining room. Service was slow but friendly on our most recent visit, and we dined off the bistro menu on an unlikely but delicious large, grilled portobello mushroom, served on a pile of garlic potatoes with basil vinaigrette ($8.95). Dinner entrées also include filet mignon ($18.50) and baked scrod.

Andiamo Ristorante (648-9107), Huckle Hill Road, Bernardston. Open for dinner. A glass-faced, hilltop building with the best views of any restaurant in the valley. Specialties include calamari in a spicy marinara sauce and bistecca alla Pepe (a 12-ounce New York cut, broiled or sautéed with peppercorns, brandy, and cream). Entrées from $9.95 for pasta to $17.95.

EATING OUT

In Northampton

Sylvester's Restaurant & Bakery (586-5343), 111 Pleasant Street. Named for and housed in the onetime home of pioneer vegetarian and whole wheat advocate Dr. Sylvester Graham (as in graham cracker). Two storefront dining rooms are cheery, good for breakfast (try the Lox-Ness

Street cafés in Northampton

Omelet), lunch (soups of the day, veggie and regular burgers, salads, quesadillas), and a wide choice of dinner entrées, beef and chicken as well as chicken and seafood, like sherried scallops in garlic with black olives and homemade marinara over pasta ($8.95); all dinners include salad and homemade bread.

Amanouz Café (585-9128), 44 Main Street. Open for lunch and dinner. A narrow but deep storefront with great falafel, salads, and sandwiches, like Shawerma (marinated lamb and beef, vegetables, and tahini). You can also dine on chicken or lamb couscous ($6.25). Beer and wine served.

Melino's Northampton (586-8900), 21 Center Street. Open for dinner, closed Mondays. A popular trattoria with a downstairs lounge, good for pasta dishes and specials such as cacciucco, a hearty seafood stew with fennel, potatoes, and crostini ($12).

Fitzwilly's (584-8666), 23 Main Street. Open daily 11:30 until midnight. One of New England's first fern bars: brick walls, plenty of copper, antiques, hanging plants. It all works, including the immense menu and sandwiches.

Paul & Elizabeth's (584-4832), 150 Main Street. Open Sunday through Wednesday 11:30–9 or 9:30, Friday and Saturday until 10. The town's oldest natural foods restaurant, specializing in vegetarian dishes, seafood, home-baked breads and pastries. Dinner entrées average $10. Beer and wine.

Cha Cha Cha (586-7311), 134 Main Street. Open daily for lunch and dinner (closed Monday). This bright, busy spot in the middle of Main Street is a good bet for burritos and salads. Try the Cajun catfish tacos (flour tortillas filled with spicy fish), served with red onions, sour cream, and salsa.

Fresh Pasta Co. (586-5875), 249 Main Street. A cheerful corner storefront with white brick walls, a varied menu including focaccia, pizza, pasta, and chicken the specialties (avoid the chicken pot pie); try the grilled eggplant with fresh basil and goat cheese; wine and beer served.

La Cazuela (586-0400), 7 Old South Street. Open Monday through Thursday for dinner from 5, Saturday and Sunday from 3 PM. Housed in the rambling old hotel that was known as a semilegal watering hole to generations of students, this cheerful place (note the seasonal patio dining) offers outstanding spicy Mexican and southwestern fare, including plenty of vegetarian dishes. Try the spinach enchiladas or pollo verde. Entrées $6–10. Full bar.

The Northampton Brewery (584-9903), 11 Brewer Court. Open Monday through Saturday 11:30–11, Sunday 1–11. The area's only microbrewery, housed in a 19th-century livery stable. A pleasant, multilevel space serving sandwiches, pizza, burgers, steaks, seafood, and stir fries. Beer changes daily; live music Wednesday and Sunday evenings.

India House (586-6344), 45 State Street. Open Monday through Saturday for lunch and dinner, Sunday 4–9. Decorated with Indian prints and featuring background sitar music, Tandoori cooking, many vegetarian dishes; the valley's original Indian restaurant. Entrées from $7.95.

In Amherst and Hadley

Judie's (253-3491), 51 North Pleasant Street, Amherst. Open Sunday through Thursday 11:30–11, Friday and Saturday until 11:30. This cheerful, glass-fronted restaurant seems to be everyone's favorite: casual, friendly, and specializing in oversized, overstuffed popovers (we recommend the lime chili chicken with mushrooms, peppers, onions, and tomatoes), creative salad and pasta dishes, and sinful desserts. Reasonably priced dinner entrées include a salad and popover. Full bar.

Amber Waves (253-9200), 63 Main Street, Amherst. Open Monday through Saturday 11:30–10:30, Sunday 12:30–9:30. A storefront restaurant with remarkably reasonably priced and delicious Thai, Vietnamese, Chinese, and Japanese noodle soups and stir fries. Plenty of vegetarian dishes.

Carmelina's at the Commons (584-8000), 96 Russell Street, Hadley. Open for dinner nightly from 5 and for Sunday brunch. Huge portions of standout Italian cuisine at reasonable rates make this a big area favorite. It's always busy, and there may be lines on weekends. Full liquor license.

El Acuna, Boltwood Walk, Amherst. A fun and funky place with Tex-Mex food and decor. You can sit on saddles and munch a grilled papaya cilantro burrito at a table that's an overturned washtub. The bucket lanterns have real bullet holes to let the light shine through.

Top of the Campus (549-6000), Murray D. Lincoln Campus Center, UMass campus. Open weekdays for lunch; inquire about dinner. A pleasant, 11th-floor dining room with a moderately priced, ho-hum menu but a spectacular view.

✐ **Classé Café** (253-2291), 168 North Pleasant Street, Amherst. Open Monday through Saturday 7 AM–10 PM, Sunday brunch 7 AM–3 PM. Kids eat free on Wednesday. A college hangout known for decent burgers (including veggie burgers) and excellent fries. Local artwork, wine and beer, smoking permitted only from 2–8.

The Pub (549-1200), 15 East Pleasant Street, Amherst. Open Monday through Saturday 11:30–9:30, Sunday brunch 11–3 and dinner to 9:30. The name says it all: a classic college-town pub with a 10-page menu featuring everything from burgers to broiled scrod; a wide choice of beer. Most dinner entrées are less than $10. There's dancing, too.

Panda East Restaurant (256-8923), 103 North Pleasant Street, Amherst. Open 11:30–10:30 daily. This is part of an excellent local chain specializing in traditional Hunan-style Chinese food. Full bar.

Atkins Farms Fruit Bowl (253-9528), corner of Route 116 and Bay Road, South Amherst. Open daily, hours vary. Probably the fanciest farm stand in New England, this handsome redwood building sits amid thousands of fruit trees on the 190 acres that the family has farmed for generations. There is a first-rate deli, but for some reason it's on the opposite side of the building from the bakery, where there's seating.

Amherst Chinese (253-7835), 62 Main Street, Amherst. Open daily for lunch and dinner. A mural in the dining room depicts the restaurant's nearby farm, source of the vegetables in its dishes. Known fondly as AmChin, this is a local favorite. Note the luncheon specials from $4.25 and the $5.75 weekday dinner specials; no MSG.

Amherst Brewing Company, 36 North Pleasant Street. Open daily for lunch and dinner; live entertainment Thursday through Saturday, 10 PM–1 AM. The town's first microbrewery, so new at this writing that the verdict isn't in. It looks good, though, with a reasonably priced menu that includes traditional pub food like Irish stew, shepherd's pie, and cock-a-leekie pie. Tell us what you think of the brew.

In and Around Greenfield

Artisan's Cafe (774-4680), 298 Federal Street, Greenfield. Open daily for lunch and dinner, Sunday brunch from 8:30. A brightly decorated dining space with changing work by local artists, part of the Lunt Design Center. Lunch on curried turkey and wild rice salad, an individual pizza, or a sauteed chicken sandwich. Dine on haddock with pesto sauce; specials.

✐ **Bill's Restaurant** (773-8331), 30 Federal Street, Greenfield. Open daily 11–11. This friendly, traditional restaurant remains a local favorite; liquor served. Lunch from $3.95, dinner from $6.95, a children's and senior's menu.

The People's Pint (773-0333), 24 Federal Street, Greenfield. From 4 PM. A first-rate brew pub that's also a great people place; good food too. Specialties include soups, breads, and "The Ploughman" (crusty sourdough topped with sharp cheddar, a pickle, and mustard). Chess, board games, and darts weekday evenings, live music Saturday night, Celtic music Sundays.

☞ **Shady Glen Restaurant** (863-9636), 7 Avenue A, Turners Falls. Open Monday through Saturday 5 AM–9 PM, Sunday 5:30–11:45 AM. A real find: good home cooking, terrific pies and atmosphere, just off Route 2, a great way-stop.

Turnbull's Sunny Farms (773-8203), Route 2/I-91 rotary, Greenfield. Open daily for lunch and dinner. Not a particularly fancy place, this restaurant is our family's favored way-stop, good for quiche, sandwiches, or seafood and steaks; great salads. Liquor served, moderately priced.

In Northfield

The Main Street Cafe, Main Street. Open Tuesday through Sunday for breakfast and lunch, Tuesday night (when Rua's across the street closes; see below) for dinner. The breads and muffins are all freshly baked in this storefront café. Service is quick and friendly and most patrons along the counter and in the booths know each other. The one-person tables are an unusual, much appreciated feature.

Rua's, Main Street. Open 5:30 AM–8 PM except Tuesday, when closing time is 2 PM. This place serves as the center of town, where news is traded along a yellow Formica counter with eight stools; there's also a small, pine-paneled space with red vinyl booths. The soup of the day is $1.50, and a great chicken salad sandwich on whole wheat is $1.95; coffee comes in solid mugs, and the service is warmly efficient.

Elsewhere

Marfrans Turkey Ranch & Restaurant (467-7440), 55 Taylor Street, Granby. Open Wednesday through Sunday 11–8:30. Well worth finding, this valley landmark should be far better known than it is. The two cheerful rooms are in a restaurant that Marion and Frank (hence Marfran) Nugent built, part of a 25-acre farm that they bought in 1963. With their six children they rebuilt the "pole barns" and have been raising quality, grain-fed birds ever since. There's also a slaughtering house and a retail store (where you can buy a turkey fresh or cooked), and the dinner turkey plate ($9.50) is about as good as it can be. Turkey pot pie, turkey croquettes, and turkey liver with onions are also specialties, but the menu ranges from haddock to baked ham, from fried clams to lobster Newburg. At lunch you can have a lobster and crab roll as well as a turkey club or turkey burger. Full liquor license.

Bub's Bar BQ (548-9630), Route 116, Sunderland. Known as the best barbecue (try the hickory-smoked ribs) in the valley, with a fixin's bar that includes collard greens, yams, salads, and more; eat inside or (weather permitting) out.

Steeplejacks (665-7980), Amherst Road, center of Sunderland. Open daily for lunch and dinner. An attractive, dependable place to dine on entrées like gingered Cornish game hen ($10.95).

Harvest Valley Country Store (532-1664), Route 141 near the Mount Tom Reservation entrance, Easthampton. Open Monday through Saturday for lunch (11–4) and dinner (4–9:30); Sunday brunch (10–2) and dinner (noon–9:30). The impressive thing here is the view—out across the valley and west to the Hilltowns. Good sandwiches, quiche, and pies like apple pecan. The dining room is glass-sided, and there's a sun deck.

Greenfield Corner Cupboard (774-2990), Main Street, Greenfield. Owned by a former chef at a well-known New York restaurant, this is a popular local gathering spot known for good food.

Wolfie's (665-7068), 106 South Main Street, South Deerfield. Open 11–10, Monday through Saturday. An appealing little family restaurant in the middle of town, good for sandwiches like a Deerfield Reuben (sliced kielbasa loaf, sauerkraut, Swiss cheese, and mustard on rye) or a Wolfieburger. Dinner begins at $6.95 for barbecued ribs, and there are daily specials; full liquor license.

Green Fields Market (773-9567), 144 Main Street, Greenfield. This natural-foods cooperative occupies a former JC Penney and includes a tempting deli and a "from-scratch" bakery with attractive seating space near the windows.

DINERING OUT

Miss Florence Diner (584-3179), 99 Main Street, Florence (Northampton). Open for early breakfast through late dinner, 3 miles west of downtown Northampton. Known locally as Miss Flo's, this is the most famous diner in western Massachusetts, in the same family since the '40s. Forget the banquet addition and stick to the stools or booths. Unexpected specialties like clam and oyster stew and baked stuffed lobster casserole, a soup and salad bar, and full liquor license. Good beef barley soup and coconut and macaroon cream pudding.

Bluebonnet Diner (584-3333), 324 King Street, Northampton. Open Monday through Friday 5:30 AM–midnight, Saturday 6 AM–midnight. A classic diner with "home cooking." Full bar, smoking section. Dinners average $6.95.

Look Restaurant (584-9850), 410 North Main Street, Leeds (Northampton). A landmark with a '50s look and menu, "homestyle cooking," breakfast available all day. Fresh-made breads, muffins, and pies.

Whately Diner, Route 5/Route 10 just off I-91, exit 24. This is a classic chrome diner, open 24 hours, adjacent to a gas station/truck stop. Try the homemade meat loaf.

ROAD FOOD

French King Restaurant (659-3328), handy to Route 2, Millers Falls. A family restaurant, open daily for lunch and dinner, breakfast in summer.

Miss Florence Diner

Four Leaf Clover Restaurant (648-9514), Route 5, Bernardston. A solid family restaurant within minutes of I-91, exit 28B.

Also see **Shady Glen Restaurant,** worth a detour but right there in Turners Falls, just off Route 2 (see *Eating Out—In and Around Greenfield*).

SNACKS

Black Sheep Deli and Bakery (253-3442), 79 Main Street, Amherst. A genuine coffeehouse/deli with exceptional deli sandwiches, baked goods; good picnic-makings. Folk music, weekends; periodic poetry readings.

Bart's in Amherst (103 North Pleasant Street) and Northampton (249 Main Street). Open Sunday through Thursday until 11, Friday and Saturday until midnight. Since 1976, milk from local cows is used for great ice cream in 100 flavors like mud pie, blueberry cheesecake, and orange Dutch chocolate.

McCray Farm (533-3714), 55 Alvord Street, South Hadley. The dairy bar, open spring through fall, features homemade ice cream. This working dairy farm is near the river, with a small petting zoo; maple breakfasts during sugaring season (see *For Families*).

The Coffee Club (774-3841), 286 Main Street, Greenfield. A good selection of coffees, teas, pastries; lunch tables.

ENTERTAINMENT

For the academic year consult the *Five College Calendar of Events,* published monthly and available at all campuses. A typical month lists more than 27 films, 30 lectures, 19 concerts, and 32 theatrical performances. Visitors welcome.

Academy of Music Opera House (584-8463), 274 Main Street, Northampton. This Renaissance-style, century-old 300-seat theater features a balcony and even graceful men's and women's lounges; shows art films and first-run movies; also a schedule of live entertainment.

Mullins Center (545-0505), UMass campus, Amherst. A 10,500-seat sports and entertainment arena with a year-round schedule of theater and concerts as well as sports.

Fine Arts Center, UMass campus (545-2511), Amherst. Performing arts series of theater, music, dance.

Northampton Center for the Arts (584-7327), New South Street. Theater, dance, art exhibits.

MUSIC

Summer music series include the **Amherst College Early Music Festival** (542-2000), **Bright Moments Music Festival** (also known as **Jazz in July**) at UMass (545-3530) in Amherst, and **Musicorda** (532-0607), Chapin Auditorium, Mount Holyoke College, South Hadley (string festival presenting distinguished guest artists and faculty on Friday, students on Sunday, Wednesday, and Thursday, July through August).

The **Mount Holyoke Summit House** (586-8686) is the scene of a sunset concert series (folk, jazz, barbershop), 7:30 Thursday; and in Northampton **Look Memorial Park Sunday Concerts** are held Sunday at 4 PM, late June through mid-August.

THEATER

Mount Holyoke Summer Theatre (538-2632), in the Festival Tent at Mount Holyoke College, South Hadley, a professional summer stock company performing late June through mid-August; also children's theater.

Hampshire Shakespeare Company (253-2576). Shakespeare Under the Stars summer festival June through August. Performances on selected nights in the garden of the Lord Jeffery Inn, Amherst.

Newworld Theater performances at the Fine Arts Center, UMass (545-1972). This outstanding series, presented during the academic year, features ethnic and minority themes.

Arena Civic Theatre (773-9891) presents musicals and comedies, mid-June through August, in various Franklin County locations.

Shea Community Theater (863-2281), 71 Avenue A, Turners Falls. Call Tuesday through Friday between noon and 3. Inquire about performances by the resident community theater and visiting professional theater companies.

Old Deerfield Productions (774-7476) presents periodic summer performances.

FILM

Tower Theaters (533-2663), 19 College Street, South Hadley. First-run and art films; seats may be reserved.

Pleasant Street Theatre (586-0935). 27 Pleasant Street, Northampton. Independent, foreign, and art films, one theater upstairs and the well-named **Little Theater** in the basement.

Amherst Cinema (253-5426), 30 Amity Street. First-run films nightly.

Hampshire 6 Theaters (584-7550), Café Square, Hampshire Mall, Route 9, and **Mountain Farms 4 Theaters,** Mountain Farms Mall, Route 9, Hadley.

NIGHTLIFE

The Iron Horse (584-0610), 20 Center Street, Northampton. Live folk, jazz, and comedy, plus 50 brands of imported beer; dinner served. According to *Billboard* magazine, the Iron Horse "boasts one of the richest musical traditions in the country."

Pearl Street (584-7771), 10 Pearl Street, Northampton. Dancing nightly, live music several nights a week. DJ.

Live music can also be heard frequently in Northampton at the **Green Street Cafe** (see *Dining Out*) and at neighboring **North Star**, and at the **Fire & Water Coffee House** (586-8336) on Old South Street (also the place for Wednesday night poetry readings).

SELECTIVE SHOPPING

ANTIQUES AND AUCTIONS

This is a particularly rich antiquing area. Auction houses include **Douglas** (665-2877), Route 5, Deerfield (Friday nights); and **Ken Miller** (498-2749), Northfield, auctions on Monday night (6:30) in summer and fall, Saturday (10–5) in the off-season, also flea markets Sundays, mid-April through October, 7–3.

Along Route 5/Route 10 in Deerfield: **Antique Center of Old Deerfield** (773-3620); **Lighthouse Antiques,** specializing in New England items; **Yesterdays Antique Center** (665-7226), 27 dealers, displaying everything from books to major furniture pieces.

Northampton has become a good place for antiques in the past few years since a half-dozen shops have opened along and around Market Street. The largest is the **Antique Center of Northampton** (584-3600), 9½ Market Street. Open five days 10–5, closed Wednesday; Sunday noon–5. A multidealer shop on three levels. **American Decorative Arts,** 3 Olive Street, has become something of a mecca for collectors of early-20th-century furniture. **Hadley Antique Center** (586-4093), Route 9, Hadley, is open daily 10–5 except Wednesday. Ninety dealers in antiques and collectibles.

ART GALLERIES

Note: In recent years Northampton has become an art center its own right as aspiring artists gather to study with established names. Many restaurants and coffeehouses also mount constantly changing work (for sale) by local artists. There's even a distinctive Northampton school of Realism.

R. Michaelson Galleries (586-3964), 132 Main Street, Northampton, and 25 South Pleasant Street, Amherst. Open Monday through Wednesday 10–6, Thursday through Saturday 10–9, Sunday noon–5. Since 1979 Richard Michaelson has maintained galleries at various locations in Northampton, in 1995 moving into the huge and handsome two-story-high space designed in 1913 for the Northampton Savings Bank. The gallery showcases work by 50 local artists, including Leonard Baskin, one of America's most respected sculptors, painters, and printmakers, with work selling here from $100 (Baskin consciously prices prints for student budgets) to $100,000. Other well-known artists whose work is usually on view include Barry Moser, Gregory Gillespie, Linda Post, and Lewis Bryden. **The Hart Gallery** (586-6343), lower level, 102 Main Street. Open daily, until 8 Thursday through Saturday, from noon on Sunday. At street level this appears to be simply an art shop, but upstairs are the Guild Art Center's studio space (the artistic heart of town); the basement-level gallery frequently showcases work by top area artists. **WM Baczek Fine Arts** (587-9880), 229 Main Street, Northampton. A recent offshoot of the Guild Art Center, a serious gallery also displaying top artists. **The Canal Gallery** (532-4141), 380 Dwight Street, Holyoke. A 19th-century mill building houses some 20 artists' studios. Shows and gallery hours vary.

CRAFT GALLERIES

In Northampton

Some 1500 craftspeople work in the valley and nearby Hilltowns, and Northampton is their major showcase, known particularly for handcrafted jewelry, pottery, and furniture. **One Cottage Street** in Easthampton, **The Cutlery Building** in Northampton, and the **Pro-Brush Building** in Florence all house artisans. For periodic tours and open houses check with the Northampton Chamber of Commerce (see *Guidance*).

Ferrin Gallery/Pinch Pottery (586-4509), 179 Main Street. The specialty here is pottery, both practical and artistic, and the back gallery is frequently filled with teapots (inquire about the annual October Tea Party).

Almost half of what you see is locally crafted. **Skera** (586-4563), 221 Main Street. Open daily, Sunday from noon, Thursday until 9. Longtime owners Harriet and Steve Rogers specialize more and more in stunning hand crafted clothing, "wearable art." **Silverscape Designs** (586-3324), 3 Pleasant Street, Northampton; also 264 North Pleasant Street, Amherst (253-3324). The Northampton store (open weekdays 10–6, Saturday until 9, Sunday noon–5) is a beauty, the Tiffany's of the valley—a former bank building with art deco detailing and a glorious stained-glass skylight. The old tellers' windows are still in place; there's also a cascading fountain. A wide variety of jewelry and accessories, also Tiffany-style lamps. **Don Muller Gallery** (586-1119), 40 Main Street, Northampton. An outstanding store displaying a wide variety of crafted items, specializing in art glass, always exhibiting the deeply colored signature orbs hand-blown by locally based Josh Simpson. **Peacework Gallery** (586-7033), 213 Main Street, Northampton, specializes in the fine arts and crafts of Native Americans and the Southwest. **Artisan Gallery** (586-1942), Thornes Market, 150 Main Street, Northampton. A quality selection of jewelry, pottery, woodwork, and glass; kaleidoscopes are a specialty. **Claytopia** (584-9323), 157 Main Street. Open daily except Monday 11–8:30, Sunday until 6. Billed as an "art studio for you to paint beautiful, unique pottery," this popular new place sells you a piece of dishwater-, microwave-, and oven-safe pottery and supplies the paints and stencils with which to can decorate it ($8 per hour). If you aren't in town long enough to pick up the final product (it takes three days to fire and process), they ship. **Sutter's** (586-1470), 233 Main Street, Northampton. A long-established custom jeweler exhibiting work by some 20 designers as well as John Sutter's own work. **Bill Brough Jewelry Designs** (586-8985), 18 Main Street, Northampton. Original jewelry designs in gold, diamonds, pearls, and special stones.

Greenfield/Northfield Area

Artspace Gallery (772-6811), corner of Main and Franklin Street, Greenfield. Open Wednesday through Friday noon–4, Saturday 10–4. Changing craft shows represent area artists and artisans. **Joel McFadden Designs** (772-1003), 24 Miles Street, Greenfield. A master goldsmith, McFadden is known for the settings he designs for brilliant stones. His attractive gallery is also the scene of changing exhibits for a variety of area craftspeople and artists. **Lunt Design Center and Marketplace** (772-0767), 298 Federal Street, Greenfield. Longtime Greenfield silversmiths, Lunt has recently added a retail wing to their factory, a handsome space displaying work by roughly one hundred craftspeople offering demonstrations in glassblowing and weaving as well as silvermaking. Hopefully, with time, it will feature more work by the area's outstanding local craftspeople. The complex also includes a café and a Silver Garden with some 2,000 perennials in white and silver hues. **Room with a Loom** (367-2062), Montague Mill (see *Scenic*

Drives). Generally open Wednesday through Sunday noon–5:30, but hours are longer at busy times and in December and shorter during slow periods, so call ahead to check. A small but exceptional gallery displaying local craftworks, also paintings by Louise Minks and Virginia Senders, whose studio is upstairs (visitors welcome when they are there). This space also doubles as a weaving studio for owner Karen Chapman. **The Northfield Carriage House** (498-2925), 158 Burnam Road, Northfield. John Nelson, working primarily in clay but also in other media, is the anchor artist in this studio, which is also home to three potters, a photographer, and other artisans. Call ahead. **Tom White Pottery** (498-2175), 205 Winchester Road, Northfield. Sited at the corner of Pierson and Winchester Roads, this studio is a source of wheel-thrown, porcelain production work that's obviously been influenced by traditional Chinese forms and glazes. Call ahead.

BOOKSTORES
Book browsing is a major pastime in this area.

In Northampton

Beyond Words Bookshop (586-6304; 1-800-442-6304), 189 Main Street. A large bookstore featuring books for inner development; also music, stationery, gifts. **Broadside Bookshop** (586-4235), 247 Main Street. A general trade bookstore with a strong emphasis on fiction and literature as well as personal advice. Owner Bruce Macmillan is usually at the counter. **Booklink** (585-9955), 150 Main Street. Wally Swist, manager of the much loved and missed former Globe Bookshop, now runs this corner of Thornes Marketplace; specialties include poetry, local books, and travel. A poet himself, Swist stages frequent poetry and other readings. **Bookends** (585-8667), 93 Main Street, Florence. Nine rooms of quality used books. **The Old Book Store** (586-0576), 32 Mason Street. Open Tuesday through Saturday, 10–5. Our copy editor's favorite source of used books. **Third Wave Bookstore** (586-7851), 90 King Street. New, used, and rare feminist and lesbian books, periodicals, and music, jewelry, cards, bumper stickers. **Metropolitan Books & Records** (586-7077), 9¾ Market Street. Specializes in used poetry and art books. **Pride and Joy** (585-0683), 20 Crafts Avenue, features books for lesbians, bisexuals, and gays. **Raven Used Books** (584-9868), 4 Old South Street, specializes in scholarly titles, women's studies, and philosophy.

In Amherst

Jeffery Amherst Bookstore (253-3381), 55 South Pleasant Street. A full-service bookstore with a strong children's book section, specializing in Emily Dickinson. **Atticus/Albion** (256-1547), 8 Main Street, has a wide selection of new and used books. **Book Marks** (549-6136), 1 East Pleasant Street (Carriage Shops). A wide selection of used books specializing in art, poetry, photography, and Emily Dickinson. **Food for Thought Books** (253-5432), 106 North Pleasant Street, featuring gay and lesbian, progressive political, and African American titles. **Laos Religious**

Montague Book Mill

Book Center (253-3909), 16 Spring Street, an ecumenical bookstore with both Christian and Jewish titles. **The University Store** (545-2619), Murray D. Lincoln Campus Center, UMass. A full-service college bookstore specializing in academic, technical reference, math, physics, and chemistry. The store also carries a large selection of UMass gift items. **Wootten's Books** (253-2722), 19 North Pleasant Street. A used bookstore specializing in art, poetry, fiction, philosophy, and cultural studies.

In South Hadley

Odyssey Bookstore (534-7307; 1-800-540-7307), Village Commons, 9 College Street. A destination bookstore, one of the largest and most attractive in the state.

In Greenfield

World Eye Bookshop (772-2186), 156 Main Street. Open daily. This well-stocked book and gift store serves a wide upcountry area. **Book Mill** (367-9206) in the Montague Mill, Greenfield and Depot Roads, Montague. Open daily 10–6. Housed in an early 19th-century mill on the Sawmill River, you'll find thousands of used and discount books on two floors. Art books, CDs, records, and video rentals.

CLOTHING

In Northampton

No longer bastions of humdrum tweed, Northampton stores that are on the cutting edge of rural chic include **Cathy Cross** (586-9398), 151 Main Street; **Country Comfort, Ltd**. (584-0042), 153 Main Street; **Square One Presents** (585-1118), 24 Pleasant Street; **Bibi Stein Handweavings** (584-7455), 225 Main Street, second floor; **25 Central** (586-8017),

150 Main Street; and **Serendipity** (584-6528), 126 Main Street.
In Amherst
Zanna (253-2563), 187 North Pleasant Street, the largest in a three-shop chain (the others are in Williamstown and Brattleboro, Vermont).

FACTORY OUTLETS
Several factory outlets are housed in Holyoke Mills. They include **ES Sports** (534-5634), 47 Jackson Street (gym bags, sweatshirts, sportswear); **Deerfield Woodworking Factory Store** (532-2377), 420 Dwight Street (wooden curtain rods and brackets, bookcases, quilt racks, shelves, nightstands); **Becker Jean Factory Store** (532-5797), 323 Main Street (Becker, Levi, and Lee jeans); and **Riverbend Woodworks and Lady Bugs Ltd.** (533-8809), 380 Dwight Street (dried flowers, wreaths, baskets, hats).

FARMSTANDS
Atkins Farms Country Market (253-9528), 1150 West Street (Route 116 south), Amherst. Open daily 8–6 except holidays, later in summer. The valley's largest and fanciest farmstand, a vast redwood market with a huge selection of quality produce, much it from the family's 290 acres and 25,000 fruit trees; the complex includes a popular deli café (see *Eating Out*) and is surrounded by apple orchards (see *Pick-Your-Own*). **Hibbard Farm** (549-5684), 311 River Drive, Hadley. Open 9–12 and 1–4 in season; offering asparagus in May and June, carrots August through December, and parsnips September through January. **Hopewell Farm Stand** (665-2030), 3 West Street, Hatfield. Open May through Columbus Day for vegetables and horticultural products. **Dion Pumpkin Farms** (584-6170), 28 Middle Street, Hadley. Pumpkins, Indian corn, Chinese lanterns, gourds, apples, farm tours, horse-drawn hay rides, and a game farm. **Golonka Farm** (247-3256), 6 State Road, Whately (Route 5/10). Open 9–6 in summer for corn, cucumbers, and watermelons. **J&J Farms** (549-6497), 324 Meadow Street, North Amherst. Sweet corn, tomatoes, peppers, squash, dairy, firewood, and flowers. **Smiarowski Farmstand and Creamery** (665-3415), 320 River Road, Sunderland. Ice cream, fruit, cut flowers, maple syrup, farm-fresh salads and desserts. **Wagon Farm Stand** (584-3678), Route 9, Hadley (next to WMECO). Open July through September for sweet corn, tomatoes, and potatoes.

FLOWERS
Blue Meadow Farm (367-2394), 184 Meadow Road, Montague Center. Open April 15 through June 15, daily 9–6, closed at 5 and on Tuesday in summer. This is one of New England's truly outstanding flower farms, featuring perennials, ornamental grasses, woody plants, annuals, and herbs. The display garden is itself worth a trip. **Baystate Perennial Farm** (665-3525), Route 5/Route 10, Whately. Open daily 9–6. **Andrew's Greenhouse** (253-2937), 1178 South East Street, Amherst.

Our copy editor's favorite source of perennials, herbs, bedding plants, and cut-your-own flowers. **Hadley Garden Center** (584-1423), 285 Russell Street, Hadley. Herbs, orchids, bulbs, bird food, indoor plants, firewood, and gardening workshops. **Wanczyk Evergreen Nursery** (584-3709), 166 Russell Street, Hadley. Open weekdays 8–6, weekends 8–5 in spring; Sundays and mornings only in summer; until 5 in fall. A great source of perennials and nursery plants.

PICK-YOUR-OWN

Atkins Farms (253-9528), 1150 West Street (Route 116 South), Amherst. Pick-your-own apples in fall. (Also see *Farmstands, Eating Out*.) **Delta Organic Farm** (253-1893), 352 East Hadley Street, Amherst. Strawberries. Also sells herbs, syrup, and organic produce. **Lakeside U-Pick Strawberries** (549-0805), 281 River Drive, Hadley. Open daily in season, 7:30–7. **Nourse Farm** (665-2650), River Road, Whately. This farmstand by the river is billed as the state's largest strawberry farm; it also offers raspberries. Pick-your-own daily in season, 8–4. **Ripka's Farm** (665-4687), Routes 5/10, Deerfield. Farm stand open daily for pick-your-own strawberries. **Sapowsky Farms** (467-7952), 436 East Street, Granby. Pick-your-own strawberries. They also sell milk, cheese, eggs, syrups, honey, jams, and firewood. **Teddy C. Smiarowski Farm** (247-5181), 378 Main Street, Hatfield. Asparagus.

SUGARHOUSES

Maple producers who welcome visitors include **Williams Farm Sugar House,** Routes 5/10 in Deerfield; **Brookledge Sugarhouse** (665-3837) and **Fairview Farms** (665-4361) in Whately; **River Maple Farm** (648-9767), Route 5, Bernardston; **Ripley's Sugarhouse** (367-2031), 195 Chestnut Hill Road, Montague; **Boisvert Farm/Hadley Sugar Shack** (585-8820), 181 River Drive, Hadley.

OTHER SPECIAL STORES AND ENTERPRISES

A2Z Science and Learning Store (586-1611), 57 King Street, Northampton. Intelligent toys, gadgets, and gifts for children of all ages. **Berkshire Brewing Co., Inc.** (665-6600), 12 Railroad Street, South Deerfield. Chris Lalli and Gary Bogoff produce a variety of tasty brews, notably Steel Rail Extra Pale Ale; tours and tastings are offered Saturday at 1 PM, but call ahead. **Lukasik Game Farm** (534-5697), Pear Street, South Hadley. Fowl and large animals (elk, deer, wild boar), cheese, jams, jellies. Christmas trees. **Mapeline Farm** (549-6174), 73 Comins Road, Hadley. Open daily, weekdays 1–6, Saturday 8–5, Sunday 8–12. Milk, cheese, and ice cream. **The Museum Store**, Historic Deerfield. The J.G. Pratt store is a trove of books, crafts, museum reproductions, gifts, and souvenirs. Open museum hours. **Northampton Wools** (586-4331), 11 Pleasant Street, Northampton. Linda Daniels's small shop just off Main Street is crammed with bright wools and knitting gear; workshops offered. **Pekarski's Sausage** (665-4537), Route 116, South Deerfield.

Homemade Polish kielbasa, breakfast sausage, smoked ham and bacon. **Thomas & Thomas Rod Makers, Inc.** (863-9727), 2 Avenue A, Turners Falls. Fine fly rods are made and sold; visitors welcome. **Twin Willows Turkey Farm** (323-6046), 51 Ludlow Road, Belchertown. All natural turkeys, pot pies, and sausages, low-cholesterol and range-reared sheep. **Wilson's**, 258 Main Street, Greenfield. The town's long-established, dependable department store with four floors of general merchandise, clothing, housewares, jewelry, books, cards, and gifts. (Also see **McCray's Farm** under *For Families*.)

SHOPPING CENTERS

Thornes Marketplace, 150 Main Street, Northampton. An incubator for many Northampton stores: a five-story, 40-shop complex with high ceilings, wood floors. **The Village Commons in South Hadley**. A whimsical, white-clapboard complex of shops designed by Boston architect Graham Gund to include a pizza place, coffeehouse, movie theater (two screens), Chinese restaurant, and pub; also boutiques and specialty shops ranging from Stonebrook Saddlery to Neuchatel chocolates. Appropriately, the anchor store is a splendid bookstore (Odyssey Bookshop). **Holyoke Mall** (536-1440) at Ingleside (I-91 exit 15, and Mass. Pike exit 4), open Monday through Saturday 10–9:30 and Sunday noon–6. The single biggest mall in western Massachusetts, with Filene's, Lord & Taylor, JCPenney, Macy's Close-Out, and Sears as anchors.

SPECIAL EVENTS

Note: Northampton maintains an events listings number: 1-800-A-FUNTOWN. Farmers' markets are held spring through fall on Saturday in Northampton (on Gothic Street) and Amherst (on the common), and in Holyoke on Thursday afternoons (2:30–5:30, Hampden Park off Dwight Street); in Greenfield, Saturdays 8–1.

March: **Annual Bulb Show,** Smith College (first two weeks). **St. Patrick's Day Parade**, Holyoke (Sunday after St. Patrick's Day).

May: **Taste of Amherst**, **Community Fair** and (the Saturday nearest the 15th) **Emily Dickinson's World Weekend**. **Western Massachusetts Appaloosa Horse Show**, Three-County Fairgrounds, Northampton.

June: **Crafts Night** in Northampton; **Old Deerfield Summer Crafts Fair** at Memorial Hall, more than 250 exhibitors (last weekend).

June through August: **Hot Summer Nights,** Wednesday night concert series on the common, Amherst.

July: **Amherst Crafts Fair** (July 1). **Fireworks** (July 4), Amherst. **Morgan Horse Show**, Northampton.

July: **Old-Fashioned Independence Day** in Old Deerfield. **Green River Festival,** a mid-July spectacle, sponsored by the Franklin County Chamber of Commerce, at Greenfield Community College.

August: **Amherst Teddy Bear Rally** (first weekend). **Taste of Northampton** (second weekend); more than 40 restaurants participate. **Three-County Fair** at the Three-County Fairgrounds, Northampton.

Weekend before Labor Day: **Celebrate Holyoke** (four-day, multicultural music festival, food, dancing) at Heritage State Park.

October: **Greenfield Fall Festival,** Main Street, Columbus Day weekend—craftspeople, music, children's entertainment, sidewalk sales. **Paradise City Arts Festival** (1-800-752-9924), Northampton, the premier arts and crafts festival in the state. *Every other year:* **Book and Plow Festival**, Amherst—three days honoring local writers and farmers.

November: **Northampton Film Festival.**

December: **First Night**, Northampton.

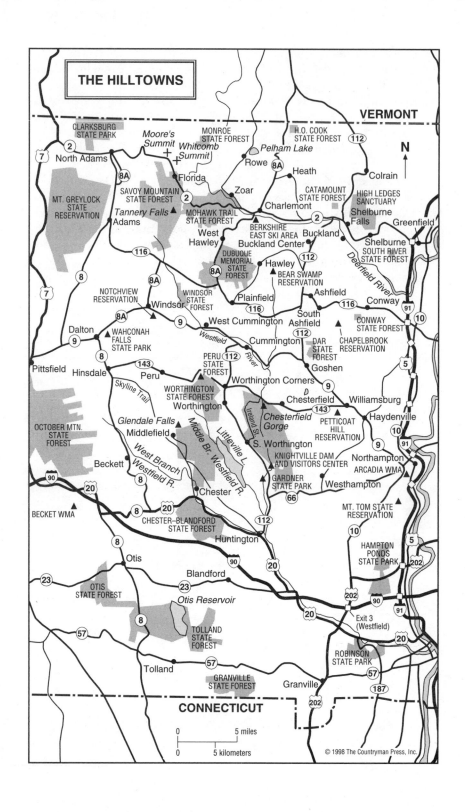

THE HILLTOWNS

N

VERMONT

CLARKSBURG STATE PARK

Moore's Summit + *Whitcomb Summit*

MONROE STATE FOREST

H.O. COOK STATE FOREST 112

North Adams 2 7

8A

Florida

Rowe 8A

Heath

Colrain

Pelham Lake

Zoar

MT. GREYLOCK STATE RESERVATION

SAVOY MOUNTAIN STATE FOREST 2

Tannery Falls Adams

CATAMOUNT STATE FOREST

Charlemont 2

HIGH LEDGES SANCTUARY

Shelburne Falls

Greenfield

116

MOHAWK TRAIL STATE FOREST

West Hawley

BERKSHIRE EAST SKI AREA

Buckland Center

Buckland

Shelburne

SOUTH RIVER STATE FOREST

8 7

NOTCHVIEW RESERVATION

8A

WINDSOR STATE FOREST

DUBUQUE MEMORIAL STATE FOREST 8A

Hawley 112

BEAR SWAMP RESERVATION

Deerfield River

Windsor

Dalton 9

WAHCONAH FALLS STATE PARK

9

Plainfield

Ashfield

116

Conway 91 10

West Cummington

South Ashfield

116

CONWAY STATE FOREST

8

143

Westfield *River*

Cummington

112

DAR STATE FOREST

CHAPELBROOK RESERVATION

5

Pittsfield Hinsdale

Peru

PERU STATE FOREST 112

Goshen

Skyline Trail

WORTHINGTON STATE FOREST

Worthington Corners

9

Worthington

Chesterfield

Williamsburg

143

Haydenville

OCTOBER MTN. STATE FOREST

Glendale Falls Middlefield

Chesterfield Gorge

PETTICOAT HILL RESERVATION

10

91

Beckett

West Branch *Westfield R.*

Middle Br. Westfield R.

Littleville L.

Ireland St.

S. Worthington

9

Northampton

ARCADIA WMA

90 20

8

Chester

20

KNIGHTVILLE DAM AND VISITORS CENTER

GARDNER STATE PARK 66

Westhampton

BECKET WMA

8

20

CHESTER–BLANDFORD STATE FOREST

112

MT. TOM STATE RESERVATION

Huntington

10

8

Otis

90

20

HAMPTON PONDS STATE PARK

5

202

23

Blandford

23

202

90

91

OTIS STATE FOREST

Otis Reservoir

8

TOLLAND STATE FOREST

Exit 3 (Westfield)

20

57

ROBINSON STATE PARK

Tolland

57

GRANVILLE STATE FOREST

Granville

57

187

CONNECTICUT

202

0 — 5 miles

0 — 5 kilometers

© 1998 The Countryman Press, Inc.

The Berkshire Hilltowns

The 500-square-mile swath of rolling terra incognita between the Connecticut River Valley and Berkshire County is known simply as "the Hilltowns." We call it the Berkshire Hilltowns because this area is as much a part of the Berkshire hills as Berkshire County to the west, where the highest hills—Mount Greylock and Mount Everett—are actually strays from New York's Taconic range.

This region is a plateau that's been sculpted by fast-flowing rivers to form many rounded hills and narrow valleys. Two major rivers, the Deerfield and the Westfield, have also cut three parallel east–west valleys, now obvious traffic conduits: Route 2, the northernmost east–west high road (highway would be an overstatement) shadows the ancient Mohawk Trail along the Deerfield River. Route 9 (the Berkshire Trail) follows the West Branch of the Westfield River across the middle of the state, while Route 20 (Jacob's Ladder Trail), hugs the main branch of the Westfield. This high ground is also the watershed between the two major north–south valleys in the Northeast. It's said that raindrops falling on the western slant of the Congregational church roof in hilltop Peru ultimately flow into the Hudson, while those on the eastern slant fall into the Connecticut.

This area looks the way much of Vermont did a couple of decades ago: Valleys are steep, alternately wooded and patched with open fields. Relatively few homes have been built in this century. In winter, cross-country skiers drive from Boston and Hartford to take advantage of the highest, most dependably snow-covered trails south of Vermont. Early spring brings sit-down breakfasts in sugarhouses and tours of the sugarbush (there are more maple producers here than in all the rest of the state put together). In late spring white-water rafters begin converging on the Deerfield River, and nationally ranked white-water canoeists compete on the Westfield. Anglers find trout in both rivers. In summer, back roads beckon bicyclists, and hikers follow trails to hilltop lookouts and deep-in-the-woods waterfalls. In fall the Mohawk Trail is thronged with leaf-peepers, but back roads receive surprisingly little use.

Although the fertile bottomland along the Deerfield and Westfield Rivers was settled in the mid-18th century, this area was mostly an out-

KIMBERLY GRANT

The birthplace of Cecil B. DeMille in Ashfield

post until after the Revolution, and many hill farms were deserted as early as the 1820s, when the Erie Canal opened the way to greener, less stony, western pastures. Too far from population centers to be bedroom towns and not close enough to Boston or New York to attract second-home owners in serious numbers, the Hilltowns are home to an unusual number of artists, craftspeople, and musicians. You'll find a poet laureate reading his works in a country church, a former director of Dublin's famed Abbey Theatre producing plays in a village town hall, and world-class pianists performing in a defunct country academy. The biggest events are still country fairs.

The Hilltowns have a long tradition of welcoming summer people (witness William Cullen Bryant's summer home, and the former 19th-century hotel in Ashfield), and throughout the past century many farms took in summer boarders. In 1916 the Mohawk Trail—38 miles of up-and-down paved road (in an era when the country boasted relatively few paved miles) through the northern, hilliest part of this region—was inaugurated as New England's first formal Tourist Route. Thousands of "tourists" came to drive it in their first cars. Let's hope the trail's surviving observation towers, Indian trading posts, and old motor courts will be preserved as historic before they disappear.

Though the Hilltown area may all look much the same to visitors, locals will tell you that the region is clearly divided along county lines. Conway, Ashfield, Hawley, and the towns to the north all fall into "West County" (of Franklin County), whereas the towns along Route 9 and south consider themselves the "Hampshire Hills," a name coined a dozen years ago by the area's bed & breakfast association.

Present lodging options in the Hilltowns include roughly three dozen widely scattered B&Bs, a rustic lodge or two, plus several farms with rental units and a half-dozen motels and campgrounds. At present, however, the only information center in this entire area is in Shelburne Falls, the most obvious way-stop on the Mohawk Trail. Nowhere else in New England is such a beautiful, easily accessible and yet unspoiled area as underpromoted. We predict this situation won't last forever, and suggest you explore it now, before the word spreads.

West County/Mohawk Trail

"Peaks of one or two thousand feet rush up either bank of the river in ranges, thrusting out their shoulders side by side. . . I have never driven through such romantic scenery, where there was such a variety and boldness of mountain shapes as this," observed Nathaniel Hawthorne about the view that you can now enjoy from the truncated, wooden observation tower at Whitcomb Summit.

The tower is one of three period pieces still staked along the original Mohawk Trail, that 38-mile stretch of Route 2 between Greenfield and North Adams that was formally dedicated in 1914. Although it shadows an ancient Native American path through the mountains, the Mohawk Trail in its present incarnation was designed specifically for "auto touring" (see "The Berkshire Hilltowns") in an era when the quickest way to North Adams was by train. The Indian trading posts, with their plastic buffalos and wooden Indians, and the '30s and '40s tourist cabins now look a bit funky and worn, but they still smack of a romantic era.

East of the Hoosac Range, the Mohawk Trail follows the Deerfield River through a narrow valley, hemmed by abrupt hills. Charlemont, the old crossroads community here, offers motel rooms and campsites, attracting fishermen in spring, white-water rafters spring through fall, and both downhill and cross-country skiers in winter. But in recent years Shelburne Falls, 8 miles east, has become the most popular way-stop on the trail. Long known for its Bridge of Flowers and glacial potholes, Shelburne now also offers great shopping and a choice of good places to eat.

Venture north off Route 2—up the roads to Zoar and Rowe, Heath or Colrain—and you will find a mix of dairy farms and orchards, backed by spruce-forested hills, harboring any number of surprises: memorable places to stay, white-water rafting, a winery, and a lively café in a former church, for starters. South of Route 2 the hills are gentler and still patterned with open meadows, fields, and orchards. Valley roads link the classic village centers of Ashfield, Conway, and Buckland, and bed & breakfasts are scattered along the old roads that web the hills.

AREA CODE: 413
GUIDANCE
Franklin County Chamber of Commerce (773-5463; daily, 24 hours), PO Box 790, Main Street, Greenfield 01302; Web site: www.do.franklin.ma.us.

Along the Mohawk Trail

The office at 395 Main Street is a year-round, walk-in information center; a seasonal information booth is maintained at the Route 2/I-91 rotary.

Shelburne Falls Village Information Center (625-2544), 75 Bridge Street, PO Box 42, Shelburne Falls 01370. A friendly, well-stocked information source for the surrounding area as well as the village, in a former fire station at the center of town.

GETTING THERE

From Boston: The obvious way is Route 2, which technically becomes the Mohawk Trail in Orange but is not evident as a tourist route until you hit the first observation platform just west of Greenfield. From points north and south, take exit 26 off I-91 at Greenfield. Coming from the Five College area, take Route 116 north from Amherst or Route 9 north to Route 112 from Northampton.

MEDICAL EMERGENCY

Franklin Medical Center (772-0211), 164 High Street, Greenfield.

VILLAGES

Ashfield. This unusually spirited town of some 1700 people publishes its own newspaper. A large, former summer hotel still stands in the middle of the village but most traffic now stops at **Elmer's Store**. The pride of Ashfield remains the Wren-style steeple on its town hall (built as a church in 1814) and its unusual number of both maple producers and craftspeople, most of whom exhibit at the annual fall festival. Ashfield is the birthplace of movie director Cecil B. DeMille (his parents happened to be staying at the hotel) and has been home for a number of artists and writers, making for an unusually interesting **Ashfield Historical Society** (open Saturday and Sunday in July and August, 2–5, or call 628-4541); it also features the glass-plate photos of New England towns and working people taken by the two Howes brothers of Ashfield around the turn of the century. In summer there is swimming at the small town beach (transients discouraged), right in the village on Ashfield Lake, and there are two outstanding Trustees of Reservations properties (see *Green Space*).

Buckland. Buckland's town hall stands just across the Bridge of Flowers in the heart of Shelburne Falls (the town's northern boundary is the Deerfield River). The village of Buckland is, however, a gathering of a classic little church, a historical society, a small brick library, and aristocratic, 18th-century homes (one of them now a bed & breakfast), all set high on a hill a dozen miles south and off Route 112. The **historical society** (open selected summer Sundays, 2–4; 625-6619) has exhibits about Mary Lyon, the Buckland woman who pioneered education for women in the early 19th century and is remembered as the founder of both Mount Holyoke College in South Hadley and Wheaton College in Norton. In the four-square, four-chimneyed **Major Joseph Griswold House** you can inspect the third-floor ballroom in which Lyon began her first female academy in 1824. The space has been restored to look as it did then, complete with appropriate books (open Tuesday in summer, but call ahead: 625-2031). The way to the site of Mary Lyon's birthplace is marked from Route 112.

Charlemont. The Deerfield River rushes down from Vermont, then slows, widens, and turns east in Charlemont, creating fertile floodplains that clearly have been farmed since the mid-18th century (judging from the age of several proud brick and clapboard farmhouses). Today the year-round population of Charlemont hovers around just 1500, and this town is the only one in New England known for both alpine skiing (Berkshire East) and white-water rafting (see *To Do*). Rafting has introduced many visitors to the high backcountry north of Route 2. **Bissel Covered Bridge,** rebuilt in 1951 and presently in danger of being deep-sixed, spans Mill Brook just off Route 2 on Route 8A. The **Charlemont Historical Society Museum** in the town hall is open June through September, Saturday 1–4:30 (339-6633).

Colrain. This town boomed with sheep raising, cotton mills, and an iron foundry in the mid-19th century. The old foundry is still in Foundry Hollow, and a covered bridge sits by the North River (waiting to be put back on its pilings). Catamount Hill, site of the first schoolhouse to fly the American flag, has old cellar holes, a covered bridge (currently under restoration), and portions of both the H.P. Cook and the Catamount State Forests (339-5504); the latter includes a 27-acre trout-stocked lake. The **Colrain Historical Society** (624-3710) is housed in the **G. William Pitt House** on Main Street. The village center with its three

Shelburne Falls "potholes"

KIMBERLY GRANT

churches (one is now the popular **Green Emporium**; see *Dining Out*)
and common is at the junction of four scenic routes, including Route
112 north to Vermont (a well-known shortcut from Route 2 to Mount
Snow). **West County Winery** is just off of Route 2 (turn at Strawberry
Fields Antiques).

Conway. Turn off Route 116 and stop long enough at the triangular green
to admire the domed **Marshall Field Memorial Library** (369-4646),
gift of the native son who founded a Chicago department store. There's
a marble rotunda and elaborate detailing within; the historical collection is open selected days. The heart of town is easy to miss: **Baker's
Store** serves lunch, great pie, and all the local news you need. Note the
covered bridge across the South River off Route 116.

Heath. Heath is worth finding, just for the fun of it: a classic hilltown with a common surrounded by the usual white-clapboard buildings. What's amazing (going and coming) are the long views. Several interesting places to stay are squirreled away up scenic roads. To come from Route 2, turn north at the line of A-frames.

Shelburne Falls. Usually rivers divide towns, but in this case the Deerfield has united the 19th-century shopping areas of two towns to form Shelburne Falls, one of the most unusual and lively villages in New England. Instead of a common, there's a bridge—an abandoned trolley bridge (now reserved for foot traffic) that local garden clubs keep flooded with flowers as a war memorial. An iron bridge also links the main streets on both sides of the river. An aberration from its rural setting, this totally Victorian shopping center has become a showcase for the fine craftswork produced in the surrounding hills. The potholes at the foot of Salmon Falls (Deerfield Avenue, off Bridge Street) are no longer considered glacial, but they are still unusual, worth a look. The **historical society** in the Arms Academy Building (corner of Maple and Church Streets) is open fairly regularly (check with the information center). Mill buffs should cross into Buckland to see the wood-and-brick Lamson & Goodnow Cutlery complex, dating back more than 150 years (its products are sold in McCuskers Market at 3 State Street). The second-floor Opera House in vintage 1897 **Memorial Hall** has recently been restored and once more serves as the town's movie house (Pot Hole Pictures) as well as the stage for live entertainment. Across the street another fine old building at 22 Bridge Street is now **Art Bank** (625-6235), a community arts center and setting for frequent art exhibits and artistic happenings.

Rowe (population 378) is known chiefly as the former home of New England's first atomic energy plant (1961–93), which has had obvious effects on the town's budget for civil amenities. Instead of the usual town dump, Rowe has a landscaped "Refuse Garden." Plaques label the sites of buildings that stood in town when it bustled: the Foliated Talc Mill (1908–22) and Eddy's Casket Shop (1846-1948), for example. The Browning Bench Tool Factory has been restored and moved to the shore of Pelham Lake, where it serves as an arts and community center. There are picnic tables in 1000-acre **Pelham Lake Park,** and a gazebo ornaments the common. The **Rowe Historical Society Museum** (open weekends July 4 through Columbus Day, 2–5) collection includes records and artifacts from 18th-century Fort Pelham (the site is marked).

TO SEE

SCENIC DRIVES

The Mohawk Trail. Every autumn the AAA and other leaf-peeping pundits advise the world to take this route—which is blessedly little-used the rest of the year. If you do drive it during foliage season, be sure to come midweek. Whenever you come, though, shift back mentally to the 1920s-to-'40s auto-touring era. Note that the first "must" stop—the "Highest Steel Observation Tower in Massachusetts" at the Longview Gift Shop—is sited not just to take advantage of the "five-state view" but also to water and cool the engines of the early automobiles making the steep climb from Greenfield. The original tower and a similar tower at the western end of the trail were built by two enterprising sisters as added attractions to their tearooms. The **Mohawk Trading Post,** with its huge buffalo outside, is the first trading post you see. The second, just beyond the turnoff to Shelburne Falls (see *Villages*), is the **Big Indian Shop,** so called because a 28-foot-tall wooden Indian guards its door. There were plenty of Indians on hand to greet 1920s tourists: Shopkeepers imported Native Americans to sell baskets and beadwork by the road. The largest of the half-dozen "trading posts" that survive is Indian Plaza in Charlemont (see *Villages*), site of periodic Indian pow-wows spring through fall. **Mohawk Park** in Charlemont is the official centerpiece of the trail, site of the bronze statue placed in 1932 to commemorate the five Native American nations that regularly used this trail, chiefly for raiding purposes. The arrowhead-shaped tablet at the base of the statue reads: HAIL TO THE SUNRISE—IN MEMORY OF THE MOHAWK INDIAN. There is a wishing pool with 100 inscribed stones from the various tribes and councils from throughout the country. Route 2 climbs steeply west from here, following the river, and then travels over Florida Mountain. This Florida, incidentally, is one of the coldest towns in the state, but it was named in 1805 just as the United States was purchasing the state of Florida from Spain. The next landmark is the Eastern Summit Gift Shop (under the same ownership for more than 20 years); then comes **Whitcomb Summit,** the site of a motel, snack bar, cluster of vintage cottages, a bronze elk (placed here by the Massachusetts Elks in 1923), and a tower (much reduced in height), from which you look back down the narrow Deerfield Valley. A path leads off to Moore's Summit (2250 feet), the highest point on the Mohawk Trail. Continue on to the Western Summit, site of the third lookout tower with its "three-state view" and of the **Wigwam** gift shop and cottages. From this point on Route 2, the well-named **Hairpin Turn** zigs and zags down the Western Summit into North Adams.

River Road to Whitcomb Summit is a worthwhile deviation from the Mohawk Trail. Take the road marked ROWE just west of the village of Charlemont, but bear left almost immediately at the fork (marked by a dead tree with numerous signs tacked to it) along **River Road.** Follow it along the river, by the **Zoar Picnic Area** in a pine grove. Continue along the river as the valley walls steepen, past Whitcomb Summit Road, over the railroad tracks. Look here for the eastern portal of the Hoosac Tunnel, opened in the 1870s by blasting through granite. Con-

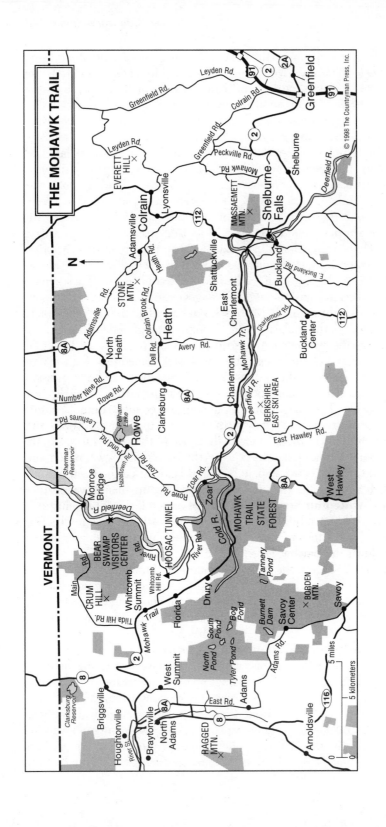

THE MOHAWK TRAIL

© 1998 The Countryman Press, Inc.

tinue a little more than 3 miles, passing a series of fishing and boating access points, until you reach the Fife Brook Dam; in another mile you will see the **Bear Swamp Visitors Center** (424-5213). It's open Memorial Day weekend through Columbus Day, except Tuesday and Wednesday, 9–5. Displays explain how underground pumps generate power from the Deerfield as it flows from the upper to lower reservoirs. The Dunbar picnic area with rest rooms and swings is another mile up the road, across from the trailheads for hiking in the **Monroe State Forest.** Return to Whitcomb Road and follow it up to Route 2 at the Whitcomb Summit. You can also continue through the village of Monroe Bridge and on to Vermont, or you might want to loop back on Monroe Hill Road past the decommissioned Yankee Rowe Nuclear Power Plant, into the village of Rowe and on back down the Zoar Road to Route 2.

TO DO

BICYCLING
Bicycles Unlimited (772-2700), 322 High Street, Greenfield, rents mountain bikes and can advise about good routes through this region's maze of back roads.

CANOEING
Zoar Outdoor (1-800-532-7483), Route 2 in Charlemont, rents canoes for use on several stretches of the Deerfield; also offers shuttle service. Canoeing and white-water clinics are offered.

FISHING
The stretch of the Deerfield River in Charlemont lures anglers from across the Northeast. There is a catch-and-release section in the village of Hoosac Tunnel. Beware of the changing depth of the water throughout this area due to releases from the dam. Fly-fishing clinics on the Deerfield River are offered by **Points North Fly Fishing Outfitters** (743-4030).

GOLF
Edge Hill Golf Course (628-6018), Barnes Road in Ashfield. This former dairy farm is now a nine-hole course with the golf shop/snack bar and lounge in the former barn overlooking a pond.

HIKING
The Mahican-Mohawk Trail runs for 7.25 miles between Shelburne Falls and Deerfield. The Mohawk Trail has always billed itself as an ancient Indian route, and in places it is. Several years ago, however, Berkshire writer and naturalist Lauren Stevens initiated a study that revealed not only the location of the old riverside path but the fact that it was still roughly maintained by the New England Power Company to access a series of hydroelectric dams. Thanks to the concerted efforts of local environmental groups, this trail is now accessible to sturdily shod hik-

ers. According to Richard Matthews, editor and publisher of the *West County News*, the hike takes at least four hours; the most impressive but rugged few miles are at the Shelburne Falls end. Trail maps are available at the **Shelburne Falls Village Information Center** (see *Guidance*). Another segment of this trail can be hiked in the **Mohawk State Forest** in Charlemont.

CROSS-COUNTRY SKIING

Stump Sprouts (339-4265), West Hill Road, West Hawley. High on the side of a mountain, this 450-acre tract offers some memorable cross-country skiing on wooded trails at 1500- to 2000-foot elevations. Snacks and rentals are available in the warming hut, which is part of Lloyd and Suzanne Crawford's home (see *Lodging*). There are 25 km of trails, lessons, and guided tours. All admission $8 per day.

Note: Also see *Green Space* for trails in the **Savoy Mountain** and **Kenneth Dubuque Memorial State Forests**.

DOWNHILL SKIING

Berkshire East (339-6617), South River Road, Charlemont. This is an unusually challenging mountain for its size. *Vertical drop:* 1180 feet. *Terrain:* 25 trails, 40 percent expert, 40 percent intermediate. *Lifts:* Four chairs, two bars. *Snowmaking:* 90 percent of terrain. *Facilities:* Nursery, two base lodges, ski school, shop; open daily; night skiing Wednesday through Saturday; snowboarding. *Rates:* Adults $35 weekends, $25 weekdays; juniors $20 weekends, $15 weekdays.

SWIMMING

See *Green Space* for the **Mohawk Trail** and **Savoy Mountain State Forests**; ask locally about swimming holes in the Deerfield River.

TUBING

Bring your own, or inquire locally about where to pick up an inner tube and coast down the Deerfield River (Charlemont is the local hub for tubing).

WHITE-WATER RAFTING

"When I first approached New England Electric they said 'No. You can't raft the river,'" Bruce Lessels recalls, adding that over the next few years, however, the power company became increasingly cooperative. In 1989 the company began releasing water from Fife Brook Dam with a regularity that makes rafting possible on most days April through October on a 10-mile stretch of the river—from Florida, through steep, green-walled, boulder-strewn Zoar Gap, and on down to Charlemont. Lessels, a former member of the US Olympic white-water team, now heads up **Zoar Outdoor** (1-800-532-7483), based in a 1750s house with 80 acres on Route 2 in Charlemont. The complex presently includes a bathhouse with changing rooms and hot showers, an orientation pavilion, and a campground.

Crab Apple (1-800-553-7238), Route 2, Charlemont. An outfitter with a larger base on Maine's Kennebec River, Crab Apple has been offering raft trips on the Deerfield since 1989 and is now also based in a former

Conway Public Library

riverside motel and restaurant. Inquire about "funyaks." Although Zoar Gap is admittedly not as visually and viscerally exciting as parts of Maine's Kennebec or Penobscot Rivers, it offers a great introduction to rafting. The day we ran it, a third of our group was under age 16 (minimum weight: 50 pounds). The Upper Deerfield Dryway, a stretch of water above the Fife Field Dam, is also a rafting and kayaking possibility on specific days.

GREEN SPACE

PICNICKING
Gardner Falls, Shelburne Falls Recreation Area. Follow North Street along the river until you see the sign. The old power canal here is a great fishing spot, and it's also a fine place for a picnic (go past the picnic tables, down by the river).

STATE FORESTS
Savoy Mountain State Forest (663-8469). From Route 2 in Florida, take Shaft Road south to the supervisor's headquarters; the more direct approach is from Route 116 in Savoy. You can swim in North Pond and camp (45 sites) at South Pond. Tannery Falls is past the camping area: At a Y in the road fork right, cross the bridge and turn left at the sign. Continue until you reach the picnic area on your left; park and take the short trail to the head of the falls. At the campground there are rest rooms, showers, picnic sites, and three log cabins. There are 24 miles of

hiking trails, two ski-touring loops, and a "crooked forest" of deformed trees. The waters are stocked with fish.

Monroe State Forest (339-5504) covers 4000 acres in the towns of Florida and Monroe. Access is on Monroe Road off Route 2 (just east of Whitcomb Summit; see River Road under *Scenic Drives*). Nine miles of hiking trails and several "pack-in" campsites are on the Dunbar Brook Falls Trail. The Roycroft Lookout takes in a panorama of the Deerfield River Valley.

Mohawk Trail State Forest (339-5504), Route 2, Charlemont, covers 6457 acres, offers more than 50 campsites and four log cabins, and allows swimming in an artificially formed pool, complete with bathhouse, scattered picnic tables, and many miles of hiking trails.

Catamount State Forest (339-5504), Route 112, Colrain. Fishing is the big attraction in this 1125-acre forest in southwestern Colrain and eastern Charlemont. Streams and a 27-acre lake are stocked. There are also hiking and riding trails.

H.O. Cook State Forest (258-4774), Route 8A, Colrain. The lure here is fishing for trout in more than 5 miles of streams. There are also hiking and riding trails. Access is off Route 8A on State Farm Road in northeastern Heath, ½ mile south of the Vermont line.

Kenneth Dubuque Memorial State Forest, also known as **Hawley State Forest** (339-5504), northwest of Plainfield on Route 8A, offers a fine loop hike starting at Moody Spring, a genuine mineral spring with a metal pipe spouting water. A sign proclaims: THIS WATER HAS PROVEN HELPFUL IN CASES OF SORE THROAT, STOMACHACHE, INTESTINAL DISORDERS, RHEUMATISM AND ALL SCROFULA DISEASES. Not far from the spring, just off East Hawley Road, stands a well-preserved charcoal kiln. The forest's many miles of dirt roads make for fine winter ski touring and summer dirt biking.

WALKS

Bear Swamp Reservation, maintained by the Trustees of Reservations, is in Ashfield on Hawley Road (less than 2 miles west of the junction of Route 116 and 112). It has 171 acres with roads and trails and is known for wildflowers: lady's slipper, painted trillium, cowslip, marsh marigold, blue gentian, wild azalea, and flowering dogwood.

High Ledges, Shelburne. A 300-acre preserve with superb views of the surrounding countryside. This Massachusetts Audubon Sanctuary is still maintained by the family that donated it. For directions, check with the **Shelburne Falls Information Center** (see *Guidance*).

WATERFALLS

Chapelbrook Reservation, maintained by the Trustees, is in South Ashfield. (Where Route 116 doglegs east, continue south on the Williamsburg Road for 2¼ miles.) Turn left to find the series of shallow falls that spill into a deep pool, perfect for sliding down. Across the road, the Chapelbrook Ledges offer long views.

LODGING

BED & BREAKFASTS

The Johnson Homestead Bed & Breakfast (625-6603), 79 East Buckland Road, Shelburne Falls 01370. Susan Grader's grandparents took in boarders for a full 40 years in this gracious 1890s farmhouse; now Susan and her husband David have revived the tradition. Sited on a quiet road, this is a homey, pleasant place with comfortable common rooms and three guest rooms (we like the one with the 1805 maple bed and hand-loomed coverlet); the rooms share two baths. $65 double, $55 single includes a full breakfast, maybe Dutch apple pancakes or stuffed crêpes; $20 per extra person, children 12 and over welcome. The House features an unusual outdoor fireplace and flower gardens.

Bull Frog Bed & Breakfast (628-4493), Route 116, South Ashfield 01330. Lucille Thibault's home was the first bed & breakfast in Ashfield (a number have come and gone since). This 200-year-old Cape sits back from Route 116 south of South Ashfield, with a lovely back garden, a frog pond, and five kinds of berry bushes. The organically grown blueberries, strawberries, blackberries, gooseberries, and currants are the ingredients for the homemade jams that are part of the full country breakfast. $75–85; $50 single.

☞ **Penfrydd Farm B&B** (624-5516), 105 Hillman Road, Colrain 01340. Thom Griffin is your host at this 160-acre hilltop farm, ringed by more hills. Resident animals include llamas and horses; guests are invited to hike with the llamas along paths through woods and meadows. There are four guest rooms, two sharing a bath ($55 per couple); one, far larger and more attractive than the others, has a whirlpool tub ($65). Plans call for reducing the number of bedrooms and increasing the number of baths. Common space is informal and attractive but nothing fancy; rates include breakfast.

The Farm at Ashfield (628-4067), 1084 Cape Street (Route 112), Ashfield 01330. Bunny Tavares and John Bos have both held high-powered jobs in Washington, D.C., among other places. Their 1790s house here is a beauty, a blend of comfort and interesting pieces. Common spaces include a hospitable country kitchen and music/TV room, as well as a parlor with a fireplace; the master bedroom has its own woodstove. $55–$65 includes a full country breakfast.

✐ **Maple House Bed and Breakfast** (339-0107), Middletown Hill Road, Rowe 01367. A 200-year-old farmhouse that took in summer boarders a century ago, Maple House sits high on a hill surrounded by fields. Becky and Michael Bradley have young children of their own and welcome families. Common rooms are comfortable rather than fancy, and the four guest rooms are on the renovated third floor, with pine floors and exposed posts and beams; they range from a double with private bath to a family suite. Full breakfasts feature homemade syrups (blueberry and raspberry as well as maple). Guests can swim in Pelham Lake. $45 single, $50–60 double; dinner available, $10 per adult, $5 per child.

The Merriams (369-4052), Conway 01341. This 1767 center-chimney classic house could easily fit into the lineup in Old Deerfield. Its paneling is exquisite, and a formal parlor is hung with family portraits. The upstairs former ballroom is still used as common space. A full breakfast is served in the formal dining room. Guest rooms include two doubles ($70) and one single ($65), divided between the main house and the barn. Bob Merriam taught English at Deerfield Academy for 25 years and now maintains an antiquarian bookshop here. Mary Merriam is a noted quilter and gives workshops.

Kinsman Homestead Bed & Breakfast (337-5712), Colrain Stage Road, Heath 01346. A distinguished looking 1860s brick house with a gothic-arched door. Guest rooms upstairs and down have working fireplaces and are tastefully decorated with family antiques, as is the large living room. There is plenty of space to relax inside and out; lawn games include croquet, badminton, and volleyball. $45–$70 includes a breakfast of muffins, fruit, and cereals in the dining room by the old-fashioned hearth.

Newhall Farm (369-4324; fax: 369-4106), 482 Newhall Road, Conway 01341. A three-room, self-contained cottage with a living room, kitchen, bath, and bedroom. Attached to the main 1790s house, it is surrounded by 100 acres of woods. $70 single, $85 per couple includes a full breakfast; hosts Thomas and Susan Dichter have lived in many exotic places.

Parson Hubbard House (625-9730), Old Village Road, Shelburne 01370. Open May through October only. Dick and Jean Bole pride themselves on preserving the beauty of this 200-year-old parsonage, which has been their home for more than 25 years. Choose from three rooms sharing 1½ baths. The view is off across fields. Note the mossy maple out front; it dates from the 1750s. $45–55 per couple.

1796 House (625-2975), Upper Street, Buckland 01338. Janet Turley's 18th-century home on the classic green is a standout. The front parlor and dining room retain their original paneling and are filled with antiques. Guests enter through the big country kitchen and tend to start chatting there, and then settle in on the ample screened-in porch. Of the three upstairs rooms, our favorite is the front one with Bermuda prints, a four-poster, and a dressing room leading to the bath. Breakfast is substantial and tasty, but best of all is the welcome you get from Janet, a motherly host who obviously enjoys her guests. $60–80 includes a very full breakfast.

MOTEL

The Oxbow (625-6011), Mohawk Trail, Charlemont 01339. A 24-room motel with a dining room, air-conditioning, TV, tennis, and a pool and fitness center. Breakfast is served in the restaurant on weekends. $39–59.

CAMPGROUNDS

Springbrook Family Camp Area (625-6618), 32 Tower Road, Shelburne 01370. We rarely list private campgrounds, but this one is a standout, set high on a hillside with a great view as well as a recreational lodge, lawn games, and a big pool. $20–22.

  ♿ **Mohawk Trail State Forest Camping Area** (339-5504), Route 2, Charlemont. Open year-round; office hours are 8 AM–10 PM. Fifty-six wooded campsites and several log cabins (campsites and a cabin are wheelchair accessible); showers, pool, hiking trails. Standard sites are $6, log cabins $8–$10 (a minimum stay of one week and a maximum of two weeks is required from late June to Labor Day; reservations accepted up to six months in advance). Reservations for campsites are accepted up to three months in advance for a stay of less than 7 days, up to six months for more than seven days; two-night minimum on all reservations.

Zoar Outdoor (1-800-532-7483), Route 2, Charlemont. Set in a wooded area surrounded by 80 acres of woods, 3 tent sites and 6 cabin tents (accommodates 44 campers); hot showers, flush toilets, pay phone; $6 per site, $13 per cabin tent.

OTHER LODGING

☞ **Stump Sprouts Guest Lodge** (339-4265), West Hill Road, Hawley 01339. Lloyd Crawford has built this modern, hilltop lodge almost entirely with his own hands, from timbers he found standing on this 450-acre spread. He also built the bunks and much of the furniture inside. A maximum of 20 can be accommodated in seven rooms, sleeping from two to five, and the common spaces are on many levels (there are lofts and corners to sit in with skylights and stained glass). Windows maximize the view of tier upon tier of wooded hills. The former barn is a great rec room with table tennis, pool, and a piano; the ceiling drops down for warmth in winter and can be raised to allow even more space (the old silo is a great aerie) in summer. There's a wonderful view from the sauna, too. Vegetable gardens supply the table, which Suzanne Crawford sets family style, or you can cook for yourself. It's possible to come singly or in couples, but it's most fun to come as a group. In winter there are the cross-country ski trails for which this place is well known (see *To Do*), and in summer the trails are still there to walk or bike. $109 per person per weekend includes six meals; from $29 per person midweek.

✎ **Rowe Conference Center** (339-4954), Kings Highway Road, Rowe 01367. The Unitarian-Universalist center consists of a farmhouse and assorted camp buildings on a quiet back road. There are 16 private and semi-private rooms with a total of 125 beds, mostly dorm-style. On most weekends throughout the year there are speakers (many of them well known) on topics ranging from "Writing from the Heart," to "Herbs, Holiness, and Menopause," to "Gardening: Making and Keeping a Private Eden." Seven summer weeks are also reserved for school-age, adult, and family camps.

✐ **Blue Heron Farm** (339-4045), Warner Hill Road, Charlemont 01339. Bill and Norma Coli offer a choice of lodging options on their 100-acre organic farm. Three rentals, a self-contained cottage (two-bedrooms, 2 baths, fireplace, sleeps up to 7), a log cabin (sleeps up to 4, one bedroom), and an attractive apartment attached to the sugarhouse (sleeps up to 3) are all good for families. Overall this place is great for families; pony-cart rides, berry picking, and helping with the horses and goats are encouraged. $75–150 per night, two-night minimum stay, cheaper by the week and month.

Hall Tavern Farm (625-9008), Route 2, Shelburne Falls 01370. This is the state's oldest privately owned tree farm (see *Selective Shopping— Farms*). A two-bedroom cottage is tucked into meadowland on the banks of the Deerfield River. Prices on request.

WHERE TO EAT

DINING OUT

Green Emporium (624-5122), Route 112, Colrain. Open for dinner Thursday through Saturday; Sunday for brunch and early dinner; reservations requested. Michael Collins, a New York chef, and Pacifico "Tony" Palumbo, a well-known neon artist, have transformed a 150-year-old former Methodist Church into an exceptional space filled with round tables, neon, painted and sculpted art, plants, fresh flowers, and the aroma of soup (maybe Bermudian chowder or Portuguese Calda Verde) and entrées like summer pasta—sautéed purple kale, roasted red peppers, and portobello mushrooms on linguine ($14)—or grilled Atlantic salmon topped with roasted sweet red pepper sauce ($17). Save room for Lillian Brigham's (of Colrain) pie. Beer and wine are served. Wednesday is pasta and performance night. Sunday brunch is an excuse to drive the scenic loop from Shelburne (stopping at the West County Winery) to Colrain and back down Route 112 to Shelburne Falls. Check out the amazing garden.

✐ **Copper Angel Café** (625-2727), 2 State Street, Shelburne Falls. Open daily 11:30–9, Sunday 9–8. Gail Beauregard and Nicol Wander have created a very special place in this dining room that seems suspended over the river, with the best view in town of the Bridge of Flowers. There are plenty of vegetarian dishes like Thai fried noodles, but if you must there's a cheeseburger platter (admittedly it's ground turkey). Dinner specialties include crabcakes served with the house tartar sauce ($10.95) and ham-wrapped scallops with maple mustard cream ($12.95), as well as lentil cutlets with gravy ($6.50). Brunch includes veggie eggs Benedict. The Kids Menu choices are less than $3. Wine is served, along with a variety of organic coffees.

The Warfield House at Valley View Farm (339-6600; 1-888-339-VIEW), 200 Warfield Road, off Route 2, Charlemont. Dinner Thursday through

Sunday, lunch Friday and Saturday, breakfast Sunday (7:30–10) and brunch (9–3). Newly opened when we dined well here on roast duckling à l'orange ($16.95), this is the most spectacularly positioned restaurant in the Hilltowns. Perched on a hill, its walls of windows overlook the slopes of Berkshire East ski area. The barnyard is home to exotic as well as farm animals; inquire about llama trek picnics and buggy rides. Dinner entrées begin at $9.95 for chicken pot pie or meatloaf and include grilled emu kabobs marinated in balsamic vinegar on a rosemary skewer ($15.95).

Charlemont Inn (339-5796), Main Street, Charlemont. Open daily 6 AM through dinner, best known for live entertainment on weekends. The big, informal room is a good bet for breakfast; lunch features burgers and sandwiches (home fries are a specialty). At dinner the menu includes a wide choice of vegetarian dishes, along with everything from Zoar steak ($12.95 for the 10-ounce), BBQ ribs ($9.95), and maple chicken, to the chef's special roast duck ($14.95). Frankly geared to fishermen, hunters, rafters, bicyclists, and other outdoorspeople, this is a genuine old upcountry inn (we didn't list the rooms but they are clean and reasonably priced).

Panini Palate (625-6221), 24 Bridge Street, Shelburne Falls, open daily for lunch and dinner. The town's first trendy cafe features panini (grilled sandwiches on focaccia bread), build-your-own sandwiches, and soups and stews, with bread and pastry made on the premises. Dinner entrées might include rosemary-roasted Cornish game hen ($13) or penne with spinach, plum tomatoes, olive oil, and roasted garlic ($10).

EATING OUT

10 Bridge Street Cafe & Restaurant (625-2345), 10 Bridge Street, Shelburne Falls. Open Monday through Thursday 6:30 AM–9 PM, Friday and Saturday 7 AM–10 PM, Sunday 7 AM–9 PM. The restaurant is closed some days, but the café is the lively center of town, good for a variety of burgers (be sure to stipulate if you want it rare) and a selection of hearty sandwiches, soups, quiches, and salads. Liquor is served.

Countrypie Pizza Company (628-4488), 343 Main Street, Ashfield. Open Wednesday through Sunday 11–9. Good pizza with plenty of veggie varieties, including eggplant, broccoli, artichoke hearts, feta, and Garden Delight, featuring fresh spinach, mushrooms, and so forth. Plenty of grinders.

Buckland Bar & Grill (625-2588), 15 State Street, Shelburne Falls. Open 10 AM–midnight. Known affectionately as "The Hole," this is the alternative to the neighboring sprouts-and-lentils menus. The subterranean room features a long bar and booths, hometown-style, and reasonably priced sandwiches and dinners like liver and onions, hot turkey, and fried fish.

Gould's Sugar House (625-6170), Route 2, Shelburne. Open March through October except May, daily 8:30–2. A great roadside stop for breakfast or lunch, featuring maple specialties.

Spruce Corner Restaurant (268-3188), Route 116, Ashfield (near the Plainfield line). Open for dinner Wednesday through Sunday, otherwise breakfast and lunch. Tina and Jerry Bird are the chef-owners of this cheery way-stop, which fills a real need in this corner of the hills; reasonably priced dinner specials like beef stew and meatloaf, liquor license.

Charlemont Pizza (339-4472), Main Street, Charlemont. Open at 11 daily, noon Sunday, until at least 9. Try the kielbasa pizza with extra cheese.

Pine Hill Orchards (624-3325), Greenfield Road, Colrain. Open weekdays 7 AM–5 PM, until 6 on Friday; weekends from 8 AM. Home-baked items are served at the counter and tables. The property also includes a petting zoo, picnic tables, and West County Winery (see *Selective Shopping*).

Ashfield Lake House, off Main Street by the lake, Ashfield. Open 4–11. Better than it looks at first: good, reasonably priced food and tables on the deck by the lake.

McCusker's Market (625-9411), 3 State Street, Shelburne Falls. Open weekdays 6 AM–8 PM, weekends 7 AM–8 PM. Booths in the back, a great place to get light food or coffee and the paper; check out the rest rooms.

ENTERTAINMENT

CONCERTS

Mohawk Trail Concerts (625-9511), 75 Bridge Street, Charlemont. Having celebrated its 25th season in 1994, this series of chamber and choral music concerts only seems to get better. Concerts are Friday at 7:30, Saturday at 8 during July and August, in the 225-seat, acoustically fine Federated Church on Route 2.

Rural Renaissance concerts (contact John Bos at 628-3323), Ashfield Town Hall, Ashfield. A series of musical offerings, presented during the winter months, ranging from country-western singers to a Gershwin trio to the 24-player Providence Mandolin Orchestra.

FILM

Pothole Pictures (625-2526), Memorial Hall Theater, Shelburne Falls. A series of popular and art films.

Zoar Outdoor (1-800-532-7483), Route 2, Charlemont. The sporting outfitter sponsors a summer film series in its outdoor pavilion, featuring films like "A Photographer's Climbing Adventures in Pakistan."

SELECTIVE SHOPPING

ANTIQUES SHOPS

The **Shelburne Falls Information Center** (see *Guidance*) publishes a list of local dealers.

BOOKSTORE

Boswell's (625-9362), 1 State Street, Shelburne Falls. Open daily. A full-service bookshop with new and used books, audio and video rentals, and pleasant reading corners.

Mohawk Trail Concerts

CRAFTS SHOPS

Salmon Falls Artisans (625-9833), 176 Ashfield Street, Shelburne Falls. Open April through December, daily 10–5, Sunday noon–5; January through March, Wednesday through Saturday 10–5, Sunday noon–5. This is an exceptional gallery showcasing much of the best work crafted in this area as well as farther afield and featuring the distinctive, widely acclaimed glass orbs by Shelburne-based Josh Simpson. **Bald Mountain Pottery** (625-8110), 28 State Street, Shelburne Falls. Open Tuesday through Saturday 10–5, Sunday noon–5; closed Monday through Wednesday off-season. The distinctive, functional pottery is made in the riverside studio, which also displays work by several other local potters. **North River Glass** (625-6422), Deerfield Avenue, Shelburne Falls. Watch glass being blown; the deeply colored resulting vases, bowls, perfume bottles, and art glass are displayed in the adjacent gallery. **Mole Hollow Candles** (625-6337), Deerfield Avenue, Shelburne Falls. Open daily 10–5, later in summer. Overlooks the potholes along the Deerfield River; candles are made on weekdays. The shop also sells gifts and cards. **Textile Arts** (625-8241), 6 Bridge Street, Shelburne Falls. A small weaving studio in which Susie Robbins displays locally woven wool blankets and shawls, cotton placemats and tablecloths, local wools; also books. **Ann Brauer Quilt Studio** (625-8605), 2 Conway Street, Shelburne Falls. Open Wednesday through Sunday; studio art quilts,wall hangings, accessories. **The Whistling Crow** (625-2595), 20 Bridge Street, Shelburne Falls. Open Wednesday through Sunday, 11–5. A combination nature store and candy shop geared to wildlife lovers (books, birding supplies) with proceeds benefiting CROW, a wildlife rehabilitation center in nearby Hawley.

Note: See *Scenic Drives—The Mohawk Trail* for more information on the trading posts and gift shops along the trail.

FARMS

Donovan Farm (339-4213), Forget Road, Hawley. The state's largest organically certified farm, with sweeping views and five kinds of potatoes, produces its own hand-cooked, organic potato chips. **Hall Tavern Farm** (625-9008), Route 2, Shelburne Falls. The state's oldest privately owned tree farm produces timbers and lumber for its sawmill and offers a variety of kiln-dried wood products, including wide-pine flooring, paneling, and wainscoting as well as ash, cherry, maple, and oak flooring from its 500 acres (also see *Lodging*). **Penfrydd Farm** (624-5516), Colrain. The Farm Store on the 160-acre farm off the byways of Colrain features hand-dyed yarns, handwoven blankets, knitted garments, sheepskins, and other farm products (also see *Lodging*). **Burnt Hill Farm** (337-4454), Burnt Hill, Heath. Pick-your-own blueberries in-season on top of a mountain with a 50-mile view. **Long Hill Farm** (339-4336), Long Hill Road, Heath. Open Tuesday through Saturday 10–5; farmer's market Saturday during the season. Wool is processed in the farm store, a former Unitarian meetinghouse (1830–60); the farm includes a picnic area, hiking trails, a sugarhouse, a cider press, lambs, and hay. **Walnut Hill Farm** (625-9002), 104 Ashfield Road, Shelburne Falls. Open daily 7:30–7. A dairy farm and vegetable stand welcome visitors. The world's largest ox, weighing 4700 pounds, was raised here at the turn of the century.

SUGARHOUSES

As already noted, the Hilltowns are the prime source of Massachusetts's maple sugar, and the sugaring season—which can begin as early as late February and extend well into April—draws locals and visitors alike to sugarhouses and to pancake breakfasts featuring the new syrup. A brochure detailing information about the sugaring process and each producer is available from the **Massachusetts Maple Producers Association**, Watson-Spruce Corner Road, Ashfield 01330. During sugaring season you can call the **Massachusetts Maple Phone** (628-3912) to get an overall view on whether the sap is flowing and producers are "boiling off." The following sugarhouses are geared toward visitors more than most, but it's still a good idea to call before coming. All also sell their syrup from their farms year-round.

In Ashfield, **Gray's Sugarhouse** (625-6559) has a dining room open on weekends during sugaring, as does **South Face Farm** (628-3268), which also exhibits antique maple-sugaring equipment. **Puringtons' Maple** (625-2780), Buckland, still use horses to collect sap. **Blue Heron Farm** (339-4045), Charlemont, welcomes visitors with rental units attached to its sugarhouse (see *Lodging*); the farm also features dairy goats, NorwegianFjord horses, and organic produce. **Boyden**

Brothers, right on Route 116 in Conway, is the big producer here, but a number of other producers using wood-burning evaporators are scattered through the hills. **Girard's Sugarhouse** (337-5788) in Heath has been operating more than 90 years.

In Shelburne, **Gould's Sugar House** (625-6170), right on Route 2, features locally made syrup on waffles; also homemade sausage and sugar-on-snow among its other items (see *Eating Out*). **Davenport Maple Farm** (625-2866), set high above the valley with a splendid view, operates a restaurant during sugaring season and sells syrup from the house year-round (a good excuse to drive up).

APPLE ORCHARDS

Mohawk Orchards (625-2874), ¼ mile north of Route 2 on the Colrain-Shelburne Road. Open year-round, daily. Pick-your-own apples Labor Day through Columbus Day, otherwise a farm stand sited in the middle of the orchard, picnic tables, small farm animals for petting. **Pine Hill Orchards** (624-3324), 248 Greenfield Road, Colrain. Open year-round daily. Pick-your-own apples in season, also bakery/restaurant (see *Eating Out*), sugarhouse, farm animals for petting.

SPECIAL SHOPS

McCusker's Market (625-9411), 3 State Street, Shelburne Falls. Aside from carrying gourmet and ecologically correct lines, McCusker's is the only outlet for Lamson & Goodnow Cutlery, manufactured in town for more than 150 years. Exceptional in quality, the cutlery ranges from a $16 bar/fruit knife to a $40 "slicer," and there are frequent sales on individual pieces and sets (see also *Eating Out*). **Bear Meadow Farm** (663-9241), Whitcomb Summit, Route 2, Florida. The quality preserves and condiments sold here are made at a neighboring farm.

WINERY

West County Winery (624-3481) at Pine Hill Orchards, Colrain (turn at **Strawberry Fields Antiques** on Route 2). Open May through December, Thursday through Sunday 11–5, and Friday through Sunday the rest of the year. Six hard ciders, dry to sweet, with alcohol 4 to 5 percent, are produced from local fruit, available for sampling in the tasting room.

SPECIAL EVENTS

May: **Indian Pow Wow** at Indian Plaza, Charlemont. **Memorial Day Parade,** Shelburne Falls.

June: **Riverfest**—daylong festival along the street and river in Shelburne Falls. **Indian Pow Wow,** Indian Plaza, Charlemont.

July: July 4th **Indian Pow Wow,** Charlemont. **July 4th parade** in Shelburne Falls.

August: **Bridge of Flowers 10K road race** and **Bridge of Flowers Festival,** Shelburne Falls. **Heath Fair** (mid-month).

September: The big event comes the last weekend with the **Conway Festival of the Hills,** one of New England's most colorful foliage festivals. The **Colrain Fair** is mid-month.

October: **Ashfield Fall Festival** on Columbus Day weekend is not to be missed. Shelburne Falls also stages a **fall foliage festival** with sidewalk sales, music, and trolley rides the first weekend.

November: **Midnight Madness** the day after Thanksgiving: tree lighting, caroling, and special sales in Shelburne Falls.

Hampshire Hills

This 225-square-mile spread of rolling hill and woodland is even farther off the tourist map than the West County hilltowns to the north. It's been blessedly bypassed by the Mass. Pike (there are no exits for the 30 miles between Westfield and Lee).

During the decades before income taxes, when wealthy Americans were building themselves summer palaces in Stockbridge and Lenox, a number of old farms around Worthington and Cummington were gentrified (the William Cullen Bryant Homestead is the most obvious surviving example). For much of this century, however, this area was just a nameless region to pass through. Then in 1982 the Hilltown Community Development Corporation placed an ad in local papers asking people with spare rooms to consider the bed & breakfast business and in short order a dozen or so households responded, forming the Hampshire Hills Bed & Breakfast Association and publishing a descriptive brochure. So it happens that the Hampshire Hills is a destination with a name and a choice of places to stay.

Since 1982 the Association has expanded to include several B&Bs in Hamden County to the south. B&B hosts direct their guests to local swimming holes, antiques shops, craftspeople, hiking trails, fishing holes, and waterfalls. This area offers few restaurants, but an unusual number of places under *Green Space*, several genuine old general stores that can supply picnic needs, and some outstanding craftspeople. Generally speaking, the hills are less steep here than in the Hilltowns to the north, more conducive to bicycling.

The Miniature Theatre of Chester and the Sevenars concerts in South Worthington (see *Entertainment*) are both widely acclaimed, but most events—auctions, agricultural fairs, and town homecomings—are promoted only locally.

AREA CODE: 413

GUIDANCE

Hampshire Hills Bed & Breakfast Association (1-888-414-7664), PO Box 553, Worthington 01908.

The Hilltown Hospitality Council (1-888-527-0570), PO Box 17, Chesterfield 01012. Request a copy of the free map/guide, *The Hidden Hills of Western Massachusetts*.

GETTING THERE
Part of the beauty of this area is in its approach. Few places in this region
are much more than a half-hour's drive from I-91 or the Mass. Pike, but
you are quickly on back roads. The principal east–west roads—Route 9
and Route 66/Route 20—follow the river valleys, while Route 57 to the
south is a high old byway. The major north–south routes, Route 112
and Route 8, also follow rivers. If you are coming from the east via the
Mass. Pike, take exit 3 in Westfield.

MEDICAL EMERGENCY
Dial 911, or check with the **Worthington Health Center** (238-5511), Old
North Road, Worthington.

VILLAGES

Chesterfield. A white-clapboard village with an 1835 Congregational
church, 1848 town hall, and the **Edward Memorial** (historical) **Museum** near the library. But the big attraction is Chesterfield Gorge (see
Green Space). The town stages a fine July 4th parade; inquire about the
Charles Bisbee Sr. Agricultural and Industrial Museum.

Cummington. The classic village center is posted from Route 9 and worth
a stop to see the **Kingman Tavern** (open Saturday 2–5 in July and
August), a lovingly restored combination tavern, fully stocked general
store, and post office. There are a dozen period rooms filled with town
mementos like the palm-leaf hats and cigars once made here. There is
also a barn full of tools and a shed full of horse-drawn vehicles. The big
annual event is the **Hillside Agricultural Society Fair**, the last weekend in August (see *Special Events*). Cummington has nurtured a number of poets over the years and is the longtime home of America's former
poet laureate Richard Wilbur. The **William Cullen Bryant Homestead** (see *To See*) offers one of the best views of the town and its valley.

Middlefield (population 392), a town in which the main road (one of the few
that's paved) is known as the Skyline Trail because it follows the edge of a
1650-foot-high plateau, offers spectacular views west to the Berkshires.
The only specific site to visit here is **Glendale Falls** (see *Green Space*),
but everywhere you walk or drive is rewarding.

Plainfield. This beautiful old farming town has a population of 466, which
swells to 2000 in summer. Roads are lined with stone walls and avenues
of maples, and the center has its mid-19th-century white Congregational church and town hall. The **Shaw-Hudson House** (634-5417),
open by appointment, was built in 1833 by Dr. Samuel Shaw, medical
partner and brother-in-law of William Cullen Bryant.

Williamsburg. The easternmost of the Hilltowns, this village is something
of a bedroom town for Northampton. The two-street center straddles
the Mill River and invites you to stroll, munching something you've
bought at the general store (see *Selective Shopping—General Stores*).

Cummington

The **historical society** (268-7332), housed in the 1841 town hall, exhibits photographs of the 1874 flood that burst a dam 3 miles above the village, killing 136 residents, collapsing buildings, and wiping out most of the mills. Note the **Brassworks** mill in Haydenville, rebuilt since the flood and recently renovated.

Worthington. The village at the heart of this town, known locally as Worthington Corners, is a classic, mid-19th-century crossroads with its general store and surrounding old homes along roads that radiate in every direction. Note the grocery (see *General Stores*), golf course (vintage 1904), B&Bs, cross-country ski center, and auctions and crafts store (see *Selective Shopping*).

TO SEE

HISTORIC HOMES

William Cullen Bryant Homestead (634-2244) in Cummington, south of Route 9 off Route 112. Open for guided tours from the last week in June through Labor Day, Friday, Saturday, Sunday, and holidays 1–5; until Columbus Day, weekends and holidays. Adults $5; $2.50 ages 6–12. This graceful mansion is filled with the spirit of an obviously tough-minded and original individual and with a sense of the era in which he was thoroughly involved. William Cullen Bryant was born in Cummington in 1794 and is remembered for his early nature poems, "Thanatopsis" and "To a Waterfowl," for example, and for his impact as editor and part owner for a half century (1829–1878) of the *New York Evening Post*. Bryant successfully advocated causes ranging from abolitionism to free trade to the creation of Central Park. He returned to his boyhood home at age 72, buying back the family homestead, adding another floor, and totally transforming it into a 23-room Victorian summer manse set atop 246 acres of farmland. The land has since been reduced to a mere 189 acres, but the expansive view remains. The house has been preserved (painted in its original chocolate browns) by the Trustees of Reservations to look as it did during Bryant's last summer here, in 1878.

SCENIC DRIVES

In the Hilltowns the drive that is not scenic is the exception. You almost can't lose, especially if you turn off the main roads in search of the waterfalls, swimming holes, crafts studios, and maple producers described in this chapter. Several drives, however, are particularly noteworthy.

The Skyline Trail, accessible from Route 143 in Hinsdale and from Route 20 in Chester, follows the edge of the Berkshire plateau through the middle of Middlefield. It's possible to make a loop from Chesterfield through Middlefield, stopping at Glendale Falls (see *Green Space*) and the River Studio (see *Selective Shopping*) and returning via Chester Hill (another high point), but it's best to ask directions locally.

Ireland Street, Chesterfield to South Worthington. A mile or so west of the village of Chesterfield turn left off Route 143 at the bridge. This is Ireland Street and best known as the way to Chesterfield Gorge (0.8 mile from Route 143 at River Road; see *Green Space*). Be sure to stop there. Then continue along Ireland Street, which is a straight, high ridge road. Stop at Ireland Street Orchards (see *Farms*) for the view, if for nothing else. Continue on to South Worthington, stopping by Stonepool Pottery (see *Selective Shopping*). If you feel like a swim, Gardner State Park (see *To Do—Swimming*) is just down Route 112.

Get Lost. Seriously. If we try to direct you from Plainfield to Buckland via the web of back roads that begin with Union Street north from the middle of Plainfield, you will have us to blame. But this is high, largely open countryside that was obviously far more populated a couple of hundred years ago than it is now. Bring a camera and compass.

TO DO

BALLOONING

Worthington Balloons (238-5514), Worthington. Paul Sena offers champagne flights May to November from a variety of local sites (including local B&Bs); sunrise and sunset flights geared to couples. Request the multicolored "Thunderbuster."

BICYCLING

Mountain bikers enthuse about the unpaved **River Road** south from Chesterfield Gorge in Worthington (see *Green Space*) to Knightville Dam.

The *Rubel Bike Map to Western Massachusetts* is an excellent guide to biking throughout this area (see "What's Where—Bicycling").

FISHING

The **Little River** and all three branches of the **Westfield River** are recognized throughout the country for the quality of their fishing. For details check with the **Hilltown Hospitality Council** (see *Guidance*).

GOLF

Chesterfield Chip & Putt (296-4767), 223 South Street, Chesterfield. A par-three, 18-hole course open daily 9–dark. Children must be 9 years old to play. **Beaver Brook Golf Club** (268-7229), 191 Haydenville Road (Route 9), Williamsburg, and the **Worthington Golf Club** (238-9731), Worthington, are both nine holes.

CROSS-COUNTRY SKIING

Hickory Hill Ski Touring Center (623-5535), Buffington Hill Road, Worthington. Open Friday through Monday in season. The lodge is an old potato barn with a bar and snack bar (both featuring homemade pretzels) and a staff of three, all related. "It's kind of funky, but people like it," observes Paul Sena, the man who cut as well as grooms the 24 km of trails on his family's 500-acre farm, a largely wooded spread. Snow-farming is Paul Sena's obsession. When we last visited, there had been virtually no new snow for more than a week and freezing rain had glazed the landscape. Sena was in his Snowcat, a large alpine groomer, chewing the surface to bits—to be subsequently smoothed with a powder-maker and ultimately tracked. Trails climb through maples, birches, beeches, and firs, skirting a large field or two, and follow several streams to an altitude of more than 1800 feet. Although a track is kept carefully groomed for skating and free-style skiing, the majority of the trails are tracked for traditional recreational skiing.

Notchview Reservation (684-3722), Route 9, Windsor. The highest cross-country trails in Massachusetts are found on this 3000-acre Trustees of Reservations property. Admittedly, it takes a new snowfall to work your way up to the summit of 2297-foot-high Judges Hill, but frequently there is snow on the former lawns of the General Budd Homesite. The panoramic view from this open area includes the notch in the hills cut by the Westfield River, for which the preserve is named. Adults $7, children $2.

Maple Corner Farm (357-6697), Beech Hill Road, Granville. Twelve miles of trails; lessons, lodge with fireplace, moonlight tours.

SWIMMING

The **West Branch**, **Middle Branch,** and **Westfield River** proper all weave their way through this area, offering countless swimming holes to which B&B hosts can direct you. More formal, public swimming spots like Plainfield Pond tend to be restricted to residents.

DAR State Forest (268-7098), Goshen, maintains a swimming area on Upper Highland Lake (see *Green Space*).

Windsor State Forest (684-9760), River Road, West Cummington, has a swimming area on a dammed portion of the river (see *Green Space*).

✐ **Gardner State Park**, Route 112, Huntington. Probably the best-known swimming hole on the Westfield River. A great spot to bring small children; there's an old-fashioned picnic pavilion in the pines.

GREEN SPACE

PICNICKING

South River State Forest (268-7098 or 339-5504), north from Conway village on the Shelburne Falls and Bardwells Ferry Roads, offers picnic tables and grills scattered along the gorge of the South River to its confluence with the Deerfield. Near the parking area, notice the South River Dam, once used to power the trolley line.

STATE FORESTS

DAR State Forest (268-7098), Goshen, provides more than 50 campsites, each with a table and fireplace. The swimming area at Upper Highland Lake, complete with bathhouses and lifeguards, also has a boat ramp (no motors allowed). Trails lead to Moore's Hill, just 1697 feet high but with an extensive view.

Windsor State Forest (684-9760). Follow signs from Route 9 in West Cummington, via River Road. There are 24 campsites. You can swim in the dammed section of the river; there are bathhouses, picnic tables, and grills here.

East Branch State Forest (268-7098), River Road, Chesterfield, offers some good fishing.

WALKS

Notchview Reservation (684-0148). The **Budd Visitor Center** on Route 9 in Windsor (1 mile east of the junction with Route 8A) is open daily year-round. There are picnic tables and trail maps for the 25 miles of hiking and cross-country trails (see *To Do—Cross-Country Skiing*) on this former 3000-acre estate maintained by the Trustees of Reservations. This is a good place for birding.

Windsor Jambs in **Windsor State Park** is a ¼-mile-long gorge with sheer cliffs, topped with hemlocks above the rushing water. A trail leads along the edge. Unfortunately, picnicking is not permitted here, but it's a beautiful walk (there's a railing). The state dams the river for swimming, and there are bathhouses, 80 picnic tables, and grills. This stretch of the Westfield River is a popular spot for white-water canoeing. There are also many miles of hiking trails.

Petticoat Hill Reservation in Williamsburg (up Petticoat Hill Road from the village). A trail leads to the summit of Scott Hill. Stone walls and cellar holes hint that this spot was the most populated part of town in the 1700s, but it's now forested, a good spot for wildflowers.

Chesterfield Gorge

Devil's Den Brook in Williamsburg is a rocky gorge off Old Goshen Road (turn right on Hemenway Road at the western fringe of the center, then branch left onto Old Goshen). If you take the next left, up Brier Hill Road, you come to 70 acres of wooded trails, good for cross-country skiing and hiking. Ask locally about **Rheena's Cave.**

WATERFALLS

Glendale Falls, Middlefield (off the Skyline Trail Road onto Clark Wright Road—which is closed in winter—some 3½ miles southeast of the village). Glendale Brook drops more than 150 feet over rocky ledges. There are 60 surrounding acres.

Chesterfield Gorge. Turn off Route 143 at the West Chesterfield Bridge, 1 mile south on River Road. A deep canyon was carved by the Westfield River and walled by sheer granite cliffs topped with hemlock, ash, and yellow birch. Swimming is not allowed, but the Trustees of Reservations provide picnic tables.

LODGING

BED & BREAKFASTS

☞ **Windfields Farm** (684-3786), 154 Windsor Bush Road, Cummington 01026. Open daily except in March and April. We put this at the head of the Hilltown listings because it was one of the first and remains among our favorites based on its location and the hospitality of its hosts. There are just two rooms (one with a massive, early-19th-century canopy bed), and these share a bath; but just behind this Federal (1830) house is a swimming pond, blueberry pastures, organic gardens, fireplace, and solar greenhouse. You can ski or walk up the road to the falls at Windsor Jambs (see *Green Space—Walks*) or hike through the 200-acre property itself; it adjoins the Audubon Society's 1500-acre West Mountain Sanctuary. Carolyn and Arnold Westwood (Arnold is a retired Unitarian minister who is still frequently called upon to perform marriages) are consummate hosts, and Carolyn's maple syrup has won top honors at the Cummington Fair (see *Special Events*). Breakfast is a marvel, featuring the farm's eggs, raspberries, breads, and jams, as well as maple syrup. Two-night minimum on most weekends. On winter weekends Arnold and Carolyn open the kitchen to a minimum of four guests, who can cook their own lunch and dinner. $70 per couple, $50 single; midweek discounts.

✐ **The Worthington Inn** (238-4441), at Four Corners Farm, Old North Road (Route 143), Worthington 01098. A striking, vintage-1780 house with wide floorboards, five fireplaces, and fine paneling, restored in 1942 by the architect responsible for much of the Old Deerfield restoration. The three bedrooms are sparely, tastefully furnished with antiques and down comforters and have private baths. The house is sited on its own 15 acres on the edge of a photogenic village. Hickory Hill Ski Touring Center (see *Cross-Country Skiing*) is less than a mile away. Children and horses are welcome. Debi Shaw is a hospitable, helpful host. $70–90.

☞ **The Seven Hearths** (296-4312), 412 Main Road, Chesterfield 01012. An 1890s house that has been renovated to look older, set in the middle of the village historic district. Doc and Denise LeDuc serve memorable multi-course breakfasts (maybe stuffed French toast prefaced by a fruit-stuffed melon) in the formal dining room. The common rooms and two of the three guest rooms have working fireplaces; the larger guest room offers sitting and writing space and a private bath. Facilities include a hot tub. $55–75.

☞ **Twin Maples** (268-7925), 106 South Street, Williamsburg 01096. This vintage 1806 house is set in its own 27 acres and surrounding farmland on a back road not far from the center of town. It's been home to Eleanor and Martin Hebert for more than 30 years. Eleanor also operates Berkshire Bed & Breakfast, a reservation service for much of Massachusetts. The three bedrooms and shared bath are clean and crisp (we like the blue room with the antique iron and brass bed), and the welcome is genuine. During March you can watch sap turn into syrup in the sugarhouse, and any season you can meet the farm animals, which included—at latest count—two Hereford heifers and two calves, a flock of Rhode Island Red hens and roosters, a number of sheep, and two dogs. $60–65.

☞ **Cumworth Farm** (634-5529), 472 West Cummington Road (Route 112), Cummington 01026. Open May through November only. This is a splendid but comfortable 18th-century, hip-roofed farmhouse, and Ed McColgan, a former state representative, still does serious farming, producing some 600 gallons of maple syrup and raising berries and sheep. The McColgans' seven children are grown and have left five spare rooms, all furnished with antiques. Amenities include a hot tub in the gazebo and breakfasts that are full farm. $60–75 double, $50–60 single.

Strawberry Banke Farm (623-6471), 140 Skyline Trail, Middlefield 01243. Middlefield is the kind of place where you might expect to find a bed & breakfast like this one, a 1780s farmhouse surrounded by flowers, painted (inside and out) and whimsically furnished by artist/host Judy Tavener Artioli, whose own paintings (Chagall is monotone by comparison) are displayed in the adjacent studio. The guest room with private bath is on the first floor, and two more rooms upstairs share a bath. The breakfast specialty of the house is Belgian waffles. $70 double or single.

Baird Tavern (848-2096), 2 Old Chester Road, Blandford 01008. This vintage-1768 house retains its original paneling and wide floorboards and conveys a sense of comfort. Host Carolyn Taylor is a local caterer, and breakfasts can as easily be quiche as blueberry pancakes. One bedroom is a double, and the other has twins and an add-on space suitable for a family. A cot and crib are available, and at least a couple of Persian Angora cats (which Carolyn raises) are usually on hand. $60 double, $50 single, $10 for a crib.

Carmelwood (667-5786), 8 Montgomery Road, Huntington 01050. Handy to the Sevenars concerts just up the road (see *Entertainment*), also to swimming in the Westfield River. This is a handsome Victorian house with a grand piano in the living room, an ample front porch, and the gardens that are Katheryn Corrigan's pride. Breakfast features home-baked breads and pastries and locally grown fruit. There are three double bedrooms, two with double beds, one with twins. $50–70 double.

The Hill Gallery (238-5914), 137 East Windsor Road, Worthington 01098. A modern home, designed and built by owner Walter Korzec, offers two rooms with private bath (cots available). The multilevel home doubles as a gallery for Korzec's prints and paintings and also showcases local pottery. $50–70 double, $45 single, less midweek; a small cottage is also available.

Cliffside Farm Bed & Breakfast (296-4022), 592 Main Road (Route 143), West Chesterfield 01084-0005. Sited in 150 acres high on a mountain ridge, a contemporary house offers two guest rooms in a private wing on the ground floor. Both rooms have a queen-size bed and either a daybed or rollout for another person or child. The two share a full bath. $70–75 per couple, $19 for an extra child, $25 for an extra adult includes breakfast. Handy to Chesterfield Gorge.

The Ruddy Duck Inn and Tavern (238-0126), Worthington 01098. A relatively recent building on Route 112 south of the village: a restaurant downstairs and five attractively antiques-furnished rooms, each with private bath, off an upstairs hall handy to downhill and cross-country skiing. $75 double, $70 single. ~~CLOSED~~

OTHER LODGING

Remington Lodge (634-5388), West Cummington 01026. Jo and Ken Cyr offer old-fashioned, no-frills hospitality to hikers, bikers, white-water canoeists, skiers, hunters—anyone willing to bring his or her own sleeping bag and sleep in a room with 4, 6, or 16 other people. The food is fine (the lodge is open to nonguests Friday evenings by reservation).

WHERE TO EAT

DINING OUT

The Squires' (268-7222), the Brassworks on Route 9, Williamsburg. Open for dinner Wednesday through Sunday from 5; call for reservations. The menu borrows from a number of cultures, but all dishes are smoked or grilled on a wood fire. Specialties include fava duck, Moroccan-style chicken, and "Blues ribs"; entrée prices are $13.95–28. The special might be a mixed grill of elk and wild boar sausage with sage ($16.95). Liquor, as well as wine and beer, is served.

Williams House (268-7300), Route 9, Williamsburg. Closed Mondays; otherwise open daily for lunch and dinner; Sunday buffet 10:30–1:30; dinner 2–8. David and Carol Majercik, who own the neighboring Williamsburg General Store (see *Selective Shopping—General Stores*), have rejuvenated this old landmark with its low-beamed dining room and large hearth. Hearty luncheon sandwiches run $5.25–7.50, and dinner entrées range from "fancy fettucine" to prime rib ($10.95–20.95). There are daily specials and full wine and liquor lists; patrons are also welcome simply for espresso and dessert.

Little River Café (238-5837), corner of Route 112 and Ireland Street, South Worthington. Open Wednesday through Sunday 5–9:30. Nothing fancy but very pleasant, with a screened porch set above the Little River, handy to Sevenars (see *Entertainment*) concerts. Entrées range from baked vegetarian manicotti ($7.95) to steak *au poivre,* pan-fried in sherry and sweet butter, served flambéed ($14.95). There's also an extensive pub menu, wine and beer lists.

EATING OUT

Woodside Restaurant (268-3685), Main Street (Route 9), Williamsburg. Open 6 AM–8 PM; until 2 PM Monday, until 9 PM Friday and Saturday. Clean, welcoming, a counter as well as several tables, homemade soups, daily specials.

The Old Creamery (634-5560), corner of Route 9 and Route 112, Cummington. Open daily 7:30–7:30, from 9 on Sunday. A spiffed-up general store with a deli, wine selection, and several tables.

Remington Lodge (634-5388), West Cummington Village. Friday night meals are open to the public by reservation and are so good and so reasonably priced that you are advised to call toward the beginning of the week. If it's stuffed baked pork chops night you may have to reserve two weeks in advance.

Also see **Spruce Corner Restaurant** under "West County/Mohawk Trail."

ENTERTAINMENT

Miniature Theatre of Chester (667-8818), PO Box 487, Huntington 01050. The season runs from early July through Labor Day weekend. Vincent Dowling, a former artistic director and still an associate director of Dublin's famed Abbey Theatre, first came to Chester to fish and swim in the Westfield River and has since built himself a house while staging a summer program of plays—a mix of lesser-known classics and original works, performed in Chester's town hall (150 seats). Casts are limited to just one or two professional actors and are generally outstanding.

Sevenars Music Festival (238-5854), Route 112 between Huntington and Worthington. Concerts are Friday evenings (at 7:30) and Sunday afternoons (at 5), mid-July through August. The seven "R"s stand for the seven Schrades, who include Robert (longtime soloist with orchestras and a member of the faculty at the Manhattan School of Music), his wife Rolande (a concert pianist in her own right and composer of more than 1000 songs), Robelyn, Rorianne, and Randolf Schrade (all with impressive degrees and concert careers). The twins Rhonda-Lee and Rolisa don't perform but Robelyn's husband, well-known New Zealand pianist David James, and their daughter, Lynelle, do. Concerts are staged in the tongue-and-groove paneled hall of a double-porched, 19th-century academy just off Route 112 by the South Worthington Cascade.

Ridgehaven Art Institute (634-8879), 156 Nash Road, Cummington, is the site of frequent concerts, poetry readings, and art shows.

SELECTIVE SHOPPING

ANTIQUES SHOPS
Sena's Auctions (238-5813), Buffington Hill Road, Worthington. Since the 1950s, auctions have taken place on Tuesday, but check to make sure. Held in the former potato barn that serves in winter as a ski-touring center. **Chesterfield Antiques** (296-4252), Route 143, Chesterfield, has a good selection.

CRAFTS SHOPS
The Basket Shop (296-4278), 513 Main Road (Route 143), Chesterfield. The shop itself is special, built by hand by Ben Higgins with an open basket-weave ceiling, woven cabinet doors, dovetailed drawers, and a variety of timeworn tools. Ben specialized in the rare art of weaving ash baskets, a skill his son-in-law Milton Lanford carries on using a variety of wooden

The work of sculptor Andrew deVries is on display in his Middlefield sculpture garden.

molds, some more than 100 years old. The baskets are striking and unusually durable. Call before making a special trip; inquire about Open Days.

Sheepgate Handwovens (848-0990), Otis Stage Road, Blandford. Open
Sunday 11–5. The sheep are at the door, and the weaver is working her
hand looms, selling one-of-a-kind clothing, shawls, bedding, pillows,
sheepskin, buttons, and jewelry.

Stonepool Pottery (238-5362), Conwell Road, Worthington, just up Ireland Street from the old academy in South Worthington (take the next
left). Open daily year-round. Distinctive. Functional work by three potters is displayed in a small gallery near a studio and above the house
now owned by potter Mark Shapiro, an old homestead in which the
Reverend Russell Conwell was born. Conwell later added an unusual
"stone pool" and built the nearby academy, but he is better known as
the founder of Philadelphia's Temple University.

Judy Tavener Artoli (623-6481), Skyline Trail, Middlefield. You don't have
to stay at Strawberry Banke Farm in order to view the original bright

oils, acrylics, pastels, hand-painted floorcloths, and clothes displayed in the studio here.

River Studio (238-7755), River Road, Middlefield. Open July, August, and September, Thursday through Saturday 1–6, or year-round by appointment. The internationally acclaimed dancing statues of Andrew deVries are a find in their own right—especially set as they are on a meadow stage in a particularly obscure and lovely corner of Middlefield.

Storybook Hill (238-5548), Buffington Hill Road, Worthington. No set hours, just ring the bell on the shop door behind the house. Florence Chamberlin takes several days to sew each of the stuffed animals for which she has become widely known over the past 30 years. Rabbits are her trademark, rabbits with beguiling faces and amazing clothing. All the creations, each one unique, are sturdy and washable. To complement the dolls, Florence's husband, Edward, builds dollhouses, also among the 1000 items for sale in the shop.

Quilts by Jane (634-5703), Route 116, Plainfield. Jane Nerri's eye-catching quilts festoon her front porch; visitors are welcome. Neri enjoys coming out to escort you into her studio (alias garage), hung with dozens of bright quilts, all made from castoff materials friends and neighbors bring her. Quilts are priced reasonably.

FARMS

In Chesterfield: **Ireland Street Orchards** (296-4014), Ireland Street. April through November, open 10–6. Pick-your-own apples and flowers; a farm stand with local produce and crafts; horse-drawn hayrides on weekends during harvest season. Annual apple festival the first weekend in October.

In Cummington: **Minority Mountain Farm** (634-5404), 133 Plainfield Road. This is a dairy operation with homegrown vegetables, maple syrup, jams, jellies, and pickles at the farm stand. **Splendorview Farm** (634-5528), 160 Bryant Road. A sheep farm with a nice view. Tours offered.

In Granville: **Gran-Val Farm/Scoop**, Route 189. Open mid-April to mid-October, 11–9:30. This is a dairy farm with an ice cream stand serving at least 24 flavors of homemade ice cream. There's also a petting zoo with goats, sheep, a donkey, rabbits, chickens, and a heifer barn. **Robert's Hillside Orchards** (357-6696), South Lane Road. Open July 15 through December 24. Pick-your-own blueberries, peaches, and apples; a cider mill, hiking trails.

In Huntington: **Sunscape Gardens** (667-5786), 8 Montgomery Road. Gifts for gardeners, from gardens, and inspired by gardeners. Features work by local artisans, books, a schedule of workshops, garden tours, in-season farm stand.

In Plainfield: **Waryjasz's Potato Farm** (634-5336), 166 East Main Street (Route 116). It's difficult to miss this hilltop barn with its painted people

KIMBERLY GRANT

The Corners Grocery in Worthington Center

and many signs. Potato lovers can choose from white, red-skinned, table stock, chilliping, and rye seed potatoes; browsers will find a flea market's worth of trash and treasure in the barn.

In Westhampton: **Outlook Farm** (529-9338), Route 66. Open weekdays 6–7, weekends 6–6. You can pick your own apples and find seasonal fruit and produce here, but the real specialties of the roadside store are homemade sausage, smoked hams, bacon, and ribs (although the pigs are no longer raised here the way they used to be, the USDA-certified slaughterhouse and smokehouse continue to operate). Sandwiches and daily specials are served. Hayrides available.

In Worthington: **Cumworth Farm** (634-5529), Route 112. Pick-your-own blueberries and raspberries; the farm also sells jam and syrup.

GENERAL STORES

Granville Country Store (1-800-356-2141), Granville, just off Route 57. Open daily 7–6:30, Sunday 7:30–5:30. A typical village store but with a difference: a store cheese (regular and sharp cheddar) that's been sold here since 1850; will ship anywhere. Lucy and Rowland Entwistle are only the third proprietors.

The High Country General Store (258-4055), Route 57, Tolland. Open daily 8–6:30, Sunday 9–5. Not particularly picturesque, but claims to be "the biggest little store in the country" and serves breakfast and lunch.

Huntington General Store (667-3232), Route 112 north of the village, Huntington. A bit hokeyed up but known for its baked goods and soups; ice cream and assorted gadgetry, local crafts are also sold.

Middlefield General Store, Skyline Trail, Middlefield. Sweeping views from the store's front door, an oasis selling good coffee as well as picnic basics.

Williamsburg General Store (268-3006), 3 Main Street, Williamsburg. Local maple products, grinders, soups and salads, fresh fruit, local crafts.

The Corners Grocery (238-5531), Worthington Center. A double-porched, extremely photogenic store in the middle of a matching village; picnic makings.

SUGARHOUSES

As already noted, the Hilltowns are the prime source of Massachusetts's maple sugar and sugaring season—which can begin as early as late February and extend well into April. Locals and visitors alike are drawn to sugarhouses and pancake breakfasts featuring the new syrup. A brochure detailing information about the sugaring process and each producer is available from the **Massachusetts Maple Producers Association**, Watson–Spruce Corner Road, Ashfield 01330. The following sugarhouses welcome visitors during sugaring-off, but call before coming. All also sell their syrup from their farms year-round:

In Chester: **High Meadow Sugar Shack** (667-3640) on the Skyline Trail offers spectacular views. **Lyman Farm Sugarhouse** (667-3463) is a 200-year-old farm. **Misty Mountain Farm** (354-6337) has a covered bridge and chapel. Sugar is collected by horses and oxen on weekends.

In Chesterfield: **Bisbee Family Maple** (296-4717) has a hand-built sugarhouse sited in the apple orchard; hot coffee and picnic tables; maple creams a specialty. **Krug Sugarbush** (549-1461), South Street, offers nature walks through the sugarbush.

In Cummington: **Cumworth Farm** (634-5529) is between Worthington and Cummington on Route 112; Ed McColgan is a longtime producer and, with his wife Mary, welcomes guests (see *Lodging—Bed & Breakfasts*) in their 200-year-old farmhouse. **Tessiers Sugarhouse** (634-5022), 60 Fairgrounds Road, is ½ mile south of Route 9.

In Worthington: **Cook's Maple Products** (238-5827) in West Worthington has a sugarhouse accessible via a marked trail; picnic tables. **High Hopes Sugarshack** (238-5919) displays work by local artists and features an "all-you-can-eat" pancake buffet. **The Red Bucket Sugar**

Shack (238-7710) features pancakes, French toast, wagon rides, and snowshoeing. **Windy Hill Farm** (238-5869) also offers a dining room with a full maple menu in season.

Other Towns: **Hillwood Farm** (268-7036), Route 9, Goshen, 3 miles west of Williamsburg center, uses Clydesdale horses to gather sap. **East Branch Sugarhouse** (667-3995), Knightville Dam Road off Route 112, Huntington; open evenings and weekends with free samples for kids. **Thatcher's Sugarhouse** (634-5582), 1 mile south of Plainfield center or 3 miles north of Route 9; the sugarhouse is set behind dairy barns. **Bridgmont Farm** (527-6193), Westhampton. A 200-year-old dairy farm; call for directions. **Paul's Sugar House** (268-3544), Route 9, 1 mile west of Williamsburg. Open March through mid-April; maple candies, also apple, cherry, and blackberry syrups.

SPECIAL EVENTS

March: **Chester Hill Maplefest.**

April: **Westfield River race,** Huntington.

May: Beginning mid-May through Columbus Day weekend, **Hilltown Farmers' Market,** Huntington town common, Saturday 9–1.

July: **Independence Day Parade,** Chesterfield. **Jacob's Ladder Days,** Chesterfield, first weekend. **Goshen Flower Show.**

August: **Littleville Fair** (first weekend). **Middlefield Fair** (second weekend). **Hillside Agricultural Society Fair (Cummington Fair)** in Cummington (last weekend).

September: **Blandford Fair** on Labor Day weekend. **Worthington Country Music Festival and Picnic** (second weekend).

October: Columbus Day weekend—**Chester Hill Harvest Festival.**

Berkshire County

SOUTH AND CENTRAL BERKSHIRE

Berkshire County is a roll of hill and valley that extends the full 56-mile length of the state. Its highest mountains, including Mt. Greylock (3491 feet high and part of a massif containing the five highest peaks in Southern New England) in North Berkshire and Mt. Everett (2264 feet) in South County, are actually strays from New York's Taconic range. But ask any resident where they live and the answer will be "the Berkshires," not even Massachusetts.

Walled from New York State on the west by the Taconics and from the rest of "the Bay State" by the rugged Hoosac range and the Berkshire Plateau, Berkshire County has always been a place apart. Its first settlers were easy-going Dutchmen rather than the dour Puritans, and while Pittsfield, the county seat, is almost equidistant from both Boston and New York City, visitors and ideas tend to flow from the south rather than the east.

North Berkshire is its own isolated landscape of steep valleys cut by the rushing Hoosic River, divided and dominated by Mount Greylock. In 1800 Timothy Dwight, president of Yale University, described the view from Greylock's 3491-foot summit as "immense and of amazing grandeur." Dwight's widely read guide book may have inspired many subsequent visitors, including Nathaniel Hawthorne, who compared the "high mountain swells" of the Taconics on the west to "immense, subsiding waves," and Henry David Thoreau, who bushwhacked up and spent the night on top, waking to "an ocean of mist . . . and undulating country of clouds." The view from the summit, now accessible by paved road, extends 70 to 100 miles on a clear day.

Berkshire County is aptly promoted as "Culture in the Country" and North Berkshire has its share. Williamstown, just northwest of Mount Greylock, is home to Williams—the state's second oldest college, a village campus with an outstanding art museum and summer theater—and to the Clark Art Museum, a destination in its own right. In North

369

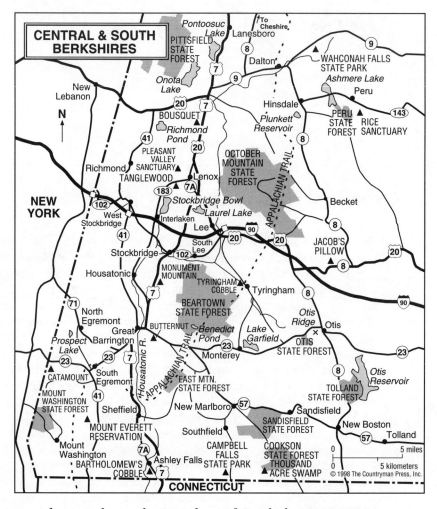

Adams, at the northeastern base of Greylock, MASS MOCA, a contemporary and multimedia art center, is currently evolving.

Admittedly, however, it's Central Berkshire and South County (distinct regions which we have merged here to facilitate cross-referencing) that visitors have come to equate with the summer cultural life—music, theater, dance, art and resident literati—for which the Berkshires are known.

Writers such as Henry Wadsworth Longfellow, Nathaniel Hawthorne, Herman Melville, and Oliver Wendell Holmes Sr. were among the first Berkshire summer residents. Their lyrical descriptions of its inspirational scenery attracted wealthy rusticators, who built great summer mansions (coyly called "cottages") and terraced cornfields into formal gardens. The stock market crash of 1929, the Depression, and the federal income tax thinned the ranks of the Berkshires' wealthy elite. The mansions remained, however, and were frequently taken over by private schools, religious orders, or cultural institutions.

In 1937 the Boston Symphony Orchestra (BSO) made Tanglewood its summer home. Dancers, musicians, actors, and writers began flocking to the Lenox area, lured by the presence of the Berkshire Playhouse, Jacob's Pillow Dance Festival, and the BSO—all presenting summer programs at former private estates.

High-culture happenings still attract a steady flow of summer visitors to central Berkshire and the tranquil countryside remains far more than a backdrop. Since the 1840s, both picnicking and hiking (along bench-spotted paths and up gentle mountains) have been considered the thing to do in the Berkshires. With more than 100,000 acres of state forest and a sizable number of other public preserves, the area remains one of the most inviting to explore on foot; bicycling and skiing are also popular.

In and around Lenox, many mansions are now inns and bed & breakfasts. Regardless of decor or degree of luxury, their rates vary wildly through the year. On weekends during "Tanglewood season" (July and August) you can pay Manhattan prices for a modest room and must stay a minimum of three, frequently four days. With the exception of fall foliage season, however, during midweek—even in August—you pay less and don't wait in line.

Stockbridge, as aristocratic as Lenox and summer home of the Berkshire Theatre Festival, draws far less traffic than Lenox during Tanglewood season and does little to encourage more, especially since the Norman Rockwell Museum has moved from its Main Street location to a hilltop three miles west.

The other resort villages are South Egremont (blink and you're through), with its clutch of restaurants and antiques shops, and Sheffield, synonymous with antiques dealers. Great Barrington is a workaday western Massachusetts town six miles south of Stockbridge, a place to buy a book or a bolt, to see a doctor, or to go to the movies. Movies are shown at the Mahaiwe Theater, a restored vaudeville house with occasional live entertainment. Restaurants are plentiful.

The quiet southwest corner of Massachusetts has its own distinctive beauty and pace. The Housatonic River is slower, and the roads are more heavily wooded, winding through classic old villages, by swimming holes, and past hiking paths that lead to waterfalls.

In winter lodging prices throughout Central Berkshire and South County drop substantially but the many museums and galleries and most of the inns and restaurants remain open. In Lenox, Canyon Ranch (New England's premier spa) and Kripalu (the region's largest yoga center) each draw hundreds of patrons every week of the off-season, and local inn and B&B guests are discovering the town's unusual wealth of day-spa services. In winter the area also offers hundreds of miles of cross-country ski trails and several major alpine areas.

AREA CODE: 413

GUIDANCE

The **Berkshire Visitors Bureau** (443-9186; outside Massachusetts 1-800-237-5747), Berkshire Common, Pittsfield 01201. Open Monday through Friday 9–5. This is the source of *The Berkshires Vacation Guide,* a thick biannual listing of attractions, lodgings, and dining. The bureau also keeps track of vacancies during crunch periods and can refer callers to inns and motels with space. The **Pittsfield Information Booth,** across Main Street at the park, is open daily mid-June through Labor Day, Monday through Thursday 9–5, Friday and Saturday 9–8, Sunday 10–2; Labor Day to Columbus Day, weekends only.

Lenox Chamber of Commerce (637-3646 or 800-25-LENOX), in the old Lenox Academy building, 75 Main Street. Open year-round. Summer: Monday through Saturday 10–6, Sunday 10–4:30. Winter: Monday 10–noon, 1–3; Tuesday through Saturday 9:30–4:30. A very helpful walk-in center with an extensive pamphlet rack. Free lodging referral, which during Tanglewood season includes many private homes.

Southern Berkshire Chamber of Commerce (528-1510), 362 Main Street at the southern edge of Great Barrington (Route 23/Route 7). Open year-round Tuesday through Saturday 9:30–12:30 and 1:30–4:30, weekends 12–3.

Stockbridge Information Booth. A kiosk-style booth on Main Street is open daily in summer months (but just noon–2 on Sunday). The **Stockbridge Chamber of Commerce** (298-5200) is good for help by phone weekdays 8:30–2:30. **The Stockbridge Lodging Association** publishes its own pamphlet brochure (write: Box 224, Stockbridge 01262) and operates a lodging hotline: 298-5327.

The **Lee Chamber of Commerce** (243-0852), Airoldi Building, Railroad Street, is open Monday, Wednesday, and Friday 9–noon. A seasonal wooden booth is conveniently positioned in the town hall parking lot on Main Street, open May through September, Monday through Saturday 11–5.

GETTING THERE

By air: Pittsfield is 37 miles from Albany County Airport, 70 miles from Bradley International Airport in Windsor Locks, Connecticut.

By bus: From Boston's bus terminal at South Station, **Peter Pan–Trailways** (1-800-343-9999) serves Lee, Lenox, and Pittsfield via Springfield. From Manhattan **Bonanza** (1-800-556-3815) runs up Route 7, stopping in Sheffield, Great Barrington (Bill's Pharmacy: 528-1590), South Egremont (the Gaslight Store), Stockbridge (Main Street), Lee (McClelland Drugs: 243-0135), Lenox (Lenox News & Variety: 637-2815), and Pittsfield (the bus terminal, 57 South Church Street: 442-4451).

By train from Boston: **AMTRAK** (1-800-USA-RAIL) stops in Pittsfield (at a shelter on Depot Street; no tickets sold) twice daily en route to and from Chicago.

By car: The obvious route from Boston is the Mass. Pike to Lee (2 hours on the button), but a more scenic drive through South Berkshire is the turnpike to Westfield (exit 3) and either Route 10/Route 202 to Route 57 west through Granville and Tolland to New Boston and New Marlboro or Route 20 to Route 23 west through Otis and Monterey. From New York City, the obvious approach is the Major Deegan Expressway or the Henry Hudson Parkway to the Saw Mill River Parkway, then to the Taconic Parkway; take the South Berkshire exit, Hillsdale, Claverack, Route 23.

GETTING AROUND

The **Berkshire Regional Transit Authority** (499-2782 or 1-800-292-2782) links Great Barrington, Lee, Lenox, and Stockbridge with Pittsfield; hours are geared to commuters rather than to visitors. Fare is $.60 per town.

Taxis: **Abbott's Limousine** (243-1645) and **Park Taxi** (243-0020) in Lee; **Alston's** (637-3676) and **Tobi's Limousine Service** (637-1224) in Lenox; **Stockbridge Livery** (298-4848) in Stockbridge; **Aarow Taxi** (499-8604), **Airport & Limousine** (443-7111), and **Rainbow Taxi** (499-4300) in Pittsfield; **Alexis Taxi & Powell Limousine Service** (442-3531; outside Berkshire County 1-800-345-3531) in Pittsfield.

MEDICAL EMERGENCY

Fairview Hospital (528-0790), 29 Lewis Avenue, Great Barrington; or dial 911.

Berkshire Medical Center (447-2000), 725 North Street, Pittsfield: 24-hour emergency care.

Lenox Ambulance (637-2345), 14 Walker Street, Lenox: 24-hour emergency service.

VILLAGES

Lenox. Lenox evolved in stages. Its 1787 status as county seat gave it graceful Federal buildings like the courthouse (the present library with its luxurious reading rooms, gallery, and outdoor reading park), the Academy (now housing the chamber of commerce), and the **Church on the Hill**. In the 1860s, county government shifted to Pittsfield and summer visitors began buying up large holdings. By the turn of the century, more than 90 elaborate summer "cottages" were scattered along every ridge in the area. Lenox's glory years as the inland Newport were brief, ended by the Great Depression and the federal income tax. The resort might have vanished entirely had it not been for the BSO's Berkshire Music Festival. Concert halls were not yet air-conditioned, and symphony music typically ceased during the summer. The orchestra selected Lenox as its summer home because **Tanglewood** (a forested estate named by Hawthorne, who wrote *Tanglewood Tales* there) was given to it by a patron. More than 50 grand "Berkshire Cottages" still cluster in and around Lenox. **The Mount,** former residence of novelist Edith

The Church on the Hill in Lenox

Wharton (whose best-known work, *Ethan Frome*, is set in the Berkshires) is now open to tours and serves as home to **Shakespeare & Company,** a theater company performing modern works as well as productions based on Wharton's own life and work and Shakespeare plays. **Bellefontaine,** another baronial cottage, is now a spa (Canyon Ranch), several are inns, and the site of one of the grandest (Andrew Carnegie's mansion unfortunately burned) is now the **Kripalu Center for Yoga and Health.**

Stockbridge was founded in 1734 to contain and educate the local Mohegans. Just four white families were permitted to settle, theoretically to "afford civilizing examples to the Indians." But predictably, the whites multiplied and the Native Americans dwindled. After distinguishing themselves as the only tribe to serve in the Revolution and the first to be given US citizenship, the Stockbridge tribe was shipped west, eventually to Wisconsin, where a few hundred descendants still live. Stockbridge boasts that the Laurel Hill Association was the country's first village-improvement society. Residents will tell you that the same number of notables have been summering in town for the past century; only the faces change periodically. The rambling, wooden **Red Lion Inn** forms the heart of the village, a short walk from the **Mission** and **Merwin** houses. **Naumkeag** is just a short way up the hill, and the **Berkshire Theatre Festival** is on the northern fringe of town. The village green is actually west of the Route 102/Route 7 junction, and many visitors miss it entirely. Here stand the imposing brick **Congregational Church** (1824), the pillared **Old Town Hall** (1839), and the

Field Chime Tower, which marks the site of the original Native American mission. The **Indian Burial Ground** is nearby—the large mound topped by a stone obelisk and overlooking the golf course. The **Village Cemetery**, across from the green, contains the remains of John Sergeant, Native American chief John Konkapot, 19th-century tycoons like Joseph Choate, and town aristocrats like the Fields and Sedgwicks.

Sheffield. This town was the first in the Berkshires to be chartered; its wide main street (Route 7) is lined with stately old homes. Its **Colonel Ashley House** (1735) is the oldest in the Berkshires (see *To See—Historic Homes*), and the town boasts the greatest number of antiques dealers of any town in the Berkshires. The 1770s brick **Dan Raymond House** (open Friday 1:30–4) in the center of town is maintained by the historical society to reflect the lifestyle of this prosperous merchant, his wife, and their nine children. The 1760 **Old Parish Church** is a beauty, the oldest church in Berkshire County and the site of the annual 3-day **Sheffield Antiques Fair,** always the second weekend in August.

Tyringham. Hemmed in on three sides by mountains and not on the way to anywhere else, this village was the site of a Shaker community from the 1790s until the 1870s (a group of privately owned Shaker buildings still stands on Jerusalem Road near Shaker Pond). The village then began attracting prominent summer residents, including Samuel Clemens. A number of 19th-century writers eulogized Tyringham but the reason most people visit today is to see **Santorella** (243-3260), 75 Main Road, rebuilt by sculptor Henry Hudson Kitson as his studio in the 1930s. The building, also known as the Gingerbread House because it resembles a fairy-tale witch's house, is open May–October daily, 10–4:30. In the village itself, note the Greek Revival (1844) **United Church of Christ**. (See also **Tyringham Cobble** under *Green Space.*)

Egremont. There is no village of Egremont; instead there's **North Egremont** and **South Egremont,** divided by **Baldwin Hill.** South Egremont is the livelier village, one of the few in the Berkshires to retain its original, rambling old inn, and though there's no longer a general store or gas station, there are plenty of antiques shops, galleries, and restaurants. Note the Egremont fan window in the **Congregational Church** and the town hall in the southern village. Don't miss **Baldwin Hill,** with its surviving farms and sense of serenity, and North Village, with its general store, inn, and lakeside campground.

Monterey. Much of this town has been absorbed into **Beartown State Forest**, and it is largely a second-home community (Lake Garfield is ringed with summer homes, and its beach is private). The **General Store**, though, is well worth a stop any day (you can lunch or snack at tables in the rear), and the **Bidwell House** on Art School Road (528-6888; open Memorial Day to mid-October, Tuesday through Sunday and holidays, 11–4; $5 adults, $1 children) is an appropriately furnished

18th-century home. This was once a dairy center producing more cheese than any other location in the county, and **Monterey Chèvre** from Rawson Brook Farm is still the county's best cheese (see *Selective Shopping*).

Mount Washington. Mount Washington looms like a solitary green island above the valleys in three states. The town is the southwesternmost, the highest, and one of the smallest in Massachusetts. Best known as the home of **Bash Bish Falls,** the state's most dramatic and photographed cascade (see *Green Space*), it is also the site of one of the highest peaks (Mount Everett) and the highest lake (Guilder Pond) in Massachusetts. The community is also arguably the oldest in Berkshire County (settled by the Dutch in the 1690s). The town is webbed with hiking trails— including one of the more dramatic, open ridgeline sections of the **Appalachian Trail**. Given that you can drive almost to the top of Mount Everett and that you can park at several other trailheads that access high-elevation trails—and paths to several waterfalls (the cascades of Race Brook and Bear Rock as well as Bash Bish)—you would assume this place was one of the better-known, more popular spots to hike. Not so. Mount Washington seems to be a well-kept hikers' secret (see *To Do—Hiking* and *Green Space*). Population is a whopping 135 and triples in summer. The center of the village is marked by the small **Union Church** (ecumenical, open summers only) and tiny town hall. Note the old cemetery on West Street and Blueberry Hill Farm (see *Selective Shopping*).

TO SEE

SCENIC DRIVES

Great Barrington to Lee is one of our favorite routes. Follow Route 23 east to Route 57, wandering through the historic village of New Marlboro and continuing on about 5 miles to the hamlet of Montville; turn left on Town Hill Road. Crossing Route 23, take the Tyringham Road (also called Main Road) into the breathtaking Tyringham Valley, which opens up before you as you approach Lee, near Route 102 and exit 2 on the Mass. Pike. Stop at **Tyringham Cobble,** parking by the cow pasture just above the village, and walk to the top of the cobble (a limestone hill); the trail also winds through forest and meadow (see *Green Space*).

Pittsfield to Williamstown. Route 20 west from Pittsfield climbs past **Hancock Shaker Village** (see *Museums*) on through state forest land. Turn off to see the classic buildings of **Mt. Lebanon Shaker Village** (see *Museums*); go north for a few miles on Route 22 (just over the New York line) and return east through a valley on Route 43 from the town of Hancock to the Five Corners section of Williamstown on Route 7.

MUSEUMS

Berkshire Museum (443-7171), 39 South Main Street (Route 7, just south of the park), Pittsfield. Open Tuesday through Saturday 10–5, Sunday 1–5 (Monday in July and August); $3 adult, $2 senior and student, $1 child 5–18. An example of what a regional museum should be, this complex was founded in 1903 by Dalton philanthropist Zenas Crane. The 18 galleries display both permanent and changing exhibits and there are frequent films, performances, lectures, and concerts in the **Little Cinema,** a 300-seat theater. The permanent collection includes Hudson River School landscapes and early American portraits by Church, Inness, and Copley, plus mobiles by Alexander Calder. There are also 15th- to 18th-century European works and ancient artifacts, including a 2000-year-old mummy. Children love the natural history collection of shells, gemstones, and fossils, and the aquarium featuring fish from throughout the world, as well as reptiles, spiders, local animals, and birds. A special Berkshire section includes a birchbark canoe.

Hancock Shaker Village (443-0188), 5 miles west of Pittsfield on Route 20, junction with Route 41; use the Mass. Pike West Stockbridge exit (take Route 41 north to Route 20 west). Open Memorial Day through mid-October 9:30-5, $12.50 adults, $5 children 5–17, family rate. Closed December through March. Open shoulder seasons daily 10–3; $10 adults, $5 children; special family rate. Inquire about special events. In 1961 the village's 20 buildings were about to be sold to a neighboring racetrack when a group of Pittsfield residents rallied and bought the entire community—including 1000 acres—from its last Shaker sisters. The buildings have been restored, including the much copied and photographed round stone barn. A scattering of tidy buildings grouped around the 1830 brick dining hall and surrounded by its own orchards and meadows, the village looks like some primitive painter's vision of the heavenly kingdom. Founded in 1790, this City of Peace prospered in the mid-19th century (some 250 brethren were divided among six "families" in the 1830s), and it survived 170 years. The guides, craftsmen, and furnishings all tell about the dancing monks and nuns who turned farming, craftsmanship, and invention into visible prayers. Note the frequent special events staged throughout the year. During July, August, and part of September, traditional Shaker dinners are served in the brick building; the cost is $38 (call for reservations). A snack bar and picnic areas are on the grounds. The gift shop sells yarn, herbs, and baked goods made on the premises. Inquire about the **Shaker Trail** leading to the adjacent **Pittsfield State Forest** (see *Green Space*), traveling past the sites of old Shaker dwellings and religious ceremonies and by the Shaker-built Great Wall of the Berkshires. You might also want to continue a few miles west on Route 20 to the **Mount Lebanon Shaker Village** (518-794-9500) in New Lebanon, New York. Far less

Hancock Shaker Village

developed as a museum than its Hancock neighbor, this village has been preserved primarily as the Darrow School; while approaching the dozen "Church Family" buildings along the quiet dirt road, it's easy to imagine away a century.

Arrowhead (442-1793), 789 Holmes Road (off Route 7/Route 20), Pittsfield. Open Memorial Day through Labor Day daily 10–5; through Halloween Friday–Monday, 10–5, otherwise by appointment. $5 adults, $4.50 seniors, $3.50 children, family rate: $15. It was in this 18th-century house, purchased in 1850 when he was 31, that Herman Melville wrote *Moby-Dick*. The grandly conceived story of the great white whale and the mad sea captain who obsessively pursues it was penned in a study overlooking the looming, probably inspiring, mass of Mount Greylock. The house is sparsely furnished, but it conveys a sense of Melville during the 13 years he lived here, writing *Moby-Dick* and a number of other works that brought him no fame or money in his lifetime. The house is headquarters for the Berkshire County Historical Society, and a film on Berkshire history is shown. The 160-acre grounds include a walking trail. *Note:* Melville buffs should also find the Herman Melville Room in the **Berkshire Athenaeum** (499-9480) on the common in Pittsfield. It contains every book about as well as by the author and such artifacts as the desk on which he wrote *Billy Budd*.

The Mount (637-1899), Plunkett Street (junction of routes 7 and 7A), Lenox. Open daily for tours Memorial Day weekend through October, 9–2, weekends in May 9–2. $6 adults, $5.50 seniors, $4.50 ages 13–18.

Novelist Edith Wharton's Georgian-style home is a turn-of-the-century copy of an English mansion designed by Christopher Wren but incorporates many of the ideas articulated in her book *The Decoration of Houses*. Wharton had a hand in designing the gardens as well as the buildings and interior; the resulting mansion is special indeed. Tours conveying a sense of Wharton's life and work are offered by Edith Wharton Restoration, Inc. Inquire about the Women of Achievement lecture series, presented in July and August Mondays at 4 PM ($15 for lecture and reception). See *The Arts* for Shakespeare & Company productions at the Mount.

Crane Museum (684-2600), off Route 8, 30 South Street, Dalton. Open year-round 10–5; closed major holidays. Free and worth a stop. Housed in the rag room of the **Old Stone Mill** (1846) by the Housatonic, the displays tell the story of paper making and include a fascinating variety of paper money. Crane Paper is the sole supplier of "money paper" to the US Mint; the company has been in the family for five generations.

Chesterwood (298-3579). Go 3 miles west of Stockbridge on Route 102 and turn left onto Route 183; follow signs. Open May through October, daily 10–5. $6.50 adults, $3.50 ages 13–18, $1.50 6–12; family rate $16. This 160-acre estate served as the summer home for 33 years to Daniel Chester French (1850–1931), whose *Minuteman* statue in Concord established his eminence as a sculptor at age 25. By 1895, when he discovered Stockbridge, he was internationally respected and able to maintain this elaborate summer home and studio, which commands, as he put it, the "best dry view" he'd ever seen. Maintained by the National Trust, the property includes the mansion, a barn gallery with special exhibits, and the studio, now exhibit space for plaster casts of many of the sculptor's works, including the statue that now sits in Washington's Lincoln Memorial. Visitors are welcome to stroll the grounds, which include a wooded path—the Hemlock Glade—overlooking Monument Mountain. Frequent events are staged throughout the summer, and there is also a November sale (at the gift store) and a Christmas tour.

The Norman Rockwell Museum (298-4100), Route 183 (0.6 mile) south of the junction of Route 183 and Route 102, three miles west of Stockbridge. Open daily 10–5 in summer; November through April, weekdays 11–4, weekends 10–5. Closed Thanksgiving, Christmas, New Year's Day. Rockwell's studio is open May through October. $8 adults, $2 ages 6–18. Norman Rockwell (1894–1978) lived his last 50 years in Stockbridge and is represented here by some 200 works, including *The Four Freedoms* and many original paintings for *Saturday Evening Post* covers. Works also include illustrations he made for *Collier's Magazine* on 1960s civil rights incidents. The handsome new museum is on a 36-acre estate with views from tranquil benches (and picnic facilities) overlooking the Housatonic River.

Main Street Stockbridge at Christmastime *by Norman Rockwell*

HISTORIC HOMES

Naumkeag (298-3239), Prospect Hill Road, Stockbridge. Open daily late
May to Labor Day, then weekends and holidays through Columbus
Day 10–4:15. $7 adults for house and garden, $5 for garden only; $2.50
ages 6–12; members free. The Trustees of Reservations maintain this
gabled and shingled 26-room "cottage." It was designed by McKim,
Mead, and White in 1885 for one of the leading lawyers of the day,
Joseph Hodges Choate, who endeared himself to his wealthy colleagues
by securing the reversal of an income-tax law that Congress had passed
in 1894. The gardens are as exceptional as the house.

Mission House (298-3239), Main Street, Stockbridge. Open Memorial
Day weekend to Columbus Day, daily 10–5. Adults $5, children $2.50.
John Sergeant, idealistic young missionary to the Stockbridge tribe,
built this house for his bride in 1739. He built it not on Route 102
where it now stands (known as the Plain at the time, this site held Native American wigwams), but up on the hill where the town's few white
families lived, among them the Williamses. Sergeant's wife was Abigail
Williams, a lady of pretensions, and the house is elaborately built for its
time and place. It was salvaged and moved to this site in 1929 and is
maintained by the Trustees of Reservations.

Colonel John Ashley House (229-8600), in Ashley Falls, well marked from
Route 7, south of Sheffield Village. Open June through Labor Day,
Wednesday–Sunday 1–5, also weekends and holidays from Memorial
Day weekend until Columbus Day. $5 adults, $2.50 children. The oldest
in Berkshire County (1735), this house was the site of the 1773 drafting
of the Sheffield Declaration denouncing the British Parliament. The
home is beautifully paneled, restored, and furnished. You learn about

Mum Bet, purportedly the first slave to sue for, and win, her freedom under due process of law. The house and nearby **Bartholomew's Cobble** (see *Green Space*) are maintained by the Trustees of Reservations.

Merwin House (298-4703), 14 Main Street, Stockbridge. Open June through mid-October, Tuesday, Thursday, Saturday, and Sunday, with tours on the hour noon–4. $4 adults, $3.50 seniors, $2 children. An 1825 home preserved to look the way it did as a late-19th-century summer home, it's maintained by the Society for the Preservation of New England Antiquities.

THE ARTS

In no other part of the country are so many quality music, dance, and theater productions found so near each other. Almost any day of the summer you can choose from a rich menu of live performances, many at prices far below what they would command in New York or Boston.

Tanglewood Music Festival (637-1600), Tanglewood, entrance on West Street (Route 183) west of Lenox village. The **Boston Symphony Orchestra's** summer concert series, June through August, has been held since the 1930s in a fan-shaped, open-sided hall understatedly referred to as **The Shed.** It actually seats more than 5000 people and has splendid acoustics. A striking new addition to Tanglewood is the 1200-seat **Seiji Ozawa Hall,** named for the BSO's longtime music director. More than 14,000 people regularly converge on Tanglewood on weekends, but a concert is never sold out—there is always room on the 500-acre grounds. Many concertgoers actually prefer sitting on the lawn and come several hours early, dressed in high resort style (or any old way at

Pilobolus Dance Theater at the Jacob's Pillow Dance Festival

all), bearing elaborate picnic hampers that have been known to include white linen tablecloths and candelabras. The lawn at Tanglewood is one of New England's great people-watching places. In addition to the symphonic concerts (Friday and Saturday evenings and Sunday afternoons), there are weekly chamber music concerts and open rehearsals, the annual **Festival of Contemporary Music,** and almost daily concerts by young musicians of the Tanglewood Music Center. The **Boston Pops** performs each summer as well. Prices for BSO shed concerts are $12–70; Ozawa Hall, $12–30. A detailed schedule and order form is available by contacting the Tanglewood Ticket Office (before May 31), Symphony Hall, Boston 02115 (617-266-1492; after May, contact Tanglewood in Lenox, 637-5165).

Berkshire Performing Arts Theater at the National Music Center (637-4718, tickets and schedule; 637-1800, information), 70 Kemble Street, Lenox. Housed in a former boys school, the center focuses on American music of all sorts. Plans call for a museum of American music, library and archive, recording studios, and residence and retirement facilities for professional musicians. The center presents a season-long program of pop, folk, blues, and jazz performances by well-known artists in its 1200-seat, air-conditioned hall.

Jacob's Pillow Dance Festival (243-0745), George Carter Road, Becket (off Route 20, eight miles east of Lee). America's oldest dance festival,

Jacob's Pillow presents a 10-week summer program of classic and experimental dance. Located on a onetime hilltop farm, the Pillow was founded in the 1930s by the famed dancer Ted Shawn as both a school for dancers and a performance center. As well as scheduled productions, informal impromptu performances are going on all the time. There is the pleasant **Pillow Cafe.** Tickets are $10–35.

Shakespeare & Company at the Mount (box office: 637-3353; off-season: 637-1197), Plunkett Street, Lenox. Productions late May through October; tickets $13–32. For more than 20 years this outstanding theater company has been performing Shakespeare plays at the Mount; the main stage is outdoors in the garden (bring your own blanket if you don't want to use the aluminum chairs). Additional productions are staged in the 200-seat Oxford Court outdoor theater, the 75-seat indoor Wharton Theater, and the 108-seat Stables Theater.

Albany-Berkshire Ballet (445-5382), 51 North Street, Pittsfield. Performances are staged periodically year-round at the Berkshire Community College Koussevitzky Theatre.

Armstrong Chamber Concerts (637-3646; 203-868-0522), Town Hall Theater, Lenox. April through November. Programs by noted artists use combinations of instruments in a wide spectrum of musical styles.

Berkshire Opera Company (243-1343), Cranwell Opera House, Route 20, Lenox. Full productions of traditional and modern operas sung in English. July and August.

The Berkshire Theatre Festival (298-5536), East Main Street (Route 102), Stockbridge. Celebrating its 70th season in 1998, the July through August festival is staged in a building designed by Stanford White in 1887 as the Stockbridge Casino, restored and moved to its present site in the 1920s by Mabel Choate (mistress of Naumkeag; see *To See—Historic Homes*). The plays are all by American playwrights, and the performers are aspiring actors; a young Katharine Hepburn, Ethel Barrymore, James Cagney, and Dustin Hoffman all performed here. Children's theater is staged Thursday and Saturday at noon under a tent.

The Berkshire Choral Festival (229-8526), 245 Undermountain Road (Berkshire School), Sheffield. A summer series of five Saturday concerts featuring as many as 200 voices and the Springfield Symphony.

Aston Magna Festival (528-3595), St. James Church, Main Street, Great Barrington. Seventeenth-, 18th-, and early-19th-century music, very professionally played on period instruments.

The Mahaiwe Theater (528-0100), 14 Castle Street, Great Barrington. This wonderfully ornate theater was built in 1905 to present original plays, something it still does along with stubbornly preserving its single movie screen. Additional movie choices are available on Railroad Street at the **Mahaiwe Triplex** (528-8885).

TO DO

BICYCLING

Rubel's *Western Massachusetts Bicycle and Road Map* (Rubel BikeMaps, Cambridge, $4.25) is an excellent investment for those intending to bike the back roads. *Short Bike Rides in the Berkshires* by Lewis C. Cuyler (Berkshire House, $9.95), describes 30 routes. *The Bicyclist's Guide to the South Berkshires* (Freewheel Publishers, Lenox, $14.95) is also an excellent book. Bicycles can be rented from **Gaffer's Outdoors** (229-0063), Route 7, Sheffield; and from **Berkshire Bike & Blade** (528-5555), 284 Main Street, Great Barrington; In Lenox, **Main Street Sports and Leisure** (637-4407 or 800-932-9171), 48 Main Street (also rents canoes, kayaks, in-line skates, snowshoes, and cross-country skis; provides information, books, and guides); and the **Arcadian Shop** (637-3010), 91 Pittsfield Road, open daily (also cross-country skis, snowshoes, backpacking equipment, and clothing). In Pittsfield, rentals are available from **Plaine's Ski and Cycle Center** (499-0294), 55 West Housatonic Street.

BIRDING

Pleasant Valley Wildlife Sanctuary (637-0320), 472 West Mountain Road, Lenox. $3 per adult, $2 children and seniors. This 730-acre Massachusetts Audubon sanctuary includes an evolving education center and year-round programs. Its 730 acres include part of Lenox Mountain, Yokun Brook, beaver ponds, a hemlock gorge, and 7 miles of trails used for cross-country skiing in winter. It harbors hooded mergansers, great blue herons, and belted kingfishers as well as beavers, snapping turtles, and many other animals.

Thousand Acre Swamp, off Norfolk Road, south of Southfield, left on Hotchkiss. A birder's delight.

Canoe Meadows Wildlife Sanctuary, Holmes Road off Route 7, south of Pittsfield. This Massachusetts Audubon sanctuary offers a mix of wetlands and croplands with 5 miles of trails. No rest rooms. $2 adults, $1 children and seniors.

Dorothy Frances Rice Wildlife Refuge in Peru: South Road off Route 143 from the town center. Three hundred acres, walking trails, and self-guiding trails owned by the New England Forestry Foundation.

BOATING

The placid **Housatonic** is ideal for lazy rides down the river. Trips are detailed in the *AMC River Guide—Central/Southern New England*. Canoe rentals and shuttle service are available from **Gaffer's Outdoors** (229-0063), 216 Main Street (Route 7), in Sheffield; and from **Clarke Outdoors** (203-672-6365), which also offers kayak lessons, not far south of the border on Route 7 in West Cornwall, Connecticut. In Lenox **Main Street Sports & Leisure** (637-4407 or 1-800-952-9197), 48 Main Street, offers canoe rentals and delivery. In Pittsfield Lew Cuyler's **Berkshire Sculling Association** (496-9160) is also well worth checking out: Cuyler rents and offers instruction in an unusually lightweight and stable scull. A variety of boats can be rented for use on Otis Reservoir in Tolland State Forest from **J&D Marine** (269-4839). Boat rentals are also available at Pontoosuc Lake in Pittsfield (**Quirk's Marine,** 447-7512); at Greenwater Pond in Becket, Laurel Lake in Lee, Hoosac Lake in Cheshire, and Richmond Pond in Richmond. **Berkshire Hiking Holidays** (637-4442), PO Box 2231, Lenox, offers canoeing/lodging/hiking packages.

CAR RACING
Lime Rock Park (203-435-0896), Lakeville, Connecticut. Open April through October Saturday and holidays. Sports-car superstars who race here include Paul Newman.

FISHING
For a detailed listing of every pond and river stocked with bass, pickerel, perch, hornpout, and trout, check the annual (free) *Berkshires Official Guide.*

GOLF
The local courses are the 18-hole **Country Club of Pittsfield** (447-8500), 639 South Street; the outstanding 18-hole **Cranwell Golf Course** (637-0441), Lee Road in Lenox; and the 18-hole **Wahconah Country Club** (684-1333), Orchard Road in Dalton. **Egremont Country Club** (528-4222), Route 23, South Egremont, offers 18 holes, moderate greens fees. **Greenock Country Club** (243-3323), West Park Street, Lee, has nine holes, moderate greens fees. **Wyantenuck Country Club** (528-3229), Sheffield Road, Great Barrington, offers 18 holes, pricey greens fees.

MINIATURE GOLF
A Berkshire trip isn't complete without a visit to the indoor **Rainbow's End Miniature Golf** (18 holes) at the **Cove Lanes** in Great Barrington (Route 7).

HIKING
More than 100,000 acres of Berkshire County (75 percent) is wooded, and 86 miles of the **Appalachian Trail** traverse the county. The number and variety of walking and hiking trails, many dating back to the 19th century, are amazing. They are described in several books, notably *Hikes & Walks in the Berkshire Hills* by Lauren R. Stevens ($9.95), *A Guide to Natural Places in the Berkshire Hills* by Rene Laubach ($9.95), and *Wildflowers of the Berkshire & Taconic Hills* by Joseph G. Strauch Jr. ($12.95), all published by Berkshire House, based in South Lee. The *Appalachian Mountain Club Guide to Massachusetts and Rhode Island* ($16.95) is also extremely helpful (get the 1995 edition), published by AMC Books.

Berkshire Hiking Holidays (499-9648), based in Lenox, offers 3–6-day trips that combine lodging, hiking, and canoeing, as well as summer cultural events for individuals and groups.

(Also see the trails described in *Green Space.*)

HORSEBACK RIDING

Aspinwall-Bayville Stables (637-0245), Route 7, Lenox; supervised trail rides. **R & C Stables** (637-0613) at Eastover Resort, East Street, Lenox; supervised trail rides. **Twin Ponds Farm** (518-733-6793), off Route 22, Stephentown, New York; trail rides, $20 an hour, $50 for 3 hours (pony rides $3).

Undermountain Farm (637-3365), Undermountain Road, Lenox. Year-round lessons, trail rides.

RAILROAD EXCURSION

Berkshire Scenic Railway (637-2210), 10 Willow Creek Road (off Housatonic Street), Lenox. Open Memorial day through October. Adults $2, $1 children and seniors. Fifteen-minute narrated train rides are offered from the grounds of this museum in the Historic Lenox Station.

CROSS-COUNTRY SKIING

Bucksteep Manor (623-5535; 1-800-645-2825), Washington Mountain Road, Washington. With an 1800-foot elevation and 25 km of trails on 400 acres, this area is usually snow-covered in winter. Trails are groomed and tracked, and there are rentals and guided tours in October Mountain State Forest (see *Green Space*); also lodging and dining on the premises. Trail fees: adults $10 on weekends, $8 midweek; $7 and $5 for juniors.

Butternut (528-2000), Great Barrington. Adjacent to the alpine area are 8 kilometers of trails connecting with **Beartown State Forest Cross-Country Skiing.** Trail fee $8.

Canterbury Farms (623-8765), Fred Snow Road, Becket. Open 9–5. Offers 121 miles of tracked wide trails over 2000 acres (which includes a lake), three levels of difficulty at an average elevation of 1700 feet, rental equipment, lessons, fireplaced room with drinks, hot soup, chili, snacks, or space for your own picnic. Adults $10, juniors $8.

Cranwell (637-1364), Lee Road, Lenox, offers snowmaking along golf course trails, equipment rentals, and instruction. Adults $11, $9 after 1 PM; seniors $10/$8; juniors $9/$7.

Some of the best cross-country skiing is to be found in the areas described under *Green Space*. The **Mount Washington State Forest** is a standout, as is **Bartholomew's Cobble** in Ashley Falls, and **Beartown State Forest** in Monterey. This past November (mid-November!) we actually found good skiing in **Kennedy Park,** Lenox: The easiest access to this extensive trail system is from the parking lot behind Lenox House Restaurant (Route 7 north); rental equipment is available next door at the Arcadian Shop.

DOWNHILL SKIING

Bousquet (442-8316), Pittsfield. Marked from Route 7/Route 20 south of town. The Berkshires' oldest ski area, founded in 1932, and the one that pioneered both the ski train and night skiing. Noted for friendly slopes ideal for beginning and intermediate skiers. Open daily in winter, also nightly except Sunday. *Vertical drop:* 750 feet. *Terrain:* 21 trails. *Rates:* Adults and juniors $20, seniors $10.

Butternut (528-2000), Great Barrington; west on Route 23. Still owned by the same family that founded it more than 40 years ago, Butternut is known for its grooming and for the beauty of its design—both on and off the slopes. Skiwee for 4–8 year olds; Butternut Mountaineer for ages 9–12. *Vertical drop*: 1000 feet. *Terrain:* 22 trails. *Lifts:* One quad, one triple, four double chairs. *Snowmaking:* 98 percent of area. *Rates:* Adults $38 weekends, $30 weekdays; juniors and seniors $25 weekends, $20 weekdays.

Catamount (528-1262; 1-800-342-1840), South Egremont, Route 23. Catamount straddles the New York/Massachusetts line, overlooking the rolling farm country of the Hudson Valley. It's been in business more than 40 years as a family area. The newly enlarged base lodge is pleasant. *Vertical drop:* 1000 feet. *Terrain:* 25 slopes and trails. *Lifts:* Four chair lifts, three T-bars. *Snowmaking:* 85 percent of area. *Rates:* Adults $39 weekends, $25 weekdays; juniors and seniors $25; night skiing Wednesday–Saturday $20.

Otis Ridge (269-4444), Route 23 in Otis. A long-established family ski area that limits lift ticket sales to 800 per day and operates a ski camp (ages 8–16) near the top of its trails. *Vertical drop*: 400 feet. *Terrain:* 10 slopes and trails. *Lifts:* One double chair, five tows. *Snowmaking:* 80 percent of area. *Facilities:* Lodging and food at the slopeside Grouse House (269-4446). *Rates:* Adults $20 weekends, $15 weekdays; seniors $10/$7; juniors $20/$15.

DAY SPAS

Lenox Myotherapy and Massage Clinic (637-0342), 21 Franklin Street, Lenox. Director Christine Ford is a longtime RN and former staff member at Canyon Ranch both in Lenox and Tucson, Arizona. Staff specialize in deep, pressure point massage that smooths out those knots in body muscles, releasing a sense of well being that's very real. Visitors can certainly profit as this one did for a one-shot session, which comes with sound advice.

The Healing Place (637-1980), 1 West Street, Lenox. Open daily, offering a customized spa day; also facials, massage, and yoga and exercise classes.

Essencials Day Spa (637-8224), Brushwood Farm, Route 7, Lenox. At first glance this seems to be your standard beauty salon but the several treatment rooms are well fitted for massage, seaweed treatments, facials, body buffing, etc. Yoga classes are next door. Spa days a specialty.

Lenox Fitness Center (637-9893), 68 Main Street, Lenox. Open daily with the full complement of fitness equipment; day membership $10.

SWIMMING

State parks and forests offer some of the most pleasant as well as most accessible swimming in this area (see *Green Space—Parks and State*

Forests). For a fee, you can also swim at **Prospect Lake Park** (528-4158), a private campground in North Egremont; at the **Egremont Country Club** (528-4222), South Egremont; at **Kinne's Grove** on Lake Garfield in Monterey; and at **Card Lake** in West Stockbridge. Under *Green Space*, check Wahconah Falls, Pittsfield, Beartown, Sandisfield, and Tolland.

TENNIS

Tennis Village School, West Stockbridge, two hard-surface courts. **Sheffield Racquet Club** (229-7968), four clay courts, clubhouse. **Greenock Country Club** (243-3323), Lee, two courts. **Egremont Country Club** (528-4222), South Egremont, four courts. **Berkshire West Athletic Club** (499-4600), Dan Fox Drive, Pittsfield, four outdoor and five indoor courts. **Cranwell Resort** (637-0441), Route 20, Lenox, two Har-Tru courts. **Ponterril/YMCA** (447-7405 or 499-0640), Route 7, Pontoosuc Lake, Pittsfield, six clay courts, fee for nonmembers.

GREEN SPACE

PARKS AND STATE FORESTS

The Massachusetts Department of Environmental Management (DEM) publishes a handy map/guide of its Berkshire holdings and maintains a visitor-friendly regional office on Route 7 south of Pittsfield (442-8928).

Beartown State Forest (528-0904), Blue Hill Road, Monterey; 10,555 acres. The high tablelands stretching northwest from Monterey are known as Beartown, the upper end dropping down to the Housatonic River in South Lee. Accessible from both Route 102 in South Lee and Route 17 in Monterey, the area includes 35-acre Benedict Pond, an artificially formed pond good for swimming (there are sanitary but no changing facilities), picnicking, and boating (no motors). There are also a dozen campsites plus lean-tos along the Appalachian Trail. You can drive or hike to the summit of Mount Wilcox; a 1½-mile trail circles the pond there.

Mount Washington State Forest (582-0330), East Street, Mount Washington. This 4500-acre tract fills the southwest corner of Massachusetts. It's best known for **Bash Bish Falls** (see *Waterfalls*), a dramatic 60-foot falls that rushes down a 1000-foot-deep gorge, finally plunging some 80 feet around two sides of a mammoth boulder and dropping into a perfect pool that's labeled NO SWIMMING. Needless to say this sign is frequently ignored (rangers are on duty weekends only) and, sad to say, divers occasionally die here. Don't swim, but do explore this special place. Access is via Route 23, Route 41, and Mt. Washington Road in South Egremont; take the wooded, winding Falls Road to "the upper parking lot"—from which a rugged ¼-mile trail meanders steeply down through pines to the falls. Continue down the road to "the lower parking lot" in New York's **Taconic State Park** if you prefer to walk a level

path to the bottom of the falls. From this lot you can also access the
steep but short trail to the upper rim of the falls—which continues (via
the South Taconic Trail) to Alander Mountain. The forest includes 15
primitive, walk-in camping sites with pit toilets, spring water, and fireplaces on the way to Alander Mountain. In June mountain laurel blooms
throughout the forest. (Also see **Mount Everett State Reservation** in
this section and **Mount Washington** under *Villages*.)

Mount Everett State Reservation (528-0330), also in the town of Mount
Washington, features a road to the top of Mount Everett, the 2602-foot-
high mountain (second highest in Massachusetts) that commands an overview of Berkshire County to the north. Dogwood blooms in spring, mountain laurel in June, and there is blueberrying in August. **Guilder Pond**,
accessible by car, is filled with pink water lilies during late July and much
of August. (Also see **Race Brook Falls** and **Bash Bish Falls** under *Waterfalls*, and, under *Villages*, **Mount Washington**.)

October Mountain State Forest (243-1178), a total of 15,710 acres accessible from Route 20 in both Lenox and Lee. Camping is the big
draw here, but there are just 50 sites. **Schermerhorn Gorge** is a popular hike and has many miles of trails also used for winter skiing and
snowmobiling. Much of this area was once impounded by Harry Payne
Whitney as a game preserve (it included buffalo, moose, and Angora
goats as well as smaller animals). **Halfway Pond** is a good fishing spot.

Otis State Forest (528-0904), off Route 23 on Nash Road in West Otis. Boating (no motors) is permitted on Upper Spectacle Pond, and there are extensive cross-country ski trails, some of which traverse the original road
that Henry Knox labored over with cannons in the winter of 1775–76.

Tolland State Forest (269-7268) off Route 8 in Otis offers 90 campsites
(85 of them for tents); also picnic space for 100, and swimming, fishing,
and boating in Otis Reservoir.

Sandisfield/Cookson State Forests (258-4774). The state forest holdings
are scattered around Sandisfield; the most popular section is just over
the New Marlboro line (Route 57) on York Lake, a 40-acre dammed
area near the headquarters of Sandy Brook. Here you can swim, boat
(no motors), and picnic (there are tables, grills, and fireplaces). There
are also 10 wilderness campsites.

Kennedy Park in Lenox on Route 7. The grounds of the former Aspinwall
Hotel offer trails for hiking and biking (also see *To Do—Cross-Country
Skiing*).

  ♾ **Pittsfield State Forest** (442-8992) totals 9695 acres. From the corner of
Route 20 and Route 7 in Pittsfield, drive west on West Street, north on
Churchill Street, and west on Cascade to the entrance. $2 day-use fee. A
5-mile circular paved road travels beside Lulu Brook to Berry Pond,
where there is camping (13 sites) and boating (no motors); 18 more sites
are located at Parker Brook, with a picnic area across the way and another
at the Lulu Brook swimming area. A ski lodge, located near the ski jump,

can be rented by groups in summer; it's used as a warming hut in winter. Trails lead to the Taconic Skyline Trail, a spectacular ridge route leading north into Vermont. Tranquillity Trail, a paved, ¾-mile loop through spruce woods, has been designed for wheelchair access. There are taped descriptions of flora and fauna. In June the forest harbors 40 acres of azaleas. Balance Rock—a 165-ton boulder poised on another rock—is accessible via Balance Rock Road from Route 7 in Lanesboro.

Wahconah Falls State Park (442-8992), off Route 9 in Dalton, 3 miles east of the town center. A 2-minute walk brings you from the parking area down to picnic tables, scattered among the smooth rocks above the falls; swimming is permitted in the small pool at their base.

Peru State Forest (442-8992), off Route 143 in Peru; south on Curtin Road, 1 mile from Peru Center. Garnet Hill (2178 feet) yields a good view of the surrounding country, and there is fishing in Garnet Lake. (Also see *To Do—Birding*.)

PICNICKING

Bowker Woods, Route 183 between Stockbridge and Chesterwood; drive in at the sign. There's a pine grove by a small pond, good for picnics.

WALKS

Monument Mountain on Route 7 north of Great Barrington. This peak is one of the most distinctive in the state: a long ridge of pinkish quartzite, scarcely 15 feet wide in some places, 1700 feet high. The climb is lovely any day, whether by the Hickey or the Monument Trail. The hillside is covered with red pine and, in June, with flowering mountain laurel. A Bryant poem tells of a Native American maiden, disappointed in love, who hurled herself from Squaw Peak. Nathaniel Hawthorne, Herman Melville, and O.W. Holmes all picnicked here in 1850.

Bartholomew's Cobble (229-8600), marked from Route 7A in Ashley Falls, south of Sheffield. This 200-acre tract takes its name from the high limestone knolls or cobbles of marble and quartzite that border the glass-smooth Housatonic River. We recommend the pine-carpeted Ledges Trail, a (theoretically) 45-minute loop with many seductive side trails down to the river or up into the rocky heights. A booklet guide is available from the naturalist when the property is open (daily year-round—naturalist on duty mid-April to mid-October, Wednesday through Sunday and holidays 9–5; $2 adults, $1 children). There are exhibits in the **Bailey Trailside Museum.**

Tyringham Cobble, ½ mile from Tyringham center on Jerusalem Road. The Appalachian Trail crosses a portion of this 206-acre property: steep upland pasture and woodland, including a part of Hop Brook, with views of the valley and village below. Note that the Trustees of Reservations also maintain 446-acre **McLennan Reservation** on Fenn Road, 2 miles south of Tyringham center: steep, wooded slopes with one of the county's most spectacular views.

Laurel Hill, Stockbridge. A path leads from the elementary school on Main Street to a stone seat designed by Daniel Chester French. Marked trails continue across the Housatonic to Ice Glen (a ravine) and to Laura's Tower (a steel tower); another trail leads along the crest of the spur of Beartown Mountain.

Berkshire Botanical Garden (298-3926), Stockbridge, junction of Routes 102 and 183. Open year-round. This botanical garden is on 15 acres that include a pond, woodland trail, and children's garden. There are shrubs, trees, perennial borders, greenhouses, herbs, and periodic lectures and workshops. Picnickers welcome. Admission charged mid-May to mid-October.

WATERFALLS

Bash Bish Falls. The area's most famous and dramatic waterfall—a 60-foot fall plunging through a sheer gorge (see also Mount Washington State Forest under *Parks and State Forests*).

Race Brook Falls in Sheffield: a series of five cascades and a picnic area. From the turnout on Route 41 north of the Stagecoach Inn, follow red blazes for 1½ miles.

Becket Falls. Two-tenths of a mile up Brooker Hill from the Becket Arts Center (Route 8 and Pittsfield Road) there is a shallow turnout in which to park. It's a steep scramble down to view the 25-foot-high cascade.

Umpachene Falls. At the New Marlboro Church in the village center, turn south; follow signs to Mill River. Just before the metal bridge there is a dirt road forking right; from here follow signs.

Campbell Falls State Park, accessible from Route 57 in New Marlboro, then a forest road to this site. The Whiting River pours over a split ledge and cascades 80 feet down a precipitous declivity. There are picnic tables, toilets, and foot trails.

Sages Ravine. A strikingly cut chasm with a series of falls, best accessed from Salisbury Road in Mount Washington.

LODGING

Note: Lodging tax varies from town to town. At this writing, in Great Barrington and Lee it is 9.7 percent; in Sheffield and Egremont it's 5.7 percent. Also note that prices tend to soar during Tanglewood season (July and August), and many inns require a minimum 2- or 3-night stay on weekends.

RESORTS

All resorts are in Lenox 01240.

Blantyre (637-3556; off-season 298-3806), Blantyre Road. Built in 1902 to replicate an ancestral home in Scotland, this magnificent, Tudor-style mansion was lovingly restored to its original glory in 1980 by Jack and Jane Fitzpatrick, owners of the Red Lion Inn in Stockbridge. There is a

baronial entry hall and a truly graceful music room with crystal chandeliers, sofas covered in petit point, a piano, and a harp. Guests enjoy
their meals in the paneled dining room, around the long formal table or
in the adjoining, smaller, octagonal room. Guest rooms are impeccably
furnished with antiques, and most have fireplaces. There are 85 well-
kept acres with four tennis courts, a swimming pool (with Jacuzzi hot
tub and sauna), and competition croquet courts (grounds and buildings
are not open to the public for viewing). Open mid-May through October. Including continental breakfast, room rates during peak season are
$255–465; suites, $465–650; cottages, $180–500; off-season rates gen-
erally $10–25 less.

Cranwell Resort & Golf Club (637-1364; 1-800-CRANWEL;
www.cranwell.com), Route 20. A 380-acre, 95-room resort with 360-
degree hilltop views. The imposing main building was built as a grand
private home in 1893. Rooms in the mansion are luxurious and furnished with period antiques. "Resort" rooms—those in various cottages
or the carriage house—are pleasant but more simply furnished: most
have coffeemakers, data ports, and desks. There are two dining rooms,
a lounge, meeting rooms (one the old chapel), two tennis courts, and a
heated outdoor pool. The cross-country ski center provides equipment,
instruction, and snowmaking on 15 km of groomed trails. The big attraction, however, is the 18-hole, PGA championship golf course, the
area's most challenging (see *To Do—Golf*). Rates vary over five periods
of the year, ranging from $89–169 (resort) and $119–229 (mansion)
from November through March to $199–319 (resort) and $269–439
(mansion) during July and August, with continental breakfast. No
charge for children under 16 sharing a room with parents; $20 for an
extra cot. Various seasonal packages available.

Wheatleigh (637-0610), West Hawthorne Road. This yellow-brick palazzo
was built in 1893 and set in 22 acres that now include a swimming pool
and tennis courts. Tanglewood (see *The Arts*) is around the corner.
There are 17 large and elegantly decorated rooms, all with private bath,
about half with fireplaces. The restaurant is expensive but award-winning. This is a special and impressive place. $155–525 in-season, $155–
375 off-season.

Seven Hills (637-0060; 1-800-869-6518), 40 Plunkett Street. This 1911
Tudor Revival mansion with its wonderfully ornate carved woodwork is
set in 27 terraced and landscaped acres, next door to Edith Wharton's
home, The Mount. The 52 rooms vary from classic old bedrooms with
flowery wallpaper and working fireplaces in the manor to bright, motel-
style doubles out in the garden annex (several are handicapped accessible); all have phones and air conditioning. We wished we could have
stayed in room #1, a corner room with leaded-glass windows and sleigh
bed, where we would read in front of the fireplace in the Victorian
loveseat, or maybe in the rocker. Room #4 is a pleasant suite with sitting

room and a sofa bed for children. There is a gourmet restaurant with bluestone dining patio and a good local reputation (see *Dining Out*). Facilities include a pool and tennis courts; a path leads down to Laurel Lake. Open year-round. Rates, with full breakfast in-season, continental breakfast in the off-season, are $75–250 in the manor house, $65–150 in the annex (depending on day and season). Ask about packages.

✐ **Eastover** (637-0625), 430 East Street. This 1000-acre hilltop estate has been offering "old-fashioned fun" since 1947. There are 165 rooms, some in a turn-of-the-century gilded "cottage," most in motel-style annexes. Facilities include a small ski slope with a chairlift, an ice rink, driving range, tennis courts, horseback riding and hayrides, archery, basketball, indoor and outdoor pools, sauna and exercise room, and a crenellated castle with swings for the kids. Other amenities include a huge dance hall, a Civil War museum, and a herd of buffalo! Weeks and weekends are tightly scheduled, with the unusual twist that some programs are geared exclusively to singles, others to families, still others to couples. Liquor is not served but guests may bring their own. Weekends are $85–117 per person per night, including all meals and almost all activities.

A SPA AND A YOGA CENTER

Lenox is arguably the spa center of the Northeast. It's said to have one masseuse for every 60 residents. Augmenting the two residential centers described below are several day spas, a resource for all visitors, especially in the off-season when inn prices are so reasonable. Nowhere else in New England is it so possible to combine the comforts of an inn or B&B with so many services that improve the health of both body and spirit. (See *To Do—Day Spas*.)

Canyon Ranch in the Berkshires (637-4100; 1-800-326-7080), Bellefontaine, 91 Kemble Street, Lenox 01240. Sister to the famous spa in Arizona, this spectacularly deluxe, 150-acre fitness resort is blessed with a superb setting. The focal point is a grand 1890s manor house that is a replica of the Petit Trianon of Louis XVI. Guests sleep in the adjoining 120-room inn, a clapboard building in traditional New England style. Just about every health and fitness program imaginable is offered, and instruction and equipment are state of the art. Meals are dietary but also gourmet and delicious. Canyon Ranch has been called "a cross between boot camp and heaven," but guests (who have included many celebrities) almost invariably depart glowing and enthusiastic. Three-night packages run $1040–1600 including meals and a wide variety of spa and sports services. The staff-to-guest ratio is nearly three to one.

✐ **Kripalu Center for Yoga and Health** (637-3280; 1-800-741-7353), Route 183, Lenox 01240. This yoga-based holistic health center offers a structured daily regimen and a variety of weekend, week-long, and longer programs. A mainstream mecca for spiritual and physical renewal, Kripalu is housed in a former Jesuit novitiate on 300 acres overlooking Lake Mahkeenac and within walking distance of Tanglewood. Founded as a yoga ashram, it is now staffed primarily by paid professionals. The country's largest holistic health center, it accommodates more than 300 guests. Facilities include whirlpools, saunas, hiking and cross-country trails, beach, boats, and tennis; also a children's program during summer months. "R&R" (Retreat and Renewal) rates, which include vegetarian meals, use of all facilities, and a minimal daily program, run from $75 a day in a dormitory to $195 for a private room with bath. Basic rates are lower ($110–$340 for two nights) when combined with tuition for various programs; two-day programs, for example, run $80–$160.

INNS

  ᐲ **The Red Lion Inn** (298-5545), Main Street, Stockbridge 01250. Probably the most famous inn in Massachusetts, the Red Lion is a rambling white-clapboard beauty built in 1897. Staying here is like stepping into a Norman Rockwell painting, and there isn't a musty or dusty corner anywhere. Even the cheapest, shared-bath rooms are carefully furnished with real and reproduction antiques and bright prints, and there are some splendid rooms with canopy beds. The inn's long porch, festooned with flowers and amply furnished with rockers in warm weather, is the true center of Stockbridge in summer, as is the hearth in its lobby in winter. There is a large, formal dining room, a cozy pub, and, in summer, a garden café by the pool. You now actually have a choice of 111 guest rooms (90 with private bath, 2 handicapped accessible) if you count rooms and suites in the annex, the newest of which is the old Stockbridge firehouse that Norman Rockwell painted. $87–355 per room; children are free but there's a $20 charge per cot.

The Old Inn on the Green and Gedney Farm (229-3131), New Marlboro 01230. Back in the '70s Bradford Wagstaff and Leslie Miller (husband and wife) restored this fine 1760 double-porched inn in a beautiful village center; more recently, they converted a turn-of-the-century, Norman-style barn at Gedney Farm down the road into 15 fantasy guest rooms and suites, many with fireplace and tiled whirlpool. In the barn, antiques, kilims, and a muted palette combine to give guest rooms, common areas, and galleries a contemporary Shaker feel. Our candlelit whirlpool tub was the highlight of a bathroom suite with a glass ceiling that was open to the barn's rafters. From $120–175 in the Old Inn and from $175–285 at Gedney Farm, with breakfast served in the restored horse barn next door. Ideal site for weddings and conferences. (Also see *Dining Out*.)

Apple Tree Inn (637-1477), 10 Richmond Mountain Road, Lenox 01240. This century-old house sits high on a hill overlooking the waters of the Stockbridge Bowl, near the main entrance to Tanglewood (see *The Arts*). The view is one of the loveliest in the Berkshires, enhanced by flowering apple trees and lush rose gardens. Each of the 12 rooms and 2 suites in the main house has been imaginatively, lovingly restored and furnished, four with working fireplace. The 21 rooms in the modern lodge are motel-style but pleasant and handy to the pool. Well-behaved children are welcome. The circular, glass-walled dining room is open to the public in season for dinner and is popular with concertgoers. Light meals are also available in the oak-beamed tavern after Tanglewood concerts, as is dinner during the off-season (see *Dining Out*); it's also where breakfast is served to inn guests. $150–300 in Tanglewood season, $75–240 the rest of the year.

The Village Inn (637-0020; 1-800-253-0917), 16 Church Street, Lenox 01240. On a quiet back street in Lenox village, this cozy old inn—built in 1770—offers 32 rooms (all with private bath and telephone, six with fireplace), a comfortable screened porch, and a Victorian-style parlor. There is usually someone sitting on the stool behind the check-in desk, which doubles as a bar. There is a stair chair to the second floor. Children over 6 are welcome. $75–185 summer and fall, $65–175 the rest of the year, with a midweek discount in winter and spring (the suite ranges from $240 in the spring to $395 in summer).

Gateways Inn (637-2532), 51 Walker Street, Lenox 01240. Built by Harley Procter of Procter & Gamble in 1912, the inn has been said to resemble a cake of Ivory soap, but it is more elegant than that, with black shutters and central skylit mahogany staircase designed by the firm of McKim, Mead and White. New owners Fabrizio and Rosemary Chiariello have made many improvements, with more under way. The 12 guest rooms all have private bath, telephone, television, and individually controlled central air-conditioning. Four are on the first floor, along with a restaurant (see *Dining Out*), wood-paneled bar, and canopied deck. Second-floor rooms include a suite with two fireplaces that was Arthur Fiedler's favorite place to stay when he conducted at Tanglewood; another has a fireplace and wonderful Eastlake furnishings ($110–195 high season) and a third, named for Romeo and Juliet, features a king-size sleigh bed under a small skylight ($105–150 January through May). A small queen-bed room called Cozy goes for $90–120. Rates for other rooms are $95–150 low season and $110–215 high season, depending on the day of the week (the suite is more). Inquire about off-season packages.

Candlelight Inn (637-1555; www.candlelightinn-lenox.com), 53 Walker Street, Lenox 01240. In the heart of the village, the Candlelight has eight attractive guest rooms upstairs, all with air-conditioning and private bath. There are four dining rooms plus a pub (see *Dining Out*). Open year-round. $65–168 depending on the day and season, including continental breakfast. Special packages available.

The Williamsville Inn (274-6118), Route 41, West Stockbridge 01266. The 1797 house is known for its fine dining (see *Dining Out;* call about days open), and its flower and sculpture gardens. The mother-daughter innkeepers, Gail and Kathleen Ryan, organize a Sunday night storytelling and dinner series in winter and in January an ice sculpture contest. Facilities include a pool and clay tennis court. All 16 guest rooms, whether in the main house or in the barn, have private bath, and many have fireplace or woodstove. $120–185. Nice for weddings, parties, and small conferences.

The Egremont Inn (528-2111), Old Sheffield Road, Box 418, South Egremont 01258. This three-story, double-porched landmark is in the middle of a classic crossroads village. The inn dates, in part, from 1780; it is a comfy, rambling place with fireplaces in each of the three first-floor sitting rooms. There are 21 rooms (all with private bath), which vary in comfort. Facilities include a dining room, pool, and two tennis courts, and Catamount ski area is just down the road (see *To Do— Downhill Skiing*). $80–165 (full breakfast on weekends, continental midweek); weekend packages available in July, August, and foliage season (includes one dinner for two).

The Morgan House Inn (243-0181; 1-800-243-0188), 33 Main Street, Lee 01238. This building has always been a downtown landmark: a stagecoach stop since 1853 and now the place where the bus stops. Since acquiring it in 1993, Lenora and Stuart Bowen have established a good reputation for the dining room (see *Dining Out;* there is also a tavern) and have been gradually renovating the rooms, six of which have private bath. There is one suite. Guests can sit and rock on the second-floor porch. Children are welcome. $80–155 per room in summer includes full country breakfast; off-season, $50–95. Inquire about rates for stays of more than 3 days.

BED & BREAKFASTS
In Lenox 01240

☞ **Garden Gables** (637-0193), 141 Main Street (Route 7). Mario and Lynn Mekinda's inn, a triple-gabled, white-clapboard house dating in part from 1780, is set well back from the road but within walking distance of the village shops and restaurants. The 18 rooms are bright and comfortable, all with private bath, telephone (with answering machine), and air-conditioning, several with whirlpools, many with fireplaces or private porches. Four suites in the garden cottages have cathedral ceilings and sitting areas. The ample grounds convey a sense of being out in the country, and the outdoor, guests-only pool is one of the biggest in Berkshire County. $90–225 in season, $70–175 off-season.

☞ **Amadeus House** (637-4770), 15 Cliffwood Street. A large, comfortable, 19th-century house with seven guest rooms and a small rentable apartment. Two rooms share a bath, the rest have their own. All rooms are named for composers. Amadeus was, of course, Mozart's middle name, and his room is unusually nice with a sitting area, woodstove, and porch. House amenities include a large collection of classical CDs. Owners Marty Gottron and John Felton are a friendly, interesting couple—both with a journalism background—who like to spend time with their guests. $85–175 July to Labor Day with a three-night minimum (four nights for larger rooms), otherwise two nights on weekends; $65–115 the rest of the year; $900 per week for the Beethoven suite during Tanglewood Season; inquire about winter packages.

☞ **Walker House** (637-1271; 1-800-235-3098), 64 Walker Street. This expanded Federal-era (1804) house has a Victorian feel inside, nicely decorated with interesting art and inviting common rooms. A long flower-garnished and wicker-furnished veranda overlooks the expansive back garden. Five of the eight guest rooms, each named for a composer, have fireplace, and all have charm. Innkeepers Peggy and Richard Houdek are casual but knowledgeable about music and art (she sings, he's been an arts critic and administrator). They know the area thoroughly and are happy to share their knowledge. There is a seven-foot screen in the library on which they show classic and current movies, operas, plays, and TV specials. Continental breakfast and afternoon tea are included in the rates. $80–190 in July and August, $70–120 the rest of the year (but weekend high of $160 for foliage season).

Cliffwood Inn (637-3330; 1-800-789-3331; www.cliffwood.com), 25 Cliffwood Street. On a quiet street just a block off Main, Cliffwood is the home of Joy and Scottie Farrelly, who speak four languages, and Valentina, a Yorkshire terrier. Built in 1904 as the summer home of the American ambassador to France, the inn is airy and elegant with seven guest rooms, six with working fireplace. (You might ask for the third floor room with skylight and king-sized bed from which you can enjoy the fireplace just inside the bathroom, with its an oak floor and Oriental rug.) In summer, breakfast is served on the veranda overlooking the garden and pool; in winter, eat by the fireplace in the gracious oval dining room. Robes are supplied to guests who wish to use the new countercurrent indoor pool and spa in the basement with a glass wall looking onto the yard. Children from 11 years are welcome, but credit cards are not. Weekend rates are $123–213 in season, $78–159 the rest of the year (lower rates midweek). Includes full breakfast except midweek low season.

Rookwood (637-9750; 1-800-223-9750), 11 Old Stockbridge Road. A turreted, 19-room Victorian inn within walking distance of Tanglewood (see *The Arts*). All 21 rooms have private bath, some have a small private balcony, and seven have fireplaces. We liked Victorian Dream on the second floor with its fainting couch, fireplace, and bath with both claw-foot tub and extra-large shower, but our favorite was Revels Retreat, a third-floor room with queen bed and an octagonal space with daybed four steps up in a turret with oval windows and incredible views. Suites have phone and TV. With advance notice, those arriving Friday evening after restaurants close can enjoy "light bites" at the inn (perhaps a bowl of stew or casserole, though not a full meal). Well-behaved, supervised children are welcome. Rates, which include afternoon tea as well as full, heart-healthy breakfast, are $100–275 July through Labor Day; $80–$225 September and October; $75–200 the rest of the year, except holidays.

Birchwood Inn (637-2600; 1-800-524-1646), 7 Hubbard Street. This grand hilltop mansion dates back to 1767. There are 10 rooms in the main house (8 with private bath and all with telephone), and two suites in the carriage house. The library parlor is a gracious, welcoming room that takes up one side of the house. Kennedy Park (good for walking and cross-country skiing) is across the street. You would be able to spread out in room #4, with its Asian and American antiques, king bed, window seat, love seat, and comfortable chair in front of the fireplace. More economical is the third-floor double with two good reading lamps, extra reading pillows, a massive pedestal sink in the bathroom, and an understated beige and white palette. Children over 12 welcome. Rates, which include afternoon wine and cheese as well as full breakfast (cranberry waffles or huevos Albuquerque are two possibilities), are $89–199 in season, $60–140 off-season. This is a lovely place for small weddings. Ask about special packages.

Brook Farm Inn (637-3013; www.brookfarm.com), 15 Hawthorne Street. A handsome yellow Victorian house on a quiet byway south of the village, Brook Farm is furnished to fit its period (1889). There are 12 guest rooms, all with private bath, four with fireplace. Breakfast is buffet-style in the elegant green dining room overlooking the garden, and afternoon tea is served. There is a pool, a comfortable lounging parlor with fireplace, and a large library of poetry books and tapes (poetry readings are a regular feature). $95–200 in-season, $80–130 in "quiet season."

☞ **The Gables Inn** (637-3416), 81 Walker Street (Route 183). This gracious old home housed Edith Wharton while she was constructing the Mount (see *Museums*). Central to everything in the village, it has 19 bedrooms with private bath. Some also have fireplace or TV and VCR. Pool, tennis court, gardens. Rates, with continental breakfast, are $90–210 in summer and fall, $75–160 the rest of the year.

♿ **The Hilltop Inn** (637-1746), 174 Main Street. This handsome old house at the crest of Main Street has six guest rooms furnished in period style, though several seem more like Victorian reproductions than the real thing. All have bathroom, fireplace, air-conditioning, and cable TV. The Norman Rockwell suite also has a canopy bed and splendiferous bath. A lovely first-floor room with fine views is fully handicapped accessible. A wraparound porch and a combination sitting and breakfast room look out on the garden. $115–205 in-season (suite $215–295), $95–160 off-season (suite $185–260).

♿ **The Kemble Inn** (637-4113; 1-800-353-4113), 2 Kemble Street. This Georgian Revival mansion was built in 1881 by US Secretary of State Frederick Freylinghuysen and named for tart-tongued actress Fanny Kemble—a frequent Lenox visitor in the last century. All 15 guest rooms have private bath, telephone, and air conditioning, and one room, which has a black marble fireplace, is handicapped accessible. Children over 12 are welcome. $85–275 with continental breakfast.

Whistler's Inn (637-0975), 5 Greenwood Street (corner of Route 7A). A mostly Tudor-style mansion with large, opulent common rooms including a ballroom, library, music room, and dining room; the grounds include 7 acres of garden and woodland. The formal garden is Italianate. The 11 guest rooms all have private bath. In the carriage house, a very large room on the second floor has wide pine floors, two sitting areas, a NordicTrack, TV, small refrigerator, and lots of light, interesting art, African artifacts, and books; the rustic suite on the first floor includes a queen bedroom with woodstove, a sitting/sleeping/TV room, and private deck. Continental breakfast is served. Innkeeper Richard Mears is a novelist; wife Joan is an artist. No surprise, then, that the library is well stocked, the walls hung with interesting art, and the atmosphere distinctly cultural. The inn is across from the Church on the Hill and an easy walk from both village shops and Kennedy Park. $80–225 in summer and fall, $70–160 off-season.

In Great Barrington 01230

Windflower (528-2720; 1-800-992-1993), 684 South Egremont Road (Route 23). We keep returning to this gracious, turn-of-the-century country mansion. The common rooms are just the right combination of elegance and comfort. Most of the 13 guest rooms have canopy or four-poster beds and fireplaces, and the plumbing is fine (check out the deep claw-foot tub in room #5). You'll have to reserve early for room #12 with its huge stone fireplace. Several of the rooms have both queen and twin beds. But what really makes this place is the welcoming family who run it: veteran innkeepers Gerry and Barbara Liebert and their daughter Claudia with her green-thumbed and handy husband, John Ryan. Facilities include a landscaped pool; golf and tennis are across the road at the Egremont Country Club (see *To Do—Golf*). $100–170 with full country breakfast. The charge for an extra person in the room is $25, less for infants.

Littlejohn Manor (528-2882), PO Box 148, Route 23 at the Newsboy Monument. Built as the gardener's cottage for a former estate, this delightful house has four guest rooms sharing two baths and scenic views. The hosts, Paul DuFour and Herb Littlejohn, pride themselves on their full English breakfasts (complete with genuine "bangers") and teas (homemade scones and all). They also bottle and sell their wine vinegar. Their other pride is the perennial and herb gardens, carefully rebuilt and replanted after the tornado that whipped through town on Memorial Day of 1995; both the house and garden have since undergone major repairs. $65–95 with breakfast. Paul is a justice of the peace, and weddings can be arranged.

Seekonk Pines (528-4192; 1-800-292-4192), 142 Seekonk Cross Road (at Route 23). This is an expansive old home with spreading gardens, hammock, pool, and picnic tables under the tall pines, and a large common room with a fireplace and piano. Hosts Bruce, Roberta, and Rita Lefkowitz serve a full country breakfast and a guest pantry is stocked with complimentary beverages. Guest rooms feature antiques and collectibles. Facilities include a VCR and game table. Well-behaved children welcome. $80–135.

The Turning Point Inn (528-4777), corner of Route 23 and Lake Buel Road, RD 2 Box 140. Open year-round. Built as the Pixley Tavern in 1800, this striking double-doored inn, nicely renovated, offers six guest rooms (four with private bath) in the main house and a two-bedroom cottage with kitchenette. There's a cheery parlor with piano, also a great country kitchen in which guests are permitted to make their coffee and tea. The Yost family serves ample, whole-grain breakfasts, perhaps with tofu scramble (or even vegan on request). Lake Buel is just down the road, and Butternut Basin ski area is a few minutes' drive (see *To Do— Downhill Skiing*). $80–100 includes full, healthy (plenty of grains) breakfasts; $200 per night for the cottage.

♿✐**Wainright Inn** (528-2062), 518 South Main Street (Route 7), south of town. Said to date from 1766, this large, Victorian-looking house was expanded to its present shape by Franklin Pope, an electrical genius recognized for a number of inventions (a couple in partnership with Thomas Edison), but who died while tinkering with a transformer in his basement here. This is an informal place, good for children. It also offers a full handicapped-accessible, ground-floor room and accepts dogs. There are eight rooms, all but two with private bath and some with working fireplaces; one has a kitchen and an extra twin bed. Dinner from a small menu is available if reserved by 3 PM. $65–175 per room.

In Egremont 01230

☞ **Baldwin Hill Farm** (528-4092), 121 Baldwin Hill Road North/South. This is a very special place: A Victorian farmhouse that commands a sweeping view of mountains. Dick Burdsall's grandfather bought the 450-acre hilltop farm as a summer place in 1912, adding touches like the mammoth fieldstone fireplace in one of the two living rooms. While Dick was growing up here (attending classes in the one-room schoolhouse), this was a serious dairy farm; now there are ducks and, every two years, sheep; the surrounding fields are still hayed. All four guest rooms (two with shared bath) have good views, but our favorite is the bay window room with chairs positioned for enjoying the sight of Mount Everett to the south; it can be arranged with twin beds or a king. Inviting common spaces include a comfortably furnished screened-in porch and seats in the landscaped garden; there's also a pool in summer and cross-country skiing in winter. Choice of full country breakfast. $75–100.

Frog Pond Hill (528-0906), 28 Warner Rd, South Egremont. A bed-and-breakfast for anyone with an international bent, this stone-and-redwood contemporary is set on 60 secluded acres with distant views, a gazebo, and a tennis court. Host Gabriele Van Zon, who speaks at least four languages, has filled her house with European and American antiques, leather sofas, and Chinese and modern art. There is an indoor pool with sauna and whirlpool. The four rooms are all different, from the second-floor queen bedroom with small balcony and a dramatic bath of wood and handmade tiles to the lower-level suite complete with billiard table. Continental breakfast is served on the terrace, the pool patio, or in the wood-paneled kitchen. $100–175.

The Weathervane Inn (528-9580), Route 23, South Egremont 01258. A gracious, 200-year-old inn on 10 acres. Its 10 rooms all have private bath, antiques, and air-conditioning. There is a bar by the living room hearth, a TV room, and a pool. $85–160 with full breakfast and afternoon tea. Children over 7 are welcome.

In Lee 01238, unless otherwise noted

☞ **Historic Merrell Tavern Inn** (243-1794; 1-800-243-1794), 1565 Pleasant Street (Route 102), South Lee 01260. This is a standout: a double-porched inn built in 1794 with a third-floor ballroom added in 1837, a stagecoach stop for much of the 19th century. Difficult as it is to believe, it stood vacant for 75 years before Chuck and Faith Reynolds purchased it in 1981 and spent years restoring the fine detailing, adding appropriate colors, wallpaper, and a mural or two. All guest rooms have private bath, and have been carefully decorated with an eye to comfort as well as style. A suite on the first floor has a river view and its own private porch. Guests breakfast in the old keeping room, and the taproom with its original birdcage bar in the corner is a cozy sitting room. Grounds slope gently in back to a gazebo beside the Housatonic River. $75–165 includes full breakfast (the suite is more) and tea; children are $15 extra.

Applegate Bed and Breakfast (243-4451; 1-800-691-9012), 279 West Park Street. This place is a winner: a 1920s mansion with a pillared portico that's spacious and comfortable. Rick Cannata is a retired pilot, and Nancy is a retired flight attendant with an obvious knack for hospitality. Common rooms are filled with photos of past guests. A grand piano is tucked into a corner of the living room, which has built-in bookcases and window seats, a fireplace, and space for reading or playing backgammon. Guest rooms vary in size from huge (room 1, with its king-sized four-poster, fireplace, and steam shower with two shower heads) to quite snug (the one we like, room 6, with its large bed tucked under the eaves). Breakfast here is by candlelight. Amenities include a pool, a guest fridge, and plenty of lawn. $85–225 depending on the room, day, and season. Inquire about winter and spring packages.

Devonfield (243-3298; 1-800-664-0880), 85 Stockbridge Road. A large, elegant house with an 18th-century core and turn-of-the-century lines (it was landscaped and modernized by George Westinghouse Jr.), Devonfield is now home for Sally and Ben Schenck. Rooms and suites are all furnished in antiques and have private baths; several have working fireplace and Jacuzzi, and a one-bedroom cottage by the pool has kitchen facilities and a hearth in the living room. There is a tennis court, and rates include full breakfast. $70–195 for rooms, $120–260 for suites. Children over 10 welcome.

☞ **Parsonage on the Green** (243-4364), 20 Park Place. Built in 1851 to house the minister of the Congregational church next door, this comfortable house is set back on a quiet corner of the town common. It's furnished with the family history of its new owners, the Mahonys (Barbara is a former history teacher, Don a retired businessman). Their collection of black-and-white and sepia photographs, antiques, china, and other mementos embraces an unusual span of generations, often with stories to match, and the effect is not at all overbearing. There is a library filled with books and games, and both a piano and fireplace grace the parlor. The four guest rooms have shared baths and many thoughtful touches. Breakfast is hearty continental, and afternoon tea and sweets are served. Children over 12 are welcome. Rates are $60–80 off-season, $90–110 in-season.

✐ **The Inn at Laurel Lake** (243-1436), Route 20 West. This inn has served Berkshire travelers since 1900. One of its nicest features is the small private beach just 150 feet downhill from the house. Current owners Tom and Heidi Fusco (they have two young children) bought the inn in 1996 and have improved and brightened it considerably. Of the 19 rooms and suites, 17 have private bath. Facilities include a music room with over 1000 classical recordings, tennis court and sauna, picnic tables on a bluff overlooking the lake, and rowboats tied up at the dock. A well-behaved dog can be accommodated in the room with a separate entrance. The Cork 'N Hearth restaurant is next door (see *Dining Out*). Supervised children are welcome. Rates include continental breakfast and afternoon tea: $80–195 in-season and $50–125 from mid-October through June.

♿ **Chambery Inn** (243-2221; 1-800-537-4321), 199 Main Street. This unlikely lodging place, a parochial school built in 1885, was rescued from the wrecker's ball and moved to its present site by Joe Toole (whose grandfather was in the first class to attend the school). As you might suspect, the rooms are huge, with 13-foot-high tin ceilings, 8-foot-tall windows—and blackboards (chalk is supplied). A continental breakfast is delivered to your room. $75–265 depending on the season and day.

In Sheffield 01257

☞ **Staveleigh House** (229-2129), 59 Main Street (Route 7). Dorothy Marosy and Marion Whitman, longtime friends, have created a truly homey Berkshire retreat. We don't mean homey as in cluttered and shabby, because every wing chair and sofa is brightly, tastefully upholstered, and every room is furnished with flair. There are five guest rooms, one with private bath and two downstairs, off by themselves overlooking the garden. My favorite is a symphony in blues and whites with a wicker chaise lounge and rocker. The house was built as a parsonage in 1818 and has inviting gardens out back. Breakfast is an event here: puffed pancakes, individually baked and topped with apple slivers, for instance. $70–95 including breakfast.

☞ **Ivanhoe Country House** (229-2143), 254 South Undermountain Road (Route 41). This is an exceptional find: gracious, friendly, comfortable. Guests are welcome to play games or the piano, watch TV, or dip into the library of the paneled Chestnut Room where a fire burns in winter and French doors create an airy feel in summer. There are nine rooms, some with kitchenettes, all with private bath and access to fridges. One two-bedroom unit with a glassed-in porch can sleep a family. Continental breakfast appears outside each bedroom in the morning (rooms all have eating space). In summer use the pool and the hiking trails up to the five cascades along the Race Brook Trail, leading to a spectacular stretch of the Appalachian Trail across Mount Race; in winter you can poke around the inn's own 25 acres on skis. $85–175 (two-bedroom unit with bath) on weekends in summer. Well-behaved, leashed (at all times) dogs are welcome for an extra $10 (Carole and Dick Maghery have golden retrievers).

☞ **Orchard Shade** (229-8463), 84 Maple Avenue. This is a find that is easy to miss, on a side street in the middle of the village. What you notice first is the expansive screened-in porch on which paying guests have been rocking since 1888. The older part of the house dates from 1841. The ten rooms (six with private bath) are attractively homey; two open directly onto the pool (one of these has two walls of windows and a cool quarry tile floor). There is also a new attic suite. Longtime hosts Debbie and Henry Thornton are welcoming; the extensive garden includes a pool and chairs overlooking marshes and the Housatonic River. Family-style dinner is served Saturday by reservation, and ski packages are available (cross-country skiers can take off from the property). $55–120 (the suite is $175).

Stagecoach Hill Inn (229-8585), 854 South Undermountain Road. A genuine old stage stop in 1829 has been a lodging and dining landmark off and on ever since. Upstairs are seven rooms furnished with a pleasing mix of family heirlooms, antiques, and period reproductions; the three third-floor rooms share a bath; four rooms, available May through October, are in the cottage out back near the pool. Innkeeper Sandra MacDougall has spiffed up the old tavern (a great little pub with a hearth and reasonably priced menu) and the formal dining room over which her son, chef David Essenfeld, presides (see *Dining Out*). The trail to the cascades along the Race Brook Trail and up to the Appalachian Trail is just next door. $50–135, depending on the room and season. Well-supervised children are welcome.

*☞**Race Brook Lodge** (229-2916), 864 South Undermountain Road (Route 41). Architect David Rothstein has transformed a 1790s barn into one of Berkshire County's more distinctive places to stay. "This is a chintz-free zone," Rothstein quips about the lack of antiques and frills in his 21 guest rooms (14 in the barn, many with private entries, and 7 more divided between cottages). The open beams and angles of the rustic old barn remain, but walls are white and stenciled; rooms are furnished with Native American rugs and quilts or spreads. As you would expect in a barn, the common room is large and multileveled, with some good artwork; a wine bar is in one corner. It serves as the setting for a summer series of Sunday jazz concerts (Rothstein was the last manager of the legendary Berkshire Music Barn). The lodge caters to hikers and walkers, encouraging guests to climb the Race Brook Trail that measures 1½ miles in distance and rises almost 2000 feet in elevation—past a series of five cascades—to Mount Race (see **Mount Washington** under *Villages*). Abundant continental breakfast with one hot special. Children are welcome, as are well-behaved dogs. And the $95–135 rates don't go up during Tanglewood season; there are even lower midweek rates and no minimum stay is required, either.

In Stockbridge 01262

* **Cherry Hill Farm Bed & Breakfast** (298-3535 or 298-5452), 24 Cherry Hill Road, west off Route 7, PO Box 1245. As we traveled up the long drive to this imposing 1890s Georgian-style mansion, we worried that a butler would shoo us away. Not so. Nick Swan couldn't have been more welcoming, explaining that the house has been in his family since the 1930s and that families—even young children—are welcome. Guests breakfast casually around the formal table in the paneled dining room and sleep in large, high-ceilinged rooms (all four units—two of them suites—have working fireplaces and two have shared bath). Views are across fields to Monument Mountain. The extensive grounds include a tennis court, trampoline, a pond for winter ice skating, and walking/ cross-country trails. $60–150 year-round with full breakfast.

& **The Inn at Stockbridge** (298-3337), Route 7, Box 2033. This white-pillared mansion was built in 1906 and set on 12 acres with ample woods and meadow to tramp around in. Flowers, comfortable chairs, and books fill the living room, where afternoon wine and cheese are served and a fire is lit on rainy days. There's an attractive pool in the garden. Full breakfast is served in the formal dining room. In addition to the eight guest rooms in the main house—each different, most with king beds and all with private bath—there are four large, new, well-appointed rooms in back near the pool. These have decorative touches of Kashmir, Scotland, Africa, or Provence, and one is fully handicapped accessible. All rooms have air-conditioning and telephone. $100–260.

Berkshire Thistle Bed & Breakfast (298-3188), PO Box 1227, Route 7. Gene Elling, a second-generation B&B host, and his wife, Diane, offer exceptional hospitality in this guest-friendly modern Colonial, which is set on 5 sloping acres with a spacious pool out back. The recently enlarged common space for guests overlooks a horse corral, and numerous bird feeders are visible from the breakfast table and the large deck. (We woke to a hummingbird hovering over the impatiens in our second-floor window box.) There are four guest rooms furnished simply but tastefully, with many pieces refinished by Gene. Breakfast is "expanded continental" midweek but on weekends is very full, all made from scratch. Children over 8 years. $65–135.

Elsewhere

The Golden Goose (243-3008), Box 123, Main Road, Tyringham 01264-0336. This inviting old house with a large deck is set on 6 acres in the middle of a peaceful valley village. Lilja and Joseph Rizzo invite amateur musicians to try their hand at the baby grand piano and all guests to spread out on Sunday morning with the newspaper (by the fire, in winter) and push open the beveled French doors to enjoy the view from the large deck. Guest rooms are furnished with antiques; breakfast, which usually includes homemade applesauce and hot biscuits, is served family-style at the oak table. There are private baths and a small studio apartment with its own entrance; guests also have access to a fridge and BBQ. They are encouraged to walk through nearby Tyringham Cobble (see *Green Space*), which connects with the Appalachian Trail. $80–125. Children are welcome in the studio for $10 additional per person.

New Boston Inn (258-4477), junction of Routes 8 and 57, Sandisfield 01255. The former ladies' parlor in this 1737 stagecoach stop is now the breakfast room, the pub is just for guests, and the ballroom upstairs is now the Gathering Room, a great space with a billiards table, TV, piano, plenty of room to read and play games, and matching fireplaces at either end of the room. The two downstairs and six upstairs guest rooms have wide floorboards and private baths. $95 includes a full country breakfast.

✐ **Country Hearts** (499-7671), 52 Broad Street, Pittsfield 01201. This Carpenter Gothic "painted lady" is just off South Street in a quiet neighborhood of older homes, within easy walking distance of the Berkshire Museum (see *Museums*). The welcome is warm, though the eclectic decor of the common rooms is rather sparse (a nice alternative, perhaps, to chintz and knickknacks). There are three guest rooms, each with private bath. The one in front has two brass beds (double and queen); we liked the one at the other end of the hall with lots of original wainscoting in the bath. Enjoy the perennial gardens in spring and summer from the deck, with barbecue grill; there's a jungle gym for the kids. $65–135 includes continental breakfast.

✐ **White Horse Inn** (442-2512; www.regionnet.com/colberk/whitehorse.html), 378 South Street (Route 7), Pittsfield 01201. Linda and Joe Kalisz have

taken over this turn-of-the-century house with eight guest rooms, all with private bath, phone, and air-conditioning. Some rooms have two double beds; fax and laundry service are also available. A full breakfast in summer is served in the glass-walled dining room or on the deck, both of which overlook a lovely yard; breakfast is usually continental off-season. Children are welcome. Weekday rates $95–130, depending on the season; rates on weekends are $110–170.

OTHER LODGING

Crown Plaza Hotel (499-2000), Berkshire common at West Street, Pittsfield. This is the Berkshires' only high-rise and very much a part of the county seat. There are 175 rooms, an indoor pool, and café. $109–199.

WHERE TO EAT

DINING OUT

In Lenox

Gateways Inn (637-2532), 751 Walker Street. Open daily for dinner, plus lunch and brunch on weekends (except Tuesday in winter). A well-known restaurant specializing in Continental and classic Italian cuisine. The menu might include lobster ravioli in a tomato-cream sauce ($16.25), rack of lamb Provençal ($22.50), and tournedos Gateways: two hand-cut filets wrapped in bacon, one topped with sauce béarnaise, the other with a piquant sauce Robert. Entrées $15–22.

Wheatleigh (637-0610), West Hawthorne Road. Open for lunch and brunch in season; closed Monday. This Florentine palazzo, within walking distance of Tanglewood, features "creative cuisine": pheasant with cognac sauce or rack of lamb, for instance. The renowned dining room has a prix fixe menu of $68, including low-fat and vegetarian options. The summer Grill Room is à la carte with entrées $15–25.

Village Inn (637-0527), 16 Church Street. The dining room has a pronounced country inn feel. The specialty is regional American cuisine with an emphasis on New England dishes. Entrées are $12–19. On summer Sundays, full breakfast and an elaborate, English-style high tea are served.

Apple Tree Inn (637-1477), 10 Richmond Mountain Road. The round corner dining room, twinkling with myriad small white lights, seems suspended above the Stockbridge Bowl, which it overlooks. Continental cuisine and homemade desserts. Open 7 days in July and August; the rest of the year dinner is served Thursday through Sunday in the large oak-beamed tavern. Entrées are $17–25. Sunday brunch is served year-round.

  ♿ **Cafe Lucia** (637-2460), 980 Church Street. Open for dinner daily except Monday, July through September, closed Sunday and Monday the rest of the year. A remodeled art gallery is the setting for appreciating fine regional Italian dishes such as osso buco con risotto ($28) and chicken Scarparello ($17), with tiramisu for dessert. Good wine list. The Caesar salad is rich and garlicky. Reservations recommended. Entrées $16–28.

The Candlelight Inn (637-1555), 35 Walker Street. Several small candlelit dining rooms—outdoor dining in summer—and a pub on the premises. American and Continental dishes; house specialties include country pâté ($6.95), gravlax ($8.95), and confit of duck with seasonal glaze ($19.95).

Church Street Cafe (637-2745), 69 Church Street. Open daily for lunch and dinner. A lively, popular restaurant with an eclectic and always interesting menu. There is a pleasant dining patio and several connecting dining rooms, the walls of which are hung with paintings by local artists. Entrées les than $20.

Spigalina (637-4455), 80 Main Street. Open daily for lunch and dinner (except Tuesday and Wednesday in the off-season). A very pleasant recent entry presenting flavors and colors of the Mediterranean. The chef co-owners are Culinary Institute of America-trained Lima Aliberti and Lausanne-bred Serge Paccaud. Our mesclun salad with grilled shrimp was excellent, and the caramel chocolate mousse was light and satisfying. Grilled sea bass was perfection. Dinner entrées, $12–$20, could include salmon en papillote with couscous and salsa verde, filet au poivre with creamy polenta, or zuppa di pesce ($38 for two or more).

Roseborough Grill (637-2700), 83 Church Street. Open daily for lunch and dinner in summer; closed Tuesday and Wednesday off-season. A casual place with varied dinner offerings, from vegetable and bean stew with corn pudding or linguine with clams to BBQ baby back ribs or a char-grilled burger with hand-cut fries. Dinner entrées are $12–19 (charcoal-grilled sirloin is $24). Lunches go for $7–10; we had a tasty shrimp cake with chipotle remoulade on a roll. All baking done on the premises.

Blantyre (637-3556), 16 Blantyre Road. Open May through November, Blantyre is a baronial mansion that epitomizes the Berkshires' Gilded Age glory; dining in its grand restaurant is a memorable (and expensive) experience. The cuisine is French (of course), prepared with care and served with flair. The wine list is vast and varied. The prix fixe menu is $65 per person. Dinner is by reservation only. In summer, lunch is also served, on the terrace overlooking the formal garden.

Seven Hills (637-0060), 40 Plunkett Street. Open for dinner daily in-season; call for weekend hours off-season. The dining room of this grand, 1911 Tudor mansion is elegant and the chef, Rico De Luca, is well respected. You might choose veal with artichokes and shiitake and oyster mushrooms with a marchand de vin sauce ($26), or duck breast with sauce Biggerard ($30). Somewhat lighter options might be sea bass in a sesame crust with sweet and sour ginger sauce ($26) or shrimp fra diablo with angelhair pasta, fresh tomato, basil, and olive oil ($36). Most entrées $25–30. Reservations recommended.

Lenox House (637-1341), 55 Pittsfield Road (Route 7/20). Open daily for lunch, dinner, and snacks. Antiques and shining copper give this restaurant a New England feeling that is also reflected in the menu.

Specialties include such dishes as bouillabaisse, roast duckling, and New England seafood pie. Most entrées are $10–17.

 ♧ **Trattoria il Vesuvio** (637-4904), 242 Pittsfield Road (Route 7/20). Though the exterior has little character, this new entry is well regarded by many. It has an interesting menu of Italian specialties including stuffed veal breast, marinated grilled salmon, and, for an appetizer, *suppli* (rice balls stuffed with prosciutto, mozzarella, mushrooms, and tomato and lightly fried).

In Great Barrington

Castle Street Cafe (528-5244), 10 Castle Street. Closed Tuesday. Next door to the Mahaiwe Theater (see *The Arts*), this casually elegant café is open for dinner and features local farm products, fresh fish, pasta, grilled meats, homemade desserts, and a good wine list. You might begin with steamed mussels ($6) and dine on a Castle burger with straw potatoes ($9) or cedar-planked salmon with maple glaze ($18). Dessert options usually include the "world's best chocolate mousse cake."

Hudson's (528-2002), 50 Stockbridge Road (Route 7). Dinner daily in-season, closed Monday and Tuesday fall and winter. Recently opened by chef-owners Geoff and Cynthia Brown, this is a sunny yellow Victorian, with tables on the open porch in warm weather. Geoff is a Lenox native with experience as a chef in New Orleans and California, and the influence shows. We had pork tenderloin with orange lime sauce, fried plantain, mango salsa, black beans, and rice ($16) though we were sorely tempted by the crawfish étouffe ($15) and the grilled salmon with smoked tomato coulis ($16).

Bizen (528-4343), 17 Railroad Street. Open noon–2:30 for lunch, 5–10 for dinner. This restaurant and sushi bar, opened in 1997 by potter Michael Marcus, brings together his unique Bizen tableware, created since 1982 in his studio and "climbing kiln" in Monterey, and the cuisine for which it was intended. More than three dozen varieties of sushi, sashimi, and maki are made from the freshest fish, seafood, and organic vegetables. Dinner entrées ($7.95–$16.95) include seafood, chicken, vegetables, tempura, and noodles. *Yaki hotate gai,* char-broiled sea scallops served on a bed of fried sweet potatoes with a dollop of garlic mayonnaise, is $15.95, and *udon* or *soba* in broth with shrimp tempura is $11.95.

Kintaro (528-5678), Great Barrington Railroad Station (turn off Main Street at the information center). Spacious and artfully decorated, this is the kind of place where you tend to linger. Although a full range of sushi, sashimi, maki, udon, soba, and other Japanese dishes are offered, the menu also retains some favorites of its predecessor in this location, including the Bronze Dog Café Roasted Garlic Plate with sun-dried tomatoes, local chèvre, white bean salad, olives, and red pepper ($7.95) and rosemary lemon–roasted chicken with garlic mashed potatoes and vegetables ($14.95).

Painted Lady Restaurant (528-1662), 785 South Main Street (Route 7). Open daily for dinner 5–10, Sunday 4–9. We have never met anyone with a bad word for this combination of Italian and Continental cuisine served in Victorian splendor. You might dine on veal caldostana (served on a bed of spinach and topped with prosciutto, artichokes, plum tomatoes, and mozzarella; $16.40) or simply on eggplant Parmesan with angelhair marinara ($12.50).

La Tomate (528-8020), 405 Stockbridge Road (Route 7). Closed Monday. Open for lunch Thursday through Saturday, dinner Tuesday through Sunday. The chef-owner has reopened after closing his Railroad Street location, turning a small Victorian house into a light, lovely restaurant with value that would be recognized as exceptional even in Provence— the source of the particular dishes and flavors in which Jean Claude Vierne specializes. Dinner pastas like linguine à l'épice (spicy pasta, chicken breast, eggplant, and peppers) are $11, while the steak au poivre with cognac sauce and shoestring potatoes is $18. A bouillabaisse of lobster, shellfish, saffron, and herbs is $17. You can lunch on "le Burger" or on a salmon, bacon, lettuce, and tomato sandwich ($6.50). The wine list is extensive.

✎ **Union Bar and Grill** (528-6228), 293 Main Street. Open for lunch and dinner. Exposed pipes, stainless steel, and bleached tabletops with lime green trim give this new storefront a loft-in-Soho feel, but the ambiance is relaxed and family-friendly and the menu nouvelle country. We had an excellent Caesar salad and perfectly roasted salmon on a mound of buttermilk mashed potatoes ($16). Children's menu.

In Egremont

The Old Mill (528-1421), Route 23, South Egremont. Dining Tuesday through Sunday. No reservations for groups of fewer than five, so come early or expect a wait in the pleasant bar (a lighter tavern menu is offered here, except Saturdays). The vintage-1797 gristmill by Hubbard Brook makes a simple, elegant setting for 85 guests. Your meal might begin with duck liver mousse pâté with red onion marmalade ($6.50) and you might dine on grilled swordfish with citrus salsa ($20) or penne with sweet sausage, tomato, arugula and light cream ($17). A grilled NY strip steak with shoestring fries is $22. Save room for desserts.

Elm Court Inn (528-0325), Route 71, North Egremont. Dinner served daily except Tuesday and Wednesday. The large, low-ceilinged dining room of this 1790 inn gleams with polished wood. Chef-owner Urs Bieri serves mouthwatering fish and seafood along the lines of broiled striped bass with pecan crust and pico de gallo or flash-seared scallops with garlic mashed potatoes and maple balsamic glaze; he also earns high praise for his classic German/Swiss dishes like filet goulash forestiere with rosti potato ($17.25) and Wiener schnitzel. Rack of lamb Provençal ($26) and roast duckling ($21.50) are also staples. There is an extensive wine list.

John Andrews (528-3469), Route 23, South Egremont. Open for dinner nightly and for Sunday brunch. We love the warm, earth-toned walls and soft lighting, not to mention the menu that includes so many of our favorite foods: starters like pan-fried oysters with mesclun greens and anchovy vinaigrette or arugula with crisp duck (each $7.50), followed by seared sea scallops with sweet corn cakes, shrimp dumplings, and a shrimp glaze for $18.50. Grilled pizza with prosciutto, fontina, and truffle oil is $11. Leave room for dessert.

Spencer's at Thornewood Inn (528-3828), junction of Routes 7 and 183. This recently enlarged dining room offers expansive views and a Sunday live jazz brunch. Starters include Brie and walnut pâté ($7.50) and marinated tuna tartare with wasabi ($8.95); entrées range from angelhair with leeks, tomatoes, clams, and garlic for $13.95 to the house specialty of roasted rack of lamb au jus with garlic–rosemary–pine nut crust.

Swiss Hutte Inn & Restaurant (528-6200), Route 23 at Catamount ski area in South Egremont. Open in the winter and summer seasons for lunch and dinner. A Swiss chef-owner; outdoor patio as well as inside seating. Specialties include Wiener schnitzel, rack of lamb, and Swiss rösti. Entrées average $19.

In Lee

Federal House (243-1824), Route 102, South Lee. Open for dinner. Rated highly, the small dining rooms in this 1824 pillared mansion are the place to dine on salmon, red pepper, and corn cake with wilted spinach and mango salsa ($18.95) or roast duckling with wild rice pancakes, pear chutney, and English mustard sauce ($22.95).

The Morgan House Inn (243-0181), Main Street. The center of town since stagecoach days, this place is a sure bet for either lunch or dinner, especially with chef-owner Lenora Bowen in the kitchen. Specialties include chicken in a popover and roast duckling with rum sauce and spiced pecans. Entrées $15–21.

Cork'n Hearth (243-0535), Route 20. Open for dinner; call ahead in the off-season. Dine overlooking Laurel Lake if you can get a table near the large glass windows; walls in the other room are lined with barnboard hung with all manner of copper pans and implements; a two-way fireplace connects the two rooms. With a new chef, new menu, and new kitchen, this casual spot specializes in seafood, plus veal, chicken, duck, and beef; there's also a children's menu. We ate good crusty rolls with our appetizer mussels in wine, garlic, and herbs (more than a dozen for $6.95) and ended by almost licking the bowl of the light but rich crème brûlée ($3.95). Entrées are $14–18. Tavern food, along with homemade soups, salad, crab-stuffed mushrooms, and steamers, is served in the bar.

In Stockbridge

The Red Lion Inn (298-5545), Main Street. Breakfast, lunch, and dinner served daily. The Lion's Den is open daily except midweek in winter, good for a reasonably priced tavern menu. The formal and quite wonderful old main dining room requires tie and jacket for dinner. You can lunch on salmon cakes or a grilled chicken salad (both $9.50) and dine on brook trout ($19.75), vegetable tart of artichokes and portobellos with frisée lettuce and chive oil ($17.50), or sirloin of venison with wild mushrooms in red wine sauce ($23.50). For dessert we recommend the Red Lion Indian pudding ($3.50). The wine list is extensive, ranging from $16.50 for a California chardonnay to $150 for a 1987 French Burgundy.

Once Upon a Table (298-3870), 36 Main Street. Chef/owners Christian and Lynne Urbain offer attentive service and a casual ambiance in a small mews. Open for lunch and dinner daily in July and August, variable days at other times, with a menu that changes with the seasons. We had a beautifully balanced Caesar salad ($4.50), rainbow trout with roasted garlic yam and Yukon Gold purée ($13.75), and minted couscous with spicy harissa and vegetables in saffron broth ($13.75).

Williamsville Inn (274-6580), Route 41, West Stockbridge. Dining by candlelight is from a country gourmet menu using local seasonal products. Recent choices included salmon basil roulade with pesto sauce served with corn pudding, and double-cut pork chop with black bean cakes and apple chutney.

Trúc Orient Express (232-4204), Harris Street, West Stockbridge. Open for lunch and dinner, weekends until 10. A Vietnamese restaurant that's been here since '79, offering an informal, pleasant, woven-straw and white-tablecloth decor, an extensive menu, and food that can be as spicy as you specify. Specialties include Trúc's special triangular shrimp rolls with crab, pork, and vegetables surrounding a large shrimp, wrapped in crisp, golden rice paper ($5.95) and many vegetarian selections. Dinner entrées begin at $11.50 for sweet-and-sour chicken or marinated beef on rice noodles and average $14.50.

La Bruschetta Ristorante (232-7141), 1 Harris Street, West Stockbridge. Most people rave about this place, but we have heard a few complaints; best to judge for yourself. You might begin with pan-roasted Wellfleet clams with spicy sausage and wine ($8.50), and dine on cioppino ($19), rack of lamb with grilled gorgonzola polenta and rosemary green peppercorn sauce ($20.50) or artichoke ravioli with summer ratatouille ($16).

In Pittsfield

Truffles and Such (442-0151), Allendale Shopping Center (Routes 8 and 9). Lunch and dinner; closed Sunday. Transcontinental cuisine in a sleek, contemporary setting. The menu includes dishes like Caribbean crabcake with green peppercorns and braised mustard- and maple-glazed pork loin. Most entrées are $14–19.

Dakota (499-7900), Route 7, Lenox/Pittsfield line. There is a large fieldstone fireplace in the dining room, which is supposed to resemble an Adirondack lodge. Specialties include seafood, hand-cut steaks, and mesquite-grilled fish, along with some heart-healthy choices. Open for dinner daily and Sunday brunch. Most entrées are $12–16.

Elsewhere

The Cottage Cafe (229-3411), The Buggy Whip Factory, Main Street, Southfield. Open every day during high season, otherwise for lunch

Friday through Monday and dinner Thursday through Sunday. Browse for antiques and collectibles next door, then lunch on smoked fish with fresh corn cakes and a creamy horseradish-aïoli or a sandwich of aged cheddar with roasted tomatoes, apples, and sprouts. Dinner (you may bring your own wine) might be grilled pork with fresh plum sauce ($15.95) or angelhair pasta with garden vegetables, fresh herbs, and local goat cheese ($14.95).

The Old Inn on the Green and Gedney Farm (229-3131), Route 57, Village Green, New Marlboro. Open for dinner in the 18th-century inn, either on the garden terrace or in the four small, candlelit (there's no other light) dining rooms, daily except Tuesday July through October, Thursday through Sunday from November through June. Saturday nights dinner is prix fixe, reservations required. Choices might include red wine–marinated lamb sirloin with rosemary potatoes, pâté-stuffed roasted onions and haricots verts, or tomato papardelle with Maine crab, smoked salmon, cilantro, and roasted garlic, followed by caramelized apple tart with green apple sorbet for dessert. Lunch is served in the Gallery Cafe only in August.

The Hillside (528-3123), Route 57, New Marlboro. Closed Monday year-round, Tuesday too in winter, otherwise open for dinner. Ask Berkshire residents what their favorite restaurants are, and this low-key but elegant place is always mentioned. Specialties are Continental classics like pâté maison and onion soup gratinée, filet of sole Oscar, melon and prosciutto, and veal dishes. Entrées $15–21.

☞ **Stagecoach Hill Inn** (229-8585), 854 South Undermountain Road (Route 41), Sheffield. Closed Wednesday; reservations for parties of 5 or more. This classic brick stage stop serves American regional fare in its formal dining room and the adjacent, pubby tavern (a bargain by Berkshire standards). Appetizers of steamed mussels in garlic-tomato-wine broth and fried corn and crabmeat wontons might precede steak and mushroom pie with garlic mashed potatoes and grilled tomatoes, grilled salmon or trout. Dinner entrées range from $15–20 (rack of lamb is $24).

EATING OUT

In Lenox

Village Snack Shop (637-2564), 35 Housatonic Street. Great breakfasts, soups, sandwiches, and luncheon specials. Inexpensive. Popular local hangout and gossip exchange (if they don't know about it at the Village Snack Shop, it didn't happen).

Lenox Pizza House (637-2590), Franklin Street. Serving up Greek-style pan pizzas, grinders, Greek salads, and so on, for more than 20 years. A liquor license, open 7 days, and they deliver.

Savori (637-2220), 60 Main Street. A casual spot for lunch or dinner; take out or eat in; hot and cold salad and entrée bar. Tortilla roll-up is $5.25 and roasted duck breast with wine glaze is $11.95. Dinner might be an interesting sandwich, shrimp and scallop en brochette, glazed salmon, or a Black Angus burger from the grill. Specialty ice creams and sorbets for dessert.

In Great Barrington

20 Railroad Street (528-9345), 20 Railroad Street. Open daily for lunch and dinner, also for Sunday brunch. Railroad Street was still dingy in 1977 when this friendly pub opened. Since then, the side street has filled with boutiques and restaurants, but this one still stands out. The menu is huge, ranging through soups, chilis, nachos, salads, pocket sandwiches, burgers, and Reubens, and featuring daily specials like chicken Marbella. The ornate, 28-foot-long bar was moved from the Commodore Hotel in Manhattan to Great Barrington in 1919 and served as the centerpiece of a speakeasy until 1933—when it became one of the first legal bars in town.

Jodi's Country Cookery (528-6064), 327 Stockbridge Road. Open daily for breakfast, lunch, and dinner. Jodi and Steven Amoruso have created a bright, attractive space that's popular with locals and visitors alike, dedicated to good food at affordable prices without being dull. The baked sole is stuffed with real, moist crabmeat ($15.95), and the chicken Florentine is layered with fresh spinach, prosciutto, and mozzarella ($14.95). Try the lox for breakfast and a grilled sandwich for lunch. Sesame noodles with Oriental vegetables is $10.95.

Hickory Bill's Barb-B-Que (528-1444), 405 Stockbridge Road (Route 7), next to the Boiler Room Cafe. Open Tuesday through Saturday for lunch and dinner. For seven years, Bill Ross has been behind the counter serving "authentic Texas-style" pork, beef back ribs, chicken, and even kielbasa that's been barbecued for 12 hours over hickory wood; it's served with a choice of sauces and collards, beans, slaw, or salad. Dinner plates are mostly $10–12. Picnic tables out back overlook the Housatonic. For dessert, try the sweet potato pie. Bill has an extensive catering business and expects to open a roadside takeout with glass-enclosed barbecue pit just over the state line on Route 7 from Williamstown in Pownal, Vermont.

Four Brothers (528-9684), Route 7. This restaurant is part of an upstate New York chain, but it doesn't seem that way. The decor is classic Greek, complete with plants and fake grape arbor. Generally regarded as having the best pizzas, Greek salads, and lasagna around; there's also fried fish and eggplant casserole ($7.45). Dinners range from a small pizza ($5.25) to $9.45 for honey-dipped fried chicken.

Martin's (528-5455), 49 Railroad Street. Open daily for breakfast and lunch. Breakfast is an all-day affair, the omelets are a feast, and the burgers are outstanding, too. Beer and herbal teas are served, and crayons are at every table; inspired customers of all ages can design their own place mats.

In South Egremont

Mom's Country Cafe (528-2414), Route 23 in the village. A great little way-stop that's open for breakfast (6:30 AM), lunch, and dinner, with friendly service and a shady deck in back overlooking a stream. A good choice of burgers, sandwiches, pastas, seafood, veal, and chicken dishes, plus homemade meat loaf and some vegetarian options. Beer and wine are served.

The Gaslight Cafe (528-0870), Main Street. This place has laid-back charm and is a good bet for breakfast (try the Shays Rebellion omelet) and lunch, and there are tables out back.

In Lee

Cactus Cafe (243-4300), 54 Main Street. Open for lunch and dinner daily. A zany storefront, middle-of-town place that uses no lard and offers good fresh salsa. We had a fabulous chili relleno, brothy chowder overflowing with seafood, and a vegetable and three-cheese quesadilla. Beers include Carta Blanca, and there's sangria or wine by the glass.

51 Park Street (243-2153), 51 Park Street. An informal eatery at one end of the Lee common, this restaurant and lounge offers wood-fired pizza ($7–10) and such wood-grilled specialties as salmon, kielbasa, and barbecued chicken ($7–9.50), along with calzones, grinders, salads, and a children's menu.

Joe's Diner (243-9756), 63 Center Street, South Lee. Open 24 hours a day (but closed Sunday and late Saturday night). Choose from a counter or a booth and watch the town saunter in and out. The food is good, too.

Sullivan Station (243-2082), Railroad Street (off Main Street behind the Chambery Inn; see *Lodging*). Open daily April through December for lunch, dinner, and anything in between. Call for winter hours.

In Stockbridge

Theresa's Stockbridge Cafe (298-5465), 40 Main Street. Open 11 AM to 9 PM. Good for lunch. Anyone who knew the old Alice's Restaurant of Arlo Guthrie's song will do a double take at the present trompe l'oeil pillars and busts in this familiar space. The deli case is full of quiche, lemon chicken with couscous, and tasty Middle Eastern delicacies. There are also sandwiches, pizza, and two soups of the day. The marble tables are a bit small, the plates are paper, and the utensils are plastic, but there is a small patio and this is still an oasis of sorts.

Shaker Mill Tavern (232-4369), Route 102, West Stockbridge. Open for lunch and dinner. This large, attractive dining place is furnished in "eclectic" (stained glass, etc.) style. The huge menu offers everything from pizzas and burgers to chicken penne pesto ($10.95) and grilled salmon ($13.95). A variety of beer is served, and there is a large deck open on weekends.

In Pittsfield

Elizabeth's Cafe Pizzeria (448-8244), 1264 East Street (across from the GE plant). A small, inexpensive but interesting eatery. Soups are great; real Italian polenta is a specialty. There are marvelous salads.

The Highland (442-2457), 100 Fenn Street. An oasis for the frugal diner since 1936. Open for lunch and dinner; closed Monday. The most expensive item on the menu is sirloin steak at $9.95. The cheapest dish, a staple since the Great Depression, is the $2.95 spaghetti, so we could afford a glass of wine or a cocktail. No credit cards, no reservations, no pretensions.

The Brewery (442-5072), 34 Depot Street. Open for lunch and dinner. Handy to the Berkshire Museum; good for soups, burgers, specialty sandwiches, pastas, and brews.

Elsewhere

Jack's Grill & Restaurant (274-1000), Main Street, Housatonic. Open for lunch only for large groups by reservation, for dinner except Monday and Tuesday. Owned by the Fitzpatricks of Red Lion Inn fame, this former company store (for the workers in this classic 19th-century mill village) is decorated with nostalgia items like tube radios and a model train and filled with sounds of the '40s and '50s. The menu ranges from hamburgers, rainbow Jell-O, and Toll House cookies to grilled salmon with tomato tarragon salsa and pizza toppings like clams and cob-smoked bacon or grilled vegetables, arugula, and mozzarella. Entrées generally $8–15.

SNACKS

Berkshire Ice Cream (232-4111), Route 102, West Stockbridge. We love the story and the taste of this creamy ice cream. The roots are in Ipswich, where Norbert V. White founded White Farms Golden Guernsey Dairy in 1953, and the update is in West Stockbridge where Norby's son Robert founded Berkshire Ice Cream, convincing a number of local residents to buy a share in the cows of his start-up herd. Son Matt makes all the ice cream, which comes from the milk of the dairy's own prizewinning Guernsey herd; and whatever the secret, the 65 flavors of ice cream, frozen yogurt, and sherbet taste pretty good—a dozen are available each day.

Mystery Cafe (229-0075), 137 Main Street (Route 7), Sheffield, occupying the lucky space formerly known as Mary's Place. The café offers a half-dozen mismatched tables, cappuccino, chocolate cheesecake, and other temptations like Death by Chocolate or carrot cake; it also has a full line of paperback mysteries. You can lunch on the soup of the day, an artichoke melt, or curried tuna with apples and golden raisins.

SELECTIVE SHOPPING

ANTIQUES SHOPS

South Berkshire is one of the antiques centers of New England. Sheffield alone harbors more than two dozen stores, and South Egremont has almost the same number. A pamphlet listing Berkshire County antiques dealers is available from every store and from the sources listed under *Guidance*.

ARTS AND CRAFTS

Great Barrington Pottery (274-6259), Route 41, Housatonic. The handsome, nicely glazed pieces are fired in a Japanese wood-burning kiln. During July and August, visitors are invited to view demonstrations of ikebana or the tea ceremony between 1 and 4 in the Kyoto-style teahouse; silk flowers are also sold.

Joyous Spring Pottery (528-4115), Art School Road, Monterey. Open daily 10–5 in summer; otherwise call ahead. Striking unglazed vases and other decorative pieces, fired once a year day and night for 12 days, an ancient Japanese technique called *yaki-shime*. (At the same time, visit the Bidwell House; see Monterey under *Villages*.)

Pond House Studio (243-2271), 85 Dublin Street, Lee. Call to check hours. Bowls handmade from sections of trees found locally. These are one-of-a-kind art forms, very special.

Fellerman & Raabe Glassworks (229-8533), South Main Street (Route 7), Sheffield. Open daily Tuesday through Friday 8–6, Saturday through Monday 11–6 (closed Mondays November through May). Don't miss this place. The showroom is a riot of brilliant colors and fascinating shapes: bowls, perfume bottles, dishes, jewelry. Visitors are welcome to watch Stephen Fellerman and other artists blow and shape these pieces of art.

Butler Sculpture Park (229-8924), 481 Shunpike Road, Sheffield. Open May through October 10–5 daily; by appointment in winter. Robert Butler fashions large, brightly colored abstract sculptures in his studio, which features a gallery with views over the Sheffield Valley. The building sits atop a hillside that's been landscaped with wooded paths into a truly remarkable sculpture garden.

Undermountain Weavers (274-6565), Route 41, West Stockbridge. A studio workshop in a barn is the source of classic men's sports jackets, women's suits and skirts, ties and scarves, ponchos and blankets. Most are designed and fabricated here from Shetland wools and rare Chinese cashmere.

October Mountain Stained Glass (528-6681), 343 Main Street, Great Barrington. A variety of quality stained glass: lampshades, bottles, jewelry, custom work.

Housatonic Galleries, Route 183, Housatonic. The old mill village of Housatonic harbors a number of interesting studios and galleries—including **Tokonoma Gallery** at the bend by the bridge, with interesting photography, craft furniture, jewelry, prints and fabric wares—that traditionally hold a monthly open house.

West Stockbridge has become a cluster point for galleries and studios. These include **Hoffman Pottery** (232-4646), #103 on Route 41, featuring brightly patterned functional pieces; **New England Stained Glass Studio** (232-7181), 5 Center Street, featuring Tiffany reproductions; **The Contemporary Sculptors Guild** (232-7187), 32 Main Street, showcasing a 3-acre sculpture garden on the Williams River; **Berkshire Center for Contemporary Glass** (232-4666), where the collection is large, varied, and stunning and where visitors may watch glassblowing or even try their hand; and **Clay Forms Studio** (232-4339; call ahead for hours), the source of Leslie Klein's ceramic visions, on Austerlitz

Road about a 10-minute drive from the village on winding roads lined with farms and fields.

Ute Stebich Gallery (637-3566), 69 Church Street, Lenox. A multilevel gallery showing contemporary, folk, and tribal art and textiles.

Berkshire Artisans (499-9348), 28 Renne Avenue, Pittsfield. Open Monday through Friday 11–5, Saturday from noon. Just behind the vest-pocket park on Main Street, a handsome gallery hosting exhibitions by nationally known professionals; also the setting for performances and concerts.

BOOKSTORES

Apple Tree Books (243-2012), 87 Main Street, Lee. A small general bookstore specializing in Native American titles; it also carries jewelry. The owner's two birds and dog are always present, making this a cozy place in which to browse. **Barnes & Noble** (496-9051), Berkshire Crossing Mall, Route 9, Pittsfield. A superstore with just about every title you can think of plus tapes and a Starbucks. **Berkshire Book Company** (229-0122), 510 South Main Street (Route 7), Sheffield. A well-stocked independent bookstore with helpful staff. **Berkshire Book Shop** (442-0165), 164 North Street, Pittsfield. Bestsellers, magazines, a Main Street book source. **The Bookloft** (528-1521), Barrington Plaza, Route 7, Great Barrington. A large, attractive, general bookstore with a wide variety of titles, both new and used; a good children's section. **The Bookstore** (637-3390), 9 Housatonic Street, Lenox. An inviting bookstore with a large and varied selection. Stocks books of regional interest and by authors with local connections, such as Edith Wharton. **The Village Bookstore** (562-7332), 47 Southwick Road, Westfield. A good stop if you take the scenic route west from turnpike exit 3. Beth Bentley is a genealogy expert with several published research guides to her credit. She stocks a small but choice selection of new and used books for adults and children, including some comics for the long car ride.

FARMS

Monterey Chèvre (528-2138), off New Marlboro Road, 2 miles from Route 23 in Monterey. Getting there is half the fun since the back roads leading to Ranson Brook Farm are beautiful. Wayne Dunlop and Susan Sellew have chosen to supply local restaurants and customers rather than go big time—an option that is very real given the quality of their goat cheese, in five varieties (plain, with chives and garlic, no salt, with thyme and olive oil, and a peppered log). The cheese is available in various sizes from the fridge at the dairy at prices well below what you pay in local stores. Children will love seeing the baby goats, but adult supervision is a must. **Blueberry Hill Farm** (528-1479), East Street, Mount Washington. If you don't happen to have your own blueberry patch, this is the next best thing: pick-your-own wild blueberries (in-season of course) in one of the Berkshires' most beautiful settings (see

At Monterey Chèvre

Mount Washington under *Villages*). **Windy Hill Farm** (298-3217), 686
Stockbridge Road, Great Barrington. Open April through Christmas
daily 9–5. Pick-your-own apples (more than 25 varieties), pies and fresh-
pressed cider in fall, extensive container-grown nursery stock and hardy
perennials; staff are very knowledgeable.

SHOPPING COMPLEXES

The Buggy Whip Factory (447-2170), Southfield. A long, picturesque,
sagging wooden tannery, said to date from 1792, now houses one of the
largest gatherings of antiques dealers in the county as well as an artisans' gallery and The Cottage Café (see *Dining Out*).

Jenifer House Commons, Route 7, north of Great Barrington. The former
Jenifer House now offers an assortment of antiques and boutiques, also
a brewpub with cheddar-ale soup and eclectic lunch and dinner choices
that are worth a stop.

Railroad Street, Great Barrington. The boutiques change frequently here
but are always worth checking out.

West Stockbridge. A village full of riverside shops.

Berkshire Outlet Village (243-8186 or 800-866-5900), at Mass. Pike exit
2 in Lee. The usual array of upscale and everyday wares, from Waterford
Crystal to Carter's children's wear, from J. Crew and Tommy Hilfiger to
Coach and Berkshire Leather.

SPECIAL SHOPS

The Flower Barn (528-3323), Route 23, South Egremont. It's difficult to
miss the display of concrete garden and lawn ornaments. Inside are
antiques and interesting garden pots. This is a local landmark. **Country
Curtains** (298-5565) at the Red Lion Inn, Stockbridge (see *Lodging*).

A phenomenon rather than just a store, nationally known through its catalog, Country Curtains is a source of a wide variety of matching curtains and beddings, beautifully displayed in the rear of the inn. **Kenver, Ltd.** (538-2330), Route 23, South Egremont. Housed in an 18th-century tavern, a long-established source of ski- and sportswear. **Naomi's Herbs** (637-0616), 11 Housatonic Street, Lenox. Dried herbs and flowers. Potpourri fragrances, herbs, and oils. **The Soap Box Factory** (800-880-SOAP), 26 Church Street, Lenox. Ask Gabrielle Shreiner how she happened to hit on her formula for pure olive oil soap—and why; it's a great story. The soap is great too. We were skeptical and wish we had bought more. **Stones Throw Antiques** (637-2733), 57 Church Street, Lenox. Prints, glass, china, and other 19th-century decorative objects. **The Cottage** (447-9643), 31 South Street, Pittsfield. A stylish shop with tableware, baskets, gourmet foods, soaps, clothing, jewelry, and more. **Yankee Candle** (499-3626), Pittsfield-Lenox Road, Lenox. Candles (including dip-your-own), gifts, and bath accessories.

SPECIAL EVENTS

May: **Chesterwood Antique Auto Show,** Stockbridge. **Memorial Day Parade,** Great Barrington.

July: **Fireworks** and Independence Day music at Tanglewood. **Independence Day** parade and celebrations, Pittsfield.

August: **Berkshire Crafts Fair,** at the high school, Great Barrington. **Annual Antiques Show**, midmonth at Berkshire Botanical Garden. **Monument Mountain Author Climb,** commemorating the day in 1850 that Melville, Hawthorne, and Holmes met and picnicked atop the mountain (see *Green Space—Walks*).

September: **Barrington Fair** at the Great Barrington Fairgrounds.

October: **Berkshire Botanical Garden Harvest Festival**, Stockbridge. **Halloween Walk Through Ice Glen** (a Stockbridge tradition), usually followed by a bonfire.

December: **Naumkeag** is decorated for Christmas (see *Historic Homes*). *A Christmas Carol* is read in Stockbridge Library.

NORTH BERKSHIRE

In the very northwest corner of Massachusetts, northern Berkshire County is a ruggedly beautiful landscape of steep-sided, wooded hills and isolated valleys veined with fast-rushing rivers. Although geographically out of the way, North Berkshire's natural beauty attracts a stream of visitors year-round.

Dividing and dominating the area is the massive presence of 3491-foot-high Mount Greylock, the state's tallest mountain. Greylock is not an isolated peak but part of a range containing the three highest mountains in Massachusetts and rising steeply above the countryside on four sides. Geologically, Mount Greylock is part of New York's Taconic Range, Berkshire's western wall. To the east, the highest peaks of the Hoosac Range hedge northern Berkshire from the Hilltowns.

Greylock is topped by Massachusetts's official war monument, from which on a clear day you can supposedly see 100 miles. It is the only New England mountain that still has a place to stay on the summit. Massively built of fieldstone in the 1930s by the Civilian Conservation Corps, Bascom Lodge is now maintained by the Appalachian Mountain Club. The surrounding 10,000-acre state reservation offers excellent hiking and some of the finest views in New England.

Given what it has to offer, the reservation is underused. Even in foliage season, when the mountain and the countryside colors are spectacular, relatively few visitors take the trouble to drive to the summit (it's accessible from both the region's major highways, Route 2 and Route 7), let alone hike up.

However, just about everyone stops in Williamstown, the area's "village beautiful." Sited at the junction of Route 2 and Route 7 and home of prestigious Williams College, Williamstown is the quintessential gracious old college town. It is also internationally known for its two superb art museums, the Sterling and Francine Clark Art Institute and the Williams College Museum of Art. In summer, the Williamstown Theater Festival draws its audience from all over.

Neighboring North Adams is, by contrast, a blue-collar mill town that has lost most of its onetime industries: shoes, textiles, rugs, boxes, bricks, biscuits, and electronic parts. Its future, however, looks more promising. Many of the former factory buildings are being put to interesting new use (one is now a shiitake mushroom farm), and the largest mill complex, the sprawling former Sprague Electric Works, is being transformed into MASS MOCA (the Massachusetts Museum of Contemporary Art), a modern art museum and a multidisciplinary cultural center that will include galleries, artists' studios, performance stages, and restaurants.

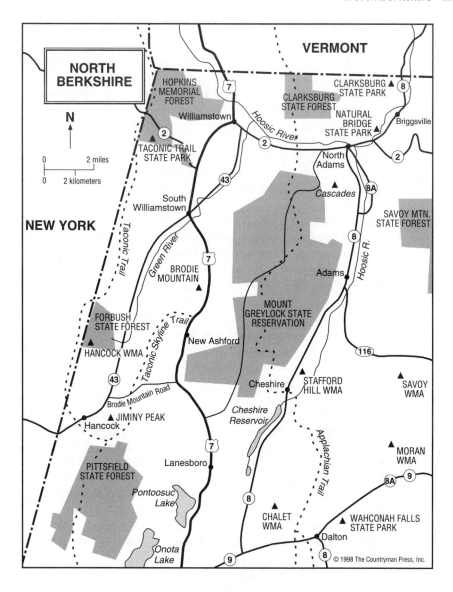

The first view of North Adams for most motorists is from the Western Summit, one of the high points on the Mohawk Trail (Route 2), just before they take the precipitous plunge down the back of the Hoosac Range along the zigs and zags of the famous (in winter, infamous) Hairpin Turn. Because the range is so steep, early locomotives were unable to climb it, which meant a railroad couldn't run directly from Boston to the west. Massachusetts's industries were handicapped, and Boston's future as a major port was in doubt until after 25 years of nonstop work, at a cost of nearly 200 lives, a 4.7-mile-long railroad tunnel was finally blasted through the Hoosac Range in 1875. The story of the Hoosac Tunnel and the boom years its construction brought to the town is well told at the Western Gateway Heritage State Park in downtown North Adams.

North Adams manufactured a variety of products but its smaller sister town of Adams was known primarily for its textile mills. The old mills, many of them imposing examples of late-19th-century industrial architecture, still stand, and some now house discount outlets.

In McKinley Square at the center of Adams stands a bronze statue of President William McKinley, arms outstretched pleadingly as they were when he asked Congress to pass a tariff protecting American textile manufacturers from foreign competition. The protective tariff was responsible for Adams's period of greatest prosperity and directly benefited a local industrialist and longtime friend of McKinley, William Plunkett, owner of the Berkshire Cotton Manufacturing Company. A grateful and grieving Plunkett erected the statue after McKinley's assassination in 1901.

Mount Greylock towers over Adams, visible everywhere. The high plateau above the town, known as Greylock Glen, has been proposed for a series of developments over the years. A four-season facility, featuring golf and cross-country skiing, is presently planned. The entire mountain is webbed with hiking trails.

AREA CODE: 413
GUIDANCE
Berkshire Visitors Bureau (443-9186; 1-800-237-5747), plaza level, Berkshire Common, West Street (next to the Hilton Hotel), Pittsfield. Berkshire County's official tourist information center offers information about lodging, dining, and cultural attractions. Maps, brochures, and guidebooks are available. A seasonal tourist information booth in Park Square, Pittsfield, is staffed and stocked with maps and brochures.

Northern Berkshire Chamber of Commerce (663-3735), in the Holiday Inn at 40 Main Street, North Adams. Open Monday through Friday 9–5. A seasonal information booth is maintained at the gatehouse to the Windsor Mill on Union Street.

Western Gateway Heritage State Park (663-6312), 9 Furnace Street Bypass (Building No. 4), North Adams. Tourist materials are available at the park information desk.

Williamstown Tourist Board Booth (458-4922 or 458-9077), intersection of Route 2 and Route 7, Williamstown. A well-stocked and usually staffed information booth in the heart of town.

MEDICAL EMERGENCY
North Adams Regional Hospital (663-6701), Hospital Avenue, North Adams. Northern **Berkshire Family Medicine** (743-7084 or 664-7785), 1 Commercial Street, Adams. **Williamstown Medical Associates** (458-8182), 197 Adams Road, Williamstown.

Williamstown

Village Ambulance Service (call 911), Williamstown.
GETTING THERE
By bus: **Bonanza** (458-9371; 1-800-556-3815) serves North Adams and
Williamstown from Boston and New York.
GETTING AROUND
Williamstown, North Adams, Adams, Cheshire, and Lanesboro are all
served by buses of **BRTA**, the **Berkshire Regional Transit Author-
ity** (499-2782; 1-800-292-6636).

VILLAGES

Williamstown. From its earliest years Williamstown has been an orderly,
elegantly planned, and education-minded community. It was founded
in 1753 as West Hoosac, and at their first meeting the seven original
proprietors passed what would now be called zoning laws. Meadows
and uplands were divided, and settlers were required to clear a minimum of 5 acres of land and build a house at least 15 by 18 feet—a
substantial dwelling by frontier standards. An exact replica of one of
these "regulation" houses, built as a town bicentennial project using
mid-18th-century tools and methods, stands in **Field Park,** a remnant
of the original town green. Two years after the settlement was founded,
Colonel Ephraim Williams Jr.—who had commanded the local fort and
first surveyed the area—wrote a will endowing "a free school forever,"
provided that the township fell within Massachusetts (New York
claimed it) and was renamed Williamstown. Shortly after making his

will, Williams was killed in upstate New York fighting the French, but the conditions of his will weren't met for many years.

Because the border between Massachusetts and New York was long disputed, the school, now **Williams College**, couldn't be founded until 1791. It quickly became central to town life, however. In 1815, when finances were shaky and the trustees considered moving the school to a less isolated location, local people pledged enough money to keep it in town. Williams College has long been one of the country's most respected liberal arts schools, and its well-endowed campus is very beautiful. Because of its small student body (about 2000) compared with the number of applicants for admission each year, it is also one of the hardest of all American colleges to get into.

The town has been a tourist destination since the mid-19th century. As early as the 1830s, local mineral springs began attracting visitors, and by the Civil War, Williamstown was an established resort with some large hotels and palatial summer homes. The old resort hotels are long gone, but there are some comfortable modern ones, plus motels and a spate of bed & breakfasts, many of the latter in fine old houses. Bucolic South Williamstown still has a number of gentlemen's farms, some quite grand.

The **Sterling and Francine Clark Art Institute** alone is worth a trip to Williamstown, and its world-class collection is complemented by that of the first-rate Williams College Museum of Art. The summer theater festival is one of the best of its kind in the country. All in all, Williamstown, a jewel of a village set within a circle of mountains, deserves more than a quick stop.

TO SEE

Williams College (597-3131) enrolls some 2000 students, almost equally divided between men and women and drawn from throughout the United States and more than 40 countries. Tours of the 450-acre campus are available at the admissions office (next to the Adams Memorial Theater; see *Entertainment*). Few other colleges are as entwined with their communities. Be sure to pick up the *Guide to the Campus,* with a map that covers half of town. Buildings of interest to the general public (in addition to the art museum) include the following entries.

Chapin Library (597-2462) of rare books, in Stetson Hall, sits behind Thompson Memorial Chapel, across Main Street from the Museum of Art (see *Museums*). It's worth visiting to see the college's priceless collection of documents from the American Revolution. Original copies of the Declaration of Independence, the Articles of Confederation, two early versions of the Bill of Rights, and a draft of the Constitution are exhibited. Closed Saturday and Sunday.

Edgar Degas's bronze Little Dancer of Fourteen Years, *at Williamstown's Sterling and Francine Clark Art Institute.*

Hopkins Observatory (597-2188), dedicated in 1838, is one of the first observatories in the country. Free shows are offered here in the Milham Planetarium most Fridays; since space is limited, make reservations.

MUSEUMS

Sterling and Francine Clark Art Institute (458-9545), 225 South Street, Williamstown. Open Tuesday through Sunday 10–5. Free. This collection rivals those of many city museums. There are medieval works like a 15th-century panel painting by Piero della Francesca and works by such masters as Fragonard, Turner, and Goya. The museum is best known for its French Impressionist paintings (Monet, Degas, Pissarro, and no fewer than 30 Renoirs) and for its American period pieces (Winslow Homer, John Singer Sargent, and Frederic Remington). The white-marble building and its modern red-granite addition contrast nicely with the meadow next door and the clapboard farmhouse across the street. In summer there is an outdoor café. The parklike lawns have picnic tables. A path (used for cross-country skiing in winter) leads over a brook and up Stone Hill. The museum sponsors a series of films and lectures.

Williams College Museum of Art (597-2429). Open Tuesday through Saturday 10–5, Sunday 1–5. Free. This striking building combines a vintage-1846, two-story octagon with a major three-story addition (full of unconventional spaces) designed by Charles Moore. The museum has an outstanding permanent collection of American 19th-and 20th-century works by Eakins, Hassam, Feininger, Rivers, and Hopper, and represents the world's largest collection of works by Maurice Prendergast. Exhibits change frequently.

Massachusetts Museum of Contemporary Art (MASS MOCA; 664-4481), 87 Marshall Street, North Adams. A multidisciplinary center for visual, performing, and media arts, MASS MOCA will be one of the world's largest art centers when completed. Housed in a sprawling factory complex built as textile mills in the last century, it is scheduled to be fully open late in 1998. The $26 million project, expected to revitalize downtown North Adams, will include exhibition galleries, performance spaces, retail shops, cafes, restaurants, and various other arts-related enterprises. Call for information about special events and guided tours.

Williamstown House of Local History, Elizabeth S. Botsford Memorial Library (458-2160), Main Street. Open Monday through Friday 10–5:30; Wednesday 10–8; Saturday 10–1. Built in 1815 as a residence for the college treasurer, this homey library building retains many original features, including a curved staircase and graceful fireplace mantels. The House of Local History wing contains an extensive and eclectic collection that includes spinning wheels, Civil War uniforms, old ice skates, photos, and much more.

FOR FAMILIES

Alpine Slide at Jiminy Peak (738-5500), Corey Road (between Route 7 and Route 43), Hancock. Open Memorial Day to Labor Day daily, weekends in May and September, 10:30 AM to 10 PM.

TO DO

BICYCLING

Rubel's *Western Massahcusetts Bicycle and Road Map* (Rubel BikeMaps, Cambridge, MA, $4.25) is highly recommended for its in-depth coverage of the area. Biking is popular on the back roads around Williamstown, especially on Route 43 along the **Green River.** Bicycles (both mountain and 10-speed) are available in Williamstown from **The Spoke** (458-3456) on Main Street and **The Mountain Goat** (458-8445) on Water Street, which also rents mountain bikes. **Jiminy Peak** (738-5500) rents bikes in summer.

CANOEING

The **Hoosic River** is good for canoeing. Canoe and kayak rentals as well as sales and guidance can be found at **Berkshire Outfitters** (743-5900), Route 8 in Adams.

FISHING

The **Green River** can be rewarding for anglers, as can town-owned **Bridges Pond** and, in Hemlock, **Broad** and **Roaring Brooks**. **Points North Outfitters** (743-4030), Route 8, North Adams, sells fly-fishing gear, runs fly-fishing schools, and offers guided trips on the Deerfield River.

GOLF

The **Taconic Golf Club** (458-3997), Meachem Street, Williamstown; open daily mid-April to mid-November; and the **Waubeeka Golf Links** (458-8355), South Williamstown, open daily April to mid-November.

HIKING

The **Hopkins Memorial Forest** (597-2346), Northwest Hill Road, Williamstown, is a 2000-acre preserve owned by Williams College with a network of hiking (and, in winter, cross-country skiing) and nature trails. Some connect with the **Taconic Crest Trail,** on which you can hike to New York and Vermont. Also here are the **Hopkins Farm Museum** and a botanical garden. (Also see **Mount Greylock State Reservation** under *Green Space.*)

HORSEBACK RIDING

Bonnie Lea Farm (458-3149), Route 7, Williamstown. Lessons $15 an hour. Guided cross-country trail rides for riders over 13 and by appointment only; $40 for 2 hours.

CROSS-COUNTRY SKIING

Brodie Mountain (443-4752), Route 7, New Ashford, maintains roughly 16 miles of trails with a good deal of variety. Wide, tracked trails are lit at night (used by the Williams College Ski Team), and less formal trails run through pastures and up into the wooded **Mount Greylock State Reservation**. Rentals are available here and in Williamstown at **The Mountain Goat** (458-8445) and at **Goff's** (458-3605). Cross-country skiers are also welcome on the **Taconic Golf Course** (see *Golf*), in Hopkins Memorial Forest, and on the **Stone Hill** trails (also see *Green Space*).

DOWNHILL SKIING

Brodie Mountain (443-4752), Route 7, New Ashford (10 minutes south of Williamstown). Named for an 18th-century Irishman, Brodie is also known as Kelly's Irish Alps (it's owned by the Kelly family), famed for its Leprechaun Lounge and its green snow on St. Patrick's Day. It's also a respectable ski hill with lodging and a year-round campground. *Vertical drop:* 1250 feet. *Terrain:* 28 miles of slopes and trails. *Lifts:* Four chairs, two tows. *Snowmaking:* 95 percent of area. *Facilities:* Night skiing; nursery (infants accepted). *Rates:* Adults $38 weekends, $24 weekdays; juniors and seniors $30 weekends, $20 weekdays.

Jiminy Peak (738-5500), Corey Road, Hancock, sits high in the Jericho Valley, a narrow corridor that runs east–west between Route 43 and Route 7. It is a self-contained winter resort with rental condos and a

105-suite inn (see *Lodging*). *Vertical drop:* 1200 feet. *Terrain:* 28 slopes and trails. *Lifts:* Seven chairs, one J-bar. *Snowmaking:* 95 percent of area. *Facilities:* Night skiing; nursery (2 years and up). *Rates:* Adults $39 weekends, $29 weekdays; juniors and seniors $28 weekends, $25 weekdays.

SWIMMING

Sands Spring Pool and Spa (458-8281), Sands Spring Road (off Route 7, north of Williamstown; turn at the Cozy Corner Motel and Restaurant; see *Eating Out*). Open May through September, weekdays 11–7:30; weekends and holidays 10–8. Admission fee. This attractive pool is fed by the town's mineral springs. Billed as the oldest spa in the United States, it was formally established in 1813. This old-fashioned complex, run by the same family since 1950, includes a snack bar, changing rooms, sauna, whirlpool, and video machines. The pool is sparkling clean, 74 degrees, and genuinely exhilarating.

The Margaret Lindley Park (Route 2 and Route 7), Williamstown, is a well-kept town pool with changing rooms and picnic tables; daily charge for nonresidents. Open summer and school vacation, daily 11–7. (See also **Clarksburg State Park** under *Green Space.*)

TENNIS

There is a free town court off Main Street, across from the **Maple Terrace Motel,** Williamstown. Williams College (597-3131) maintains 12 clay and 12 hard-top tennis courts (fee and reservations). For a fee you can also use the indoor courts at **Brodie Mountain Tennis and Racquetball Club** (458-4677) in New Ashford and at **Jiminy Peak** (738-5500) in Hancock, both on Route 7.

GREEN SPACE

STATE PARKS AND FORESTS

Mount Greylock State Reservation (499-4262 or 499-4263), Rockwell Road (between Route 7 and Route 8), Lanesboro. There are two main approaches to the summit, one from Lanesboro and the other from North Adams. From Route 7 in Lanesboro, follow the MOUNT GREYLOCK RESERVATION signs to the Park Visitors Center and continue up Rockwell Road another 9 miles. We recommend this route because the information center offers guidance on this 10,000-acre reservation with its 45 miles of trails, 35 rustic campsites, and a picnic area with a dramatic overlook (at nearby Stony Ledge). From North Adams, one road to the top is marked from Route 8 at the **Western Gateway Heritage State Park** (see below), and the other is the Notch Road from Route 2. The **Appalachian Trail** crosses the summit of Mount Greylock, which at 3491 feet is the roof of Massachusetts. The reservation's chief points of interest include the **Summit Veterans Memorial Tower**, a 92-foot-high granite tower built in 1933 as a memorial to all Bay State men

Bascom Lodge, atop Mount Greylock

killed in the nation's wars. On a clear day, five states can be seen from the top of the tower. **Bascom Lodge** is a handsome fieldstone lodge built on the summit in the 1930s by the Civilian Conservation Corps and now run by the Appalachian Mountain Club. It is one of the nicest stops along the Appalachian Trail, welcoming motorists, day hikers, and trail walkers alike. A shop sells trail snacks, maps, and guides, and there is a snack bar with a gourmet view. Accommodations include both private and dorm-style rooms (see *Lodging*). **The Cascades:** A waterfall formed by Notch Brook as it tumbles into a pool below, this is a popular 1-hour hike from Route 2. Park on Marion Avenue and pick up the path at the end of the street. Cross the footbridge and follow the trail.

Western Heritage Gateway State Park (663-6312), Furnace Street (Route 8), downtown North Adams. Open daily 10–5. Free. Housed in a former railroad freight yard, the park tells the epic story of the construction of the 4.7-mile-long Hoosac Tunnel, one of 19th-century America's greatest engineering feats. The tunnel took 25 years to build, from 1850 to 1875, claimed nearly 200 lives, pioneered use of the explosive nitroglycerine, and cost $20 million—a vast sum for the time. In a replica of a section of tunnel, an audiovisual presentation takes visitors back in time with the sounds of dripping water, pickaxes striking stone, nitroglycerin explosions, and a political debate about the merits of the massive project. There are also changing arts and crafts exhibits. Other buildings in the complex contain restaurants and shops.

Natural Bridge State Park (663-6392 summer; 663-8469 winter), Route 8, North Adams. The centerpiece of this 49-acre park is an unusual natural formation, a white-marble bridge spanning a steep gorge. The only one of its kind in North America, the bridge was created aeons ago by melting glaciers. There are picnic tables and nature trails, and in summer a park interpreter is on hand to explain the geological forces that created the bridge.

Clarksburg State Park and **Clarksburg State Forest** (664-8345 summer; 442-8928 winter), Middle Road, Clarksburg. Together, the park and forest cover 3250 wooded acres that are particularly beautiful in foliage season. The park's **Mauserts Pond** has a day-use area with swimming, picnic facilities, and a pavilion. There is a scenic nature trail around the pond and 50 campsites nearby (nominal fee). (In "West Franklin County/Mohawk Trail," also see **Savoy Mountain State Forest,** with its beautiful **Tannery Falls,** swimming in North Pond, and camping at South Pond, all not far from Adams.)

PICNICKING

Stone Hill. A 55-acre town park, accessible from Stone Hill Road off South Street, Williamstown, offers wooded trails and a stone seat with a view.

Mount Hope Park. Sixteen acres on Route 43, Williamstown. Mount Hope Park has picnic tables by the confluence of the Hopper and Green Rivers (see *Fishing*).

LODGING

INNS

The Williams Inn (458-9371), Main Street (junction of Route 2 and Route 7), Williamstown 01267. A modern, Colonial Revival–style hostelry in the heart of town with 100 guest rooms, all with full bath, TV, and air-conditioning. Amenities include an indoor swimming pool and sauna. The dining room is open for breakfast, lunch, and dinner, and lighter fare is served in the tavern lounge. Doubles are $100–150.

The Orchards (458-9611), 222 Adams Road (off Route 2), Williamstown 01267. Located in a commercial strip on the edge of town, the Orchards is a sand-colored complex that includes both a 49-room hotel and a large and popular restaurant (see *Dining Out*). The contemporary exterior doesn't even suggest the interior, which is that of an English country house and filled with antiques, including a collection of 65 vintage silver teapots. Rooms overlook interior courtyards and feature four-poster beds, goosefeather and down pillows, and tasteful touches like TVs concealed in armoires. $125–225.

The Country Inn (738-5500; outside Massachusetts 1-800-882-8859), Jiminy Peak, Corey Road, Hancock 01237. There are 105 one-bedroom efficiency suites in this complex, part of a four-season resort. Downhill skiing in winter, miniature golf, tennis, and an alpine slide in summer. Year-round amenities include a restaurant and lounge. $99–219.

LODGE
Bascom Lodge (443-0011), Mount Greylock Reservation, Lanesboro 01237. Open mid-May to mid-October. Located just below the highest point in Massachusetts—the summit of Greylock—Bascom Lodge is a handsome fieldstone building erected in the 1930s to house the US Army officers who ran the local Civilian Conservation Corps forestry program. It accommodates up to 36 guests in both private rooms and dorms. Sheets, blankets, and towels are provided. The entire lodge can be rented, and it's a great place for weddings. A full breakfast ($6) and dinner ($12) are served. Private rooms are $62; dormitory bunks $20 weekdays, $25 weekends.

BED & BREAKFASTS
In Williamstown 01267

Riverbend Farm (458-3121), 643 Simonds Road (Route 7). Many B&Bs try to cultivate a colonial ambiance but Riverbend Farm doesn't have to try: It's an authentic 1770 former tavern listed on the National Register of Historic Places. The present cozy parlor was originally the tavern taproom, where the Battle of Bennington was planned and where Colonel Ephraim Williams signed his will endowing Williams College. Owners David and Judy Loomis have lovingly restored the place, preserving the wood paneling, wide floorboards, and massive central chimney serving five working fireplaces. Breakfast is served at a long table by the hearth in the old "keeping room" or kitchen. Four guest rooms share two baths. $90 double occupancy.

Williamstown Bed and Breakfast (458-9202), 30 Cold Spring Road. A spacious 1880s house nicely but unfussily furnished in period style. Three good-sized guest rooms with private bath. The full breakfast always includes a hot entrée and home-baked bread and muffins. $80–85 double.

The House on Main Street (458-3031), 1120 Main Street. Built in the early 1700s, this house was moved to its present site in the 1830s, enlarged and Victorianized in the 1870s, and remodeled and modernized by the Riley family in 1986. There are six large, sunny, and cheerfully decorated guest rooms, three with private bath and the others sharing 1½ baths. A full breakfast is served in the country-style kitchen. Guests have the use of a parlor and a large screened porch. $75–95.

Goldberry's (458-3935), 39 Cold Spring Road. An elegant Federal house, built in the 1830s as a girls school or "female seminary." The three bedrooms all have private bath. The full breakfast includes fresh fruit, and tea or cider is served in the afternoon. A deck looks out on the garden. $80 for two.

Little Farm (458-5492), 2708 Hancock Road. Set in a narrow valley that provides an especially dramatic setting in autumn, this contemporary farmhouse has lots of old oak, old telephones (his), and old clocks (hers).

Sit and rock on the wide front porch with its several nooks, watch for deer or wild turkeys from the Adirondack chairs on the back deck, or relax in front of the brick hearth and enjoy the smells of whatever is simmering on the cast-iron stove in the kitchen. $55 with shared bath, $65 with private bath; continental breakfast.

In South Williamstown 01267

Field Farm Guest House (458-3135), 554 Sloan Road (off Route 43, near the intersection with Route 7). The only B&B run by the Trustees of Reservations, this is a jewel. Built in 1948 as the country home of a wealthy Williams College alumnus, the beautifully appointed, California-style ranch house is surrounded by 300 acres of gardens and meadows that include a fishpond and a sweeping view of Mount Greylock and the Taconic Range. The five guest rooms all have private bath, views, and balcony or deck. Doubles are $125 with full breakfast.

In North Adams 01247

Blackinton Manor (663-5795), 1391 Massachusetts Avenue, Blackinton Village. An elegant, Federal-style mansion with Italianate embellishments built in 1849 by Sanford Blackinton, a wealthy textile manufacturer whose mill was nearby. Musician owners Dan and Betsey Epstein—Dan a classical pianist, Betsey an opera singer and cantor—bought the nearly derelict manor in 1992 and have completely restored it. There are five guest rooms furnished with antiques. All have private bath and air-conditioning. The Epsteins frequently give concerts in the manor. There is an in-ground pool. Rooms are $95–125 with full breakfast, served in the formal dining room.

Twin Sisters Inn (663-6933), 1111 South Street/Curran Highway (Route 8). A former turn-of-the-century carriage house was remodeled into a country retreat in the 1930s. Now it is surrounded by 10 acres of lawns and garden. Four pleasant guest rooms, one with private bath; the others share two full baths. Full breakfast. $60–85 double occupancy.

WHERE TO EAT

DINING OUT

In Williamstown

Robin's Restaurant (458-4489), 117 Latham (foot of Spring Street). Open for lunch and dinner. An elegant eating place anytime, but with a large pine tree–shaded deck that makes it particularly pleasant in warm weather. The cuisine blends Mediterranean and innovative American cooking in dishes such as a mixed grill of duck leg confit and sausages, and grilled salmon steak with red and green pestos. Most entrées are in the $15–25 range.

Water Street Grill (458-2175), 123 Water Street. Open Tuesday through Sunday for dinner 4–10. A cozy, tavern atmosphere. Steak, grilled salmon, and pasta dishes are particular specialties. Most entrées are $10–25.

Hobson's Choice (458-9101), 159 Water Street. Open for lunch and dinner. A friendly, unpretentious roadhouse-style restaurant with old-fashioned wooden booths. Very popular with the college crowd, and there is often a line to get in. Prime ribs are served nightly but there are always seafood and vegetarian dishes on the menu. Entrées are usually $10–20.

The Orchards (458-9611), Route 2, Williamstown. Open for lunch and dinner; Sunday brunch. An elegant formal dining room serving basically Continental cuisine. Tables are set with Irish linen and decorated with fresh flowers. The dining room walls are covered with plush velvet. Dinner entrées are in the $20–30 range.

Cobble Cafe (458-5930), 27 Spring Street. Open for breakfast (usually around 6:30 AM), lunch, and dinner. A pleasant, intimate restaurant right downtown. The menu is innovative and contemporary with great salads and interesting pasta dishes. Dinner entrées in the $12–20 range.

In North Adams

Due Baci Ristorante (664-6581), 40 Main Street (the Holiday Inn). A serious but unstuffy restaurant run by local dentist John Moresi—a chef by avocation—and his son, John Jr. The menu is basically northern Italian with veal in white wine sauce a specialty. Open for breakfast, lunch, and dinner. Lunch features an all-you-can-eat buffet for $5.25. Most dinner entrées are $10–15.

EATING OUT
In Williamstown

Cozy Corner Restaurant (458-3854), 850 Simonds Road (Route 7). Breakfast, lunch, and dinner daily. An unpretentious roadhouse with low prices and a loyal following. Fish-and-chips and pizza are specialties.

Purple Pub (458-3306), Bank Street (just off Spring Street). Open for lunch and dinner. This hospitable little place really feels like a pub. You'll get good sandwiches and burgers, daily specials, and fast and friendly service. There is a small outdoor dining area.

Misty Moonlight Diner (458-3305), 408 Main Street (Route 2). A family restaurant with a 1950s atmosphere. Open 7 AM–10 PM, and serves breakfast all day.

Chopsticks (458-5750), 412 Main Street (Route 2). Open daily for lunch and dinner. An established and popular restaurant with a large menu featuring dishes from different regions of China. The lounge specializes in "exotic tropical drinks" (not easy to find in the Northern Berkshires) and also carries imported Chinese beers.

In Adams

Miss Adams Diner (743–5300), 53 Park Street. A classic diner (delivered to the spot by the Worcester Lunch Car Co. in 1949) with old-fashioned prices: The breakfast special is $2.95, the blue plate special

$5.95. Breakfast is served all day and includes Polish specialties such as the breakfast casserole and a kielbasa, eggs, grilled cabbage, and home fries combination plate.

In North Adams

Freight Yard Pub (663-6547), Western Gateway Heritage State Park. Open for lunch and dinner. An informal place, this pub has something of a sports-bar atmosphere. Burgers, seafood, and Italian dishes are always on the menu. Locally made kielbasa is a specialty, and there is an outdoor dining patio.

Jack's Hot Dogs (664-9006), 12 Eagle Street (off Main Street). Lunch, dinner, and noshing in between. A local institution that's been in the same family for more than seven decades. If you like hot dogs with all the trimmings (including sauerkraut), Jack's is the place.

ENTERTAINMENT

Williamstown Theater Festival (597-3399), PO Box 517, Williamstown. For more than 40 years this festival has offered some of the best theater in the Northeast from the last week of June through August. Both new and classic plays are presented, featuring top actors and actresses. Most performances (some 240 each July and August) are on the main stage of the 521-seat **Adams Memorial Theater,** but other venues are also used.

The Williamstown Community Theatre and the college's **Williams Theater** perform during winter months.

The Sterling and Francine Clark Art Institute (see *To See—Museums*) presents a variety of films, lectures, and plays throughout the year.

Images Cinema (458-5612), 40 Spring Street, Williamstown. A classic college-town movie house showing foreign films and interesting domestic ones.

SELECTIVE SHOPPING

Delftree Farm (664-4907), 2340 Main Street, North Adams. Housed in an old brick factory building, Delftree Farm grows some 8000 pounds of prized shiitake mushrooms a week. Here, at the source, the mushrooms sell for $8–10 a pound, depending on quality—far less than the price in a big-city gourmet shop.

Pottery Plus (458-2143), 25 Spring Street, Williamstown. Handmade jewelry, crafted wooden items, pottery, glass, and such.

ANTIQUES SHOPS

Collector's Warehouse (458-9686), 105 North Street (Route 7), Williamstown. Open Wednesday through Friday 10–3; Saturday 10–5. Miscellaneous antiques and collectibles, including glassware, jewelry, frames, dolls, linen, and furniture.

The Library Antiques (458-3436), 70 Spring Street, Williamstown. Open daily. A series of rooms filled with antiques of all sorts. Browsers welcome.

Saddleback Antique (458-5852), Route 7, Williamstown. A dealers' group shop in an old schoolhouse. All manner of antiques, including furniture, pottery, and posters.

Amber Springs Antiques (442-1237), Main Street (Route 7), Lanesboro. Open daily year-round. American furnishings and tools, pottery, advertising, country store items, and trivia.

BOOKSTORE

Water Street Books (458-8071), 26 Water Street, Williamstown. This well-stocked general bookstore has a particularly good selection of books on the Berkshires and by area authors.

FACTORY OUTLETS

Old Stone Mill (743-1042), 5 Hoosac Street, Adams. Save up to 75 percent on a wide variety of wallpapers, many with matching fabrics, comforters.

Novtex (664-4207), 510 State Road (Route 2), North Adams. Lace, ribbons, crafts supplies, and notions at big savings.

Interior Alternatives Outlet (743-1986), 5 Hoosac Street, Adams. Waverly fabrics, wallpaper, bedding, Oriental and area rugs.

Berkshire Sportswear (664-4931), 121 Union Street, Windsor Mill. Factory firsts and seconds of women's sportswear, specialty knits.

SPECIAL EVENTS

June: **La Festa,** a multiethnic festival in North Adams, features entertainment, crafts, and food (last three weekends).

Late July through early August: **Susan B. Anthony Days** commemorate the suffragette, who was born in Adams. Main Street is closed off and filled with booths, games, and food stalls.

Mid- to late August: **Adams Agricultural Fair.**

First weekend in October: **Northern Berkshire Fall Foliage Festival** in North Adams. Includes races, games, suppers, and sales, and culminates with a big parade that traditionally coincides with peak foliage colors.

Columbus Day weekend: **Mount Greylock Ramble**—a traditional mass climb of "their" mountain by Adams residents.

Lodging Index

General Index

Books from The Countryman Press

EXPLORER'S GUIDES

The alternative to mass-market guides with their paid listings, *Explorer's Guides* focus on independently owned inns, B&Bs, and restaurants, and on family and cultural activities reflecting the character and unique qualities of the area.

Cape Cod: An Explorer's Guide Second Edition
Connecticut: An Explorer's Guide Second Edition
The Best of the Hudson Valley and Catskill Mountains: An Explorer's Guide Third Edition
Maine: An Explorer's Guide Eighth Edition
New Hampshire: An Explorer's Guide Third Edition
Rhode Island: An Explorer's Guide Second Edition
Vermont: An Explorer's Guide Seventh Edition

A SELECTION OF OUR BOOKS ABOUT MASSACHUSETTS AND THE NORTHEAST

50 Hikes in Massachusetts
Walks and Rambles on Cape Cod and the Islands
25 Bicycle Tours on Cape Cod and the Islands
25 Mountain Bike Tours in Massachusetts
Canoeing Massachusetts, Rhode Island, and Connecticut
In-Line Skate New England
The Architecture of the Shakers
Seasoned with Grace: My Generation of Shaker Cooking
The Story of the Shakers
The New England Herb Gardener
Living with Herbs

We offer many more books on hiking, fly-fishing, travel, nature, and other subjects. Our books are available at bookstores and outdoor stores everywhere. For more information or a free catalog, please call 1-800-245-4151 or write to us at The Countryman Press, PO Box 748, Woodstock, Vermont 05091. You can find us on the Internet at www.countrymanpress.com.